Nathaniel Hawthorne (July 4, 1804 – May 19, 1864) was an American novelist, dark romantic, and short story writer. His works often focus on history, morality, and religion. He was born in 1804 in Salem, Massachusetts, to Nathaniel Hathorne and the former Elizabeth Clarke Manning. His ancestors include John Hathorne, the only judge involved in the Salem witch trials who never repented of his actions. He entered Bowdoin College in 1821, was elected to Phi Beta Kappa in 1824, and graduated in 1825. He published his first work in 1828, the novel Fanshawe; he later tried to suppress it, feeling that it was not equal to the standard of his later work. He published several short stories in periodicals, which he collected in 1837 as Twice-Told Tales. The next year, he became engaged to Sophia Peabody. He worked at the Boston Custom House and joined Brook Farm, a transcendentalist community, before marrying Peabody in 1842. The couple moved to The Old Manse in Concord, Massachusetts, later moving to Salem, the Berkshires, then to The Wayside in Concord. (Source: Wikipedia)

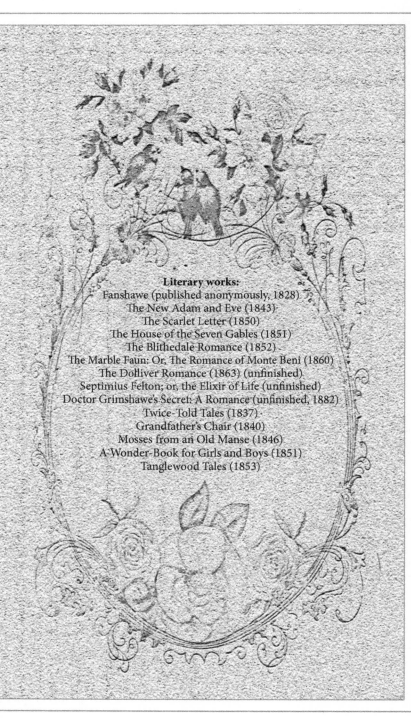

Literary works:

Fanshawe (published anonymously, 1828)
The New Adam and Eve (1843)
The Scarlet Letter (1850)
The House of the Seven Gables (1851)
The Blithedale Romance (1852)
The Marble Faun: Or, The Romance of Monte Beni (1860)
The Dolliver Romance (1863) (unfinished)
Septimius Felton; or, the Elixir of Life (unfinished)
Doctor Grimshawe's Secret: A Romance (unfinished, 1882)
Twice-Told Tales (1837)
Grandfather's Chair (1840)
Mosses from an Old Manse (1846)
A Wonder-Book for Girls and Boys (1851)
Tanglewood Tales (1853)

PASSAGES
FROM THE
ENGLISH NOTEBOOKS

NATHANIEL HAWTHORNE

PRINCE CLASSICS

PRINCE CLASSICS

This is a work of fiction. Names, characters, places, and incidents either are the product of the author's imagination or are used fictitiously. Any resemblance to actual persons, living or dead, events, or locales is entirely coincidental.

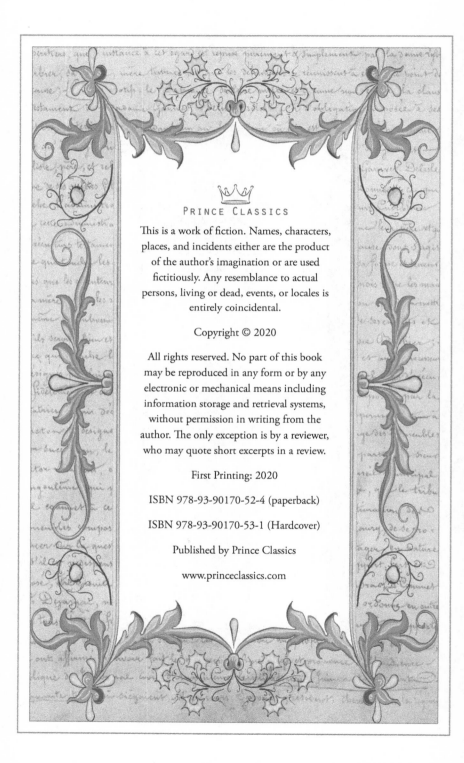

First Printing: 2020

ISBN 978-93-90170-52-4 (paperback)

ISBN 978-93-90170-53-1 (Hardcover)

Published by Prince Classics

www.princeclassics.com

Contents

PASSAGES
FROM THE
ENGLISH NOTEBOOKS

To Francis Bennoch, Esq.,

The dear and valued friend, who, by his generous and genial hospitality and unfailing sympathy, contributed so largely (as is attested by the book itself) to render Mr. Hawthorne's residence in England agreeable and homelike, these ENGLISH NOTES are dedicated, with sincere respect and regard, by The Editor.

PREFACE

It seems justly due to Mr. Hawthorne that the occasion of any portion of his private journals being brought before the Public should be made known, since they were originally designed for his own reference only.

There had been a constant and an urgent demand for a life or memoir of Mr. Hawthorne; yet, from the extreme delicacy and difficulty of the subject, the Editor felt obliged to refuse compliance with this demand. Moreover, Mr. Hawthorne had frequently and emphatically expressed the hope that no one would attempt to write his Biography; and the Editor perceived that it would be impossible for any person, outside of his own domestic circle, to succeed in doing it, on account of his extreme reserve. But it was ungracious to do nothing, and therefore the Editor, believing that Mr. Hawthorne himself was alone capable of satisfactorily answering the affectionate call for some sketch of his life, concluded to publish as much as possible of his private records, and even extracts from his private letters, in order to gratify the desire of his friends and of literary artists to become more intimately acquainted with him. The Editor has been severely blamed and wondered at, in some instances, for allowing many things now published to see the light; but it has been a matter both of conscience and courtesy to withhold nothing that could be given up. Many of the journals were doubtless destroyed; for the earliest date found in his American papers was that of 1835.

The Editor has transcribed the manuscripts just as they were left, without making any new arrangement or altering any sequence,—merely omitting some passages, and being especially careful to preserve whatever could throw any light upon his character. To persons on a quest for characteristics, however, each of his books reveals a great many, and it is believed that with the aid of the Notes (both American and English) the Tales and Romances will make out a very complete and true picture of his individuality; and the Notes are often an open sesame to the artistic works.

Several thickly written pages of observations—fine and accurate etchings—have been omitted, sometimes because too personal with regard to himself or others, and sometimes because they were afterwards absorbed into one or another of the Romances or papers in Our Old Home. It seemed a pity not to give these original cartoons fresh from his mind, because they are so carefully finished at the first stroke. Yet, as Mr. Hawthorne chose his own way of presenting them to the public, it was thought better not to exhibit what he himself withheld. Besides, to any other than a fellow-artist they might seem mere repetitions.

It is very earnestly hoped that these volumes of notes—American, English, and presently Italian—will dispel an often-expressed opinion that Mr. Hawthorne was gloomy and morbid. He had the inevitable pensiveness and gravity of a person who possessed what a friend of his called "the awful power of insight"; but his mood was always cheerful and equal, and his mind peculiarly healthful, and the airy splendor of his wit and humor was the light of his home. He saw too far to be despondent, though his vivid sympathies and shaping imagination often made him sad in behalf of others. He also perceived morbidness, wherever it existed, instantly, as if by the illumination of his own steady cheer; and he had the plastic power of putting himself into each person's situation, and of looking from every point of view, which made his charity most comprehensive. From this cause he necessarily attracted confidences, and became confessor to very many sinning and suffering souls, to whom he gave tender sympathy and help, while resigning judgment to the Omniscient and All-wise.

Throughout his journals it will be seen that Mr. Hawthorne is entertaining, and not asserting, opinions and ideas. He questions, doubts, and reflects with his pen, and, as it were, instructs himself. So that these Note-Books should be read, not as definitive conclusions of his mind, but merely as passing impressions often. Whatever conclusions be arrived at are condensed in the works given to the world by his own hand, in which will never be found a careless word. He was so extremely scrupulous about the value and effect of every expression that the Editor has felt great compunction in allowing a single sentence to be printed. unrevised by himself; but, with the consideration of the above remarks always kept in mind, these volumes are intrusted to the generous interpretation of the reader. If any one must be harshly criticised, it ought certainly to be the Editor.

When a person breaks in, unannounced, upon the morning hours of an artist, and finds him not in full dress, the intruder, and not the surprised artist, is doubtless at fault. S. H.

Dresden, April, 1870.

PASSAGES FROM HAWTHORNE'S ENGLISH NOTE-BOOKS

Liverpool, August 4th, 1853.—A month lacking two days since we left America,—a fortnight and some odd days since we arrived in England. I began my services, such as they are, on Monday last, August 1st, and here I sit in my private room at the Consulate, while the Vice-Consul and clerk are carrying on affairs in the outer office.

The pleasantest incident of the morning is when Mr. Pearce (the Vice-Consul) makes his appearance with the account-books, containing the receipts and expenditures of the preceding day, and deposits on my desk a little rouleau of the Queen's coin, wrapped up in a piece of paper. This morning there were eight sovereigns, four half-crowns, and a shilling,—a pretty fair day's work, though not more than the average ought to be. This forenoon, thus far, I have had two calls, not of business,—one from an American captain and his son, another from Mr. H—— B——, whom I met in America, and who has showed us great attention here. He has arranged for us to go to the theatre with some of his family this evening.

Since I have been in Liverpool we have hardly had a day, until yesterday, without more or less of rain, and so cold and shivery that life was miserable. I am not warm enough even now, but am gradually getting acclimated in that respect.

Just now I have been fooled out of half a crown by a young woman, who represents herself as an American and destitute, having come over to see an uncle whom she found dead, and she has no means of getting back again. Her accent is not that of an American, and her appearance is not particularly prepossessing, though not decidedly otherwise. She is decently dressed and modest in deportment, but I do not quite trust her face. She has been separated from her husband, as I understand her, by course of law, has had two children, both now dead. What she wants is to get back to America, and perhaps arrangements may be made with some shipmaster to take her as stewardess or in some subordinate capacity. My judgment, on the whole, is that she is an English woman, married to and separated from an American husband,—of no very decided virtue. I might as well have kept my half-crown, and yet I might have bestowed it worse. She is very decent in manner, cheerful, at least not despondent.

At two o'clock I went over to the Royal Rock Hotel, about fifteen or twenty minutes' steaming from this side of the river. We are going there on Saturday to reside for a while. Returning, I found that, Mr. B., from the American Chamber of Commerce, had called to arrange the time and place of a visit to the Consul from a delegation of that body. Settled for to-morrow at quarter past one at Mr. Blodgett's.

August 5th.—An invitation this morning from the Mayor to dine at the Town Hall on Friday next. Heaven knows I had rather dine at the humblest inn in the city, inasmuch as a speech will doubtless be expected from me. However, things must be as they may.

At a quarter past one I was duly on hand at Mr. Blodgett's to receive the deputation from the Chamber of Commerce. They arrived pretty seasonably, in two or three carriages, and were ushered into the drawing-room,—seven or eight gentlemen, some of whom I had met before. Hereupon ensued a speech from Mr. B., the Chairman of the delegation, short and sweet, alluding to my literary reputation and other laudatory matters, and occupying only a minute or two. The speaker was rather embarrassed, which encouraged me a little, and yet I felt more diffidence on this occasion than in my effort at Mr. Crittenden's lunch, where, indeed, I was perfectly self-possessed. But here, there being less formality, and more of a conversational character in what was said, my usual diffidence could not so well be kept in abeyance. However, I did not break down to an intolerable extent, and, winding up my eloquence as briefly as possible, we had a social talk. Their whole stay could not have been much more than a quarter of an hour.

A call, this morning, at the Consulate, from Dr. Bowrug, who is British minister, or something of the kind, in China, and now absent on a twelvemonth's leave. The Doctor is a brisk person, with the address of a man of the world,—free, quick to smile, and of agreeable manners. He has a good face, rather American than English in aspect, and does not look much above fifty, though he says he is between sixty and seventy. I should take him rather for an active lawyer or a man of business than for a scholar and a literary man. He talked in a lively way for ten or fifteen minutes, and then took his leave, offering me any service in his power in London,—as, for instance, to introduce me to the Athenaeum Club.

August 8th.—Day before yesterday I escorted my family to Rock Ferry, two miles either up or down the Mersey (and I really don't know which) by steamer, which runs every half-hour. There are steamers going continually to Birkenhead and other landings, and almost always a great many passengers on the transit. At this time the boat was crowded so as to afford scanty standing-room; it being Saturday, and therefore a kind of gala-day. I think I have never seen a populace before coming to England; but this crowd afforded a specimen of one, both male and female. The women were the most remarkable; though they seemed not disreputable, there was in them a coarseness, a freedom, an—I don't know what, that was purely English. In fact, men and women here do things that would at least make them ridiculous in America. They are not afraid to enjoy themselves in their own way, and have no pseudo-gentility to support. Some girls danced upon the crowded deck, to the miserable music of a little fragment of a band which goes up and down the river on each trip of the boat. Just before the termination of the voyage a man goes round with a bugle turned upwards to receive the eleemosynary pence and half-pence of the passengers. I gave one of them, the other day, a silver fourpence, which fell into the vitals of the instrument, and compelled the man to take it to pieces.

At Rock Ferry there was a great throng, forming a scene not unlike one of our muster-days or a Fourth of July, and there were bands of music and banners, and small processions after them, and a school of charity children, I believe, enjoying a festival. And there was a club of respectable persons, playing at bowls on the bowling-green of the hotel, and there were children, infants, riding on donkeys at a penny a ride, while their mothers walked alongside to prevent a fall. Yesterday, while we were at dinner, Mr. B. came in his carriage to take us to his residence, Poulton Hall. He had invited us to dine; but I misunderstood him, and thought he only intended to give us a drive. Poulton Hall is about three miles from Rock Ferry, the road passing through some pleasant rural scenery, and one or two villages, with houses standing close together, and old stone or brick cottages, with thatched roofs, and now and then a better mansion, apart among trees. We passed an old church, with a tower and spire, and, half-way up, a patch of ivy, dark green, and some yellow wall-flowers, in full bloom, growing out of the crevices of the stone. Mr. B. told us that the tower was formerly quite clothed with ivy from bottom to top, but that it had fallen away for lack of the nourishment that it used to find in the lime between the stones. This old church answered to my Transatlantic fancies of England better than anything I have yet seen. Not far from it was the Rectory, behind a deep grove of ancient trees; and there lives the Rector, enjoying a thousand pounds a year and his nothing-to-do, while a curate performs the real duty on a stipend of eighty pounds.

We passed through a considerable extent of private road, and finally drove over a lawn, studded with trees and closely shaven, till we reached the door of Poulton Hall. Part of the mansion is three or four hundred years old; another portion is about a hundred and fifty, and still another has been built during the present generation. The house is two stories high, with a sort of beetle-browed roof in front. It is not very striking, and does not look older than many wooden houses which I have seen in America. There is a curious stately staircase, with a twisted balustrade much like that of the old Province House in Boston. The drawing-room is a handsome modern apartment, being beautifully painted and gilded and paper-hung, with a white marble fireplace and rich furniture, so that the impression is that of newness, not of age. It is the same with the dining-room, and all the rest of the interior so far as I saw it.

Mr. B. did not inherit this old hall, nor, indeed, is he the owner, but only the tenant of it. He is a merchant of Liverpool, a bachelor, with two sisters residing with him. In the entrance-hall, there was a stuffed fox with glass eyes, which I never should have doubted to be an actual live fox except for his keeping so quiet; also some grouse and other game. Mr. B. seems to be a sportsman, and is setting out this week on an excursion to Scotland, moor-fowl shooting.

While the family and two or three guests went to dinner, we walked out to see the place. The gardener, an Irishman, showed us through the garden, which is large and well cared for. They certainly get everything from Nature which she can possibly be persuaded to give them, here in England. There were peaches and pears growing against the high brick southern walls,—the trunk and branches of the trees being spread out perfectly flat against the wall, very much like the skin of a dead animal nailed up to dry, and not a single branch protruding. Figs were growing in the same way. The brick wall, very probably, was heated within, by means of pipes, in order to re-enforce the insufficient heat of the sun. It seems as if there must be something unreal and unsatisfactory in fruit that owes its existence to such artificial methods. Squashes were growing under glass, poor things! There were immensely large gooseberries in the garden; and in this particular berry, the English, I believe, have decidedly the advantage over ourselves. The raspberries, too, were large and good. I espied one gigantic hog-weed in the garden; and, really, my heart warmed to it, being strongly reminded of the principal product of my own garden at Concord. After viewing the garden sufficiently, the gardener led us to other parts of the estate, and we had glimpses of a delightful valley, its sides shady with beautiful trees, and a rich, grassy meadow at the bottom. By means of a steam-engine and subterranean pipes and hydrants, the liquid manure from the barn-yard is distributed wherever it is wanted over the estate, being spouted in rich showers from the hydrants. Under this influence, the meadow at the bottom of the valley had already been made to produce three crops of grass during the present season, and would produce another.

The lawn around Poulton Hall, like thousands of other lawns in England, is very beautiful, but requires great care to keep it so, being shorn every three or four days. No other country will ever have this charm, nor the charm of lovely verdure, which almost makes up for the absence of sunshine. Without the constant rain and shadow which strikes us as so dismal, these lawns would be as brown as an autumn leaf. I have not, thus far, found any such magnificent trees as I expected. Mr. B. told me that three oaks, standing in a row on his lawn, were the largest in the county. They were very good trees, to be sure, and perhaps four feet in diameter near the ground, but with no very noble spread of foliage. In Concord there are, if not oaks, yet certainly elms, a great deal more stately and beautiful. But, on the whole, this lawn, and the old Hall in the midst of it, went a good way towards realizing some of my fancies of English life.

By and by a footman, looking very quaint and queer in his livery coat, drab breeches, and white stockings, came to invite me to the table, where I found Mr. B. and his sisters and guests sitting at the fruit and wine. There were port, sherry, madeira, and one bottle of claret, all very good; but they take here much heavier wines than we drink now in America. After a tolerably long session we went to the tea-room, where I drank some coffee, and at about the edge of dusk the carriage drew up to the door to take us home. Mr. B. and his sisters have shown us genuine kindness, and they gave us a hearty invitation to come and ramble over the house whenever we pleased, during their absence in Scotland. They say that there are many legends and ghost-stories connected with the house; and there is an attic chamber, with a skylight, which is called the Martyr's chamber, from the fact of its having, in old times, been tenanted by a lady, who was imprisoned there, and persecuted to death for her religion. There is an old black-letter library, but the room containing it is shut, barred, and padlocked,—the owner of the house refusing to let it be opened, lest some of the books should be stolen. Meanwhile the rats are devouring them, and the damps destroying them.

August 9th.—A pretty comfortable day, as to warmth, and I believe there is sunshine overhead; but a sea-cloud, composed of fog and coal-smoke, envelops Liverpool. At Rock Ferry, when I left it at half past nine, there was promise of a cheerful day. A good many gentlemen (or, rather, respectable business people) came in the boat, and it is not unpleasant, on these fine mornings, to take the breezy atmosphere of the river. The huge steamer Great Britain, bound for Australia, lies right off the Rock Ferry landing; and at a little distance are two old hulks of ships of war, dismantled, roofed over, and anchored in the river, formerly for quarantine purposes, but now used chiefly or solely as homes for old seamen, whose light labor it is to take care of these condemned ships. There are a great many steamers plying up and down the river to various landings in the vicinity; and a good many steam-tugs; also, many boats, most of which have dark-red or tan-colored sails, being oiled to resist the wet; also, here and there, a yacht or pleasure-boat, and a few ships riding stately at their anchors, probably on the point of sailing. The river, however, is by no means crowded; because the immense multitude of ships are ensconced in the docks, where their masts make an intricate forest for miles up and down the Liverpool shore. The small black steamers, whizzing industriously along, many of them crowded with passengers, snake up the chief life of the scene. The Mersey has the color of a mud-puddle, and no atmospheric effect, as far as I have seen, ever gives it a more agreeable tinge.

Visitors to-day, thus far, have been H. A. B., with whom I have arranged to dine with us at Rock Ferry, and then he is to take us on board the Great Britain, of which his father is owner (in great part). Secondly, Monsieur H., the French Consul, who can speak hardly any English, and who was more powerfully scented with cigar-smoke than any man I ever encountered; a polite, gray-haired, red-nosed gentleman, very courteous and formal. Heaven keep him from me! At one o'clock, or thereabouts, I walked into the city, down through Lord Street, Church Street, and back to the Consulate through various untraceable crookednesses. Coming to Chapel Street, I crossed the graveyard of the old Church of St. Nicholas. This is, I suppose, the oldest sacred site in Liverpool, a church having stood here ever since the Conquest, though, probably, there is little or nothing of the old edifice in the present one, either the whole of the edifice or else the steeple, being thereto shaken by a chime of bells,— perhaps both, at different times,—has tumbled down; but the present church is what we Americans should call venerable. When the first church was built, and long afterwards, it must have stood on the grassy verge of the Mersey; but now there are pavements and warehouses, and the thronged Prince's and George's Docks, between it and the river; and all around it is the very busiest bustle of commerce, rumbling wheels, hurrying men, porter-shops, everything that pertains to the grossest and most practical life. And, notwithstanding, there is the broad churchyard extending on three sides of it, just as it used to be a thousand years ago. It is absolutely paved from border to border with flat tombstones, on a level with the soil and with each other, so that it is one floor of stone over the whole space, with grass here and there sprouting between the crevices. All these stones, no doubt, formerly had inscriptions; but as many people continually pass, in various directions, across the churchyard, and as the tombstones are not of a very hard material, the records on many of them are effaced. I saw none very old. A quarter of a century is sufficient to obliterate the letters, and make all smooth, where the direct pathway from gate to gate lies over the stones. The climate and casual footsteps rub out any inscription in less than a hundred years. Some of the monuments are cracked. On many is merely cut "The burial place of" so and so; on others there is a long list of half-readable names; on some few a laudatory epitaph, out of which, however, it were far too tedious to pick the meaning. But it really is interesting and suggestive to think of this old church, first built when Liverpool was a small village, and remaining, with its successive dead of ten centuries around it, now that the greatest commercial city in the world has its busiest centre there. I suppose people still continue to be buried in the cemetery. The greatest upholders of burials in cities are those whose progenitors have been deposited around or within the city churches. If this spacious churchyard stood in a similar position in one of our American cities, I rather suspect that long ere now it would have run the risk of being laid out in building-lots, and covered with warehouses; even if the church itself escaped,—but it would not escape longer than till its disrepair afforded excuse for tearing it down. And why should it, when its purposes might be better served in another spot?

We went on board the Great Britain before dinner, between five and six o'clock,—a great structure, as to convenient arrangement and adaptation, but giving me a strong impression of the tedium and misery of the long voyage to Australia. By way of amusement, she takes over fifty pounds' worth of playing-cards, at two shillings per pack, for the use of passengers; also, a small, well-selected library. After a considerable time spent on board, we returned to the hotel and dined, and Mr. B. took his leave at nine o'clock.

August 10th.—I left Rock Ferry for the city at half past nine. In the boat which arrived thence, there were several men and women with baskets on their heads, for this is a favorite way of carrying burdens; and they trudge onward beneath them, without any apparent fear of an overturn, and seldom putting up a hand to steady them. One woman, this morning, had a heavy load of crockery; another, an immense basket of turnips, freshly gathered, that seemed to me as much as a man could well carry on his back. These must be a stiff-necked people. The women step sturdily and freely, and with not ungraceful strength. The trip over to town was pleasant, it being a fair morning, only with a low-hanging fog. Had it been in America, I should have anticipated a day of burning heat.

Visitors this morning. Mr. Ogden of Chicago, or somewhere in the Western States, who arrived in England a fortnight ago, and who called on me at that time. He has since been in Scotland, and is now going to London and the Continent; secondly, the Captain of the Collins steamer Pacific, which sails to-day; thirdly, an American shipmaster, who complained that he had never, in his heretofore voyages, been able to get sight of the American Consul.

Mr. Pearce's customary matutinal visit was unusually agreeable to-day, inasmuch as he laid on my desk nineteen golden sovereigns and thirteen shillings. It being the day of the steamer's departure, an unusual number of invoice certificates had been required,—my signature to each of which brings me two dollars.

The autograph of a living author has seldom been so much in request at so respectable a price. Colonel Crittenden told me that he had received as much as fifty pounds on a single day. Heaven prosper the trade between America and Liverpool!

August 15th.—Many scenes which I should have liked to record have occurred; but the pressure of business has prevented me from recording them from day to day.

On Thursday I went, on invitation from Mr. B., to the prodigious steamer Great Britain, down the harbor, and some miles into the sea, to escort her off a little way on her voyage to Australia. There is an immense enthusiasm among the English people about this ship, on account of its being the largest in the world. The shores were lined with people to see her sail, and there were innumerable small steamers, crowded with men, all the way out into the ocean. Nothing seems to touch the English nearer than this question of nautical superiority; and if we wish to hit them to the quick, we must hit them there.

On Friday, at 7 P.M., I went to dine with the Mayor. It was a dinner given to the Judges and the Grand Jury. The Judges of England, during the time of holding an Assize, are the persons first in rank in the kingdom. They take precedence of everybody else,—of the highest military officers, of the Lord Lieutenants, of the Archbishops,—of the Prince of Wales,—of all except the Sovereign, whose authority and dignity they represent. In case of a royal dinner, the Judge would lead the Queen to the table.

The dinner was at the Town Hall, and the rooms and the whole affair were all in the most splendid style. Nothing struck me more than the footmen in the city livery. They really looked more magnificent in their gold-lace and breeches and white silk stockings than any officers of state. The rooms were beautiful; gorgeously painted and gilded, gorgeously lighted, gorgeously hung with paintings,—the plate was gorgeous, and the dinner gorgeous in the English fashion.

After the removal of the cloth the Mayor gave various toasts, prefacing each with some remarks,—the first, of course, the Sovereign, after which "God save the Queen" was sung, the company standing up and joining in the chorus, their ample faces glowing with wine, enthusiasm, and loyalty. Afterwards the Bar, and various other dignities and institutions were toasted; and by and by came the toast to the United States, and to me, as their Representative. Hereupon either "Hail Columbia," or "Yankee Doodle," or some other of our national tunes (but Heaven knows which), was played; and at the conclusion, being at bay, and with no alternative, I got upon my legs, and made a response. They received me and listened to my nonsense with a good deal of rapping, and my speech seemed to give great satisfaction; my chief difficulty being in not knowing how to pitch my voice to the size of the room. As for the matter, it is not of the slightest consequence. Anybody may make an after-dinner speech who will be content to talk onward without saying anything. My speech was not more than two or three inches long; and, considering that I did not know a soul there, except the Mayor himself, and that I am wholly unpractised in all sorts of oratory, and that I had nothing to say, it was quite successful. I hardly thought it was in me, but, being once started, I felt no embarrassment, and went through it as coolly as if I were going to be hanged.

Yesterday, after dinner, I took a walk with my family. We went through by-ways and private roads, and saw more of rural England, with its hedge-rows, its grassy fields, and its whitewashed old stone cottages, than we have before seen since our arrival.

August 20th.—This being Saturday, there early commenced a throng of visitants to Rock Ferry. The boat in which I came over brought from the city a multitude of factory-people. They had bands of music, and banners inscribed with the names of the mills they belong to, and other devices: pale-looking people, but not looking exactly as if they were underfed. They are brought on reduced terms by the railways and steamers, and come from great distances in the interior. These, I believe, were from Preston. I have not yet had an opportunity of observing how they amuse themselves during these excursions.

At the dock, the other day, the steamer arrived from Rock Ferry with a countless multitude of little girls, in coarse blue gowns, who, as they landed, formed in procession, and walked up the dock. These girls had been taken from the workhouses and educated at a charity-school, and would by and by be apprenticed as servants. I should not have conceived it possible that so many children could have been collected together, without a single trace of beauty or scarcely of intelligence in so much as one individual; such mean, coarse, vulgar features and figures betraying unmistakably a low origin, and ignorant and brutal parents. They did not appear wicked, but only stupid, animal, and soulless. It must require many generations of better life to wake the soul in them. All America could not show the like.

August 22d.—A Captain Auld, an American, having died here yesterday, I went with my clerk and an American shipmaster to take the inventory of his effects. His boarding-house was in a mean street, an old dingy house, with narrow entrance,—the class of boarding-house frequented by mates of vessels, and inferior to those generally patronized by masters. A fat elderly landlady, of respectable and honest aspect, and her daughter, a pleasing young woman enough, received us, and ushered us into the deceased's bedchamber. It was a dusky back room, plastered and painted yellow; its one window looking into the very narrowest of back-yards or courts, and out on a confused multitude of back buildings, appertaining to other houses, most of them old, with rude chimneys of wash-rooms and kitchens, the bricks of which seemed half loose.

The chattels of the dead man were contained in two trunks, a chest, a sail-cloth bag, and a barrel, and consisted of clothing, suggesting a thickset, middle-sized man; papers relative to ships and business, a spyglass, a loaded iron pistol, some books of navigation, some charts, several great pieces of tobacco, and a few cigars; some little plaster images, that he had probably bought for his children, a cotton umbrella, and other trumpery of no great value. In one of the trunks we found about twenty pounds' worth of English and American gold and silver, and some notes of hand, due in America. Of all these things the clerk made an inventory; after which we took possession of the money and affixed the consular seal to the trunks, bag, and chest.

While this was going on, we heard a great noise of men quarrelling in an adjoining court; and, altogether, it seemed a squalid and ugly place to live in, and a most undesirable one to die in. At the conclusion of our labors, the young woman asked us if we would not go into another chamber, and look at the corpse, and appeared to think that we should be rather glad than otherwise of the privilege. But, never having seen the man during his lifetime, I declined to commence his acquaintance now.

His bills for board and nursing amount to about the sum which we found in his trunk; his funeral expenses will be ten pounds more; the surgeon has sent in a bill of eight pounds, odd shillings; and the account of another medical man is still to be rendered. As his executor, I shall pay his landlady and nurse; and for the rest of the expenses, a subscription must be made (according to the custom in such cases) among the shipmasters, headed by myself. The funeral pomp will consist of a hearse, one coach, four men, with crape hatbands, and a few other items, together with a grave at five pounds, over which his friends will be entitled to place a stone, if they choose to do so, within twelve months.

As we left the house, we looked into the dark and squalid dining-room, where a lunch of cold meat was set out; but having no associations with the house except through this one dead man, it seemed as if his presence and attributes pervaded it wholly. He appears to have been a man of reprehensible habits, though well advanced in years. I ought not to forget a brandy-flask (empty) among his other effects. The landlady and daughter made a good impression on me, as honest and respectable persons.

August 24th.—Yesterday, in the forenoon, I received a note, and shortly afterwards a call at the Consulate from Miss H——, whom I apprehend to be a lady of literary tendencies. She said that Miss L. had promised her an introduction, but that, happening to pass through Liverpool, she had snatched the opportunity to make my acquaintance. She seems to be a mature lady, rather plain, but with an honest and intelligent face. It was rather a singular freedom, methinks, to come down upon a perfect stranger in this way,—to sit with him in his private office an hour or two, and then walk about the streets with him, as she did; for I did the honors of Liverpool, and showed her the public buildings. Her talk was sensible, but not particularly brilliant nor interesting; a good, solid personage, physically and intellectually. She is an English woman.

In the afternoon, at three o'clock, I attended the funeral of Captain Auld. Being ushered into the dining-room of his boarding-house, I found brandy, gin, and wine set out on a tray, together with some little spicecakes. By and by came in a woman, who asked if I were going to the funeral; and then proceeded to put a mourning-band on my hat,—a black-silk band, covering the whole hat, and streaming nearly a yard behind. After waiting the better part of an hour, nobody else appeared, although several shipmasters had promised to attend. Hereupon, the undertaker was anxious to set forth; but the landlady, who was arrayed in shining black silk, thought it a shame that the poor man should be buried with such small attendance. So we waited a little longer, during which interval I heard the landlady's daughter sobbing and wailing in the entry; and but for this tender-heartedness there would have been no tears at all. Finally we set forth,—the undertaker, a friend of his, and a young man, perhaps the landlady's son, and myself, in the black-plumed coach, and the landlady, her daughter, and a female friend, in the coach behind. Previous to this, however, everybody had taken some wine or spirits; for it seemed to be considered disrespectful not to do so.

Before us went the plumed hearse, a stately affair, with a bas-relief of funereal figures upon its sides. We proceeded quite across the city to the Necropolis, where the coffin was carried into a chapel, in which we found already another coffin, and another set of mourners, awaiting the clergyman. Anon he appeared,—a stern, broad-framed, large, and bald-headed man, in a black-silk gown. He mounted his desk, and read the service in quite a feeble and unimpressive way, though with no lack of solemnity. This done, our four bearers took up the coffin, and carried it out of the chapel; but, descending the steps, and, perhaps, having taken a little too much brandy, one of them stumbled, and down came the coffin,—not quite to the ground, however; for they grappled with it, and contrived, with a great struggle, to prevent the misadventure. But I really expected to see poor Captain Auld burst forth among us in his grave-clothes.

The Necropolis is quite a handsome burial-place, shut in by high walls, so overrun with shrubbery that no part of the brick or stone is visible. Part of the space within is an ornamental garden, with flowers and green turf; the rest is strewn with flat gravestones, and a few raised monuments; and straight avenues run to and fro between. Captain Auld's grave was dug nine feet deep. It is his own for twelve months; but, if his friends do not choose to give him a stone, it will become a common grave at the end of that time; and four or five more bodies may then be piled upon his. Every one seemed greatly to admire the grave; the undertaker praised it, and also the dryness of its site, which he took credit to himself for having chosen. The grave-digger, too, was very proud of its depth, and the neatness of his handiwork. The clergyman, who had marched in advance of us from the chapel, now took his stand at the head of the grave, and, lifting his hat, proceeded with what remained of the service, while we stood bareheaded around. When he came to a particular part, "ashes to ashes, dust to dust," the undertaker lifted a handful of earth, and threw it rattling on the coffin,—so did the landlady's son, and so did I. After the funeral the undertaker's friend, an elderly, coarse-looking man, looked round him, and remarked that "the grass had never grown on the parties who died in the cholera year"; but at this the undertaker laughed in scorn.

As we returned to the gate of the cemetery, the sexton met us, and pointed to a small office, on entering which we found the clergyman, who was waiting for his burial-fees. There was now a dispute between the clergyman and the undertaker; the former wishing to receive the whole amount for the gravestone, which the undertaker, of course, refused to pay. I explained how the matter stood; on which the clergyman acquiesced, civilly enough; but it was very strange to see the worldly, business-like way in which he entered into this squabble, so soon after burying poor Captain Auld.

During our drive back in the mourning-coach, the undertaker, his friend, and the landlady's son still kept descanting on the excellence of the grave,—"Such a fine grave,"—"Such a nice grave,"—"Such a splendid grave,"—and, really, they seemed almost to think it worth while to die, for the sake of being buried there. They deemed it an especial pity that such a grave should ever become a common grave. "Why," said they to me, "by paying the extra price you may have it for your own grave, or for your family!" meaning that we should have a right to pile ourselves over the defunct Captain. I wonder how the English ever attain to any conception of a future existence, since they so overburden themselves with earth and mortality in their ideas of funerals. A drive with an undertaker, in a sable-plumed coach!—talking about graves!—and yet he was a jolly old fellow, wonderfully corpulent, with a smile breaking out easily all over his face,—although, once in a while, he looked professionally lugubrious.

All the time the scent of that horrible mourning-coach is in my nostrils, and I breathe nothing but a funeral atmosphere.

Saturday, August 27th.—This being the gala-day of the manufacturing people about Liverpool, the steamboats to Rock Ferry were seasonably crowded with large parties of both sexes. They were accompanied with two bands of music, in uniform; and these bands, before I left the hotel, were playing, in competition and rivalry with each other in the coach-yard, loud martial strains from shining brass instruments. A prize is to be assigned to one or to the other of these bands, and I suppose this was a part of the competition. Meanwhile the merry-making people who thronged the courtyard were quaffing coffee from blue earthen mugs, which they brought with them,—as likewise they brought the coffee, and had it made in the hotel.

It had poured with rain about the time of their arrival, notwithstanding which they did not seem disheartened; for, of course, in this climate, it enters into all their calculations to be drenched through and through. By and by the sun shone out, and it has continued to shine and shade every ten minutes ever since. All these people were decently dressed; the men generally in dark clothes, not so smartly as Americans on a festal day, but so as not to be greatly different as regards dress. They were paler, smaller, less wholesome-looking and less intelligent, and, I think, less noisy, than so many Yankees would have been. The women and girls differed much more from what American girls and women would be on a pleasure-excursion, being so shabbily dressed, with no kind of smartness, no silks, nothing but cotton gowns, I believe, and ill-looking bonnets,— which, however, was the only part of their attire that they seemed to care about guarding from the rain. As to their persons, they generally looked better developed and healthier than the men; but there was a woful lack of beauty and grace, not a pretty girl among them, all coarse and vulgar. Their bodies, it seems to me, are apt to be very long in proportion to their limbs,—in truth, this kind of make is rather characteristic of both sexes in England. The speech of these folks, in some instances, was so broad Lancashire that I could not well understand it.

A WALK TO BEBBINGTON.

Rock Ferry, August 29th.—Yesterday we all took a walk into the country. It was a fine afternoon, with clouds, of course, in different parts of the sky, but a clear atmosphere, bright sunshine, and altogether a Septembrish feeling. The ramble was very pleasant, along the hedge-lined roads in which there were flowers blooming, and the varnished holly, certainly one of the most beautiful shrubs in the world, so far as foliage goes. We saw one cottage which I suppose was several hundred years old. It was of stone, filled into a wooden frame, the black-oak of which was visible like an external skeleton; it had a thatched roof, and was whitewashed. We passed through a village,—higher Bebbington, I believe,—with narrow streets and mean houses all of brick or stone, and not standing wide apart from each other as in American country villages, but conjoined. There was an immense almshouse in the midst; at least, I took it to be so. In the centre of the village, too, we saw a moderate-sized brick house, built in imitation of a castle with a tower and turret, in which an upper and an under row of small cannon were mounted,—now green with moss. There were also battlements along the roof of the house, which looked as if it might have been built eighty or a hundred years ago. In the centre of it there was the dial of a clock, but the inner machinery had been removed, and the hands, hanging listlessly, moved to and fro in the wind. It was quite a novel symbol of decay and neglect. On the wall, close to the street, there were certain eccentric inscriptions cut into slabs of stone, but I could make no sense of them. At the end of the house opposite the turret, we peeped through the bars of an iron gate and beheld a little paved court-yard, and at the farther side of it a small piazza, beneath which seemed to stand the figure of a man. He appeared well advanced in years, and was dressed in a blue coat and buff breeches, with a white or straw hat on his head. Behold, too, in a kennel beside the porch, a large dog sitting on his hind legs, chained! Also, close beside the gateway, another man, seated in a kind of arbor! All these were wooden images; and the whole castellated, small, village-dwelling, with the inscriptions and the queer statuary, was probably the whim of some half-crazy person, who has now, no doubt, been long asleep in Bebbington churchyard.

The bell of the old church was ringing as we went along, and many respectable-looking people and cleanly dressed children were moving towards the sound. Soon we reached the church, and I have seen nothing yet in England that so completely answered my idea of what such a thing was, as this old village church of Bebbington.

It is quite a large edifice, built in the form of a cross, a low peaked porch in the side, over which, rudely cut in stone, is the date 1300 and something. The steeple has ivy on it, and looks old, old, old; so does the whole church, though portions of it have been renewed, but not so as to impair the aspect of heavy, substantial endurance, and long, long decay, which may go on hundreds of years longer before the church is a ruin. There it stands, among the surrounding graves, looking just the same as it did in Bloody Mary's days; just as it did in Cromwell's time. A bird (and perhaps many birds) had its nest in the steeple, and flew in and out of the loopholes that were opened into it. The stone framework of the windows looked particularly old.

There were monuments about the church, some lying flat on the ground, others elevated on low pillars, or on cross slabs of stone, and almost all looking dark, moss-grown, and very antique. But on reading some of the inscriptions, I was surprised to find them very recent; for, in fact, twenty years of this climate suffices to give as much or more antiquity of aspect, whether to gravestone or edifice, than a hundred years of our own,—so soon do lichens creep over the surface, so soon does it blacken, so soon do the edges lose their sharpness, so soon does Time gnaw away the records. The only really old monuments (and those not very old) were two, standing close together, and raised on low rude arches, the dates on which were 1684 and 1686. On one a cross was rudely cut into the stone. But there may have been hundreds older than this, the records on which had been quite obliterated, and the stones removed, and the graves dug over anew. None of the monuments commemorate people of rank; on only one the buried person was recorded as "Gent."

While we sat on the flat slabs resting ourselves, several little girls, healthy-looking and prettily dressed enough, came into the churchyard, and began to talk and laugh, and to skip merrily from one tombstone to another. They stared very broadly at us, and one of them, by and by, ran up to U. and J., and gave each of them a green apple, then they skipped upon the tombstones again, while, within the church, we heard them singing, sounding pretty much as I have heard it in our pine-built New England meeting-houses. Meantime the rector had detected the voices of these naughty little girls, and perhaps had caught glimpses of them through the windows; for, anon, out came the sexton, and, addressing himself to us, asked whether there had been any noise or disturbance in the churchyard. I should not have borne testimony against these little villagers, but S. was so anxious to exonerate our own children that she pointed out these poor little sinners to the sexton, who forthwith turned them out. He would have done the same to us, no doubt, had my coat been worse than it was; but, as the matter stood, his demeanor was rather apologetic than menacing, when he informed us that the rector had sent him.

We stayed a little longer, looking at the graves, some of which were between the buttresses of the church and quite close to the wall, as if the sleepers anticipated greater comfort and security the nearer they could get to the sacred edifice.

As we went out of the churchyard, we passed the aforesaid little girls, who were sitting behind the mound of a tomb, and busily babbling together. They called after us, expressing their discontent that we had betrayed them to the sexton, and saying that it was not they who made the noise. Going homeward, we went astray in a green lane, that terminated in the midst of a field, without outlet, so that we had to retrace a good many of our footsteps.

Close to the wall of the church, beside the door, there was an ancient baptismal font of stone. In fact, it was a pile of roughly hewn stone steps, five or six feet high, with a block of stone at the summit, in which was a hollow about as big as a wash-bowl. It was full of rainwater.

The church seems to be St. Andrew's Church, Lower Bebbington, built in 1100.

September 1st.—To-day we leave the Rock Ferry Hotel, where we have spent nearly four weeks. It is a comfortable place, and we have had a good table and have been kindly treated. We occupied a large parlor, extending through the whole breadth of the house, with a bow-window, looking towards Liverpool, and adown the intervening river, and to Birkenhead, on the hither side. The river would be a pleasanter object, if it were blue and transparent, instead of such a mud-puddly hue; also, if it were always full to its brine; whereas it generally presents a margin, and sometimes a very broad one, of glistening mud, with here and there a small vessel aground on it.

Nevertheless, the parlor-window has given us a pretty good idea of the nautical business of Liverpool; the constant objects being the little black steamers puffing unquietly along, sometimes to our own ferry, sometimes beyond it to Eastham, and sometimes towing a long string of boats from Runcorn or otherwhere up the river, laden with goods, and sometimes gallanting a tall ship in or out. Some of these ships lie for days together in the river, very majestic and stately objects, often with the flag of the stars and stripes waving over them. Now and then, after a gale at sea, a vessel comes in with her masts broken short off in the midst, and with marks of rough handling about the hull. Once a week comes a Cunard steamer, with its red funnel pipe whitened by the salt spray; and, firing off cannon to announce her arrival, she moors to a large iron buoy in the middle of the river, and a few hundred yards from the stone pier of our ferry. Immediately comes poring towards her a little mail-steamer, to take away her mail-bags and such of the passengers as choose to land; and for several hours afterwards the Cunard lies with the smoke and steam coming out of her, as if she were smoking her pipe after her toilsome passage across the Atlantic. Once a fortnight comes an American steamer of the Collins line; and then the Cunard salutes her with cannon, to which the Collins responds, and moors herself to another iron buoy, not far from the Cunard. When they go to sea, it is with similar salutes; the two vessels paying each other the more ceremonious respect, because they are inimical and jealous of each other.

Besides these, there are other steamers of all sorts and sizes, for pleasure-excursions, for regular trips to Dublin, the Isle of Man, and elsewhither; and vessels which are stationary, as floating lights, but which seem to relieve one another at intervals; and small vessels, with sails looking as if made of tanned leather; and schooners, and yachts, and all manner of odd-looking craft, but none so odd as the Chinese junk. This junk lies by our own pier, and looks as if it were copied from some picture on an old teacup. Beyond all these objects we see the other side of the Mersey, with the delectably green fields opposite to us, while the shore becomes more and more thickly populated, until about two miles off we see the dense centre of the city, with the dome of the Custom House, and steeples and towers; and, close to the water, the spire of St. Nicholas; and above, and intermingled with the whole city scene, the duskiness of the coal-smoke gushing upward. Along the bank we perceive the warehouses of the Albert dock, and the Queen's tobacco warehouses, and other docks, and, nigher to us, a shipyard or two. In the evening all this sombre picture gradually darkens out of sight, and in its place appear only the lights of the city, kindling into a galaxy of earthly stars, for a long distance, up and down the shore; and, in one or two spots, the bright red gleam of a furnace, like the "red planet Mars"; and once in a while a bright, wandering beam gliding along the river, as a steamer cones or goes between us and Liverpool.

ROCK PARK.

September 2d.—We got into our new house in Rock Park yesterday. It is quite a good house, with three apartments, beside kitchen and pantry on the lower floor; and it is three stories high, with four good chambers in each story. It is a stone edifice, like almost all the English houses, and handsome in its design. The rent, without furniture, would probably have been one hundred pounds; furnished, it is one hundred and sixty pounds. Rock Park, as the locality is called, is private property, and is now nearly covered with residences for professional people, merchants, and others of the upper middling class; the houses being mostly built, I suppose, on speculation, and let to those who occupy them. It is the quietest place imaginable, there being a police station at the entrance, and the officer on duty allows no ragged or ill-looking person to pass. There being a toll, it precludes all unnecessary passage of carriages; and never were there more noiseless streets than those that give access to these pretty residences. On either side there is thick shrubbery, with glimpses through it of the ornamented portals, or into the trim gardens with smooth-shaven lawns, of no large extent, but still affording reasonable breathing-space. They are really an improvement on anything, save what the very rich can enjoy, in America. The former occupants of our house (Mrs. Campbell and family) having been fond of flowers, there are many rare varieties in the garden, and we are told that there is scarcely a month in the year when a flower will not be found there.

The house is respectably, though not very elegantly, furnished. It was a dismal, rainy day yesterday, and we had a coal-fire in the sitting-room, beside which I sat last evening as twilight came on, and thought, rather sadly, how many times we have changed our home since we were married. In the first place, our three years at the Old Manse; then a brief residence at Salem, then at Boston, then two or three years at Salem again; then at Lenox, then at West Newton, and then again at Concord, where we imagined that we were fixed for life, but spent only a year. Then this farther flight to England, where we expect to spend four years, and afterwards another year or two in Italy, during all which time we shall have no real home. For, as I sat in this English house, with the chill, rainy English twilight brooding over the lawn, and a coal-fire to keep me comfortable on the first evening of September, and the picture of a stranger—the dead husband of Mrs. Campbell—gazing down at me from above the mantel-piece,—I felt that I never should be quite at home here. Nevertheless, the fire was very comfortable to look at, and the shape of the fireplace—an arch, with a deep cavity—was an improvement on the square, shallow opening of an American coal-grate.

September 7th.—It appears by the annals of Liverpool, contained in Gore's Directory, that in 1076 there was a baronial castle built by Roger de Poictiers on the site of the present St. George's Church. It was taken down in 1721. The church now stands at one of the busiest points of the principal street of the city. The old Church of St. Nicholas, founded about the time of the Conquest, and more recently rebuilt, stood within a quarter of a mile of the castle.

In 1150, Birkenhead Priory was founded on the Cheshire side of the Mersey. The monks used to ferry passengers across to Liverpool until 1282, when Woodside Ferry was established,—twopence for a horseman, and a farthing for a foot-passenger. Steam ferry-boats now cross to Birkenhead, Monk's Ferry, and Woodside every ten minutes; and I believe there are large hotels at all these places, and many of the business men of Liverpool have residences in them.

In 1252 a tower was built by Sir John Stanley, which continued to be a castle of defence to the Stanley family for many hundred years, and was not finally taken down till 1820, when its site had become the present Water Street, in the densest commercial centre of the city.

There appear to have been other baronial castles and residences in different parts of the city, as a hall in old Hall Street, built by Sir John de la More, on the site of which a counting-house now stands. This knightly family of De la More sometimes supplied mayors to the city, as did the family of the Earls of Derby.

About 1582, Edward, Earl of Derby, maintained two hundred and fifty citizens of Liverpool, fed sixty aged persons twice a day, and provided twenty-seven hundred persons with meat, drink, and money every Good Friday.

In 1644, Prince Rupert besieged the town for twenty-four days, and finally took it by storm. This was June 26th, and the Parliamentarians, under Sir John Meldrum, repossessed it the following October.

In 1669 the Mayor of Liverpool kept an inn.

In 1730 there was only one carriage in town, and no stage-coach came nearer than Warrington, the roads being impassable.

In 1734 the Earl of Derby gave a great entertainment in the tower.

In 1737 the Mayor was George Norton, a saddler, who frequently took, the chair with his leather apron on. His immediate predecessor seems to have been the Earl of Derby, who gave the above-mentioned entertainment during his mayoralty. Where George's Dock now is, there used to be a battery of fourteen eighteen-pounders for the defence of the town, and the old sport of bull-baiting was carried on in that vicinity, close to the Church of St. Nicholas.

September 12th.—On Saturday a young man was found wandering about in West Derby, a suburb of Liverpool, in a state of insanity, and, being taken before a magistrate, he proved to be an American. As he seemed to be in a respectable station of life, the magistrate sent the master of the workhouse to me, in order to find out whether I would take the responsibility of his expenses, rather than have him put in the workhouse. My clerk went to investigate the matter, and brought me his papers. His name proves to be —— ———, belonging to ———, twenty-five years of age. One of the papers was a passport from our legation in Naples; likewise there was a power of attorney from his mother (who seems to have been married a second time) to dispose of some property of hers abroad; a hotel bill, also, of some length, in which were various charges for wine; and, among other evidences of low funds, a pawnbroker's receipt for a watch, which he had pledged at five pounds. There was also a ticket for his passage to America, by the screw steamer Andes, which sailed on Wednesday last. The clerk found him to the last degree incommunicative; and nothing could be discovered from him but what the papers disclosed. There were about a dozen utterly unintelligible notes among the papers, written by himself since his derangement.

I decided to put him into the insane hospital, where he now accordingly is, and to-morrow (by which time he may be in a more conversable mood) I mean to pay him a visit.

The clerk tells me that there is now, and has been for three years, an American lady in the Liverpool almshouse, in a state of insanity. She is very accomplished, especially in music; but in all this time it has been impossible to find out who she is, or anything about her connections or previous life. She calls herself Jenny Lind, and as for any other name or identity she keeps her own secret.

September 14th.—It appears that Mr. ——— (the insane young gentleman) being unable to pay his bill at the inn where he was latterly staying, the landlord had taken possession of his luggage, and satisfied himself in that way. My clerk, at my request, has taken his watch out of pawn. It proves to be not a very good one, though doubtless worth more than five pounds, for which it was pledged. The Governor of the Lunatic Asylum wrote me yesterday, stating that the patient was in want of a change of clothes, and that, according to his own account, he had left his luggage at the American Hotel. After office-hours, I took a cab, and set out with my clerk, to pay a visit to the Asylum, taking the American Hotel in our way.

The American Hotel is a small house, not at all such a one as American travellers of any pretension would think of stopping at, but still very respectable, cleanly, and with a neat sitting-room, where the guests might assemble, after the American fashion. We asked for the landlady, and anon down she came, a round, rosy, comfortable-looking English dame of fifty or thereabouts. On being asked whether she knew a Mr. ———, she readily responded that he had been there, but, had left no luggage, having taken it away before paying his bill; and that she had suspected him of meaning to take his departure without paying her at all. Hereupon she had traced him to the hotel before mentioned, where she had found that he had stayed two nights,—but was then, I think, gone from thence. Afterwards she encountered him again, and, demanding her due, went with him to a pawnbroker's, where he pledged his watch and paid her. This was about the extent of the landlady's knowledge of the matter. I liked the woman very well, with her shrewd, good-humored, worldly, kindly disposition.

Then we proceeded to the Lunatic Asylum, to which we were admitted by a porter at the gate. Within doors we found some neat and comely servant-women, one of whom showed us into a handsome parlor, and took my card to the Governor. There was a large bookcase, with a glass front, containing handsomely bound books, many of which, I observed, were of a religious character. In a few minutes the Governor came in, a middle-aged man, tall, and thin for an Englishman, kindly and agreeable enough in aspect, but not with the marked look of a man of force and ability. I should not judge from his conversation that he was an educated man, or that he had any scientific acquaintance with the subject of insanity.

He said that Mr. ——— was still quite incommunicative, and not in a very promising state; that I had perhaps better defer seeing him for a few days; that it would not be safe, at present, to send him home to America without an attendant, and this was about all. But on returning home I learned from my wife, who had had a call from Mrs. Blodgett, that Mrs. Blodgett knew Mr. ——— and his mother, who has recently been remarried to a young husband, and is now somewhere in Italy. They seemed to have boarded at Mrs. Blodgett's house on their way to the Continent, and within a week or two, an acquaintance and pastor of Mr. ———, the Rev. Dr. ———, has sailed for America. If I could only have caught him, I could have transferred the care, expense, and responsibility of the patient to him. The Governor of the Asylum mentioned, by the way, that Mr. ——— describes himself as having been formerly a midshipman in the navy.

I walked through the St. James's cemetery yesterday. It is a very pretty place, dug out of the rock, having formerly, I believe, been a stone-quarry. It is now a deep and spacious valley, with graves and monuments on its level and grassy floor, through which run gravel-paths, and where grows luxuriant shrubbery. On one of the steep sides of the valley, hewn out of the rock, are tombs, rising in tiers, to the height of fifty feet or more; some of them cut directly into the rock with arched portals, and others built with stone. On the other side the bank is of earth, and rises abruptly, quite covered with trees, and looking very pleasant with their green shades. It was a warm and sunny day, and the cemetery really had a most agreeable aspect. I saw several gravestones of Americans; but what struck me most was one line of an epitaph on an English woman, "Here rests in peace a virtuous wife." The statue of Huskisson stands in the midst of the valley, in a kind of mausoleum, with a door of plate-glass, through which you look at the dead statesman's effigy.

September 22d.—. . . . Some days ago an American captain came to the office, and said he had shot one of his men, shortly after sailing from New Orleans, and while the ship was still in the river. As he described the event, he was in peril of his life from this man, who was an Irishman; and he fired his pistol only when the man was coming upon him, with a knife in one hand, and some other weapon of offence in the other, while he himself was struggling with one or two more of the crew. He was weak at the time, having just recovered from the yellow fever. The shots struck the man in the pit of the stomach, and he lived only about a quarter of an hour. No magistrate in England has a right to arrest or examine the captain, unless by a warrant from the Secretary of State, on the charge of murder. After his statement to me, the mother of the slain man went to the police officer, and accused him of killing her son. Two or three days since, moreover, two of the sailors came before me, and gave their account of the matter; and it looked very differently from that of the captain. According to them, the man had no idea of attacking the captain, and was so drunk that he could not keep himself upright without assistance. One of these two men was actually holding him up when the captain fired two barrels of his pistol, one immediately after the other, and lodged two balls in the pit of his stomach. The man sank down at once, saying, "Jack, I am killed,"—and died very shortly. Meanwhile the captain drove this man away, under threats of shooting him likewise. Both the seamen described the captain's conduct, both then and during the whole voyage, as outrageous, and I do not much doubt that it was so. They gave their evidence like men who wished to tell the truth, and were moved by no more than a natural indignation at the captain's wrong.

I did not much like the captain from the first,—a hard, rough man, with little education, and nothing of the gentleman about him, a red face and a loud voice. He seemed a good deal excited, and talked fast and much about the event, but yet not as if it had sunk deeply into him. He observed that he "would not have had it happen for a thousand dollars," that being the amount of detriment which he conceives himself to suffer by the ineffaceable blood-stain on his hand. In my opinion it is little short of murder, if at all; but what would be murder on shore is almost a natural occurrence when done in such a hell on earth as one of these ships, in the first hours of the voyage. The men are then all drunk,— some of them often in delirium tremens; and the captain feels no safety for his life except in making himself as terrible as a fiend. It is the universal testimony that there is a worse set of sailors in these short voyages between Liverpool and America than in any other trade whatever.

There is no probability that the captain will ever be called to account for this deed. He gave, at the time, his own version of the affair in his log-book; and this was signed by the entire crew, with the exception of one man, who had hidden himself in the hold in terror of the captain. His mates will sustain his side of the question; and none of the sailors would be within reach of the American courts, even should they be sought for.

October 1st.—On Thursday I went with Mr. Ticknor to Chester by railway. It is quite an indescribable old town, and I feel at last as if I had had a glimpse of old England. The wall encloses a large space within the town, but there are numerous houses and streets not included within its precincts. Some of the principal streets pass under the ancient gateways; and at the side there are flights of steps, giving access to the summit. Around the top of the whole wall, a circuit of about two miles, there runs a walk, well paved with flagstones, and broad enough for three persons to walk abreast. On one side—that towards the country—there is a parapet of red freestone three or four feet high. On the other side there are houses, rising up immediately from the wall, so that they seem a part of it. The height of it, I suppose, may be thirty or forty feet, and, in some parts, you look down from the parapet into orchards, where there are tall apple-trees, and men on the branches, gathering fruit, and women and children among the grass, filling bags or baskets. There are prospects of the surrounding country among the buildings outside the wall; at one point, a view of the river Dee, with an old bridge of arches. It is all very strange, very quaint, very curious to see how the town has overflowed its barrier, and how, like many institutions here, the ancient wall still exists, but is turned to quite another purpose than what it was meant for,—so far as it serves any purpose at all. There are three or four towers in the course of the circuit; the most interesting being one from the top of which King Charles the First is said to have seen the rout of his army by the Parliamentarians. We ascended the short flight of steps that led up into the tower, where an old man pointed out the site of the battle-field, now thickly studded with buildings, and told us what we had already learned from the guide-book. After this we went into the cathedral, which I will perhaps describe on some other occasion, when I shall have seen more of it, and to better advantage. The cloisters gave us the strongest impression of antiquity; the stone arches being so worn and blackened by time. Still an American must always have imagined a better cathedral than this. There were some immense windows of painted glass, but all modern. In the chapter-house we found a coal-fire burning in a grate, and a large heap of old books—the library of the cathedral—in a discreditable state of decay,—mildewed, rotten, neglected for years. The sexton told us that they were to be arranged and better ordered. Over the door, inside, hung two failed and tattered banners, being those of the Cheshire regiment.

The most utterly indescribable feature of Chester is the Rows, which every traveller has attempted to describe. At the height of several feet above some of the oldest streets, a walk runs through the front of the houses, which project over it. Back of the walk there are shops; on the outer side is a space of two or three yards, where the shopmen place their tables, and stands, and show-cases; overhead, just high enough for persons to stand erect, a ceiling. At frequent intervals little narrow passages go winding in among the houses, which all along are closely conjoined, and seem to have no access or exit, except through the shops, or into these narrow passages, where you can touch each side with your elbows, and the top with your hand. We penetrated into one or two of them, and they smelt anciently and disagreeably. At one of the doors stood a pale-looking, but cheerful and good-natured woman, who told us that she had come to that house when first married, twenty-one years before, and had lived there ever since; and that she felt as if she had been buried through the best years of her life. She allowed us to peep into her kitchen and parlor,—small, dingy, dismal, but yet not wholly destitute of a home look. She said that she had seen two or three coffins in a day, during cholera times, carried out of that narrow passage into which her door opened. These avenues put me in mind of those which run through ant-hills, or those which a mole makes underground. This fashion of Rows does not appear to be going out; and, for aught I can see, it may last hundreds of years longer. When a house becomes so old as to be untenantable, it is rebuilt, and the new one is fashioned like the old, so far as regards the walk running through its front. Many of the shops are very good, and even elegant, and these Rows are the favorite places of business in Chester. Indeed, they have many advantages, the passengers being sheltered from the rain, and there being within the shops that dimmer light by which tradesmen like to exhibit their wares.

A large proportion of the edifices in the Rows must be comparatively modern; but there are some very ancient ones, with oaken frames visible on the exterior. The Row, passing through these houses, is railed with oak, so old that it has turned black, and grown to be as hard as stone, which it might be mistaken for, if one did not see where names and initials have been cut into it with knives at some bygone period. Overhead, cross-beams project through the ceiling so low as almost to hit the head. On the front of one of these buildings was the inscription, "GOD'S PROVIDENCE IS MINE INHERITANCE," said to have been put there by the occupant of the house two hundred years ago, when the plague spared this one house only in the whole city. Not improbably the inscription has operated as a safeguard to prevent the demolition of the house hitherto; but a shopman of an adjacent dwelling told us that it was soon to be taken down.

Here and there, about some of the streets through which the Rows do not run, we saw houses of very aged aspect, with steep, peaked gables. The front gable-end was supported on stone pillars, and the sidewalk passed beneath. Most of these old houses seemed to be taverns,—the Black Bear, the Green Dragon, and such names. We thought of dining at one of them, but, on inspection, they looked rather too dingy and close, and of questionable neatness. So we went to the Royal Hotel, where we probably fared just as badly at much more expense, and where there was a particularly gruff and crabbed old waiter, who, I suppose, thought himself free to display his surliness because we arrived at the hotel on foot. For my part, I love to see John Bull show himself. I must go again and again and again to Chester, for I suppose there is not a more curious place in the world.

Mr. Ticknor, who has been staying at Rock Park with us since Tuesday, has steamed away in the Canada this morning. His departure seems to make me feel more abroad, more dissevered from my native country, than before.

October 3d.—Saturday evening, at six, I went to dine with Mr. Aiken, a wealthy merchant here, to meet two of the sons of Burns. There was a party of ten or twelve, Mr. Aiken and his two daughters included. The two sons of Burns have both been in the Indian army, and have attained the ranks of Colonel and Major; one having spent thirty, and the other twenty-seven years in India. They are now old gentlemen of sixty and upwards, the elder with a gray head, the younger with a perfectly white one,—rather under than above the middle stature, and with a British roundness of figure,—plain, respectable, intelligent-looking persons, with quiet manners. I saw no resemblance in either of them to any portrait of their father. After the ladies left the table, I sat next to the Major, the younger of the two, and had a good deal of talk with him. He seemed a very kindly and social man, and was quite ready to speak about his father, nor was he at all reluctant to let it be seen how much he valued the glory of being descended from the poet. By and by, at Mr. Aiken's instance, he sang one of Burns's songs,—the one about "Annie" and the "rigs of barley." He sings in a perfectly simple style, so that it is little more than a recitative, and yet the effect is very good as to humor, sense, and pathos. After rejoining the ladies, he sang another, "A posie for my ain dear May," and likewise "A man's a man for a' that." My admiration of his father, and partly, perhaps, my being an American, gained me some favor with him, and he promised to give me what he considered the best engraving of Burns, and some other remembrance of him. The Major is that son of Burns who spent an evening at Abbotsford with Sir Walter Scott, when, as Lockhart writes, "the children sang the ballads of their sires." He spoke with vast indignation of a recent edition of his father's works by Robert Chambers, in which the latter appears to have wronged the poet by some misstatements.—I liked them both and they liked me, and asked me to go and see there at Cheltenham, where they reside. We broke up at about midnight.

The members of this dinner-party were of the more liberal tone of thinking here in Liverpool. The Colonel and Major seemed to be of similar principles; and the eyes of the latter glowed, when he sang his father's noble verse, "The rank is but the guinea's stamp," etc. It would have been too pitiable if Burns had left a son who could not feel the spirit of that verse.

October 8th.—Coning to my office, two or three mornings ago, I found Mrs. ———, the mother of Mr. ———, the insane young man of whom I had taken charge. She is a lady of fifty or thereabouts, and not very remarkable anyway, nor particularly lady-like. However, she was just come off a rapid journey, having travelled from Naples, with three small children, without taking rest, since my letter reached her. A son (this proved to be her new husband) of about twenty had come with her to the Consulate. She was, of course, infinitely grieved about the young man's insanity, and had two or three bursts of tears while we talked the matter over. She said he was the hope of her life,—the best, purest, most innocent child that ever was, and wholly free from every kind of vice. But it appears that he had a previous attack of insanity, lasting three months, about three years ago.

After I had told her all I knew about him, including my personal observations at a visit a week or two since, we drove in a cab to the Asylum. It must have been a dismal moment to the poor lady, as we entered the gateway through a tall, prison-like wall. Being ushered into the parlor, the Governor soon appeared, and informed us that Mr. ——— had had a relapse within a few days, and was not now so well as when I saw him. He complains of unjust confinement, and seems to consider himself, if I rightly understand, under persecution for political reasons. The Governor, however, proposed to call him down, and I took my leave, feeling that it would be indelicate to be present at his first interview with his mother. So here ended my guardianship of the poor young fellow.

In the afternoon I called at the Waterloo Hotel, where Mrs. ——— was staying, and found her in the coffee-room with the children. She had determined to take a lodging in the vicinity of the Asylum, and was going to remove thither as soon as the children had had something to eat. They seemed to be pleasant and well-behaved children, and impressed me more favorably than the mother, whom I suspect to be rather a foolish woman, although her present grief makes her appear in a more respectable light than at other times. She seemed anxious to impress me with the respectability and distinction of her connections in America, and I had observed the same tendency in the insane patient, at my interview with him. However, she has undoubtedly a mother's love for this poor shatterbrain, and this may weigh against the folly of her marrying an incongruously youthful second husband, and many other follies.

This was day before yesterday, and I have heard nothing of her since. The same day I had applications for assistance in two other domestic affairs; one from an Irishman, naturalized in America, who wished me to get him a passage thither, and to take charge of his wife and family here, at my own private expense, until he could remit funds to carry them across. Another was from an Irishman, who had a power of attorney from a countrywoman of his in America, to find and take charge of an infant whom she had left in the Liverpool work-house, two years ago. I have a great mind to keep a list of all the business I am consulted about and employed in. It would be very curious. Among other things, all penniless Americans, or pretenders to Americanism, look upon me as their banker; and I could ruin myself any week, if I had not laid down a rule to consider every applicant for assistance an impostor until he prove himself a true and responsible man,—which it is very difficult to do. Yesterday there limped in a very respectable-looking old man, who described himself as a citizen of Baltimore, who had been on a trip to England and elsewhere, and, being detained longer than he expected, and having had an attack of rheumatism, was now short of funds to pay his passage home, and hoped that I would supply the deficiency. He had quite a plain, homely, though respectable manner, and, for aught I know, was the very honestest man alive; but as he could produce no kind of proof of his character and responsibility, I very quietly explained the impossibility of my helping him. I advised him to try to obtain a passage on board of some Baltimore ship, the master of which might be acquainted with him, or, at all events, take his word for payment, after arrival. This he seemed inclined to do, and took his leave. There was a decided aspect of simplicity about this old man, and yet I rather judge him to be an impostor.

It is easy enough to refuse money to strangers and unknown people, or whenever there may be any question about identity; but it will not be so easy when I am asked for money by persons whom I know, but do not like to trust. They shall meet the eternal "No," however.

October 13th.—In Ormerod's history of Chester it is mentioned that Randal, Earl of Chester, having made an inroad into Wales about 1225, the Welshmen gathered in mass against him, and drove him into the castle of Nothelert in Flintshire. The Earl sent for succor to the Constable of Chester, Roger Lacy, surnamed "Hell," on account of his fierceness. It was then fair-time at Chester, and the constable collected a miscellaneous rabble of fiddlers, players, cobblers, tailors, and all manner of debauched people, and led them to the relief of the Earl. At sight of this strange army the Welshmen fled; and forever after the Earl assigned to the constable of Chester power over all fiddlers, shoemakers, etc., within the bounds of Cheshire. The constable retained for himself and his heirs the control of the shoemakers; and made over to his own steward, Dutton, that of the fiddlers and players, and for many hundreds of years afterwards the Duttons of Dutton retained the power. On midsummer-day, they used to ride through Chester, attended by all the minstrels playing on their several instruments, to the Church of St. John, and there renew their licenses. It is a good theme for a legend. Sir Peter Leycester, writing in Charles the Second's time, copies the Latin deed from the constable to Dutton; rightly translated, it seems to mean "the magisterial power over all the lewd people . . . . in the whole of Cheshire," but the custom grew into what is above stated. In the time of Henry VII., the Duttons claimed, by prescriptive right, that the Cheshire minstrels should deliver them, at the feast of St. John, four bottles of wine and a lance, and that each separate minstrel should pay fourpence halfpenny. . . .

Another account says Ralph Dutton was the constable's son-in-law, and "a lusty youth."

October 19th.—Coming to the ferry this morning a few minutes before the boat arrived from town, I went into the ferry-house, a small stone edifice, and found there an Irishman, his wife and three children, the oldest eight or nine years old, and all girls. There was a good fire burning in the room, and the family was clustered round it, apparently enjoying the warmth very much; but when I went in both husband and wife very hospitably asked me to come to the fire, although there was not more than room at it for their own party. I declined on the plea that I was warm enough, and then the woman said that they were very cold, having been long on the road. The man was gray-haired and gray-bearded, clad in an old drab overcoat, and laden with a huge bag, which seemed to contain bedclothing or something of the kind. The woman was pale, with a thin, anxious, wrinkled face, but with a good and kind expression. The children were quite pretty, with delicate faces, and a look of patience and endurance in them, but yet as if they had suffered as little as they possibly could. The two elder were cuddled up close to the father, the youngest, about four years old, sat in its mother's lap, and she had taken off its small shoes and stockings, and was warming its feet at the fire. Their little voices had a sweet and kindly sound as they talked in low tones to their parents and one another. They all looked very shabby, and yet had a decency about them; and it was touching to see how they made themselves at home at this casual fireside, and got all the comfort they could out of the circumstances. By and by two or three market-women came in and looked pleasantly at them, and said a word or two to the children.

They did not beg of me, as I supposed they would; but after looking at them awhile, I pulled out a piece of silver, and handed it to one of the little girls. She took it very readily, as if she partly expected it, and then the father and mother thanked me, and said they had been travelling a long distance, and had nothing to subsist upon, except what they picked up on the road. They found it impossible to live in England, and were now on their way to Liverpool, hoping to get a passage back to Ireland, where, I suppose, extreme poverty is rather better off than here. I heard the little girl say that she should buy bread with the money. There is not much that can be caught in the description of this scene; but it made me understand, better than before, how poor people feel, wandering about in such destitute circumstances, and how they suffer; and yet how they have a life not quite miserable, after all, and how family love goes along with them. Soon the boat arrived at the pier, and we all went on board; and as I sat in the cabin, looking up through a broken pane in the skylight, I saw the woman's thin face, with its anxious, motherly aspect; and the youngest child in her arms, shrinking from the chill wind, but yet not impatiently; and the eldest of the girls standing close by with her expression of childish endurance, but yet so bright and intelligent that it would evidently take but a few days to make a happy and playful child of her. I got into the interior of this poor family, and understand, through sympathy, more of them than I can tell. I am getting to possess some of the English indifference as to beggars and poor people; but still, whenever I come face to face with them, and have any intercourse, it seems as if they ought to be the better for me. I wish, instead of sixpence, I had given the poor family ten shillings, and denied it to a begging subscriptionist, who has just fleeced me to that amount. How silly a man feels in this latter predicament!

I have had a good many visitors at the Consulate from the United States within a short time,—among others, Mr. D. D. Barnard, our late minister to Berlin, returning homeward to-day by the Arctic; and Mr. Sickles, Secretary of Legation to London, a fine-looking, intelligent, gentlemanly young man. . . . With him came Judge Douglas, the chosen man of Young America. He is very short, extremely short, but has an uncommonly good head, and uncommon dignity without seeming to aim at it, being free and simple in manners. I judge him to be a very able man, with the Western sociability and free-fellowship. Generally I see no reason to be ashamed of my countrymen who come out here in public position, or otherwise assuming the rank of gentlemen.

October 20th.—One sees incidents in the streets here, occasionally, which could not be seen in an American city. For instance, a week or two since, I was passing a quiet-looking, elderly gentleman, when, all of a sudden, without any apparent provocation, he uplifted his stick, and struck a black-gowned boy a smart blow on the shoulders. The boy looked at him wofully and resentfully, but said nothing, nor can I imagine why the thing was done. In Tythebarne Street to-day I saw a woman suddenly assault a man, clutch at his hair, and cuff him about the ears. The man, who was of decent aspect enough, immediately took to his heels, full speed, and the woman ran after him, and, as far as I could discern the pair, the chase continued.

October 22d.—At a dinner-party at Mr. Holland's last evening, a gentleman, in instance of Charles Dickens's unweariability, said that during some theatrical performances in Liverpool he acted in play and farce, spent the rest of the night making speeches, feasting, and drinking at table, and ended at seven o'clock in the morning by jumping leap-frog over the backs of the whole company.

In Moore's diary he mentions a beautiful Guernsey lily having been given to his wife, and says that the flower was originally from Guernsey. A ship from there had been wrecked on the coast of Japan, having many of the lilies on board, and the next year the flowers appeared,—springing up, I suppose, on the wave-beaten strand.

Wishing to send a letter to a dead man, who may be supposed to have gone to Tophet,—throw it into the fire.

Sir Arthur Aston had his brains beaten out with his own wooden leg, at the storming of Tredagh in Ireland by Cromwell.

In the county of Cheshire, many centuries ago, there lived a half-idiot, named Nixon, who had the gift of prophecy, and made many predictions about places, families, and important public events, since fulfilled. He seems to have fallen into fits of insensibility previous to uttering his prophecies.

The family of Mainwaring (pronounced Mannering), of Bromborough, had an ass's head for a crest.

"Richard Dawson, being sick of the plague, and perceiving he must die, rose out of his bed and made his grave, and caused his nephew to cast straw into the grave, which was not far from the house, and went and laid him down in the said grave, and caused clothes to be laid upon him, and so departed out of this world. This he did because he was a strong man, and heavier than his said nephew and a serving-wench were able to bury. He died about the 24th of August. Thus was I credibly told he did, 1625." This was in the township of Malpas, recorded in the parish register.

At Bickley Hall, taken down a few years ago, used to be shown the room where the body of the Earl of Leicester was laid for a whole twelvemonth,—1659 to 1660,—he having been kept unburied all that time, owing to a dispute which of his heirs should pay his funeral expenses.

November 5th.—We all, together with Mr. Squarey, went to Chester last Sunday, and attended the cathedral service. A great deal of ceremony, and not unimposing, but rather tedious before it was finished,—occupying two hours or more. The Bishop was present, but did nothing except to pronounce the benediction. In America the sermon is the principal thing; but here all this magnificent ceremonial of prayer and chanted responses and psalms and anthems was the setting to a short, meagre discourse, which would not have been considered of any account among the elaborate intellectual efforts of New England ministers. While this was going on, the light came through the stained glass windows and fell upon the congregation, tingeing them with crimson. After service we wandered about the aisles, and looked at the tombs and monuments,—the oldest of which was that of some nameless abbot, with a staff and mitre half obliterated from his tomb, which was under a shallow arch on one side of the cathedral. There were also marbles on the walls, and lettered stones in the pavement under our feet; but chiefly, if not entirely, of modern date. We lunched at the Royal Hotel, and then walked round the city walls, also crossing the bridge of one great arch over the Dee, and penetrating as far into Wales as the entrance of the Marquis of Westminster's Park at Eaton. It was, I think, the most lovely day as regards weather that I have seen in England.

I passed, to-day, a man chanting a ballad in the street about a recent murder, in a voice that had innumerable cracks in it, and was most lugubrious. The other day I saw a man who was reading in a loud voice what seemed to be an account of the late riots and loss of life in Wigan. He walked slowly along the street as he read, surrounded by a small crowd of men, women, and children; and close by his elbow stalked a policeman, as if guarding against a disturbance.

November 14th.—There is a heavy dun fog on the river and over the city to-day, the very gloomiest atmosphere that ever I was acquainted with.

On the river the steamboats strike gongs or ring bells to give warning of their approach. There are lamps burning in the counting-rooms and lobbies of the warehouses, and they gleam distinctly through the windows.

The other day, at the entrance of the market-house, I saw a woman sitting in a small hand-wagon, apparently for the purpose of receiving alms. There was no attendant at hand; but I noticed that one or two persons who passed by seemed to inquire whether she wished her wagon to be moved. Perhaps this is her mode of making progress about the city, by the voluntary aid of boys and other people who help to drag her. There is something in this—I don't yet well know what—that has impressed me, as if I could make a romance out of the idea of a woman living in this manner a public life, and moving about by such means.

November 29th.—Mr. H. A. B. told me of his friend Mr. ——— (who was formerly attache to the British Legation at Washington, and whom I saw at Concord), that his father, a clergyman, married a second wife. After the marriage, the noise of a coffin being nightly carried down the stairs was heard in the parsonage. It could be distinguished when the coffin reached a certain broad lauding and rested on it. Finally, his father had to remove to another residence. Besides this, Mr. ——— had had another ghostly experience,—having seen a dim apparition of an uncle at the precise instant when the latter died in a distant place. The attache is a credible and honorable fellow, and talks of these matters as if he positively believed them. But Ghostland lies beyond the jurisdiction of veracity.

In a garden near Chester, in taking down a summer-house, a tomb was discovered beneath it, with a Latin inscription to the memory of an old doctor of medicine, William Bentley, who had owned the place long ago, and died in 1680. And his dust and bones had lain beneath all the merry times in the summer-house.

December 1st.—It is curious to observe how many methods people put in practice here to pick up a halfpenny. Yesterday I saw a man standing bareheaded and barelegged in the mud and misty weather, playing on a fife, in hopes to get a circle of auditors. Nobody, however, seemed to take any notice.

Very often a whole band of musicians will strike up,— passing a hat round after playing a tune or two. On board the ferry, until the coldest weather began, there were always some wretched musicians, with an old fiddle, an old clarinet, and an old verdigrised brass bugle, performing during the passage, and, as the boat neared the shore, sending round one of their number to gather contributions in the hollow of the brass bugle. They were a very shabby set, and must have made a very scanty living at best. Sometimes it was a boy with an accordion, and his sister, a smart little girl, with a timbrel,—which, being so shattered that she could not play on it, she used only to collect halfpence in. Ballad-singers, or rather chanters or croakers, are often to be met with in the streets, but hand-organ players are not more frequent than in our cities.

I still observe little girls and other children barelegged and barefooted on the wet sidewalks. There certainly never was anything so dismal as the November weather has been; never any real sunshine; almost always a mist; sometimes a dense fog, like slightly rarefied wool, pervading the atmosphere.

An epitaph on a person buried on a hillside in Cheshire, together with some others, supposed to have died of the plague, and therefore not admitted into the churchyards:—

"Think it not strange our bones ly here,

Thine may ly thou knowst not where."

Elizabeth Hampson.

These graves were near the remains of two rude stone crosses, the purpose of which was not certainly known, although they were supposed to be boundary marks. Probably, as the plague-corpses were debarred from sanctified ground, the vicinity of these crosses was chosen as having a sort of sanctity.

"Bang beggar,"—an old Cheshire term for a parish beadle.

Hawthorne Hall, Cheshire, Macclesfield Hundred, Parish of Wilmslow, and within the hamlet of Morley. It was vested at an early period in the Lathoms of Irlam, Lancaster County, and passed through the Leighs to the Pages of Earlshaw. Thomas Leigh Page sold it to Mr. Ralph Bower of Wilmslow, whose children owned it in 1817. The Leighs built a chancel in the church of Wilmslow, where some of them are buried, their arms painted in the windows. The hall is an "ancient, respectable mansion of brick."

December 2d.—Yesterday, a chill, misty December day, yet I saw a woman barefooted in the street, not to speak of children.

Cold and uncertain as the weather is, there is still a great deal of small trade carried on in the open air. Women and men sit in the streets with a stock of combs and such small things to sell, the women knitting as if they sat by a fireside. Cheap crockery is laid out in the street, so far out that without any great deviation from the regular carriage-track a wheel might pass straight through it. Stalls of apples are innumerable, but the apples are not fit for a pig. In some streets herrings are very abundant, laid out on boards. Coals seem to be for sale by the wheelbarrowful. Here and there you see children with some small article for sale,—as, for instance, a girl with two linen caps. A somewhat overladen cart of coal was passing along and some small quantity of the coal fell off; no sooner had the wheels passed than several women and children gathered to the spot, like hens and chickens round a handful of corn, and picked it up in their aprons. We have nothing similar to these street-women in our country.

December 10th.—I don't know any place that brings all classes into contiguity on equal ground so completely as the waiting-room at Rock Ferry on these frosty days. The room is not more than eight feet, square, with walls of stone, and wooden benches ranged round them, and an open stove in one corner, generally well furnished with coal. It is almost always crowded, and I rather suspect that many persons who have no fireside elsewhere creep in here and spend the most comfortable part of their day.

This morning, when I looked into the room, there were one or two gentlemen and other respectable persons; but in the best place, close to the fire, and crouching almost into it, was an elderly beggar, with the raggedest of overcoats, two great rents in the shoulders of it disclosing the dingy lining, all bepatched with various stuff covered with dirt, and on his shoes and trousers the mud of an interminable pilgrimage. Owing to the posture in which he sat, I could not see his face, but only the battered crown and rim of the very shabbiest hat that ever was worn. Regardless of the presence of women (which, indeed, Englishmen seldom do regard when they wish to smoke), he was smoking a pipe of vile tobacco; but, after all, this was fortunate, because the man himself was not personally fragrant. He was terribly squalid,— terribly; and when I had a glimpse of his face, it well befitted the rest of his development,— grizzled, wrinkled, weather-beaten, yet sallow, and down-looking, with a watchful kind of eye turning upon everybody and everything, meeting the glances of other people rather boldly, yet soon shrinking away; a long thin nose, a gray beard of a week's growth; hair not much mixed with gray, but rusty and lifeless;—a miserable object; but it was curious to see how he was not ashamed of himself, but seemed to feel that he was one of the estates of the kingdom, and had as much right to live as other men. He did just as he pleased, took the best place by the fire, nor would have cared though a nobleman were forced to stand aside for him. When the steamer's bell rang, he shouldered a large and heavy pack, like a pilgrim with his burden of sin, but certainly journeying to hell instead of heaven. On board he looked round for the best position, at first stationing himself near the boiler-pipe; but, finding the deck damp underfoot, he went to the cabin-door, and took his stand on the stairs, protected from the wind, but very incommodiously placed for those who wished to pass. All this was done without any bravado or forced impudence, but in the most quiet way, merely because he was seeking his own comfort, and considered that he had a right to seek it. It was an Englishman's spirit; but in our country, I imagine, a beggar considers himself a kind of outlaw, and would hardly assume the privileges of a man in any place of public resort. Here beggary is a system, and beggars are a numerous class, and make themselves, in a certain way, respected as such. Nobody evinced the slightest disapprobation of the man's proceedings. In America, I think, we should see many aristocratic airs on such provocation, and probably the ferry people would there have rudely thrust the beggar aside; giving him a shilling, however, which no Englishman would ever think of doing. There would also have been a great deal of fun made of his squalid and ragged figure; whereas nobody smiled at him this morning, nor in any way showed the slightest disrespect. This is good; but it is the result of a state of things by no means good. For many days there has been a great deal of fog on the river, and the boats have groped their way along, continually striking their bells, while, on all sides, there are responses of bell and gong; and the vessels at anchor look shadow-like as we glide past them, and the master of one steamer shouts a warning to the master of another which he meets. The Englishmen, who hate to run any risk without an equivalent object, show a good deal of caution and timidity on these foggy days.

December 13th.—Chill, frosty weather; such an atmosphere as forebodes snow in New England, and there has been a little here. Yet I saw a barefooted young woman yesterday. The feet of these poor creatures have exactly the red complexion of their hands, acquired by constant exposure to the cold air.

At the ferry-room, this morning, was a small, thin, anxious-looking woman, with a bundle, seeming in rather poor circumstances, but decently dressed, and eying other women, I thought, with an expression of slight ill-will and distrust; also, an elderly, stout, gray-haired woman, of respectable aspect, and two young lady-like persons, quite pretty, one of whom was reading a shilling volume of James's "Arabella Stuart." They talked to one another with that up-and-down intonation which English ladies practise, and which strikes an unaccustomed ear as rather affected, especially in women of size and mass. It is very different from an American lady's mode of talking: there is the difference between color and no color; the tone variegates it. One of these young ladies spoke to me, making some remark about the weather,—the first instance I have met with of a gentlewoman's speaking to an unintroduced gentleman. Besides these, a middle-aged man of the lower class, and also a gentleman's out-door servant, clad in a drab great-coat, corduroy breeches, and drab cloth gaiters buttoned from the knee to the ankle. He complained to the other man of the cold weather; said that a glass of whiskey, every half-hour, would keep a man comfortable; and, accidentally hitting his coarse foot against one of the young lady's feet, said, "Beg pardon, ma'am,"—which she acknowledged with a slight movement of the head. Somehow or other, different classes seem to encounter one another in an easier manner than with us; the shock is less palpable. I suppose the reason is that the distinctions are real, and therefore need not be continually asserted.

Nervous and excitable persons need to talk a great deal, by way of letting off their steam.

On board the Rock Ferry steamer, a gentleman coming into the cabin, a voice addresses him from a dark corner, "How do you do, sir?"—"Speak again!" says the gentleman. No answer from the dark corner; and the gentleman repeats, "Speak again!" The speaker now comes out of the dark corner, and sits down in a place where he can be seen. "Ah!" cries the gentleman, "very well, I thank you. How do you do? I did not recognize your voice." Observable, the English caution, shown in the gentleman's not vouchsafing to say, "Very well, thank you!" till he knew his man.

What was the after life of the young man, whom Jesus, looking on, "loved," and bade him sell all that he had, and give to the poor, and take up his cross and follow him? Something very deep and beautiful might be made out of this.

December 31st.—Among the beggars of Liverpool, the hardest to encounter is a man without any legs, and, if I mistake not, likewise deficient in arms. You see him before you all at once, as if he had sprouted halfway out of the earth, and would sink down and reappear in some other place the moment he has done with you. His countenance is large, fresh, and very intelligent; but his great power lies in his fixed gaze, which is inconceivably difficult to bear. He never once removes his eye from you till you are quite past his range; and you feel it all the same, although you do not meet his glance. He is perfectly respectful; but the intentness and directness of his silent appeal is far worse than any impudence. In fact, it is the very flower of impudence. I would rather go a mile about than pass before his battery. I feel wronged by him, and yet unutterably ashamed. There must be great force in the man to produce such an effect. There is nothing of the customary squalidness of beggary about him, but remarkable trimness and cleanliness. A girl of twenty or thereabouts, who vagabondizes about the city on her hands and knees, possesses, to a considerable degree, the same characteristics. I think they hit their victims the more effectually from being below the common level of vision.

January 3d, 1854.—Night before last there was a fall of snow, about three or four inches, and, following it, a pretty hard frost. On the river, the vessels at anchor showed the snow along their yards, and on every ledge where it could lie. A blue sky and sunshine overhead, and apparently a clear atmosphere close at hand; but in the distance a mistiness became perceptible, obscuring the shores of the river, and making the vessels look dim and uncertain. The steamers were ploughing along, smoking their pipes through the frosty air. On the landing stage and in the streets, hard-trodden snow, looking more like my New England Home than anything I have yet seen. Last night the thermometer fell as low as 13 degrees, nor probably is it above 20 degrees to-day. No such frost has been known in England these forty years! and Mr. Wilding tells me that he never saw so much snow before.

January 6th.—I saw, yesterday, stopping at a cabinet-maker's shop in Church Street, a coach with four beautiful white horses, and a postilion on each near-horse; behind, in the dicky, a footman; and on the box a coachman, all dressed in livery. The coach-panel bore a coat-of-arms with a coronet, and I presume it must have been the equipage of the Earl of Derby. A crowd of people stood round, gazing at the coach and horses; and when any of them spoke, it was in a lower tone than usual. I doubt not they all had a kind of enjoyment of the spectacle, for these English are strangely proud of having a class above them.

Every Englishman runs to "The Times" with his little grievance, as a child runs to his mother.

I was sent for to the police court the other morning, in the case of an American sailor accused of robbing a shipmate at sea. A large room, with a great coal-fire burning on one side, and above it the portrait of Mr. Rushton, deceased, a magistrate of many years' continuance. A long table, with chairs, and a witness-box. One of the borough magistrates, a merchant of the city, sat at the head of the table, with paper and pen and ink before him; but the real judge was the clerk of the court, whose professional knowledge and experience governed all the proceedings. In the short time while I was waiting, two cases were tried, in the first of which the prisoner was discharged. The second case was of a woman,—a thin, sallow, hard-looking, careworn, rather young woman,—for stealing a pair of slippers out of a shop: The trial occupied five minutes or less, and she was sentenced to twenty-one days' imprisonment,—whereupon, without speaking, she looked up wildly first into one policeman's face, then into another's, at the same time wringing her hands with no theatric gesture, but because her torment took this outward shape,—and was led away. The Yankee sailor was then brought up,—an intelligent, but ruffian-like fellow,—and as the case was out of the jurisdiction of the English magistrates, and as it was not worth while to get him sent over to America for trial, he was forthwith discharged. He stole a comforter.

If mankind were all intellect, they would be continually changing, so that one age would be entirely unlike another. The great conservative is the heart, which remains the same in all ages; so that commonplaces of a thousand years' standing are as effective as ever.

Monday, February 20th.—At the police court on Saturday, I attended the case of the second mate and four seamen of the John and Albert, for assaulting, beating, and stabbing the chief mate. The chief mate has been in the hospital ever since the assault, and was brought into the court to-day to give evidence,—a man of thirty, black hair, black eyes, a dark complexion, disagreeable expression; sallow, emaciated, feeble, apparently in pain, one arm disabled. He sat bent and drawn upward, and had evidently been severely hurt, and was not yet fit to be out of bed. He had some brandy-and-water to enable him to sustain himself. He gave his evidence very clearly, beginning (sailor-like) with telling in what quarter the wind was at the time of the assault, and which sail was taken in. His testimony bore on one man only, at whom he cast a vindictive look; but I think he told the truth as far as he knew and remembered it. Of the prisoners the second mate was a mere youth, with long sandy hair, and an intelligent and not unprepossessing face, dressed as neatly as a three or four weeks' captive, with small, or no means, could well allow, in a frock-coat, and with clean linen,—the only linen or cotton shirt in the company. The other four were rude, brutish sailors, in flannel or red-baize shirts. Three of them appeared to give themselves little concern; but the fourth, a red-haired and red-bearded man,—Paraman, by name,—evidently felt the pressure of the case upon himself. He was the one whom the mate swore to have given him the first blow; and there was other evidence of his having been stabbed with a knife. The captain of the ship, the pilot, the cook, and the steward, all gave their evidence; and the general bearing of it was, that the chief mate had a devilish temper, and had misused the second mate and crew,—that the four seamen had attacked him, and that Paraman had stabbed him; while all but the steward concurred in saying that the second mate had taken no part in the affray. The steward, however, swore to having seen him strike the chief mate with a wooden marlinspike, which was broken by the blow. The magistrate dismissed all but Paraman, whom I am to send to America for trial. In my opinion the chief mate got pretty nearly what he deserved, under the code of natural justice. While business was going forward, the magistrate, Mr. Mansfield, talked about a fancy ball at which he had been present the evening before, and of other matters grave and gay. It was very informal; we sat at the table, or stood with our backs to the fire; policemen came and went; witnesses were sworn on the greasiest copy of the Gospels I ever saw, polluted by hundreds and thousands of perjured kisses; and for hours the prisoners were kept standing at the foot of the table, interested to the full extent of their capacity, while all others were indifferent. At the close of the case, the police officers and witnesses applied to me about their expenses.

Yesterday I took a walk with my wife and two children to Bebbington Church. A beautifully sunny morning. My wife and U. attended church, J. and I continued our walk. When we were at a little distance from the church, the bells suddenly chimed out with a most cheerful sound, and sunny as the morning. It is a pity we have no chimes of bells, to give the churchward summons, at home. People were standing about the ancient church-porch and among the tombstones. In the course of our walk, we passed many old thatched cottages, built of stone, and with what looked like a cow-house or pigsty at one end, making part of the cottage; also an old stone farm-house, which may have been a residence of gentility in its day. We passed, too, a small Methodist chapel, making one of a row of low brick edifices. There was a sound of prayer within. I never saw a more unbeautiful place of worship; and it had not even a separate existence for itself, the adjoining tenement being an alehouse.

The grass along the wayside was green, with a few daisies. There was green holly in the hedges, and we passed through a wood, up some of the tree-trunks of which ran clustering ivy.

February 23d.—There came to see me the other day a young gentleman with a mustache and a blue cloak, who announced himself as William Allingham, and handed me a copy of his poems, a thin volume, with paper covers, published by Routledge. I thought I remembered hearing his name, but had never seen any of his works. His face was intelligent, dark, pleasing, and not at all John-Bullish. He said that he had been employed in the Customs in Ireland, and was now going to London to live by literature,—to be connected with some newspaper, I imagine. He had been in London before, and was acquainted with some of the principal literary people,—among others, Tennyson and Carlyle. He seemed to have been on rather intimate terms with Tennyson. We talked awhile in my dingy and dusky Consulate, and he then took leave. His manners are good, and he appears to possess independence of mind.

Yesterday I saw a British regiment march down to George's Pier, to embark in the Niagara for Malta. The troops had nothing very remarkable about them; but the thousands of ragged and squalid wretches, who thronged the pier and streets to gaze on them, were what I had not seen before in such masses. This was the first populace I have beheld; for even the Irish, on the other side of the water, acquire a respectability of aspect. John Bull is going with his whole heart into the Turkish war. He is very foolish. Whatever the Czar may propose to himself, it is for the interest of democracy that he should not be easily put down. The regiment, on its way to embark, carried the Queen's colors, and, side by side with them, the banner of the 28th,—yellow, with the names of the Peninsular and other battles in which it had been engaged inscribed on it in a double column. It is a very distinguished regiment; and Mr. Henry Bright mentioned as one of its distinctions, that Washington had formerly been an officer in it. I never heard of this.

February 27th.—We walked to Woodside in the pleasant forenoon, and thence crossed to Liverpool. On our way to Woodside, we saw the remains of the old Birkenhead Priory, built of the common red freestone, much time-worn, with ivy creeping over it, and birds evidently at hone in its old crevices. These ruins are pretty extensive, and seem to be the remains of a quadrangle. A handsome modern church, likewise of the same red freestone, has been built on part of the site occupied by the Priory; and the organ was sounding within, while we walked about the premises. On some of the ancient arches, there were grotesquely carved stone faces. The old walls have been sufficiently restored to make them secure, without destroying their venerable aspect. It is a very interesting spot; and so much the more so because a modern town, with its brick and stone houses, its flags and pavements, has sprung up about the ruins, which were new a thousand years ago. The station of the Chester railway is within a hundred yards. Formerly the monks of this Priory kept the only ferry that then existed on the Mersey.

At a dinner at Mr. Bramley Moore's a little while ago, we had a prairie-hen from the West of America. It was a very delicate bird, and a gentleman carved it most skilfully to a dozen guests, and had still a second slice to offer to them.

Aboard the ferry-boat yesterday, there was a laboring man eating oysters. He took them one by one from his pocket in interminable succession, opened them with his jack-knife, swallowed each one, threw the shell overboard, and then sought for another. Having concluded his meal, he took out a clay tobacco-pipe, filled it, lighted it with a match, and smoked it,—all this, while the other passengers were looking at him, and with a perfect coolness and independence, such as no single man can ever feel in America. Here a man does not seem to consider what other people will think of his conduct, but only whether it suits his own convenience to do so and so. It may be the better way.

A French military man, a veteran of all Napoleon's wars, is now living, with a false leg and arm, both movable by springs, false teeth, a false eye, a silver nose with a flesh-colored covering, and a silver plate replacing part of the skull. He has the cross of the Legion of Honor.

March 18th.—On Saturday I went with Mr. B—— to the Dingle, a pleasant domain on the banks of the Mersey almost opposite to Rock Ferry. Walking home, we looked into Mr. Thorn's Unitarian Chapel, Mr. B——'s family's place of worship. There is a little graveyard connected with the chapel, a most uninviting and unpicturesque square of ground, perhaps thirty or forty yards across, in the midst of back fronts of city buildings. About half the space was occupied by flat tombstones, level with the ground, the remainder being yet vacant. Nevertheless, there were perhaps more names of men generally known to the world on these few tombstones than in any other churchyard in Liverpool,—Roscoe, Blanco White, and the Rev. William Enfield, whose name has a classical sound in my ears, because, when a little boy, I used to read his "Speaker" at school. In the vestry of the chapel there were many books, chiefly old theological works, in ancient print and binding, much mildewed and injured by the damp. The body of the chapel is neat, but plain, and, being not very large, has a kind of social and family aspect, as if the clergyman and his people must needs have intimate relations among themselves. The Unitarian sect in Liverpool have, as a body, great wealth and respectability.

Yesterday I walked with my wife and children to the brow of a hill, overlooking Birkenhead and Tranmere, and commanding a fine view of the river, and Liverpool beyond. All round about new and neat residences for city people are springing up, with fine names,—Eldon Terrace, Rose Cottage, Belvoir Villa, etc., etc., with little patches of ornamented garden or lawn in front, and heaps of curious rock-work, with which the English are ridiculously fond of adorning their front yards. I rather think the middling classes—meaning shopkeepers, and other respectabilities of that level—are better lodged here than in America; and, what I did not expect, the houses are a great deal newer than in our new country! Of course, this can only be the case in places circumstanced like Liverpool and its suburbs. But, scattered among these modern villas, there are old stone cottages of the rudest structure, and doubtless hundreds of years old, with thatched roofs, into which the grass has rooted itself, and now looks verdant. These cottages are in themselves as ugly as possible, resembling a large kind of pigsty; but often, by dint of the verdure on their thatch and the shrubbery clustering about them, they look picturesque.

The old-fashioned flowers in the gardens of New England—blue-bells, crocuses, primroses, foxglove, and many others—appear to be wild flowers here on English soil. There is something very touching and pretty in this fact, that the Puritans should have carried their field and hedge flowers, and nurtured theme in their gardens, until, to us, they seem entirely the product of cultivation.

March 16th.—Yesterday, at the coroner's court, attending the inquest on a black sailor who died on board an American vessel, after her arrival at this port. The court-room is capable of accommodating perhaps fifty people, dingy, with a pyramidal skylight above, and a single window on one side, opening into a gloomy back court. A private room, also lighted with a pyramidal skylight, is behind the court-room, into which I was asked, and found the coroner, a gray-headed, grave, intelligent, broad, red-faced man, with an air of some authority, well mannered and dignified, but not exactly a gentleman,—dressed in a blue coat, with a black cravat, showing a shirt-collar above it. Considering how many and what a variety of cases of the ugliest death are constantly coming before him, he was much more cheerful than could be expected, and had a kind of formality and orderliness which I suppose balances the exceptionalities with which he has to deal. In the private room with him was likewise the surgeon, who professionally attends the court. We chatted about suicide and such matters,—the surgeon, the coroner, and I,—until the American case was ready, when we adjourned to the court-room, and the coroner began the examination. The American captain was a rude, uncouth Down-Easter, about thirty years old, and sat on a bench, doubled and bent into an indescribable attitude, out of which he occasionally straightened himself, all the time toying with a ruler, or some such article. The case was one of no interest; the man had been frost-bitten, and died from natural causes, so that no censure was deserved or passed upon the captain. The jury, who had been examining the body, were at first inclined to think that the man had not been frostbitten, but that his feet had been immersed in boiling water; but, on explanation by the surgeon, readily yielded their opinion, and gave the verdict which the coroner put into their mouths, exculpating the captain from all blame. In fact, it is utterly impossible that a jury of chance individuals should not be entirely governed by the judgment of so experienced and weighty a man as the coroner. In the court-room were two or three police officers in uniform, and some other officials, a very few idle spectators, and a few witnesses waiting to be examined. And while the case was going forward, a poor-looking woman came in, and I heard her, in an undertone, telling an attendant of a death that had just occurred. The attendant received the communication in a very quiet and matter-of-course way, said that it should be attended to, and the woman retired.

THE DIARY OF A CORONER would be a work likely to meet with large popular acceptance. A dark passageway, only a few yards in extent, leads from the liveliest street in Liverpool to this coroner's court-room, where all the discussion is about murder and suicide. It seems, that, after a verdict of suicide, the corpse can only be buried at midnight, without religious rites.

"His lines are cast in pleasant places,"—applied to a successful angler.

A woman's chastity consists, like an onion, of a series of coats. You may strip off the outer ones without doing much mischief, perhaps none at all; but you keep taking off one after another, in expectation of coming to the inner nucleus, including the whole value of the matter. It proves however, that there is no such nucleus, and that chastity is diffused through the whole series of coats, is lessened with the removal of each, and vanishes with the final one, which you supposed would introduce you to the hidden pearl.

March 23d.—Mr. B. and I took a cab Saturday afternoon, and drove out of the city in the direction of Knowsley. On our way we saw many gentlemen's or rich people's places, some of them dignified with the title of Halls,—with lodges at their gates, and standing considerably removed from the road. The greater part of them were built of brick,—a material with which

I have not been accustomed to associate ideas of grandeur; but it was much in use here in Lancashire, in the Elizabethan age,—more, I think, than now. These suburban residences, however, are of much later date than Elizabeth's time. Among other places, Mr. B. called at the Hazels, the residence of Sir Thomas Birch, a kinsman of his. It is a large brick mansion, and has old trees and shrubbery about it, the latter very fine and verdant,—hazels, holly, rhododendron, etc. Mr. B. went in, and shortly afterwards Sir Thomas Birch came out,—a very frank and hospitable gentleman,—and pressed me to enter and take luncheon, which latter hospitality I declined.

His house is in very nice order. He had a good many pictures, and, amongst them, a small portrait of his mother, painted by Sir Thomas Lawrence, when a youth. It is unfinished, and when the painter was at the height of his fame, he was asked to finish it. But Lawrence, after looking at the picture, refused to retouch it, saying that there was a merit in this early sketch which he could no longer attain. It was really a very beautiful picture of a lovely woman.

Sir Thomas Birch proposed to go with us and get us admittance into Knowsley Park, where we could not possibly find entrance without his aid. So we went to the stables, where the old groom had already shown hospitality to our cabman, by giving his horse some provender, and himself some beer. There seemed to be a kindly and familiar sort of intercourse between the old servant and the Baronet, each of them, I presume, looking on their connection as indissoluble.

The gate-warden of Knowsley Park was an old woman, who readily gave us admittance at Sir Thomas Birch's request. The family of the Earl of Derby is not now at the Park. It was a very bad time of year to see it; the trees just showing the earliest symptoms of vitality, while whole acres of ground were covered with large, dry, brown ferns,—which I suppose are very beautiful when green. Two or three hares scampered out of these ferns, and sat on their hind legs looking about them, as we drove by. A sheet of water had been drawn off, in order to deepen its bed. The oaks did not seem to me so magnificent as they should be in an ancient noble property like this. A century does not accomplish so much for a tree, in this slow region, as it does in ours.

I think, however, that they were more individual and picturesque, with more character in their contorted trunks; therein somewhat resembling apple-trees. Our forest-trees have a great sameness of character, like our people,— because one and the other grow too closely.

In one part of the Park we came to a small tower, for what purpose I know not, unless as an observatory; and near it was a marble statue on a high pedestal. The statue had been long exposed to the weather, and was overgrown and ingrained with moss and lichens, so that its classic beauty was in some sort gothicized. A half-mile or so from this point, we saw the mansion of Knowsley, in the midst of a very fine prospect, with a tolerably high ridge of hills in the distance. The house itself is exceedingly vast, a front and two wings, with suites of rooms, I suppose, interminable. The oldest part, Sir Thomas Birch told us, is a tower of the time of Henry VII. Nevertheless, the effect is not overwhelming, because the edifice looks low in proportion to its great extent over the ground; and besides, a good deal of it is built of brick, with white window-frames, so that, looking at separate parts, I might think them American structures, without the smart addition of green Venetian blinds, so universal with us. Portions, however, were built of red freestone; and if I had looked at it longer, no doubt I should have admired it more. We merely drove round it from the rear to the front. It stands in my memory rather like a college or a hospital, than as the ancestral residence of a great English noble.

We left the Park in another direction, and passed through a part of Lord Sefton's property, by a private road.

By the by, we saw half a dozen policemen, in their blue coats and embroidered collars, after entering Knowsley Park; but the Earl's own servants would probably have supplied their place, had the family been at home. The mansion of Croxteth, the seat of Lord Sefton, stands near the public road, and, though large, looked of rather narrow compass after Knowsley.

The rooks were talking together very loquaciously in the high tops of the trees near Sir Thomas Birch's house, it being now their building-time. It was a very pleasant sound, the noise being comfortably softened by the remote height. Sir Thomas said that more than half a century ago the rooks used to inhabit another grove of lofty trees, close in front of the house; but being noisy, and not altogether cleanly in their habits, the ladies of the family grew weary of them and wished to remove them. Accordingly, the colony was driven away, and made their present settlement in a grove behind the house. Ever since that time not a rook has built in the ancient grove; every year, however, one or another pair of young rooks attempt to build among the deserted tree-tops, but the old rooks tear the new nest to pieces as often as it is put together. Thus, either the memory of aged individual rooks or an authenticated tradition in their society has preserved the idea that the old grove is forbidden and inauspicious to them.

A soil of General Arnold, named William Fitch Arnold, and born in 1794, now possesses the estate of Little Messenden Abbey, Bucks County, and is a magistrate for that county. He was formerly Captain of the 19th Lancers. He has now two sons and four daughters. The other three sons of General Arnold, all older than this one, and all military men, do not appear to have left children; but a daughter married to Colonel Phipps, of the Mulgrave family, has a son and two daughters. I question whether any of our true-hearted Revolutionary heroes have left a more prosperous progeny than this arch-traitor. I should like to know their feelings with respect to their ancestor.

April 3d.—I walked with J——, two days ago, to Eastham, a village on the road to Chester, and five or six miles from Rock Ferry. On our way we passed through a village, in the centre of which was a small stone pillar, standing on a pedestal of several steps, on which children were sitting and playing. I take it to have been an old Catholic cross; at least, I know not what else it is. It seemed very ancient. Eastham is the finest old English village I have seen, with many antique houses, and with altogether a rural and picturesque aspect, unlike anything in America, and yet possessing a familiar look, as if it were something I had dreamed about. There were thatched stone cottages intermixed with houses of a better kind, and likewise a gateway and gravelled walk, that perhaps gave admittance to the Squire's mansion. It was not merely one long, wide street, as in most New England villages, but there were several crooked ways, gathering the whole settlement into a pretty small compass. In the midst of it stood a venerable church of the common red freestone, with a most reverend air, considerably smaller than that of Bebbington, but more beautiful, and looking quite as old. There was ivy on its spire and elsewhere. It looked very quiet and peaceful, and as if it had received the people into its low arched door every Sabbath for many centuries. There were many tombstones about it, some level with the ground, some raised on blocks of stone, on low pillars, moss-grown and weather-worn; and probably these were but the successors of other stones that had quite crumbled away, or been buried by the accumulation of dead men's dust above them. In the centre of the churchyard stood an old yew-tree, with immense trunk, which was all decayed within, so that it is a wonder how the tree retains any life,—which, nevertheless, it does. It was called "the old Yew of Eastham," six hundred years ago!

After passing through the churchyard, we saw the village inn on the other side. The doors were fastened, but a girl peeped out of the window at us, and let us in, ushering us into a very neat parlor. There was a cheerful fire in the grate, a straw carpet on the floor, a mahogany sideboard, and a mahogany table in the middle of the room; and, on the walls, the portraits of mine host (no doubt) and of his wife and daughters,—a very nice parlor, and looking like what I might have found in a country tavern at home, only this was an ancient house, and there is nothing at home like the glimpse, from the window, of the church, and its red, ivy-grown tower. I ordered some lunch, being waited on by the girl, who was very neat, intelligent, and comely,—and more respectful than a New England maid. As we came out of the inn, some village urchins left their play, and ran to me begging, calling me "Master!" They turned at once from play to begging, and, as I gave them nothing, they turned to their play again.

This village is too far from Liverpool to have been much injured as yet by the novelty of cockney residences, which have grown up almost everywhere else, so far as I have visited. About a mile from it, however, is the landing-place of a steamer (which runs regularly, except in the winter months), where a large, new hotel is built. The grounds about it are extensive and well wooded. We got some biscuits at the hotel, and I gave the waiter (a splendid gentleman in black) four halfpence, being the surplus of a shilling.

He bowed and thanked me very humbly. An American does not easily bring his mind to the small measure of English liberality to servants; if anything is to be given, we are ashamed not to give more, especially to clerical-looking persons, in black suits and white neckcloths.

I stood on the Exchange at noon, to-day, to see the 18th Regiment, the Connaught Rangers, marching down to embark for the East. They were a body of young, healthy, and cheerful-looking men, and looked greatly better than the dirty crowd that thronged to gaze at them. The royal banner of England, quartering the lion, the leopard, and the harp, waved on the town-house, and looked gorgeous and venerable. Here and there a woman exchanged greetings with an individual soldier, as he marched along, and gentlemen shook hands with officers with whom they happened to be acquainted. Being a stranger in the land, it seemed as if I could see the future in the present better than if I had been an Englishman; so I questioned with myself how many of these ruddy-cheeked young fellows, marching so stoutly away, would ever tread English ground again. The populace did not evince any enthusiasm, yet there could not possibly be a war to which the country could assent more fully than to this. I somewhat doubt whether the English populace really feels a vital interest in the nation.

Some years ago, a piece of rude marble sculpture, representing St. George and the Dragon, was found over the fireplace of a cottage near Rock Ferry, on the road to Chester. It was plastered over with pipe-clay, and its existence was unknown to the cottagers, until a lady noticed the projection and asked what it was. It was supposed to have originally adorned the walls of the Priory at Birkenhead. It measured fourteen and a half by nine inches, in which space were the heads of a king and queen, with uplifted hands, in prayer; their daughters also in prayer, and looking very grim; a lamb, the slain dragon, and St. George, proudly prancing on what looks like a donkey, brandishing a sword over his head.

The following is a legend inscribed on the inner margin of a curious old box:—

"From Birkenhead into Hilbree

A squirrel might leap from tree to tree."

I do not know where Hilbree is; but all round Birkenhead a squirrel would scarcely find a single tree to climb upon. All is pavement and brick buildings now.

Good Friday.—The English and Irish think it good to plant on this day, because it was the day when our Saviour's body was laid in the grave. Seeds, therefore, are certain to rise again.

At dinner the other day, Mrs. ——— mentioned the origin of Franklin's adoption of the customary civil dress, when going to court as a diplomatist. It was simply that his tailor had disappointed him of his court suit, and he wore his plain one with great reluctance, because he had no other. Afterwards, gaining great success and praise by his mishap, he continued to wear it from policy.

The grandmother of Mrs. ——— died fifty years ago, at the age of twenty-eight. She had great personal charms, and among them a head of beautiful chestnut hair. After her burial in the family tomb, the coffin of one of her children was laid on her own, so that the lid seems to have decayed, or been broken from this cause; at any rate, this was the case when the tomb was opened about a year ago. The grandmother's coffin was then found to be filled with beautiful, glossy, living chestnut ringlets, into which her whole substance seems to have been transformed, for there was nothing else but these shining curls, the growth of half a century in the tomb. An old man, with a ringlet of his youthful mistress treasured on his heart, might be supposed to witness this wonderful thing.

Madam ———, who is now at my house, and very infirm, though not old, was once carried to the grave, and on the point of being buried. It was in Barbary, where her husband was Consul-General. He was greatly attached to her, and told the pall-bearers at the grave that he must see her once more. When her face was uncovered, he thought he discerned signs of life, and felt a warmth. Finally she revived, and for many years afterwards supposed the funeral procession to have been a dream; she having been partially conscious throughout, and having felt the wind blowing on her, and lifting the shroud from her feet,—for I presume she was to be buried in Oriental style, without a coffin. Long after, in London, when she was speaking of this dream, her husband told her the facts, and she fainted away. Whenever it is now mentioned, her face turns white. Mr. ———, her son, was born on shipboard, on the coast of Spain, and claims four nationalities,—those of Spain, England, Ireland, and the United States; his father being Irish, his mother a native of England, himself a naturalized citizen of the United States, and his father having registered his birth and baptism in a Catholic church of Gibraltar, which gives him Spanish privileges. He has hereditary claims to a Spanish countship. His infancy was spent in Barbary, and his lips first lisped in Arabic. There has been an unsettled and wandering character in his whole life.

The grandfather of Madam ———, who was a British officer, once horsewhipped Paul Jones,—Jones being a poltroon. How singular it is that the personal courage of famous warriors should be so often called in question!

May 20th.—I went yesterday to a hospital to take the oath of a mate to a protest. He had met with a severe accident by a fall on shipboard. The hospital is a large edifice of red freestone, with wide, airy passages, resounding with footsteps passing through them. A porter was waiting in the vestibule. Mr. Wilding and myself were shown to the parlor, in the first instance,—a neat, plainly furnished room, with newspapers and pamphlets lying on the table and sofas. Soon the surgeon of the house came,—a brisk, alacritous, civil, cheerful young man, by whom we were shown to the apartment where the mate was lying. As we went through the principal passage, a man was borne along in a chair looking very pale, rather wild, and altogether as if he had just been through great tribulation, and hardly knew as yet whereabouts he was. I noticed that his left arm was but a stump, and seemed done up in red baize,—at all events it was of a scarlet line. The surgeon shook his right hand cheerily, and he was carried on. This was a patient who had just had his arm cut off. He had been a rough person apparently, but now there was a kind of tenderness about him, through pain and helplessness.

In the chamber where the mate lay, there were seven beds, all of them occupied by persons who had met with accidents. In the centre of the room was a stationary pine table, about the length of a man, intended, I suppose, to stretch patients upon for necessary operations. The furniture of the beds was plain and homely. I thought that the faces of the patients all looked remarkably intelligent, though they were evidently men of the lower classes. Suffering had educated them morally and intellectually. They gazed curiously at Mr. Wilding and me, but nobody said a word. In the bed next to the mate lay a little boy with a broken thigh. The surgeon observed that children generally did well with accidents; and this boy certainly looked very bright and cheerful. There was nothing particularly interesting about the mate.

After finishing our business, the surgeon showed us into another room of the surgical ward, likewise devoted to cases of accident and injury. All the beds were occupied, and in two of them lay two American sailors who had recently been stabbed. They had been severely hurt, but were doing very well. The surgeon thought that it was a good arrangement to have several cases together, and that the patients kept up one another's spirits,—being often merry together. Smiles and laughter may operate favorably enough from bed to bed; but dying groans, I should think, must be somewhat of a discouragement. Nevertheless, the previous habits and modes of life of such people as compose the more numerous class of patients in a hospital must be considered before deciding this matter. It is very possible that their misery likes such bedfellows as it here finds.

As we were taking our leave, the surgeon asked us if we should not like to see the operating-room; and before we could reply he threw open the door, and behold, there was a roll of linen "garments rolled in blood,"— and a bloody fragment of a human arm! The surgeon glanced at me, and smiled kindly, but as if pitying my discomposure.

Gervase Elwes, son of Sir Gervase Elwes, Baronet, of Stoke, Suffolk, married Isabella, daughter of Sir Thomas Hervey, Knight, and sister of the first Earl of Bristol. This Gervase died before his father, but left a son, Henry, who succeeded to the Baronetcy. Sir Henry died without issue, and was succeeded by his sister's son, John Maggott Twining, who assumed the name of Elwes. He was the famous miser, and must have had Hawthorne blood in him, through his grandfather, Gervase, whose mother was a Hawthorne. It was to this Gervase that my ancestor, William Hawthorne, devised some land in Massachusetts, "if he would come over, and enjoy it." My ancestor calls him his nephew.

June 12th.—Barry Cornwall, Mr. Procter, called on me a week or more ago, but I happened not to be in the office. Saturday last he called again, and as I had crossed to Rock Park he followed me thither. A plain, middle-sized, English-looking gentleman, elderly, with short, white hair, and particularly quiet in his manners. He talks in a somewhat low tone without emphasis, scarcely distinct. His head has a good outline, and would look well in marble. I liked him very well. He talked unaffectedly, showing an author's regard to his reputation, and was evidently pleased to hear of his American celebrity. He said that in his younger days he was a scientific pugilist, and once took a journey to have a sparring encounter with the Game-Chicken. Certainly, no one would have looked for a pugilist in this subdued old gentleman. He is now Commissioner of Lunacy, and makes periodical circuits through the country, attending to the business of his office. He is slightly deaf, and this may be the cause of his unaccented utterance,—owing to his not being able to regulate his voice exactly by his own ear. He is a good man, and much better expressed by his real name, Procter, than by his poetical one, Barry Cornwall. . . . He took my hand in both of his at parting. . . .

June 17th.—At eleven, at this season (and how much longer I know not), there is still a twilight. If we could only have such dry, deliciously warm evenings as we used to have in our own land, what enjoyment there might be in these interminable twilights! But here we close the window-shutters, and make ourselves cosey by a coal-fire.

All three of the children, and, I think, my wife and myself, are going through the hooping-cough. The east-wind of this season and region is most horrible. There have been no really warm days; for though the sunshine is sometimes hot, there is never any diffused heat throughout the air. On passing from the sunshine into the shade, we immediately feel too cool.

June 20th.—The vagabond musicians about town are very numerous. On board the steam ferry-boats, I have heretofore spoken of them. They infest them from May to November, for very little gain apparently. A shilling a day per man must be the utmost of their emolument. It is rather sad to see somewhat respectable old men engaged in this way, with two or three younger associates. Their instruments look much the worse for wear, and even my unmusical ear can distinguish more discord than harmony. They appear to be a very quiet and harmless people. Sometimes there is a woman playing on a fiddle, while her husband blows a wind instrument. In the streets it is not unusual to find a band of half a dozen performers, who, without any provocation or reason whatever, sound their brazen instruments till the houses re-echo. Sometimes one passes a man who stands whistling a tune most unweariably, though I never saw anybody give him anything. The ballad-singers are the strangest, from the total lack of any music in their cracked voices. Sometimes you see a space cleared in the street, and a foreigner playing, while a girl— weather-beaten, tanned, and wholly uncomely in face and shabby in attire dances ballets. The common people look on, and never criticise or treat any of these poor devils unkindly or uncivilly; but I do not observe that they give them anything.

A crowd—or, at all events, a moderate-sized group—is much more easily drawn together here than with us. The people have a good deal of idle and momentary curiosity, and are always ready to stop when another person has stopped, so as to see what has attracted his attention. I hardly ever pause to look at a shop-window, without being immediately incommoded by boys and men, who stop likewise, and would forthwith throng the pavement if I did not move on.

June 30th.—If it is not known how and when a man dies, it makes a ghost of him for many years thereafter, perhaps for centuries. King Arthur is an example; also the Emperor Frederic, and other famous men, who were thought to be alive ages after their disappearance. So with private individuals. I had an uncle John, who went a voyage to sea about the beginning of the War of 1812, and has never returned to this hour. But as long as his mother lived, as many as twenty years, she never gave up the hope of his return, and was constantly hearing stories of persons whose description answered to his. Some people actually affirmed that they had seen him in various parts of the world. Thus, so far as her belief was concerned, he still walked the earth. And even to this day I never see his name, which is no very uncommon one, without thinking that this may be the lost uncle.

Thus, too, the French Dauphin still exists, or a kind of ghost of him; the three Tells, too, in the cavern of Uri.

July 6th.—Mr. Cecil, the other day, was saying that England could produce as fine peaches as any other country. I asked what was the particular excellence of a peach, and he answered, "Its cooling and refreshing quality, like that of a melon!" Just think of this idea of the richest, most luscious, of all fruits! But the untravelled Englishman has no more idea of what fruit is than of what sunshine is; he thinks he has tasted the first and felt the last, but they are both alike watery. I heard a lady in Lord Street talking about the "broiling sun," when I was almost in a shiver. They keep up their animal heat by means of wine and ale, else they could not bear this climate.

July 19th.—A week ago I made a little tour in North Wales with Mr. Bright. We left Birkenhead by railway for Chester at two o'clock; thence for Bangor; thence by carriage over the Menai bridge to Beaumaris. At Beaumaris, a fine old castle,—quite coming up to my idea of what an old castle should be. A gray, ivy-hung exterior wall, with large round towers at intervals; within this another wall, the place of the portcullis between; and again, within the second wall the castle itself, with a spacious green court-yard in front. The outer wall is so thick that a passage runs in it all round the castle, which covers a space of three acres. This passage gives access to a chapel, still very perfect, and to various apartments in the towers,—all exceedingly dismal, and giving very unpleasant impressions of the way in which the garrison of the castle lived. The main castle is entirely roofless, but the hall and other rooms are pointed out by the guide, and the whole is tapestried with abundant ivy, so that my impression is of gray walls, with here and there a vast green curtain; a carpet of green over the floors of halls and apartments; and festoons around all the outer battlement, with an uneven and rather perilous foot-path running along the top. There is a fine vista through the castle itself, and the two gateways of the two encompassing walls. The passage within the wall is very rude, both underfoot and on each side, with various ascents and descents of rough steps,—sometimes so low that your head is in danger; and dark, except where a little light comes through a loophole or window in the thickness of the wall. In front of the castle a tennis-court was fitted up, by laying a smooth pavement on the ground, and casing the walls with tin or zinc, if I recollect aright. All this was open to the sky; and when we were there, some young men of the town were playing at the game. There are but very few of these tennis-courts in England; and this old castle was a very strange place for one.

The castle is the property of Sir Richard Bulkely, whose seat is in the vicinity, and who owns a great part of the island of Anglesea, on which Beaumaris lies. The hotel where we stopped was the Bulkely Arms, and Sir Richard has a kind of feudal influence in the town.

In the morning we walked along a delightful road, bordering on the Menai Straits, to Bangor Ferry. It was really a very pleasant road, overhung by a growth of young wood, exceedingly green and fresh. English trees are green all about their stems, owing to the creeping plants that overrun them. There were some flowers in the hedges, such as we cultivate in gardens. At the ferry, there was a whitewashed cottage; a woman or two, some children, and a fisherman-like personage, walking to and fro before the door. The scenery of the strait is very beautiful and picturesque, and directly opposite to us lay Bangor,—the strait being here almost a mile across. An American ship from Boston lay in the middle of it. The ferry-boat was just putting off for the Bangor side, and, by the aid of a sail, soon neared the shore.

At Bangor we went to a handsome hotel, and hired a carriage and two horses for some Welsh place, the name of which I forget; neither can I remember a single name of the places through which we posted that day, nor could I spell them if I heard them pronounced, nor pronounce them if I saw them spelt. It was a circuit of about forty miles, bringing us to Conway at last. I remember a great slate-quarry; and also that many of the cottages, in the first part of our drive, were built of blocks of slate. The mountains were very bold, thrusting themselves up abruptly in peaks,—not of the dumpling formation, which is somewhat too prevalent among the New England mountains. At one point we saw Snowdon, with its bifold summit. We also visited the smaller waterfall (this is a translation of an unpronounceable Welsh name), which is the largest in Wales. It was a very beautiful rapid, and the guide-book considers it equal in sublimity to Niagara. Likewise there were one or two lakes which the guide-book greatly admired, but which to me, who remembered a hundred sheets of blue water in New England, seemed nothing more than sullen and dreary puddles, with bare banks, and wholly destitute of beauty. I think they were nowhere more than a hundred yards across. But the hills were certainly very good, and, though generally bare of trees, their outlines thereby were rendered the stronger and more striking.

Many of the Welsh women, particularly the older ones, wear black beaver hats, high-crowned, and almost precisely like men's. It makes them look ugly and witchlike. Welsh is still the prevalent language, and the only one spoken by a great many of the inhabitants. I have had Welsh people in my office, on official business, with whom I could not communicate except through an interpreter.

At some unutterable village we went into a little church, where we saw an old stone image of a warrior, lying on his back, with his hands clasped. It was the natural son (if I remember rightly) of David, Prince of Wales, and was doubtless the better part of a thousand years old. There was likewise a stone coffin of still greater age; some person of rank and renown had mouldered to dust within it, but it was now open and empty. Also, there were monumental brasses on the walls, engraved with portraits of a gentleman and lady in the costumes of Elizabeth's time. Also, on one of the pews, a brass record of some persons who slept in the vault beneath; so that, every Sunday, the survivors and descendants kneel and worship directly over their dead ancestors. In the churchyard, on a flat tombstone, there was the representation of a harp. I supposed that it must be the resting-place of a bard; but the inscription was in memory of a merchant, and a skilful manufacturer of harps.

This was a very delightful town. We saw a great many things which it is now too late to describe, the sharpness of the first impression being gone; but I think I can produce something of the sentiment of it hereafter.

We arrived at Conway late in the afternoon, to take the rail for Chester. I must see Conway, with its old gray wall and its unrivalled castle, again. It was better than Beaumaris, and I never saw anything more picturesque than the prospect from the castle-wall towards the sea. We reached Chester at 10 P. M. The next morning, Mr. Bright left for Liverpool before I was awake. I visited the Cathedral, where the organ was sounding, sauntered through the Rows, bought some playthings for the children, and left for home soon after twelve.

Liverpool, August 8th.—Visiting the Zoological Gardens the other day with J———, it occurred to me what a fantastic kind of life a person connected with them might be depicted as leading,—a child, for instance. The grounds are very extensive, and include arrangements for all kinds of exhibitions calculated to attract the idle people of a great city. In one enclosure is a bear, who climbs a pole to get cake and gingerbread from the spectators. Elsewhere, a circular building, with compartments for lions, wolves, and tigers. In another part of the garden is a colony of monkeys, the skeleton of an elephant, birds of all kinds. Swans and various rare water-fowl were swimming on a piece of water, which was green, by the by, and when the fowls dived they stirred up black mud. A stork was parading along the margin, with melancholy strides of its long legs, and came slowly towards us, as if for companionship. In one apartment was an obstreperously noisy society of parrots and macaws, most gorgeous and diversified of hue. These different colonies of birds and beasts were scattered about in various parts of the grounds, so that you came upon them unexpectedly. Also, there were archery and shooting-grounds, and a sewing. A theatre, also, at which a rehearsal was going on,—we standing at one of the doors, and looking in towards the dusky stage where the company, in their ordinary dresses, were rehearsing something that had a good deal of dance and action in it. In the open air there was an arrangement of painted scenery representing a wide expanse of mountains, with a city at their feet, and before it the sea, with actual water, and large vessels upon it, the vessels having only the side that would be presented to the spectator. But the scenery was so good that at a first casual glance I almost mistook it for reality. There was a refreshment-room, with drinks and cakes and pastry, but, so far as I saw, no substantial victual. About in the centre of the garden there was an actual, homely-looking, small dwelling-house, where perhaps the overlookers of the place live. Now this might be wrought, in an imaginative description, into a pleasant sort of a fool's paradise, where all sorts of unreal delights should cluster round some suitable personage; and it would relieve, in a very odd and effective way, the stern realities of life on the outside of the garden-walls. I saw a little girl, simply dressed, who seemed to have her habitat within the grounds. There was also a daguerreotypist, with his wife and family, carrying on his business in a shanty, and perhaps having his home in its inner room. He seemed to be an honest, intelligent, pleasant young man, and his wife a pleasant woman; and I had J———'s daguerreotype taken for three shillings, in a little gilded frame. In the description of the garden, the velvet turf, of a charming verdure, and the shrubbery and shadowy walks and large trees, and the slopes and inequalities of ground, must not be forgotten. In one place there was a maze and labyrinth, where a person might wander a long while in the vain endeavor to get out, although all the time looking at the exterior garden, over the low hedges that border the walks of the maze. And this is like the inappreciable difficulties that often beset us in life.

I will see it again before long, and get some additional record of it.

August 10th.—We went to the Isle of Man, a few weeks ago, where S——— and the children spent a fortnight. I spent two Sundays with them.

I never saw anything prettier than the little church of Kirk Madden there. It stands in a perfect seclusion of shadowy trees,—a plain little church, that would not be at all remarkable in another situation, but is most picturesque in its solitude and bowery environment. The churchyard is quite full and overflowing with graves, and extends down the gentle slope of a hill, with a dark mass of shadow above it. Some of the tombstones are flat on the ground, some erect, or laid horizontally on low pillars or masonry. There were no very old dates on any of these stones; for the climate soon effaces inscriptions, and makes a stone of fifty years look as old as one of five hundred,—unless it be slate, or something harder than the usual red freestone. There was an old Runic monument, however, near the centre of the churchyard, that had some strange sculpture on it, and an inscription still legible by persons learned in such matters. Against the tower of the church, too, there is a circular stone, with carving on it, said to be of immemorial antiquity. There is likewise a tall marble monument, as much as fifty feet high, erected some years ago to the memory of one of the Athol family by his brother-officers of a local regiment of which he was colonel. At one of the side-entrances of the church, and forming the threshold within the thickness of the wall, so that the feet of all who enter must tread on it, is a flat tombstone of somebody who felt himself a sinner, no doubt, and desired to be thus trampled upon. The stone is much worn.

The structure is extremely plain inside and very small. On the walls, over the pews, are several monumental sculptures,—a quite elaborate one to a Colonel Murray, of the Coldstreamn Guards; his military profession being designated by banners and swords in marble.—Another was to a farmer.

On one side of the church-tower there was a little penthouse, or lean-to,—merely a stone roof, about three or four feet high, and supported by a single pillar, beneath which was once deposited the bier.

I have let too much time pass before attempting to record my impressions of the Isle of Man; but, as regards this church, no description can come up to its quiet beauty, its seclusion, and its every requisite for an English country church.

Last Sunday I went to Eastham, and, entering the churchyard, sat down on a tombstone under the yew-tree which has been known for centuries as the Great Tree of Eastham. Some of the village people were sitting on the graves near the door; and an old woman came towards me, and said, in a low, kindly, admonishing tone, that I must not let the sexton see me, because he would not allow any one to be there in sacrament-time. I inquired why she and her companions were there, and she said they were waiting for the sacrament. So I thanked her, gave her a sixpence, and departed. Close under the eaves, I saw two upright stones, in memory of two old servants of the Stanley family,—one over ninety, and the other over eighty years of age.

August 12th.—J——- and I went to Birkenhead Park yesterday. There is a large ornamental gateway to the Park, and the grounds within are neatly laid out, with borders of shrubbery. There is a sheet of water, with swans and other aquatic fowl, which swim about, and are fed with dainties by the visitors. Nothing can be more beautiful than a swan. It is the ideal of a goose,—a goose beautified and beatified. There were not a great many visitors, but some children were dancing on the green, and a few lover-like people straying about. I think the English behave better than the Americans at similar places.

There was a camera-obscure, very wretchedly indistinct. At the refreshment-room were ginger-beer and British wines.

August 21st.—I was in the Crown Court on Saturday, sitting in the sheriff's seat. The judge was Baron ———, an old gentleman of sixty, with very large, long features. His wig helped him to look like some strange kind of animal,—very queer, but yet with a sagacious, and, on the whole, beneficent aspect. During the session some mischievous young barrister occupied himself with sketching the judge in pencil; and, being handed about, it found its way to me. It was very like and very laughable, but hardly caricatured. The judicial wig is an exceedingly odd affair; and as it covers both ears, it would seem intended to prevent his Lordship, and justice in his person, from hearing any of the case on either side, that thereby he may decide the better. It is like the old idea of blindfolding the statue of Justice.

It seems to me there is less formality, less distance between the judge, jury, witnesses, and bar, in the English courts than in our own. The judge takes a very active part in the trial, constantly asking a question of the witness on the stand, making remarks on the conduct of the trial, putting in his word on all occasions, and allowing his own sense of the matter in hand to be pretty plainly seen; so that, before the trial is over, and long before his own charge is delivered, he must have exercised a very powerful influence over the minds of the jury. All this is done, not without dignity, yet in a familiar kind of way. It is a sort of paternal supervision of the whole matter, quite unlike the cold awfulness of an American judge. But all this may be owing partly to the personal characteristics of Baron ———. It appeared to me, however, that, from the closer relations of all parties, truth was likely to be arrived at and justice to be done. As an innocent man, I should not be afraid to be tried by Baron ———.

EATON HALL.

August 24th.—I went to Eaton Hall yesterday with my wife and Mr. G. P. Bradford, via Chester. On our way, at the latter place, we visited St. John's Church. It is built of the same red freestone as the cathedral, and looked exceedingly antique, and venerable; this kind of stone, from its softness, and its liability to be acted upon by the weather, being liable to an early decay. Nevertheless, I believe the church was built above a thousand years ago,—some parts of it, at least,—and the surface of the tower and walls is worn away and hollowed in shallow sweeps by the hand of Time. There were broken niches in several places, where statues had formerly stood. All, except two or three, had fallen or crumbled away, and those which remained were much damaged. The face and details of the figure were almost obliterated. There were many gravestones round the church, but none of them of any antiquity. Probably, as the names become indistinguishable on the older stones, the graves are dug over again, and filled with new occupants and covered with new stones, or perhaps with the old ones newly inscribed.

Closely connected with the church was the clergyman's house, a comfortable-looking residence; and likewise in the churchyard, with tombstones all about it, even almost at the threshold, so that the doorstep itself might have been a tombstone, was another house, of respectable size and aspect. We surmised that this might be the sexton's dwelling, but it proved not to be so; and a woman, answering our knock, directed us to the place where he might be found. So Mr. Bradford and I went in search of him, leaving S—— seated on a tombstone. The sexton was a jolly-looking, ruddy-faced man, a mechanic of some sort, apparently, and he followed us to the churchyard with much alacrity. We found S—— standing at a gateway, which opened into the most ancient, and now quite ruinous, part of the church, the present edifice covering much less ground than it did some centuries ago. We went through this gateway, and found ourselves in an enclosure of venerable walls, open to the sky, with old Norman arches standing about, beneath the loftiest of which the sexton told us the high altar used to stand. Of course, there were weeds and ivy growing in the crevices, but not so abundantly as I have seen them elsewhere. The sexton pointed out a piece of a statue that had once stood in one of the niches, and which he himself, I think, had dug up from several feet below the earth; also, in a niche of the walls, high above our heads, he showed us an ancient wooden coffin, hewn out of a solid log of oak, the hollow being made rudely in the shape of a human figure. This too had been dug up, and nobody knew how old it was. While we looked at all this solemn old trumpery, the curate, quite a young man, stood at the back door of his house, elevated considerably above the ruins, with his young wife (I presume) and a friend or two, chatting cheerfully among themselves. It was pleasant to see them there. After examining the ruins, we went inside of the church, and found it a dim and dusky old place, quite paved over with tombstones, not an inch of space being left in the aisles or near the altar, or in any nook or corner, uncovered by a tombstone. There were also mural monuments and escutcheons, and close against the wall lay the mutilated statue of a Crusader, with his legs crossed, in the style which one has so often read about. The old fellow seemed to have been represented in chain armor; but he had been more battered and bruised since death than even during his pugnacious life, and his nose was almost knocked away. This figure had been dug up many years ago, and nobody knows whom it was meant to commemorate.

The nave of the church is supported by two rows of Saxon pillars, not very lofty, but six feet six inches (so the sexton says) in diameter. They are covered with plaster, which was laid on ages ago, and is now so hard and smooth that I took the pillars to be really composed of solid shafts of gray stone. But, at one end of the church, the plaster had been removed from two of the pillars, in order to discover whether they were still sound enough to support the building; and they prove to be made of blocks of red freestone, just as sound as when it came from the quarry; for though this stone soon crumbles in the open air, it is as good as indestructible when sheltered from the weather. It looked very strange to see the fresh hue of these two pillars amidst the dingy antiquity of the rest of the structure.

The body of the church is covered with pews, the wooden enclosures of which seemed of antique fashion. There were also modern stoves; but the sexton said it was very cold there, in spite of the stoves. It had, I must say, a disagreeable odor pervading it, in which the dead people of long ago had doubtless some share,—a musty odor, by no means amounting to a stench, but unpleasant, and, I should think, unwholesome. Old wood-work, and old stones, and antiquity of all kinds, moral and physical, go to make up this smell. I observed it in the cathedral, and Chester generally has it, especially under the Rows. After all, the necessary damp and lack of sunshine, in such a shadowy old church as this, have probably more to do with it than the dead people have; although I did think the odor was particularly strong over some of the tombstones. Not having shillings to give the sexton, we were forced to give him half a crown.

The Church of St. John is outside of the city walls. Entering the East gate, we walked awhile under the Rows, bought our tickets for Eaton Hall and its gardens, and likewise some playthings for the children; for this old city of Chester seems to me to possess an unusual number of toy-shops. Finally we took a cab, and drove to the Hall, about four miles distant, nearly the whole of the way lying through the wooded Park. There are many sorts of trees, making up a wilderness, which looked not unlike the woods of our own Concord, only less wild. The English oak is not a handsome tree, being short and sturdy, with a round, thick mass of foliage, lying all within its own bounds. It was a showery day. Had there been any sunshine, there might doubtless have been many beautiful effects of light and shadow in these woods. We saw one or two herds of deer, quietly feeding, a hundred yards or so distant. They appeared to be somewhat wilder than cattle, but, I think, not much wilder than sheep. Their ancestors have probably been in a half-domesticated state, receiving food at the hands of man, in winter, for centuries. There is a kind of poetry in this, quite as much as if they were really wild deer, such as their forefathers were, when Hugh Lupus used to hunt them.

Our miserable cab drew up at the steps of Eaton Hall, and, ascending under the portico, the door swung silently open, and we were received very civilly by two old men,—one, a tall footman in livery; the other, of higher grade, in plain clothes. The entrance-hall is very spacious, and the floor is tessellated or somehow inlaid with marble. There was statuary in marble on the floor, and in niches stood several figures in antique armor, of various dates; some with lances, and others with battle-axes and swords. There was a two-handed sword, as much as six feet long; but not nearly so ponderous as I have supposed this kind of weapon to be, from reading of it. I could easily have brandished it.

I don't think I am a good sight-seer; at least, I soon get satisfied with looking at the sights, and wish to go on to the next.

The plainly dressed old man now led us into a long corridor, which goes, I think, the whole length of the house, about five hundred feet, arched all the way, and lengthened interminably by a looking-glass at the end, in which I saw our own party approaching like a party of strangers. But I have so often seen this effect produced in dry-goods stores and elsewhere, that I was not much impressed. There were family portraits and other pictures, and likewise pieces of statuary, along this arched corridor; and it communicated with a chapel with a scriptural altar-piece, copied from Rubens, and a picture of St. Michael and the Dragon, and two, or perhaps three, richly painted windows. Everything here is entirely new and fresh, this part having been repaired, and never yet inhabited by the family. This brand-newness makes it much less effective than if it had been lived in; and I felt pretty much as if I were strolling through any other renewed house. After all, the utmost force of man can do positively very little towards making grand things or beautiful things. The imagination can do so much more, merely on shutting one's eyes, that the actual effect seems meagre; so that a new house, unassociated with the past, is exceedingly unsatisfactory, especially when you have heard that the wealth mud skill of man has here done its best. Besides, the rooms, as we saw them, did not look by any means their best, the carpets not being down, and the furniture being covered with protective envelopes. However, rooms cannot be seen to advantage by daylight; it being altogether essential to the effect, that they should be illuminated by artificial light, which takes them somewhat out of the region of bare reality. Nevertheless, there was undoubtedly great splendor, for the details of which I refer to the guide-book. Among the family portraits, there was one of a lady famous for her beautiful hand; and she was holding it up to notice in the funniest way, —and very beautiful it certainly was. The private apartments of the family were not shown us. I should think it impossible for the owner of this house to imbue it with his personality to such a degree as to feel it to be his home. It must be like a small lobster in a shell much too large for him.

After seeing what was to be seen of the rooms, we visited the gardens, in which are noble conservatories and hot-houses, containing all manner of rare and beautiful flowers, and tropical fruits. I noticed some large pines, looking as if they were really made of gold. The gardener (under-gardener I suppose he was) who showed this part of the spectacle was very intelligent as well as kindly, and seemed to take an interest in his business. He gave S—— a purple everlasting flower, which will endure a great many years, as a memento of our visit to Eaton Hall. Finally, we took a view of the front of the edifice, which is very fine, and much more satisfactory than the interior,—and returned to Chester.

We strolled about under the unsavory Rows, sometimes scudding from side to side of the street, through the shower; took lunch in a confectioner's shop, and drove to the railway station in time for the three-o'clock train. It looked picturesque to see two little girls, hand in hand, racing along the ancient passages of the Rows; but Chester has a very evil smell.

At the railroad station, S—— saw a small edition of "Twice-Told Tales," forming a volume of the Cottage Library; and, opening it, there was the queerest imaginable portrait of myself,—so very queer that we could not but buy it. The shilling edition of "The Scarlet Letter" and "Seven Gables" are at all the book-stalls and shop-windows; but so is "The Lamplighter," and still more trashy books.

August 26th.—All past affairs, all home conclusions, all people whom I have known in America and meet again here, are strangely compelled to undergo a new trial. It is not that they suffer by comparison with circumstances of English life and forms of English manhood or womanhood; but, being free from my old surroundings, and the inevitable prejudices of home, I decide upon them absolutely.

I think I neglected to record that I saw Miss Martineau a few weeks since. She is a large, robust, elderly woman, and plainly dressed; but withal she has so kind, cheerful, and intelligent a face that she is pleasanter to look at than most beauties. Her hair is of a decided gray, and she does not shrink from calling herself old. She is the most continual talker I ever heard; it is really like the babbling of a brook, and very lively and sensible too; and all the while she talks, she moves the bowl of her ear-trumpet from one auditor to another, so that it becomes quite an organ of intelligence and sympathy between her and yourself. The ear-trumpet seems a sensible part of her, like the antennae of some insects. If you have any little remark to make, you drop it in; and she helps you to make remarks by this delicate little appeal of the trumpet, as she slightly directs it towards you; and if you have nothing to say, the appeal is not strong enough to embarrass you. All her talk was about herself and her affairs; but it did not seem like egotism, because it was so cheerful and free from morbidness. And this woman is an Atheist, and thinks that the principle of life will become extinct when her body is laid in the grave! I will not think so; were it only for her sake. What! only a few weeds to spring out of her mortality, instead of her intellect and sympathies flowering and fruiting forever!

September 13th.—My family went to Rhyl last Thursday, and on Saturday I joined them there, in company with O'Sullivan, who arrived in the Behama from Lisbon that morning. We went by way of Chester, and found S——- waiting for us at the Rhyl station. Rhyl is a most uninteresting place, —a collection of new lodging-houses and hotels, on a long sand-beach, which the tide leaves bare almost to the horizon. The sand is by no means a marble pavement, but sinks under the foot, and makes very heavy walking; but there is a promenade in front of the principal range of houses, looking on the sea, whereon we have rather better footing. Almost all the houses were full, and S—— had taken a parlor and two bedrooms, and is living after the English fashion, providing her own table, lights, fuel, and everything. It is very awkward to our American notions; but there is an independence about it, which I think must make it agreeable on better acquaintance. But the place is certainly destitute of attraction, and life seems to pass very heavily. The English do not appear to have a turn for amusing themselves.

Sunday was a bright and hot day, and in the forenoon I set out on a walk, not well knowing whither, over a very dusty road, with not a particle of shade along its dead level. The Welsh mountains were before me, at the distance of three or four miles,—long ridgy hills, descending pretty abruptly upon the plain; on either side of the road, here and there, an old whitewashed, thatched stone cottage, or a stone farm-house, with an aspect of some antiquity. I never suffered so much before, on this side of the water, from heat and dust, and should probably have turned back had I not espied the round towers and walls of an old castle at some distance before me. Having looked at a guide-book, previously to setting out, I knew that this must be Rhyddlan Castle, about three miles from Rhyl; so I plodded on, and by and by entered an antiquated village, on one side of which the castle stood. This Welsh village is very much like the English villages, with narrow streets and mean houses or cottages, built in blocks, and here and there a larger house standing alone; everything far more compact than in our rural villages, and with no grassy street-margin nor trees; aged and dirty also, with dirty children staring at the passenger, and an undue supply of mean inns; most, or many of the men in breeches, and some of the women, especially the elder ones, in black beaver hats. The streets were paved with round pebbles, and looked squalid and ugly.

The children and grown people stared lazily at me as I passed, but showed no such alert and vivacious curiosity as a community of Yankees would have done. I turned up a street that led me to the castle, which looked very picturesque close at hand,—more so than at a distance, because the towers and walls have not a sufficiently broken outline against the sky. There are several round towers at the angles of the wall very large in their circles, built of gray stone, crumbling, ivy-grown, everything that one thinks of in an old ruin. I could not get into the inner space of the castle without climbing over a fence, or clambering down into the moat; so I contented myself with walking round it, and viewing it from the outside. Through the gateway I saw a cow feeding on the green grass in the inner court of the castle. In one of the walls there was a large triangular gap, where perhaps the assailants had made a breach. Of course there were weeds on the ruinous top of the towers, and along the summit of the wall. This was the first castle built by Edward I. in Wales, and he resided here during the erection of Conway Castle, and here

Queen Eleanor gave birth to a princess. Some few years since a meeting of Welsh bards was held within it.

After viewing it awhile, and listening to the babble of some children who lay on the grass near by, I resumed my walk, and, meeting a Welshman in the village street, I asked him my nearest way back to Rhyl. "Dim Sassenach," said he, after a pause. How odd that an hour or two on the railway should have brought me amongst a people who speak no English! Just below the castle, there is an arched stone bridge over the river Clwyd, and the best view of the edifice is from hence. It stands on a gentle eminence, commanding the passage of the river, and two twin round towers rise close beside one another, whence, I suppose, archers have often drawn their bows against the wild Welshmen, on the river-banks. Behind was the line of mountains; and this was the point of defence between the hill country and the lowlands. On the bridge stood a good many idle Welshmen, leaning over the parapet, and looking at some small vessels that had come up the river from the sea. There was the frame of a new vessel on the stocks near by.

As I returned, on my way home, I again inquired my way of a man in breeches, who, I found, could speak English very well. He was kind, and took pains to direct me, giving me the choice of three ways, viz. the one by which I came, another across the fields, and a third by the embankment along the river-side. I chose the latter, and so followed the course of the Clwyd, which is very ugly, with a tidal flow and wide marshy banks. On its farther side was Rhyddlan marsh, where a battle was fought between the Welsh and Saxons a thousand years ago. I have forgotten to mention that the castle and its vicinity was the scene of the famous battle of the fiddlers, between De Blandeville, Earl of Chester, and the Welsh, about the time of the Conqueror.

CONWAY CASTLE.

September 13th.—On Monday we went with O'Sullivan to Conway by rail. Certainly this must be the most perfect specimen of a ruinous old castle in the whole world; it quite fills up one's idea. We first walked round the exterior of the wall, at the base of which are hovels, with dirty children playing about them, and pigs rambling along, and squalid women visible in the doorways; but all these things melt into the picturesqueness of the scene, and do not harm it. The whole town of Conway is built in what was once the castle-yard, and the whole circuit of the wall is still standing in a delightful state of decay. At the angles, and at regular intervals, there are round towers, having half their circle on the outside of the walls, and half within. Most of these towers have a great crack pervading them irregularly from top to bottom; the ivy hangs upon them,—the weeds grow on the tops. Gateways, three or four of them, open through the walls, and streets proceed from them into the town. At some points, very old cottages or small houses are close against the sides, and, old as they are, they must have been built after the whole structure was a ruin. In one place I saw the sign of an alehouse painted on the gray stones of one of the old round towers. As we entered one of the gates, after making the entire circuit, we saw an omnibus coming down the street towards us, with its horn sounding. Llandudno was its place of destination; and, knowing no more about it than that it was four miles off, we took our seats. Llandudno is a watering-village at the base of the Great Orme's Head, at the mouth of the Conway River. In this omnibus there were two pleasant-looking girls, who talked Welsh together,—a guttural, childish kind of a babble. Afterwards we got into conversation with them, and found them very agreeable. One of them was reading Tupper's "Proverbial Philosophy." On reaching Llandudno, S——- waited at the hotel, while O'Sullivan, U——, and I ascended the Great Orme's Head. There are copper-mines here, and we heard of a large cave, with stalactites, but did not go so far as that. We found the old shaft of a mine, however, and threw stones down it, and counted twenty before we heard them strike the bottom. At the base of the Head, on the side opposite the village, we saw a small church with a broken roof, and horizontal gravestones of slate within the stone enclosure around it. The view from the hill was most beautiful,—a blue summer sea, with the distant trail of smoke from a steamer, and many snowy sails; in another direction the mountains, near and distant, some of them with clouds below their peaks.

We went to one of the mines which are still worked, and boys came running to meet us with specimens of the copper ore for sale. The miners were not now hoisting ore from the shaft, but were washing and selecting the valuable fragments from great heaps of crumbled stone and earth. All about this spot there are shafts and well-holes, looking fearfully deep and black, and without the slightest protection, so that we might just as easily have walked into them as not. Having examined these matters sufficiently, we descended the hill towards the village, meeting parties of visitors, mounted on donkeys, which is a much more sensible way of ascending in a hot day than to walk. On the sides and summit of the hill we found yellow gorse,—heath of two colors, I think, and very beautiful,—and here and there a harebell. Owing to the long-continued dry weather, the grass was getting withered and brown, though not so much so as on American hill-pastures at this season. Returning to the village, we all went into a confectioner's shop, and made a good luncheon. The two prettiest young ladies whom I have seen in England came into the shop and ate cakes while we were there. They appeared to be living together in a lodging-house, and ordered some of their housekeeping articles from the confectioner.

Next we went into the village bazaar,—a sort of tent or open shop, full of knick-knacks and gewgaws, and bought some playthings for the children. At half past one we took our seats in the omnibus, to return to Conway.

We had as yet only seen the castle wall and the exterior of the castle; now we were to see the inside. Right at the foot of it an old woman has her stand for the sale of lithographic views of Conway and other places; but these views are ridiculously inadequate, so that we did not buy any of them. The admittance into the castle is by a wooden door of modern construction, and the present seneschal is, I believe, the sexton of a church. He remembered me as having been there a month or two ago; and probably, considering that

I was already initiated, or else because he had many other visitors, he left us to wander about the castle at will. It is altogether impossible to describe Conway Castle. Nothing ever can have been so perfect in its own style, and for its own purposes, when it was first built; and now nothing else can be so perfect as a picture of ivy-grown, peaceful ruin. The banqueting-hall, all open to the sky and with thick curtains of ivy tapestrying the walls, and grass and weeds growing on the arches that overpass it, is indescribably beautiful. The hearthstones of the great old fireplaces, all about the castle, seem to be favorite spots for weeds to grow. There are eight large round towers, and out of four of them, I think, rise smaller towers, ascending to a much greater height, and once containing winding staircases, all of which are now broken, and inaccessible from below, though, in at least one of the towers, the stairs seemed perfect, high aloft. It must have been the rudest violence that broke down these stairs; for each step was a thick and heavy slab of stone, built into the wall of the tower. There is no such thing as a roof in any part; towers, hall, kitchen, all are open to the sky. One round tower, directly overhanging the railway, is so shattered by the falling away of the lower part, that you can look quite up into it and through it, while sitting in the cars; and yet it has stood thus, without falling into complete ruin, for more than two hundred years. I think that it was in this tower that we found the castle oven, an immense cavern, big enough to bake bread for an army. The railway passes exactly at the base of the high rock, on which this part of the castle is situated, and goes into the town through a great arch that has been opened in the castle wall. The tubular bridge across the Conway has been built in a style that accords with the old architecture, and I observed that one little sprig of ivy had rooted itself in the new structure.

There are numberless intricate passages in the thickness of the castle walls, forming communications between tower and tower,—damp, chill passages, with rough stone on either hand, darksome, and very likely leading to dark pitfalls. The thickness of the walls is amazing; and the people of those days must have been content with very scanty light, so small were the apertures,—sometimes merely slits and loopholes, glimmering through many feet of thickness of stone. One of the towers was said to have been the residence of Queen Eleanor; and this was better lighted than the others, containing an oriel-window, looking out of a little oratory, as it seemed to be, with groined arches and traces of ornamental sculpture, so that we could dress up some imperfect image of a queenly chamber, though the tower was roofless and floorless. There was another pleasant little windowed nook, close beside the oratory, where the Queen might have sat sewing or looking down the river Conway at the picturesque headlands towards the sea. We imagined her stately figure in antique robes, standing beneath the groined arches of the oratory. There seem to have been three chambers, one above another, in these towers, and the one in which was the embowed window was the middle one. I suppose the diameter of each of these circular rooms could not have been more than twenty feet on the inside. All traces of wood-work and iron-work are quite gone from the whole castle. These are said to have been taken away by a Lord Conway in the reign of Charles II. There is a grassy space under the windows of Queen Eleanor's tower,—a sort of outwork of the castle, where probably, when no enemy was near, the Queen used to take the open air in summer afternoons like this. Here we sat down on the grass of the ruined wall, and agreed that nothing in the world could be so beautiful and picturesque as Conway Castle, and that never could there have been so fit a time to see it as this sunny, quiet, lovely afternoon. Sunshine adapts itself to the character of a ruin in a wonderful way; it does not "flout the ruins gray," as Scott says, but sympathizes with their decay, and saddens itself for their sake. It beautifies the ivy too.

We saw, at the corner of this grass-plot around Queen Eleanor's tower, a real trunk of a tree of ivy, with so stalwart a stem, and such a vigorous grasp of its strong branches, that it would be a very efficient support to the wall, were it otherwise inclined to fall. O that we could have ivy in America! What is there to beautify us when our time of ruin comes?

Before departing, we made the entire circuit of the castle on its walls, and O'Sullivan and I climbed by a ladder to the top of one of the towers. While there, we looked down into the street beneath, and saw a photographist preparing to take a view of the castle, and calling out to some little girl in some niche or on some pinnacle of the walls to stand still that he might catch her figure and face. I think it added to the impressiveness of the old castle, to see the streets and the kitchen-gardens and the homely dwellings that had grown up within the precincts of this feudal fortress, and the people of to-day following their little businesses about it. This does not destroy the charm; but tourists and idle visitors do impair it. The earnest life of to-day, however, petty and homely as it may be, has a right to its place alongside of what is left of the life of other days; and if it be vulgar itself, it does not vulgarize the scene. But tourists do vulgarize it; and I suppose we did so, just like others.

We took the train back to Rhyl, where we arrived at about four o'clock, and, having dined, we again took the rail for Chester, and thence to Rock Park (that is, O'Sullivan and I), and reached home at about eleven o'clock.

Yesterday, September 13th, I began to wear a watch from Bennet's, 65 Cheapside, London. W. C. Bennet warrants it as the best watch which they can produce. If it prove as good and as durable as he prophesies, J—— will find it a perfect time-keeper long after his father has done with Time. If I had not thought of his wearing it hereafter, I should have been content with a much inferior one. No. 39,620.

September 20th.—I went back to Rhyl last Friday in the steamer. We arrived at the landing-place at nearly four o'clock, having started at twelve, and I walked thence to our lodgings, 18 West Parade. The children and their mother were all gone out, and I sat some time in our parlor before anybody came. The next morning I made an excursion in the omnibus as far as Ruthin, passing through Rhyddlan, St. Asaph, Denbigh, and reaching Ruthin at one o'clock. All these are very ancient places. St. Asaph has a cathedral which is not quite worthy of that name, but is a very large and stately church in excellent repair. Its square battlemented tower has a very fine appearance, crowning the clump of village houses on the hill-top, as you approach from Rhyddlan. The ascent of the hill is very steep; so it is at Denbigh and at Ruthin,—the steepest streets, indeed, that I ever climbed. Denbigh is a place of still more antique aspect than St. Asaph; it looks, I think, even older than Chester, with its gabled houses, many of their windows opening on hinges, and their fronts resting on pillars, with an open porch beneath. The castle makes an admirably ruinous figure on the hill, higher than the village. I had come hither with the purpose of inspecting it, but as it began to rain just then, I concluded to get into the omnibus and go to Ruthin. There was another steep ascent from the commencement of the long street of Ruthin, till I reached the market-place, which is of nearly triangular shape, and an exceedingly old-looking place. Houses of stone or plastered brick; one or two with timber frames; the roofs of an uneven line, and bulging out or sinking in; the slates moss-grown. Some of them have two peaks and even three in a row, fronting on the streets, and there is a stone market-house with a table of regulations. In this market-place there is said to be a stone on which King Arthur beheaded one of his enemies; but this I did not see. All these villages were very lively, as the omnibus drove in; and I rather imagine it was market-day in each of them,—there being quite a bustle of Welsh people. The old women came round the omnibus courtesying and intimating their willingness to receive alms,—witch-like women, such as one sees in pictures or reads of in romances, and very unlike anything feminine in America. Their style of dress cannot have changed for centuries. It was quite unexpected to me to hear Welsh so universally and familiarly spoken. Everybody spoke it. The omnibus-driver could speak but imperfect English; there was a jabber of Welsh all through the streets and market-places; and it flowed out with a freedom quite different from the way in which they expressed themselves in English. I had had an idea that Welsh was spoken rather as a freak and in fun than as a native language; it was so strange to find another language the people's actual and earnest medium of thought within so short a distance of England. But English is scarcely more known to the body of the Welsh people than to the peasantry of France. However, they sometimes pretend to ignorance, when they might speak it fairly enough.

I took luncheon at the hotel where the omnibus stopped, and then went to search out the castle. It appears to have been once extensive, but the remains of it are now very few, except a part of the external wall. Whatever other portion may still exist, has been built into a modern castellated mansion, which has risen within the wide circuit of the fortress,—a handsome and spacious edifice of red freestone, with a high tower, on which a flag was flying. The grounds were well laid out in walks, and really I think the site of the castle could not have been turned to better account. I am getting tired of antiquity. It is certainly less interesting in the long run than novelty; and so I was well content with the fresh, warm, red hue of the modern house, and the unworn outline of its walls, and its cheerful, large windows; and was willing that the old ivy-grown ruins should exist now only to contrast with the modernisms. These ancient walls, by the by, are of immense thickness. There is a passage through the interior of a portion of them, the width from this interior passage to the outer one being fifteen feet on one side, and I know not how much on the other.

It continued showery all day; and the omnibus was crowded. I had chosen the outside from Rhyl to Denbigh, but, all the rest of the journey, imprisoned myself within. On our way home, an old lady got into the omnibus,—a lady of tremendous rotundity; and as she tumbled from the door to the farthest part of the carriage, she kept advising all the rest of the passengers to get out. "I don't think there will be much rain, gentlemen," quoth she, "you'll be much more comfortable on the outside." As none of us complied, she glanced along the seats. "What! are you all Saas'uach?" she inquired. As we drove along, she talked Welsh with great fluency to one of the passengers, a young woman with a baby, and to as many others as could understand her. It has a strange, wild sound, like a language half blown away by the wind. The lady's English was very good; but she probably prided herself on her proficiency in Welsh. My excursion to-day had been along the valley of the Clwyd, a very rich and fertile tract of country.

The next day we all took a long walk on the beach, picking up shells.

On Monday we took an open carriage and drove to Rhyddlan; whence we sent back the carriage, meaning to walk home along the embankment of the river Clwyd, after inspecting the castle. The fortress is very ruinous, having been dismantled by the Parliamentarians. There are great gaps,—two, at least, in the walls that connect the round towers, of which there were six, one on each side of a gateway in front, and the same at a gateway towards the river, where there is a steep descent to a wall and square tower, at the water-side. Great pains and a great deal of gunpowder must have been used in converting this castle into a ruin. There were one or two fragments lying where they had fallen more than two hundred years ago, which, though merely a conglomeration of small stones and mortar, were just as hard as if they had been solid masses of granite. The substantial thickness of the walls is composed of these agglomerated small stones and mortar, the casing being hewn blocks of red freestone. This is much worn away by the weather, wherever it has been exposed to the air; but, under shelter, it looks as if it might have been hewn only a year or two ago. Each of the round towers had formerly a small staircase turret rising beside and ascending above it, in which a warder might be posted, but they have all been so battered and shattered that it is impossible for an uninstructed observer to make out a satisfactory plan of then. The interior of each tower was a small room, not more than twelve or fifteen feet across; and of these there seem to have been three stories, with loop-holes for archery and not much other light than what came through them. Then there are various passages and nooks and corners and square recesses in the stone, some of which must have been intended for dungeons, and the ugliest and gloomiest dungeons imaginable, for they could not have had any light or air. There is not, the least, splinter of wood-work remaining in any part of the castle,—nothing but bare stone, and a little plaster in one or two places, on the wall. In the front gateway we looked at the groove on each side, in which the portcullis used to rise and fall; and in each of the contiguous round towers there was a loop-hole, whence an enemy on the outer side of the portcullis might be shot through with an arrow.

The inner court-yard is a parallelogram, nearly a square, and is about forty-five of my paces across. It is entirely grass-grown, and vacant, except for two or three trees that have been recently set out, and which are surrounded with palings to keep away the cows that pasture in and about the place. No window looks from the walls or towers into this court-yard; nor are there any traces of buildings having stood within the enclosure, unless it be what looks something like the flue of a chimney within one of the walls. I should suppose, however, that there must have been, when the castle was in its perfect state, a hall, a kitchen, and other commodious apartments and offices for the King and his train, such as there were at Conway and Beaumaris. But if so, all fragments have been carried away, and all hollows of the old foundations scrupulously filled up. The round towers could not have comprised all the accommodation of the castle. There is nothing more striking in these ruins than to look upward from the crumbling base, and see flights of stairs, still comparatively perfect, by which you might securely ascend to the upper heights of the tower, although all traces of a staircase have disappeared below, and the upper portion cannot be attained. On three sides of the fortress is a moat, about sixty feet wide, and cased with stone. It was probably of great depth in its day, but it is now partly filled up with earth, and is quite dry and grassy throughout its whole extent. On the inner side of the moat was the outer wall of the castle, portions of which still remain. Between the outer wall and the castle itself the space is also about sixty feet.

The day was cloudy and lowering, and there were several little spatterings of rain, while we rambled about. The two children ran shouting hither and thither, and were continually clambering into dangerous places, racing along ledges of broken wall. At last they altogether disappeared for a good while; their voices, which had heretofore been plainly audible, were hushed, nor was there any answer when we began to call them, while making ready for our departure. But they finally appeared, coming out of the moat, where they had been picking and eating blackberries,—which, they said, grew very plentifully there, and which they were very reluctant to leave. Before quitting the castle, I must not forget the ivy, which makes a perfect tapestry over a large portion of the walls.

We walked about the village, which is old and ugly; small, irregular streets, contriving to be intricate, though there are few of them; mean houses, joining to each other. We saw, in the principal one, the parliament house in which Edward I. gave a Charter, or allowed rights of some kind to his Welsh subjects. The ancient part of its wall is entirely distinguishable from what has since been built upon it.

Thence we set out to walk along the embankment, although the sky looked very threatening. The wind, however, was so strong, and had such a full sweep at us, on the top of the bank, that we decided on taking a path that led from it across the moor. But we soon had cause to repent of this; for, which way soever we turned, we found ourselves cut off by a ditch or a little stream; so that here we were, fairly astray on Rhyddlan moor, the old battle-field of the Saxons and Britons, and across which, I suppose, the fiddlers and mountebanks had marched to the relief of the Earl of Chester. Anon, too, it began to shower; and it was only after various leaps and scramblings that we made our way to a large farm-house, and took shelter under a cart-shed. The back of the house to which we gained access was very dirty and ill-kept; some dirty children peeped at us as we approached, and nobody had the civility to ask us in; so we took advantage of the first cessation of the shower to resume our way. We were shortly overtaken by a very intelligent-looking and civil man, who seemed to have come from Rhyddlan, and said he was going to Rhyl. We followed his guidance over stiles and along hedge-row paths which we never could have threaded rightly by ourselves.

By and by our kind guide had to stop at an intermediate farm; but he gave us full directions how to proceed, and we went on till it began to shower again pretty briskly, and we took refuge in a little bit of old stone cottage, which, small as it was, had a greater antiquity than any mansion in America. The door was open, and as we approached, we saw several children gazing at us; and their mother, a pleasant-looking woman, who seemed rather astounded at the visit that was about to befall her, tried to draw a tattered curtain over a part of her interior, which she fancied even less fit to be seen than the rest. To say the truth, the house was not at all better than a pigsty; and while we sat there, a pig came familiarly to the door, thrust in his snout, and seemed surprised that he should be driven away, instead of being admitted as one of the family. The floor was of brick; there was no ceiling, but only the peaked gable overhead. The room was kitchen, parlor, and, I suppose, bedroom for the whole family; at all events, there was only the tattered curtain between us and the sleeping accommodations. The good woman either could not or would not speak a word of English, only laughing when S—— said, "Dim Sassenach?" but she was kind and hospitable, and found a chair for each of us. She had been making some bread, and the dough was on the dresser. Life with these people is reduced to its simplest elements. It is only a pity that they cannot or do not choose to keep themselves cleaner. Poverty, except in cities, need not be squalid. When the shower abated a little, we gave all the pennies we had to the children, and set forth again. By the by, there were several colored prints stuck up against the walls, and there was a clock ticking in a corner and some paper-hangings pinned upon the slanting roof.

It began to rain again before we arrived at Rhyl, and we were driven into a small tavern. After staying there awhile, we set forth between the drops; but the rain fell still heavier, so that we were pretty well damped before we got to our lodgings. After dinner, I took the rail for Chester and Rock Park, and S—— and the children and maid followed the next day.

September 22d.—I dined on Wednesday evening at Mr. John Heywood's, Norris Green. Mr. Mouckton Mimes and lady were of the company. Mr. Mimes is a very agreeable, kindly man, resembling Longfellow a good deal in personal appearance; and he promotes, by his genial manners, the same pleasant intercourse which is so easily established with Longfellow. He is said to be a very kind patron of literary men, and to do a great deal of good among young and neglected people of that class. He is considered one of the best conversationists at present in society: it may very well be so; his style of talking being very simple and natural, anything but obtrusive, so that you might enjoy its agreeableness without suspecting it. He introduced me to his wife (a daughter of Lord Crewe), with whom and himself I had a good deal of talk. Mr. Milnes told me that he owns the land in Yorkshire, whence some of the pilgrims of the Mayflower emigrated to Plymouth, and that Elder Brewster was the Postmaster of the village. . . . He also said that in the next voyage of the Mayflower, after she carried the Pilgrims, she was employed in transporting a cargo of slaves from Africa,—to the West Indies, I suppose. This is a queer fact, and would be nuts for the Southerners.

Mem.—An American would never understand the passage in Bunyan about Christian and Hopeful going astray along a by-path into the grounds of Giant Despair,—from there being no stiles and by-paths in our country.

September 26th.—On Saturday evening my wife and I went to a soiree given by the Mayor and Mrs. Lloyd at the Town Hall to receive the Earl of Harrowby. It was quite brilliant, the public rooms being really magnificent, and adorned for the occasion with a large collection of pictures, belonging to Mr. Naylor. They were mostly, if not entirely, of modern artists,—of Turner, Wilkie, Landseer, and others of the best English painters. Turner's seemed too ethereal to have been done by mortal hands.

The British Scientific Association being now in session here, many distinguished strangers were present.

September 29th.—Mr. Monekton Milnes called on me at the Consulate day before yesterday. He is pleasant and sensible. Speaking of American politicians, I remarked that they were seldom anything but politicians, and had no literary or other culture beyond their own calling. He said the case was the same in England, and instanced Sir ———, who once called on him for information when an appeal had been made to him respecting two literary gentlemen. Sir ——— had never heard the names of either of these gentlemen, and applied to Mr. Milnes as being somewhat conversant with the literary class, to know whether they were distinguished and what were their claims. The names of the two literary men were James Sheridan Knowles and Alfred Tennyson.

October 5th.—Yesterday I was present at a dejeuner on board the James Barnes, on occasion of her coming under the British flag, having been built for the Messrs. Barnes by Donald McKay of Boston. She is a splendid vessel, and magnificently fitted up, though not with consummate taste. It would be worth while that ornamental architects and upholsterers should study this branch of art, since the ship-builders seem willing to expend a good deal of money on it. In fact, I do not see that there is anywhere else so much encouragement to the exercise of ornamental art. I saw nothing to criticise in the solid and useful details of the ship; the ventilation, in particular, being free and abundant, so that the hundreds of passengers who will have their berths between decks, and at a still lower depth, will have good air and enough of it.

There were four or five hundred persons, principally Liverpool merchants and their wives, invited to the dejeuner; and the tables were spread between decks, the berths for passengers not being yet put in. There was not quite light enough to make the scene cheerful, it being an overcast day; and, indeed, there was an English plainness in the arrangement of the festal room, which might have been better exchanged for the flowery American taste, which I have just been criticising. With flowers, and the arrangement of flags, we should have made something very pretty of the space between decks; but there was nothing to hide the fact that in a few days hence there would be crowded berths and sea-sick steerage passengers where we were now feasting. The cheer was very good,—cold fowl and meats; cold pies of foreign manufacture very rich, and of mysterious composition; and champagne in plenty, with other wines for those who liked them.

I sat between two ladies, one of them Mrs. ———, a pleasant young woman, who, I believe, is of American provincial nativity, and whom I therefore regarded as half a countrywoman. We talked a good deal together, and I confided to her my annoyance at the prospect of being called up to answer a toast; but she did not pity me at all, though she felt, much alarm about her husband, Captain ———, who was in the same predicament. Seriously, it is the most awful part of my official duty,— this necessity of making dinner-speeches at the Mayor's, and other public or semi-public tables. However, my neighborhood to Mrs. ——— was good for me, inasmuch as by laughing over the matter with her came to regard it in a light and ludicrous way; and so, when the time actually came, I stood up with a careless dare-devil feeling. The chairman toasted the president immediately after the Queen, and did me the honor to speak of myself in a most flattering manner, something like this: "Great by his position under the Republic,—greater still, I am bold to say, in the Republic of letters!" I made no reply at all to this; in truth, I forgot all about it when I began to speak, and merely thanked the company in behalf of the President, and my countrymen, and made a few remarks with no very decided point to them. However, they cheered and applauded, and I took advantage of the applause to sit down, and Mrs. ——— informed me that I had succeeded admirably. It was no success at all, to be sure; neither was it a failure, for I had aimed at nothing, and I had exactly hit it. But after sitting down, I was conscious of an enjoyment in speaking to a public assembly, and felt as if I should like to rise again. It is something like being under fire,—a sort of excitement, not exactly pleasure, but more piquant than most pleasures. I have felt this before, in the same circumstances; but, while on my legs, my impulse is to get through with my remarks and sit down again as quickly as possible. The next speech, I think, was by Rev. Dr. ———, the celebrated Arctic gentleman, in reply to a toast complimentary to the clergy. He turned aside from the matter in hand, to express his kind feelings towards America, where he said he had been most hospitably received, especially at Cambridge

University. He also made allusions to me, and I suppose it would have been no more than civil in me to have answered with a speech in acknowledgment, but I did not choose to make another venture, so merely thanked him across the corner of the table, for he sat near me. He is a venerable-looking, white-haired gentleman, tall and slender, with a pale, intelligent, kindly face.

Other speeches were made; but from beginning to end there was not one breath of eloquence, nor even one neat sentence; and I rather think that Englishmen would purposely avoid eloquence or neatness in after-dinner speeches. It seems to be no part of their object. Yet any Englishman almost, much more generally than Americans, will stand up and talk on in a plain way, uttering one rough, ragged, and shapeless sentence after another, and will have expressed himself sensibly, though in a very rude manner, before he sits down. And this is quite satisfactory to his audience, who, indeed, are rather prejudiced against the man who speaks too glibly.

The guests began to depart shortly after three o'clock. This morning I have seen two reports of my little speech,—one exceedingly incorrect; another pretty exact, but not much to my taste, for I seem to have left out everything that would have been fittest to say.

October 6th.—The people, for several days, have been in the utmost anxiety, and latterly in the highest exultation about Sebastopol,—and all England, and Europe to boot, have been fooled by the belief that it had fallen. This, however, now turns out to be incorrect; and the public visage is somewhat grim, in consequence. I am glad of it. In spite of his actual sympathies, it is impossible for a true American to be otherwise than glad. Success makes an Englishman intolerable; and, already, on the mistaken idea that the way was open to a prosperous conclusion of the war, The Times had begun to throw out menaces against America. I shall never love England till she sues to us for help, and, in the mean time, the fewer triumphs she obtains, the better for all parties. An Englishman in adversity is a very respectable character; he does not lose his dignity, but merely comes to a proper conception of himself. It is rather touching to an observer to see how much the universal heart is in this matter,—to see the merchants gathering round the telegraphic messages, posted on the pillars of the Exchange news-room, the people in the street who cannot afford to buy a paper clustering round the windows of the news-offices, where a copy is pinned up,—the groups of corporals and sergeants at the recruiting rendezvous, with a newspaper in the midst of them and all earnest and sombre, and feeling like one man together, whatever their rank. I seem to myself like a spy or a traitor when I meet their eyes, and am conscious that I neither hope nor fear in sympathy with them, although they look at me in full confidence of sympathy. Their heart "knoweth its own bitterness," and as for me, being a stranger and all alien, I "intermeddle not with their joy."

October 9th.—My ancestor left England in 1630. I return in 1853. I sometimes feel as if I myself had been absent these two hundred and twenty-three years, leaving England just emerging from the feudal system, and finding it, on my return, on the verge of republicanism. It brings the two far-separated points of time very closely together, to view the matter thus.

October 16th.—A day or two ago arrived the sad news of the loss of the Arctic by collision with a French steamer off Newfoundland, and the loss also of three or four hundred people. I have seldom been more affected by anything quite alien from my personal and friendly concerns, than by the death of Captain Luce and his son. The boy was a delicate lad, and it is said that he had never been absent from his mother till this time, when his father had taken him to England to consult a physician about a complaint in his hip. So his father, while the ship was sinking, was obliged to decide whether he would put the poor, weakly, timorous child on board the boat, to take his hard chance of life there, or keep him to go down with himself and the ship. He chose the latter; and within half an hour, I suppose, the boy was among the child-angels. Captain Luce could not do less than die, for his own part, with the responsibility of all those lost lives upon him. He may not have been in the least to blame for the calamity, but it was certainly too heavy a one for him to survive. He was a sensible man, and a gentleman, courteous, quiet, with something almost melancholy in his address and aspect. Oftentimes he has come into my inner office to say good-by before his departures, but I cannot precisely remember whether or no he took leave of me before this latest voyage. I never exchanged a great many words with him; but those were kind ones.

October 19th.—It appears to be customary for people of decent station, but in distressed circumstances, to go round among their neighbors and the public, accompanied by a friend, who explains the case. I have been accosted in the street in regard to one of these matters; and to-day there came to my office a grocer, who had become security for a friend, and who was threatened with an execution,—with another grocer for supporter and advocate. The beneficiary takes very little active part in the affair, merely looking careworn, distressed, and pitiable, and throwing in a word of corroboration, or a sigh, or an acknowledgment, as the case may demand. In the present instance, the friend, a young, respectable-looking tradesman, with a Lancashire accent, spoke freely and simply of his client's misfortunes, not pressing the case unduly, but doing it full justice, and saying, at the close of the interview, that it was no pleasant business for himself. The broken grocer was an elderly man, of somewhat sickly aspect. The whole matter is very foreign to American habits. No respectable American would think of retrieving his affairs by such means, but would prefer ruin ten times over; no friend would take up his cause; no public would think it worth while to prevent the small catastrophe. And yet the custom is not without its good side as indicating a closer feeling of brotherhood, a more efficient sense of neighborhood, than exists among ourselves, although, perhaps, we are more careless of a fellow-creature's ruin, because ruin with us is by no means the fatal and irretrievable event that it is in England.

I am impressed with the ponderous and imposing look of an English legal document,—an assignment of real estate in England, for instance,—engrossed on an immense sheet of thickest paper, in a formal hand, beginning with "This Indenture" in German text, and with occasional phrases of form, breaking out into large script,—very long and repetitious, fortified with the Mayor of Manchester's seal, two or three inches in diameter, which is certified by a notary-public, whose signature, again, is to have my consular certificate and official seal.

November 2d.—A young Frenchman enters, of gentlemanly aspect, with a grayish cloak or paletot overspreading his upper person, and a handsome and well-made pair of black trousers and well-fitting boots below. On sitting down, he does not throw off nor at all disturb the cloak. Eying him more closely, one discerns that he has no shirt-collar, and that what little is visible of his shirt-bosom seems not to be of to-day nor of yesterday,—perhaps not even of the day before. His manner is not very good; nevertheless, he is a coxcomb and a jackanapes. He avers himself a naturalized citizen of America, where he has been tutor in several families of distinction, and has been treated like a son. He left America on account of his health, and came near being tutor in the Duke of Norfolk's family, but failed for lack of testimonials; he is exceedingly capable and accomplished, but reduced in funds, and wants employment here, of the means of returning to America, where he intends to take a situation under government, which he is sure of obtaining. He mentioned a quarrel which he had recently had with an Englishman in behalf of America, and would have fought a duel had such been the custom of the country. He made the Englishman foam at the mouth, and told him that he had been twelve years at a military school, and could easily kill him. I say to him that I see little or no prospect of his getting employment here, but offer to inquire whether any situation, as clerk or otherwise, can be obtained for him in a vessel returning to America, and ask his address. He has no address. Much to my surprise, he takes his leave without requesting pecuniary aid, but hints that he shall call again. He is a very disagreeable young fellow, like scores of others who call on me in the like situation. His English is very good for a Frenchman, and he says he speaks it the least well of five languages. He has been three years in America, and obtained his naturalization papers, he says, as a special favor, and by means of strong interest. Nothing is so absolutely odious as the sense of freedom and equality pertaining to an American grafted on the mind of a native of any other country in the world. A naturalized citizen is HATEFUL. Nobody has a right to our ideas, unless born to them.

November 9th.—I lent the above Frenchman a small sum; he advertised for employment as a teacher; and he called this morning to thank me for my aid, and says Mr. C——— has engaged him for his children, at a guinea a week, and that he has also another engagement. The poor fellow seems to have been brought to a very low ebb. He has pawned everything, even to his last shirt, save the one he had on, and had been living at the rate of twopence a day. I had procured him a chance to return to America, but he was ashamed to go back in such poor circumstances, and so determined to seek better fortune here. I like him better than I did,—partly, I suppose, because I have helped him.

November 14th.—The other day I saw an elderly gentleman walking in Dale Street, apparently in a state of mania; for as he limped along (being afflicted with lameness) he kept talking to himself, and sometimes breaking out into a threat against some casual passenger. He was a very respectable-looking man; and I remember to have seen him last summer, in the steamer, returning from the Isle of Man, where he had been staying at Castle Mona. What a strange and ugly predicament it would be for a person of quiet habits to be suddenly smitten with lunacy at noonday in a crowded street, and to walk along through a dim maze of extravagances,— partly conscious of then, but unable to resist the impulse to give way to them! A long-suppressed nature might be represented as bursting out in this way, for want of any other safety-valve.

In America, people seem to consider the government merely as a political administration; and they care nothing for the credit of it, unless it be the administration of their own political party. In England, all people, of whatever party, are anxious for the credit of their rulers. Our government, as a knot of persons, changes so entirely every four years, that the institution has come to be considered a temporary thing.

Looking at the moon the other evening, little R——- said, "It blooms out in the morning!" taking the moon to be the bud of the sun.

The English are a most intolerant people. Nobody is permitted, nowadays, to have any opinion but the prevalent one. There seems to be very little difference between their educated and ignorant classes in this respect; if any, it is to the credit of the latter, who do not show tokens of such extreme interest in the war. It is agreeable, however, to observe how all Englishmen pull together,—how each man comes forward with his little scheme for helping on the war,—how they feel themselves members of one family, talking together about their common interest, as if they were gathered around one fireside; and then what a hearty meed of honor they award to their soldiers! It is worth facing death for. Whereas, in America, when our soldiers fought as good battles, with as great proportionate loss, and far more valuable triumphs, the country seemed rather ashamed than proud of them.

Mrs. Heywood tells me that there are many Catholics among the lower classes in Lancashire and Cheshire,—probably the descendants of retainers of the old Catholic nobility and gentry, who are more numerous in these shires than in other parts of England. The present Lord Sefton's grandfather was the first of that race who became Protestant.

December 25th.—Commodore P——— called to see me this morning,—a brisk, gentlemanly, offhand, but not rough, unaffected and sensible man, looking not so elderly as he ought, on account of a very well made wig. He is now on his return from a cruise in the East Indian seas, and goes home by the Baltic, with a prospect of being very well received on account of his treaty with Japan. I seldom meet with a man who puts himself more immediately on conversable terms than the Commodore. He soon introduced his particular business with me,—it being to inquire whether I would recommend some suitable person to prepare his notes and materials for the publication of an account of his voyage. He was good enough to say that he had fixed upon me, in his own mind, for this office; but that my public duties would of course prevent me from engaging in it. I spoke of Herman Melville, and one or two others; but he seems to have some acquaintance with the literature of the day, and did not grasp very cordially at any name that I could think of; nor, indeed, could I recommend any one with full confidence. It would be a very desirable task for a young literary man, or, for that matter, for an old one; for the world can scarcely have in reserve a less hackneyed theme than Japan.

This is a most beautiful day of English winter; clear and bright, with the ground a little frozen, and the green grass along the waysides at Rock Ferry sprouting up through the frozen pools of yesterday's rain. England is forever green. On Christmas day, the children found wall-flowers, pansies, and pinks in the garden; and we had a beautiful rose from the garden of the hotel grown in the open air. Yet one is sensible of the cold here, as much as in the zero atmosphere of America. The chief advantage of the English climate is that we are not tempted to heat our rooms to so unhealthy a degree as in New England.

I think I have been happier this Christmas than ever before,—by my own fireside, and with my wife and children about me,—more content to enjoy what I have,—less anxious for anything beyond it in this life.

My early life was perhaps a good preparation for the declining half of life; it having been such a blank that any thereafter would compare favorably with it. For a long, long while, I have occasionally been visited with a singular dream; and I have an impression that I have dreamed it ever since I have been in England. It is, that I am still at college,—or, sometimes, even at school,—and there is a sense that I have been there unconscionably long, and have quite failed to make such progress as my contemporaries have done; and I seem to meet some of them with a feeling of shame and depression that broods over me as I think of it, even when awake. This dream, recurring all through these twenty or thirty years, must be one of the effects of that heavy seclusion in which I shut myself up for twelve years after leaving college, when everybody moved onward, and left me behind. How strange that it should come now, when I may call myself famous and prosperous!—when I am happy, too!

January 3d, 1855.—The progress of the age is trampling over the aristocratic institutions of England, and they crumble beneath it. This war has given the country a vast impulse towards democracy. The nobility will never hereafter, I think, assume or be permitted to rule the nation in peace, or command armies in war, on any ground except the individual ability which may appertain to one of their number, as well as to a commoner. And yet the nobles were never positively more noble than now; never, perhaps, so chivalrous, so honorable, so highly cultivated; but, relatively to the rest of the world, they do not maintain their old place. The pressure of the war has tested and proved this fact, at home and abroad. At this moment it would be an absurdity in the nobles to pretend to the position which was quietly conceded to them a year ago. This one year has done the work of fifty ordinary ones; or, more accurately, it has made apparent what has long been preparing itself.

January 6th.—The American ambassador called on me to-day and stayed a good while,—an hour or two. He is visiting at Mr. William Browne's, at Richmond Hill, having come to this region to bring his niece, who is to be bride's-maid at the wedding of an American girl. I like Mr. ———. He cannot exactly be called gentlemanly in his manners, there being a sort of rusticity about him; moreover, he has a habit of squinting one eye, and an awkward carriage of his head; hut, withal, a dignity in his large person, and a consciousness of high position and importance, which gives him ease and freedom. Very simple and frank in his address, he may be as crafty as other diplomatists are said to be; but I see only good sense and plainness of speech,—appreciative, too, and genial enough to make himself conversable. He talked very freely of himself and of other public people, and of American and English affairs. He returns to America, he says, next October, and then retires forever from public life, being sixty-four years of age, and having now no desire except to write memoirs of his times, and especially of the administration of Mr. Polk. I suggested a doubt whether the people would permit him to retire; and he immediately responded to my hint as regards his prospects for the Presidency. He said that his mind was fully made up, and that he would never be a candidate, and that he had expressed this decision to his friends in such a way as to put it out of his own power to change it. He acknowledged that he should have been glad of the nomination for the Presidency in 1852, but that it was now too late, and that he was too old,—and, in short, he seemed to be quite sincere in his nolo episcopari; although, really, he is the only Democrat, at this moment, whom it would not be absurd to talk of for the office. As he talked, his face flushed, and he seemed to feel inwardly excited. Doubtless, it was the high vision of half his lifetime which he here relinquished. I cannot question that he is sincere; but, of course, should the people insist upon having him for President, he is too good a patriot to refuse. I wonder whether he can have had any object in saying all this to me. He might see that it would be perfectly natural for me to tell it to General Pierce. But it is a very vulgar idea,—this of seeing craft and subtlety, when there is a plain and honest aspect.

January 9th.—I dined at Mr. William Browne's (M. P.) last, evening with a large party. The whole table and dessert service was of silver. Speaking of Shakespeare, Mr. ——— said that the Duke of Somerset, who is now nearly fourscore, told him that the father of John and Charles Kemble had made all possible research into the events of Shakespeare's life, and that he had found reason to believe that Shakespeare attended a certain revel at Stratford, and, indulging too much in the conviviality of the occasion, he tumbled into a ditch on his way home, and died there! The Kemble patriarch was an aged man when he communicated this to the Duke; and their ages, linked to each other; would extend back a good way; scarcely to the beginning of the last century, however. If I mistake not, it was from the traditions of Stratford that Kemble had learned the above. I do not remember ever to have seen it in print,—which is most singular.

Miss L—— has an English rather than an American aspect,—being of stronger outline than most of our young ladies, although handsomer than English women generally, extremely self-possessed and well poised without affectation or assumption, but quietly conscious of rank, as much so as if she were an Earl's daughter. In truth, she felt pretty much as an Earl's daughter would do towards the merchants' wives and daughters who made up the feminine portion of the party.

I talked with her a little, and found her sensible, vivacious, and firm-textured, rather than soft and sentimental. She paid me some compliments; but I do not remember paying her any.

Mr. J———'s daughters, two pale, handsome girls, were present. One of them is to be married to a grandson of Mr. ———, who was also at the dinner. He is a small young man, with a thin and fair mustache, ... and a lady who sat next me whispered that his expectations are 6,000 pounds per annum. It struck me, that, being a country gentleman's son, he kept himself silent and reserved, as feeling himself too good for this commercial dinner-party; but perhaps, and I rather think so, he was really shy and had nothing to say, being only twenty-one, and therefore quite a boy among Englishmen. The only man of cognizable rank present, except Mr. ——— and the Mayor of Liverpool, was a Baronet, Sir Thomas Birch.

January 17th.—S—— and I were invited to be present at the wedding of Mr. J———'s daughter this morning, but we were also bidden to the funeral services of Mrs. G———, a young American lady; and we went to the "house of mourning," rather than to the "house of feasting." Her death was very sudden. I crossed to Rock Ferry on Saturday, and met her husband in the boat. He said his wife was rather unwell, and that he had just been sent for to see her; but he did not seem at all alarmed. And yet, on reaching home, he found her dead! The body is to be conveyed to America, and the funeral service was read over her in her house, only a few neighbors and friends being present. We were shown into a darkened room, where there was a dim gaslight burning, and a fire glimmering, and here and there a streak of sunshine struggling through the drawn curtains. Mr. G——— looked pale, and quite overcome with grief,—this, I suppose, being his first sorrow,—and he has a young baby on his hands, and no doubt, feels altogether forlorn in this foreign land. The clergyman entered in his canonicals, and we walked in a little procession into another room, where the coffin was placed.

Mr. G——— sat down and rested his head on the coffin: the clergyman read the service; then knelt down, as did most of the company, and prayed with great propriety of manner, but with no earnestness,—and we separated.

Mr. G——— is a small, smooth, and pretty young man, not emphasized in any way; but grief threw its awfulness about him to-day in a degree which I should not have expected.

January 20th.—Mr. Steele, a gentleman of Rock Ferry, showed me this morning a pencil-case formerly belonging to Dr. Johnson. It is six or seven inches long, of large calibre, and very clumsily manufactured of iron, perhaps plated in its better days, but now quite bare. Indeed, it looks as rough as an article of kitchen furniture. The intaglio on the end is a lion rampant. On the whole, it well became Dr. Johnson to have used such a stalwart pencil-case. It had a six-inch measure on a part of it, so that it must have been at least eight inches long. Mr. Steele says he has seen a cracked earthen teapot, of large size, in which Miss Williams used to make tea for Dr. Johnson.

God himself cannot compensate us for being born for any period short of eternity. All the misery endured here constitutes a claim for another life, and, still more, all the happiness; because all true happiness involves something more than the earth owns, and needs something more than a mortal capacity for the enjoyment of it.

After receiving an injury on the head, a person fancied all the rest of his life that he heard voices flouting, jeering, and upbraiding him.

February 19th.—I dined with the Mayor at the Town Hall last Friday evening. I sat next to Mr. W. J———, an Irish-American merchant, who is in very good standing here. He told me that he used to be very well acquainted with General Jackson, and that he was present at the street fight between him and the Bentons, and helped to take General Jackson off the ground. Colonel Benton shot at him from behind; but it was Jesse Benton's ball that hit him and broke his arm. I did not understand him to infer any treachery or cowardice from the circumstance of Colonel Benton's shooting at Jackson from behind, but, suppose it occurred in the confusion and excitement of a street fight. Mr. W. J——— seems to think that, after all, the reconciliation between the old General and Benton was merely external, and that they really hated one another as before. I do not think so.

These dinners of the Mayors are rather agreeable than otherwise, except for the annoyance, in my case, of being called up to speak to a toast, and that is less disagreeable than at first. The suite of rooms at the Town House is stately and splendid, and all the Mayors, as far as I have seen, exercise hospitality in a manner worthy of the chief magistrates of a great city. They are supposed always to spend much more than their salary (which is 2,000 pounds) in these entertainments. The town provides the wines, I am told, and it might be expected that they should be particularly good,—at least, those which improve by age, for a quarter of a century should be only a moderate age for wine from the cellars of centuries-long institutions, like a corporate borough. Each Mayor might lay in a supply of the best vintage he could find, and trust his good name to posterity to the credit of that wine; and so he would be kindly and warmly remembered long after his own nose had lost its rubicundity. In point of fact, the wines seem to be good, but not remarkable.

The dinner was good, and very handsomely served, with attendance enough, both in the hall below—where the door was wide open at the appointed hour, notwithstanding the cold—and at table; some being in the rich livery of the borough, and some in plain clothes. Servants, too, were stationed at various points from the hall to the reception-room; and the last one shouted forth the name of the entering guest. There were, I should think, about fifty guests at this dinner. Two bishops were present. The Bishops of Chester and New South Wales, dressed in a kind of long tunics, with black breeches and silk stockings, insomuch that I first fancied they were Catholics. Also Dr. McNeil, in a stiff-collared coat, looking more like a general than a divine. There were two officers in blue uniforms; and all the rest of us were in black, with only two white waistcoats,—my own being one,—and a rare sprinkling of white cravats. How hideously a man looks in them! I should like to have seen such assemblages as must have gathered in that reception-room, and walked with stately tread to the dining-hall, in times past, the Mayor and other civic dignitaries in their robes, noblemen in their state dresses, the Consul in his olive-leaf embroidery, everybody in some sort of bedizenment,—and then the dinner would have been a magnificent spectacle, worthy of the gilded hall, the rich table-service, and the powdered and gold-laced servitors. At a former dinner I remember seeing a gentleman in small-clothes, with a dress-sword; but all formalities of the kind are passing away. The Mayor's dinners, too, will no doubt be extinct before many years go by. I drove home from the Woodside Ferry in a cab with Bishop Burke and two other gentlemen. The Bishop is nearly seven feet high.

After writing the foregoing account of a civic banquet, where I ate turtle-soup, salmon, woodcock, oyster patties, and I know not what else, I have been to the News-room and found the Exchange pavement densely thronged with people of all ages and of all manner of dirt and rags. They were waiting for soup-tickets, and waiting very patiently too, without outcry or disturbance, or even sour looks,—only patience and meekness in their faces. Well, I don't know that they have a right to be impatient of starvation; but, still there does seem to be an insolence of riches and prosperity, which one day or another will have a downfall. And this will be a pity, too.

On Saturday I went with my friend Mr. Bright to Otterpool and to Larkhill to see the skaters on the private waters of those two seats of gentlemen; and it is a wonder to behold—and it is always a new wonder to me—how comfortable Englishmen know how to make themselves; locating their dwellings far within private grounds, with secure gateways and porters' lodges, and the smoothest roads and trimmest paths, and shaven lawns, and clumps of trees, and every bit of the ground, every hill and dell, made the most of for convenience and beauty, and so well kept that even winter cannot cause disarray; and all this appropriated to the same family for generations, so that I suppose they come to believe it created exclusively and on purpose for them. And, really, the result is good and beautiful. It is a home,—an institution which we Americans have not; but then I doubt whether anybody is entitled to a home in this world, in so full a sense.

The day was very cold, and the skaters seemed to enjoy themselves exceedingly. They were, I suppose, friends of the owners of the grounds, and Mr. Bright said they were treated in a jolly way, with hot luncheons. The skaters practise skating more as an art, and can perform finer manoeuvres on the ice, than our New England skaters usually can, though the English have so much less opportunity for practice. A beggar-woman was haunting the grounds at Otterpool, but I saw nobody give her anything. I wonder how she got inside of the gate.

Mr. W. J——— spoke of General Jackson as having come from the same part of Ireland as himself, and perhaps of the same family. I wonder whether he meant to say that the General was born in Ireland,—that having been suspected in America.

February 21st.—Yesterday two companies of work-people came to our house in Rock Park, asking assistance, being out of work and with no resource other than charity. There were a dozen or more in each party. Their deportment was quiet and altogether unexceptionable,—no rudeness, no gruffness, nothing of menace. Indeed, such demonstrations would not have been safe, as they were followed about by two policemen; but they really seem to take their distress as their own misfortune and God's will, and impute it to nobody as a fault. This meekness is very touching, and makes one question the more whether they have all their rights. There have been disturbances, within a day or two, in Liverpool, and shops have been broken open and robbed of bread and money; but this is said to have been done by idle vagabonds, and not by the really hungry work-people. These last submit to starvation gently and patiently, as if it were an every-day matter with them, or, at least, nothing but what lay fairly within their horoscope. I suppose, in fact, their stomachs have the physical habit that makes hunger not intolerable, because customary. If they had been used to a full meat diet, their hunger would be fierce, like that of ravenous beasts; but now they are trained to it.

I think that the feeling of an American, divided, as I am, by the ocean from his country, has a continual and immediate correspondence with the national feeling at home; and it seems to be independent of any external communication. Thus, my ideas about the Russian war vary in accordance with the state of the public mind at home, so that I am conscious whereabouts public sympathy is.

March 7th.—J——- and I walked to Tranmere, and passed an old house which I suppose to be Tranmere Hall. Our way to it was up a hollow lane, with a bank and hedge on each side, and with a few thatched stone cottages, centuries old, their ridge-poles crooked and the stones time-worn, scattered along. At one point there was a wide, deep well, hewn out of the solid red freestone, and with steps, also hewn in solid rock, leading down to it. These steps were much hollowed by the feet of those who had come to the well; and they reach beneath the water, which is very high. The well probably supplied water to the old cotters and retainers of Tranmere Hall five hundred years ago. The Hall stands on the verge of a long hill which stretches behind Tranmere and as far as Birkenhead.

It is an old gray stone edifice, with a good many gables, and windows with mullions, and some of them extending the whole breadth of the gable. In some parts of the house, the windows seem to have been built up; probably in the days when daylight was taxed. The form of the Hall is multiplex, the roofs sloping down and intersecting one another, so as to make the general result indescribable. There were two sun-dials on different sides of the house, both the dial-plates of which were of stone; and on one the figures, so far as

I could see, were quite worn off, but the gnomon still cast a shadow over it in such a way that I could judge that it was about noon. The other dial had some half-worn hour-marks, but no gnomon. The chinks of the stones of the house were very weedy, and the building looked quaint and venerable; but it is now converted into a farm-house, with the farm-yard and outbuildings closely appended. A village, too, has grown up about it, so that it seems out of place among modern stuccoed dwellings, such as are erected for tradesmen and other moderate people who have their residences in the neighborhood of a great city. Among these there are a few thatched cottages, the homeliest domiciles that ever mortals lived in, belonging to the old estate. Directly across the street is a Wayside Inn, "licensed to sell wine, spirits, ale, and tobacco." The street itself has been laid out since the land grew valuable by the increase of Liverpool and Birkenhead; for the old Hall would never have been built on the verge of a public way.

March 27th.—I attended court to day, at St. George's Hall, with my wife, Mr. Bright, and Mr. Channing, sitting in the High Sheriff's seat. It was the civil side, and Mr. Justice Cresswell presided. The lawyers, as far as aspect goes, seemed to me inferior to an American bar, judging from their countenances, whether as intellectual men or gentlemen. Their wigs and gowns do not impose on the spectator, though they strike him as an imposition. Their date is past. Mr. Warren, of the "Ten Thousand a Year," was in court,—a pale, thin, intelligent face, evidently a nervous man, more unquiet than anybody else in court,—always restless in his seat, whispering to his neighbors, settling his wig, perhaps with an idea that people single him out.

St. George's Hall—the interior hall itself, I mean—is a spacious, lofty, and most rich and noble apartment, and very satisfactory. The pavement is made of mosaic tiles, and has a beautiful effect.

April 7th.—I dined at Mr. J. P. Heywood's on Thursday, and met there Mr. and Mrs. ——— of Smithell's Hall. The Hall is an old edifice of some five hundred years, and Mrs. ——— says there is a bloody footstep at the foot of the great staircase. The tradition is that a certain martyr, in Bloody Mary's time, being examined before the occupant of the Hall, and committed to prison, stamped his foot, in earnest protest against the injustice with which he was treated. Blood issued from his foot, which slid along the stone pavement, leaving a long footmark, printed in blood. And there it has remained ever since, in spite of the scrubbings of all succeeding generations. Mrs. ——— spoke of it with much solemnity, real or affected. She says that they now cover the bloody impress with a carpet, being unable to remove it. In the History of Lancashire, which I looked at last night, there is quite a different account,—according to which the footstep is not a bloody one, but is a slight cavity or inequality in the surface of the stone, somewhat in the shape of a man's foot with a peaked shoe. The martyr's name was George Marsh. He was a curate, and was afterwards burnt. Mrs. ——— asked me to go and see the Hall and the footmark; and as it is in Lancashire, and not a great way off, and a curious old place, perhaps I may.

April 12th.—The Earl of ———, whom I saw the other day at St. George's Hall, has a somewhat elderly look,—a pale and rather thin face, which strikes one as remarkably short, or compressed from top to bottom. Nevertheless, it has great intelligence, and sensitiveness too, I should think, but a cold, disagreeable expression. I should take him to be a man of not very pleasant temper,—not genial. He has no physical presence nor dignity, yet one sees him to be a person of rank and consequence. But, after all, there is nothing about him which it need have taken centuries of illustrious nobility to produce, especially in a man of remarkable ability, as Lord ——— certainly is. S———, who attended court all through the Hapgood trial, and saw Lord ——— for hours together every day, has come to conclusions quite different from mine. She thinks him a perfectly natural person, without any assumption, any self-consciousness, any scorn of the lower world. She was delighted with his ready appreciation and feeling of what was passing around him,— his quick enjoyment of a joke,—the simplicity and unaffectedness of his emotion at whatever incidents excited his interest,—the genial acknowledgment of sympathy, causing him to look round and exchange glances with those near him, who were not his individual friends, but barristers and other casual persons. He seemed to her all that a nobleman ought to be, entirely simple and free from pretence and self-assertion, which persons of lower rank can hardly help bedevilling themselves with. I saw him only for a very few moments, so cannot put my observation against hers, especially as I was influenced by what I had heard the Liverpool people say of him.

I do not know whether I have mentioned that the handsomest man I have seen in England was a young footman of Mr. Heywood's. In his rich livery, he was a perfect Joseph Andrews.

In my Romance, the original emigrant to America may have carried away with him a family secret, whereby it was in his power, had he so chosen, to have brought about the ruin of the family. This secret he transmits to his American progeny, by whom it is inherited throughout all the intervening generations. At last, the hero of the Romance comes to England, and finds, that, by means of this secret, he still has it in his power to procure the downfall of the family. It would be something similar to the story of Meleager, whose fate depended on the firebrand that his mother had snatched from the flames.

April 24th.—On Saturday I was present at a dejeuner on board the Donald McKay; the principal guest being Mr. Layard, M. P. There were several hundred people, quite filling the between decks of the ship, which was converted into a saloon for the occasion. I sat next to Mr. Layard, at the head of the table, and so had a good opportunity of seeing and getting acquainted with him. He is a man in early middle age,—of middle stature, with an open, frank, intelligent, kindly face. His forehead is not expansive, but is prominent in the perceptive regions, and retreats a good deal. His mouth is full,—I liked him from the first. He was very kind and complimentary to me, and made me promise to go and see him in London.

It would have been a very pleasant entertainment, only that my pleasure in it was much marred by having to acknowledge a toast, in honor of the President. However, such things do not trouble me nearly so much as they used to do, and I came through it tolerably enough. Mr. Layard's speech was the great affair of the day. He speaks with much fluency (though he assured me that he had to put great force upon himself to speak publicly), and, as he warms up, seems to engage with his whole moral and physical man,—quite possessed with what he has to say. His evident earnestness and good faith make him eloquent, and stand him instead of oratorical graces. His views of the position of England and the prospects of the war were as dark as well could be; and his speech was exceedingly to the purpose, full of common-sense, and with not one word of clap-trap. Judging from its effect upon the audience, he spoke the voice of the whole English people,—although an English Baronet, who sat next below me, seemed to dissent, or at least to think that it was not exactly the thing for a stranger to hear. It concluded amidst great cheering. Mr. Layard appears to be a true Englishman, with a moral force and strength of character, and earnestness of purpose, and fulness of common-sense, such as have always served England's turn in her past successes; but rather fit for resistance than progress. No doubt, he is a good and very able man; but I question whether he could get England out of the difficulties which he sees so clearly, or could do much better than Lord Palmerston, whom he so decries.

April 25th.—Taking the deposition of sailors yesterday, in a case of alleged ill-usage by the officers of a vessel, one of the witnesses was an old seaman of sixty. In reply to some testimony of his, the captain said, "You were the oldest man in the ship, and we honored you as such." The mate also said that he never could have thought of striking an old man like that. Indeed, the poor old fellow had a kind of dignity and venerableness about him, though he confessed to having been drunk, and seems to have been a mischief-maker, what they call a sea-preacher,— promoting discontent and grumbling. He must have been a very handsome man in his youth, having regular features of a noble and beautiful cast. His beard was gray; but his dark hair had hardly a streak of white, and was abundant all over his head. He was deaf, and seemed to sit in a kind of seclusion, unless when loudly questioned or appealed to. Once he broke forth from a deep silence thus, "I defy any man!" and then was silent again. It had a strange effect, this general defiance, which he meant, I suppose, in answer to some accusation that he thought was made against him. His general behavior throughout the examination was very decorous and proper; and he said he had never but once hitherto been before a consul, and that was in 1819, when a mate had ill-used him, and, "being a young man then, I gave him a beating,"—whereupon his face gleamed with a quiet smile, like faint sunshine on an old ruin. "By many a tempest has his beard been shook"; and I suppose he must soon go into a workhouse, and thence, shortly, to his grave. He is now in a hospital, having, as the surgeon certifies, some ribs fractured; but there does not appear to have been any violence used upon him aboard the ship of such a nature as to cause this injury, though he swears it was a blow from a rope, and nothing else. What struck me in the case was the respect and rank that his age seemed to give him, in the view of the officers; and how, as the captain's expression signified, it lifted him out of his low position, and made him a person to be honored. The dignity of his manner is perhaps partly owing to the ancient mariner, with his long experience, being an oracle among the forecastle men.

May 3d.—It rains to-day, after a very long period of east-wind and dry weather. The east-wind here, blowing across the island, seems to be the least damp of all the winds; but it is full of malice and mischief, of an indescribably evil temper, and stabs one like a cold, poisoned dagger. I never spent so disagreeable a spring as this, although almost every day for a month has been bright.

Friday, May 11th.—A few weeks ago, a sailor, a most pitiable object, came to my office to complain of cruelty from his captain and mate. They had beaten him shamefully, of which he bore grievous marks about his face and eyes, and bruises on his head and other parts of his person: and finally the ship had sailed, leaving him behind. I never in my life saw so forlorn a fellow, so ragged, so wretched; and even his wits seemed to have been beaten out of him, if perchance he ever had any. He got an order for the hospital; and there he has been, off and on, ever since, till yesterday, when I received a message that he was dying, and wished to see the Consul; so I went with Mr. Wilding to the hospital. We were ushered into the waiting-room,—a kind of parlor, with a fire in the grate, and a centre-table, whereon lay one or two medical journals, with wood engravings; and there was a young man, who seemed to be an official of the house, reading. Shortly the surgeon appeared,—a brisk, cheerful, kindly sort of person, whom I have met there on previous visits. He told us that the man was dying, and probably would not be able to communicate anything, but, nevertheless, ushered us up to the highest floor, and into the room where he lay. It was a large, oblong room, with ten or twelve beds in it, each occupied by a patient. The surgeon said that the hospital was often so crowded that they were compelled to lay some of the patients on the floor. The man whom we came to see lay on his bed in a little recess formed by a projecting window; so that there was a kind of seclusion for him to die in. He seemed quite insensible to outward things, and took no notice of our approach, nor responded to what was said to him,—lying on his side, breathing with short gasps,—his apparent disease being inflammation of the chest, although the surgeon said that he might be found to have sustained internal injury by bruises. he was restless, tossing his head continually, mostly with his eyes shut, and much compressed and screwed up, but sometimes opening them; and then they looked brighter and darker than when I first saw them. I think his face was not at any time so stupid as at his first interview with me; but whatever intelligence he had was rather inward than outward, as if there might be life and consciousness at a depth within, while as to external matters he was in a mist. The surgeon felt his wrist, and said that there was absolutely no pulsation, and that he might die at any moment, or might perhaps live an hour, but that there was no prospect of his being able to communicate with me. He was quite restless, nevertheless, and sometimes half raised himself in bed, sometimes turned himself quite over, and then lay gasping for an instant. His woollen shirt being thrust up on his arm, there appeared a tattooing of a ship and anchor, and other nautical emblems, on both of them, which another sailor-patient, on examining them, said must have been done years ago. This might be of some importance, because the dying man had told me, when I first saw him, that he was no sailor, but a farmer, and that, this being his first voyage, he had been beaten by the captain for not doing a sailor's duty, which he had had no opportunity of learning. These sea-emblems indicated that he was probably a seaman of some years' service.

While we stood in the little recess, such of the other patients as were convalescent gathered near the foot of the bed; and the nurse came and looked on, and hovered about us,—a sharp-eyed, intelligent woman of middle age, with a careful and kind expression, neglecting nothing that was for the patient's good, yet taking his death as coolly as any other incident in her daily business. Certainly, it was a very forlorn death-bed; and I felt—what I have heretofore been inclined to doubt— that it might, be a comfort to have persons whom one loves, to go with us to the threshold of the other world, and leave us only when we are fairly across it. This poor fellow had a wife and two children on the other side of the water.

At first he did not utter any sound; but by and by he moaned a little, and gave tokens of being more sensible to outward concerns,—not quite so misty and dreamy as hitherto. We had been talking all the while—myself in a whisper, but the surgeon in his ordinary tones—about his state, without his paying any attention. But now the surgeon put his mouth down to the man's face and said, "Do you know that you are dying?" At this the patient's head began to move upon the pillow; and I thought at first that it was only the restlessness that he had shown all along; but soon it appeared to be an expression of emphatic dissent, a negative shake of the head. He shook it with all his might, and groaned and mumbled, so that it was very evident how miserably reluctant he was to die. Soon after this he absolutely spoke. "O, I want you to get me well! I want to get away from here!" in a groaning and moaning utterance. The surgeon's question had revived him, but to no purpose; for, being told that the Consul had come to see him, and asked whether he had anything to communicate, he said only, "O, I want him to get me well!" and the whole life that was left in him seemed to be unwillingness to die. This did not last long; for he soon relapsed into his first state, only with his face a little more pinched and screwed up, and his eyes strangely sunken. And lost in his head; and the surgeon said that there would be no use in my remaining. So I took my leave. Mr. Wilding had brought a deposition of the man's evidence, which he had clearly made at the Consulate, for him to sign, and this we left with the surgeon, in case there should be such an interval of consciousness and intelligence before death as to make it possible for him to sign it. But of this there is no probability.

I have just received a note from the hospital, stating that the sailor, Daniel Smith, died about three quarters of an hour after I saw him.

May 18th.—The above-mentioned Daniel Smith had about him a bundle of letters, which I have examined. They are all very yellow, stained with sea-water, smelling of bad tobacco-smoke, and much worn at the folds. Never were such ill-written letters, nor such incredibly fantastic spelling. They seem to be from various members of his family,—most of them from a brother, who purports to have been a deck-hand in the coasting and steamboat trade between Charleston and other ports; others from female relations; one from his father, in which he inquires how long his son has been in jail, and when the trial is to come on,—the offence, however, of which he was accused, not being indicated. But from the tenor of his brother's letters, it would appear that he was a small farmer in the interior of South Carolina, sending butter, eggs, and poultry to be sold in Charleston by his brother, and receiving the returns in articles purchased there. This was his own account of himself; and he affirmed, in his deposition before me, that he had never had any purpose of shipping for Liverpool, or anywhere else; but that, going on board the ship to bring a man's trunk ashore, he was compelled to remain and serve as a sailor. This was a hard fate, certainly, and a strange thing to happen in the United States at this day,—that a free citizen should be absolutely kidnapped, carried to a foreign country, treated with savage cruelty during the voyage, and left to die on his arrival. Yet all this has unquestionably been done, and will probably go unpunished.

The seed of the long-stapled cotton, now cultivated in America, was sent there in 1786 from the Bahama Islands, by some of the royalist refugees, who had settled there. The inferior short-stapled cotton had been previously cultivated for domestic purposes. The seeds of every other variety have been tried without success. The kind now grown was first introduced into Georgia. Thus to the refugees America owes as much of her prosperity as is due to the cotton-crops, and much of whatever harm is to result from slavery.

May 22d.—Captain J——— says that he saw, in his late voyage to Australia and India, a vessel commanded by an Englishman, who had with him his wife and thirteen children. This ship was the home of the family, and they had no other. The thirteen children had all been born on board, and had been brought up on board, and knew nothing of dry land, except by occasionally setting foot on it.

Captain J——— is a very agreeable specimen of the American shipmaster, —a pleasant, gentlemanly man, not at all refined, and yet with fine and honorable sensibilities. Very easy in his manners and conversation, yet gentle,—talking on freely, and not much minding grammar; but finding a sufficient and picturesque expression for what he wishes to say; very cheerful and vivacious; accessible to feeling, as yesterday, when talking about the recent death of his mother. His voice faltered, and the tears came into his eyes, though before and afterwards he smiled merrily, and made us smile; fond of his wife, and carrying her about the world with him, and blending her with all his enjoyments; an excellent and sagacious man of business; liberal in his expenditure; proud of his ship and flag; always well dressed, with some little touch of sailor-like flashiness, but not a whit too much; slender in figure, with a handsome face, and rather profuse brown beard and whiskers; active and alert; about thirty-two. A daguerreotype sketch of any conversation of his would do him no justice, for its slang, its grammatical mistakes, its mistaken words (as "portable" for "portly"), would represent a vulgar man, whereas the impression he leaves is by no means that of vulgarity; but he is a character quite perfect within itself, fit for the deck and the cabin, and agreeable in the drawing-room, though not amenable altogether to its rules. Being so perfectly natural, he is more of a gentleman for those little violations of rule, which most men, with his opportunities, might escape.

The men whose appeals to the Consul's charity are the hardest to be denied are those who have no country,—-Hungarians, Poles, Cubans, Spanish-Americans, and French republicans. All exiles for liberty come to me, if the representative of America were their representative. Yesterday, came an old French soldier, and showed his wounds; to-day, a Spaniard, a friend of Lopez,—bringing his little daughter with him. He said he was starving, and looked so. The little girl was in good condition enough, and decently dressed.—May 23d.

May 30th.—The two past days have been Whitsuntide holidays; and they have been celebrated at Tranmere in a manner very similar to that of the old "Election" in Massachusetts, as I remember it a good many years ago, though the festival has now almost or quite died out. Whitsuntide was kept up on our side of the water, I am convinced, under pretence of rejoicings at the election of Governor. It occurred at precisely the same period of the year,—the same week; the only difference being, that Monday and Tuesday are the Whitsun festival days, whereas, in Massachusetts, Wednesday was "Election day," and the acme of the merry-making.

I passed through Tranmere yesterday forenoon, and lingered awhile to see the sports. The greatest peculiarity of the crowd, to my eye, was that they seemed not to have any best clothes, and therefore had put on no holiday suits,—a grimy people, as at all times, heavy, obtuse, with thick beer in their blood. Coarse, rough-complexioned women and girls were intermingled, the girls with no maiden trimness in their attire, large and blowsy. Nobody seemed to have been washed that day. All the enjoyment was of an exceedingly sombre character, so far as I saw it, though there was a richer variety of sports than at similar festivals in America. There were wooden horses, revolving in circles, to be ridden a certain number of rounds for a penny; also swinging cars gorgeously painted, and the newest named after Lord Raglan; and four cars balancing one another, and turned by a winch; and people with targets and rifles,— the principal aim being to hit an apple bobbing on a string before the target; other guns for shooting at the distance of a foot or two, for a prize of filberts; and a game much in fashion, of throwing heavy sticks at earthen mugs suspended on lines, three throws for a penny. Also, there was a posture-master, showing his art in the centre of a ring of miscellaneous spectators, and handing round his bat after going through all his attitudes. The collection amounted to only one halfpenny, and, to eke it out, I threw in three more. There were some large booths with tables placed the whole length, at which sat men and women drinking and smoking pipes; orange-girls, a great many, selling the worst possible oranges, which had evidently been boiled to give them a show of freshness. There were likewise two very large structures, the walls made of boards roughly patched together, and rooted with canvas, which seemed to have withstood a thousand storms. Theatres were there, and in front there were pictures of scenes which were to be represented within; the price of admission being twopence to one theatre, and a penny to the other. But, small as the price of tickets was, I could not see that anybody bought them. Behind the theatres, close to the board wall, and perhaps serving as the general dressing-room, was a large windowed wagon, in which I suppose the company travel and live together. Never, to my imagination, was the mysterious glory that has surrounded theatrical representation ever since my childhood brought down into such dingy reality as this. The tragedy queens were the same coarse and homely women and girls that surrounded me on the green. Some of the people had evidently been drinking more than was good for them; but their drunkenness was silent and stolid, with no madness in it. No ebullition of any sort was apparent.

May 31st.—Last Sunday week, for the first time, I heard the note of the cuckoo. "Cuck-oo—cuck-oo" it says, repeating the word twice, not in a brilliant metallic tone, but low and flute-like, without the excessive sweetness of the flute,—without an excess of saccharine juice in the sound. There are said to be always two cuckoos seen together. The note is very soft and pleasant. The larks I have not yet heard in the sky; though it is not infrequent to hear one singing in a cage, in the streets of Liverpool.

Brewers' draymen are allowed to drink as much of their master's beverage as they like, and they grow very brawny and corpulent, resembling their own horses in size, and presenting, one would suppose, perfect pictures of physical comfort and well-being. But the least bruise, or even the hurt of a finger, is liable to turn to gangrene or erysipelas, and become fatal.

When the wind blows violently, however clear the sky, the English say, "It is a stormy day." And, on the other hand, when the air is still, and it does not actually rain, however dark and lowering the sky may be, they say, "The weather is fine!"

June 2d.—The English women of the lower classes have a grace of their own, not seen in each individual, but nevertheless belonging to their order, which is not to be found in American women of the corresponding class. The other day, in the police court, a girl was put into the witness-box, whose native graces of this sort impressed me a good deal. She was coarse, and her dress was none of the cleanest, and nowise smart. She appeared to have been up all night, too, drinking at the Tranmere wake, and had since ridden in a cart, covered up with a rug. She described herself as a servant-girl, out of place; and her charm lay in all her manifestations,—her tones, her gestures, her look, her way of speaking and what she said, being so appropriate and natural in a girl of that class; nothing affected; no proper grace thrown away by attempting to appear lady-like,—which an American girl would have attempted,—and she would also have succeeded in a certain degree. If each class would but keep within itself, and show its respect for itself by aiming at nothing beyond, they would all be more respectable. But this kind of fitness is evidently not to be expected in the future; and something else must be substituted for it.

These scenes at the police court are often well worth witnessing. The controlling genius of the court, except when the stipendiary magistrate presides, is the clerk, who is a man learned in the law. Nominally the cases are decided by the aldermen, who sit in rotation, but at every important point there comes a nod or a whisper from the clerk; and it is that whisper which sets the defendant free or sends him to prison. Nevertheless, I suppose the alderman's common-sense and native shrewdness are not without their efficacy in producing a general tendency towards the right; and, no doubt, the decisions of the police court are quite as often just as those of any other court whatever.

June 11th.—I walked with J—— yesterday to Bebington Church. When I first saw this church, nearly two years since, it seemed to me the fulfilment of my ideal of an old English country church. It is not so satisfactory now, although certainly a venerable edifice. There used some time ago to be ivy all over the tower; and at my first view of it, there was still a little remaining on the upper parts of the spire. But the main roots, I believe, were destroyed, and pains were taken to clear away the whole of the ivy, so that now it is quite bare,—nothing but homely gray stone, with marks of age, but no beauty. The most curious thing about the church is the font. It is a massive pile, composed of five or six layers of freestone in an octagon shape, placed in the angle formed by the projecting side porch and the wall of the church, and standing under a stained-glass window. The base is six or seven feet across, and it is built solidly up in successive steps, to the height of about six feet,—an octagonal pyramid, with the basin of the font crowning the pile hewn out of the solid stone, and about a foot in diameter and the same in depth. There was water in it from the recent rains,—water just from heaven, and therefore as holy as any water it ever held in old Romish times. The aspect of this aged font is extremely venerable, with moss in the basin and all over the stones; grass, and weeds of various kinds, and little shrubs, rooted in the chinks of the stones and between the successive steps.

At each entrance of Rock Park, where we live, there is a small Gothic structure of stone, each inhabited by a policeman and his family; very small dwellings indeed, with the main apartment opening directly out-of-doors; and when the door is open, one can see the household fire, the good wife at work, perhaps the table set, and a throng of children clustering round, and generally overflowing the threshold. The policeman walks about the Park in stately fashion, with his silver-laced blue uniform and snow-white gloves, touching his hat to gentlemen who reside in the Park. In his public capacity he has rather an awful aspect, but privately he is a humble man enough, glad of any little job, and of old clothes for his many children, or, I believe, for himself. One of the two policemen is a shoemaker and cobbler. His pay, officially, is somewhere about a guinea a week.

The Park, just now, is very agreeable to look at, shadowy with trees and shrubs, and with glimpses of green leaves and flower-gardens through the branches and twigs that line the iron fences. After a shower the hawthorn blossoms are delightfully fragrant. Golden tassels of the laburnum are abundant.

I may have mentioned elsewhere the traditional prophecy, that, when the ivy should reach the top of Bebbington spire, the tower was doomed to fall. It lies still, therefore, a chance of standing for centuries. Mr. Turner tells me that the font now used is inside of the church, but the one outside is of unknown antiquity, and that it was customary, in papistical time, to have the font without the church.

There is a little boy often on board the Rock Ferry steamer with an accordion,—an instrument I detest; but nevertheless it becomes tolerable in his hands, not so much for its music, as for the earnestness and interest with which he plays it. His body and the accordion together become one musical instrument on which his soul plays tunes, for he sways and vibrates with the music from head to foot and throughout his frame, half closing his eyes and uplifting his face, as painters represent St. Cecilia and other famous musicians; and sometimes he swings his accordion in the air, as if in a perfect rapture. After all, my ears, though not very nice, are somewhat tortured by his melodies, especially when confined within the cabin. The boy is ten years old, perhaps, and rather pretty; clean, too, and neatly dressed, very unlike all other street and vagabond children whom I have seen in Liverpool. People give him their halfpence more readily than to any other musicians who infest the boat.

J——, the other day, was describing a soldier-crab to his mother, he being much interested in natural history, and endeavoring to give as strong an idea as possible of its warlike characteristics, and power to harm those who molest it. Little R—— sat by, quietly listening and sewing, and at last, lifting her head, she remarked, "I hope God did not hurt himself, when he was making him!"

LEAMINGTON.

June 21st.—We left Rock Ferry and Liverpool on Monday the 18th by the rail for this place; a very dim and rainy day, so that we had no pleasant prospects of the country; neither would the scenery along the Great Western Railway have been in any case very striking, though sunshine would have made the abundant verdure and foliage warm and genial. But a railway naturally finds its way through all the common places of a country, and is certainly a most unsatisfactory mode of travelling, the only object being to arrive. However, we had a whole carriage to ourselves, and the children enjoyed the earlier part of the journey very much. We skirted Shrewsbury, and I think I saw the old tower of a church near the station, perhaps the same that struck Falstaff's "long hour." As we left the town I saw the Wrekin, a round, pointed hill of regular shape, and remembered the old toast, "To all friends round the Wrekin!" As we approached Birmingham, the country began to look somewhat Brummagemish, with its manufacturing chimneys, and pennons of flame quivering out of their tops; its forges, and great heaps of mineral refuse; its smokiness and other ugly symptoms. Of Birmingham itself we saw little or nothing, except the mean and new brick lodging-houses, on the outskirts of the town. Passing through Warwick, we had a glimpse of the castle,—an ivied wall and two turrets, rising out of imbosoming foliage; one's very idea of an old castle. We reached Leamington at a little past six, and drove to the Clarendon Hotel,—a very spacious and stately house, by far the most splendid hotel I have yet seen in England. The landlady, a courteous old lady in black, showed my wife our rooms, and we established ourselves in an immensely large and lofty parlor, with red curtains and ponderous furniture, perhaps a very little out of date. The waiter brought me the book of arrivals, containing the names of all visitors for from three to five years back. During two years I estimated that there had been about three hundred and fifty persons only, and while we were there, I saw nobody but ourselves to support the great hotel. Among the names were those of princes, earls, countesses, and baronets; and when the people of the house heard from R——'s nurse that I too was a man of office, and held the title of Honorable in my own country, they greatly regretted that I entered myself as plain "Mister" in the book. We found this hotel very comfortable, and might doubtless have made it luxurious, had we chosen to go to five times the expense of similar luxuries in America; but we merely ordered comfortable things, and so came off at no very extravagant rate,—and with great honor, at all events, in the estimation of the waiter.

During the afternoon we found lodgings, and established ourselves in them before dark.

This English custom of lodgings, of which we had some experience at Rhyl last year, has its advantages; but is rather uncomfortable for strangers, who, in first settling themselves down, find that they must undertake all the responsibility of housekeeping at an instant's warming, and cannot get even a cup of tea till they have made arrangements with the grocer. Soon, however, there comes a sense of being at home, and by our exclusive selves, which never can be attained at hotels nor boarding-houses. Our house is well situated and respectably furnished, with the dinginess, however, which is inseparable from lodging-houses,—as if others had used these things before and would use them again after we had gone,—a well-enough adaptation, but a lack of peculiar appropriateness; and I think one puts off real enjoyment from a sense of not being truly fitted.

July 1st.—On Friday I took the rail with J—— for Coventry. It was a bright and very warm day, oppressively so, indeed; though I think that there is never in this English climate the pervading warmth of an American summer day. The sunshine may be excessively hot, but an overshadowing cloud or the shade of a tree or of a building at once affords relief; and if the slightest breeze stirs, you feel the latent freshness of the air.

Coventry is some nine or ten miles from Leamington. The approach to it from the railway presents nothing very striking,—a few church-towers, and one or two tall steeples; and the houses first seen are of modern and unnoticeable aspect. Getting into the interior of the town, however, you find the streets very crooked, and some of them very narrow. I saw one place where it seemed possible to shake hands from one jutting storied old house to another. There were whole streets of the same kind of houses, one story impending over another, such as used to be familiar to me in Salem, and in some streets of Boston. In fact, the whole aspect of the town—its irregularity and continual indirectness—reminded me very much of Boston, as I used to see it, in rare visits thither, when a child.

These Coventry houses, however, many of them, are much larger than any of similar style that I have seen elsewhere, and they spread into greater bulk as they ascend, by means of one story jutting over the other. Probably the New-Englanders continued to follow this fashion of architecture after it had been abandoned in the mother country. The old house built, by Philip English, in Salem, dated about 1692; and it was in this style,—many gabled, and impending. Here the edifices of such architecture seem to be Elizabethan, and of earlier date. A woman in Stratford told us that the rooms, very low on the ground-floor, grew loftier from story to story to the attic. The fashion of windows, in Coventry, is such as I have not hitherto seen. In the highest story, a window of the ordinary height extends along the whole breadth of the house, ten, fifteen, perhaps twenty feet, just like any other window of a commonplace house, except for this inordinate width. One does not easily see what the inhabitants want of so much window-light; but the fashion is very general, and in modern houses, or houses that have been modernized, this style of window is retained. Thus young people who grow up amidst old people contract quaint and old-fashioned manners and aspect.

I imagine that these ancient towns—such as Chester and Stratford, Warwick and Coventry—contain even a great deal more antiquity than meets the eye. You see many modern fronts; but if you peep or penetrate inside, you find an antique arrangement,—old rafters, intricate passages, and ancient staircases, which have put on merely a new outside, and are likely still to prove good for the usual date of a new house. They put such an immense and stalwart ponderosity into their frameworks, that I suppose a house of Elizabeth's time, if renewed, has at least an equal chance of durability with one that is new in every part. All the hotels in Coventry, so far as I noticed them, are old, with new fronts; and they have an archway for the admission of vehicles into the court-yard, and doors opening into the rooms of the building on each side of the arch. Maids and waiters are seen darting across the arched passage from door to door, and it requires a guide (in my case, at least) to show you the way to the coffee-room or the bar. I have never been up stairs in any of them, but can conceive of infinite bewilderment of zigzag corridors between staircase and chamber.

It was fair-day in Coventry, and this gave what no doubt is an unusual bustle to the streets. In fact, I have not seen such crowded and busy streets in any English town; various kinds of merchandise being for sale in the open air, and auctioneers disposing of miscellaneous wares, pretty much as they do at musters and other gatherings in the United States. The oratory of the American auctioneer, however, greatly surpasses that of the Englishman in vivacity and fun. But this movement and throng, together with the white glow of the sun on the pavements, make the scene, in my recollection, assume an American aspect, and this is strange in so antique and quaint a town as Coventry.

We rambled about without any definite aim, but found our way, I believe, to most of the objects that are worth seeing. St. Michael's Church was most magnificent,—so old, yet enduring; so huge, so rich; with such intricate minuteness in its finish, that, look as long as you will at it, you can always discover something new directly before your eyes. I admire this in Gothic architecture,—that you cannot master it all at once, that it is not a naked outline; but, as deep and rich as human nature itself, always revealing new ideas. It is as if the builder had built himself and his age up into it, and as if the edifice had life. Grecian temples are less interesting to me, being so cold and crystalline. I think this is the only church I have seen where there are any statues still left standing in the niches of the exterior walls. We did not go inside. The steeple of St. Michael's is three hundred and three feet high, and no doubt the clouds often envelop the tip of the spire. Trinity, another church with a tall spire, stands near St. Michael's, but did not attract me so much; though I, perhaps, might have admired it equally, had I seen it first or alone. We certainly know nothing of church-building in America, and of all English things that I have seen, methinks the churches disappoint me least. I feel, too, that there is something much more wonderful in them than I have yet had time to know and experience.

In the course of the forenoon, searching about everywhere in quest of Gothic architecture, we found our way into St. Mary's Hall. The doors were wide open; it seemed to be public,—there was a notice on the wall desiring visitors to give nothing to attendants for showing it, and so we walked in. I observed, in the guide-books, that we should have obtained an order for admission from some member of the town council; but we had none, and found no need of it. An old woman, and afterwards an old man, both of whom seemed to be at home on the premises, told us that we might enter, and troubled neither themselves nor us any further.

St. Mary's Hall is now the property of the Corporation of Coventry, and seems to be the place where the Mayor and Council hold their meetings. It was built by one of the old guilds or fraternities of merchants and tradesmen The woman shut the kitchen door when I approached, so that I did not see the great fireplaces and huge cooking-utensils which are said to be there. Whether these are ever used nowadays, and whether the Mayor of Coventry gives such hospitable banquets as the Mayor of Liverpool, I do not know.

We went to the Red Lion, and had a luncheon of cold lamb and cold pigeon-pie. This is the best way of dining at English hotels,—to call the meal a luncheon, in which case you will get as good or better a variety than if it were a dinner, and at less than half the cost. Having lunched, we again wandered about town, and entered a quadrangle of gabled houses, with a church, and its churchyard on one side. This proved to be St. John's Church, and a part of the houses were the locality of Bond's Hospital, for the reception of ten poor men, and the remainder was devoted to the Bablake School. Into this latter I peered, with a real American intrusiveness, which I never found in myself before, but which I must now assume, or miss a great many things which I am anxious to see. Running along the front of the house, under the jut of the impending story, there was a cloistered walk, with windows opening on the quadrangle. An arched oaken door, with long iron hinges, admitted us into a school-room about twenty feet square, paved with brick tiles, blue and red. Adjoining this there is a larger school-room which we did not enter, but peeped at, through one of the inner windows, from the cloistered walk. In the room which we entered, there were seven scholars' desks, and an immense arched fireplace, with seats on each side, under the chimney, on a stone slab resting on a brick pedestal. The opening of the fireplace was at least twelve feet in width. On one side of the room were pegs for fifty-two boys' hats and clothes, and there was a boy's coat, of peculiar cut, hanging on a peg, with the number "50" in brass upon it. The coat looked ragged and shabby. An old school-book was lying on one of the desks, much tattered, and without a title; but it seemed to treat wholly of Saints' days and festivals of the Church. A flight of stairs, with a heavy balustrade of carved oak, ascended to a gallery, about eight or nine feet from the lower floor, which runs along two sides of the room, looking down upon it. The room is without a ceiling, and rises into a peaked gable, about twenty feet high. There is a large clock in it, and it is lighted by two windows, each about ten feet wide,—one in the gallery, and the other beneath it. Two benches or settles, with backs, stood one on each side of the fireplace. An old woman in black passed through the room while I was making my observations, and looked at me, but said nothing. The school was founded in 1563, by Thomas Whealby, Mayor of Coventry; the revenue is about 900 pounds, and admits children of the working-classes at eleven years old, clothes and provides for them, and finally apprentices them for seven years. We saw some of the boys playing in the quadrangle, dressed in long blue coats or gowns, with cloth caps on their heads. I know not how the atmosphere of antiquity, and massive continuance from age to age, which was the charm to me in this scene of a charity school-room, can be thrown over it in description. After noting down these matters, I looked into the quiet precincts of Bond's Hospital, which, no doubt, was more than equally interesting; but the old men were lounging about or lolling at length, looking very drowsy, and I had not the heart nor the face to intrude among them. There is something altogether strange to an American in these charitable institutions,—in the preservation of antique modes and customs which is effected by them, insomuch that, doubtless, without at all intending it, the founders have succeeded in preserving a model of their own long-past age down into the midst of ours, and how much later nobody can know.

We were now rather tired, and went to the railroad, intending to go home; but we got into the wrong train, and were carried by express, with hurricane speed, to Bradon, where we alighted, and waited a good while for the return train to Coventry. At Coventry again we had more than an hour to wait, and therefore wandered wearily up into the city, and took another look at its bustling streets, in which there seems to be a good emblem of what England itself really is,—with a great deal of antiquity in it, and which is now chiefly a modification of the old. The new things are based and supported on the sturdy old things, and often limited and impeded by them; but this antiquity is so massive that there seems to be no means of getting rid of it without tearing society to pieces.

July 2d.—To-day I shall set out on my return to Liverpool, leaving my family here.

TO THE LAKES.

July 4th.—I left Leamington on Monday, shortly after twelve, having been accompanied to the railway station by U—— and J——-, whom I sent away before the train started. While I was waiting, a rather gentlemanly, well-to-do, English-looking man sat down by me, and began to talk of the Crimea, of human affairs in general, of God and his Providence, of the coming troubles of the world, and of spiritualism, in a strange free way for an Englishman, or, indeed, for any man. It was easy to see that he was an enthusiast of some line or other. He being bound for Birmingham and I for Rugby, we soon had to part; but he asked my name, and told me his own, which I did not much attend to, and immediately forgot.

[Here follows a long account of a visit to Lichfield and Uttoxeter, condensed in "Our Old Home."]

July 6th.—The day after my arrival, by way of Lichfield and Uttoxeter, at Liverpool, the door of the Consulate opened, and in came the very sociable personage who accosted me at the railway station at Leamington. He was on his way towards Edinburgh, to deliver a course of lectures or a lecture, and had called, he said, to talk with me about spiritualism, being desirous of having the judgment of a sincere mind on the subject. In his own mind, I should suppose, he is past the stage of doubt and inquiry; for he told me that in every action of his life he is governed by the counsels received from the spiritual world through a medium. I did not inquire whether this medium (who is a small boy) had suggested his visit to me. My remarks to him were quite of a sceptical character in regard to the faith to which he had surrendered himself. He has formerly lived in America, and had had a son born there. He gave me a pamphlet written by himself, on the cure of consumption and other diseases by antiseptic remedies. I hope he will not bore me any more, though he seems to be a very sincere and good man; but these enthusiasts who adopt such extravagant ideas appear to one to lack imagination, instead of being misled by it, as they are generally supposed to be.

NEWBY BRIDGE.—FOOT OF WINDERMERE.

July 13th.—I left Liverpool on Saturday last, by the London and Northwestern Railway, for Leamington, spent Sunday there, and started on Monday for the English lakes, with the whole family. We should not have taken this journey just now, but I had an official engagement which it was convenient to combine with a pleasure-excursion. The first night we arrived at Chester, and put up at the Albion Hotel, where we found ourselves very comfortable. We took the rail at twelve the next day, and went as far as Milnethorpe station, where we engaged seats in an old-fashioned stage-coach, and came to Newby Bridge. I suppose there are not many of these coaches now running on any road in Great Britain; but this appears to be the genuine machine, in all respects, and especially in the round, ruddy coachman, well moistened with ale, good-natured, courteous, and with a proper sense of his dignity and important position. U———, J———, and I mounted atop, S——— , nurse, and R——— got inside, and we bowled off merrily towards the hearts of the hills. It was more than half past nine when we arrived at Newby Bridge, and alighted at the Swan Hotel, where we now are.

It is a very agreeable place: not striking as to scenery, but with a pleasant rural aspect. A stone bridge of five arches crosses the river Severn (which is the communication between Windermere Lake and Morecambe Bay) close to the house, which sits low—and well sheltered in the lap of hills,—an old-fashioned inn, where the landlord and his people have a simple and friendly way of dealing with their guests, and yet provide them with all sorts of facilities for being comfortable. They load our supper and breakfast tables with trout, cold beef, ham, toast, and muffins; and give us three fair courses for dinner, and excellent wine, the cost of all which remains to be seen. This is not one of the celebrated stations among the lakes; but twice a day the stage-coach passes from Milnethorpe towards Ulverton, and twice returns, and three times a little steamer passes to and fro between our hotel and the head of the lake. Young ladies, in broad-brimmed hats, stroll about, or row on the river in the light shallops, of which there are abundance; sportsmen sit on the benches under the windows of the hotel, arranging their fishing-tackle; phaetons and post-chaises, with postilions in scarlet jackets and white breeches, with one high-topped boot, and the other leathered far up on the leg to guard against friction between the horses, dash up to the door. Morning and night comes the stage-coach, and we inspect the outside passengers, almost face to face with us, from our parlor-windows, up one pair of stairs. Little boys, and J—— among them, spend hours on hours fishing in the clear, shallow river for the perch, chubs, and minnows that may be seen flashing, like gleams of light over the flat stones with which the bottom is paved. I cannot answer for the other boys, but J—— catches nothing.

There are a good many trees on the hills and roundabout, and pleasant roads loitering along by the gentle river-side, and it has been so sunny and warm since we came here that we shall have quite a genial recollection of the place, if we leave it before the skies have time to frown. The day after we came, we climbed a high and pretty steep hill, through a path shadowed with trees and shrubbery, up to a tower, from the summit of which we had a wide view of mountain scenery and the greater part of Windermere. This lake is a lovely little pool among the hills, long and narrow, beautifully indented with tiny bays and headlands; and when we saw it, it was one smile (as broad a smile as its narrowness allowed) with really brilliant sunshine. All the scenery we have yet met with is in excellent taste, and keeps itself within very proper bounds,— never getting too wild and rugged to shock the sensibilities of cultivated people, as American scenery is apt to do. On the rudest surface of English earth, there is seen the effect of centuries of civilization, so that you do not quite get at naked Nature anywhere. And then every point of beauty is so well known, and has been described so much, that one must needs look through other people's eyes, and feels as if he were seeing a picture rather than a reality. Man has, in short, entire possession of Nature here, and I should think young men might sometimes yearn for a fresher draught. But an American likes it.

FURNESS ABBEY.

Yesterday, July 12th, we took a phaeton and went to Furness Abbey,—a drive of about sixteen miles, passing along the course of the Leam to Morecambe Bay, and through Ulverton and other villages. These villages all look antique, and the smallest of them generally are formed of such close, contiguous clusters of houses, and have such narrow and crooked streets, that they give you an idea of a metropolis in miniature. The houses along the road (of which there are not many, except in the villages) are almost invariably old, built of stone, and covered with a light gray plaster; generally they have a little flower-garden in front, and, often, honeysuckles, roses, or some other sweet and pretty rustic adornment, are flowering over the porch. I have hardly had such images of simple, quiet, rustic comfort and beauty, as from the look of these houses; and the whole impression of our winding and undulating road, bordered by hedges, luxuriantly green, and not too closely clipped, accords with this aspect. There is nothing arid in an English landscape; and one cannot but fancy that the same may be true of English rural life. The people look wholesome and well-to-do,—not specimens of hard, dry, sunburnt muscle, like our yeomen,—and are kind and civil to strangers, sometimes making a little inclination of the head in passing. Miss Martineau, however, does not seem to think well of their mental and moral condition.

We reached Furness Abbey about twelve. There is a railway station close by the ruins; and a new hotel stands within the precincts of the abbey grounds; and continually there is the shriek, the whiz, the rumble, the bell-ringing, denoting the arrival of the trains; and passengers alight, and step at once (as their choice may be) into the refreshment-room, to get a glass of ale or a cigar,—or upon the gravelled paths of the lawn, leading to the old broken walls and arches of the abbey. The ruins are extensive, and the enclosure of the abbey is stated to have covered a space of sixty-five acres. It is impossible to describe them. The most interesting part is that which was formerly the church, and which, though now roofless, is still surrounded by walls, and retains the remnants of the pillars that formerly supported the intermingling curves of the arches. The floor is all overgrown with grass, strewn with fragments and capitals of pillars. It was a great and stately edifice, the length of the nave and choir having been nearly three hundred feet, and that of the transept more than half as much. The pillars along the nave were alternately a round, solid one and a clustered one. Now, what remains of some of them is even with the ground; others present a stump just high enough to form a seat; and others are, perhaps, a man's height from the ground,—and all are mossy, and with grass and weeds rooted into their chinks, and here and there a tuft of flowers, giving its tender little beauty to their decay. The material of the edifice is a soft red stone, and it is now extensively overgrown with a lichen of a very light gray line, which, at a little distance, makes the walls look as if they had long ago been whitewashed, and now had partially returned to their original color. The arches of the nave and transept were noble and immense; there were four of them together, supporting a tower which has long since disappeared,—arches loftier than I ever conceived to have been made by man. Very possibly, in some cathedral that I have seen, or am yet to see, there may be arches as stately as these; but I doubt whether they can ever show to such advantage in a perfect edifice as they do in this ruin,—most of them broken, only one, as far as I recollect, still completing its sweep. In this state they suggest a greater majesty and beauty than any finished human work can show; the crumbling traces of the half-obliterated design producing somewhat of the effect of the first idea of anything admirable, when it dawns upon the mind of an artist or a poet,—an idea which, do what he may, he is sure to fall short of in his attempt to embody it.

In the middle of the choir is a much-dilapidated monument of a cross-legged knight (a crusader, of course) in armor, very rudely executed; and, against the wall, lie two or three more bruised and battered warriors, with square helmets on their heads and visors down. Nothing can be uglier than these figures; the sculpture of those days seems to have been far behind the architecture. And yet they knew how to put a grotesque expression into the faces of their images, and we saw some fantastic shapes and heads at the lower points of arches which would do to copy into Punch. In the chancel, just at the point below where the high altar stands, was the burial-place of the old Barons of Kendal. The broken crusader, perhaps, represents one of them; and some of their stalwart bones might be found by digging down. Against the wall of the choir, near the vacant space where the altar was, are some stone seats with canopies richly carved in stone, all quite perfectly preserved, where the priests used to sit at intervals, during the celebration of mass. Conceive all these shattered walls, with here and there an arched door, or the great arched vacancy of a window; these broken stones and monuments scattered about; these rows of pillars up and down the nave; these arches, through which a giant might have stepped, and not needed to bow his head, unless in reverence to the sanctity of the place,—conceive it all, with such verdure and embroidery of flowers as the gentle, kindly moisture of the English climate procreates on all old things, making them more beautiful than new,—conceive it with the grass for sole pavement of the long and spacious aisle, and the sky above for the only roof. The sky, to be sure, is more majestic than the tallest of those arches; and yet these latter, perhaps, make the stronger impression of sublimity, because they translate the sweep of the sky to our finite comprehension. It was a most beautiful, warm, sunny day, and the ruins had all the pictorial advantage of bright light and deep shadows. I must not forget that birds flew in and out among the recesses, and chirped and warbled, and made themselves at home there. Doubtless, the birds of the present generation are the posterity of those who first settled in the ruins, after the Reformation; and perhaps the old monks of a still earlier day may have watched them building about the abbey, before it was a ruin at all.

We had an old description of the place with us, aided by which we traced out the principal part of the edifice, such as the church, as already mentioned, and, contiguous to this, the Chapter-house, which is better preserved than the church; also the kitchen, and the room where the monks met to talk; and the range of wall, where their cells probably were. I never before had given myself the trouble to form any distinct idea of what an abbey or monastery was,—a place where holy rites were daily and continually to be performed, with places to eat and sleep contiguous and convenient, in order that the monks might always be at hand to perform those rites. They lived only to worship, and therefore lived under the same roof with their place of worship, which, of course, was the principal object in the edifice, and hallowed the whole of it. We found, too, at one end of the ruins, what is supposed to have been a school-house for the children of the tenantry or villeins of the abbey. All round this room is a bench of stone against the wall, and the pedestal also of the master's seat. There are, likewise, the ruins of the mill; and the mill-stream, which is just as new as ever it was, still goes murmuring and babbling, and passes under two or three old bridges, consisting of a low gray arch overgrown with grass and shrubbery. That stream was the most fleeting and vanishing thing about the ponderous and high-piled abbey; and yet it has outlasted everything else, and might still outlast another such edifice, and be none the worse for wear.

There is not a great deal of ivy upon the walls, and though an ivied wall is a beautiful object, yet it is better not to have too much,—else it is but one wall of unbroken verdure, on which you can see none of the sculptural ornaments, nor any of the hieroglyphics of Time. A sweep of ivy here and there, with the gray wall everywhere showing through, makes the better picture; and I think that nothing is so effective as the little bunches of flowers, a mere handful, that grow in spots where the seeds have been carried by the wind ages ago.

I have made a miserable botch of this description; it is no description, but merely an attempt to preserve something of the impression it made on me, and in this I do not seem to have succeeded at all. I liked the contrast between the sombreness of the old walls, and the sunshine falling through them, and gladdening the grass that floored the aisles; also, I liked the effect of so many idle and cheerful people, strolling into the haunts of the dead monks, and going babbling about, and peering into the dark nooks; and listening to catch some idea of what the building was from a clerical-looking personage, who was explaining it to a party of his friends. I don't know how well acquainted this gentleman might be with the subject; but he seemed anxious not to impart his knowledge too extensively, and gave a pretty direct rebuff to an honest man who ventured an inquiry of him. I think that the railway, and the hotel within the abbey grounds, add to the charm of the place. A moonlight solitary visit might be very good, too, in its way; but I believe that one great charm and beauty of antiquity is, that we view it out of the midst of quite another mode of life; and the more perfectly this can be done, the better. It can never be done more perfectly than at Furness Abbey, which is in itself a very sombre scene, and stands, moreover, in the midst of a melancholy valley, the Saxon name of which means the Vale of the Deadly Nightshade.

The entrance to the stable-yard of the hotel is beneath a pointed arch of Saxon architecture, and on one side of this stands an old building, looking like a chapel, but which may have been a porter's lodge. The Abbot's residence was in this quarter; and the clerical personage, before alluded to, spoke of these as the oldest part of the ruins.

About half a mile on the hither side of the abbey stands the village of Dalton, in which is a castle built on a Roman foundation, and which was afterwards used by the abbots (in their capacity of feudal lords) as a prison. The abbey was founded about 1027 by King Stephen, before he came to the throne; and the faces of himself and of his queen are still to be seen on one of the walls.

We had a very agreeable drive home (our drive hither had been uncomfortably sunny and hot), and we stopped at Ulverton to buy a pair of shoes for J—— and some drawing-books and stationery. As we passed through the little town in the morning, it was all alive with the bustle and throng of the weekly market; and though this had ceased on our return, the streets still looked animated, because the heat of the day drew most of the population, I should imagine, out of doors. Old men look very antiquated here in their old-fashioned coats and breeches, sunning themselves by the wayside.

We reached home somewhere about eight o'clock,—home I see I have called it; and it seems as homelike a spot as any we have found in England,—the old inn, close by the bridge, beside the clear river, pleasantly overshadowed by trees. It is entirely English, and like nothing that one sees in America; and yet. I feel as if I might have lived here a long while ago, and had now come back because I retained pleasant recollections of it. The children, too, make themselves at home. J—— spends his time from morning to night fishing for minnows or trout, and catching nothing at all, and U—— and R—— have been riding between fields and barn in a hay-cart. The roads give us beautiful walks along the river-side, or wind away among the gentle hills; and if we had nothing else to look at in these walks, the hedges and stone fences would afford interest enough, so many and pretty are the flowers, roses, honeysuckles, and other sweet things, and so abundantly does the moss and ivy grow among the old stones of the fences, which would never have a single shoot of vegetation on them in America till the very end of time. But here, no sooner is a stone fence built, than Nature sets to work to make it a part of herself. She adopts it and adorns it, as if it were her own child. A little sprig of ivy may be seen creeping up the side, and clinging fast with its many feet; a tuft of grass roots itself between two of the stones, where a little dust from the road has been moistened into soil for it: a small bunch of fern grows in another such crevice; a deep, soft, green moss spreads itself over the top and all along the sides of the fence; and wherever nothing else will grow, lichens adhere to the stones and variegate their lines. Finally, a great deal of shrubbery is sure to cluster along its extent, and take away all hardness from the outline; and so the whole stone fence looks as if God had had at least as much to do with it as man. The trunks of the trees, too, exhibit a similar parasitical vegetation. Parasitical is an unkind phrase to bestow on this beautiful love and kindness which seems to exist here between one plant and another; the strong thing—being always ready to give support and sustenance, and the weak thing to repay with beauty, so that both are the richer,—as in the case of ivy and woodbine, clustering up the trunk of a tall tree, and adding Corinthian grace to its lofty beauty.

Mr. W———, our landlord, has lent us a splendid work with engravings, illustrating the antiquities of Furness Abbey. I gather from it that the hotel must have been rebuilt or repaired from an old manor-house, which was itself erected by a family of Prestons, after the Reformation, and was a renewal from the Abbot's residence. Much of the edifice probably, as it exists now, may have been part of the original one; and there are bas-reliefs of Scripture subjects, sculptured in stone, and fixed in the wall of the dining-room, which have been there since the Abbot's time. This author thinks that what we had supposed to be the school-house (on the authority of an old book) was really the building for the reception of guests, with its chapel. He says that the tall arches in the church are sixty feet high. The Earl of Burlington, I believe, is the present proprietor of the abbey.

THE LAKES.

July 16th.—On Saturday, we left Newby Bridge, and came by steamboat up Windermere Lake to Lowwood Hotel, where we now are. The foot of the lake is just above Newby Bridge, and it widens from that point, but never to such a breadth that objects are not pretty distinctly visible from shore to shore. The steamer stops at two or three places in the course of its voyage, the principal one being Bowness, which has a little bustle and air of business about it proper to the principal port of the lake. There are several small yachts, and many skiffs rowing about. The banks are everywhere beautiful, and the water, in one portion, is strewn with islands; few of which are large enough to be inhabitable, but they all seem to be appropriated, and kept in the neatest order. As yet, I have seen no wildness; everything is perfectly subdued and polished and imbued with human taste, except, indeed, the outlines of the hills, which continue very much the same as God made them. As we approached the head of the lake, the congregation of great hills in the distance became very striking. The shapes of these English mountains are certainly far more picturesque than those which I have seen in Eastern America, where their summits are almost invariably rounded, as I remember them. They are great hillocks, great bunches of earth, similar to one another in their developments. Here they have variety of shape, rising into peaks, falling in abrupt precipices, stretching along in zigzag outlines, and thus making the most of their not very gigantic masses, and producing a remarkable effect.

We arrived at the Lowwood Hotel, which is very near the head of the lake, not long after two o'clock. It stands almost on the shore of Windermere, with only a green lawn between,—an extensive hotel, covering a good deal of ground; but low, and rather village-inn-like than lofty. We found the house so crowded as to afford us no very comfortable accommodations, either as to parlor or sleeping-rooms, and we find nothing like the home-feeling into which we at once settled down at Newby Bridge. There is a very pretty vicinity, and a fine view of mountains to the northwest, sitting together in a family group, sometimes in full sunshine, sometimes with only a golden gleam on one or two of them, sometimes all in a veil of cloud, from which here and there a great, dusky head raises itself, while you are looking at a dim obscurity. Nearer, there are high, green slopes, well wooded, but with such decent and well-behaved wood as you perceive has grown up under the care of man; still no wildness, no ruggedness,—as how should there be, when, every half-mile or so, a porter's lodge or a gentleman's gateway indicates that the whole region is used up for villas. On the opposite shore of the lake there is a mimic castle, which I suppose I might have mistaken for a real one two years ago. It is a great, foolish toy of gray stone.

A steamboat comes to the pier as many as six times a day, and stage-coaches and omnibuses stop at the door still oftener, communicating with Ambleside and the town of Windermere, and with the railway, which opens London and all the world to us. We get no knowledge of our fellow-guests, all of whom, like ourselves, live in their own circles, and are just as remote from us as if the lake lay between. The only words I have spoken since arriving here have been to my own family or to a waiter, save to one or two young pedestrians who met me on a walk, and asked me the distance to Lowwood Hotel. "Just beyond here," said I, and I might stay for months without occasion to speak again.

Yesterday forenoon J—— and I walked to Ambleside,—distant barely two miles. It is a little town, chiefly of modern aspect, built on a very uneven hillside, and with very irregular streets and lanes, which bewilder the stranger as much as those of a larger city. Many of the houses look old, and are probably the cottages and farm-houses which composed the rude village a century ago; but there are stuccoed shops and dwellings, such as may have been built within a year or two; and three hotels, one of which has the look of a good old village inn; and the others are fashionable or commercial establishments. Through the midst of the village comes tumbling and rumbling a mountain streamlet, rushing through a deep, rocky dell, gliding under an old stone inch, and turning, when occasion calls, the great block of a water-mill. This is the only very striking feature of the village,—the stream taking its rough pathway to the lake as it used to do before the poets had made this region fashionable.

In the evening, just before eight o'clock, I took a walk alone, by a road which goes up the hill, back of our hotel, and which I supposed might be the road to the town of Windermere. But it went up higher and higher, and for the mile or two that it led me along, winding up, I saw no traces of a town; but at last it turned into a valley between two high ridges, leading quite away from the lake, within view of which the town of Windermere is situated. It was a very lonely road, though as smooth, hard, and well kept as any thoroughfare in the suburbs of a city; hardly a dwelling on either side, except one, half barn, half farm-house, and one gentleman's gateway, near the beginning of the road, and another more than a mile above. At, two or three points there were stone barns, which are here built with great solidity. At one place there was a painted board, announcing that a field of five acres was to be sold, and referring those desirous of purchasing to a solicitor in London. The lake country is but a London suburb. Nevertheless, the walk was lonely and lovely; the copses and the broad hillside, the glimpses of the lake, the great misty company of pikes and fells, beguiled me into a sense of something like solitude; and the bleating of the sheep, remote and near, had a like tendency. Gaining the summit of the hill, I had the best view of Windermere which I have yet attained,—the best, I should think, that can be had, though, being towards the south, it brings the softer instead of the more striking features of the landscape into view. But it shows nearly the whole extent of the lake, all the way from Lowwood, beyond Newby Bridge, and I think there can hardly be anything more beautiful in the world. The water was like a strip and gleam of sky, fitly set among lovely slopes of earth. It was no broader than many a river, and yet you saw at once that it could be no river, its outline being so different from that of a running stream, not straight nor winding, but stretching to one side or the other, as the shores made room for it.

This morning it is raining, and we are not very comfortable nor contented, being all confined to our little parlor, which has a broken window, against which I have pinned The Times to keep out the chill damp air. U—— has been ill, in consequence of having been overheated at Newby Bridge. We have no books, except guide-books, no means of amusement, nothing to do. There are no newspapers, and I shall remember Lowwood not very agreeably. As far as we are concerned, it is a scrambling, ill-ordered hotel, with insufficient attendance, wretched sleeping-accommodations, a pretty fair table, but German-silver forks and spoons; our food does not taste very good, and yet there is really no definite fault to be found with it.

Since writing the above, I have found the first volume of Sir Charles Grandison, and two of G. P. R. James's works, in the coffee-room. The days pass heavily here, and leave behind them a sense of having answered no very good purpose. They are long enough, at all events, for the sun does not set till after eight o'clock, and rises I know not when. One of the most remarkable distinctions between England and the United States is the ignorance into which we fall of whatever is going on in the world the moment we get away from the great thoroughfares and centres of life. In Leamington we heard no news from week's end to week's end, and knew not where to find a newspaper; and here the case is neither better nor worse. The rural people really seem to take no interest in public affairs; at all events, they have no intelligence on such subjects. It is possible that the cheap newspapers may, in time, find their way into the cottages, or, at least, into the country taverns; but it is not at all so now. If they generally know that Sebastopol is besieged, it is the extent of their knowledge. The public life of America is lived through the mind and heart of every man in it; here the people feel that they have nothing to do with what is going forward, and, I suspect, care little or nothing about it. Such things they permit to be the exclusive concern of the higher classes.

In front of our hotel, on the lawn between us and the lake, there are two trees, which we have hitherto taken to be yews; but on examining them more closely, I find that they are pine-trees, and quite dead and dry, although they have the aspect of dark rich life. But this is caused by the verdure of two great ivy-vines, which have twisted round them like gigantic snakes, and, clambering up and throttling the life out of them, have put out branches, and made crowns of thick green leaves, so that, at a little distance, it is quite impossible not to take them for genuine trees. The trunks of the ivy-vines must be more than a foot in circumference, and one feels they have stolen the life that belonged to the pines. The dead branches of one of the pines stick out horizontally through the ivy-boughs. The other shows nothing but the ivy, and in shape a good deal resembles a poplar. When the pine trunks shall have quite crumbled away, the ivy-stems will doubtless have gained sufficient strength to sustain themselves independently.

July 19th.—Yesterday S—— went down the lake in the steamboat to take U——, baby, and nurse to Newby Bridge, while the three rest of us should make a tour through the lake region. After mamma's departure, and when I had finished some letters, J—— and I set out on a walk, which finally brought us to Bowness, through much delightful shade of woods, and past beautiful rivulets or brooklets, and up and down many hills. This chief harbor of the lakes seemed alive and bustling with tourists, it being a sunny and pleasant day, so that they were all abroad, like summer insects. The town is a confused and irregular little place, of very uneven surface. There is an old church in it, and two or three large hotels. We stayed there perhaps half an hour, and then went to the pier, where shortly a steamer arrived, with music sounding,—on the deck of which, with her back to us, sat a lady in a gray travelling-dress. J—— cried out, "Mamma! mamma!" to which the lady deigned no notice, but, he repeating it, she turned round, and was as much surprised, no doubt, to see her husband and son, as if this little lake had been the great ocean, and we meeting each other from opposite shores of it. We soon steamed back to Lowwood, and took a car thence for Rydal and Grasmere, after a cold luncheon. At Bowness I met Miss Charlotte Cushman, who has been staying at the Lowwood Hotel with us since Monday, without either party being aware of it.

Our road to Rydal lay through Ambleside, which is certainly a very pretty town, and looks cheerfully in a sunny day. We saw Miss Martineau's residence, called "The Knoll," standing high up on a hillock, and having at its foot a Methodist chapel, for which, or whatever place of Christian worship, this good lady can have no occasion. We stopped a moment in the street below her house, and deliberated a little whether to call on her; but concluded we would not.

After leaving Ambleside, the road winds in and out among the hills, and soon brings us to a sheet (or napkin, rather than a sheet) of water, which the driver tells us is Rydal Lake! We had already heard that it was but three quarters of a mile long, and one quarter broad; still, it being an idea of considerable size in our minds, we had inevitably drawn its ideal, physical proportions on a somewhat corresponding scale. It certainly did look very small; and I said, in my American scorn, that I could carry it away easily in a porringer; for it is nothing more than a grass-bordered pool among the surrounding hills which ascend directly from its margin; so that one might fancy it, not, a permanent body of water, but a rather extensive accumulation of recent rain. Moreover, it was rippled with a breeze, and so, as I remember it, though the sun shone, it looked dull and sulky, like a child out of humor. Now, the best thing these small ponds can do is to keep perfectly calm and smooth, and not attempt to show off any airs of their own, but content themselves with serving as a mirror for whatever of beautiful or picturesque there may be in the scenery around them. The hills about Rydal Water are not very lofty, but are sufficiently so as objects of every-day view,— objects to live with; and they are craggier than those we have hitherto seen, and bare of wood, which indeed would hardly grow on some of their precipitous sides.

On the roadside, as we reach the foot of the lake, stands a spruce and rather large house of modern aspect, but with several gables and much overgrown with ivy,—a very pretty and comfortable house, built, adorned, and cared for with commendable taste. We inquired whose it was, and the coachman said it was "Mr. Wordsworth's," and that "Mrs. Wordsworth was still residing there." So we were much delighted to have seen his abode, and as we were to stay the night at Grasmere, about two miles farther on, we determined to come back and inspect it as particularly as should be allowable. Accordingly, after taking rooms at Brown's Hotel, we drove back in our return car, and, reaching the head of Rydal Water, alighted to walk through this familiar scene of so many years of Wordsworth's life. We ought to have seen De Quincey's former residence and Hartley Coleridge's cottage, I believe, on our way, but were not aware of it at the time. Near the lake there is a stone-quarry, and a cavern of some extent, artificially formed, probably by taking out the stone. Above the shore of the lake, not a great way from Wordsworth's residence, there is a flight of steps hewn in a rock and ascending to a rock seat where a good view of the lake may be attained; and, as Wordsworth has doubtless sat there hundreds of times, so did we ascend and sit down, and look at the hills and at the flags on the lake's shore.

Reaching the house that had been pointed out to us as Wordsworth's residence, we began to peer about at its front and gables, and over the garden wall, on both sides of the road, quickening our enthusiasm as much as we could, and meditating to pilfer some flower or ivy-leaf from the house or its vicinity, to be kept as sacred memorials. At this juncture a man approached, who announced himself as the gardener of the place, and said, too, that this was not Wordsworth's house at all, but the residence of Mr. Ball, a Quaker gentleman; but that his ground adjoined Wordsworth's, and that he had liberty to take visitors through the latter. How absurd it would have been if we had carried away ivy-leaves and tender recollections from this domicile of a respectable Quaker! The gardener was an intelligent man, of pleasant, sociable, and respectful address; and as we went along he talked about the poet, whom he had known, and who, he said, was very familiar with the country people. He led us through Mr. Ball's grounds, up a steep hillside, by winding, gravelled walks, with summer-houses at points favorable for them. It was a very shady and pleasant spot, containing about an acre of ground, and all turned to good account by the manner of laying it out; so that it seemed more than it really is. In one place, on a small, smooth slab of slate, let into a rock, there is an inscription by Wordsworth, which I think I have read in his works, claiming kindly regards from those who visit the spot after his departure, because many trees had been spared at his intercession. His own grounds, or rather his ornamental garden, is separated from Mr. Ball's only by a wire fence, or some such barrier, and the gates have no fastening, so that the whole appears like one possession, and doubtless was so as regarded the poet's walks and enjoyments. We approached by paths so winding that I hardly know how the house stands in relation to the road; but, after much circuity, we really did see Wordsworth's residence,—an old house with an uneven ridge-pole, built of stone, no doubt, but plastered over with some neutral tint,—a house that would not have been remarkably pretty in itself, but so delightfully situated, so secluded, so hedged about with shrubbery, and adorned with flowers, so ivy-grown on one side, so beautified with the personal care of him who lived in it and loved it, that it seemed the very place for a poet's residence; and as if, while he lived so long in it, his poetry had manifested itself in flowers, shrubbery, and ivy. I never smelt such a delightful fragrance of flowers as there was all through the garden. In front of the house there is a circular terrace of two ascents, in raising which Wordsworth had himself performed much of the labor; and here there are seats, from which we obtained a fine view down the valley of the Rothay, with Windermere in the distance,—a view of several miles, and which we did not suppose could be seen, after winding among the hills so far from the lake. It is very beautiful and picture-like. While we sat here, S——- happened to refer to the ballad of little Barbara Lewthwaite, and J——- began to repeat the poem concerning her, and the gardener said that "little Barbara" had died not a great while ago, an elderly woman, leaving grown-up children behind her. Her marriage-name was Thompson, and the gardener believed there was nothing remarkable in her character.

There is a summer-house at one extremity of the grounds, in deepest shadow, but with glimpses of mountain views through trees which shut it in, and which have spread intercepting boughs since Wordsworth died. It is lined with pine-cones, in a pretty way enough, but of doubtful taste. I rather wonder that people of real taste should help Nature out, and beautify her, or perhaps rather prettify her so much as they do,—opening vistas, showing one thing, hiding another, making a scene picturesque, whether or no. I cannot rid myself of the feeling that there is something false—a kind of humbug—in all this. At any rate, the traces of it do not contribute to my enjoyment, and, indeed, it ought to be done so exquisitely as to leave no trace. But I ought not to criticise in any way a spot which gave me so much pleasure, and where it is good to think of Wordsworth in quiet, past days, walking in his home-shadow of trees which he knew, and training flowers, and trimming shrubs, and chanting in an undertone his own verses up and down the winding walks.

The gardener gave J—— a cone from the summer-house, which had fallen on the seat, and S—— got some mignonette, and leaves of laurel and ivy, and we wended our way back to the hotel. Wordsworth was not the owner of this house; it being the property of Lady Fleming. Mrs. Wordsworth still lives there, and is now at home.

Five o'clock.—All day it has been cloudy and showery, with thunder now and then; the mists hang low on the surrounding hills, adown which, at various points, we can see the snow-white fall of little streamlets ("forces" they call them here) swollen by the rain. An overcast day is not so gloomy in the hill-country as in the lowlands; there are more breaks, more transfusion of skylight through the gloom, as has been the case to-day, and as I found in Lenox; we get better acquainted with clouds by seeing at what height they be on the hillsides, and find that the difference betwixt a fair day and a cloudy and rainy one is very superficial, after all. Nevertheless, rain is rain, and wets a man just as much among the mountains as anywhere else; so we have been kept within doors all day, till an hour or so ago, when J——- and I went down to the village in quest of the post-office.

We took a path that leads from the hotel across the fields, and, coming into a wood, crosses the Rothay by a one-arched bridge and passes the village church. The Rothay is very swift and turbulent to-day, and hurries along with foam-specks on its surface, filling its banks from brim to brim,—a stream perhaps twenty feet wide, perhaps more; for I am willing that the good little river should have all it can fairly claim. It is the St. Lawrence of several of these English lakes, through which it flows, and carries off their superfluous waters. In its haste, and with its rushing sound, it was pleasant both to see and hear; and it sweeps by one side of the old churchyard where Wordsworth lies buried,—- the side where his grave is made. The church of Grasmere is a very plain structure, with a low body, on one side of which is a small porch with a pointed arch. The tower is square and looks ancient; but the whole is overlaid with plaster of a buff or pale yellow hue. It was originally built, I suppose, of rough shingly stones, as many of the houses hereabouts are now, and, like many of them, the plaster is used to give a finish. We found the gate of the churchyard wide open; and the grass was lying on the graves, having probably been mowed yesterday. It is but a small churchyard, and with few monuments of any pretension in it, most of them being slate headstones, standing erect. From the gate at which we entered, a distinct foot-track leads to the corner nearest the riverside, and I turned into it by a sort of instinct, the more readily as I saw a tourist-looking man approaching from that point, and a woman looking among the gravestones. Both of these persons had gone by the time I came up, so that J——- and I were left to find Wordsworth's grave all by ourselves.

At this corner of the churchyard there is a hawthorn bush or tree, the extremest branches of which stretch as far as where Wordsworth lies. This whole corner seems to be devoted to himself and his family and friends; and they all lie very closely together, side by side, and head to foot, as room could conveniently be found. Hartley Coleridge lies a little behind, in the direction of the church, his feet being towards Wordsworth's head, who lies in the row of those of his own blood. I found out Hartley Coleridge's grave sooner than Wordsworth's; for it is of marble, and, though simple enough, has more of sculptured device about it, having been erected, as I think the inscription states, by his brother and sister. Wordsworth has only the very simplest slab of slate, with "William Wordsworth" and nothing else upon it. As I recollect it, it is the midmost grave of the row. It is or has been well grass-grown, but the grass is quite worn away from the top, though sufficiently luxuriant at the sides. It looks as if people had stood upon it, and so does the grave next to it, which I believe is one of his children. I plucked some grass and weeds from it, and as he was buried within so few years they may fairly be supposed to have drawn their nutriment from his mortal remains, and I gathered them from just above his head. There is no fault to be found with his grave,—within view of the hills, within sound of the river, murmuring near by,—no fault except that he is crowded so closely with his kindred; and, moreover, that, being so old a churchyard, the earth over him must all have been human once. He might have had fresh earth to himself; but he chose this grave deliberately. No very stately and broad-based monument can ever be erected over it without infringing upon, covering, and overshadowing the graves, not only of his family, but of individuals who probably were quite disconnected with him. But it is pleasant to think and know—were it but on the evidence of this choice of a resting-place—that he did not care for a stately monument.

After leaving the churchyard, we wandered about in quest of the post-office, and for a long time without success. This little town of Grasmere seems to me as pretty a place as ever I met with in my life. It is quite shut in by hills that rise up immediately around it, like a neighborhood of kindly giants. These hills descend steeply to the verge of the level on which the village stands, and there they terminate at once, the whole site of the little town being as even as a floor. I call it a village; but it is no village at all,—all the dwellings standing apart, each in its own little domain, and each, I believe, with its own little lane leading to it, independently of the rest. Most of these are old cottages, plastered white, with antique porches, and roses and other vines trained against them, and shrubbery growing about them; and some are covered with ivy. There are a few edifices of more pretension and of modern build, but not so strikingly so as to put the rest out of countenance. The post-office, when we found it, proved to be an ivied cottage, with a good deal of shrubbery round it, having its own pathway, like the other cottages. The whole looks like a real seclusion, shut out from the great world by these encircling hills, on the sides of which, whenever they are not too steep, you see the division lines of property, and tokens of cultivation,—taking from them their pretensions to savage majesty, but bringing them nearer to the heart of man.

Since writing the above, I have been again with S——- to see Wordsworth's grave, and, finding the door of the church open, we went in. A woman and little girl were sweeping at the farther end, and the woman came towards us out of the cloud of dust which she had raised. We were surprised at the extremely antique appearance of the church. It is paved with bluish-gray flagstones, over which uncounted generations have trodden, leaving the floor as well laid as ever. The walls are very thick, and the arched windows open through them at a considerable distance above the floor. There is no middle aisle; but first a row of pews next either wall, and then an aisle on each side of the pews, occupying the centre of the church,—then, two side aisles, but no middle one. And down through the centre or the church runs a row of five arches, very rude and round-headed, all of rough stone, supported by rough and massive pillars, or rather square, stone blocks, which stand in the pews, and stood in the same places probably, long before the wood of those pews began to grow. Above this row of arches is another row, built upon the same mass of stone, and almost as broad, but lower; and on this upper row rests the framework, the oaken beams, the black skeleton of the roof. It is a very clumsy contrivance for supporting the roof, and if it were modern, we certainly should condemn it as very ugly; but being the relic of a simple age it comes in well with the antique simplicity of the whole structure. The roof goes up, barn-like, into its natural angle, and all the rafters and cross-beams are visible. There is an old font; and in the chancel is a niche, where (judging from a similar one in Furness Abbey) the holy water used to be placed for the priest's use while celebrating mass. Around the inside of the porch is a stone bench, against the wall, narrow and uneasy, but where a great many people had sat, who now have found quieter resting-places.

The woman was a very intelligent-looking person, not of the usual English ruddiness, but rather thin and somewhat pale, though bright, of aspect. Her way of talking was very agreeable. She inquired if we wished to see Wordsworth's monument, and at once showed it to us,—a slab of white marble fixed against the upper end of the central row of stone arches, with a pretty long inscription, and a profile bust, in bas-relief, of his aged countenance. The monument, is placed directly over Wordsworth's pew, and could best be seen and read from the very corner seat where he used to sit. The pew is one of those occupying the centre of the church, and is just across the aisle from the pulpit, and is the best of all for the purpose of seeing and hearing the clergyman, and likewise as convenient as any, from its neighborhood to the altar. On the other side of the aisle, beneath the pulpit, is Lady Fleming's pew. This and one or two others are curtained, Wordsworth's was not. I think I can bring up his image in that corner seat of his pew—a white-headed, tall, spare man, plain in aspect—better than in any other situation. The woman said that she had known him very well, and that he had made some verses on a sister of hers. She repeated the first lines, something about a lamb, but neither S——— nor I remembered them.

On the walls of the chancel there are monuments to the Flemings, and painted escutcheons of their arms; and along the side walls also, and on the square pillars of the row of arches, there are other monuments, generally of white marble, with the letters of the inscription blackened. On these pillars, likewise, and in many places in the walls, were hung verses from Scripture, painted on boards. At one of the doors was a poor-box,—an elaborately carved little box, of oak, with the date 1648, and the name of the church—St. Oswald's—upon it. The whole interior of the edifice was plain, simple, almost to grimness,—or would have been so, only that the foolish church-wardens, or other authority, have washed it over with the same buff color with which they have overlaid the exterior. It is a pity; it lightens it up, and desecrates it greatly, especially as the woman says that there were formerly paintings on the walls, now obliterated forever. I could have stayed in the old church much longer, and could write much more about it, but there must be an end to everything. Pacing it from the farther end to the elevation before the altar, I found that it was twenty-five paces long.

On looking again at the Rothay, I find I did it some injustice; for at the bridge, in its present swollen state, it is nearer twenty yards than twenty feet across. Its waters are very clear, and it rushes along with a speed which is delightful to see, after an acquaintance with the muddy and sluggish Avon and Leam.

Since tea I have taken a stroll from the hotel in a different direction from heretofore, and passed the Swan Inn, where Scott used to go daily to get a draught of liquor, when he was visiting Wordsworth, who had no wine nor other inspiriting fluid in his house. It stands directly on the wayside,—a small, whitewashed house, with an addition in the rear that seems to have been built since Scott's time. On the door is the painted sign of a swan, and the name "Scott's Swan Hotel." I walked a considerable distance beyond it, but, a shower cooling up, I turned back, entered the inn, and, following the mistress into a snug little room, was served with a glass of bitter ale. It is a very plain and homely inn, and certainly could not have satisfied Scott's wants if he had required anything very far-fetched or delicate in his potations. I found two Westmoreland peasants in the room, with ale before them. One went away almost immediately; but the other remained, and, entering into conversation with him, he told me that he was going to New Zealand, and expected to sail in September. I announced myself as an American, and he said that a large party had lately gone from hereabouts to America; but he seemed not to understand that there was any distinction between Canada and the States. These people had gone to Quebec. He was a very civil, well-behaved, kindly sort of person, of a simple character, which I took to belong to the class and locality, rather than to himself individually. I could not very well understand all that he said, owing to his provincial dialect; and when he spoke to his own countrymen, or to the women of the house, I really could but just catch a word here and there. How long it takes to melt English down into a homogeneous mass! He told me that there was a public library in Grasmere to which he has access in common with the other inhabitants, and a reading-room connected with it, where he reads The Times in the evening. There was no American smartness in his mind. When I left the house, it was showering briskly; but the drops quite ceased, and the clouds began to break away before I reached my hotel, and I saw the new moon over my right shoulder.

July 21st.—We left Grasmere yesterday, after breakfast; it being a delightful morning, with some clouds, but the cheerfullest sunshine on great part of the mountainsides and on ourselves. We returned, in the first place, to Ambleside, along the border of Grasmere Lake, which would be a pretty little piece of water, with its steep and high surrounding hills, were it not that a stubborn and straight-lined stone fence, running along the eastern shore, by the roadside, quite spoils its appearance. Rydal Water, though nothing can make a lake of it, looked prettier and less diminutive than at the first view; and, in fact, I find that it is impossible to know accurately how any prospect or other thing looks, until after at least a second view, which always essentially corrects the first. This, I think, is especially true in regard to objects which we have heard much about, and exercised our imagination upon; the first view being a vain attempt to reconcile our idea with the reality, and at the second we begin to accept the thing for what it really is. Wordsworth's situation is really a beautiful one; and Nab Scaur behind his house rises with a grand, protecting air. We passed Nab's cottage, in which De Quincey formerly lived, and where Hartley Coleridge lived and died. It is a small, buff-tinted, plastered stone cottage, immediately on the roadside, and originally, I should think, of a very humble class; but it now looks as if persons of taste might some time or other have sat down in it, and caused flowers to spring up about it. It is very agreeably situated under the great, precipitous hill, and with Rydal Water close at band, on the other side of the road. An advertisement of lodgings to let was put up on this cottage.

I question whether any part of the world looks so beautiful as England—this part of England, at least—on a fine summer morning. It makes one think the more cheerfully of human life to see such a bright universal verdure; such sweet, rural, peaceful, flower-bordered cottages,—not cottages of gentility, but dwellings of the laboring poor; such nice villas along the roadside, so tastefully contrived for comfort and beauty, and adorned more and more, year after year, with the care and after-thought of people who mean to live in them a great while, and feel as if their children might live in them also, and so they plant trees to overshadow their walks, and train ivy and all beautiful vines up against their walls, and thus live for the future in another sense than we Americans do. And the climate helps them out, and makes everything moist, and green, and full of tender life, instead of dry and arid, as human life and vegetable life is so apt to be with us. Certainly, England can present a more attractive face than we can; even in its humbler modes of life, to say nothing of the beautiful lives that might be led, one would think, by the higher classes, whose gateways, with broad, smooth gravelled drives leading through them, one sees every mile or two along the road, winding into some proud seclusion. All this is passing away, and society most assume new relations; but there is no harm in believing that there has been something very good in English life,— good for all classes while the world was in a state out of which these forms naturally grew.

Passing through Ambleside, our phaeton and pair turned towards Ullswater, which we were to reach through the Pass of Kirkstone. This is some three or four miles from Ambleside, and as we approached it the road kept ascending higher and higher, the hills grew more bare, and the country lost its soft and delightful verdure. At last the road became so steep that J——— and I alighted to walk. This is the aspiring road that Wordsworth speaks of in his ode; it passes through the gorge of precipitous hills,—or almost precipitous,—too much so for even the grass to grow on many portions, which are covered with gray smugly stones; and I think this pass, in its middle part, must have looked just the same when the Romans marched through it as it looks now. No trees could ever have grown on the steep hillsides, whereon even the English climate can generate no available soil. I do not know that I have seen anything more impressive than the stern gray sweep of these naked mountains, with nothing whatever to soften or adorn them. The notch of the White Mountains, as I remember it in my youthful days, is more wonderful and richly picturesque, but of quite a different character.

About the centre and at the highest point of the pass stands an old stone building of mean appearance, with the usual sign of an alehouse, "Licensed to retail foreign spirits, ale, and tobacco," over the door, and another small sign, designating it as the highest inhabitable house in England. It is a chill and desolate place for a residence. They keep a visitor's book here, and we recorded our names in it, and were not too sorry to leave the mean little hovel, smelling as it did of tobacco-smoke, and possessing all other characteristics of the humblest alehouse on the level earth.

The Kirkstone, which gives the pass its name, is not seen in approaching from Ambleside, until some time after you begin to descend towards Brothers' Water. When the driver first pointed it out, a little way up the hill on our left, it looked no more than a bowlder of a ton or two in weight, among a hundred others nearly as big; and I saw hardly any resemblance to a church or church-spire, to which the fancies of past generations have likened it. As we descended the pass, however, and left the stone farther and farther behind, it continued to show itself, and assumed a more striking and prominent aspect, standing out clearly relieved against the sky, so that no traveller would fail to observe it, where there are so few defined objects to attract notice, amid the naked monotony of the stern hills; though, indeed, if I had taken it for any sort of an edifice, it would rather have been for a wayside inn or a shepherd's hut than for a church. We lost sight of it, and again beheld it more and more brought out against the sky, by the turns of the road, several times in the course of our descent. There is a very fine view of Brothers' Water, shut in by steep hills, as we go down Kirkstone Pass.

At about half past twelve we reached Patterdale, at the foot of Ullswater, and here took luncheon. The hotels are mostly very good all through this region, and this deserved that character. A black-coated waiter, of more gentlemanly appearance than most Englishmen, yet taking a sixpence with as little scruple as a lawyer would take his fee; the mistress, in lady-like attire, receiving us at the door, and waiting upon us to the carriage-steps; clean, comely housemaids everywhere at hand,— all appliances, in short, for being comfortable, and comfortable, too, within one's own circle. And, on taking leave, everybody who has done anything for you, or who might by possibility have done anything, is to be feed. You pay the landlord enough, in all conscience; and then you pay all his servants, who have been your servants for the time. But, to say the truth, there is a degree of the same kind of annoyance in an American hotel, although it is not so much an acknowledged custom. Here, in the houses where attendance is not charged in the bill, no wages are paid by the host to those servants—chambermaid, waiter, and boots—who come into immediate contact with travellers. The drivers of the cars, phaetons, and flys are likewise unpaid, except by their passengers, and claim threepence a mile with the same sense of right as their masters in charging for the vehicles and horses. When you come to understand this claim, not as an appeal to your generosity, but as an actual and necessary part of the cost of the journey, it is yielded to with a more comfortable feeling; and the traveller has really option enough, as to the amount which he will give, to insure civility and good behavior on the driver's part.

Ullswater is a beautiful lake, with steep hills walling it about, so steep, on the eastern side, that there seems hardly room for a road to run along the base. We passed up the western shore, and turned off from it about midway, to take the road towards Keswick. We stopped, however, at Lyulph's Tower, while our chariot went on up a hill, and took a guide to show us the way to Airey Force,—a small cataract, which is claimed as private property, and out of which, no doubt, a pretty little revenue is raised. I do not think that there can be any rightful appropriation, as private property, of objects of natural beauty. The fruits of the land, and whatever human labor can produce from it, belong fairly enough to the person who has a deed or a lease; but the beautiful is the property of him who can hive it and enjoy it. It is very unsatisfactory to think of a cataract under lock and key. However, we were shown to Airey Force by a tall and graceful mountain-maid, with a healthy cheek, and a step that had no possibility of weariness in it. The cascade is an irregular streak of foamy water, pouring adown a rude shadowy glen. I liked well enough to see it; but it is wearisome, on the whole, to go the rounds of what everybody thinks it necessary to see. It makes me a little ashamed. It is somewhat as if we were drinking out of the same glass, and eating from the same dish, as a multitude of other people.

Within a few miles of Keswick, we passed along at the foot of Saddleback, and by the entrance of the Vale of St. John, and down the valley, on one of the slopes, we saw the Enchanted Castle. Thence we drove along by the course of the Greta, and soon arrived at Keswick, which lies at the base of Skiddaw, and among a brotherhood of picturesque eminences, and is itself a compact little town, with a market-house, built of the old stones of the Earl of Derwentwater's ruined castle, standing in the centre,—the principal street forking into two as it passes it. We alighted at the King's Arms, and went in search of Southey's residence, which we found easily enough, as it lies just on the outskirts of the town. We inquired of a group of people, two of whom, I thought, did not seem to know much about the matter; but the third, an elderly man, pointed it out at once,—a house surrounded by trees, so as to be seen only partially, and standing on a little eminence, a hundred yards or so from the road.

We went up a private lane that led to the rear of the place, and so penetrated quite into the back-yard without meeting anybody,—passing a small kennel, in which were two hounds, who gazed at us, but neither growled nor wagged their tails. The house is three stories high, and seems to have a great deal of room in it, so as not to discredit its name, "Greta Hall,"—a very spacious dwelling for a poet. The windows were nearly all closed; there were no signs of occupancy, but a general air of neglect. S———, who is bolder than I in these matters, ventured through what seemed a back garden gate, and I soon heard her in conversation with some man, who now presented himself, and proved to be a gardener. He said he had formerly acted in that capacity for Southey, although a gardener had not been kept by him as a regular part of his establishment. This was an old man with an odd crookedness of legs, and strange, disjointed limp. S——— had told him that we were Americans, and he took the idea that we had come this long distance, over sea and land, with the sole purpose of seeing Southey's residence, so that he was inclined to do what he could towards exhibiting it. This was but little; the present occupant (a Mr. Radday, I believe the gardener called him) being away, and the house shut up.

But he showed us about the grounds, and allowed us to peep into the windows of what had been Southey's library, and into those of another of the front apartments, and showed us the window of the chamber in the rear, in which Southey died. The apartments into which we peeped looked rather small and low,—not particularly so, but enough to indicate an old building. They are now handsomely furnished, and we saw over one of the fireplaces an inscription about Southey; and in the corner of the same room stood a suit, of bright armor. It is taller than the country-houses of English gentlemen usually are, and it is even stately. All about, in front, beside it and behind, there is a great profusion of trees, most of which were planted by Southey, who came to live here more than fifty years ago, and they have, of course, grown much more shadowy now than he ever beheld them; for he died about fourteen years since. The grounds are well laid out, and neatly kept, with the usual lawn and gravelled walks, and quaint little devices in the ornamental way. These may be of later date than Southey's time. The gardener spoke respectfully of Southey, and of his first wife, and observed that "it was a great loss to the neighborhood when that family went down."

The house stands directly above the Greta, the murmur of which is audible all about it; for the Greta is a swift little river, and goes on its way with a continual sound, which has both depth and breadth. The gardener led us to a walk along its banks, close by the Hall, where he said Southey used to walk for hours and hours together. He might, indeed, get there from his study in a moment. There are two paths, one above the other, well laid out on the steep declivity of the high bank; and there is such a very thick shade of oaks and elms, planted by Southey himself over the bank, that all the ground and grass were moist, although it had been a sunny day. It is a very sombre walk; not many glimpses of the sky through those dense boughs. The Greta is here, perhaps, twenty yards across, and very dark of hue, and its voice is melancholy and very suggestive of musings and reveries; but I should question whether it were favorable to any settled scheme of thought. The gardener told us that there used to be a pebbly beach on the margin of the river, and that it was Southey's habit to sit and write there, using a tree of peculiar shape for a table. An alteration in the current of the river has swept away the beach, and the tree, too, has fallen. All these things were interesting to me, although Southey was not, I think, a picturesque man, —not one whose personal character takes a strong hold on the imagination. In these walks he used to wear a pair of shoes heavily clamped with iron; very ponderous they must have been, from the particularity with which the gardener mentioned them.

The gardener took leave of us at the front entrance of the grounds, and, returning to the King's Arms, we ordered a one-horse fly for the fall of Lodore. Our drive thither was along the banks of Derwentwater, and it is as beautiful a road, I imagine, as can be found in England or anywhere else. I like Derwentwater the best of all the lakes, so far as I have yet seen them. Skiddaw lies at the head of a long even ridge of mountains, rising into several peaks, and one higher than the rest. On the eastern side there are many noble eminences, and on the west, along which we drove, there is a part of the way a lovely wood, and nearly the whole distance a precipitous range of lofty cliffs, descending sheer down without any slope, except what has been formed in the lapse of ages by the fall of fragments, and the washing down of smaller stones. The declivity thus formed along the base of the cliffs is in some places covered with trees or shrubs; elsewhere it is quite bare and barren. The precipitous parts of the cliffs are very grand; the whole scene, indeed, might be characterized as one of stern grandeur with an embroidery of rich beauty, without lauding it too much. All the sternness of it is softened by vegetative beauty wherever it can possibly be thrown in; and there is not here, so strongly as along Windermere, evidence that human art has been helping out Nature. I wish it were possible to give any idea of the shapes of the hills; with these, at least, man has nothing to do, nor ever will have anything to do. As we approached the bottom of the lake, and of the beautiful valley in which it lies, we saw one hill that seemed to crouch down like a Titanic watch-dog, with its rear towards the spectator, guarding the entrance to the valley. The great superiority of these mountains over those of New England is their variety and definiteness of shape, besides the abundance everywhere of water prospects, which are wanting among our own hills. They rise up decidedly, and each is a hill by itself, while ours mingle into one another, and, besides, have such large bases that you can tell neither where they begin nor where they end. Many of these Cumberland mountains have a marked vertebral shape, so that they often look like a group of huge lions, lying down with their backs turned toward each other. They slope down steeply from narrow ridges; hence their picturesque seclusions of valleys and dales, which subdivide the lake region into so many communities. Our hills, like apple-dumplings in a dish, have no such valleys as these.

There is a good inn at Lodore,—a small, primitive country inn, which has latterly been enlarged and otherwise adapted to meet the convenience of the guests brought thither by the fame of the cascade; but it is still a country inn, though it takes upon itself the title of hotel.

We found pleasant rooms here, and established ourselves for the night. From this point we have a view of the beautiful lake, and of Skiddaw at the head of it. The cascade is within three or four minutes' walk, through the garden gate, towards the cliff, at the base of which the inn stands. The visitor would need no other guide than its own voice, which is said to be audible sometimes at the distance of four miles. As we were coming from Keswick, we caught glimpses of its white foam high up the precipice; and it is only glimpses that can be caught anywhere, because there is no regular sheet of falling water. Once, I think, it must have fallen abruptly over the edge of the long line of precipice that here extends along parallel with the shore of the lake; but, in the course of time, it has gnawed and sawed its way into the heart of the cliff,—this persistent little stream,—so that now it has formed a rude gorge, adown which it hurries and tumbles in the wildest way, over the roughest imaginable staircase. Standing at the bottom of the fall, you have a far vista sloping upward to the sky, with the water everywhere as white as snow, pouring and pouring down, now on one side of the gorge, now on the other, among immense bowlders, which try to choke its passage. It does not attempt to leap over these huge rocks, but finds its way in and out among then, and finally gets to the bottom after a hundred tumbles. It cannot be better described than in Southey's verses, though it is worthy of better poetry than that. After all, I do not know that the cascade is anything more than a beautiful fringe to the grandeur of the scene; for it is very grand,—this fissure through the cliff,—with a steep, lofty precipice on the right hand, sheer up and down, and on the other hand, too, another lofty precipice, with a slope of its own ruin on which trees and shrubbery have grown. The right-hand precipice, however, has shelves affording sufficient hold for small trees, but nowhere does it slant. If it were not for the white little stream falling gently downward, and for the soft verdure upon either precipice, and even along the very pathway of the cascade, it would be a very stern vista up that gorge.

I shall not try to describe it any more. It has not been praised too much, though it may have been praised amiss. I went thither again in the morning, and climbed a good way up, through the midst of its rocky descent, and I think I could have reached the top in this way. It is remarkable that the bounds of the water, from one step of its broken staircase to another, give an impression of softness and gentleness; but there are black, turbulent pools among the great bowlders, where the stream seems angry at the difficulties which it meets with. Looking upward in the sunshine, I could see a rising mist, and I should not wonder if a speck of rainbow were sometimes visible. I noticed a small oak in the bed of the cascade, and there is a lighter vegetation scattered about.

At noon we took a car for Portinscale, and drove back along the road to Keswick, through which we passed, stopping to get a perhaps of letters at the post-office, and reached Portinscale, which is a mile from Keswick. After dinner we walked over a bridge, and through a green lane, to the church where Southey is buried. It is a white church, of Norman architecture, with a low, square tower. As we approached, we saw two persons entering the portal, and, following them in, we found the sexton, who was a tall, thin old man, with white hair, and an intelligent, reverent face, showing the edifice to a stout, red-faced, self-important, good-natured John Bull of a gentleman. Without any question on our part, the old sexton immediately led us to Southey's monument, which is placed in a side aisle, where there is not breadth for it to stand free of the wall; neither is it in a very good light. But, it seemed to me a good work of art,—a recumbent figure of white marble, on a couch, the drapery of which he has drawn about him,—being quite enveloped in what may be a shroud. The sculptor has not intended to represent death, for the figure lies on its side, and has a book in its hand, and the face is lifelike, and looks full of expression,—a thin, high-featured, poetic face, with a finely proportioned head and abundant hair. It represents Southey rightly, at whatever age he died, in the full maturity of manhood, when he was strongest and richest. I liked the statue, and wished that it lay in a broader aisle, or in the chancel, where there is an old tomb of a knight and lady of the Ratcliffe family, who have held the place of honor long enough to yield it now to a poet. Southey's sculptor was Lough. I must not forget to mention that John Bull, climbing on a bench, to get a better view of the statue, tumbled off with a racket that resounded irreverently through the church.

The old, white-headed, thin sexton was a model man of his class, and appeared to take a loving and cheerful interest in the building, and in those who, from age to age, have worshipped and been buried there. It is a very ancient and interesting church. Within a few years it has been thoroughly repaired as to the interior, and now looks as if it might endure ten more centuries; and I suppose we see little that is really ancient, except the double row of Norman arches, of light freestone, that support the oaken beams and rafters of the roof. All the walls, however, are venerable, and quite preserve the identity of the edifice. There is a stained-glass window of modern manufacture, and in one of the side windows, set amidst plain glass, there is a single piece, five hundred years old, representing St. Anthony, very finely executed, though it looks a little faded. Along the walls, on each side, between the arched windows, there are marble slabs affixed, with inscriptions to the memories of those who used to occupy the seats beneath. I remember none of great antiquity, nor any old monument, except that in the chancel, over the knight and lady of the Ratcliffe family. This consists of a slab of stone, on four small stone pillars, about two feet high. The slab is inlaid with a brass plate, on which is sculptured the knight in armor, and the lady in the costume of Elizabeth's time, exceedingly well done and well preserved, and each figure about eighteen inches in length. The sexton showed us a rubbing of them on paper. Under the slab, which, supported by the low stone pillars, forms a canopy for them, lie two sculptured figures of stone, of life size, and at full length, representing the same persons; but I think the sculptor was hardly equal in his art to the engraver.

The most-curious antique relic in the church is the font. The bowl is very capacious, sufficiently so to admit of the complete immersion of a child of two or three months old. On the outside, in several compartments, there are bas-reliefs of Scriptural and symbolic subjects, —such as the tree of life, the word proceeding out of God's mouth, the crown of thorns,—all in the quaintest taste, sculptured by some hand of a thousand years ago, and preserving the fancies of monkish brains, in stone. The sexton was very proud of this font and its sculpture, and took a kindly personal interest, in showing it; and when we had spent as much time as we could inside, he led us to Southey's grave in the churchyard. He told us that he had known Southey long and well, from early manhood to old age; for he was only twenty-nine when he came to Keswick to reside. He had known Wordsworth too, and Coleridge, and Lovell; and he had seen Southey and Wordsworth walking arm in arm together in that churchyard. He seemed to revere Southey's memory, and said that he had been much lamented, and that as many as a hundred people came to the churchyard when he was buried. He spoke with great praise of Mrs. Southey, his first wife, telling of her charity to the poor, and how she was a blessing to the neighborhood; but he said nothing in favor of the second Mrs. Southey, and only mentioned her selling the library, and other things, after her husband's death, and going to London. Yet I think she was probably a good woman, and meets with less than justice because she took the place of another good woman, and had not time and opportunity to prove herself as good. As for Southey himself, my idea is, that few better or more blameless men have ever lived; but he seems to lack color, passion, warmth, or something that should enable me to bring him into close relation with myself. The graveyard where his body lies is not so rural and picturesque as that where Wordsworth is buried; although Skiddaw rises behind it, and the Greta is murmuring at no very great distance away. But the spot itself has a somewhat bare and bold aspect, with no shadow of trees, no shrubbery.

Over his grave there is a ponderous, oblong block of slate, a native mineral of this region, as hard as iron, and which will doubtless last quite as long as Southey's works retain any vitality in English literature. It is not a monument fit for a poet. There is nothing airy or graceful about it,—and, indeed, there cannot be many men so solid and matter-of-fact as to deserve a tomb like that. Wordsworth's grave is much better, with only a simple headstone, and the grass growing over his mortality, which, for a thousand years, at least, it never can over Southey's. Most of the monuments are of this same black slate, and some erect headstones are curiously sculptured, and seem to have been recently erected.

We now returned to the hotel, and took a car for the valley of St. John. The sky seemed to portend rain in no long time, and Skiddaw had put on his cap; but the people of the hotel and the driver said that there would be no rain this afternoon, and their opinion proved correct. After driving a few miles, we again cane within sight of the Enchanted Castle. It stands rather more than midway adown the declivity of one of the ridges that form the valley to the left, as you go southward, and its site would have been a good one for a fortress, intended to defend the lower entrance of this mountain defile. At a proper distance, it looks not unlike the gray dilapidation of a Gothic castle, which has been crumbling and crumbling away for ages, until Time might be supposed to have imperceptibly stolen its massive pile from man, and given it back to Nature; its towers and battlements and arched entrances being so much defaced and decayed that all the marks of human labor had nearly been obliterated, and the angles of the hewn stone rounded away, while mosses and weeds and bushes grow over it as freely as over a natural ledge of rocks. It is conceivable that in some lights, and in some states of the atmosphere, a traveller, at the entrance of the valley, might really imagine that he beheld a castle here; but, for myself, I must acknowledge that it required a willing fancy to make me see it. As we drew nearer, the delusion did not immediately grow less strong; but, at length, we found ourselves passing at the foot of the declivity, and, behold! it was nothing but an enormous ledge of rock, coming squarely out of the hillside, with other parts of the ledge cropping out in its vicinity. Looking back, after passing, we saw a knoll or hillock, of which the castled rock is the bare face. There are two or three stone cottages along the roadside, beneath the magic castle, and within the enchanted ground. Scott, in the Bridal of Triermain, locates the castle in the middle of the valley, and makes King Arthur ride around it, which any mortal would have great difficulty in doing. This vale of St. John has very striking scenery. Blencathra shuts it in to the northward, lying right across the entrance; and on either side there are lofty crags and declivities, those to the west being more broken and better wooded than the ridge to the eastward, which stretches along for several miles, steep, high, and bare, producing only grass enough for sheep pasture, until it rises into the dark brow of Helvellyn. Adown this ridge, seen afar, like a white ribbon, comes here and there a cascade, sending its voice before it, which distance robs of all its fury, and makes it the quietest sound in the world; and while you see the foamy leap of its upper course a mile or two away, you may see and hear the selfsame little brook babbling through a field, and passing under the arch of a rustic bridge beneath your feet. It is a deep seclusion, with mountains and crags on all sides.

About a mile beyond the castle we stopped at a little wayside inn, the King's Head, and put up for the night. This, I believe, is the only inn which I have found in England—the only one where I have eaten and slept — that does not call itself a hotel. It is very primitive in its arrangements,—a long, low, whitewashed, unadorned, and ugly cottage of two stories. At one extremity is a barn and cow-house, and next to these the part devoted to the better class of guests, where we had our parlor and chambers, contiguous to which is the kitchen and common room, paved with flagstones,—and, lastly, another barn and stable; all which departments are not under separate roofs, but under the same long contiguity, and forming the same building. Our parlor opens immediately upon the roadside, without any vestibule. The house appears to be of some antiquity, with beams across the low ceilings; but the people made us pretty comfortable at bed and board, and fed us with ham and eggs, veal-steaks, honey, oatcakes, gooseberry-tarts, and such cates and dainties,—making a moderate charge for all. The parlor was adorned with rude engravings. I remember only a plate of the Duke of Wellington, at three stages of his life; and there were minerals, delved, doubtless, out of the hearts of the mountains, upon the mantel-piece. The chairs were of an antiquated fashion, and had very capacious seats. We were waited upon by two women, who looked and acted not unlike the countryfolk of New England,—say, of New Hampshire,—except that these may have been more deferential.

While we remained here, I took various walks to get a glimpse of Helvellyn, and a view of Thirlmere,—which is rather two lakes than one, being so narrow at one point as to be crossed by a foot-bridge. Its shores are very picturesque, coming down abruptly upon it, and broken into crags and prominences, which view their shaggy faces in its mirror; and Helvellyn slopes steeply upward, from its southern shore, into the clouds. On its eastern bank, near the foot-bridge, stands Armboth House, which Miss Martineau says is haunted; and I saw a painted board at the entrance of the road which leads to it advertising lodgings there. The ghosts, of course, pay nothing for their accommodations.

At noon, on the day after our arrival, J—— and I went to visit the Enchanted Castle; and we were so venturesome as to turn aside from the road, and ascend the declivity towards its walls, which indeed we hoped to surmount. It proved a very difficult undertaking, the site of the fortress being much higher and steeper than we had supposed; but we did clamber upon what we took for the most elevated portion, when lo! we found that we had only taken one of the outworks, and that there was a gorge of the hill betwixt us and the main walls; while the citadel rose high above, at more than twice the elevation which we had climbed. J—— wished to go on, and I allowed him to climb, till he appeared to have reached so steep and lofty a height that he looked hardly bigger than a monkey, and I should not at all have wondered had he come rolling down to the base of the rock where I sat. But neither did he get actually within the castle, though he might have done so but for a high stone fence, too difficult for him to climb, which runs from the rock along the hillside. The sheep probably go thither much oftener than any other living thing, and to them we left the castle of St. John, with a shrub waving from its battlements, instead of a banner.

After dinner we ordered a car for Ambleside, and while it was getting ready, I went to look at the river of St. John, which, indeed, flows close beside our inn, only just across the road, though it might well be overlooked unless you specially sought for it. It is a brook brawling over the stones, very much as brooks do in New England, only we never think of calling them rivers there. I could easily have made a leap from shore to shore, and J—— scrambled across on no better footing than a rail. I believe I have complained of the want of brooks in other parts of England, but there is no want of them here, and they are always interesting, being of what size they may.

We drove down the valley, and gazed at the vast slope of Helvellyn, and at Thirlmere beneath it, and at Eagle's Crag and Raven's Crag, which beheld themselves in it, and we cast many a look behind at Blencathra, and that noble brotherhood of mountains out of the midst of which we came. But, to say the truth, I was weary of fine scenery, and it seemed to me that I had eaten a score of mountains, and quaffed as many lakes, all in the space of two or three days,—and the natural consequence was a surfeit. There was scarcely a single place in all our tour where I should not have been glad to spend a month; but, by flitting so quickly from one point to another, I lost all the more recondite beauties, and had come away without retaining even the surface of much that I had seen. I am slow to feel,—slow, I suppose, to comprehend, and, like the anaconda, I need to lubricate any object a great deal before I can swallow it and actually make it my own. Yet I shall always enjoy having made this journey, and shall wonder the more at England, which comprehends so much, such a rich variety, within its narrow bounds. If England were all the world, it still would have been worth while for the Creator to have made it, and mankind would have had no cause to find fault with their abode; except that there is not room enough for so many as might be happy here.

We left the great inverted arch of the valley behind us, looking back as long as we could at Blencathra, and Skiddaw over its shoulder, and the clouds were gathering over them at our last glimpse. Passing by Dummail Raise (which is a mound of stones over an old British king), we entered Westmoreland, and soon had the vale of Grasmere before us, with the church where Wordsworth lies, and Nab Scaur and Rydal Water farther on. At Ambleside we took another car for Newby Bridge, whither we drove along the eastern shore of Windermere. The superb scenery through which we had been passing made what we now saw look tame, although a week ago we should have thought it more than commonly interesting. Hawkshead is the only village on our road,—a small, whitewashed old town, with a whitewashed old Norman church, low, and with a low tower, on the same pattern with others that we have seen hereabouts. It was between seven and eight o'clock when we reached Newby Bridge, and heard U——'s voice greeting us, and saw her head, crowned with a wreath of flowers, looking down at us, out of the window of our parlor.

And to-day, July 23d, I have written this most incomplete and unsatisfactory record of what we have done and seen since Wednesday last. I am pretty well convinced that all attempts at describing scenery, especially mountain scenery, are sheer nonsense. For one thing, the point of view being changed, the whole description, which you made up from the previous point of view, is immediately falsified. And when you have done your utmost, such items as those setting forth the scene in a play,—"a mountainous country, in the distance a cascade tumbling over a precipice, and in front a lake; on one side an ivy-covered cottage,"— this dry detail brings the matter before one's mind's eyes more effectually than all the art of word-painting.

July 27th.—We are still at Newby Bridge, and nothing has occurred of remarkable interest, nor have we made any excursions, beyond moderate walks. Two days have been rainy, and to-day there is more rain. We find such weather as tolerable here as it would probably be anywhere; but it passes rather heavily with the children,—and for myself, I should prefer sunshine. Though Mr. White's books afford me some entertainment, especially an odd volume of Ben Jonson's plays, containing "Volpone," "The Alchemist," "Bartholomew Fair," and others. "The Alchemist" is certainly a great play. We watch all arrivals and other events from our parlor window,—a stage-coach driving up four times in the twenty-four hours, with its forlorn outsiders, all saturated with rain; the steamer, from the head of the lake, landing a crowd of passengers, who stroll up to the hotel, drink a glass of ale, lean over the parapet of the bridge, gaze at the flat stones which pave the bottom of the Liver, and then hurry back to the steamer again; cars, phaetons, horsemen, all damped and disconsolate. There are a number of young men staying at the hotel, some of whom go forth in all the rain, fishing, and come back at nightfall, trudging heavily, but with creels on their backs that do not seem very heavy. Yesterday was fair, and enlivened us a good deal. Returning from a walk in the forenoon, I found a troop of yeomanry cavalry in the stable-yard of the hotel. They were the North Lancashire Regiment, and were on their way to Liverpool for the purpose of drill. Not being old campaigners, their uniforms and accoutrements were in so much the finer order, all bright, and looking span-new, and they themselves were a body of handsome and stalwart young men; and it was pleasant to look at their helmets, and red jackets and carbines, and steel scabbarded swords, and gallant steeds,—all so martial in aspect,—and to know that they were only play-soldiers, after all, and were never likely to do nor suffer any warlike mischief. By and by their bugles sounded, and they trotted away, wheeling over the ivy-grown stone bridge, and disappearing behind the trees on the Milnethorpe road. Our host comes forth from the bar with a bill, which he presents to an orderly-sergeant. He, the host, then tells me that he himself once rode many years, a trooper, in this regiment, and that all his comrades were larger men than himself. Yet Mr. Thomas White is a good-sized man, and now, at all events, rather overweight for a dragoon.

Yesterday came one of those bands of music that seem to itinerate everywhere about the country. It consisted of a young woman who played the harp, a bass-viol player, a fiddler, a flutist, and a bugler, besides a little child, of whom, I suppose, the woman was the mother. They sat down on a bench by the roadside, opposite the house, and played several tunes, and by and by the waiter brought them a large pitcher of ale, which they quaffed with apparent satisfaction; though they seemed to be foreigners by their mustachios and sallow hue, and would perhaps have preferred a vinous potation. One would like to follow these people through their vagrant life, and see them in their social relations, and overhear their talk with each other. All vagrants are interesting; and there is a much greater variety of them here than in America,—people who cast themselves on Fortune, and take whatever she gives without a certainty of anything. I saw a travelling tinker yesterday,—a man with a leather apron, and a string of skewers hung at his girdle, and a pack over his shoulders, in which, no doubt, were his tools and materials of trade.

It is remarkable what a natural interest everybody feels in fishing. An angler from the bridge immediately attracts a group to watch his luck. It is the same with J——, fishing for minnows, on the platform near which the steamer lands its passengers. By the by, U—— caught a minnow last evening, and, immediately after, a good-sized perch,—her first fish.

July 30th.—We left Newby Bridge, all of us, on Saturday, at twelve o'clock, and steamed up the lake to Ambleside; a pretty good day as to weather, but with a little tendency to shower. There was nothing new on the lake, and no new impressions, as far as I can remember. At Ambleside, S—— and nurse went shopping, after which we took a carriage for Grasmere, and established ourselves at Brown's Hotel. I find that my impressions from our previous sight of all these scenes do not change on revision. They are very beautiful; but, if I must say it, I am a little weary of them. We soon tire of things which we visit merely by way of spectacle, and with which we have no real and permanent connection. In such cases we very quickly wish the spectacle to be taken away, and another substituted; at all events I do not care about seeing anything more of the English lakes for at least a year.

Perhaps a part of my weariness is owing to the hotel-life which we lead. At an English hotel the traveller feels as if everybody, from the landlord downward, united in a joint and individual purpose to fleece him, because all the attendants who come in contact with him are to be separately considered. So, after paying, in the first instance, a very heavy bill, for what would seem to cover the whole indebtedness, there remain divers dues still to be paid, to no trifling amount, to the landlord's servants,—dues not to be ascertained, and which you never can know whether you have properly satisfied. You can know, perhaps, when you have less than satisfied them, by the aspect of the waiter, which I wish I could describe, not disrespectful in the slightest degree, but a look of profound surprise, a gaze at the offered coin (which he nevertheless pockets) as if he either did not see it, or did not know it, or could not believe his eyesight;—all this, however, with the most quiet forbearance, a Christian-like non-recognition of an unmerited wrong and insult; and finally, all in a moment's space indeed, he quits you and goes about his other business. If you have given him too much, you are made sensible of your folly by the extra amount of his gratitude, and the bows with which he salutes you from the doorstep. Generally, you cannot very decidedly say whether you have been right or wrong; but, in almost all cases, you decidedly feel that you have been fleeced. Then the living at the best of English hotels, so far as my travels have brought me acquainted with them, deserves but moderate praise, and is especially lacking in variety. Nothing but joints, joints, joints; sometimes, perhaps, a meat-pie, which, if you eat it, weighs upon your conscience, with the idea that you have eaten the scraps of other people's dinners. At the lake hotels, the fare is lamb and mutton and grout,—the latter not always fresh, and soon tired of. We pay like nabobs, and are expected to be content with plain mutton.

We spent the day yesterday at Grasmere, in quiet walks about the hotel; and at a little past six in the afternoon, I took my departure in the stage-coach for Windermere. The coach was greatly overburdened with outside passengers,—fifteen in all, besides the four insiders, and one of the fifteen formed the apex of an immense pile of luggage on the top. It seems to me miraculous that we did not topple over, the road being so hilly and uneven, and the driver, I suspect, none the steadier for his visits to all the tap-rooms along the route from Cockermouth. There was a tremendous vibration of the coach now and then; and I saw that, in case of our going over, I should be flung headlong against the high stone fence that bordered most of the road. In view of this I determined to muffle my head in the folds of my thick shawl at the moment of overturn, and as I could do no better for myself, I awaited my fate with equanimity. As far as apprehension goes, I had rather travel from Maine to Georgia by rail, than from Grasmere to Windermere by stage-coach.

At Lowwood, the landlady espied me from the window, and sent out a large packet that had arrived by mail; but as it was addressed to some person of the Christian name of William, I did not venture to open it. She said, also, that a gentleman had been there, who very earnestly desired to see me, and I have since had reason to suppose that this was Allingham, the poet. We arrived at Windermere at half past seven, and waited nearly an hour for the train to start. I took a ticket for Lancaster, and talked there about the war with a gentleman in the coffee-room, who took me for an Englishman, as most people do nowadays, and I heard from him—as you may from all his countrymen—an expression of weariness and dissatisfaction with the whole business. These fickle islanders! How differently they talked a year ago! John Bull sees now that he never was in a worse predicament in his life; and yet it would not take much to make him roar as bellicosely as ever. I went to bed at eleven, and slept unquietly on feathers.

I had purposed to rise betimes, and see the town of Lancaster before breakfast. But here I reckoned without my host; for, in the first place, I had no water for my ablutions, and my boots were not brushed; and so I could not get down stairs till the hour I named for my coffee and chops; and, secondly, the breakfast was delayed half an hour, though promised every minute. In fine, I had but just time to take a hasty walk round Lancaster Castle, and see what I could of the town on my way,—a not very remarkable town, built of stone, with taller houses than in the middle shires of England, narrow streets up and down an eminence on which the castle is situated, with the town immediately about it. The castle is a satisfactory edifice, but so renovated that the walls look almost entirely modern, with the exception of the fine old front, with the statue of an armed warrior, very likely John of Gaunt himself, in a niche over the Norman arch of the entrance. Close beside the castle stands an old church.

The train left Lancaster at half past nine, and reached Liverpool at twelve, over as flat and uninteresting a country as I ever travelled. I have betaken myself to the Rock Ferry Hotel, where I am as comfortable as I could be anywhere but at home; but it is rather comfortless to think of hone as three years off, and three thousand miles away. With what a sense of utter weariness, not fully realized till then, we shall sink down on our own threshold, when we reach it. The moral effect of being without a settled abode is very wearisome.

Our coachman from Grasmere to Windermere looked like a great beer-barrel, oozy with his proper liquor. I suppose such solid soakers never get upset.

THE LAUNCH.

August 2d.—Mr. ——— has urged me very much to go with his father and family to see the launch of a great ship which has been built for their house, and afterwards to partake of a picnic; so, on Tuesday morning I presented myself at the landing-stage, and met the party, to take passage for Chester. It was a showery morning, and looked wofully like a rainy day; but nothing better is to be expected in England; and, after all, there is seldom such a day that you cannot glide about pretty securely between the drops of rain. This, however, did not turn out one of those tolerable days, but grew darker and darker, and worse and worse; and was worst of all when we had passed about six miles beyond Chester, and were just on the borders of Wales, on the hither side of the river Dee, where the ship was to be launched. Here the train stopped, and absolutely deposited our whole party of excursionists, under a heavy shower, in the midst of a muddy potato-field, whence we were to wade through mud and mire to the ship-yard, almost half a mile off. Some kind Christian, I know not whom, gave me half of his umbrella, and half of his cloak, and thereby I got to a shed near the ship, without being entirely soaked through.

The ship had been built on the banks of the Dee, at a spot where it is too narrow for her to be launched directly across, and so she lay lengthwise of the river, and was so arranged as to take the water parallel with the stream. She is, for aught I know, the largest ship in the world; at any rate, longer than the Great Britain,—an iron-screw steamer,—and looked immense and magnificent, and was gorgeously dressed out in flags. Had it been a pleasant day, all Chester and half Wales would have been there to see the launch; and, in spite of the rain, there were a good many people on the opposite shore, as well as on our side; and one or two booths, and many of the characteristics of a fair,—that is to say, men and women getting intoxicated without any great noise and confusion.

The ship was expected to go off at about twelve o'clock, and at that juncture all Mr. ———'s friends assembled under the bows of the ship, where we were a little sheltered from the rain by the projection of that part of the vessel over our heads. The bottle of port-wine with which she was to be christened was suspended from the bows to the platform where we stood by a blue ribbon; and the ceremony was to be performed by Mrs. ———, who, I could see, was very nervous in anticipation of the ceremony. Mr. ——— kept giving her instructions in a whisper, and showing her how to throw the bottle; and as the critical moment approached, he took hold of it along with her. All this time we were waiting in momentary expectation of the ship going off, everything being ready, and only the touch of a spring, as it were, needed to make her slide into the water. But the chief manager kept delaying a little longer, and a little longer; though the pilot on board sent to tell him that it was time she was off. "Yes, yes; but I want as much water as I can get," answered the manager; and so he held on till, I suppose, the tide had raised the river Dee to its very acme of height. At last the word was given; the ship began slowly to move; Mrs. ——— threw the bottle against the bow with a spasmodic effort that dashed it into a thousand pieces, and diffused the fragrance of the old port all around, where it lingered several minutes. I did not think that there could have been such a breathless moment in an affair of this kind.

The ship moved majestically down toward the river; and unless it were Niagara, I never saw anything grander and more impressive than the motion of this mighty mass as she departed from us. We on the platform, and everybody along both shores of the Dee, took off our hats in the rain, waved handkerchiefs, cheered, shouted,—"Beautiful!" "What a noble launch!" "Never was so fair a sight!"—and, really, it was so grand, that calm, majestic movement, that I felt the tears come into my eyes. The wooden pathway adown which she was gliding began to smoke with the friction; when all at once, when we expected to see her plunge into the Dee, she came to a full stop. Mr. ———, the father of my friend, a gentleman with white hair, a dark, expressive face, bright eyes, and an Oriental cast of features, immediately took the alarm. A moment before his countenance had been kindled with triumph; but now he turned pale as death, and seemed to grow ten years older while I was looking at him. Well he might, for his noble ship was stuck fast in the land of the Dee, and without deepening the bed of the river, I do not see how her vast iron hulk is ever to be got out.

[This steamer was afterwards successfully floated off on the 29th of the same month.]

There was no help for it. A steamboat was hitched on to the stranded vessel, but broke two or three cables without stirring her an inch. So, after waiting long after we had given up all hope, we went to the office of the ship-yard, and there took a lunch; and still the rain was pouring, pouring, pouring, and I never experienced a blacker affair in all my days. Then we had to wait a great while for a train to take us back, so that it was almost five o'clock before we arrived at Chester, where I spent an hour in rambling about the old town, under the Rows; and on the walls, looking down on the treetops, directly under my feet, and through their thick branches at the canal, which creeps at the base, and at the cathedral; walking under the dark intertwining arches of the cloisters, and looking up at the great cathedral tower, so wasted away externally by time and weather that it looks, save for the difference of color between white snow and red freestone, like a structure of snow, half dissolved by several warm days.

At the lunch I met with a graduate of Cambridge (England), tutor of a grandson of Percival, with his pupil (Percival, the assassinated minister, I mean). I should not like this position of tutor to a young Englishman; it certainly has an ugly twang of upper servitude. I observed that the tutor gave his pupil the best seat in the railway carriage, and in all respects provided for his comfort before thinking of his own; and this, not as a father does for his child, out of love, but from a sense of place and duty, which I did not quite see how a gentleman could consent to feel. And yet this Mr. C——— was evidently a gentleman, and a quiet, intelligent, agreeable, and, no doubt, learned man. K——— being mentioned, Mr. C——— observed that he had known him well at college, having been his contemporary there. He did not like him, however,—thought him a "dangerous man," as well as I could gather; he thinks there is some radical defect in K———'s moral nature, a lack of sincerity; and, furthermore, he believes him to be a sensualist in his disposition, in support of which view he said Mr. K——— had made drawings, such as no pure man could have made, or could allow himself to show or look at. This was the only fact which Mr. C——— adduced, bearing on his opinion of K———; otherwise, it seemed to be one of those early impressions which a collegian gets of his fellow-students, and which he never gets rid of, whatever the character of the person may turn out to be in after years. I have judged several persons in this way, and still judge them so, though the world has cone to very different conclusions. Which is right?—the world, which has the man's whole mature life on its side; or his early companion, who has nothing for it but some idle passages of his youth?

Mr. M——— remarked of newspaper reporters, that they may be known at all celebrations, and of any public occasion, by the enormous quantity of luncheon they eat.

August 12th.—Mr. B——— dined with us at the Rock Ferry Hotel the day before yesterday. Speaking of Helvellyn, and the death of Charles Cough, about whom Wordsworth and Scott have both sung, Mr. B——— mentioned a version of that story which rather detracts from the character of the faithful dog.

But somehow it lowers one's opinion of human nature itself, to be compelled so to lower one's standard of a dog's nature. I don't intend to believe the disparaging story, but it reminds me of the story of the New-Zealander who was asked whether he loved a missionary who had been laboring for his soul and those of his countrymen. "To be sure I loved him. Why, I ate a piece of him for my breakfast this morning!"

For the last week or two I have passed my time between the hotel and the Consulate, and a weary life it is, and one that leaves little of profit behind it. I am sick to death of my office,—brutal captains and brutal sailors; continual complaints of mutual wrong, which I have no power to set right, and which, indeed, seem to have no right on either side; calls of idleness or ceremony from my travelling countrymen, who seldom know what they are in search of at the commencement of their tour, and never have attained any desirable end at the close of it; beggars, cheats, simpletons, unfortunates, so mixed up that it is impossible to distinguish one from another, and so, in self-defence, the Consul distrusts them all. . . .

At the hotel, yesterday, there was a large company of factory people from Preston, who marched up from the pier with a band of military music playing before them. They spent the day in the gardens and ball-room of the hotel, dancing and otherwise merry-making; but I saw little of them, being at the Consulate. Towards evening it drizzled, and the assemblage melted away gradually; and when the band marched down to the pier, there were few to follow, although one man went dancing before the musicians, flinging out his arms, and footing it with great energy and gesticulation. Some young women along the road likewise began to dance as the music approached.

Thackeray has a dread of servants, insomuch that he hates to address them, or to ask them for anything. His morbid sensibility, in this regard, has perhaps led him to study and muse upon them, so that he may be presumed to have a more intimate knowledge of this class than any other man.

Carlyle dresses so badly, and wears such a rough outside, that the flunkies are rude to him at gentlemen's doors.

In the afternoon J—— and I took a walk towards Tranmere Hall, and beyond, as far as Oxton. This part of the country, being so near Liverpool and Birkenhead, is all sprinkled over with what they call "Terraces," "Bellevues," and other pretty names for semi-detached villas ("Recluse Cottage" was one) for a somewhat higher class. But the old, whitewashed stone cottage is still frequent, with its roof of slate or thatch, which perhaps is green with weeds or grass. Through its open door, you see that it has a pavement of flagstones, or perhaps of red freestone; and hogs and donkeys are familiar with the threshold. The door always opens directly into the kitchen, without any vestibule; and, glimpsing in, you see that a cottager's life must be the very plainest and homeliest that ever was lived by men and women. Yet the flowers about the door often indicate a native capacity for the beautiful; but often there is only a pavement of round stones or of flagstones, like those within. At one point where there was a little bay, as it were, in the hedge fence, we saw something like a small tent or wigwam,—an arch of canvas three or four feet high, and open in front, under which sat a dark-complexioned woman and some children. The woman was sewing, and I took them for gypsies.

August 17th.—Yesterday afternoon J—— and I went to Birkenhead Park, which I have already described. . . . It so happened that there was a large school spending its holiday there; a school of girls of the lower classes, to the number of a hundred and fifty, who disported themselves on the green, under the direction of the schoolmistresses and of an old gentleman. It struck me, as it always has, to observe how the lower orders of this country indicate their birth and station by their aspect and features. In America there would be a good deal of grace and beauty among a hundred and fifty children and budding girls, belonging to whatever rank of life. But here they had universally a most plebeian look,—stubbed, sturdy figures, round, coarse faces, snub-noses,—the most evident specimens of the brown bread of human nature. They looked wholesome and good enough, and fit to sustain their rough share of life; but it would have been impossible to make a lady out of any one of them. Climate, no doubt, has most to do with diffusing a slender elegance over American young-womanhood; but something, perhaps, is also due to the circumstance of classes not being kept apart there as they are here: they interfuse, amid the continual ups and downs of our social life; and so, in the lowest stations of life, you may see the refining influence of gentle blood. At all events, it is only necessary to look at such an assemblage of children as I saw yesterday, to be convinced that birth and blood do produce certain characteristics. To be sure, I have seen no similar evidence in England or elsewhere of old gentility refining and elevating the race.

These girls were all dressed in black gowns, with white aprons and neckerchiefs, and white linen caps on their heads,—a very dowdyish attire, and well suited to their figures. I saw only two of their games,—in one, they stood in a circle, while two of their number chased one another within and without the ring of girls, which opened to let the fugitive pass, but closed again to impede the passage of the pursuer. The other was blind-man's-buff on a new plan: several of the girls, sometimes as many as twenty, being blinded at once, and pursuing a single one, who rang a hand-bell to indicate her whereabouts. This was very funny; the bell-girl keeping just beyond their reach, and drawing them after her in a huddled group, so that they sometimes tumbled over one another and lay sprawling. I think I have read of this game in Strutt's "English Sports and Pastimes."

We walked from the Park home to Rock Ferry, a distance of three or four miles,—a part of which was made delightful by a foot-path, leading us through fields where the grass had just been mown, and others where the wheat harvest was commenced. The path led us into the very midst of the rural labor that was going forward; and the laborers rested a moment to look at us; in fact, they seemed to be more willing to rest than American laborers would have been. Children were loitering along this path or sitting down beside it; and we met one little maid, passing from village to village, intent on some errand. Reaching Tranmere, I went into an alehouse, nearly opposite the Hall, and called for a glass of ale. The doorstep before the house, and the flagstone floor of the entry and tap-room, were chalked all over in corkscrew lines,—an adornment that gave an impression of care and neatness, the chalked lines being evidently freshly made. It was a low, old-fashioned room ornamented with a couple of sea-shells, and an earthen-ware figure on the mantel-piece; also with advertisements of Allsop's ale, and other drinks, and with a pasteboard handbill of "The Ancient Order of Foresters"; any member of which, paying sixpence weekly, is entitled to ten shillings per week, and the attendance of a first-rate physician in sickness, and twelve pounds to be paid to his friends in case of death. Any member of this order, when travelling, is sure (says the handbill) to meet with a brother member to lend him a helping hand, there being nearly three thousand districts of this order, and more than a hundred and nine thousand members in Great Britain, whence it has extended to Australia, America, and other countries.

Looking up at the gateway of Tranmere Hall, I discovered an inscription on the red freestone lintel, and, though much time-worn, I succeeded in reading it. "Labor omnia vincit. 1614." There were likewise some initials which I could not satisfactorily make out. The sense of this motto would rather befit the present agricultural occupants of the house than the idle gentlefolks who built and formerly inhabited it.

SMITHELL'S HALL.

August 25th.—On Thursday I went by invitation to Smithell's Hall in Bolton le Moors to dine and spend the night. The Hall is two or three miles from the town of Bolton, where I arrived by railway from Liverpool, and which seems to be a pretty large town, though the houses are generally modern, or with modernized fronts of brick or stucco. It is a manufacturing town, and the tall brick chimneys rise numerously in the neighborhood, and are so near Smithell's Hall that I suspect the atmosphere is somewhat impregnated with their breath. Mr. ——— can comfort himself with the rent which he receives from the factories erected upon his own grounds; and I suppose the value of his estate has greatly increased by the growth of manufactories; although, unless he wish to sell it, I do not see what good this can do him.

Smithell's Hall is one of the oldest residences of England, and still retains very much the aspect that it must have had several centuries ago. The house formerly stood around all four sides of a quadrangle, enclosing a court, and with an entrance through an archway. One side of this quadrangle was removed in the time of the present Mr. ———'s father, and the front is now formed by the remaining three sides. They look exceedingly ancient and venerable, with their range of gables and lesser peaks. The house is probably timber-framed throughout, and is overlaid with plaster, and its generally light line is painted with a row of trefoils in black, producing a very quaint effect. The wing, forming one side of the quadrangle, is a chapel, and has been so from time immemorial; and Mr. ——— told me that he had a clergyman, and even a bishop, in his own diocese. The drawing-room is on the opposite side of the quadrangle; and through an arched door, in the central portion, there is a passage to the rear of the house. It is impossible to describe such an old rambling edifice as this, or to get any clear idea of its plan, even by going over it, without the aid of a map. Mr. ——— has added some portions, and altered others, but with due regard to harmony with the original structure, and the great body of it is still mediaeval.

The entrance-hall opens right upon the quadrangular court; and is a large, low room, with a settle of carved old oak, and other old oaken furniture,—a centre-table with periodicals and newspapers on it,—some family pictures on the walls,—and a large, bright coal-fire in the spacious grate. The fire is always kept up, throughout summer and winter, and it seemed to me an excellent plan, and rich with cheerful effects; insuring one comfortable place, and that the most central in the house, whatever may be the inclemency of the weather. It was a cloudy, moist, showery day, when I arrived; and this fire gave me the brightest and most hospitable smile, and took away any shivery feeling by its mere presence. The servant showed me thence into a low-studded dining-room, where soon Mrs. ——— made her appearance, and, after some talk, brought me into the billiard-room, opening from the hall, where Mr. ——— and a young gentleman were playing billiards, and two ladies looking on. After the game was finished, Mr. ——— took me round to see the house and grounds.

The peculiarity of this house is what is called "The Bloody Footstep." In the time of Bloody Mary, a Protestant clergyman—George Marsh by name—was examined before the then proprietor of the Hall, Sir Roger Barton, I think, and committed to prison for his heretical opinions, and was ultimately burned at the stake. As his guards were conducting him from the justice-room, through the stone-paved passage that leads from front to rear of Smithell's Hall, he stamped his foot upon one of the flagstones in earnest protestation against the wrong which he was undergoing. The foot, as some say, left a bloody mark in the stone; others have it, that the stone yielded like wax under his foot, and that there has been a shallow cavity ever since. This miraculous footprint is still extant; and Mrs. ——— showed it to me before her husband took me round the estate. It is almost at the threshold of the door opening from the rear of the house, a stone two or three feet square, set among similar ones, that seem to have been worn by the tread of many generations. The footprint is a dark brown stain in the smooth gray surface of the flagstone; and, looking sidelong at it, there is a shallow cavity perceptible, which Mrs. ——— accounted for as having been worn by people setting their feet just on this place, so as to tread the very spot, where the martyr wrought the miracle. The mark is longer than any mortal foot, as if caused by sliding along the stone, rather than sinking into it; and it might be supposed to have been made by a pointed shoe, being blunt at the heel, and decreasing towards the toe. The blood-stained version of the story is more consistent with the appearance of the mark than the imprint would be; for if the martyr's blood oozed out through his shoe and stocking, it might have made his foot slide along the stone, and thus have lengthened the shape. Of course it is all a humbug,—a darker vein cropping up through the gray flagstone; but, it is probably a fact, and, for aught I know, may be found in Fox's Book of Martyrs, that George Marsh underwent an examination in this house [There is a full and pathetic account of the examination and martyrdom of George Marsh in the eleventh section of Fox's Book of Martyrs, as I have just found (June 9, 1867). He went to Smithell's hall, among other places, to be questioned by Mr. Barton.—ED.]; and the tradition may have connected itself with the stone within a short time after the martyrdom; or, perhaps, when the old persecuting knight departed this life, and Bloody Mary was also dead, people who had stood at a little distance from the Hall door, and had seen George Marsh lift his hand and stamp his foot just at this spot,—perhaps they remembered this action and gesture, and really believed that Providence had thus made an indelible record of it on the stone; although the very stone and the very mark might have lain there at the threshold hundreds of years before. But, even if it had been always there, the footprint might, after the fact, be looked upon as a prophecy, from the time when the foundation of the old house was laid, that a holy and persecuted man should one day set his foot here, on the way that was to lead him to the stake. At any rate, the legend is a good one.

Mrs. ——— tells me that the miraculous stone was once taken up from the pavement, and flung out of doors, where it remained many years; and in proof of this, it is cracked quite across at one end. This is a pity, and rather interferes with the authenticity, if not of the stone itself, yet of its position in the pavement. It is not far from the foot of the staircase, leading up to Sir Roger Barton's examination-room, whither we ascended, after examining the footprint. This room now opens sideways on the Chapel, into which it looks down, and which is spacious enough to accommodate a pretty large congregation. On one of the walls of the Chapel there is a marble tablet to the memory of one of the present family,—Mr.———'s father, I suppose;

he being the first of the name who possessed the estate. The present owners, however, seem to feel pretty much the same pride in the antiquity and legends of the house as if it had come down to them in an unbroken succession of their own forefathers. It has, in reality, passed several times from one family to another, since the Conquest.

Mr. ——— led me through a spacious old room, which was formerly panelled with carved oak, but which is converted into a brew-house, up a pair of stairs, into the garret of one of the gables, in order to show me the ancient framework of the house. It is of oak, and preposterously ponderous,—immense beams and rafters, which no modern walls could support,—a gigantic old skeleton, which architects say must have stood a thousand years; and, indeed, it is impossible to ascertain the date of the original foundation, though it is known to have been repaired and restored between five and six centuries ago. Of course, in the lapse of ages, it must continually have been undergoing minor changes, but without at all losing its identity. Mr. ——— says that this old oak wood, though it looks as strong and as solid as ever, has really lost its strength, and that it would snap short off, on application of any force.

After this we took our walk through the grounds, which are well wooded, though the trees will bear no comparison with those which I have seen in the midland parts of England. It takes, I suspect, a much longer time for trees to attain a good size here than in America; and these trees, I think Mr. ——— told me, were principally set out by himself. He is upwards of sixty,—a good specimen of the old English country-gentleman, sensible, loving his land and his trees and his dogs and his game, doing a little justice-business, and showing a fitness for his position; so that you feel satisfied to have him keep it. He was formerly a member of Parliament. I had met him before at dinner at Mrs. H———'s. . . . He took pleasure in showing me his grounds, through which he has laid out a walk, winding up and down through dells and over hillocks, and now and then crossing a rustic bridge; so that you have an idea of quite an extensive domain.

Beneath the trees there is a thick growth of ferns, serving as cover for the game. A little terrier-dog, who had hitherto kept us company, all at once disappeared; and soon afterwards we heard the squeak of some poor victim in the cover, whereupon Mr. ——— set out with agility, and ran to the rescue.—By and by the terrier came back with a very guilty look. From the wood we passed into the open park, whence we had a distant view of the house; and, returning thither, we viewed it in other aspects, and on all sides. One portion of it is occupied by Mr. ———'s gardener, and seems not to have been repaired, at least as to its exterior, for a great many years,—showing the old wooden frame, painted black, with plaster in the interstices; and broad windows, extending across the whole breadth of the rooms, with hundreds of little diamond-shaped panes of glass. Before dinner I was shown to my room, which opens from an ancient gallery, lined with oak, and lighted by a row of windows along one side of the quadrangle. Along this gallery are the doors of several sleeping-chambers, one of which—I think it is here—is called "The Dead Man's Chamber." It is supposed to have been the room where the corpses of persons connected with the household used to be laid out. My own room was called "The Beam Chamber," from am immense cross-beam that projects from the ceiling, and seems to be an entire tree, laid across, and left rough-hewn, though at present it is whitewashed. The but of the tree (for it diminishes from one end of the chamber to the other) is nearly two feet square, in its visible part.

We dined, at seven o'clock, in a room some thirty-five or forty feet long, and proportionably broad, all panelled with the old carved oak which Mr. ——— took from the room which he had converted into a brew-house. The oak is now of a very dark brown hue, and, being highly polished, it produces a sombre but rich effect. It is supposed to be of the era of Henry the Seventh, and when I examined it the next morning, I found it very delicately and curiously wrought. There are carved profiles of persons in the costume of the times, done with great skill; also foliage, intricate puzzles of intersecting lines, sacred devices, anagrams, and, among others, the device of a bar across a tun, indicating the name of Barton. Most of the carving, however, is less elaborate and intricate than these specimens, being in a perpendicular style, and on one pattern. Before the wood grew so very dark, the beauty of the work must have been much more easily seen than now, as to particulars, though I hardly think that the general effect could have been better; at least, the sombre richness that overspreads the entire square of the room is suitable to such an antique house. An elaborate Gothic cornice runs round the whole apartment. The sideboard and other furniture are of Gothic patterns, and, very likely, of genuine antiquity; but the fireplace is perhaps rather out of keeping, being of white marble with the arms of this family sculptured on it.

Though hardly sunset when we sat down to dinner, yet, it being an overcast day, and the oaken room so sombre, we had candles burning on the table; and, long before dinner was over, the candle-light was all the light we had. It is always pleasanter to dine by artificial light. Mrs. ———'s dinner was a good one, and Mr. ———'s wines were very good. I had Mrs. ——— on one side, and another lady on the other side. . . .

After dinner there were two card-parties formed in the dining-room, at one of which there was a game of Vingt-et-un, and at the other a game of whist, at which Mrs. ——— and I lost several shillings to a Mrs. Halton and Mr. Gaskell. . . . After finishing our games at cards, Mrs. Halton drove off in a pony-chaise to her own house; the other ladies retired, and the gentlemen sat down to chat awhile over the hall fire, occasionally sipping a glass of wine-and-water, and finally we all went off to our rooms. It was past twelve o'clock when I composed myself to sleep, and I could not have slept long, when a tremendous clap of thunder woke me just in time to see a vivid flash of lightning. I saw no ghosts, though Mrs. ——— tells me there is one, which makes a disturbance, unless religious services are regularly kept up in the Chapel.

In the morning, before breakfast, we had prayers, read by Mr. ———, in the oak dining-room, all the servants coming in, and everybody kneeling down. I should like to know how much true religious feeling is indicated by this regular observance of religious rites in English families. In America, if people kneel down to pray, it is pretty certain that they feel a genuine interest in the matter, and their daily life is supposed to be in accordance with their devotions. If an American is an infidel, he knows it; but an Englishman is often so without suspecting it,—being kept from that knowledge by this formality of family prayer, and his other regularities of external worship. . . .

There was a parrot in a corner of the dining-room, and, when prayers were over, Mrs. ——— praised it very highly for having been so silent; it being Poll's habit, probably, to break in upon the sacred exercises with unseemly interjections and remarks. While we were at breakfast, Poll began to whistle and talk very vociferously, and in a tone and with expressions that surprised me, till I learned that the bird is usually kept in the kitchen and servants' hall, and is only brought into the dining-room at prayer-time and breakfast. Thus its mouth is full of kitchen talk, which flows out before the gentlefolks with the queerest effect.

After breakfast I examined the carvings of the room. Mr. ——— has added to its decorations the coats of arms of all the successive possessors of the house, with those of the families into which they married, including the Ratcliffes, Stanleys, and others. From the dining-room I passed into the library, which contains books enough to make a rainy day pass pleasantly. I remember nothing else that I need to record; and as I sat by the hall fire, talking with Mr. Gaskell, at about eleven o'clock, the butler brought me word that a fly, which I had bespoken, was ready to convey me to the railway. I took leave of Mrs. ———, her last request being that I would write a ghost-story for her house,—and drove off.

SHREWSBURY

September 5th.—Yesterday we all of us set forth from Rock Ferry at half past twelve, and reached Shrewsbury between three and four o'clock, and took up our quarters at the Lion Hotel. We found Shrewsbury situated on an eminence, around which the Severn winds, making a peninsula of it, quite densely covered by the town. The streets ascend, and curve about, and intersect each other with the customary irregularity of these old English towns, so that it is quite impossible to go directly to any given point, or for a stranger to find his way to a place which he wishes to reach, though, by what seems a singular good fortune, the sought-for place is always offering itself when least expected. On this account I never knew such pleasant walking as in old streets like those of Shrewsbury. And there are passages opening under archways, and winding up between high edifices, very tempting to the explorer, and generally leading to some court, or some queer old range of buildings or piece of architecture, which it would be the greatest pity to miss seeing. There was a delightful want of plan in the laying out of these ancient towns. In fact, they never were laid out at all, nor were restrained by any plan whatever, but grew naturally, with streets as eccentric as the pathway of a young child toddling about the floor.

The first curious thing we particularly noticed, when we strolled out after dinner, was the old market-house, which stands in the midst of an oblong square; a gray edifice, elevated on pillars and arches, and with the statue of an armed knight, Richard Plantagenet, Duke of York, in a central niche, in its front. The statue is older than the market-house, having been moved thither from one of the demolished towers of the city wall in 1795. The market-house was erected in 1595. There are other curious sculptures and carvings and quirks of architecture about this building; and the houses that stand about the square are, many of them, very striking specimens of what dwelling-houses used to be in Elizabeth's time, and earlier. I have seen no such stately houses, in that style, as we found here in Shrewsbury. There were no such fine ones in Coventry, Stratford, Warwick, Chester, nor anywhere else where we have been. Their stately height and spaciousness seem to have been owing to the fact that Shrewsbury was a sort of metropolis of the country round about, and therefore the neighboring gentry had their town-houses there, when London was several days' journey off, instead of a very few hours; and, besides, it was once much the resort of kings, and the centre-point of great schemes of war and policy. One such house, formerly belonging to a now extinct family, that of Ireland, rises to the height of four stories, and has a front consisting of what look like four projecting towers. There are ranges of embowered windows, one above another, to the full height of the house, and these are surmounted by peaked gables. The people of those times certainly did not deny themselves light; and while window-glass was an article of no very remote introduction, it was probably a point of magnificence and wealthy display to have enough of it. One whole side of the room must often have been formed by the window. This Ireland mansion, as well as all the rest of the old houses in Shrewsbury, is a timber house,—that is, a skeleton of oak, filled up with brick, plaster, or other material, and with the beams of the timber marked out with black paint; besides which, in houses of any pretension, there are generally trefoils, and other Gothic-looking ornaments, likewise painted black. They have an indescribable charm for me,—the more, I think, because they are wooden; but, indeed, I cannot tell why it is that I like them so well, and am never tired of looking at them. A street was a development of human life, in the days when these houses were built, whereas a modern street is but the cold plan of an architect, without individuality or character, and without the human emotion which a man kneads into the walls which he builds on a scheme of his own.

We strolled to a pleasant walk under a range of trees, along the shore of the Severn. It is called the Quarry Walk. The Severn is a pretty river, the largest, I think (unless it be such an estuary as the Mersey), that I have met with in England; that is to say, about a fair stone's-throw across. It is very gentle in its course, and winds along between grassy and sedgy banks, with a good growth of weeds in some part of its current. It has one stately bridge, called the English Bridge, of several arches, and, as we sauntered along the Quarry Walk, we saw a ferry where the boat seemed to be navigated across by means of a rope, stretched from bank to bank of the river. After leaving the

Quarry Walk, we passed an old tower of red freestone, the only one remaining of those formerly standing at intervals along the whole course of the town wall; and we also went along what little is now left of the wall itself. And thence, through the irregular streets, which gave no account of themselves, we found our way, I know not how, back to our hotel. It is an uncheerful old hotel, which takes upon itself to be in the best class of English country hotels, and charges the best price; very dark in the lower apartments, pervaded with a musty odor, but provided with a white-neckclothed waiter, who spares no ceremony in serving the joints of mutton.

J—— and I afterwards walked forth again, and went this time to the castle, which stands exactly above the railway station. A path, from its breadth quite a street, leads up to the arched gateway; but we found a board, giving notice that these are private grounds, and no strangers admitted; so that we only passed through the gate a few steps, and looked about us, and retired, on perceiving a man approaching us through the trees and shrubbery. A private individual, it seems, has burrowed in this old warlike den, and turned the keep, and any other available apartment, into a modern dwelling, and laid out his pleasure-grounds within the precincts of the castle wall, which allows verge enough for the purpose. The ruins have been considerably repaired. This castle was built at various times, the keep by Edward I., and other portions at an earlier period, and it stands on the isthmus left by the Severn in its wandering course about the town. The Duke of Cleveland now owns it. I do not know who occupies it.

In the course of this walk, we passed St. Mary's Church,—a very old church indeed, no matter how old, but say, eight hundred or a thousand years. It has a very tall spire, and the spire is now undergoing repairs; and, seeing the door open, I went into the porch, but found no admission further. Then, walking around it, through the churchyard, we saw that all the venerable Gothic windows—one of them grand in size— were set with stained glass, representing coats of arms and ancient armor, and kingly robes, and saints with glories about their heads, and Scriptural people; but all of these, as far as our actual perception was concerned, quite colorless, and with only a cold outline, dimly filled up. Yet, had we been within the church, and had the sunlight been streaming through, what a warm, rich, gorgeous, roseate, golden life would these figures have showed!

In the churchyard, close upon the street, so that its dust must be continually scattered over the spot, I saw a heavy gray tombstone, with a Latin inscription, purporting that Bishop Butler, the author of the Analogy, in his lifetime had chosen this as a burial-place for himself and his family. There is a statue of him within the church. From the top of the spire a man, above a hundred years ago, attempted to descend, by means of a rope, to the other side of the Severn; but the rope broke, and he fell in his midway flight, and was killed. It was an undertaking worthy of Sam Patch. There is a record of the fact on the outside of the tower.

I remember nothing more that we saw yesterday; but, before breakfast, J——— and I sallied forth again, and inspected the gateway and interior court of the Council House,—a very interesting place, both in itself and for the circumstances connected with it, it having been the place where the councillors for the Welsh marches used to reside during their annual meetings; and Charles the First also lived here for six weeks in 1612. James II. likewise held his court here in 1687. The house was originally built in 1501,—that is, the Council House itself,—the gateway, and the house through which it passes, being of as late date as 1620. This latter is a fine old house, in the usual style of timber architecture, with the timber lines marked out, and quaint adornments in black paint; and the pillars of the gateway which passes beneath the front chamber are of curiously carved oak, which has probably stood the action of English atmosphere better than marble would have done. Passing through this gateway, we entered a court, and saw some old buildings more or less modernized, but without destroying their aged stateliness, standing round three sides of it, with arched entrances and bow-windows, and windows in the roofs, and peaked gables, and all the delightful irregularity and variety that these houses have, and which make them always so fresh,—and with so much detail that every minute you see something heretofore unseen. It must have been no unfit residence for a king and his court, when those three sides of the square, all composing one great fantastic house, were in their splendor. The square itself, too, must have been a busy and cheerful scene, thronged with attendants, guests, horses, etc.

After breakfast, we all walked out, and, crossing the English Bridge, looked at the Severn over its parapet. The river is here broader than elsewhere, and very shallow, and has an island covered with bushes, about midway across. Just over the bridge we saw a church, of red freestone, and evidently very ancient. This is the Church of the Holy Cross, and is a portion of the Abbey of St. Peter and St. John, which formerly covered ten acres of ground. We did not have time to go into the church; but the windows and other points of architecture, so far as we could discern them, and knew how to admire them, were exceedingly venerable and beautiful. On the other side of the street, over a wide space, there are other remains of the old abbey; and the most interesting was a stone pulpit, now standing in the open air, seemingly in a garden, but which originally stood in the refectory of the abbey, and was the station whence one of the monks read to his brethren at their meals. The pulpit is much overgrown with ivy. We should have made further researches among these remains, though they seem now to be in private grounds; but a large mastiff came nut of his kennel, and, approaching us to the length of his iron chain, began barking very fiercely. Nor had we time to see half that we would gladly have seen and studied here and elsewhere about Shrewsbury. It would have been very interesting to have visited Hotspur's and Falstaff's battle-field, which is four miles from the town; too distant, certainly, for Falstaff to have measured the length of the fight by Shrewsbury clock. There is now a church, built there by Henry IV., and said to cover the bones of those slain in the battle.

Returning into the town, we penetrated some narrow lanes, where, as the old story goes, people might almost shake hands across from the top windows of the opposite houses, impending towards each other. Emerging into a wider street, at a spot somewhat more elevated than other parts of the town, we went into a shop to buy some Royal Shrewsbury cakes, which we had seen advertised at several shop windows. They are a very rich cake, with plenty of eggs, sugar, and butter, and very little flour.

A small public building of stone, of modern date, was close by; and asking the shopwoman what it was, she said it was the Butter Cross, or market for butter, eggs, and poultry. It is a remarkable site, for here, in ancient times, stood a stone cross, where heralds used to make proclamation, and where criminals of state used to be executed. David, the last of the Welsh princes, was here cruelly put to death by Edward I., and many noblemen were beheaded on this spot, after being taken prisoners in the battle of Shrewsbury.

I can only notice one other memorable place in Shrewsbury, and that is the Raven Inn, where Farquhar wrote his comedy of "The Recruiting Officer" in 1701. The window of the room in which he wrote is said to look into the inn yard, and I went through the arched entrance to see if I could distinguish it. The hostlers were currying horses in the yard, and so stared at me that I gave but the merest glance. The Shrewsbury inns have not only the customary names of English inns,—as the Lion, the Stag,—but they have also the carved wooden figures of the object named, whereas, in all other towns, the name alone remains.

We left Shrewsbury at half past ten, and arrived in London at about four in the afternoon.

LONDON.

September 7th.—On Wednesday, just before dusk, J——- and I walked forth, for the first time, in London. Our lodgings are in George Street, Hanover Square, No. 21; and St. George's Church, where so many marriages in romance and in fashionable life have been celebrated, is a short distance below our house, in the same street. The edifice seems to be of white marble, now much blackened with London smoke, and has a Grecian pillared portico. In the square, just above us, is a statue of William Pitt. We went down Bond Street, and part of Regent Street, just estraying a little way from our temporary nest, and taking good account of landmarks and corners, so as to find our way readily back again. It is long since I have had such a childish feeling; but all that I had heard and felt about the vastness of London made it seem like swimming in a boundless ocean, to venture one step beyond the only spot I knew. My first actual impression of London was of stately and spacious streets, and by no means so dusky and grimy as I had expected,—not merely in the streets about this quarter of the town, which is the aristocratic quarter, but in all the streets through which we had passed from the railway station. If I had not first been so imbued with the smoke and dinginess of Liverpool, I should doubtless have seen a stronger contrast betwixt dusky London and the cheerful glare of our American cities. There are no red bricks here; all are of a dark hue, and whatever of stone or stucco has been white soon clothes itself in mourning.

Yesterday forenoon I went out alone, and plunged headlong into London, and wandered about all day, without any particular object in view, but only to lose myself for the sake of finding myself unexpectedly among things that I had always read and dreamed about. The plan was perfectly successful, for, besides vague and unprofitable wanderings, I saw, in the course of the day, Hyde Park, Regent's Park, Whitehall, the two new Houses of Parliament, Charing Cross, St. Paul's, the, Strand, Fleet Street, Cheapside, Whitechapel, Leadenhall Street, the Haymarket, and a great many other places, the names of which were classic in my memory. I think what interests me most here, is the London of the writers of Queen Anne's age,—whatever Pope, The Spectator, De Foe, and down as late as Johnson and Goldsmith, have mentioned. The Monument, for instance, which is of no great height nor beauty compared with that on Bunker Hill, charmed me prodigiously. St. Paul's appeared to me unspeakably grand and noble, and the more so from the throng and bustle continually going on around its base, without in the least disturbing the sublime repose of its great dome, and, indeed, of all its massive height and breadth. Other edifices may crowd close to its foundation, and people may tramp as they like about it; but still the great cathedral is as quiet and serene as if it stood in the middle of Salisbury Plain. There cannot be anything else in its way so good in the world as just this effect of St. Paul's in the very heart and densest tumult of London. I do not know whether the church is built of marble, or of whatever other white or nearly white material; but in the time that it has been standing there, it has grown black with the smoke of ages, through which there are nevertheless gleams of white, that make a most picturesque impression on the whole. It is much better than staring white; the edifice would not be nearly so grand without this drapery of black.

I did not find these streets of the old city so narrow and irregular as I expected. All the principal ones are sufficiently broad, and there are few houses that look antique, being, I suppose, generally modern-fronted, when not actually of modern substance. There is little or no show or pretension in this part of London; it has a plain, business air,—an air of homely, actual life, as of a metropolis of tradesmen, who have been carrying on their traffic here, in sober earnest, for hundreds of years. You observe on the sign-boards, "Established ninety years in Threadneedle Street," "Established in 1109,"—denoting long pedigrees of silk-mercers and hosiers,—De Foe's contemporaries still represented by their posterity, who handle the hereditary yardstick on the same spot.

I must not forget to say that I crossed the Thames over a bridge which, I think, is near Charing Cross. Afterwards, I found my way to London Bridge, where there was a delightful density of throng. The Thames is not so wide and majestic as I had imagined,—nothing like the Mersey, for example. As a picturesque object, however, flowing through the midst of a city, it would lose by any increase of width.

Omnibuses are a most important aid to wanderers about London. I reached home, well wearied, about six o'clock. In the course of the day, I had seen one person whom I knew,—Mr. Clarke, to whom Henry B——— introduced me, when we went to see the great ship launched on the Dee. This, I believe, was in Regent Street. In that street, too, I saw a company of dragoons, beautifully mounted, and defensively armed, in brass helmets and steel cuirasses, polished to the utmost excess of splendor. It was a pretty sight. At one of the public edifices, on each side of the portal, sat a mounted trooper similarly armed, and with his carbine resting on his knee, just as motionless as a statue. This, too, as a picturesque circumstance, was very good, and really made an impression on me with respect to the power and stability of the government, though I could not help smiling at myself for it. But then the thought, that for generations an armed warrior has always sat just there, on his war-steed, and with his weapon in his hand, is pleasant to the imagination,—although it is questionable whether his carbine be loaded; and, no doubt, if the authorities had any message to send, they would choose some other messenger than this heavy dragoon,—the electric wire, for instance. Still, if he and his horse were to be withdrawn from their post, night or day (for I suppose the sentinels are on duty all night), it seems as if the monarchy would be subverted, and the English constitution crumble into rubbish; and, in honest fact, it will signify something like that, when guard is relieved there for the last time.

September 8th.—Yesterday forenoon S———, the two eldest children, and I went forth into London streets, and proceeded down Regent Street, and thence to St. James's Park, at the entrance of which is a statue of somebody,—I forget whom. On the very spacious gravel-walks, covering several acres, in the rear of the Horse Guards, some soldiers were going through their exercise; and, after looking at them awhile, we strolled through the Park, alongside of a sheet of water, in which various kinds of ducks, geese, and rare species of waterfowl were swimming. There was one swan of immense size, which moved about among the lesser fowls like a stately, full-rigged ship among gunboats. By and by we found ourselves near what we since have discovered to be Buckingham Palace,—a long building, in the Italian style, but of no impressiveness, and which one soon wearies of looking at. The Queen having gone to Scotland the day before, the palace now looked deserted, although there was a one-horse cab, of shabby aspect, standing at the principal front, where doubtless the carriages of princes and the nobility draw up. There is a fountain playing before the palace, and water-fowl love to swim under its perpetual showers. These ducks and geese are very tame, and swim to the margin of the pond to be fed by visitors, looking up at you with great intelligence.

S——- asked a man in a sober suit of livery (of whom we saw several about the Park), whose were some of the large mansions which we saw, and he pointed out Stafford House, the residence of the Duke of Sutherland, —a very noble edifice, much more beautiful than the palace, though not so large; also the house of the Earl of Ellesmere, and residences of other noblemen. This range of mansions, along the park, from the spot whence we viewed them, looks very much like Beacon Street, in Boston, bordering on the Common, allowing for a considerable enlargement of scale in favor of the Park residences. The Park, however, has not the beautiful elms that overshadow Boston Common, nor such a pleasant undulation of surface, nor the fine off-view of the country, like that across Charles River. I doubt whether London can show so delightful a spot as that Common, always excepting the superiority of English lawns, which, however, is not so evident in the London parks, there being less care bestowed on the grass than I should have expected.

From this place we wandered into what I believe to be Hyde Park, attracted by a gigantic figure on horseback, which loomed up in the distance. The effect of this enormous steed and his rider is very grand, seen in the misty atmosphere. I do not understand why we did not see St. James's Palace, which is situated, I believe, at the extremity of the same range of mansions of which Stafford House is the opposite end. From the entrance of Hyde Park, we seem to have gone along Piccadilly, and, making two or three turns, and getting bewildered, I put S——- and the children into a cab, and sent them home. Continuing my wanderings, I went astray among squares of large aristocratic-looking edifices, all apparently new, with no shops among them, some yet unfinished, and the whole seeming like a city built for a colony of gentlefolks, who might be expected to emigrate thither in a body. It was a dreary business to wander there, turning corner after corner, and finding no way of getting into a less stately and more genial region. At last, however, I passed in front of the Queen's Mews, where sentinels were on guard, and where a jolly-looking man, in a splendidly laced scarlet coat and white-topped boots, was lounging at the entrance. He looked like the prince of grooms or coachmen. . . .

The corner of Hyde Park was within a short distance, and I took a Hansom at the cab-stand there, and drove to the American Despatch Agency, 26 Henrietta Street, Covent Garden, having some documents of state to be sent by to-day's steamer. The business of forwarding despatches to America, and distributing them to the various legations and consulates in Europe, must be a pretty extensive one; for Mr. Miller has a large office, and two clerks in attendance.

From this point I went through Covent Garden Market, and got astray in the city, so that I can give no clear account of my afternoon's wanderings. I passed through Holborn, however, and I think it was from that street that I passed through an archway (which I almost invariably do, when I see one), and found myself in a very spacious, gravelled square, surrounded on the four sides by a continuous edifice of dark brick, very plain, and of cold and stern aspect. This was Gray's Inn, all tenanted by a multitude of lawyers. Passing thence, I saw "Furnival's Inn" over another archway, but, being on the opposite side of the street, I did not go thither. In Holborn, still, I went through another arched entrance, over which was "Staples Inn," and here likewise seemed to be offices; but, in a court opening inwards from this, there was a surrounding seclusion of quiet dwelling-houses, with beautiful green shrubbery and grass-plots in the court, and a great many sunflowers in full bloom. The windows were open; it was a lovely summer afternoon, and I have a sense that bees were humming in the court, though this may have been suggested by my fancy, because the sound would have been so well suited to the scene. A boy was reading at one of the windows. There was not a quieter spot in England than this, and it was very strange to have drifted into it so suddenly out of the bustle and rumble of Holborn; and to lose all this repose as suddenly, on passing through the arch of the outer court. In all the hundreds of years since London was built, it has not been able to sweep its roaring tide over that little island of quiet. In Holborn I saw the most antique-looking houses that I have yet met with in London, but none of very remarkable aspect.

I think I must have been under a spell of enchantment to-day, connecting me with St. Paul's; for, trying to get away from it by various avenues, I still got bewildered, and again and again saw its great dome and pinnacles before me. I observe that the smoke has chiefly settled on the lower part of the edifice, leaving its loftier portions and its spires much less begrimed. It is very beautiful, very rich. I did not think that anything but Gothic architecture could so have interested me. The statues, the niches, the embroidery, as it were, of sculpture traced around it, produced a delightful effect. In front of St. Paul's there is a statue of Queen Anne, which looks rather more majestic, I doubt not, than that fat old dame ever did. St. Paul's churchyard had always been a place of immense interest in my imagination. It is merely the not very spacious street, running round the base of the church,—at least, this street is included in the churchyard, together with the enclosure immediately about the church, sowed with tombstones. I meant to look for the children's book-shop, but forgot it, or neglected it, from not feeling so much interest in a thing near at hand as when it seemed unattainable.

I watched a man tearing down the brick wall of a house that did not appear very old; but it surprised me to see how crumbly the brick-work was, one stroke of his pick often loosening several bricks in a row. It is my opinion that brick houses, after a moderate term of years, stand more by habit and courtesy than through any adhesive force of the old mortar.

I recommenced my wanderings; but I remember nothing else particularly claiming to be mentioned, unless it be Paternoster Row,—a little, narrow, darksome lane, in which, it being now dusk in that density of the city, I could not very well see what signs were over the doors. In this street, or thereabouts, I got into an omnibus, and, being set down near Regent's Circus, reached home well wearied.

September 9th.—Yesterday, having some tickets to the Zoological Gardens, we went thither with the two eldest children. It was a most beautiful sunny day, the very perfection of English weather,—which is as much as to say, the best weather in the world, except, perhaps, some few days in an American October. These gardens are at the end of Regent's Park, farthest from London, and they are very extensive; though, I think, not quite worthy of London,—not so good as one would expect them to be,—not so fine and perfect a collection of beasts, birds, and fishes, as one might fairly look for, when the greatest metropolis of the world sets out to have such a collection at all.—My idea was, that here every living thing was provided for, in the way best suited to its nature and habits, and that the refinement of civilization had here restored a garden of Eden, where all the animal kingdom had regained a happy home. This is not quite the case; though, I believe, the creatures are as comfortable as could be expected, and there are certainly a good many strange beasts here. The hippopotamus is the chief treasure of the collection,—an immense, almost misshapen, mass of flesh. At this moment I do not remember anything that interested me except a sick monkey,—a very large monkey, and elderly he seemed to be. His keeper brought him some sweetened apple and water, and some tea; for the monkey had quite lost his appetite, and refused all ordinary diet. He came, however, quite eagerly, and smelt of the tea and apple, the keeper exhorting him very tenderly to eat. But the poor monkey shook his head slowly, and with the most pitiable expression, at the same time extending his hand to take the keeper's, as if claiming his sympathy and friendship. By and by the keeper (who is rather a surly fellow) essayed harsher measures, and insisted that the monkey should eat what had been brought for him, and hereupon ensued somewhat of a struggle, and the tea was overturned upon the straw of the bed. Then the keeper scolded him, and, seizing him by one arm, drew him out of his little bedroom into the larger cage, upon which the wronged monkey began a loud, dissonant, reproachful chatter, more expressive of a sense of injury than any words could be.

Observing the spectators in front of the cage, he seemed to appeal to them, and addressed his chatter thitherward, and stretched out his long, lean arm and black hand between the bars, as if claiming the grasp of any one friend he might have in the whole world. He was placable, however; for when the keeper called him in a gentler tone, he hobbled towards him with a very stiff and rusty movement, and the scene closed with their affectionately hugging one another. But I fear the poor monkey will die. In a future state of being, I think it will be one of my inquiries, in reference to the mysteries of the present state, why monkeys were made. The Creator could not surely have meant to ridicule his own work. It might rather be fancied that Satan had perpetrated monkeys, with a malicious purpose of parodying the masterpiece of creation!

The Aquarium, containing, in some of its compartments, specimens of the animal and vegetable life of the sea, and, in others, those of the fresh water, was richly worth inspecting; but not nearly so perfect as it might be. Now I think we have a right to claim, in a metropolitan establishment of this kind, in all its departments, a degree of perfection that shall quite outdo the unpractised thought of any man on that particular subject.

There were a good many well-dressed people and children in the gardens, Saturday being a fashionable day for visiting them. One great amusement was feeding some bears with biscuits and cakes, of which they seemed exceedingly fond. One of the three bears clambered to the top of a high pole, whence he invited the spectators to hand him bits of cake on the end of a stick, or to toss them into his mouth, which he opened widely for that purpose. Another, apparently an elderly bear, not having skill nor agility for these gymnastics, sat on the ground, on his hinder end, groaning most pitifully. The third took what stray bits he could get, without earning them by any antics.

At four o'clock there was some music from the band of the First Life-Guards, a great multitude of chairs being set on the greensward in the sunshine and shade, for the accommodation of the auditors. Here we had the usual exhibition of English beauty, neither superior nor otherwise to what I have seen in other parts of England. Before the music was over, we walked slowly homeward, along beside Regent's Park, which is very prettily laid out, but lacks some last touch of richness and beauty; though, after all, I do not well see what more could be done with grass, trees, and gravel-walks. The children, especially J——, who had raced from one thing to another all day long, grew tired; so we put them into a cab, and walked slowly through

Portland Place, where are a great many noble mansions, yet no very admirable architecture; none that possessed, nor that ever can possess, the indefinable charm of some of those poor old timber houses in Shrewsbury. The art of domestic architecture is lost. We can rear stately and beautiful dwellings (though we seldom do), but they do not seem proper to the life of man, in the same way that his shell is proper to the lobster; nor, indeed, is the mansion of the nobleman proper to him, in the same kind and degree, that a hut is proper to a peasant.

From Portland Place we passed into Regent Street, and soon reached home.

September 10th.—Yesterday forenoon we walked out with the children, intending for Charing Cross; but, missing our way, as usual, we went down a rather wide and stately street, and saw before us an old brick edifice with a pretty extensive front, over which rose a clock-tower,—the whole dingy, and looking both gloomy and mean. There was an arched entrance beneath the clock-tower, at which two Guardsmen, in their bear-skin caps, were stationed as sentinels; and from this circumstance, and our having some guess at the locality, we concluded the old brick building to be St. James's Palace. Otherwise we might have taken it for a prison, or for a hospital, which, in truth, it was at first intended for. But, certainly, there are many paupers in England who live in edifices of far more architectural pretension externally than this principal palace of the English sovereigns.

Seeing other people go through the archway, we also went, meeting no impediment from the sentinels, and found ourselves in a large paved court, in the centre of which a banner was stuck down, with a few soldiers standing near it. This flag was the banner of the regiment of guards on duty. The aspect of the interior court was as naked and dismal as the outside, the brick being of that dark hue almost universal in England. On one side of the court there was a door which seemed to give admission to a chapel, into which several persons went, and probably we might have gone too, had we liked. From this court, we penetrated into at least two or three others; for the palace is very extensive, and all of it, so far as I could see, on the same pattern,—large, enclosed courts, paved, and quite bare of grass, shrubbery, or any beautiful thing,—

dark, stern, brick walls, without the slightest show of architectural beauty, or even an ornament over the square, commonplace windows, looking down on those forlorn courts. A carriage-drive passes through it, if I remember aright, from the principal front, emerging by one of the sides; and I suppose that the carriages roll through the palace, at the levees and drawing-rooms. There was nothing to detain us here any long time, so we went from court to court, and came out through a side-opening. The edifice is battlemented all round, and this, with somewhat of fantastic in the shape of the clock-tower, is the only attempt at ornament in the whole.

Then we skirted along St. James's Park, passing Marlborough House,—a red brick building,—and a very long range of stone edifices, which, whether they were public or private, one house or twenty, we knew not. We ascended the steps of the York column, and soon reached Charing Cross and Trafalgar Square, where there are more architectural monuments than in any other one place in London; besides two fountains, playing in large reservoirs of water, and various edifices of note and interest.

Northumberland House, now, and for a long while, the town residence of the Percys, stands on the Strand side,—over the entrance a lion, very spiritedly sculptured, flinging out his long tail. On another side of the square is Morley's Hotel, exceedingly spacious, and looking more American than anything else in the hotel line that I have seen here.

The Nelson monument, with Lord Nelson, in a cocked hat, on its top, is very grand in its effect. All about the square there were sundry loungers, people looking at the bas-reliefs on Nelson's Column, children paddling in the reservoirs of the fountains; and, it being a sunny day, it was a cheerful and lightsome, as well as an impressive scene. On second thoughts, I do not know but that London should have a far better display of architecture and sculpture than this, on its finest site, and in its very centre; for, after all, there is nothing of the very best. But I missed nothing at the time.

In the afternoon S——- and I set out to attend divine service in Westminster Abbey. On our way thither we passed through Pall Mall, which is full of club-houses, and we were much struck with the beauty of the one lately erected for the Carleton Club. It is built of a buff-colored or yellowish stone, with pillars or pilasters of polished Aberdeen granite, wonderfully rich and beautiful; and there is a running border of sculptured figures all round the upper part of the building, besides other ornament and embroidery, wherever there was room or occasion for it. It being an oblong square, the smooth and polished aspect in this union of two rich colors in it,—this delicacy and minuteness of finish, this lavish ornament—made me think of a lady's jewel-box; and if it could be reduced to the size of about a foot square, or less, it would make the very prettiest one that ever was seen. I question whether it have any right to be larger than a jewel-box; but it is certainly a most beautiful edifice. We turned down Whitehall, at the head of which, over the very spot where the Regicides were executed, stands the bronze equestrian statue of Charles I.,—the statue that was buried under the earth during the whole of Cromwell's time, and emerged after the Restoration. We saw the Admiralty and the Horse-Guards, and, in front of the latter, the two mounted sentinels, one of whom was flirting and laughing with some girls. On the other side of the street stands the Banqueting-House, built by Inigo Jones; from a window of which King Charles stepped forth, wearing a kingly head, which, within a few minutes afterwards, fell with a dead thump on the scaffold. It was nobly done,— and nobly suffered. How rich is history in the little space around this spot!

I find that the day after I reached London, I entirely passed by Westminster Abbey without knowing it, partly because my eyes were attracted by the gaudier show of the new Houses of Parliament, and partly because this part of the Abbey has been so much repaired and renewed that it has not the marks of age. Looking at its front, I now found it very grand and venerable; but it is useless to attempt a description: these things are not to be translated into words; they can be known only by seeing them, and, until seen, it is well to shape out no idea of them. Impressions, states of mind, produced by noble spectacles of whatever kind, are all that it seems worth while to attempt reproducing with the pen.

After coming out of the Abbey, we looked at the two Houses of Parliament, directly across the way,—an immense structure, and certainly most splendid, built of a beautiful warm-colored stone. The building has a very elaborate finish, and delighted me at first; but by and by I began to be sensible of a weariness in the effect, a lack of variety in the plan and ornament, a deficiency of invention; so that instead of being more and more interested the longer one looks, as is the case with an old Gothic edifice, and continually reading deeper into it, one finds that one has seen all in seeing a little piece, and that the magnificent palace has nothing better to show one or to do for one. It is wonderful how the old weather-stained and smoke-blackened Abbey shames down this brand-newness; not that the Parliament houses are not fine objects to look at, too.

Yesterday morning we walked to Charing Cross, with U—— and J——, and there took a cab to the Tower, driving thither through the Strand, Fleet Street, past St. Paul's, and amid all the thickest throng of the city. I have not a very distinct idea of the Tower, but remember that our cab drove within an outer gate, where we alighted at a ticket-office; the old royal fortress being now a regular show-place, at sixpence a head, including the sight of armory and crown-jewels. We saw about the gate several warders or yeomen of the guard, or beefeaters, dressed in scarlet coats of antique fashion, richly embroidered with golden crowns, both on the breast and back, and other royal devices and insignia; so that they looked very much like the kings on a pack of cards, or regular trumps, at all events. I believe they are old soldiers, promoted to this position for good conduct. One of them took charge of us, and when a sufficient number of visitors had collected with us, he led us to see what very small portion of the Tower is shown.

There is a great deal of ground within the outer precincts; and it has streets and houses and inhabitants and a church within it; and, going up and down behind the warder, without any freedom to get acquainted with the place by strolling about, I know little more about it than when I went in,—only recollecting a mean and disagreeable confusion of brick walls, barracks, paved courts, with here and there a low bulky turret, of rather antique aspect, and, in front of one of the edifices, a range of curious old cannon, lying on the ground, some of them immensely large and long, and beautifully wrought in brass. I observed by a plan, however, that the White Tower, containing the armory, stands about in the centre of the fortress, and that it is a square, battlemented structure, having a turret at each angle. We followed the warder into the White Tower, and there saw, in the first place, a long gallery of mounted knights, and men at arms, which has been so often described that when I wish to recall it to memory I shall turn to some other person's account of it. I was much struck, however, with the beautiful execution of a good many of the suits of armor, and the exquisite detail with which they were engraved. The artists of those days attained very great skill, in this kind of manufacture. The figures of the knights, too, in full array, undoubtedly may have shown a combination of stateliness and grace which heretofore I have not believed in,—not seeing how it could be compatible with iron garments. But it is quite incomprehensible how, in the time of the heaviest armor, they could strike a blow, or possess any freedom of movement, except such as a turtle is capable of; and, in truth, they are said not to have been able to rise up when overthrown. They probably stuck out their lances, and rode straight at the enemy, depending upon upsetting him by their mass and weight. In the row of knights is Henry VIII.; also Charles Brandon, Duke of Suffolk, who must have been an immensely bulky man; also, a splendid suit of armor, gilded all over, presented by the city of London to Charles I.; also, two or three suits of boys' armor, for the little princes of the House of Stuart. They began to wear these burdens betimes, in order that their manhood might be the more tolerant of them. We went through this gallery so hastily that it would have been about as well not to have seen it at all.

Then we went up a winding stair to another room, containing armor and weapons, and beautiful brass cannon, that appeared to have been for ornament rather than use, some of them being quite covered with embossed sculpture, marvellously well wrought. In this room was John of Gaunt's suit, indicating a man seven feet high, and the armor seems to bear the marks of much wear; but this may be owing to great scrubbing, throughout the centuries since John of Gaunt died. There, too, we saw the cloak in which Wolfe fell, on the Plains of Abraham,—a coarse, faded, threadbare, light-colored garment, folded up under a glass case. Many other things we might have seen, worthy of being attended to, had there been time to look at them.

Following into still another room, we were told that this was Sir Walter Raleigh's apartment, while confined in the Tower, so that it was within these walls that he wrote the History of the World. The room was formerly lighted by lancet windows, and must have been very gloomy; but, if he had the whole length of it to himself, it was a good space to walk and meditate in. On one side of the apartment is a low door, giving admittance, we were told, to the cell where Raleigh slept; so we went in, and found it destitute of any window, and so dark that we could not estimate its small extent except by feeling about. At the threshold of this sleeping-kennel, there were one or two inscriptions, scratched in the wall, but not, I believe, by Raleigh.

In this apartment, among a great many other curious things, are shown the devilish instruments of torture which the Spaniards were bringing to England in their Armada; and, at the end of the room, sits Queen Elizabeth on horseback, in her high ruff and faded finery. Very likely none of these clothes were ever on her actual person. Here, too, we saw a headsman's block,—not that on which Raleigh was beheaded, which I would have given gold to see, but the one which was used for the Scotch Lords Kilmarnock, Lovat, and others, executed on account of the Rebellion of 1745. It is a block of oak, about two feet high, with a large knot in it, so that it would not easily be split by a blow of the axe; hewn and smoothed in a very workmanlike way, and with a hollow to accommodate the head and shoulders on each side. There were two or three very strong marks of the axe in the part over which the neck lay, and several smaller cuts; as if the first stroke nearly severed the head, and then the chopping off was finished by smaller blows, as we see a butcher cutting meat with his cleaver. A headsman's axe was likewise shown us,—its date unknown.

In the White Tower we were shown the Regalia, under a glass, and within an iron cage. Edward the Confessor's golden staff was very finely wrought; and there were a great many pretty things; but I have a suspicion, I know not why, that these are not the real jewels,—at least, that such inestimable ones as the Koh-i-noor (or however it is spelt) are less freely exhibited.

The warder then led us into a paved court, which he said was the place of execution of all royal personages and others, who, from motives of fear or favor, were beheaded privately. Raleigh was among these, and so was Anne Boleyn. We then followed to the Beauchamp Tower, where many state prisoners of note were confined, and where, on the walls of one of the chambers, there are several inscriptions and sculptures of various devices, done by the prisoners,—and very skilfully done, too, though perhaps with no better instrument than an old nail. These poor wretches had time and leisure enough to spend upon their work. This chamber is lighted by small lancet windows, pierced at equal intervals round the circle of the Beauchamp Tower; and it contains a large, square fireplace, in which is now placed a small modern stove. We were hurried away, before we could even glance at the inscriptions, and we saw nothing else, except the low, obscure doorway in the Bloody Tower, leading to the staircase, under which were found the supposed bones of the little princes; and lastly, the round, Norman arch, opening to the water passage, called the Traitor's Gate. Finally, we ate some cakes and buns in the refreshment-room connected with the ticket-office, and then left the fortress. The ancient moat, by the way, has been drained within a few years, and now forms a great hollow space, with grassy banks, round about the citadel.

We now wished to see the Thames, and therefore threaded our way along Thames Street, towards London Bridge, passing through a fish-market, which I suppose to be the actual Billingsgate, whence originated all the foul language in England. Under London Bridge there is a station for steamers running to Greenwich and Woolwich. We got on board one of these, not very well knowing, nor much caring, whither it might take us, and steamed down the river, which is bordered with the shabbiest, blackest, ugliest, meanest buildings: it is the back side of the town; and, in truth, the muddy tide of the Thames deserves to see no better. There was a great deal of shipping in the river, and many steamers, and it was much more crowded than the Mersey, where all the ships go into docks; but the vessels were not so fine. By and by we reached Greenwich, and went ashore there, proceeding up from the quay, past beer-shops and eating-houses in great numbers and variety. Greenwich Hospital is here a very prominent object, and after passing along its extensive front, facing towards the river, we entered one of the principal gates, as we found ourselves free to do.

We now left the hospital, and steamed back to London Bridge, whence we went up into the city, and, to finish the labors of the day, ascended the Monument. This seems to be still a favorite adventure with the cockneys; for we heard one woman, who went up with us, saying that she had been thinking of going up all her life, and another said that she had gone up thirty years ago. There is an iron railing, or rather a cage, round the top, through which it would be impossible for people to force their way, in order to precipitate themselves, as six persons have heretofore done. There was a mist over London, so that we did not gain a very clear view, except of the swarms of people running about, like ants, in the streets at the foot of the Monument.

Descending, I put S——- and the children into a cab, and I myself wandered about the city. Passing along Fleet Street, I turned in through an archway, which I rightly guessed to be the entrance to the Temple. It is a very large space, containing many large, solemn, and serious edifices of dark brick, and no sooner do you pass under the arch than all the rumble and bustle of London dies away at once; and it seems as if a person might live there in perfect quiet, without suspecting that it was not always a Sabbath. People appear to have their separate residences here; but I do not understand what is the economy of their lives. Quite in the deepest interior of this region, there is a large garden, bordering on the Thames, along which it has a gravel-walk, and benches where it would be pleasant to sit. On one edge of the garden, there is some scanty shrubbery, and flowers of no great brilliancy; and the greensward, with which the garden is mostly covered, is not particularly rich nor verdant.

Emerging from the Temple, I stopped at a tavern in the Strand, the waiter of which observed to me, "They say Sebastopol is taken, sir!" It was only such an interesting event that could have induced an English waiter to make a remark to a stranger, not called for in the way of business.

The best view we had of the town—in fact, the only external view, and the only time we really saw the White Tower—was from the river, as we steamed past it. Here the high, square, battlemented White Tower, with the four turrets at its corners, rises prominently above all other parts of the fortress.

September 13th.—Mr. ———, the American Minister, called on me on Tuesday, and left his card; an intimation that I ought sooner to have paid my respects to him; so yesterday forenoon I set out to find his residence, 56 Harley Street. It is a street out of Cavendish Square, in a fashionable quarter, although fashion is said to be ebbing away from it. The ambassador seems to intend some little state in his arrangements; but, no doubt, the establishment compares shabbily enough with those of the legations of other great countries, and with the houses of the English aristocracy. A servant, not in livery, or in a very unrecognizable one, opened the door for me, and gave my card to a sort of upper attendant, who took it in to Mr. ———. He had three gentlemen with him, so desired that I should be ushered into the office of the legation, until he should be able to receive me. Here I found a clerk or attache, Mr. M———, who has been two or three years on this side of the water; an intelligent person, who seems to be in correspondence with the New York Courier and Enquirer. By and by came in another American to get a passport for the Continent, and soon the three gentlemen took leave of the ambassador, and I was invited to his presence.

The tall, large figure of Mr. ——— has a certain air of state and dignity; he carries his head in a very awkward way, but still looks like a man of long and high authority, and, with his white hair, is now quite venerable. There is certainly a lack of polish, a kind of rusticity, notwithstanding which you feel him to be a man of the world. I should think he might succeed very tolerably in English society, being heavy and sensible, cool, kindly, and good-humored, with a great deal of experience of life. We talked about various matters, politics among the rest; and he observed that if the President had taken the advice which he gave him in two long letters, before his inauguration, he would have had a perfectly quiet and successful term of office. The advice was, to form a perfectly homogeneous cabinet of Union men, and to satisfy the extremes of the party by a fair distribution of minor offices; whereas he formed his cabinet of extreme men, on both sides, and gave the minor offices to moderate ones. But the antislavery people, surely, had no representative in the cabinet. Mr. ——— further observed, that he thought the President had a fair chance of re-nomination, for that the South could not, in honor, desert him; to which I replied that the South had been guilty of such things heretofore. Mr. ——— thinks that the next Presidential term will be more important and critical, both as to our foreign relations and internal affairs, than any preceding one,—which I should judge likely enough to be the case, although I heard the sane prophecy often made respecting the present term.

The ambassador dined with us at Rock Park a year or two ago, and I then felt, and always feel, as if he were a man of hearty feeling and simplicity, and certainly it would be unjust to conclude otherwise, merely from the fact (very suspicious, it is true) of his having been a life-long politician. After we had got through a little matter of business (respecting a young American who has enlisted at Liverpool), the Minister rang his bell, and ordered another visitor to be admitted; and so I took my leave. In the other room I found the Secretary of Legation,—a tall, slender man of about forty, with a small head and face,—gentlemanly enough, sensible, and well informed, yet I should judge, not quite up to his place. There was also a Dr. B——— from Michigan present, and I rather fancy the ambassador is quite as much bored with visitors as the consul at Liverpool. Before I left the office, Mr. ——— came in with Miss Sarah Clarke on his arm. She had come thither to get her passport vised; and when her business was concluded, we went out together.

She was going farther towards the West End, and I into the city; so we soon parted, and I lost myself among the streets and squares, arriving at last at Oxford Street, though even then I did not know whether my face were turned cityward or in the opposite direction. Crossing Regent Street, however, I became sure of my whereabout, and went on through Holborn, and sought hither and thither for Grace Church Street, in order to find the American Consul, General Campbell; for I needed his aid to get a bank post-bill cashed. But I could not find the street, go where I would; so at last I went to No. 65 Cheapside, and introduced myself to Mr. ———, whom I already knew by letter, and by a good many of his poems, which he has sent me, and by two excellent watches, which I bought of him. This establishment, though it has the ordinary front of dingy brick, common to buildings in the city, looks like a time-long stand, the old shop of a London tradesman, with a large figure of a watch over the door, a great many watches (and yet no gorgeous show of them) in the window, a low, dark front shop, and a little room behind, where there was a chair or two. Mr. ——— is a small, slender young man, quite un-English in aspect, with black, curly hair, a thin, dark, colorless visage, very animated and of quick expression, with a nervous temperament. . . . He dismounted from a desk when my card was handed to him, and turned to me with a vivid, glad look of recognition.

We talked, in the first place, about poetry and such matters, about England and America, and the nature and depth of their mutual dislike, and, of course, the slavery question came up, as it always does, in one way or another. Anon, I produced my bank post-bill; and Mr. ——— kindly engaged to identify me at the bank, being ready to swear to me, he said, on the strength of my resemblance to my engraved portrait. So we set out for the Bank of England, and, arriving there, were directed to the proper clerk, after much inquiry; but he told us that the bill was not yet due, having been drawn at seven days, and having two still to run,—which was the fact. As I was almost shillingless, Mr. ——— now offered to cash it for me. He is very kind and good. . . . Arriving at his shop again, he went out to procure the money, and soon returned with it. At my departure he gave me a copy of a new poem of his, entitled "Verdicts," somewhat in the manner of Lowell's satire. . . . Mr. ——— resides now at Greenwich, whither he hoped I would come and see him on my return to London. Perhaps I will, for I like him. It seems strange to see an Englishman with so little physical ponderosity and obtuseness of nerve.

After parting from him, it being three o'clock or thereabouts, I resumed my wanderings about the city, of which I never weary as long as I can put one foot before the other.

Seeing that the door of St. Paul's, under one of the semicircular porches, was partially open, I went in, and found that the afternoon service was about to be performed; so I remained to hear it, and to see what I could of the cathedral. What a total and admirable contrast between this and a Gothic church! the latter so dim and mysterious, with its various aisles, its intricacy of pointed arches, its dark walls and columns and pavement, and its painted glass windows, bedimming even what daylight might otherwise get into its eternal evening. But this cathedral was full of light, and light was proper to it.

There were no painted windows, no dim recesses, but a wide and airy space beneath the dome; and even through the long perspective of the nave there was no obscurity, but one lofty and beautifully rounded arch succeeding to another, as far as the eye could reach. The walls were white, the pavement constructed of squares of gray and white marble. It is a most grand and stately edifice, and its characteristic stems to be to continue forever fresh and new; whereas such a church as Westminster Abbey must have been as venerable as it is now from the first day when it grew to be an edifice at all. How wonderful man is in his works! How glad I am that there can be two such admirable churches, in their opposite styles, as St. Paul's and Westminster Abbey!

The organ was played while I was there, and there was an anthem beautifully chanted by voices that came from afar off and remotely above, as if out of a sunny sky. Meanwhile I looked at such monuments as were near; chiefly those erected to military or naval men,—Picton, General Ponsonby, Lord St. Vincent, and others; but against one of the pillars stands a statue of Dr. Johnson,—a noble and thoughtful figure, with a development of muscle befitting an athlete. I doubt whether sculptors do not err in point of taste, by making all their statues models of physical perfection, instead of expressing by them the individual character and habits of the man. The statue in the market-place at Lichfield has more of the homely truth of Johnson's actual personality than this.

St. Paul's, as yet, is by no means crowded with monuments; there is, indeed, plenty of room for a mob of the illustrious, yet to come. But it seems to me that the character of the edifice would be injured by allowing the monuments to be clustered together so closely as at Westminster, by incrusting the walls with them, or letting the statues throng about the pedestals of columns. There must be no confusion in such a cathedral as this, and I question whether the effect will ever be better than it is now, when each monument has its distinct place, and as your eye wanders around, you are not distracted from noting each marble man, in his niche against the wall, or at the base of a marble pillar. Space, distance, light, regularity, are to be preserved, even if the result should be a degree of nakedness.

I saw Mr. Appleton of the Legation, and Dr. Brown, on the floor of the cathedral. They were about to go over the whole edifice, and had engaged a guide for that purpose; but, as I intend to go thither again with S——, I did not accompany them, but went away the quicker that one of the gentlemen put on his hat, and I was ashamed of being seen in company with a man who could wear his hat in a cathedral. Not that he meant any irreverence; but simply felt that he was in a great public building,—as big, nearly, as all out of doors,—and so forgot that it was a consecrated place of worship. The sky is the dome of a greater cathedral than St. Paul's, and built by a greater architect than Sir Christopher Wren, and yet we wear our hats unscrupulously beneath it.

I remember no other event of importance, except that I penetrated into a narrow lane or court, either in the Strand or Fleet Street, where was a tavern, calling itself the "Old Thatched House," and purporting to have been Nell Gwyn's dairy. I met with a great many alleys and obscure archways, in the course of the day's wanderings.

September 14th.—Yesterday, in the earlier part of the day, it poured with rain, and I did not go out till five o'clock in the afternoon; nor did I then meet with anything interesting. I walked through Albemarle Street, for the purpose of looking at Murray's shop, but missed it entirely, at my first inquisition. The street is one of hotels, principally, with only a few tradesmen's shops, and has a quiet, aristocratic aspect. On my return, down the other sidewalk, I did discover the famous publisher's locality; but merely by the name "Mr. Murray," engraved on a rather large brass plate, such as doctors use, on the door. There was no sign of a book, nor of its being a place of trade in any way; and I should have taken the house to be, if not a private mansion, then a lawyer's office.

At seven o'clock S——, U——, and I went to dine with Mr. R—— S—— in Portland Place. . . . Mr. S——'s house is a very fine one, and he gave us a very quiet, elegant, and enjoyable dinner, in much better taste and with less fuss than some others we have attended elsewhere. Mr. S—— is a friend of Thackeray, and, speaking of the last number of The Newcomes,—so touching that nobody can read it aloud without breaking down,—he mentioned that Thackeray himself had read it to James Russell Lowell and William Story in a cider-cellar! I read all the preceding numbers of The Newcomes to my wife, but happened not to have an opportunity to read this last, and was glad of it,—knowing that my eyes would fill, and my voice quiver. Mr. S——— likes Thackeray, and thinks him a good fellow. Mr. S——— has a—or I don't know but I ought better to say the—beautiful full-length picture of Washington by Stuart, and I was proud to see that noblest face and figure here in England. The picture of a man beside whom, considered physically, any English nobleman whom I have seen would look like common clay.

Speaking of Thackeray, I cannot but wonder at his coolness in respect to his own pathos, and compare it with my emotions, when I read the last scene of The Scarlet Letter to my wife, just after writing it,—tried to read it rather, for my voice swelled and heaved, as if I were tossed up and down on an ocean as it subsides after a storm. But I was in a very nervous state then, having gone through a great diversity of emotion, while writing it, for many months. I think I have never overcome my own adamant in any other instance.

Tumblers, hand-organists, puppet-showmen, bagpipers, and all such vagrant mirth-makers, are very numerous in the streets of London. The other day, passing through Fleet Street, I saw a crowd filling up a narrow court, and high above their heads a tumbler, standing on his head, on the top of a pole, that reached as high as the third story of the neighboring Houses. Sliding down the pole head foremost, he disappeared out of my sight. A multitude of Punches go the mounds continually. Two have passed through Hanover Street, where we reside, this morning. The first asked two shillings for his performance; so we sent him away. The second demanded, in the first place, half a crown; but finally consented to take a shilling, and gave us the show at that price, though much maimed in its proportions. Besides the spectators in our windows, he had a little crowd on the sidewalk, to whom he went round for contributions, but I did not observe that anybody gave him so much as a halfpenny. It is strange to see how many people are aiming at the small change in your pocket. In every square a beggar-woman meets you, and turns back to follow your steps with her miserable murmur. At the street-crossings there are old men or little girls with their brooms; urchins propose to brush your boots; and if you get into a cab, a man runs to open the door for you, and touches his hat for a fee, as he closes it again.

September 15th.—It was raining yesterday, and I kept within doors till after four o'clock, when J—— and I took a walk into the city. Seeing the entrance to Clement's Inn, we went through it, and saw the garden, with a kneeling bronze figure in it; and when just in the midst of the Inn, I remembered that Justice Shallow was of old a student there. I do not well understand these Inns of Court, or how they differ from other places. Anybody seems to be free to reside in them, and a residence does not seem to involve any obligation to study law, or to have any connection therewith. Clement's Inn consists of large brick houses, accessible by narrow lanes and passages, but, by some peculiar privilege or enchantment, enjoying a certain quiet and repose, though in close vicinity to the noisiest part of the city. I got bewildered in the neighborhood of St. Paul's, and, try how I might to escape from it, its huge dusky dome kept showing itself before me, through one street and another. In my endeavors to escape it, I at one time found myself in St. John's Street, and was in hopes to have seen the old St. John's gate, so familiar for above a century on the cover of the Gentleman's Magazine. But I suppose it is taken down, for we went through the entire street, I think, and saw no trace of it. Either afterwards or before this we came upon Smithfield, a large irregular square, filled up with pens for cattle, of which, however, there were none in the market at that time. I leaned upon a post, at the western end of the square, and told J—— how the martyrs had been burnt at Smithfield in Bloody Mary's days. Again we drifted back to St. Paul's; and, at last, in despair of ever getting out of this enchanted region, I took a Hansom cab to Charing Cross, whence we easily made our way home.

LIVERPOOL.

September 16th.—I took the ten-o'clock train yesterday morning from the Euston station, and arrived at Liverpool at about five, passing through the valley of Trent, without touching at Birmingham. English scenery, on the tracks, is the tamest of the tame, hardly a noticeable hill breaking the ordinary gentle undulation of the landscape, but still the verdure and finish of the fields and parks make it worth while to throw out a glance now and then, as you rush by. Few separate houses are seen, as in America; but sometimes a village, with the square, gray, battlemented tower of its Norman church, and rows of thatched cottages, reminding one of the clustered mud-nests of swallows, under the eaves of a barn; here and there a lazy little river, like the Trent; perhaps, if you look sharply where the guide-book indicates, the turrets of an old castle in the distance; perhaps the great steeple and spires of a cathedral; perhaps the tall chimney of a manufactory; but, on the whole, the traveller comes to his journey's end unburdened with a single new idea. I observe that the harvest is not all gathered in as yet, and this rainy weather must look very gloomy to the farmer. I saw gleaners, yesterday, in the stubble-fields. There were two gentlemen in the same railway-carriage with me, and we did not exchange half a dozen words the whole day.

I am here, established at Mrs. Blodgett's boarding-house, which I find quite full; insomuch that she had to send one of her sea-captains to sleep in another house, in order to make room for me. It is exclusively American society: four shipmasters, and a doctor from Pennsylvania, who has been travelling a year on the Continent, and who seems to be a man of very active intelligence, interested in everything, and especially in agriculture. . . . He asserted that we are fifty years ahead of England in agricultural science, and that he could cultivate English soil to far better advantage than English farmers do, and at vastly less expense. Their tendency to cling to old ideas, which retards them in everything else, keeps them behindhand in this matter too. Really, I do not know any other place in England where a man can be made so sensible that he lives in a progressive world as here in Mrs. Blodgett's boarding-house.

The captains talk together about their voyages, and how they manage with their unruly mates and crews; and how freights are in America, and the prospects of business; and of equinoctial gales, and the qualities of different ships, and their commanders, and how crews, mates, and masters have all deteriorated since their remembrance. . . . But these men are alive, and talk of real matters, and of matters which they know. The shipmasters who come to Mrs. Blodgett's are favorable specimens of their class; being all respectable men, in the employ of good houses, and raised by their capacity to the command of first-rate ships. In my official intercourse with them, I do not generally see their best side; as they are seldom before me except as complainants, or when summoned to answer to some complaint made by a seaman. But hearing their daily talk, and listening to what is in their minds, and their reminiscences of what they have gone through, one becomes sensible that they are men of energy and ability, fit to be trusted, and retaining a hardy sense of honor, and a loyalty to their own country, the stronger because they have compared it with many others. Most of them are gentlemen, too, to a certain extent,—some more than others, perhaps; and none to a very exquisite point, or, if so, it is none the better for them as sailors or as men.

September 17th.—It is singular to feel a sense of my own country returning upon me with the intercourse of the people whom I find here. . . .

The doctor is much the most talkative of our company, and sometimes bores me thereby; though he seldom says anything that is not either instructive or amusing. He tells a curious story of Prince Albert, and how he avails himself of American sharp-shooting. During the doctor's tour in Scotland, which he has just finished, he became acquainted with one of the Prince's attaches, who invited him very earnestly to join his Royal highness's party, promising him a good gun, and a keeper to load it for him, two good dogs, besides as many cigars as he could smoke and as much wine as he could drink, on the condition that whatever game he shot should be the Prince's. "The Prince," said the attache, "is very fond of having Americans in his shooting-parties, on account of their being such excellent shots; and there was one with him last year who shot so admirably that his Royal Highness himself left off shooting in utter astonishment." The attache offered to introduce the doctor to the Prince, who would be certain to receive him very graciously. . . .

I think, perhaps, we talk of kings and queens more at our table than people do at other tables in England; not, of course, that we like them better, or admire them more, but that they are curiosities. Yet I would not say that the doctor may not be susceptible on the point of royal attentions; for he told us with great complacency how emphatically, on two or three occasions, Louis Napoleon had returned his bow, and the last time had turned and made some remark (evidently about the doctor) to the Empress. . . .

I ought not to omit mentioning that he has been told in France that he personally resembles the Emperor, and I suspect he is trying to heighten the resemblance by training his mustache on the pattern of that which adorns the imperial upper lip. He is a genuine American character, though modified by a good deal of travel; a very intelligent man, full of various ability, with eyes all over him for any object of interest,—a little of the bore, sometimes,—quick to appreciate character, with a good deal of tact, gentlemanly in his manners, but yet lacking a deep and delicate refinement. Not but that Americans are as capable of this last quality as other people are; but what with the circumstances amid which we grow up, and the peculiar activity of our minds, we certainly do often miss it. By the by, he advanced a singular proposition the other evening, namely, that the English people do not so well understand comfort, or attain it so perfectly in their domestic arrangements, as we do. I thought he hardly supported this opinion so satisfactorily as some of his other new ideas.

I saw in an American paper yesterday, that an opera, still unfinished, had been written on the story of The Scarlet Letter, and that several scenes of it had been performed successfully in New York. I should think it might possibly succeed as an opera, though it would certainly fail as a play.

LONDON.

September 24th.—On Saturday, at half past three o'clock, I left Liverpool by the London and Northwest Railway for London. Mrs. Blodgett's table had been thinned by several departures during the week. . . . My mind had been considerably enlivened, and my sense of American superiority renewed, by intercourse with these people; and there is no danger of one's intellect becoming a standing pool in such society. I think better of American shipmasters, too, than I did from merely meeting them in my office. They keep up a continual discussion of professional matters, and of all things having any reference to their profession; the laws of insurance, the rights of vessels in foreign ports, the authority and customs of vessels of war with regard to merchantmen, etc.,—with stories and casual anecdotes of their sea-adventures, gales, shipwrecks, icebergs, and collisions of vessels, and hair-breadth escapes. Their talk runs very much on the sea, and on the land as connected with the sea; and their interest does not seem to extend very far beyond the wide field of their professional concerns.

Nothing remarkable occurred on the journey to London. The greater part of the way there were only two gentlemen in the same compartment with me; and we occupied each our corner, with little other conversation than in comparing watches at the various stations. I got out of the carriage only once, at Rugby, I think, and for the last seventy or eighty miles the train did not stop. There was a clear moon the latter part of the journey, and the mist lay along the ground, looking very much like a surface of water. We reached London at about ten, and I found S—— expecting me.

Yesterday the children went with Fanny to the Zoological Gardens; and, after sending them off, S—— and I walked to Piccadilly, and there took a cab for Kensington Gardens. It was a delightful day,—the best of all weather, the real English good weather,—more like an Indian summer than anything else within my experience; a mellow sunshine, with great warmth in it,—a soft, balmy air, with a slight haze through it. If the sun made us a little too warm, we had but to go into the shade to be immediately refreshed. The light of these days is very exquisite, so gently bright, without any glare,—a veiled glow. In short, it is the kindliest mood of Nature, and almost enough to compensate for chill and dreary months. Moreover, there is more of such weather here than the English climate has ever had credit for.

Kensington Gardens form an eminently beautiful piece of artificial woodland and park scenery. The old palace of Kensington, now inhabited by the Duchess of Inverness, stands at one extremity; an edifice of no great mark, built of brick, covering much ground, and low in proportion to its extent. In front of it, at a considerable distance, there is a sheet of water; and in all directions there are vistas of wide paths among noble trees, standing in groves, or scattered in clumps; everything being laid out with free and generous spaces, so that you can see long streams of sunshine among the trees, and there is a pervading influence of quiet and remoteness. Tree does not interfere with tree; the art of man is seen conspiring with Nature, as if they had consulted together how to make a beautiful scene, and had taken ages of quiet thought and tender care to accomplish it. We strolled slowly along these paths, and sometimes deviated from them, to walk beneath the trees, many of the leaves of which lay beneath our feet, yellow and brown, and with a pleasant smell of vegetable decay. These were the leaves of chestnut-trees; the other trees (unless elms) have yet, hardly begun to shed their foliage, although you can discern a sober change of line in the woodland masses; and the trees individualize themselves by assuming each its own tint, though in a very modest way. If they could have undergone the change of an American autumn, it would have been like putting on a regal robe. Autumn often puts one on in America, but it is apt to be very ragged.

There were a good many well-dressed people scattered through the grounds,—young men and girls, husbands with their wives and children, nursery-maids and little babes playing about in the grass. Anybody might have entered the gardens, I suppose; but only well-dressed people were there not, of the upper classes, but shop-keepers, clerks, apprentices, and respectability of that sort. It is pleasant to think that the people have the freedom, and therefore the property, of parks like this, more beautiful and stately than a nobleman can keep to himself. The extent of Kensington Gardens, when reckoned together with Hyde Park, from which it is separated only by a fence of iron rods, is very great, comprising miles of greensward and woodland. The large artificial sheet of water, called the Serpentine River, lies chiefly in Hyde Park, but comes partly within the precincts of the gardens. It is entitled to honorable mention among the English lakes, being larger than some that are world-celebrated,—several miles long, and perhaps a stone's-throw across in the widest part. It forms the paradise of a great many ducks of various breeds, which are accustomed to be fed by visitors, and come flying from afar, touching the water with their wings, and quacking loudly when bread or cake is thrown to them. I bought a bun of a little hunchbacked man, who kept a refreshment-stall near the Serpentine, and bestowed it pied-meal on these ducks, as we loitered along the bank. We left the park by another gate, and walked homeward, till we came to Tyburnia, and saw the iron memorial which marks where the gallows used to stand. Thence we turned into Park Lane, then into Upper Grosvenor Street, and reached Hanover Square sooner than we expected.

In the evening I walked forth to Charing Cross, and thence along the Strand and Fleet Street, where I made no new discoveries, unless it were the Mitre Tavern. I mean to go into it some day. The streets were much thronged, and there seemed to be a good many young people,—lovers, it is to be hoped,—who had spent the day together, and were going innocently home. Perhaps so,—perhaps not.

September 25th.—Yesterday forenoon J——- and I walked out, with no very definite purpose; but, seeing a narrow passageway from the Strand down to the river, we went through it, and gained access to a steamboat, plying thence to London Bridge. The fare was a halfpenny apiece, and the boat almost too much crowded for standing-room. This part of the river presents the water-side of London in a rather pleasanter aspect than below London Bridge,—the Temple, with its garden, Somerset House,—and generally, a less tumble-down and neglected look about the buildings; although, after all, the metropolis does not see a very stately face in its mirror. I saw Alsatia betwixt the Temple and Blackfriar's Bridge. Its precincts looked very narrow, and not particularly distinguishable, at this day, from the portions of the city on either side of it. At London Bridge we got aboard of a Woolwich steamer, and went farther down the river, passing the Custom-House and the Tower, the only prominent objects rising out of the dreary range of shabbiness which stretches along close to the water's edge.

From this remote part of London we walked towards the heart of the city; and, as we went, matters seemed to civilize themselves by degrees, and the streets grew crowded with cabs, omnibuses, drays, and carts. We passed, I think, through Whitechapel, and, reaching St. Paul's, got into an omnibus, and drove to Regent Street, whence it was but a step or two home.

In the afternoon, at four o'clock, S——- and I went to call on the American Ambassador and Miss L———. The lady was not at home, but we went in to see Mr. ——— and were shown into a stately drawing-room, the furniture of which was sufficiently splendid, but rather the worse for wear,—being hired furniture, no doubt. The ambassador shortly appeared, looking venerable, as usual,—or rather more so than usual,—benign, and very pale. His deportment towards ladies is highly agreeable and prepossessing, and he paid very kind attention to S——-, thereby quite confirming her previous good feeling towards him. She thinks that he is much changed since she saw him last, at dinner, at our house,—more infirm, more aged, and with a singular depression in his manner. I, too, think that age has latterly come upon him with great rapidity. He said that Miss L——— was going home on the 6th of October, and that he himself had long purposed going, but had received despatches which obliged him to put off his departure. The President, he said, had just written, requesting him to remain till April, but this he was determined not to do. I rather think that he does really wish to return, and not for any ambitious views concerning the Presidency, but from an old man's natural desire to be at home, and among his own people.

S——- spoke to him about an order from the Lord Chamberlain for admission to view the two Houses of Parliament; and the ambassador drew from his pocket a colored silk handkerchief, and made a knot in it, in order to remind himself to ask the Lord Chamberlain. The homeliness of this little incident has a sort of propriety and keeping with much of Mr. ———'s manner, but I would rather not have him do so before English people. He arranged to send a close carriage for us to come and see him socially this evening. After leaving his house we drove round Hyde Park, and thence to Portland Place, where we left cards for Mrs. Russell Sturgis; thence into Regent's Park, thence home. U—— and J—— accompanied us throughout these drives, but remained in the carriage during our call on Mr. ———. In the evening I strolled out, and walked as far as St. Paul's,—never getting enough of the bustle of London, which may weary, but can never satisfy me. By night London looks wild and dreamy, and fills me with a sort of pleasant dread. It was a clear evening, with a bright English moon,—that is to say, what we Americans should call rather dim.

September 26th.—Yesterday, at eleven, I walked towards Westminster Abbey, and as I drew near the Abbey bells were clamorous for joy, chiming merrily, musically, and, obstreperously,—the most rejoicing sound that can be conceived; and we ought to have a chime of bells in every American town and village, were it only to keep alive the celebration of the Fourth of July. I conjectured that there might have been another victory over the Russians, that perhaps the northern side of Sebastopol had surrendered; but soon I saw the riddle that these merry bells were proclaiming. There were a great many private carriages, and a large concourse of loungers and spectators, near the door of the church that stands close under the eaves of the Abbey. Gentlemen and ladies, gayly dressed, were issuing forth, carriages driving away, and others drawing up to the door in their turn; and, in short, a marriage had just been celebrated in the church, and this was the wedding-party. The last time I was there, Westminster was flinging out its great voice of joy for a national triumph; now, for the happy union of two lovers. What a mighty sympathizer is this old Abbey!

It is pleasant to recognize the mould and fashion of English features through the marble of many of the statues and busts in the Abbey, even though they may be clad in Roman robes. I am inclined to think them, in many cases, faithful likenesses; and it brings them nearer to the mind, to see these original sculptures,—you see the man at but one remove, as if you caught his image in a looking-glass. The bust of Gay seemed to me very good,—a thoughtful and humorous sweetness in the face. Goldsmith has as good a position as any poet in the Abbey, his bust and tablet filling the pointed arch over a door that seems to lead towards the cloisters. No doubt he would have liked to be assured of so conspicuous a place. There is one monument to a native American, "Charles Wragg, Esq., of South Carolina,"—the only one, I suspect, in Westminster Abbey, and he acquired this memorial by the most un-American of qualities, his loyalty to his king. He was one of the refugees leaving America in 1777, and being shipwrecked on his passage the monument was put up by his sister. It is a small tablet with a representation of Mr. Wragg's shipwreck at the base. Next to it is the large monument of Sir Cloudesley Shovel, which I think Addison ridicules,—the Admiral, in a full-bottomed wig and Roman dress, but with a broad English face, reclining with his head on his hand, and looking at you with great placidity. I stood at either end of the nave, and endeavored to take in the full beauty and majesty of the edifice; but apparently was not in a proper state of mind, for nothing came of it. It is singular how like an avenue of overarching trees are these lofty aisles of a cathedral.

Leaving the Abbey about one o'clock, I walked into the city as far as Grace Church Street, and there called on the American Consul, General ———, who had been warmly introduced to me last year by a letter from the President. I like the General; a kindly and honorable man, of simple manners and large experience of life. Afterwards I called on Mr. Oakford, an American connected in business with Mr. Crosby, from whom I wanted some information as to the sailing of steamers from Southampton to Lisbon. Mr. Crosby was not in town. . . .

At eight o'clock Mr. ——— sent his carriage, according to previous arrangement, to take us to spend the evening socially. Miss L——— received us with proper cordiality, and looked quite becomingly,—more sweet and simple in aspect than when I have seen her in full dress. Shortly the ambassador appeared, and made himself highly agreeable; not that he is a brilliant conversationist, but his excellent sense and good-humor, and all that he has seen and been a part of, are sufficient resources to draw upon. We talked of the Queen, whom he spoke of with high respect; . . . . of the late Czar, whom he knew intimately while minister to Russia,—and he quite confirms all that has been said about the awful beauty of his person. Mr. ———'s characterization of him was quite favorable; he thought better of his heart than most people, and adduced his sports with a school of children,—twenty of whom, perhaps, he made to stand rigidly in a row, like so many bricks,—then, giving one a push, would laugh obstreperously to see the whole row tumble down. He would lie on his back, and allow the little things to scramble over him. His Majesty admitted Mr. ——— to great closeness of intercourse, and informed him of a conspiracy which was then on foot for the Czar's murder. On the evening, when the assassination was to take place, the Czar did not refrain from going to the public place where it was to be perpetrated, although, indeed, great precautions had been taken to frustrate the schemes of the conspirators. Mr. ——— said, that, in case the plot had succeeded, all the foreigners, including himself, would likewise have been murdered, the native Russians having a bitter hatred against foreigners. He observed that he had been much attached to the Czar, and had never joined in the English abuse of him. His sympathies, however, are evidently rather English than Russian, in this war. Speaking of the present emperor, he said that Lord Heytebury, formerly English ambassador in Russia, lately told him that he complimented the Czar Nicholas on the good qualities of his son, saying that he was acknowledged by all to be one of the most amiable youths in the world. "Too amiable, I fear, for his position," answered the Czar. "He has too much of his mother in him."

September 27th.—Yesterday, much earlier than English people ever do such things, General ——— made us a call on his way to the Consulate, and sat talking a stricken hour or thereabouts. Scarcely had he gone when Mrs. Oakford and her daughter came. After sitting a long while, they took U—— to their house, near St. John's Wood, to spend the night. I had been writing my journal and official correspondence during such intervals as these calls left me; and now, concluding these businesses, S——, J——, and I went out and took a cab for the terminus of the Crystal Palace Railway, whither we proceeded over Waterloo Bridge, and reached the palace not far from three o'clock. It was a beautifully bright day, such as we have in wonderful succession this month. The Crystal Palace gleamed in the sunshine; but I do not think a very impressive edifice can be built of glass,—light and airy, to be sure, but still it will be no other than an overgrown conservatory. It is unlike anything else in England; uncongenial with the English character, without privacy, destitute of mass, weight, and shadow, unsusceptible of ivy, lichens, or any mellowness from age.

The train of carriages stops within the domain of the palace, where there is a long ascending corridor up into the edifice. There was a very pleasant odor of heliotrope diffused through the air; and, indeed, the whole atmosphere of the Crystal Palace is sweet with various flower-scents, and mild and balmy, though sufficiently fresh and cool. It would be a delightful climate for invalids to spend the winter in; and if all England could be roofed over with glass, it would be a great improvement on its present condition.

The first thing we did, before fairly getting into the palace, was to sit down in a large ante-hall, and get some bread and butter and a pint of Bass's pale ale, together with a cup of coffee for S———. This was the best refreshment we could find at that spot; but farther within we found abundance of refreshment-rooms, and John Bull and his wife and family at fifty little round tables, busily engaged with cold fowl, cold beef, ham, tongue, and bottles of ale and stout, and half-pint decanters of sherry. The English probably eat with more simple enjoyment than any other people; not ravenously, as we often do, and not exquisitely and artificially, like the French, but deliberately and vigorously, and with due absorption in the business, so that nothing good is lost upon them. . . . It is remarkable how large a feature the refreshment-rooms make in the arrangements of the Crystal Palace.

The Crystal Palace is a gigantic toy for the English people to play with. The design seems to be to reproduce all past ages, by representing the features of their interior architecture, costume, religion, domestic life, and everything that can be expressed by paint and plaster; and, likewise, to bring all climates and regions of the earth within these enchanted precincts, with their inhabitants and animals in living semblance, and their vegetable productions, as far as possible, alive and real. Some part of the design is already accomplished to a wonderful degree. The Indian, the Egyptian, and especially the Arabian, courts are admirably executed. I never saw or conceived anything so gorgeous as the Alhambra. There are Byzantine and mediaeval representations, too,—reproductions of ancient apartments, decorations, statues from tombs, monuments, religious and funereal,—that gave me new ideas of what antiquity has been. It takes down one's overweening opinion of the present time, to see how many kinds of beauty and magnificence have heretofore existed, and are now quite passed away and forgotten; and to find that we, who suppose that, in all matters of taste, our age is the very flower-season of the time,—that we are poor and meagre as to many things in which they were rich. There is nothing gorgeous now. We live a very naked life. This was the only reflection I remember making, as we passed from century to century, through the succession of classic, Oriental, and mediaeval courts, adown the lapse of time,—seeing all these ages in as brief a space as the Wandering Jew might glance along them in his memory. I suppose a Pompeian house with its courts and interior apartments was as faithfully shown as it was possible to do it. I doubt whether I ever should feel at home in such a house.

In the pool of a fountain, of which there are several beautiful ones within the palace, besides larger ones in the garden before it, we saw tropical plants growing,—large water-lilies of various colors, some white, like our Concord pond-lily, only larger, and more numerously leafed. There were great circular green leaves, lying flat on the water, with a circumference equal to that of a centre-table. Tropical trees, too, varieties of palm and others, grew in immense pots or tubs, but seemed not to enjoy themselves much. The atmosphere must, after all, be far too cool to bring out their native luxuriance; and this difficulty can never be got over at a less expense than that of absolutely stewing the visitors and attendants. Otherwise, it would be very practicable to have all the vegetable world, at least, within these precincts.

The palace is very large, and our time was short, it being desirable to get home early; so, after a stay of little more than two hours, we took the rail back again, and reached Hanover Square at about six. After tea I wandered forth, with some thought of going to the theatre, and, passing the entrance of one, in the Strand, I went in, and found a farce in progress. It was one of the minor theatres, very minor indeed; but the pieces, so far as I saw them, were sufficiently laughable. There were some Spanish dances, too, very graceful and pretty. Between the plays a girl from the neighboring saloon came to the doors of the boxes, offering lemonade and ginger-beer to the occupants. A person in my box took a glass of lemonade, and shared it with a young lady by his side, both sipping out of the same glass. The audience seemed rather heavy,—not briskly responsive to the efforts of the performers, but good-natured, and willing to be pleased, especially with some patriotic dances, in which much waving and intermingling of the French and English flags was introduced. Theatrical performances soon weary me of late years; and I came away before the curtain rose on the concluding piece.

September 28th.—8—— and I walked to Charing Cross yesterday forenoon, and there took a Hansom cab to St. Paul's Cathedral. It had been a thick, foggy morning, but had warmed and brightened into one of the balmiest and sunniest of noons. As we entered the cathedral, the long bars of sunshine were falling from its upper windows through the great interior atmosphere, and were made visible by the dust, or mist, floating about in it. It is a grand edifice, and I liked it quite as much as on my first view of it, although a sense of coldness and nakedness is felt when we compare it with Gothic churches. It is more an external work than the Gothic churches are, and is not so made out of the dim, awful, mysterious, grotesque, intricate nature of man. But it is beautiful and grand. I love its remote distances, and wide, clear spaces, its airy massiveness; its noble arches, its sky-like dome, which, I think, should be all over light, with ground-glass, instead of being dark, with only diminutive windows.

We walked round, looking at the monuments, which are so arranged, at the bases of columns and in niches, as to coincide with the regularity of the cathedral, and be each an additional ornament to the whole, however defective individually as works of art. We thought that many of these monuments were striking and impressive, though there was a pervading sameness of idea,—a great many Victorys and Valors and Britannias, and a great expenditure of wreaths, which must have cost Victory a considerable sum at any florist's whom she patronizes. A very great majority of the memorials are to naval and military men, slain in Bonaparte's wars; men in whom one feels little or no interest (except Picton, Abercrombie, Moore, Nelson, of course, and a few others really historic), they having done nothing remarkable, save having been shot, nor shown any more brains than the cannonballs that killed them. All the statues have the dust of years upon then, strewn thickly in the folds of their marble garments, and on any limb stretched horizontally, and on their noses, so that the expression is much obscured. I think the nation might employ people to brush away the dust from the statues of its heroes. But, on the whole, it is very fine to look through the broad arches of the cathedral, and see, at the foot of some distant pillar, a group of sculptured figures, commemorating some man and deed that (whether worth remembering or not) the nation is so happy as to reverence. In Westminster Abbey, the monuments are so crowded, and so oddly patched together upon the walls, that they are ornamental only in a mural point of view; and, moreover, the quaint and grotesque taste of many of them might well make the spectator laugh,—an effect not likely to be produced by the monuments in St. Paul's. But, after all, a man might read the walls of the Abbey day after day with ever-fresh interest, whereas the cold propriety of the cathedral would weary him in due time.

We did not ascend to the galleries and other points of interest aloft, nor go down into the vaults, where Nelson's sarcophagus is shown, and many monuments of the old Gothic cathedral, which stood on this site, before the great fire. They say that these lower regions are comfortably warm and dry; but as we walked round in front, within the iron railing of the churchyard, we passed an open door, giving access to the crypt, and it breathed out a chill like death upon us.

It is pleasant to stand in the centre of the cathedral, and hear the noise of London, loudest all round this spot,—how it is calmed into a sound as proper to be heard through the aisles as the tones of its own organ. If St. Paul's were to be burnt again (having already been bunt and risen three or four times since the sixth century), I wonder whether it would ever be rebuilt in the same spot! I doubt whether the city and the nation are so religious as to consecrate their midmost heart for the site of a church, where land would be so valuable by the square inch.

Coming from the cathedral, we went through Paternoster Row, and saw Ave Mary Lane; all this locality appearing to have got its nomenclature from monkish personages. We now took a cab for the British Museum, but found this to be one of the days on which strangers are not admitted; so we slowly walked into Oxford Street, and then strolled homeward, till, coming to a sort of bazaar, we went in and found a gallery of pictures. This bazaar proved to be the Pantheon, and the first picture we saw in the gallery was Haydon's Resurrection of Lazarus,—a great height and breadth of canvas, right before you as you ascend the stairs. The face of Lazarus is very awful, and not to be forgotten; it is as true as if the painter had seen it, or had been himself the resurrected man and felt it; but the rest of the picture signified nothing, and is vulgar and disagreeable besides. There are several other pictures by Haydon in this collection,—the Banishment of Aristides, Nero with his Harp, and the Conflagration of Rome; but the last is perfectly ridiculous, and all of them are exceedingly unpleasant. I should be sorry to live in a house that contained one of them. The best thing of Haydon was a hasty dash of a sketch for a small, full-length portrait of Wordsworth, sitting on the crag of a mountain. I doubt whether Wordsworth's likeness has ever been so poetically brought out. This gallery is altogether of modern painters, and it seems to be a receptacle for pictures by artists who can obtain places nowhere else,—at least, I never heard of their names before. They were very uninteresting, almost without exception, and yet some of the pictures were done cleverly enough. There is very little talent in this world, and what there is, it seems to me, is pretty well known and acknowledged. We don't often stumble upon geniuses in obscure corners.

Leaving the gallery, we wandered through the rest of the bazaar, which is devoted to the sale of ladies' finery, jewels, perfumes, children's toys, and all manner of small and pretty rubbish. . . . In the evening I again sallied forth, and lost myself for an hour or two; at last recognizing my whereabouts in Tottenham Court Road. In such quarters of London it seems to be the habit of people to take their suppers in the open air. You see old women at the corners, with kettles of hot water for tea or coffee; and as I passed a butcher's open shop, he was just taking out large quantities of boiled beef, smoking hot. Butchers' stands are remarkable for their profuse expenditure of gas; it belches forth from the pipes in great flaring jets of flame, uncovered by any glass, and broadly illuminating the neighborhood. I have not observed that London ever goes to bed.

September 29th.—Yesterday we walked to the British Museum. A sentinel or two kept guard before the gateway of this extensive edifice in Great Russell Street, and there was a porter at the lodge, and one or two policemen lounging about, but entrance was free, and we walked in without question. Officials and policemen were likewise scattered about the great entrance-hall, none of whom, however, interfered with us; so we took whatever way we chose, and wandered about at will. It is a hopeless, and to me, generally, a depressing business to go through an immense multifarious show like this, glancing at a thousand things, and conscious of some little titillation of mind from them, but really taking in nothing, and getting no good from anything. One need not go beyond the limits of the British Museum to be profoundly accomplished in all branches of science, art, and literature; only it would take a lifetime to exhaust it in any one department; but to see it as we did, and with no prospect of ever seeing it more at leisure, only impressed me with the truth of the old apothegm, "Life is short, and Art is long." The fact is, the world is accumulating too many materials for knowledge. We do not recognize for rubbish what is really rubbish; and under this head might be reckoned very many things one sees in the British Museum; and, as each generation leaves its fragments and potsherds behind it, such will finally be the desperate conclusion of the learned.

We went first among some antique marbles,—busts, statues, terminal gods, with several of the Roman emperors among them. We saw here the bust whence Haydon took his ugly and ridiculous likeness of Nero,—a foolish thing to do. Julius Caesar was there, too, looking more like a modern old man than any other bust in the series. Perhaps there may be a universality in his face, that gives it this independence of race and epoch. We glimpsed along among the old marbles,—Elgin and others, which are esteemed such treasures of art;—the oddest fragments, many of them smashed by their fall from high places, or by being pounded to pieces by barbarians, or gnawed away by time; the surface roughened by being rained upon for thousands of years; almost always a nose knocked off; sometimes a headless form; a great deficiency of feet and hands,—poor, maimed veterans in this hospital of incurables. The beauty of the most perfect of them must be rather guessed at, and seen by faith, than with the bodily eye; to look at the corroded faces and forms is like trying to see angels through mist and cloud. I suppose nine tenths of those who seem to be in raptures about these fragments do not really care about them; neither do I. And if I were actually moved, I should doubt whether it were by the statues or by my own fancy.

We passed, too, through Assyrian saloons and Egyptian saloons,—all full of monstrosities and horrible uglinesses, especially the Egyptian, and all the innumerable relics that I saw of them in these saloons, and among the mummies, instead of bringing me closer to them, removed me farther and farther; there being no common ground of sympathy between them and us. Their gigantic statues are certainly very curious. I saw a hand and arm up to the shoulder fifteen feet in length, and made of some stone that seemed harder and heavier than granite, not having lost its polish in all the rough usage that it has undergone. There was a fist on a still larger scale, almost as big as a hogshead. Hideous, blubber-lipped faces of giants, and human shapes with beasts' heads on them. The Egyptian controverted Nature in all things, only using it as a groundwork to depict, the unnatural upon. Their mummifying process is a result of this tendency. We saw one very perfect mummy,—a priestess, with apparently only one more fold of linen betwixt us and her antique flesh, and this fitting closely to her person from head to foot, so that we could see the lineaments of her face and the shape of her limbs as perfectly as if quite bare. I judge that she may have been very beautiful in her day,—whenever that was. One or two of the poor thing's toes (her feet were wonderfully small and delicate) protruded from the linen, and, perhaps, not having been so perfectly embalmed, the flesh had fallen away, leaving only some little bones. I don't think this young woman has gained much by not turning to dust in the time of the Pharaohs. We also saw some bones of a king that had been taken out of a pyramid; a very fragmentary skeleton. Among the classic marbles I peeped into an urn that once contained the ashes of dead people, and the bottom still had an ashy hue. I like this mode of disposing of dead bodies; but it would be still better to burn them and scatter the ashes, instead of hoarding them up,—to scatter them over wheat-fields or flowerbeds.

Besides these antique halls, we wandered through saloons of antediluvian animals, some set up in skeletons, others imprisoned in solid stone; also specimens of still extant animals, birds, reptiles, shells, minerals,— the whole circle of human knowledge and guess-work,—till I wished that the whole Past might be swept away, and each generation compelled to bury and destroy whatever it had produced, before being permitted to leave the stage. When we quit a house, we are expected to make it clean for the next occupant; why ought we not to leave a clean world for the next generation? We did not see the library of above half a million of volumes; else I suppose I should have found full occasion to wish that burnt and buried likewise. In truth, a greater part of it is as good as buried, so far as any readers are concerned. Leaving the Museum, we sauntered home. After a little rest, I set out for St. John's Wood, and arrived thither by dint of repeated inquiries. It is a pretty suburb, inhabited by people of the middling class. U—— met me joyfully, but seemed to have had a good time with Mrs. Oakford and her daughter; and, being pressed to stay to tea, I could not well help it. Before tea I sat talking with Mrs. Oakford and a friend of hers, Miss Clinch, about the Americans and the English, especially dwelling on the defects of the latter,—among which we reckoned a wretched meanness in money transactions, a lack of any embroidery of honor and liberality in their dealings, so that they require close watching, or they will be sure to take you at advantage. I hear this character of them from Americans on all hands, and my own experience confirms it as far as it goes, not merely among tradespeople, but among persons who call themselves gentlefolks. The cause, no doubt, or one cause, lies in the fewer chances of getting money here, the closer and sharper regulation of all the modes of life; nothing being left to liberal and gentlemanly feelings, except fees to servants. They are not gamblers in England, as we to some extent are; and getting their money painfully, or living within an accurately known income, they are disinclined to give up so much as a sixpence that they can possibly get. But the result is, they are mean in petty things.

By and by Mr. Oakford came in, well soaked with the heaviest shower that I ever knew in England, which had been rattling on the roof of the little side room where we sat, and had caught him on the outside of the omnibus. At a little before eight o'clock I came home with U—— in a cab,—the gaslight glittering on the wet streets through which we drove, though the sky was clear overhead.

September 30th.—Yesterday, a little before twelve, we took a cab, and went to the two Houses of Parliament,—the most immense building, methinks, that ever was built; and not yet finished, though it has now been occupied for years. Its exterior lies hugely along the ground, and its great unfinished tower is still climbing towards the sky; but the result (unless it be the riverfront, which I have not yet seen) seems not very impressive. The interior is much more successful. Nothing can be more magnificent and gravely gorgeous than the Chamber of Peers,—a large oblong hall, panelled with oak, elaborately carved, to the height of perhaps twenty feet. Then the balustrade of the gallery runs around the hall, and above the gallery are six arched windows on each side, richly painted with historic subjects. The roof is ornamented and gilded, and everywhere throughout there is embellishment of color and carving on the broadest scale, and, at the same time, most minute and elaborate; statues of full size in niches aloft; small heads of kings, no bigger than a doll; and the oak is carved in all parts of the panelling as faithfully as they used to do it in Henry VII's time,—as faithfully and with as good workmanship, but with nothing like the variety and invention which I saw in the dining-room of Smithell's Hall. There the artist wrought with his heart and head; but much of this work, I suppose, was done by machinery. Be that as it may, it is a most noble and splendid apartment, and, though so fine, there is not a touch of finery; it glistens and glows with even a sombre magnificence, owing to the rich, deep lines, and the dim light, bedimmed with rich colors by coming through the painted windows. In arched recesses, that serve as frames, at each end of the hall, there are three pictures by modern artists from English history; and though it was not possible to see them well as pictures, they adorned and enriched the walls marvellously as architectural embellishments. The Peers' seats are four rows of long sofas on each side, covered with red morocco; comfortable seats enough, but not adapted to any other than a decorously exact position. The woolsack is between these two divisions of sofas, in the middle passage of the floor,—a great square seat, covered with scarlet, and with a scarlet cushion set up perpendicularly for the Chancellor to lean against. In front of the woolsack there is another still larger ottoman, on which he might be at full length,—for what purpose intended, I know not. I should take the woolsack to be not a very comfortable seat, though I suppose it was originally designed to be the most comfortable one that could be contrived, in view of the Chancellor's much sitting.

The throne is the first object you see on entering the hall, being close to the door; a chair of antique form, with a high, peaked back, and a square canopy above, the whole richly carved and quite covered with burnished gilding, besides being adorned with rows of rock crystals,— which seemed to me of rather questionable taste.

It is less elevated above the floor than one imagines it ought to be. While we were looking at it, I saw two Americans,—Western men, I should judge,—one of them with a true American slouch, talking to the policeman in attendance, and describing our Senate Chamber in contrast with the House of Lords. The policeman smiled and ah-ed, and seemed to make as courteous and liberal responses as he could. There was quite a mixed company of spectators, and, I think, other Americans present besides the above two and ourselves. The Lord Chamberlain's tickets appear to be distributed with great impartiality. There were two or three women of the lower middle class, with children or babies in arms, one of whom lifted up its voice loudly in the House of Peers.

We next, after long contemplating this rich hall, proceeded through passages and corridors to a great central room, very beautiful, which seems to be used for purposes of refreshment, and for electric telegraphs; though I should not suppose this could be its primitive and ultimate design. Thence we went into the House of Commons, which is larger than the Chamber of Peers, and much less richly ornamented, though it would have appeared splendid had it come first in order. The speaker's chair, if I remember rightly, is loftier and statelier than the throne itself. Both in this hall and in that of the Lords, we were at first surprised by the narrow limits within which the great ideas of the Lords and Commons of England are physically realized; they would seem to require a vaster space. When we hear of members rising on opposite sides of the House, we think of them as but dimly discernible to their opponents, and uplifting their voices, so as to be heard afar; whereas they sit closely enough to feel each other's spheres, to note all expression of face, and to give the debate the character of a conversation. In this view a debate seems a much more earnest and real thing than as we read it in a newspaper. Think of the debaters meeting each other's eyes, their faces flushing, their looks interpreting their words, their speech growing into eloquence, without losing the genuineness of talk! Yet, in fact, the Chamber of Peers is ninety feet long and half as broad, and high, and the Chamber of Commons is still larger.

Thence we went to Westminster Hall, through a gallery with statues on each side,—beautiful statues too, I thought; seven of them, of which four were from the times of the civil wars,—Clarendon, Falkland, Hampden, Selden, Somers, Mansfield, and Walpole. There is room for more in this corridor, and there are niches for hundreds of their marble brotherhood throughout the edifice; but I suppose future ages will have to fill the greater part of them. Yet I cannot help imagining that this rich and noble edifice has more to do with the past than with the future; that it is the glory of a declining empire; and that the perfect bloom of this great stone flower, growing out of the institutions of England, forbodes that they have nearly lived out their life. It sums up all. Its beauty and magnificence are made out of ideas that are gone by.

We entered Westminster Hall (which is incorporated into this new edifice, and forms an integral part of it) through a lofty archway, whence a double flight of broad steps descends to the stone pavement. After the elaborate ornament of the rooms we had just been viewing, this venerable hall looks extremely simple and bare,—a gray stone floor, gray and naked stone walls, but a roof sufficiently elaborate, its vault being filled with carved beams and rafters of chestnut, very much admired and wondered at for the design and arrangement. I think it would have pleased me more to have seen a clear vaulted roof, instead of this intricacy of wooden points, by which so much skylight space is lost. They make (be it not irreverently said) the vast and lofty apartment look like the ideal of an immense barn. But it is a noble space, and all without the support of a single pillar. It is about eighty of my paces from the foot of the steps to the opposite end of the hall, and twenty-seven from side to side; very high, too, though not quite proportionately to its other dimensions. I love it for its simplicity and antique nakedness, and deem it worthy to have been the haunt and home of History through the six centuries since it was built. I wonder it does not occur to modern ingenuity to make a scenic representation, in this very hall, of the ancient trials for life or death, pomps, feasts, coronations, and every great historic incident in the lives of kings, Parliaments, Protectors, and all illustrious men, that have occurred here. The whole world cannot show another hall such as this, so tapestried with recollections of whatever is most striking in human annals.

Westminster Abbey being just across the street, we went thither from the hall, and sought out the cloisters, which we had not yet visited. They are in excellent preservation,—broad walks, canopied with intermingled arches of gray stone, on which some sort of lichen, or other growth of ages (which seems, however, to have little or nothing vegetable in it), has grown. The pavement is entirely made of flat tombstones, inscribed with half-effaced names of the dead people beneath; and the wall all round bears the marble tablets which give a fuller record of their virtues. I think it was from a meditation in these cloisters that Addison wrote one of his most beautiful pieces in the Spectator. It is a pity that this old fashion of a cloistered walk is not retained in our modern edifices; it was so excellent for shelter and for shade during a thoughtful hour,—this sombre corridor beneath an arched stone roof, with the central space of richest grass, on which the sun might shine or the shower fall, while the monk or student paced through the prolonged archway of his meditations.

As we came out from the cloisters, and walked along by the churchyard of the Abbey, a woman came begging behind us very earnestly. "A bit of bread," she said, "and I will give you a thousand blessings! Hunger is hard to bear. O kind gentleman and kind lady, a penny for a bit of bread! It is a hard thing that gentlemen and ladies should see poor people wanting bread, and make no difference whether they are good or bad." And so she followed us almost all round the Abbey, assailing our hearts in most plaintive terms, but with no success; for she did it far too well to be anything but an impostor, and no doubt she had breakfasted better, and was likely to have a better dinner, than ourselves. And yet the natural man cries out against the philosophy that rejects beggars. It is a thousand to one that they are impostors, but yet we do ourselves a wrong by hardening our hearts against them. At last, without turning round, I told her that I should give her nothing,—with some asperity, doubtless, for the effort to refuse creates a bitterer repulse than is necessary. She still followed us a little farther, but at last gave it up, with a deep groan. I could not have performed this act of heroism on my first arrival from America.

Whether the beggar-woman had invoked curses on us, and Heaven saw fit to grant some slight response, I know not, but it now began to rain on my wife's velvet; so I put her and J—— into a cab, and hastened to ensconce myself in Westminster Abbey while the shower should last. Poets' Corner has never seemed like a strange place to me; it has been familiar from the very first; at all events, I cannot now recollect the previous conception, of which the reality has taken the place. I seem always to have known that somewhat dim corner, with the bare brown stone-work of the old edifice aloft, and a window shedding down its light on the marble busts and tablets, yellow with time, that cover the three walls of the nook up to a height of about twenty feet. Prior's is the largest and richest monument. It is observable that the bust and monument of Congreve are in a distant part of the Abbey. His duchess probably thought it a degradation to bring a gentleman among the beggarly poets.

I walked round the aisles, and paced the nave, and came to the conclusion that Westminster Abbey, both in itself and for the variety and interest of its monuments, is a thousand times preferable to St. Paul's. There is as much difference as between a snow-bank and a chimney-corner in their relation to the human heart. By the by, the monuments and statues in the Abbey seem all to be carefully dusted.

The shower being over, I walked down into the city, where I called on Mr. B——— and left S——-'s watch to be examined and put in order. He told me that he and his brother had lately been laying out and letting a piece of land at Blackheath, that had been left them by their father, and that the ground-rent would bring them in two thousand pounds per annum. With such an independent income, I doubt whether any American would consent to be anything but a gentleman,—certainly not an operative watchmaker. How sensible these Englishmen are in some things!

Thence I went at a venture, and lost myself, of course. At one part of my walk I came upon St. Luke's Hospital, whence I returned to St. Paul's, and thence along Fleet Street and the Strand. Contiguous to the latter is Holywell Street,—a narrow lane, filled up with little bookshops and bookstalls, at some of which I saw sermons and other works of divinity, old editions of classics, and all such serious matters, while at stalls and windows close beside them (and, possibly, at the same stalls) there were books with title-pages displayed, indicating them to be of the most indecent kind.

October 2d.—Yesterday forenoon I went with J—— into the city to 67 Grace Church Street, to get a bank post-note cashed by Mr. Oakford, and afterwards to the offices of two lines of steamers, in Moorgate Street and Leadenhall Street. The city was very much thronged. It is a marvel what sets so many people a going at all hours of the day. Then it is to be considered that these are but a small portion of those who are doing the business of the city; much the larger part being occupied in offices at desks, in discussions of plans of enterprise, out of sight of the public, while these earnest hurriers are merely the froth in the pot.

After seeing the steam-officials, we went to London Bridge, which always swarms with more passengers than any of the streets. Descending the steps that lead to the level of the Thames, we took passage in a boat bound up the river to Chelsea, of which there is one starting every ten minutes, the voyage being of forty minutes' duration. It began to sprinkle a little just as we started; but after a slight showeriness, lasting till we had passed Westminster Bridge, the day grew rather pleasant.

At Westminster Bridge we had a good view of the river-front of the two Houses of Parliament, which look very noble from this point,—a long and massive extent, with a delightful promenade for the legislative people exactly above the margin of the river. This is certainly a magnificent edifice, and yet

I doubt whether it is so impressive as it might and ought to have been made, considering its immensity. It makes no more impression than you can well account to yourself for, and you rather wonder that it does not make more. The reason must be that the architect has not "builded better than he knew." He felt no power higher and wiser than himself, making him its instrument. He reckoned upon and contrived all his effects with malice aforethought, and therefore missed the crowning glory,—that being a happiness which God, out of his pure grace, mixes up with only the simple-hearted, best efforts of men.

October 3d.—I again went into the city yesterday forenoon, to settle about the passages to Lisbon, taking J——— with me. From Hungerford Bridge we took the steamer to London Bridge, that being an easy and speedy mode of accomplishing distances that take many footsteps through the crowded thoroughfares. After leaving the steamer-office, we went back through the Strand, and, crossing Waterloo Bridge, walked a good way on to the Surrey side of the river; a coarse, dingy, disagreeable suburb, with shops apparently for country produce, for old clothes, second-hand furniture, for ironware, and other things bulky and inelegant. How many scenes and sorts of life are comprehended within London! There was much in the aspect of these streets that reminded me of a busy country village in America on an immensely magnified scale.

Growing rather weary anon, we got into an omnibus, which took us as far as the Surrey Zoological Gardens, which J———- wished very much to see. They proved to be a rather poor place of suburban amusement; poor, at least, by daylight, their chief attraction for the public consisting in out-of-door representations of battles and sieges. The storming of Sebastopol (as likewise at the Cremorne Gardens) was advertised for the evening, and we saw the scenery of Sebastopol, painted on a vast scale, in the open air, and really looking like miles and miles of hill and water; with a space for the actual manoeuvring of ships on a sheet of real water in front of the scene, on which some ducks were now swimming about, in place of men-of-war. The climate of England must often interfere with this sort of performance; and I can conceive of nothing drearier for spectators or performers than a drizzly evening. Convenient to this central spot of entertainment there were liquor and refreshment rooms, with pies and cakes. The menagerie, though the ostensible staple of the gardens, is rather poor and scanty; pretty well provided with lions and lionesses, also one or two giraffes, some camels, a polar bear,—who plunged into a pool of water for bits of cake,—and two black bears, who sat on their haunches or climbed poles; besides a wilderness of monkeys, some parrots and macaws, an ostrich, various ducks, and other animal and ornithological trumpery; some skins of snakes so well stuffed that I took them for living serpents till J—— discovered the deception, and an aquarium, with a good many common fishes swimming among sea-weed.

The garden is shaded with trees, and set out with greensward and gravel-walks, from which the people were sweeping the withered autumnal leaves, which now fall every day. Plaster statues stand here and there, one of them without a head, thus disclosing the hollowness of the trunk; there were one or two little drizzly fountains, with the water dripping over the rock-work, of which the English are so fond; and the buildings for the animals and other purposes had a flimsy, pasteboard aspect of pretension. The garden was in its undress; few visitors, I suppose, coming hither at this time of day,—only here and there a lady and children, a young man and girl, or a couple of citizens, loitering about. I take pains to remember these small items, because they suggest the day-life or torpidity of what may look very brilliant at night. These corked-up fountains, slovenly greensward, cracked casts of statues, pasteboard castles, and duck-pond Bay of Balaclava then shining out in magic splendor, and the shabby attendants whom we saw sweeping and shovelling probably transformed into the heroes of Sebastopol.

J—— thought it a delightful place; but I soon grew very weary, and came away about four o'clock, and, getting into a city omnibus, we alighted on the hither side of Blackfriar's Bridge. Turning into Fleet Street, I looked about for a place to dine at, and chose the Mitre Tavern, in memory of Johnson and Boswell. It stands behind a front of modern shops, through which is an archway, giving admittance into a narrow court-yard, which, I suppose, was formerly open to Fleet Street. The house is of dark brick, and, comparing it with other London edifices, I should take it to have been at least refronted since Johnson's time; but within, the low, sombre coffee-room which we entered might well enough have been of that era or earlier. It seems to be a good, plain, respectable inn; and the waiter gave us each a plate of boiled beef, and, for dessert, a damson tart, which made up a comfortable dinner. After dinner, we zigzagged homeward through Clifford's link passage, Holborn, Drury Lane, the Strand, Charing Cross, Pall Mall, and Regent Street; but I remember only an ancient brick gateway as particularly remarkable. I think it was the entrance to Lincoln's Inn. We reached home at about six.

There is a woman who has several times passed through this Hanover Street, in which we live, stopping occasionally to sing songs under the windows; and last evening, between nine and ten o'clock, she came and sang "Kathleen O'Moore" richly and sweetly. Her voice rose up out of the dim, chill street, and made our hearts throb in unison with it as we sat in our comfortable drawing-room. I never heard a voice that touched me more deeply. Somebody told her to go away, and she stopped like a nightingale suddenly shot; but, finding that S—— wished to know something about her, Fanny and one of the maids ran after her, and brought her into the hall. It seems she was educated to sing at the opera, and married an Italian opera-singer, who is now dead; lodging in a model lodging-house at threepence a night, and being a penny short to-night, she tried this method, in hope of getting this penny. She takes in plain sewing when she can get any, and picks up a trifle about the street by means of her voice, which, she says, was once sweet, but has now been injured by the poorness of her living. She is a pale woman, with black eyes, Fanny says, and may have been pretty once, but is not so now. It seems very strange, that with such a gift of Heaven, so cultivated, too, as her voice is, making even an unsusceptible heart vibrate like a harp-string, she should not have had an engagement among the hundred theatres and singing-rooms of London; that she should throw away her melody in the streets for the mere chance of a penury, when sounds not a hundredth part so sweet are worth from other lips purses of gold.

October 5th.—It rained almost all day on Wednesday, so that I did not go out till late in the afternoon, and then only took a stroll along Oxford Street and Holborn, and back through Fleet Street and the Strand. Yesterday, at a little after ten, I went to the ambassador's to get my wife's passport for Lisbon.

While I was talking with the clerk, Mr. ——— made his appearance in a dressing-gown, with a morning cheerfulness and alacrity in his manner. He was going to Liverpool with his niece, who returns to America by the steamer of Saturday. She has had a good deal of success in society here; being pretty enough to be remarked among English women, and with cool, self-possessed, frank, and quiet manners, which look very like the highest breeding.

I next went to Westminster Abbey, where I had long promised myself another quiet visit; for I think I never could be weary of it; and when I finally leave England, it will be this spot which I shall feel most unwilling to quit forever. I found a party going through the seven chapels (or whatever their number may be), and again saw those stately and quaint old tombs,—ladies and knights stretched out on marble slabs, or beneath arches and canopies of stone, let into the walls of the Abbey, reclining on their elbows, in ruff and farthingale or riveted armor, or in robes of state, once painted in rich colors, of which only a few patches of scarlet now remain; bearded faces of noble knights, whose noses, in many cases, had been smitten off; and Mary, Queen of Scots, had lost two fingers of her beautiful hands, which she is clasping in prayer. There must formerly have been very free access to these tombs; for I observed that all the statues (so far as I examined them) were scratched with the initials of visitors, some of the names being dated above a century ago. The old coronation-chair, too, is quite covered, over the back and seat, with initials cut into it with pocket-knives, just as Yankees would do it; only it is not whittled away, as would have been its fate in our hands. Edward the Confessor's shrine, which is chiefly of wood, likewise abounds in these inscriptions, although this was esteemed the holiest shrine in England, so that pilgrims still come to kneel and kiss it. Our guide, a rubicund verger of cheerful demeanor, said that this was true in a few instances.

There is a beautiful statue in memory of Horace Walpole's mother; and I took it to be really a likeness, till the verger said that it was a copy of a statue which her son had admired in Italy, and so had transferred it to his mother's grave. There is something characteristic in this mode of filial duty and honor. In all these chapels, full of the tombs and effigies of kings, dukes, arch-prelates, and whatever is proud and pompous in mortality, there is nothing that strikes me more than the colossal statue of plain Mr. Watt, sitting quietly in a chair, in St. Paul's Chapel, and reading some papers. He dwarfs the warriors and statesmen; and as to the kings, we smile at them. Telford is in another of the chapels. This visit to the chapels was much more satisfactory than my former one; although I in vain strove to feel it adequately, and to make myself sensible how rich and venerable was what I saw. This realization must come at its own time, like the other happinesses of life. It is unaccountable that I could not now find the seat of Sir George Downing's squire, though I examined particularly every seat on that side of Henry VII's Chapel, where I before found it. I must try again. . . .

October 6th.—Yesterday was not an eventful day. I took J—— with me to the city, called on Mr. Sturgis at the Barings' House, and got his checks for a bank post-note. The house is at 8 Bishopsgate Street, Within. It has no sign of any kind, but stands back from the street, behind an iron-grated fence. The firm appears to occupy the whole edifice, which is spacious, and fit for princely merchants. Thence I went and paid for the passages to Lisbon (32 pounds) at the Peninsular Steam Company's office, and thence to call on General ———. I forgot to mention, that, first of all, I went to Mr. B———'s, whom I found kind and vivacious as usual. It now rained heavily, and, being still showery when we came to Cheapside again, we first stood under an archway (a usual resort for passengers through London streets), and then betook ourselves to sanctuary, taking refuge in St. Paul's Cathedral. The afternoon service was about to begin, so, after looking at a few of the monuments, we sat down in the choir, the richest and most ornamented part of the cathedral, with screens or partitions of oak, cunningly carved. Small white-robed choristers were flitting noiselessly about, making preparations for the service, which by and by began. It is a beautiful idea, that, several times in the course of the day, a man can slip out of the thickest throng and bustle of London into this religious atmosphere, and hear the organ, and the music of young, pure voices; but, after all, the rites are lifeless in our day. We found, on emerging, that we had escaped a very heavy shower, and it still sprinkled and misted as we went homeward through Holborn and Oxford Street.

SOUTHAMPTON

October 11th.—We all left London on Sunday morning, between ten and eleven, from the Waterloo station, and arrived in Southampton about two, without meeting with anything very remarkable on the way. We put up at Chapple's Castle Hotel, which is one of the class styled "commercial," and, though respectable, not such a one as the nobility and gentry usually frequent. I saw little difference in the accommodation, except that young women attended us instead of men,—a pleasant change. It was a showery day, but J——- and I walked out to see the shore and the town and the docks, and, if possible, the ship in which S——- was to sail. The most noteworthy object was the remains of an old castle, near the water-side; the square, gray, weed grown, weird keep of which shows some modern chimney-pots above its battlements, while remaining portions of the fortress are made to seem as one of the walls for coal-depots, and perhaps for small dwellings. The English characteristically patch new things into old things in this manner, materially, legally, constitutionally, and morally. Walking along the pier, we observed some pieces of ordnance, one of which was a large brass cannon of Henry VIII.'s time, about twelve feet long, and very finely made. The bay of Southampton presents a pleasant prospect, and I believe it is the great rendezvous of the yacht-club. Old and young seafaring people were strolling about, and lounging at corners, just as they do on Sunday afternoons in the minor seaports of America.

From the shore we went up into the town, which is handsome, and of a cheerful aspect, with streets generally wide and well paved,—a cleanly town, not smoke-begrimed. The houses, if not modern, are, at least with few exceptions, new fronted. We saw one relic of antiquity,—a fine mediaeval gateway across the principal street, much more elevated than the gates of Chester, with battlements at the top, and a spacious apartment over the great arch for the passage of carriages, and the smaller one on each side for foot-passengers. There were two statues in armor or antique costume on the hither side of the gateway, and two old paintings on the other. This, so far as I know, is the only remnant of the old wall of Southampton.

On Monday the morning was bright, alternating with a little showeriness. U——, J——, and I went into the town to do some shopping before the steamer should sail; and a little after twelve we drove down to the dock. The Madeira is a pleasant-looking ship enough, not very large, but accommodating, I believe, about seventy passengers. We looked at my wife's little stateroom, with its three berths for herself and the two children; and then sat down in the saloon, and afterwards on deck, to spend the irksome and dreary hour or two before parting. Many of the passengers seemed to be Portuguese, undersized, dark, mustachioed people, smoking cigars. John Bull was fairly represented too. . . . U—— was cheerful, and R—— seemed anxious to get off. Poor Fanny was altogether cast down, and shed tears, either from regret at leaving her native land, or dread of sea-sickness, or general despondency, being a person of no spring of spirits. I waited till the captain came on board, —a middle-aged or rather elderly man, with a sensible expression, but, methought, with a hard, cold eye, to whom I introduced my wife, recommending her to his especial care, as she was unattended by any gentleman; and then we thought it best to cut short the parting scene. So we bade one another farewell; and, leaving them on the deck of the vessel, J—— and I returned to the hotel, and, after dining at the table d'hote, drove down to the railway. This is the first great parting that we have ever had.

It was three o'clock when we left Southampton. In order to get to Worcester, where we were to spend the night, we strode, as it were, from one line of railway to another, two or three times, and did not arrive at our journey's end till long after dark.

At Worcester we put ourselves into the hands of a cabman, who drove us to the Crown Hotel,—one of the old-fashioned hotels, with an entrance through an arched passage, by which vehicles were admitted into the inn-yard, which has also an exit, I believe, into another street. On one side of the arch was the coffee-room, where, after looking at our sleeping-chambers on the other side of the arch, we had some cold pigeon-pie for supper, and for myself a pint of ale.

It should be mentioned, that, in the morning, before embarking S—— and the children on board the steamer, I saw a fragment of a rainbow among the clouds, and remembered the old adage bidding "sailors take warning." In the afternoon, as J—— and I were railing from Southampton, we saw another fragmentary rainbow, which, by the same adage, should be the "sailor's delight." The weather has rather tended to confirm the first omen, but the sea-captains tell me that the steamer must have gone beyond the scope of these winds.

WORCESTER.

October 14th.—-In the morning of Tuesday, after breakfast in the coffee-room, J——- and I walked about to see the remarkables of Worcester. It is not a particularly interesting city, compared with other old English cities; the general material of the houses being red brick, and almost all modernized externally, whatever may be the age of their original framework. We saw a large brick jail in castellated style, with battlements,—a very barren and dreary-looking edifice; likewise, in the more central part of the town, a Guildhall with a handsome front, ornamented with a statue of Queen Anne above the entrance, and statues of Charles I. and Charles II. on either side of the door, with the motto, "Floreat semper civitas fidelis." Worcester seems to pride itself upon its loyalty. We entered the building, and in the large interior hall saw some old armor hanging on the wall at one end,— corselets, helmets, greaves, and a pair of breeches of chain mail. An inscription told us that these suits of armor had been left by Charles I. after the battle of Worcester, and presented to the city at a much later date by a gentleman of the neighborhood. On the stone floor of the hall, under the armor, were two brass cannon, one of which had been taken from the French in a naval battle within the present century; the other was a beautiful piece, bearing, I think, the date of 1632, and manufactured in Brussels for the Count de Burgh, as a Latin inscription testified. This likewise was a relic of the battle of Worcester, where it had been lost by Charles. Many gentlemen—connected with the city government, I suppose—were passing through the hall; and, looking through its interior doors, we saw stately staircases and council-rooms panelled with oak or other dark wood. There seems to be a good deal of state in the government of these old towns.

Worcester Cathedral would have impressed me much had I seen it earlier; though its aspect is less venerable than that of Chester or Lichfield, having been faithfully renewed and repaired, and stone-cutters and masons were even now at work on the exterior. At our first visit, we found no entrance; but coming again at ten o'clock, when the service was to begin, we found the door open, and the chorister-boys, in their white robes, standing in the nave and aisles, with elder people in the same garb, and a few black-robed ecclesiastics and an old verger. The interior of the cathedral has been covered with a light-colored paint at some recent period. There is, as I remember, very little stained glass to enrich and bedim the light; and the effect produced is a naked, daylight aspect, unlike what I have seen in any other Gothic cathedral. The plan of the edifice, too, is simple; a nave and side aisles, with great clustered pillars, from which spring the intersecting arches; and, somehow or other, the venerable mystery which I have found in Westminster Abbey and elsewhere does not lurk in these arches and behind these pillars. The choir, no doubt, is richer and more beautiful; but we did not enter it. I remember two tombs, with recumbent figures on there, between the pillars that divide the nave from the side aisles, and there were also mural monuments,—one, well executed, to an officer slain in the Peninsular war, representing him falling from his horse; another by a young widow to her husband, with an inscription of passionate grief, and a record of her purpose finally to sleep beside him. He died in 1803. I did not see on the monument any record of the consummation of her purpose; and so perhaps she sleeps beside a second husband. There are more antique memorials than these two on the wall, and I should have been interested to examine them; but the service was now about to begin in the choir, and at the far-off end of the nave the old verger waved his hand to banish us from the cathedral. At the same time he moved towards us, probably to say that he would show it to us after service; but having little time, and being so moderately impressed with what I had already seen, I took my departure, and so disappointed the old man of his expected shilling or half-crown. The tomb of King John is somewhere in this cathedral.

We renewed our rambles through the town, and, passing the Museum of the Worcester Natural History Society, I yielded to J———'s wish to go in. There are three days in the week, I believe, on which it is open to the public; but this being one of the close days, we were admitted on payment of a shilling. It seemed a very good and well-arranged collection in most departments of Natural History, and J———, who takes more interest in these matters than I do, was much delighted. We were left to examine the hall and galleries quite at our leisure. Besides the specimens of beasts, birds, shells, fishes, minerals, fossils, insects, and all other natural things before the flood and since, there was a stone bearing a Roman inscription, and various antiquities, coins, and medals, and likewise portraits, some of which were old and curious.

Leaving the museum, we walked down to the stone bridge over the Severn, which is here the largest river I have seen in England, except, of course, the Mersey and the Thames. A flight of steps leads from the bridge down to a walk along the river-side, and this we followed till we reached the spot where an angler was catching chubs and dace, under the walls of the bishop's palace, which here faces the river. It seems to be an old building, but with modern repairs and improvements. The angler had pretty good success while we were looking at him, drawing out two or three silvery fish, and depositing them in his basket, which was already more than half full. The Severn is not a transparent stream, and looks sluggish, but has really movement enough to carry the angler's float along pretty fast. There were two vessels of considerable size (that is, as large as small schooners) lying at the bridge. We now passed under an old stone archway, through a lane that led us from the river-side up past the cathedral, whence a gentleman and lady were just emerging, and the verger was closing the door behind them.

We returned to our hotel, and ordered luncheon,—some cold chicken, cold ham, and ale, and after paying the bill (about fifteen shillings, to which I added five shillings for attendance) we took our departure in a fly for the railway. The waiter (a young woman), chambermaid, and boots, all favored us with the most benign and deferential looks at parting, whence it was easy to see that I had given them more than they had any claim to receive. Nevertheless, this English system of fees has its good side, and I never travel without finding the advantage of it, especially on railways, where the officials are strictly forbidden to take fees, and where, in consequence, a fee secures twice as much good service as anywhere else. Be it recorded, that I never knew an Englishman to refuse a shilling,—or, for that matter, a halfpenny.

From Worcester we took tickets to Wolverhampton, and thence to Birkenhead. It grew dark before we reached Chester, and began to rain; and when we got to Birkenhead it was a pitiless, pelting storm, under which, on the deck of the steamboat, we crossed the detestable Mersey, two years' trial of which has made me detest it every day more and more. It being the night of rejoicing for the taking of Sebastopol and the visit of the Duke of Cambridge, we found it very difficult to get a cab on the Liverpool side; but after much waiting in the rain, and afterwards in one of the refreshment-rooms, on the landing stage, we took a Hansom and drove off. The cloudy sky reflected the illuminations, and we saw some gas-lighted stars and other devices, as we passed, very pretty, but much marred by the wind and rain. So we finally arrived at Mrs. Blodgett's, and made a good supper of ham and cold chicken, like our luncheon, after which, wet as we were, and drizzling as the weather was, and though it was two hours beyond his bedtime, I took J——- out to see the illuminations. I wonder what his mother would have said. But the boy must now begin to see life and to feel it.

There was a crowd of people in the street; such a crowd that we could hardly make a passage through them, and so many cabs and omnibuses that it was difficult to cross the ways. Some of the illuminations were very brilliant; but there was a woful lack of variety and invention in the devices. The star of the garter, which kept flashing out from the continual extinguishment of the wind and rain,—V and A, in capital letters of light,—were repeated a hundred times; as were loyal and patriotic mottoes,—crowns formed by colored lamps. In some instances a sensible tradesman had illuminated his own sign, thereby at once advertising his loyalty and his business. Innumerable flags were suspended before the houses and across the streets, and the crowd plodded on, silent, heavy, and without any demonstration of joy, unless by the discharge of pistols close at one's ear. The rain, to be sure, was quite sufficient to damp any joyous ebullition of feeling; but the next day, when the rain had ceased, and when the streets were still thronged with people, there was the same heavy, purposeless strolling from place to place, with no more alacrity of spirit than while it rained. The English do not know how to rejoice; and, in their present circumstances, to say the truth, have not much to rejoice for. We soon came home; but I believe it was nearly, if not quite, eleven.

At Mrs. Blodgett's, Mr. Archer (surgeon to some prison or house of correction here in Liverpool) spoke of an attorney who many years ago committed forgery, and, being apprehended, took a dose of prussic acid.

Mr. Archer came with the stomach-pump, and asked the patient how much prussic acid he had taken. "Sir," he replied, attorney-like, "I decline answering that question!" He recovered, and afterwards arrived at great wealth in New South Wales.

November 14th.—At dinner at Mr. Bright's, a week or two ago, Mr. Robertson Gladstone spoke of a magistrate of Liverpool, many years since, Sir John ———. Of a morning, sitting on the bench in the police court, he would take five shillings out of his pocket and say, "Here, Mr. Clerk, so much for my fine. I was drunk last night!" Mr. Gladstone witnessed this personally.

November 16th.—I went to the North Hospital yesterday, to take the deposition of a dying man as to his ill treatment by the second and third mates of the ship Assyria, on the voyage from New Orleans. This hospital is a very gloomy place, with its wide bleak entries and staircases, which may be very good for summer weather, but which are most congenial at this bleak November season. I found the physicians of the house laughing and talking very cheerfully with Mr. Wilding, who had preceded me. We went forthwith, up two or three pairs of stairs, to the ward where the sick man lay, and where there were six or eight other beds, in almost each of which was a patient,—narrow beds, shabbily furnished. The man whom I came to see was the only one who was not perfectly quiet; neither was he very restless. The doctor, informing him of my presence, intimated that his disease might be lethal, and that I was come to hear what he had to say as to the causes of his death. Afterwards, a Testament was sought for, in order to swear him, and I administered the oath, and made him kiss the book. He then (in response to Mr. Wilding's questions) told how he had been beaten and ill-treated, hanged and thwacked, from the moment he came on board, to which usage he ascribed his death. Sometimes his senses seemed to sink away, so that I almost thought him dead; but by and by the questions would appear to reach him, and bring him back, and he went on with his evidence, interspersing it, however, with dying groans, and almost death rattles. In the midst of whatever he was saying, he often recurred to a sum of four dollars and a half, which he said he had put into the hands of the porter of the hospital, and which he wanted to get back. Several times he expressed his wish to return to America (of which he was not a native), and, on the whole, I do not think he had any real sense of his precarious condition, notwithstanding that he assented to the doctor's hint to that effect. He sank away so much at one time, that they brought him wine in a tin cup, with a spout to drink out of, and he mustered strength to raise himself in his bed and drink; then hemmed, with rather a disappointed air, as if it did not stimulate and refresh him, as drink ought to do. When he had finished his evidence (which Mr. Wilding took down in writing from his mouth), he marked his cross at the foot of the paper, and we ceased to torment him with further question. His deposition will probably do no good, so far as the punishment of the persons implicated is concerned; for he appears to have come on board in a sickly state, and never to have been well during the passage. On a pallet, close by his bed, lay another seaman of the same ship, who had likewise been abused by the same men, and bore more ostensible marks of ill usage than this man did, about the head and face. There is a most dreadful state of things aboard our ships. Hell itself can be no worse than some of them, and I do pray that some New-Englander with the rage of reform in him may turn his thoughts this way. The first step towards better things—the best practicable step for the present—is to legalize flogging on shipboard; thereby doing away with the miscellaneous assaults and batteries, kickings, fisticuffings, ropes'-endings, marline-spikings, which the inferior officers continually perpetrate, as the only mode of keeping up anything like discipline. As in many other instances, philanthropy has overshot itself by the prohibition of flogging, causing the captain to avoid the responsibility of solemn punishment, and leave his mates to make devils of themselves, by habitual and hardly avoidable ill treatment of the seamen.

After I left the dying sailor, his features seemed to contract and grow sharp. Some young medical students stood about the bed, watching death creep upon him, and anticipating, perhaps, that in a day or two they would have the poor fellow's body on the dissecting-table. Dead patients, I believe, undergo this fate, unless somebody chooses to pay their funeral expenses; but the captain of the Assyria (who seems to be respectable and kind-hearted, though master of a floating hell) tells me that he means to bury the man at his own cost. This morning there is a note from the surgeon of the hospital, announcing his death, and likewise the dangerous state of his shipmate whom I saw on the pallet beside him.

Sea-captains call a dress-coat a "claw-hammer."

November 22d.—I went on board the ship William Lapscott, lying in the river, yesterday, to take depositions in reference to a homicide committed in New York. I sat on a sofa in the cabin, and Mr. Wilding at a table, with his writing-materials before him, and the crew were summoned, one by one,—rough, piratical-looking fellows, contrasting strongly with the gewgaw cabin in which I received them. There is no such finery on land as in the cabin of one of these ships in the Liverpool trade, finished off with a complete panelling of rosewood, mahogany, and bird's-eye maple, polished and varnished, and gilded along the cornices and the edges of the panels. It is all a piece of elaborate cabinet-work; and one does not altogether see why it should be given to the gales, and the salt-sea atmosphere, to be tossed upon the waves, and occupied by a rude shipmaster in his dreadnaught clothes, when the fairest lady in the land has no such boudoir. A telltale compass hung beneath the skylight, and a clock was fastened near it, and ticked loudly. A stewardess, with the aspect of a woman at home, went in and out of the cabin, about her domestic calls. Through the cabin door (it being a house on deck) I could see the arrangement of the ship.

The first sailor that I examined was a black-haired, powerful fellow, in an oil-skin jacket, with a good face enough, though he, too, might have been taken for a pirate. In the affray in which the homicide occurred, he had received a cut across the forehead, and another slantwise across his nose, which had quite cut it in two, on a level with the face, and had thence gone downward to his lower jaw. But neither he nor any one else could give any testimony elucidating the matter into which I had come to inquire. A seaman had been stabbed just before the vessel left New York, and had been sent on shore and died there. Most of these men were in the affray, and all of then were within a few yards of the spot where it occurred; but those actually present all pleaded that they were so drunk that the whole thing was now like a dream, with no distinct images; and, if any had been sober, they took care to know nothing that could inculpate any individual. Perhaps they spoke truth; they certainly had a free and honest-like way of giving their evidence, as if their only object was to tell all the truth they knew. But I rather think, in the forecastle, and during the night-watches, they have whispered to one another a great deal more than they told me, and have come to a pretty accurate conclusion as to the man who gave the stab.

While the examination proceeded, there was a drawing of corks in a side closet; and, at its conclusion, the captain asked us to stay to dinner, but we excused ourselves, and drank only a glass of wine. The captain apologized for not joining us, inasmuch as he had drunk no wine for the last seventeen years. He appears to be a particularly good and trustworthy man, and is the only shipmaster whom I have met with, who says that a crew can best be governed by kindness. In the inner closet there was a cage containing two land-birds, who had come aboard him, tired almost to death, three or four hundred miles from shore; and he had fed them and been tender of them, from a sense of what was due to hospitality. He means to give them to J———.

November 28th.—I have grown wofully aristocratic in my tastes, I fear, since coming to England; at all events, I am conscious of a certain disgust at going to dine in a house with a small entrance-hall and a narrow staircase, parlor with chintz curtains, and all other arrangements on a similar scale. This is pitiable. However, I really do not think I should mind these things, were it not for the bustle, the affectation, the intensity, of the mistress of the house. It is certain that a woman in England is either decidedly a lady or decidedly not a lady. There seems to be no respectable medium. Bill of fare: broiled soles, half of a roast pig, a haricot of mutton, stewed oysters, a tart, pears, figs, with sherry and port wine, both good, and the port particularly so. I ate some pig, and could hardly resist the lady's importunities to eat more; though to my fancy it tasted of swill,—had a flavor of the pigsty. On the parlor table were some poor editions of popular books, Longfellow's poems and others. The lady affects a literary taste, and bothered me about my own productions.

A beautiful subject for a romance, or for a sermon, would be the subsequent life of the young man whom Jesus bade to sell all he had and give to the poor; and he went away sorrowful, and is not recorded to have done what he was bid.

December 11th.—This has been a foggy morning and forenoon, snowing a little now and then, and disagreeably cold. The sky is of an inexpressibly dreary, dun color. It is so dark at times that I have to hold my book close to my eyes, and then again it lightens up a little. On the whole, disgustingly gloomy; and thus it has been for a long while past, although the disagreeableness seems to be very near the earth, and just above the steeples and house-tops very probably there may be a bright, sunshiny day. At about twelve there is a faint glow of sunlight, like the gleaming reflection from a not highly polished copper kettle.

December 26th.—On Christmas eve and yesterday, there were little branches of mistletoe hanging in several parts of the house, in the kitchen, the entries, the parlor, and the smoking-room,—suspended from the gas-fittings. The maids of the house did their utmost to entrap the gentlemen boarders, old and young; under the privileged places, and there to kiss them, after which they were expected to pay a shilling. It is very queer, being customarily so respectful, that they should assume this license now, absolutely trying to pull the gentlemen into the kitchen by main force, and kissing the harder and more abundantly the more they were resisted. A little rosy-checked Scotch lass—at other times very modest —was the most active in this business. I doubt whether any gentleman but myself escaped. I heard old Mr. S——— parleying with the maids last evening, and pleading his age; but he seems to have met with no mercy, for there was a sound of prodigious smacking immediately afterwards. J——- was assaulted, and fought, most vigorously; but was outrageously kissed,—receiving some scratches, moreover, in the conflict. The mistletoe has white, wax-looking berries, and dull green leaves, with a parasitical stem.

Early in the morning of Christmas day, long before daylight, I heard music in the street, and a woman's voice, powerful and melodious, singing a Christmas hymn. Before bedtime I presume one half of England, at a moderate calculation, was the worse for liquor.

The market-houses, at this season, show the national taste for heavy feeding,—carcasses of prize oxen, immensely fat, and bulky; fat sheep, with their woolly heads and tails still on, and stars and other devices ingeniously wrought on the quarters; fat pigs, adorned with flowers, like corpses of virgins; hares, wild-fowl, geese, ducks, turkeys; and green boughs and banners suspended about the stalls,—and a great deal of dirt and griminess on the stone floor of the market-house, and on the persons of the crowd.

There are some Englishmen whom I like,—one or two for whom I might say I have an affection; but still there is not the same union between us as if they were Americans. A cold, thin medium intervenes betwixt our most intimate approaches. It puts me in mind of Alnaschar and his princess, with the cold steel blade of his scimitar between them. Perhaps if I were at home I might feel differently; but in a foreign land I can never forget the distinction between English and American.

January 1st, 1856.—Last night, at Mrs. Blodgett's, we sat up till twelve o'clock to open the front door, and let the New Year in. After the coming guest was fairly in the house, the back door was to be opened, to let the Old Year out; but I was tired, and did not wait for the latter ceremony. When the New Year made its entrance, there was a general shaking of hands, and one of the shipmasters said that it was customary to kiss the ladies all round; but to my great satisfaction, we did not proceed to such extremity. There was singing in the streets, and many voices of people passing, and when twelve had struck, all the bells of the town, I believe, rang out together. I went up stairs, sad and lonely, and, stepping into J———'s little room, wished him a Happy New Year, as he slept, and many of them.

To a cool observer, a country does not show to best advantage during a time of war. All its self-conceit is doubly visible, and, indeed, is sedulously kept uppermost by direct appeals to it. The country must be humbugged, in order to keep its courage up.

Sentiment seems to me more abundant in middle-aged ladies in England than in the United States. I don't know how it may be with young ladies.

The shipmasters bear testimony to the singular delicacy of common sailors in their behavior in the presence of women; and they say that this good trait is still strongly observable even in the present race of seamen, greatly deteriorated as it is. On shipboard, there is never an indecorous word or unseemly act said or done by sailors when a woman can be cognizant of it; and their deportment in this respect differs greatly from that of landsmen of similar position in society. This is remarkable, considering that a sailor's female acquaintances are usually and exclusively of the worst kind, and that his intercourse with them has no relation whatever to morality or decency. For this very reason, I suppose, he regards a modest woman as a creature divine and to be reverenced.

January 16th.—-I have suffered wofully from low spirits for some time past; and this has not often been the case since I grew to be a man, even in the least auspicious periods of my life. My desolate bachelor condition, I suppose, is the cause. Really, I have no pleasure in anything, and I feel my tread to be heavier, and my physical movement more sluggish, than in happier times. A weight is always upon me. My appetite is not good. I sleep ill, lying awake till late at night, to think sad thoughts and to imagine sombre things, and awaking before light with the same thoughts and fancies still in my mind. My heart sinks always as I ascend the stairs to my office, from a dim augury of ill news from Lisbon that I may perhaps hear,—of black-sealed letters, or some such horrors. Nothing gives me any joy. I have learned what the bitterness of exile is, in these days; and I never should have known it but for the absence of "Remote, unfriended, melancholy, slow,"—I can perfectly appreciate that line of Goldsmith; for it well expresses my own torpid, unenterprising, joyless state of mind and heart. I am like an uprooted plant, wilted and drooping. Life seems so purposeless as not to be worth the trouble of carrying it on any further.

I was at a dinner, the other evening, at Mr. B———'s, where the entertainment was almost entirely American,—New York oysters, raw, stewed, and fried; soup of American partridges, particularly good; also terrapin soup, rich, but not to my taste; American pork and beans, baked in Yankee style; a noble American turkey, weighing thirty-one pounds; and, at the other end of the table, an American round of beef, which the Englishmen present allowed to be delicious, and worth a guinea an ounce. I forget the other American dishes, if there were any more,—O yes! canvas-back ducks, coming on with the sweets, in the usual English fashion. We ought to have had Catawba wine;

but this was wanting, although there was plenty of hock, champagne, sherry, madeira, port, and claret. Our host is a very jolly man, and the dinner was a merrier and noisier one than any English dinner within my experience.

February 8th.—I read to-day, in the little office-Bible (greasy with perjuries) St. Luke's account of the agony, the trial, the crucifixion, and the resurrection; and how Christ appeared to the two disciples, on their way to Emmaus, and afterwards to a company of disciples. On both these latter occasions he expounded the Scriptures to them, and showed the application of the old prophecies to himself; and it is to be supposed that he made them fully, or at least sufficiently, aware what his character was,—whether God, or man, or both, or something between, together with all other essential points of doctrine. But none of this doctrine or of these expositions is recorded, the mere facts being most simply stated, and the conclusion to which he led them, that, whether God himself, or the Son of God, or merely the Son of man, he was, at all events, the Christ foretold in the Jewish Scriptures. This last, therefore, must have been the one essential point.

February 18th.—On Saturday there called on me an elderly Robinson-Crusoe sort of man, Mr. H———, shipwright, I believe, of Boston, who has lately been travelling in the East. About a year ago he was here, after being shipwrecked on the Dutch coast, and I assisted him to get home. Again, I have supplied him with five pounds, and my credit for an outside garment. He is a spare man, with closely cropped gray, or rather white hair, close-cropped whiskers fringing round his chin, and a close-cropped white mustache, with his under lip and a portion of his chin bare beneath,—sunburnt and weather-worn. He has been in Syria and Jerusalem, through the Desert, and at Sebastopol; and says he means to get Ticknor to publish his travels, and the story of his whole adventurous life, on his return home. A free-spoken, confiding, hardy, religious, unpolished, simple, yet world-experienced man; very talkative, and boring me with longer visits than I like. He has brought home, among other curiosities, "a lady's arm," as he calls it, two thousand years old,—a piece of a mummy, of course; also some coins, one of which, a gold coin of Vespasian, he showed me, and said he bought it of an Arab of the desert. The Bedouins possess a good many of these coins, handed down immemorially from father to son, and never sell them unless compelled by want. He had likewise a Hebrew manuscript of the Book of Ruth, on a parchment roll, which was put into his care to be given to Lord Haddo.

He was at Sebastopol during the siege, and nearly got his head knocked off by a cannon-ball. His strangest statement is one in reference to Lord Raglan. He says that an English officer told him that his Lordship shut himself up, desiring not to be disturbed, as he needed sleep. When fifteen hours had gone by, his attendants thought it time to break open the door; and Lord Raglan was found dead, with a bottle of strychnine by the bedside. The affair, so far as the circumstances indicated suicide, was hushed up, and his death represented as a natural one. The English officer seems to have been an unscrupulous fellow, jesting thus with the fresh memory of his dead commander; for it is impossible to believe a word of the story. Even if Lord Raglan had wished for death, he would hardly have taken strychnine, when there were so many chances of being honorably shot. In Wood's Narrative of the Campaign, it is stated that he died surrounded by the members of his staff, after having been for some time ill. It appears, however, by the same statement, that no serious apprehensions had been entertained, until, one afternoon, he shut himself in, desiring not to be disturbed till evening. After two or three hours he called Lord Burghersh,—"Frank, Frank!" and was found to be almost in a state of collapse, and died that evening. Mr. H———'s story might very well have been a camp rumor.

It seems to me that the British Ministry, in its notion of a life-peerage, shows an entire misunderstanding of what makes people desire the peerage. It is not for the immediate personal distinction; but because it removes the peer and his consanguinity from the common rank of men, and makes a separate order of them, as if they should grow angelic. A life-peer is but a mortal amid the angelic throng.

February 28th.—I went yesterday with Mrs. ——— and another lady, and Mr. M———, to the West Derby Workhouse. . . .

[Here comes in the visit to the West Derby Workhouse, which was made the subject of a paper in Our Old Home, called "Outside Glimpses of English

Poverty." As the purpose in publishing these passages from the private notebooks is to give to those who ask for a memoir of Mr. Hawthorne every possible incident recorded by himself which shows his character and nature, the editor thinks it proper to disclose the fact that Mr. Hawthorne was himself the gentleman of that party who took up in his arms the little child, so fearfully repulsive in its condition. And it seems better to quote his own words in reference to it, than merely to say it was he.

Under date February 28, 1856.

"After this, we went to the ward where the children were kept, and, on entering this, we saw, in the first place, two or three unlovely and unwholesome little imps, who were lazily playing together. One of them (a child about six years old, but I know not whether girl or boy) immediately took the strangest fancy for me. It was a wretched, pale, half-torpid little thing, with a humor in its eyes which the Governor said was the scurvy. I never saw, till a few moments afterwards, a child that I should feel less inclined to fondle.

"But this little, sickly, humor-eaten fright prowled around me, taking hold of my skirts, following at my heels, and at last held up its hands, smiled in my face, and, standing directly before me, insisted on my taking it up! Not that it said a word, for I rather think it was underwitted, and could not talk; but its face expressed such perfect confidence that it was going to be taken up and made much of, that it was impossible not to do it. It was as if God had promised the child this favor on my behalf, and that I must needs fulfil the contract. I held my undesirable burden a little while; and, after setting the child down, it still followed me, holding two of my fingers and playing with them, just as if it were a child of my own. It was a foundling, and out of all human kind it chose me to be its father! We went up stairs into another ward; and, on coming down again, there was this same child waiting for me, with a sickly smile round its defaced mouth, and in its dim red eyes. . . . I never should have forgiven myself if I had repelled its advances."—ED.]

After leaving the workhouse, we drove to Norris Green; and Mrs. ——— showed me round the grounds, which are very good and nicely kept. O these English homes, what delightful places they are! I wonder how many people live and die in the workhouse, having no other home, because other people have a great deal more home than enough. . . . We had a very pleasant dinner, and Mr. M——— and I walked back, four miles and a half, to Liverpool, where we arrived just before midnight.

Why did Christ curse the fig-tree? It was not in the least to blame; and it seems most unreasonable to have expected it to bear figs out of season. Instead of withering it away, it would have been as great a miracle, and far more beautiful, and, one would think, of more beneficent influence, to have made it suddenly rich with ripe fruit. Then, to be sure, it might have died joyfully, having answered so good a purpose. I have been reminded of this miracle by the story of a man in Heywood, a town in Lancashire, who used such horribly profane language that a plane-tree in front of his cottage is said to have withered away from that hour. I can draw no moral from the incident of the fig-tree, unless it be that all things perish from the instant when they cease to answer some divine purpose.

March 6th.—Yesterday I lunched on board Captain Russell's ship, the Princeton. These daily lunches on shipboard might answer very well the purposes of a dinner; being, in fact, noontide dinners, with soup, roast mutton, mutton-chops, and a macaroni pudding,—brandy, port and sherry wines. There were three elderly Englishmen at table, with white heads, which, I think, is oftener the predicament of elderly heads here than in America. One of these was a retired Custom-House officer, and the other two were connected with shipping in some way. There is a satisfaction in seeing Englishmen eat and drink, they do it so heartily, and, on the whole, so wisely,—trusting so entirely that there is no harm in good beef and mutton, and a reasonable quantity of good liquor; and these three hale old men, who had acted on this wholesome faith for so long, were proofs that it is well on earth to live like earthly creatures. In America, what squeamishness, what delicacy, what stomachic apprehension, would there not be among three stomachs of sixty or seventy years' experience! I think this failure of American stomachs is partly owing to our ill usage of our digestive powers, and partly to our want of faith in them.

After lunch, we all got into an omnibus, and went to the Mersey Iron Foundry, to see the biggest piece of ordnance in the world, which is almost finished. The overseer of the works received us, and escorted us courteously throughout the establishment; which is very extensive, giving employment to a thousand men, what with night-work and day-work. The big gun is still on the axle, or turning-machine, by means of which it has been bored. It is made entirely of wrought and welded iron, fifty tons of which were originally used; and the gun, in its present state, bored out and smoothed away, weighs nearly twenty-three tons. It has, as yet, no trunnions, and does not look much like a cannon, but only a huge iron cylinder, immensely solid, and with a bore so large that a young man of nineteen shoved himself into it, the whole length, with a light, in order to see whether it is duly smooth and regular. I suppose it will have a better effect, as to the impression of size, when it is finished, polished, mounted, aid fully equipped, after the fashion of ordinary cannon. It is to throw a ball of three hundred pounds' weight five miles, and woe be to whatever ship or battlement shall bear the brunt!

After inspecting the gun we went through other portions of the establishment, and saw iron in various stages of manufacture. I am not usually interested in manufacturing processes, being quite unable to understand them, at least in cotton-machinery and the like; but here there were such exhibitions of mighty strength, both of men and machines, that I had a satisfaction in looking on. We saw lumps of iron, intensely white-hot, and in all but a melting state, passed through rollers of various size and pressure, and speedily converted into long bars, which came curling and waving out of the rollers like great red ribbons, or like fiery serpents wriggling out of Tophet; and finally, being straightened out, they were laid to cool in heaps. Trip-hammers are very pleasant things to look at, working so massively as they do, and yet so accurately; chewing up the hot iron, as it were, and fashioning it into shape, with a sort of mighty and gigantic gentleness in their mode of action. What great things man has contrived, and is continually performing! What a noble brute he is!

Also, I found much delight in looking at the molten iron, boiling and bubbling in the furnace, and sometimes slopping over, when stirred by the attendant. There were numberless fires on all sides, blinding us with their intense glow; and continually the pounding strokes of huge hammers, some wielded by machinery and others by human arms. I had a respect for these stalwart workmen, who seemed to be near kindred of the machines amid which they wrought,—mighty men, smiting stoutly, and looking into the fierce eyes of the furnace fearlessly, and handling the iron at a temperature which would have taken the skin off from ordinary fingers. They looked strong, indeed, but pale; for the hot atmosphere in which they live cannot but be deleterious, and I suppose their very strength wears them quickly out. But I would rather live ten years as an iron-smith than fifty as a tailor.

So much heat can be concentrated into a mass of iron, that a lump a foot square heats all the atmosphere about it, and burns the face at a considerable distance. As the trip-hammer strikes the lump, it seems still more to intensify the heat by squeezing it together, and the fluid iron oozes out like sap or juice.

"He was ready for the newest fashions!"—this expression was used by Mrs. Blodgett in reference to Mr. ——— on his first arrival in England, and it is a very tender way of signifying that a person is rather poorly off as to apparel.

March 15th.—Mr. ———, our new ambassador, arrived on Thursday afternoon by the Atlantic, and I called at the Adelphi Hotel, after dinner, to pay him my respects. I found him and his family at supper. . . . They seem to be plain, affable people. . . . The ambassador is a venerable old gentleman, with a full head of perfectly white hair, looking not unlike an old-fashioned wig; and this, together with his collarless white neckcloth and his brown coat, gave him precisely such an aspect as one would expect in a respectable person of pre-revolutionary days. There was a formal simplicity, too, in his manners, that might have belonged to the same era. He must have been a very handsome man in his youthful days, and is now comely, very erect, moderately tall, not overburdened with flesh; of benign and agreeable address, with a pleasant smile; but his eyes, which are not very large, impressed me as sharp and cold. He did not at all stamp himself upon me as a man of much intellectual or characteristic vigor. I found no such matter in his conversation, nor did I feel it in the indefinable way by which strength always makes itself acknowledged.

B———, though, somehow, plain and uncouth, yet vindicates himself as a large man of the world, able, experienced, fit to handle difficult circumstances of life; dignified, too, and able to hold his own in any society. Mr. ——— has a kind of venerable dignity; but yet, if a person could so little respect himself as to insult him, I should say that there was no innate force in Mr. ——— to prevent it. It is very strange that he should have made so considerable a figure in public life, filling offices that the strongest men would have thought worthy of their highest ambition. There must be something shrewd and sly under his apparent simplicity; narrow, cold, selfish, perhaps. I fancied these things in his eyes. He has risen in life by the lack of too powerful qualities, and by a certain tact, which enables him to take advantage of circumstances and opportunities, and avail himself of his unobjectionableness, just at the proper time. I suppose he must be pronounced a humbug, yet almost or quite an innocent one. Yet he is a queer representative to be sent from brawling and boisterous America at such a critical period. It will be funny if England sends him back again, on hearing the news of———'s dismissal. Mr. ——— gives me the impression of being a very amiable man in his own family. He has brought his son with him, as Secretary of Legation,—a small young man, with a little mustache. It will be a feeble embassy.

I called again the next morning, and introduced Mrs. ———, who, I believe, accompanied the ladies about town. This simplicity in Mr. ———'s manner puzzles and teases me; for, in spite of it, there was a sort of self-consciousness, as if he were being looked at,—as if he were having his portrait taken.

LONDON.

March 22d.—Yesterday,—no, day before yesterday,—I left Liverpool for London by rail, from the Lime Street station. The journey was a dull and monotonous one, as usual. Three passengers were in the same carriage with me at starting; but they dropped off; and from Rugby I was alone. We reached London after ten o'clock; and I took a cab for St. James's Place, No. 32, where I found Mr. B——— expecting me. He had secured a bedroom for me at this lodging-house, and I am to be free of his drawing-room during my stay. We breakfasted at nine, and then walked down to his counting-room, in Old Broad Street, in the city. It being a dim, dingy morning, London looked very dull, the more so as it was Good Friday, and therefore the streets were comparatively thin of people and vehicles, and had on their Sunday aspect. If it were not for the human life and bustle of London, it would be a very stupid place, with a heavy and dreary-monotony of unpicturesque streets. We went up Bolt Court, where Dr. Johnson used to live; and this was the only interesting site we saw. After spending some time in the counting-room, while Mr. ——— read his letters, we went to London Bridge, and took the steamer for Waterloo Bridge, with partly an intent to go to Richmond, but the day was so damp and dusky that we concluded otherwise. So we came home, visiting, on our way, the site of Covent Garden Theatre, lately burnt down. The exterior walls still remain perfect, and look quite solid enough to admit of the interior being renewed, but I believe it is determined to take them down.

After a slight lunch and a glass of wine, we walked out, along Piccadilly, and to Hyde Park, which already looks very green, and where there were a good many people walking and driving, and rosy-faced children at play. Somehow or other the shine and charm are gone from London, since my last visit; and I did not very much admire, nor feel much interested in anything. We returned (and I, for my part, was much wearied) in time for dinner at five. The evening was spent at home in various talk, and I find Mr. ——— a very agreeable companion, and a young man of thought and information, with a self-respecting character, and I think him a safe person to live with.

This St. James's Place is in close vicinity to St. James's Palace, the gateway and not very splendid front of which we can see from the corner. The club-houses and the best life of the town are near at hand. Addison, before his marriage, used to live in St. James's Place, and the house where Mr. Rogers recently died is up the court, not that this latter residence excites much interest in my mind. I remember nothing else very noteworthy in this first day's experience, except that on Sir Watkins Williams Wynn's door, not far from this house, I saw a gold knocker, which is said to be unscrewed every night lest it should be stolen. I don't know whether it be really gold; for it did not look so bright as the generality of brass ones. I received a very good letter from J—— this morning. He was to go to Mr. Bright's at Sandhays yesterday, and remain till Monday.

After writing the above, I walked along the Strand, Fleet Street, Ludgate Hill and Cheapside to Wood Street,—a very narrow street, insomuch that one has to press close against the wall to escape being grazed when a cart is passing. At No. 77 I found the place of business of Mr. Bennoch, who came to see me at Rock Ferry with Mr. Jerdan, not long after my arrival in England. I found him in his office; but he did not at first recognize me, so much stouter have I grown during my residence in England,—a new man, as he says. Mr. Bennoch is a kindly, frank, very good man, and was bounteous in his plans for making my time pass pleasantly. We talked of———, from whom he has just received a letter, and who says he will fight for England in case of a war. I let Bennoch know that I, at least, should take the other side.

After arranging to go to Greenwich Fair, and afterwards to dine with Bennoch, I left him and went to Mr. ———'s office, and afterwards strayed forth again, and crossed London Bridge. Thence I rambled rather drearily along through several shabby and uninteresting streets on the other side of the Thames; and the dull streets in London are really the dullest and most disheartening in the world. By and by I found my way to Southwark Bridge, and so crossed to Upper Thames Street, which was likewise very stupid, though I believe Clenman's paternal house in "Little Dorrit" stands thereabouts. . . . Next, I got into Ludgate Hill, near St. Paul's, and being quite foot-weary, I took a Paddington omnibus, and rode up into Regent Street, whence I came home.

March 24th.—Yesterday being a clear day for England, we determined upon an expedition to Hampton Court; so walked out betimes towards the Waterloo station; but first crossed the Thames by Westminster Bridge, and went to Lambeth Palace. It stands immediately on the bank of the river, not far above the bridge. We merely walked round it, and saw only an old stone tower or two, partially renewed with brick, and a high connecting wall, within which appeared gables and other portions of the palace, all of an ancient plan and venerable aspect, though evidently much patched up and restored in the course of the many ages since its foundation. There is likewise a church, part of which looks old, connected with the palace. The streets surrounding it have many gabled houses, and a general look of antiquity, more than some other parts of London.

We then walked to the Waterloo station, on the same side of the river; and at twenty minutes past one took the rail for Hampton Court, distant some twelve or fifteen miles. On arriving at the terminus, we beheld Hampton Palace, on the other side of the Thames,—an extensive structure, with a front of red brick, long and comparatively low, with the great Hall which Wolsey built rising high above the rest. We crossed the river (which is here but a narrow stream) by a stone bridge. The entrance to the palace is about half a quarter of a mile from the railway, through arched gates, which give a long perspective into the several quadrangles. These quadrangles, one beyond another, are paved with stone, and surrounded by the brick walls of the palace, the many windows of which look in upon them. Soldiers were standing sentinel at the exterior gateways, and at the various doors of the palace; but they admitted everybody without question and without fee. Policemen, or other attendants, were in most of the rooms, but interfered with no one; so that, in this respect, it was one of the pleasantest places to visit that I have found in England. A good many people, of all classes, were strolling through the apartments.

We first went into Wolsey's great Hall, up a most spacious staircase, the walls and ceiling of which were covered with an allegorical fresco by Verrio, wonderfully bright and well preserved; and without caring about the design or execution, I greatly liked the brilliancy of the colors. The great Hall is a most noble and beautiful room, above a hundred feet long and sixty high and broad. Most of the windows are of stained or painted glass, with elaborate designs, whether modern or ancient I know not, but certainly brilliant in effect. The walls, from the floor to perhaps half their height, are covered with antique tapestry, which, though a good deal faded, still retains color enough to be a very effective adornment, and to give an idea of how rich a mode of decking a noble apartment this must have been. The subjects represented were from Scripture, and the figures seemed colossal. On looking closely at this tapestry, you could see that it was thickly interwoven with threads of gold, still glistening. The windows, except one or two that are long, do not descend below the top of this tapestry, and are therefore twenty or thirty feet above the floor; and this manner of lighting a great room seems to add much to the impressiveness of the enclosed space. The roof is very magnificent, of carved oak, intricately and elaborately arched, and still as perfect to all appearance as when it was first made. There are banners, so fresh in their hues, and so untattered, that I think they must be modern, suspended along beneath the cornice of the hall, and exhibiting Wolsey's arms and badges. On the whole, this is a perfect sight, in its way.

Next to the hall there is a withdrawing-room, more than seventy feet long, and twenty-five feet high. The walls of this apartment, too, are covered with ancient tapestry, of allegorical design, but more faded than that of the hall. There is also a stained-glass window; and a marble statue of Venus on a couch, very lean and not very beautiful; and some cartoons of Carlo Cignani, which have left no impression on my memory; likewise, a large model of a splendid palace of some East Indian nabob.

I am not sure, after all, that Verrio's frescoed grand staircase was not in another part of the palace; for I remember that we went from it through an immensely long suite of apartments, beginning with the Guard-chamber. All these rooms are wainscoted with oak, which looks new, being, I believe, of the date of King William's reign. Over many of the doorways, or around the panels, there are carvings in wood by Gibbons, representing wreaths of flowers, fruit, and foliage, the most perfectly beautiful that can be conceived; and the wood being of a light hue (lime-wood, I believe), it has a fine effect on the dark oak panelling. The apartments open one beyond another, in long, long, long succession,— rooms of state, and kings' and queens' bedchambers, and royal closets bigger than ordinary drawing-rooms, so that the whole suite must be half a mile, or it may be a mile, in extent. From the windows you get views of the palace-grounds, broad and stately walks, and groves of trees, and lawns, and fountains, and the Thames and adjacent country beyond. The walls of all these rooms are absolutely covered with pictures, including works of all the great masters, which would require long study before a new eye could enjoy them; and, seeing so many of them at once, and having such a nothing of time to look at them all, I did not even try to see any merit in them. Vandyke's picture of Charles I., on a white horse beneath an arched gateway, made more impression on me than any other, and as I recall it now, it seems as if I could see the king's noble, melancholy face, and armed form, remembered not in picture, but in reality. All Sir Peter Lely's lewd women, and Kneller's too, were in these rooms; and the jolly old stupidity of George III. and his family, many times repeated; and pictures by Titian, Rubens, and other famous hands, intermixed with many by West, which provokingly drew the eye away from their betters. It seems to me that a picture, of all other things, should be by itself; whereas people always congregate them in galleries. To endeavor really to see them, so arranged, is like trying to read a hundred poems at once,—a most absurd attempt. Of all these pictures, I hardly recollect any so well as a ridiculous old travesty of the Resurrection and Last Judgment, where the dead people are represented as coming to life at the sound of the trumpet,—the flesh re-establishing itself on the bones, one man picking up his skull, and putting it on his shoulders,—and all appearing greatly startled, only half awake, and at a loss what to do next. Some devils are dragging away the damned by the heels and on sledges, and above sits the Redeemer and some angelic and sainted people, looking complacently down upon the scene!

We saw, in one of the rooms, the funeral canopy beneath which the Duke of Wellington lay in state,—very gorgeous, of black velvet embroidered with silver and adorned with escutcheons; also, the state bed of Queen Anne, broad, and of comfortable appearance, though it was a queen's,—the materials of the curtains, quilt, and furniture, red velvet, still brilliant in hue; also King

William's bed and his queen Mary's, with enormously tall posts, and a good deal the worse for time and wear.

The last apartment we entered was the gallery containing Raphael's cartoons, which I shall not pretend to admire nor to understand. I can conceive, indeed, that there is a great deal of expression in them, and very probably they may, in every respect, deserve all their fame; but on this point I can give no testimony. To my perception they were a series of very much faded pictures, dimly seen (for this part of the palace was now in shadow), and representing figures neither graceful nor beautiful, nor, as far as I could discern, particularly grand. But I came to them with a wearied mind and eye; and also I had a previous distaste to them through the medium of engravings.

But what a noble palace, nobly enriched, is this Hampton Court! The English government does well to keep it up, and to admit the people freely into it, for it is impossible for even a Republican not to feel something like awe—at least a profound respect—for all this state, and for the institutions which are here represented, the sovereigns whose moral magnificence demands such a residence; and its permanence, too, enduring from age to age, and each royal generation adding new splendors to those accumulated by their predecessors. If one views the matter in another way, to be sure, we may feel indignant that such dolt-heads, rowdies, and every way mean people, as many of the English sovereigns have been, should inhabit these stately halls, contrasting its splendors with their littleness; but, on the whole, I readily consented within myself to be impressed for a moment with the feeling that royalty has its glorious side. By no possibility can we ever have such a place in America.

Leaving Hampton Court at about four o'clock, we walked through Bushy Park,—a beautiful tract of ground, well wooded with fine old trees, green with moss, all up their twisted trunks,—through several villages, Twickenham among the rest, to Richmond. Before entering Twickenham, we passed a lath-and-plaster castellated edifice, much time-worn, and with the plaster peeling off from the laths, which I fancied might be Horace Walpole's toy-castle. Not that it really could have been; but it was like the image, wretchedly mean and shabby, which one forms of such a place, in its decay. From Hampton Court to the Star and Garter, on Richmond Hill, is about six miles. After glancing cursorily at the prospect, which is famous, and doubtless very extensive and beautiful if the English mistiness would only let it be seen, we took a good dinner in the large and handsome coffee-room of the hotel, and then wended our way to the rail-station, and reached home between eight and nine o'clock. We must have walked not far from fifteen miles in the course of the day.

March 25th.—Yesterday, at one o'clock, I called by appointment on Mr. Bennoch, and lunched with him and his partners and clerks. This lunch seems to be a legitimate continuation of the old London custom of the master living at the same table with his apprentices. The meal was a dinner for the latter class. The table was set in an upper room of the establishment; and the dinner was a large joint of roast mutton, to which ten people sat down, including a German silk-merchant as a guest besides myself. Mr. Bennoch was at the head of the table, and one of his partners at the foot. For the apprentices there was porter to drink, and for the partners and guests some sparkling Moselle, and we had a sufficient dinner with agreeable conversation. Bennoch said that G. G——— used to be very fond of these lunches while in England.

After lunch, Mr. Bennoch took me round the establishment, which is quite extensive, occupying, I think, two or three adjacent houses, and requiring more. He showed me innumerable packages of ribbons, and other silk manufactures, and all sorts of silks, from the raw thread to the finest fabrics. He then offered to show me some of the curiosities of old London, and took me first to Barber-Surgeons' Hall, in Monkwell Street. It was at this place that the first anatomical studies were instituted in England. At the time of its foundation, the Barbers and Surgeons were one company; but the latter, I believe, are now the exclusive possessors of the Hall. The edifice was built by Inigo Jones, and the principal room is a fine one, with finely carved wood-work on the ceiling and walls. There is a skylight in the roof, letting down a sufficient radiance on the long table beneath, where, no doubt, dead people have been dissected, and where, for many generations, it has been the custom of the society to hold its stated feasts. In this room hangs the most valuable picture by Holbein now in existence, representing the company of Barber-

Surgeons kneeling before Henry VIII., and receiving their charter from his hands. The picture is about six feet square. The king is dressed in scarlet, and quite fulfils one's idea of his aspect. The Barber-Surgeons, all portraits, are an assemblage of grave-looking personages, in dark costumes. The company has refused five thousand pounds for this unique picture; and the keeper of the Hall told me that Sir Robert Peel had offered a thousand pounds for liberty to take out only one of the heads, that of a person named Pen, he conditioning to have a perfect fac-simile painted in. I did not see any merit in this head over the others.

Beside this great picture hung a most exquisite portrait by Vandyke; an elderly, bearded man, of noble and refined countenance, in a rich, grave dress. There are many other pictures of distinguished men of the company, in long past times, and of some of the kings and great people of England, all darkened with age, and producing a rich and sombre effect, in this stately old hall. Nothing is more curious in London than these ancient localities and customs of the City Companies,—each trade and profession having its own hall, and its own institutions. The keeper next showed us the plate which is used at the banquets.

I should like to be present at one of these feasts. I saw also an old vellum manuscript, in black-letter, which appeared to be a record of the proceedings of the company; and at the end there were many pages ruled for further entries, but none had been made in the volume for the last three or four hundred years.

I think it was in the neighborhood of Barber-Surgeons' Hall, which stands amid an intricacy of old streets, where I should never have thought of going, that I saw a row of ancient almshouses, of Elizabethan structure. They looked wofully dilapidated. In front of one of them was an inscription, setting forth that some worthy alderman had founded this establishment for the support of six poor men; and these six, or their successors, are still supported, but no larger number, although the value of the property left for that purpose would now suffice for a much larger number.

Then Mr. Bennoch took me to Cripplegate, and, entering the door of a house, which proved to be a sexton's residence, we passed by a side entrance into the church-porch of St. Giles, of which the sexton's house seems to be an indivisible contiguity. This is a very ancient church, that escaped the great fire of London. The galleries are supported by arches, the pillars of which are cased high upwards with oak; but all this oaken work and the oaken pews are comparatively modern, though so solid and dark that they agree well enough with the general effect of the church. Proceeding to the high altar, we found it surrounded with many very curious old monuments and memorials, some in carved oak, some in marble; grim old worthies, mostly in the costume of Queen Elizabeth's time. Here was the bust of Speed, the historian; here was the monument of Fox, author of The Book of Martyrs. High up on the wall, beside the altar, there was a black wooden coffin, and a lady sitting upright within it, with her hands clasped in prayer, it being her awakening moment at the Resurrection. Thence we passed down the centre aisle, and about midway we stopped before a marble bust, fixed against one of the pillars. And this was the bust of Milton! Yes, and Milton's bones lay beneath our feet; for he was buried under the pew over the door of which I was leaning. The bust, I believe, is the original of the one in Westminster Abbey.

Treading over the tombstones of the old citizens of London, both in the aisles and the porch, and within doors and without, we went into the churchyard, one side of which is fenced in by a portion of London Wall, very solid, and still high, though the accumulation of human dust has covered much of its base. This is the most considerable portion now remaining of the ancient wall of London. The sexton now asked us to go into the tower of the church, that he might show us the oldest part of the structure, and we did so, and, looking down from the organ gallery, I saw a woman sitting alone in the church, waiting for the rector, whose ghostly consolation, I suppose, she needed.

This old church-tower was formerly lighted by three large windows,—one of them of very great size; but the thrifty church-wardens of a generation or two ago had built them up with brick, to the great disfigurement of the church. The sexton called my attention to the organ-pipe, which is of sufficient size, I believe, to admit three men.

From Cripplegate we went to Milton Street (as it is now called), through which we walked for a very excellent reason; for this is the veritable Grub Street, where my literary kindred of former times used to congregate. It is still a shabby-looking street, with old-fashioned houses, and inhabited chiefly by people of the poorer classes, though not by authors. Next we went to Old Broad Street, and, being joined by Mr. B———, we set off for London Bridge, turning out of our direct course to see London stone in Watling Street. This famous stone appears now to be built into the wall of St. Swithin's Church, and is so encased that you can only see and touch the top of it through a circular hole. There are one or two long cuts or indentations in the top, which are said to have been made by Jack Cade's sword when he struck it against the stone. If so, his sword was of a redoubtable temper. Judging by what I saw, London stone was a rudely shaped and unhewn post.

At the London Bridge station, we took the rail for Greenwich, and, it being only about five miles off, we were not long in reaching the town. It was Easter Monday; and during the first three days of Easter, from time immemorial, a fair has been held at Greenwich, and this was what we had come to see.

[This fair is described in Our Old Home, in "A Loudon Suburb."]

Reaching Mr. Bennoch's house, we found it a pretty and comfortable one, and adorned with many works of art; for he seems to be a patron of art and literature, and a warm-hearted man, of active benevolence and vivid sympathies in many directions. His face shows this. I have never seen eyes of a warmer glow than his. On the walls of one room there were a good many sketches by Haydon, and several artists' proofs of fine engravings, presented by persons to whom he had been kind. In the drawing-room there was a marble bust of Mrs. ———, and one, I think, of himself, and one of the Queen, which Mr. Bennoch said was very good, and it is unlike any other I have seen. It is intended as a gift, from a number of subscribers, to Miss Nightingale. Likewise a crayon sketch of———, looking rather morbid and unwholesome, as the poor lady really is. Also, a small picture of Mr. Bennoch in a military dress, as an officer, probably of city-horse. By and by came in a young gentleman, son of Haydon, the painter of high art, and one or two ladies staying in the house, and anon Mrs. ———. And so we went in to dinner.

Bennoch is an admirable host, and warms his guests like a household fire by the influence of his kindly face and glowing eyes, and by such hospitable demeanor as best suits this aspect. After the cloth was removed, came in Mr. Newton Crosland, a young man who once called on me in Liverpool,—the husband of a literary lady, formerly Camilla Toulmin. The lady herself was coming to spend the evening. The husband (and I presume the wife) is a decided believer in spiritual manifestations. We talked of politics and spiritualism and literature; and before we rose from table, Mr. Bennoch drank the health of the ladies, and especially of Mrs. ———, in terms very kind towards her and me. I responded in her behalf as well as I could, and left it to Mr. Bowman, as a bachelor, to respond for the ladies generally,—which he did briefly, toasting Mrs. B———.

We had heard the sound of the piano in the drawing-room for some time, and now adjourning thither, I had the pleasure to be introduced to Mrs. Newton Crosland,—a rather tall, thin, pale, and lady-like person, looking, I thought, of a sensitive character. She expressed in a low tone and quiet way great delight at seeing my distinguished self! for she is a vast admirer of The Scarlet Letter, and especially of the character of Hester; indeed, I remember seeing a most favorable criticism of the book from her pen, in one of the London magazines. . . .

At eleven o'clock Mrs. Crosland entered the tiniest pony-carriage, and set forth for her own residence, with a lad walking at the pony's head, and carrying a lantern. . . .

March 26th.—Yesterday was not a very eventful day. After writing in my journal I went out at twelve, and visited, for the first time, the National Gallery. It is of no use for me to criticise pictures, or to try to describe them, but I have an idea that I might acquire a taste, with a little attention to the subject, for I find I already begin to prefer some pictures to others. This is encouraging. Of those that I saw yesterday, I think I liked several by Murillo best. There were a great many people in the gallery, almost entirely of the middle, with a few of the lower classes; and I should think that the effect of the exhibition must at least tend towards refinement. Nevertheless, the only emotion that I saw displayed was in broad grins on the faces of a man and two women, at sight of a small picture of Venus, with a Satyr peeping at her with an expression of gross animal delight and merriment. Without being aware of it, this man and the two women were of that same Satyr breed.

If I lived in London, I would endeavor to educate myself in this and other galleries of art; but as the case stands, it would be of no use. I saw two of Turner's landscapes; but did not see so much beauty in them as in some of Claude's. A view of the grand canal in Venice, by Canaletto, seemed to me wonderful,—absolutely perfect,—a better reality, for I could see the water of the canal moving and dimpling; and the palaces and buildings on each side were quite as good in their way.

Leaving the gallery, I walked down into the city, and passed through Smithfield, where I glanced at St. Bartholomew's Hospital. . . . Then I went into St. Paul's, and walked all round the great cathedral, looking, I believe, at every monument on the floor. There is certainly nothing very wonderful in any of them, and I do wish it would not so generally happen that English warriors go into battle almost nude; at least, we must suppose so, from their invariably receiving their death-wounds in that condition. I will not believe that a sculptor or a painter is a man of genius unless he can wake the nobleness of his subject, illuminate and transfigure any given pattern of coat and breeches. Nevertheless, I never go into St. Paul's without being impressed anew with the grandeur of the edifice, and the general effect of these same groups of statuary ranged in their niches and at the bases of the pillars as adornments of the cathedral.

Coming homeward, I went into the enclosure of the Temple, and near the entrance saw "Dr. Johnson's staircase" printed over a doorway; so I not only looked in, but went up the first flight, of some broad, well-worn stairs, passing my hand over a heavy, ancient, broken balustrade, on which, no doubt, Johnson's hand had often rested. It was here that Boswell used to visit him, in their early acquaintance. Before my lunch, I had gone into Bolt Court, where he died.

This morning there have been letters from Mr. Wilding, enclosing an invitation to me to be one of the stewards of the anniversary dinner of the Literary Fund.

No, I thank you, gentlemen!

March 27th.—Yesterday I went out at about twelve, and visited the British Museum; an exceedingly tiresome affair. It quite crushes a person to see so much at once, and I wandered from hall to hall with a weary and heavy heart, wishing (Heaven forgive me!) that the Elgin marbles and the frieze of the Parthenon were all burnt into lime, and that the granite Egyptian statues were hewn and squared into building-stones, and that the mummies had all turned to dust two thousand years ago; and, in fine, that all the material relics of so many successive ages had disappeared with the generations that produced them. The present is burdened too much with the past. We have not time, in our earthly existence, to appreciate what is warm with life, and immediately around us; yet we heap up these old shells, out of which human life has long emerged, casting them off forever. I do not see how future ages are to stagger onward under all this dead weight, with the additions that will be continually made to it.

After leaving the Museum, I went to see Bennoch, and arrange with him our expedition of to-day; and he read me a letter from Topper, very earnestly inviting me to come and spend a night or two with him. Then I wandered about the city, and was lost in the vicinity of Holborn; so that for a long while I was under a spell of bewilderment, and kept returning, in the strangest way, to the same point in Lincoln's Inn Fields. . . .

Mr. Bowman and I went to the Princess's Theatre in the evening. Charles Kean performed in Louis XI. very well indeed,—a thoughtful and highly skilled actor,—much improved since I saw him, many years ago, in America.

ALDERSHOTT CAMP.

April 1st.—After my last date on Thursday, I visited the National Gallery. At three o'clock, having packed a travelling-bag, I went to Bennoch's office, and lunched with him; and at about five we took the rail from the Waterloo station for Aldershott Camp. At Tamborough we were cordially received by Lieutenant Shaw, of the North Cork Rifles, and were escorted by him, in a fly, to his quarters. The camp is a large city, composed of numberless wooden barracks, arranged in regular streets, on a wide, bleak heath, with an extensive and dreary prospect on all sides. Lieutenant Shaw assigned me one room in his hut, and Bennoch another, and made us as comfortable as kind hospitality could; but the huts are very small, and the rooms have no size at all; neither are they air-tight, and the sharp wind whistles in at the crevices; and, on the whole, of all discomfortable places, I am inclined to reckon Aldershott Camp the most so. I suppose the government has placed the camp on that windy heath, and built such wretched huts, for the very purpose of rendering life as little desirable as may be to the soldiers, so that they should throw it away the more willingly.

At seven o'clock we dined at the regimental mess, with the officers of the North Cork. The mess-room is by far the most endurable place to be found in camp. The hut is large, and the mess-room is capable of receiving between thirty and forty guests, besides the officers of the regiment, when a great dinner-party is given. As I saw it, the whole space was divided into a dining-room and two anterooms by red curtains drawn across; and the second anteroom seems to be a general rendezvous for the officers, where they meet at all times, and talk, or look over the newspapers and the army-register, which constitute the chief of their reading. The Colonel and Lieutenant-Colonel of the regiment received Bennoch and me with great cordiality, as did all the other officers, and we sat down to a splendid dinner.

All the officers of the regiment are Irishmen, and all of them, I believe, men of fortune; and they do what they can towards alleviating their hardships in camp by eating and drinking of the best that can be obtained of all good things. The table service and plate were as fine as those in any nobleman's establishment; the dishes numerous and admirably got up; and the wines delectable and genuine,—as they had need to be; for there is a great consumption of them. I liked these Irish officers exceedingly;—not that it would be possible to live long among them without finding existence a bore; for they have no thought, no intellectual movement, no ideas, that I was aware of, beyond horses, dogs, drill, garrisons, field-days, whist, wine, cigars, and all that kind of thing; yet they were really gentlemen living on the best terms with one another,—courteous, kind, most hospitable, with a rich Irish humor, softened down by social refinements,—not too refined either, but a most happy sort of behavior, as natural as that of children, and with a safe freedom that made one feel entirely at my ease. I think well of the Irish gentlemen, for their sakes; and I believe I might fairly attribute to Lieutenant-Colonel Stowell (next whom I sat) a higher and finer cultivation than the above description indicates. Indeed, many of them may have been capable of much more intellectual intercourse than that of the mess-table; but I suppose it would not have been in keeping with their camp life, nor suggested by it. Several of the elder officers were men who had been long in the army; and the Colonel—a bluff, hearty old soldier, with a profile like an eagle's head and beak—was a veteran of the Peninsula, and had a medal on his breast with clasps for three famous battles besides that of Waterloo.

The regimental band played during dinner, and the Lieutenant-Colonel apologized to me for its not playing "Hail Columbia," the tune not coning within their musical accomplishments. It was no great matter, however; for I should not have distinguished it from any other tune; but, to do me what honor was possible, in the way of national airs, the band was ordered to play a series of negro melodies, and I was entirely satisfied. It is really funny that the "wood-notes wild" of those poor black slaves should have been played in a foreign laud as an honorable compliment to one of their white countrymen.

After dinner we played whist, and then had some broiled bones for supper, and finally went home to our respective huts not much earlier than four o'clock. But I don't wonder these gentlemen sit up as long as they can keep their eyes open; for never was there anything so utterly comfortless as their camp-beds. They are really worse than the bed of honor, no wider, no softer, no warmer, and affording not nearly so sound sleep. Indeed, I got hardly any sleep at all, and almost as soon as I did close my eyes, the bugles sounded, and the drums beat reveille, and from that moment the camp was all astir; so I pretty soon uprose, and went to the mess-room for my breakfast, feeling wonderfully fresh and well, considering what my night had been.

Long before this, however, this whole regiment, and all the other regiments, marched off to take part in a general review, and Bennoch and I followed, as soon as we had eaten a few mutton-chops. It was a bright, sunshiny day; but with a strong east-wind, as piercing and pitiless as ever blew; and this wide, undulating plain of Aldershott seemed just the place where the east-wind was at home. Still, it acted, on the whole, like an invigorating cordial; and whereas in pleasanter circumstances I should have lain down, and gone to sleep, I now felt as if I could do without sleep for a month.

In due time we found out the place of the North Cork Regiment in the general battle-array, and were greeted as old comrades by the Colonel and other officers. Soon the soldiers (who, when we first reached them, were strolling about, or standing at ease) were called into order; and anon we saw a group of mounted officers riding along the lines, and among them a gentleman in a civilian's round hat, and plain frock and trousers, riding on a white horse. This group of riders turned the front of the regiment, and then passed along the rear, coming close to where we stood; and as the plainly dressed gentleman rode by, he bent towards me, and I tried to raise my hat, but did not succeed very well, because the fierce wind had compelled me to jam it tightly upon my head. The Duke of Cambridge (for this was he) is a comely-looking gentlemanly man, of bluff English face, with a great deal of brown beard about it. Though a pretty tall man, he appears, on horseback, broad and round in proportion to his height. I looked at him with a certain sort of interest, and a feeling of kindness; for one does feel kindly to whatever human being is anywise marked out from the rest, unless it be by his disagreeable qualities.

The troops, from twelve to fifteen thousand, now fell into marching order, and went to attack a wood, where we were to suppose the enemy to be stationed. The sham-fight seemed to me rather clumsily managed, and without any striking incident or result. The officers had prophesied, the night before, that General K———, commanding in the camp, would make a muddle of it; and probably he did. After the review, the Duke of Cambridge with his attendant officers took their station, and all the regiments marched in front of him, saluting as they passed. As each colonel rode by, and as the banner of each regiment was lowered, the Duke lifted his hat.

The most splendid effect of this parade was the gleam of the sun upon the long line of bayonets,—the sheen of all that steel appearing like a wavering fringe of light upon the dark masses of troops below. It was very fine. But I was glad when all was done, and I could go back to the mess-room, whither I carried an excellent appetite for luncheon. After this we walked about the camp,—looked at some model tents, inspected the arrangements and modes of living in the huts of the privates; and thus gained more and more adequate ideas of the vile uncomfortableness of a military life. Finally, I went to the anteroom and turned over the regimental literature,—a peerage and baronetage,—an army and militia register, a number of the Sporting Magazine, and one of the United Service, while Bennoch took another walk. Before dinner we both tried to catch a little nap by way of compensation for last night's deficiencies; but, for my part, the attempt was fruitless.

The dinner was as splendid and as agreeable as that of the evening before; and I believe it was nearly two o'clock when Bennoch and I bade farewell to our kind entertainers. For my part I fraternized with these military gentlemen in a way that augurs the very best things for the future peace of the two countries. They all expressed the warmest sympathies towards America and it was easy to judge from their conversation that there is no real friendliness on the part of the military towards the French. The old antipathy is just as strong as ever,—stronger than ever, perhaps, on account of the comparatively more brilliant success of the French in this Russian war. So, with most Christian sentiments of peace and brotherly love, we returned to our hut, and lay down, each in his narrow bed.

Early in the morning the drums and bugles began the usual bedevilment; and shortly after six I dressed, and we had breakfast at the mess-room, shook hands with Lieutenant Shaw (our more especial host), and drove off to the railway station at Ash.

I know not whether I have mentioned that the villages neighboring to the camp have suffered terribly as regards morality from the vicinity of the soldiers. Quiet old English towns, that till within a little time ago had kept their antique simplicity and innocence, have now no such thing as female virtue in them, so far as the lower classes are concerned. This is expressing the matter too strongly, no doubt; but there is too much truth in it, nevertheless; and one of the officers remarked that even ladies of respectability had grown much more free in manners and conversation than at first. I have heard observations similar to this from a Nova-Scotian, in reference to the moral influence of soldiers when stationed in the provinces.

WOOTON.

Wooton stands in a hollow, near the summit of one of the long swells that here undulate over the face of the country. There is a good deal of wood behind it, as should be the case with the residence of the author of the Sylva; but I believe few, if any, of these trees are known to have been planted by John Evelyn, or even to have been coeval with his time. The house is of brick, partly ancient, and consists of a front and two projecting wings, with a porch and entrance in the centre. It has a desolate, meagre aspect, and needs something to give it life and stir and jollity. The present proprietor is of the old Evelyn family, and is now one of the two members of Parliament for Surrey; but he is a very shy and retiring man, unmarried, sees little company, and seems either not to know how to make himself comfortable or not to care about it. A servant told us that Mr. ——— had just gone out, but Tupper, who is apparently on intimate terms with him, thought it best that we should go into the house, while he went in search of the master. So the servant ushered us through a hall,—where were many family pictures by Lely, and, for aught I know, by Vandyke, and by Kneller, and other famous painters,—up a grand staircase, and into the library, the inner room of which contained the ponderous volumes which John Evelyn used to read. Nevertheless, it was a room of most barren aspect, without a carpet on the floor, with pine bookcases, with a common whitewashed ceiling, with no luxurious study-chairs, and without a fire. There was an open folio on the table, and a sheet of manuscript that appeared to have been recently written. I took down a book from the shelves (a volume of annals, connected with English history), and Tupper afterwards told us that this one single volume, for its rarity, was worth either two or three hundred pounds. Against one of the windows of this library there grows a magnolia-tree, with a very large stem, and at least fifty years old.

Mrs. Tupper and I waited a good while, and then Bennoch and Tupper came back, without having found Mr. ———. Tupper wished very much to show the prayer-book used by King Charles at his execution, and some curious old manuscript volumes; but the servant said that his master always kept these treasures locked up, and trusted the key to nobody. We therefore had to take our leave without seeing them; and I have not often entered a house that one feels to be more forlorn than Wooton,—although we did have a glimpse of a dining-room, with a table laid for three or four guests, and looking quite brilliant with plate and glass and snowy napery. There was a fire, too, in this one room. Mr. ——— is making extensive alterations in the house, or has recently done so, and this is perhaps one reason of its ungenial meagreness and lack of finish.

Before our departure from Wooton, Tupper had asked me to leave my card for Mr. ———; but I had no mind to overstep any limit of formal courtesy in dealing with an Englishman, and therefore declined. Tupper, however, on his own responsibility, wrote his name, Bennoch's, and mine on a piece of paper, and told the servant to show them to Mr. ———. We soon had experience of the good effect of this; for we had scarcely got back before somebody drove up to Tupper's door, and one of the girls, looking out, exclaimed that there was Mr. ——— himself, and another gentleman. He had set out, the instant he heard of our call, to bring the three precious volumes for me to see. This surely was most kind; a kindness which I should never have dreamed of expecting from a shy, retiring man like Mr. ———.

So he and his friend were ushered into the dining-room, and introduced. Mr. ——— is a young-looking man, dark, with a mustache, rather small, and though he has the manners of a man who has seen the world, it evidently requires an effort in him to speak to anybody; and I could see his whole person slightly writhing itself, as it were, while he addressed me. This is strange in a man of his public position, member for the county, necessarily mixed up with life in many forms, the possessor of sixteen thousand pounds a year, and the representative of an ancient name. Nevertheless, I liked him, and felt as if I could become intimately acquainted with him, if circumstances were favorable; but, at a brief interview like this, it was hopeless to break through two great reserves; so I talked more with his companion—a pleasant young man, fresh from college, I should imagine—than with Mr. ——— himself.

The three books were really of very great interest. One was an octavo volume of manuscript in John Evelyn's own hand, the beginning of his published diary, written as distinctly as print, in a small, clear character. It can be read just as easily as any printed book. Another was a Church of England prayer-book, which King Charles used on the scaffold, and which was stained with his sacred blood, and underneath are two or three lines in John Evelyn's hand, certifying this to be the very book. It is an octavo, or small folio, and seems to have been very little used, scarcely opened, except in one spot; its leaves elsewhere retaining their original freshness and elasticity. It opens most readily at the commencement of the common service; and there, on the left-hand page, is a discoloration, of a yellowish or brownish hue, about two thirds of an inch large, which, two hundred years ago and a little more, was doubtless red. For on that page had fallen a drop of King Charles's blood.

The other volume was large, and contained a great many original letters, written by the king during his troubles. I had not time to examine them with any minuteness, and remember only one document, which Mr. ——— pointed out, and which had a strange pathos and pitifulness in it. It was a sort of due-bill, promising to pay a small sum for beer, which had been supplied to his Majesty, so soon as God should enable him, or the distracted circumstances of his kingdom make it possible,—or some touching and helpless expression of that kind. Prince Hal seemed to consider it an unworthy matter, that a great prince should think of "that poor creature, small beer," at all; but that a great prince should not be able to pay for it is far worse.

Mr. ——— expressed his regret that I was not staying longer in this part of the country, as he would gladly have seen me at Wooten, and he succeeded in saying something about my books; and I hope I partly succeeded in showing him that I was very sensible of his kindness in letting me see those relics. I cannot say whether or no I expressed it sufficiently. It is better with such a man, or, indeed, with any man, to say too little than too much; and, in fact, it would have been indecorous in me to take too much of his kindness to my own share, Bennoch being likewise in question.

We had a cup of coffee, and then took our leave; Tupper accompanying us part way down the village street, and bidding us an affectionate farewell.

BATTLE ABBEY.

Bennoch and I recommenced our travels, and, changing from one railway to another, reached Tunbridge Wells at nine or ten in the evening. . . . The next day was spent at Tunbridge Wells, which is famous for a chalybeate spring, and is a watering-place of note, most healthily situated on a high, breezy hill, with many pleasant walks in the neighborhood. . . . From Tunbridge Wells we transported ourselves to Battle,—the village in which is Battle Abbey. It is a large village, with many antique houses and some new ones; and in its principal street, on one side, with a wide, green space before it, you see the gray, embattled, outer wall, and great, square, battlemented entrance tower (with a turret at each corner), of the ancient Abbey. It is the perfect reality of a Gothic battlement and gateway, just as solid and massive as when it was first built, though hoary and venerable with the many intervening centuries. There are only two days in the week on which visitors are allowed entrance, and this was not one of them. Nevertheless, Bennoch was determined to get in, and he wished me to send Lady Webster my card with his own; but this I utterly refused, for the honor of America and for my own honor; because I will not do anything to increase the reputation we already have as a very forward people. Bennoch, however, called at a bookshop on the other side of the street, near the gateway of the castle; and making friends, as he has a marvellous tact in doing, with the bookseller, the latter offered to take in his card to the housekeeper, and see if Lady Webster would not relax her rule in our favor. Meanwhile, we went into the old church of Battle, which was built in Norman times, though subsequently to the Abbey. As we entered the church door, the bell rang for joy at the news of peace, which had just been announced by the London papers.

The church has been whitewashed in modern times, and does not look so venerable as it ought, with its arches and pillared aisles. In the chancel stands a marble tomb, heavy, rich, and elaborate, on the top of which lie the broken-nosed statues of Sir Anthony Browne and his lady, who were the Lord and Lady of Battle Abbey in Henry VIII.'s time. The knight is in armor, and the lady in stately garb, and (save for their broken noses) they are in excellent preservation. The pavement of the chancel and aisles is all laid with tombstones, and on two or three of these there were engraved brasses, representing knights in armor, and churchmen, with inscriptions in Latin. Some of them are very old. On the walls, too, there are various monuments, principally of dignitaries connected with the Abbey. Two hatchments, in honor of persons recently dead, were likewise suspended in the chancel. The best pew of the church is, of course, that of the Webster family. It is curtained round, carpeted, furnished with chairs and footstools, and more resembles a parlor than a pew; especially as there is a fireplace in one of the pointed archways, which I suppose has been bricked up in order to form it. On the opposite side of the aisle is the pew of some other magnate, containing a stove. The rest of the parishioners have to keep themselves warm with the fervor of their own piety. I have forgotten what else was interesting, except that we were shown a stone coffin, recently dug up, in which was hollowed a place for the head of the corpse.

Returning to the bookshop, we found that Lady Webster had sent her compliments, and would be very happy to have us see the Abbey. How thoroughly kind these English people can be when they like, and how often they like to be so!

We lost no time in ringing the bell at the arched entrance, under the great tower, and were admitted by an old woman who lives, I believe, in the thickness of the wall. She told us her room used to be the prison of the Abbey, and under the great arch she pointed to a projecting beam, where she said criminals used to be hanged.

At two of the intersecting points of the arches, which form the roof of the gateway, were carved faces of stone, said to represent King Harold and William the Conqueror. The exterior wall, of which this tower is the gateway, extends far along the village street, and encloses a very large space, within which stands the mansion, quite secluded from unauthorized visitors, or even from the sight of those without, unless it be at very distant eyeshot.

We rang at the principal door of the edifice (it is under a deep arch, in the Norman style, but of modern date), and a footman let its in, and then delivered us over to a respectable old lady in black. She was a Frenchwoman by birth, but had been very long in the service of the family, and spoke English almost without an accent; her French blood being indicated only by her thin and withered aspect, and a greater gentility of manner than would have been seen in an Englishwoman of similar station. She ushered us first into a grand and noble hall, the arched and carved oaken roof of which ascended into the gable. It was nearly sixty feet long, and its height equal to its length,—as stately a hall, I should imagine, as is anywhere to be found in a private mansion. It was lighted, at one end, by a great window, beneath which, occupying the whole breadth of the hall, hung a vast picture of the Battle of Hastings; and whether a good picture or no, it was a rich adornment of the hall. The walls were wainscoted high upward with oak: they were almost covered with noble pictures of ancestry, and of kings and great men, and beautiful women; there were trophies of armor hung aloft; and two armed figures, one in brass mail, the other in bright steel, stood on a raised dais, underneath the great picture. At the end of the hall, opposite the picture, a third of the way up towards the roof, was a gallery. All these things that I have enumerated were in perfect condition, without rust, untouched by decay or injury of any kind; but yet they seemed to belong to a past age, and were mellowed, softened in their splendor, a little dimmed with time,—toned down into a venerable magnificence. Of all domestic things that I have seen in England, it satisfied me most.

Then the Frenchwoman showed us into various rooms and offices, most of which were contrived out of the old abbey-cloisters, and the vaulted cells and apartments in which the monks used to live. If any house be haunted, I should suppose this might be. If any church-property bring a curse with it, as people say, I do not see how the owners of Battle Abbey can escape it, taking possession of and dwelling in these holy precincts, as they have done, and laying their kitchen hearth with the stones of overthrown altars. The Abbey was first granted, I believe, to Sir Anthony Browne, whom I saw asleep with his lady in the church. It was his first wife. I wish it had been his second; for she was Surrey's Geraldine. The posterity of Sir Anthony kept the place till

1719, and then sold it to the Websters, a family of Baronets, who are still the owners and occupants. The present proprietor is Sir Augustus Webster, whose mother is the lady that so kindly let us into the Abbey.

Mr. Bennoch gave the nice old French lady half a crown, and we next went round among the ruined portions of the Abbey, under the gardener's guidance. We saw two ivied towers, insulated from all other ruins; and an old refectory, open to the sky, and a vaulted crypt, supported by pillars; and we saw, too, the foundation and scanty remains of a chapel, which had been long buried out of sight of man, and only dug up within present memory,—about forty years ago. There had always been a tradition that this was the spot where Harold had planted his standard, and where his body was found after the battle; and the discovery of the ruined chapel confirmed the tradition.

I might have seen a great deal more, had there been time; and I have forgotten much of what I did see; but it is an exceedingly interesting place. There is an avenue of old yew-trees, which meet above like a cloistered arch; and this is called the Monks' Walk. I rather think they were ivy, though growing unsupported.

As we were retiring, the gardener suddenly stopped, as if he were alarmed, and motioned to us to do the same, saying, "I believe it is my lady!" And so it was,—a tall and stately lady in black, trimming shrubs in the garden. She bowed to us very graciously,—we raised our hats, and thus we met and parted without more ado. As we went through the arch of the entrance tower, Bennoch gave the old female warder a shilling, and the gardener followed us to get half a crown.

HASTINGS.

We took a fly and driver from the principal hotel of Battle, and drove off for Hastings, about seven miles distant. Hastings is now a famous watering and sea-bathing place, and seems to be well sheltered from the winds, though open to the sea, which here stretches off towards France. We climbed a high and steep hill, terraced round its base with streets of modern lodging-houses, and crowned on its summit with the ruins of a castle, the foundation of which was anterior to the Conquest. This castle has no wall towards the sea, the precipice being too high and sheer to admit of attack on that side. I have quite exhausted my descriptive faculty for the present, so shall say nothing of this old castle, which indeed (the remains being somewhat scanty and scraggling) is chiefly picturesque and interesting from its bold position on such a headlong hill.

Clambering down on another side from that of our ascent, we entered the town of Hastings, which seems entirely modern, and made up of lodging-houses, shops, hotels, parades, and all such makings up of watering-places generally. We took a delightful warm bath, washing off all weariness and naughtiness, and coming out new men. Then we walked to St. Leonard's,—a part of Hastings, I believe, but a mile or two from the castle, and there called at the lodgings of two friends of Bennoch.

These were Mr. Martin, the author of Bon Gaultier's ballads, and his wife, the celebrated actress, Helen Faucett. Mr. Martin is a barrister, a gentleman whose face and manners suited me at once; a simple, refined, sincere, not too demonstrative person. His wife, too, I liked; a tall, dark, fine, and lady-like woman, with the simplest manners, that give no trouble at all, and so must be perfect. With these two persons I felt myself, almost in a moment, on friendly terms, and in true accord, and so I talked, I think, more than I have at any time since coming to London.

We took a pleasant lunch at their house; and then they walked with us to the railway station, and there they took leave of Bennoch affectionately and of me hardly less so; for, in truth, we had grown to be almost friends in this very little while. And as we rattled away, I said to Bennoch earnestly, "What good people they are!"—and Bennoch smiled, as if he had known perfectly well that I should think and say so. And thus we rushed onward to London; and I reached St. James's Place between nine and ten o'clock, after a very interesting tour, the record of which I wish I could have kept as we went along, writing each day's history before another day's adventures began.

END OF VOL. I.

LONDON.—MILTON-CLUB DINNER.

April 4th, 1856.—On Tuesday I went to No. 14 Ludgate Hill, to dine with Bennoch at the Milton Club; a club recently founded for dissenters, nonconformists, and people whose ideas, religious or political, are not precisely in train with the establishment in church and state. I was shown into a large reading-room, well provided with periodicals and newspapers, and found two or three persons there; but Bennoch had not yet arrived. In a few moments, a tall gentleman with white hair came in,—a fine and intelligent-looking man, whom I guessed to be one of those who were to meet me. He walked about, glancing at the periodicals; and soon entered Mr. Tupper, and, without seeing me, exchanged warm greetings with the white-haired gentleman. "I suppose," began Mr. Tupper, "you have come to meet—" Now, conscious that my name was going to be spoken, and not knowing but the excellent Mr. Tupper might say something which he would not, quite like me to overhear, I advanced at once, with outstretched hand, and saluted him. He expressed great joy at the recognition, and immediately introduced me to Mr. Hall.

The dining-room was pretty large and lofty, and there were sixteen guests at table, most of them authors, or people connected with the press; so that the party represented a great deal of the working intellect of London at this present day and moment,—the men whose plays, whose songs, whose articles, are just now in vogue. Mr. Tom Taylor was one of the very few whose writings I had known anything about. He is a tall, slender, dark young man, not English-looking, and wearing colored spectacles, so that I should readily have taken him for an American literary man. I did not have much opportunity of talking with him, nor with anybody else, except Dr. ———, who seemed a shrewd, sensible man, with a certain slight acerbity of thought. Mr. Herbert Ingram, recently elected member of Parliament, was likewise present, and sat on Bennoch's left.

It was a very good dinner, with an abundance of wine, which Bennoch sent round faster than was for the next day's comfort of his guests. It is singular that I should thus far have quite forgotten W——— H————, whose books I know better than those of any other person there. He is a white-headed, stout, firm-looking, and rather wrinkled-faced old gentleman, whose temper, I should imagine, was not the very sweetest in the world. There is all abruptness, a kind of sub-acidity, if not bitterness, in his address; he seemed not to be, in short, so genial as I should have anticipated from his books.

As soon as the cloth was removed, Bennoch, without rising from his chair, made a speech in honor of his eminent and distinguished guest, which illustrious person happened to be sitting in the selfsame chair that I myself occupied. I have no recollection of what he said, nor of what I said in reply, but I remember that both of us were cheered and applauded much more than the occasion deserved. Then followed about fifty other speeches; for every single individual at table was called up (as Tupper said, "toasted and roasted"), and, for my part, I was done entirely brown (to continue T——'s figure). Everybody said something kind, not a word or idea of which can I find in my memory. Certainly, if I never get any more praise in my life, I have had enough of it for once. I made another little bit of a speech, too, in response to something that was said in reference to the present difficulties between England and America, and ended, as a proof that I deemed war impossible, with drinking success to the British army, and calling on Lieutenant Shaw, of the Aldershott Camp, to reply. I am afraid I must have said something very wrong, for the applause was vociferous, and I could hear the gentlemen whispering about the table, "Good!" "Good!" "Yes, he is a fine fellow,"—and other such ill-earned praises; and I took shame to myself, and held my tongue (publicly) the rest of the evening. But in such cases something must be allowed to the excitement of the moment, and to the effect of kindness and goodwill, so broadly and warmly displayed; and even a sincere man must not be held to speak as if he were under oath.

We separated, in a blessed state of contentment with one another, at about eleven; and (lest I should starve before morning) I went with Mr. D——— to take supper at his house in Park Lane. Mr. D——— is a pale young gentleman, of American aspect, being a West-Indian by birth. He is one of the principal writers of editorials for the Times. We were accompanied in the carriage by another gentleman, Mr. M———, who is connected with the management of the same paper. He wrote the letters from Scutari, which drew so much attention to the state of the hospitals. Mr. D——— is the husband of the former Miss ———, the actress, and when we reached his house, we found that she had just come home from the theatre, and was taking off her stage-dress. Anon she came down to the drawing-room,—a seemingly good, simple, and intelligent lady, not at all pretty, and, I should think, older than her husband. She was very kind to me, and told me that she had read one of my books—The House of the Seven Gables—thirteen years ago; which I thought remarkable, because I did not write it till eight or nine years afterwards.

The principal talk during supper (which consisted of Welsh-rabbit and biscuits, with champagne and sodawater) was about the Times, and the two contributors expressed vast admiration of Mr. ———, who has the chief editorial management of the paper. It is odd to find how little we outsiders know of men who really exercise a vast influence on affairs, for this Mr. ——— is certainly of far more importance in the world than a minister of state. He writes nothing himself; but the character of the Times seems to depend upon his intuitive, unerring judgment; and if ever he is absent from his post, even for a day or two, they say that the paper immediately shows it. In reply to my questions, they appeared to acknowledge that he was a man of expediency, but of a very high expediency, and that he gave the public the very best principles which it was capable of receiving. Perhaps it may be so: the Times's articles are certainly not written in so high a moral vein as might be wished; but what they lack in height they gain in breadth. Every sensible man in England finds his own best common-sense there; and, in effect, I think its influence is wholesome.

Apropos of public speaking, Dr. ——— said that Sir Lytton Bulwer asked him (I think the anecdote was personal to himself) whether he felt his heart beat when he was going to speak. "Yes." "Does your voice frighten you?" "Yes." "Do all your ideas forsake you?" "Yes." "Do you wish the floor to open and swallow you?" "Yes." "Why, then, you'll make an orator!" Dr. ——— told of Canning, too, how once, before rising to speak in the House of Commons, he bade his friend feel his pulse, which was throbbing terrifically. "I know I shall make one of my best speeches," said Canning, "because I'm in such an awful funk!" President Pierce, who has a great deal of oratorical power, is subject to a similar horror and reluctance.

REFORM-CLUB DINNER.

April 5th.—On Thursday, at eight o'clock, I went to the Reform Club, to dine with Dr. ———. The waiter admitted me into a great basement hall, with a tessellated or mosaic or somehow figured floor of stone, and lighted from a dome of lofty height. In a few minutes Dr. ——— appeared, and showed me about the edifice, which is very noble and of a substantial magnificence that was most satisfactory to behold,—no wood-work imitating better materials, but pillars and balustrades of marble, and everything what it purports to be. The reading-room is very large, and luxuriously comfortable, and contains an admirable library: there are rooms and conveniences for every possible purpose; and whatever material for enjoyment a bachelor may need, or ought to have, he can surely find it here, and on such reasonable terms that a small income will do as much for him as a far greater one on any other system.

In a colonnade, on the first floor, surrounding the great basement hall, there are portraits of distinguished reformers, and black niches for others yet to come. Joseph Hume, I believe, is destined to fill one of these blanks; but I remarked that the larger part of the portraits, already hung up, are of men of high rank,—the Duke of Sussex, for instance; Lord Durham, Lord Grey; and, indeed, I remember no commoner. In one room, I saw on the wall the fac-simile, so common in the United States, of our Declaration of Independence.

Descending again to the basement hall, an elderly gentleman came in, and was warmly welcomed by Dr. ———. He was a very short man, but with breadth enough, and a back excessively bent,—bowed almost to deformity; very gray hair, and a face and expression of remarkable briskness and intelligence. His profile came out pretty boldly, and his eyes had the prominence that indicates, I believe, volubility of speech, nor did he fail to talk from the instant of his appearance; and in the tone of his voice, and in his glance, and in the whole man, there was something racy,—a flavor of the humorist. His step was that of an aged man, and he put his stick down very decidedly at every footfall; though as he afterwards told me that he was only fifty-two, he need not yet have been infirm. But perhaps he has had the gout; his feet, however, are by no means swollen, but unusually small. Dr. ——— introduced him as Mr. Douglas Jerrold, and we went into the coffee-room to dine.

The coffee-room occupies one whole side of the edifice, and is provided with a great many tables, calculated for three or four persons to dine at; and we sat down at one of these, and Dr. ——— ordered some mulligatawny soup, and a bottle of white French wine. The waiters in the coffee-room are very numerous, and most of them dressed in the livery of the Club, comprising plush breeches and white-silk stockings; for these English Reformers do not seem to include Republican simplicity of manners in their system. Neither, perhaps, is it anywise essential.

After the soup, we had turbot, and by and by a bottle of Chateau Margaux, very delectable; and then some lambs' feet, delicately done, and some cutlets of I know not what peculiar type; and finally a ptarmigan, which is of the same race of birds as the grouse, but feeds high up towards the summits of the Scotch mountains. Then some cheese, and a bottle of Chambertin. It was a very pleasant dinner, and my companions were both very agreeable men; both taking a shrewd, satirical, yet not ill-natured, view of life and people, and as for Mr. Douglas Jerrold, he often reminded me of E—— C———, in the richer veins of the latter, both by his face and expression, and by a tincture of something at once wise and humorously absurd in what he said. But I think he has a kinder, more genial, wholesomer nature than E——, and under a very thin crust of outward acerbity I grew sensible of a very warm heart, and even of much simplicity of character in this man, born in London, and accustomed always to London life.

I wish I had any faculty whatever of remembering what people say; but, though I appreciate anything good at the moment, it never stays in my memory; nor do I think, in fact, that anything definite, rounded, pointed, separable, and transferable from the general lump of conversation was said by anybody. I recollect that they laughed at Mr. ———, and at his shedding a tear into a Scottish river, on occasion of some literary festival. . . . They spoke approvingly of Bulwer, as valuing his literary position, and holding himself one of the brotherhood of authors; and not so approvingly of Charles Dickens, who, born a plebeian, aspires to aristocratic society. But I said that it was easy to condescend, and that Bulwer knew he could not put off his rank, and that he would have all the advantages of it in spite of his authorship. We talked about the position of men of letters in England, and they said that the aristocracy hated and despised and feared them; and I asked why it was that literary men, having really so much power in their hands, were content to live unrecognized in the State.

Douglas Jerrold talked of Thackeray and his success in America, and said that he himself purposed going and had been invited thither to lecture. I asked him whether it was pleasant to a writer of plays to see them performed; and he said it was intolerable, the presentation of the author's idea being so imperfect; and Dr. ——— observed that it was excruciating to hear one of his own songs sung. Jerrold spoke of the Duke of Devonshire with great warmth, as a true, honest, simple, most kind-hearted man, from whom he himself had received great courtesies and kindnesses (not, as I understood, in the way of patronage or essential favors); and I (Heaven forgive me!) queried within myself whether this English reforming author would have been quite so sensible of the Duke's excellence if his Grace had not been a duke. But indeed, a nobleman, who is at the same time a true and whole-hearted man, feeling his brotherhood with men, does really deserve some credit for it.

In the course of the evening, Jerrold spoke with high appreciation of Emerson; and of Longfellow, whose Hiawatha he considered a wonderful performance; and of Lowell, whose Fable for Critics he especially admired. I mentioned Thoreau, and proposed to send his works to Dr. ———, who, being connected with the Illustrated News, and otherwise a writer, might be inclined to draw attention to then. Douglas Jerrold asked why he should not have them too. I hesitated a little, but as he pressed me, and would have an answer, I said that I did not feel quite so sure of his kindly judgment on Thoreau's books; and it so chanced that I used the word "acrid" for lack of a better, in endeavoring to express my idea of Jerrold's way of looking at men and books. It was not quite what I meant; but, in fact, he often is acrid, and has written pages and volumes of acridity, though, no doubt, with an honest purpose, and from a manly disgust at the cant and humbug of the world. Jerrold said no more, and I went on talking with Dr. ———; but, in a minute or two, I became aware that something had gone wrong, and, looking at Douglas Jerrold, there was an expression of pain and emotion on his face. By this time a second bottle of Burgundy had been opened (Clos Vougeot, the best the Club could produce, and far richer than the Chambertin), and that warm and potent wine may have had something to do with the depth and vivacity of Mr. Jerrold's feelings. But he was indeed greatly hurt by that little word "acrid." "He knew," he said, "that the world considered him a sour, bitter, ill-natured man; but that such a man as I should have the sane opinion was almost more than he could bear." As he spoke, he threw out his arms, sank back in his seat, and I was really a little apprehensive of his actual dissolution into tears. Hereupon I spoke, as was good need, and though, as usual, I have forgotten everything I said, I am quite sure it was to the purpose, and went to this good fellow's heart, as it came warmly from my own. I do remember saying that I felt him to be as genial as the glass of Burgundy which I held in my hand; and I think that touched the very right spot; for he smiled, and said he was afraid the Burgundy was better than he, but yet he was comforted. Dr. ——— said that he likewise had a reputation for bitterness; and I assured him, if I might venture to join myself to the brotherhood of two such men, that I was considered a very ill-natured person by many people in my own country. Douglas Jerrold said he was glad of it.

We were now in sweetest harmony, and Jerrold spoke more than it would become me to repeat in praise of my own books, which he said he admired, and he found the man more admirable than his books! I hope so, certainly.

We now went to the Haymarket Theatre, where Douglas Jerrold is on the free list; and after seeing a ballet by some Spanish dancers, we separated, and betook ourselves to our several homes. I like Douglas Jerrold very much.

April 8th.—On Saturday evening, at ten o'clock, I went to a supper-party at Mr. D———'s, and there met five or six people,—Mr. Faed, a young and distinguished artist; Dr. Eliotson, a dark, sombre, taciturn, powerful-looking man, with coal-black hair, and a beard as black, fringing round his face; Mr. Charles Reade, author of Christie Johnstone and other novels, and many plays,—a tall man, more than thirty, fair-haired, and of agreeable talk and demeanor.

On April 6th, I went to the Waterloo station, and there meeting Bennoch and Dr. ———, took the rail for Woking, where we found Mr. Hall's carriage waiting to convey us to Addlestone, about five miles off. On arriving we found that Mr. and Mrs. Hall had not yet returned from church. Their place is an exceedingly pretty one, and arranged in very good taste. The house is not large; but is filled, in every room, with fine engravings, statuettes, ingenious prettinesses or beautifulnesses in the way of flower-stands, cabinets, and things that seem to have bloomed naturally out of the characters of its occupants. There is a conservatory connected with the drawing-room, and enriched with lovely plants, one of which has a certain interest as being the plant on which Coleridge's eyes were fixed when he died. This conservatory is likewise beautified with several very fine casts of statues by modern sculptors, among which was the Greek Slave of Powers, which my English friends criticised as being too thin and meagre; but I defended it as in accordance with American ideas of feminine beauty. From the conservatory we passed into the garden, but did not minutely examine it, knowing that Mr. Hall would wish to lead us through it in person. So, in the mean time, we took a walk in the neighborhood, over stiles and along by-paths, for two or three miles, till we reached the old village of Chertsey. In one of its streets stands an ancient house, gabled, and with the second story projecting over the first, and bearing an inscription to the purport that the poet Cowley had once resided, and, I think, died there. Thence we passed on till we reached a bridge over the Thames, which at this point, about twenty-five miles from London, is a narrow river, but looks clean and pure, and unconscious what abominations the city sewers will pour into it anon. We were caught in two or three showers in the course of our walk; but got back to Firfield without being very much wetted.

Our host and hostess had by this time returned from church, and Mrs. Hall came frankly and heartily to the door to greet us, scolding us (kindly) for having got wet. . . . I liked her simple, easy, gentle, quiet manners, and I liked her husband too.

He has a wide and quick sympathy, and expresses it freely. . . . The world is the better for him.

The shower being now over, we went out upon the beautiful lawn before his house, where there were a good many trees of various kinds, many of which have been set out by persons of great or small distinction, and are labelled with their names. Thomas Moore's name was appended to one; Maria Edgeworth's to another; likewise Fredrika Bremer's, Jenny Lind's; also Grace Greenwood's, and I know not whose besides. This is really a pleasant method of enriching one's grounds with memorials of friends, nor is there any harm in making a shrubbery of celebrities. Three holes were already dug, and three new trees lay ready to be planted, and for me there was a sumach to plant,—a tree I never liked; but Mr. Hall said that they had tried to dig up a hawthorn, but found it clung too fast to the soil. So, since better might not be, and telling Mr. Hall that I supposed I should have a right to hang myself on this tree whenever I chose, I seized a spade, and speedily shovelled in a great deal of dirt; and there stands my sumach, an object of interest to posterity! Bennoch also and Dr. ——— set out their trees, and indeed, it was in some sense a joint affair, for the rest of the party held up each tree, while its godfather shovelled in the earth; but, after all, the gardener had more to do with it than we. After this important business was over, Mr. Hall led us about his rounds, which are very nicely planned and ordered; and all this he has bought, and built, and laid out, from the profits of his own and his wife's literary exertions.

We dined early, and had a very pleasant dinner, and, after the cloth was removed, Mr. Hall was graciously pleased to drink my health, following it with a long tribute to my genius. I answered briefly; and one half of my short speech was in all probability very foolish. . . .

After the ladies (there were three, one being a girl of seventeen, with rich auburn hair, the adopted daughter of the Halls) had retired, Dr. ——— having been toasted himself, proposed Mrs. Hall's health.

I did not have a great deal of conversation with Mrs. Hall; but enough to make me think her a genuine and good woman, unspoilt by a literary career, and retaining more sentiment than even most girls keep beyond seventeen. She told me that it had been the dream of her life to see Longfellow and myself! . . . . Her dream is half accomplished now, and, as they say Longfellow is coming over this summer, the remainder may soon be rounded out. On taking leave, our kind hosts presented me with some beautiful flowers, and with three volumes of a work, by themselves, on Ireland; and Dr. ——— was favored also with some flowers, and a plant in a pot, and Bennoch too had his hands full, ... and we went on our way rejoicing.

[Here follows an account of the Lord Mayor's dinner, taken mostly for Our Old Home; but I think I will copy this more exact description of the lady mentioned in "Civic Banquets."—ED.]

. . . . My eyes were mostly drawn to a young lady, who sat nearly opposite me, across the table. She was, I suppose, dark, and yet not dark, but rather seemed to be of pure white marble, yet not white; but the purest and finest complexion, without a shade of color in it, yet anything but sallow or sickly. Her hair was a wonderful deep raven-black, black as night, black as death; not raven-black, for that has a shiny gloss, and hers had not, but it was hair never to be painted nor described,—wonderful hair, Jewish hair. Her nose had a beautiful outline, though I could see that it was Jewish too; and that, and all her features, were so fine that sculpture seemed a despicable art beside her, and certainly my pen is good for nothing. If any likeness could be given, however; it must be by sculpture, not painting. She was slender and youthful, and yet had a stately and cold, though soft and womanly grace; and, looking at her, I saw what were the wives of the old patriarchs in their maiden or early-married days,—what Judith was, for, womanly as she looked, I doubt, not she could have slain a man in a just cause,—what Bathsheba was, only she seemed to have no sin in her,— perhaps what Eve was, though one could hardly think her weak enough to eat the apple. . . . Whether owing to distinctness of race, my sense that she was a Jewess, or whatever else, I felt a sort of repugnance, simultaneously with my perception that she was an admirable creature.

THE HOUSE OF COMMONS.

At ten o'clock the next day [after the Lord Mayor's dinner] I went to lunch with Bennoch, and afterwards accompanied him to one of the government offices in Downing Street. He went thither, not on official business, but on a matter connected with a monument to Miss Mitford, in which Mr. Harness, a clergyman and some sort of a government clerk, is interested. I gathered from this conversation that there is no great enthusiasm about the monumental affair among the British public. It surprised me to hear allusions indicating that Miss Mitford was not the invariably amiable person that her writings would suggest; but the whole drift of what they said tended, nevertheless, towards the idea that she was an excellent and generous person, loved most by those who knew her best.

From Downing Street we crossed over and entered Westminster Hall, and passed through it, and up the flight of steps at its farthest end, and along the avenue of statues, into the vestibule of the House of Commons. It was now somewhat past five, and we stood at the inner entrance of the House, to see the members pass in, Bennoch pointing out to me the distinguished ones. I was not much impressed with the appearance of the members generally; they seemed to me rather shabbier than English gentlemen usually, and I saw or fancied in many of them a certain self-importance, as they passed into the interior, betokening them to be very full of their dignity. Some of them looked more American—more like American politicians—than most Englishmen do. There was now and then a gray-headed country gentleman, the very type of stupidity; and two or three city members came up and spoke to Bennoch, and showed themselves quite as dull, in their aldermanic way, as the country squires. . . . Bennoch pointed out Lord John Russell, a small, very short, elderly gentleman, in a brown coat, and so large a hat—not large of brim, but large like a peck-measure—that I saw really no face beneath it. By and by came a rather tall, slender person, in a black frock-coat, buttoned up, and black pantaloons, taking long steps, but I thought rather feebly or listlessly. His shoulders were round, or else he had a habitual stoop in them.

He had a prominent nose, a thin face, and a sallow, very sallow complexion; . . . . and had I seen him in America I should have taken him for a hard-worked editor of a newspaper, weary and worn with night-labor and want of exercise,—aged before his time. It was Disraeli, and I never saw any other Englishman look in the least like him; though, in America, his appearance would not attract notice as being unusual. I do not remember any other noteworthy person whom we saw enter; in fact, the House had already been some time in session, and most of the members were in their places.

We were to dine at the Refectory of the House with the new member for Boston; and, meanwhile, Bennoch obtained admittance for us into the Speaker's gallery, where we had a view of the members, and could hear what was going on. A Mr. Muntz was speaking on the Income Tax, and he was followed by Sir George Cornewall Lewis and others; but it was all very uninteresting, without the slightest animation or attempt at oratory,—which, indeed, would have been quite out of place. We saw Lord Palmerston; but at too great a distance to distinguish anything but a gray head. The House had daylight in it when we entered, and for some time afterwards; but, by and by, the roof, which I had taken to be a solid and opaque ceiling, suddenly brightened, and showed itself to be transparent; a vast expanse of tinted and figured glass, through which came down a great, mild radiance on the members below.

The character of the debate, however, did not grow more luminous or vivacious; so we went down into the vestibule, and there waited for Mr. ———, who soon came and led us into the Refectory. It was very much like the coffee-room of a club. The strict rule forbids the entrance of any but members of Parliament; but it seems to be winked at, although there is another room, opening beyond this, where the law of seclusion is strictly enforced.

The dinner was good, not remarkably so, but good enough,—a soup, some turbot or salmon, cutlets, and I know not what else, and claret, sherry, and port; for, as Mr. ——— said, "he did not wish to be stingy." Mr. ——— is a self-made man, and a strong instance of the difference between the Englishman and the American, when self-made, and without early education.

He is no more a gentleman now than when he began life, —not a whit more refined, either outwardly or inwardly; while the American would have been, after the same experience, not distinguishable outwardly, and perhaps as refined within, as nine tenths of the gentlemen born, in the House of Commons. And, besides, an American comes naturally to any distinctions to which success in life may bring him; he takes them as if they were his proper inheritance, and in no wise to be wondered at. Mr. ———, on the other hand, took evidently a childish delight in his position, and felt a childish wonder in having arrived at it; nor did it seem real to him, after all. . . .

We again saw Disraeli, who has risen from the people by modes perhaps somewhat like those of Mr. ———. He came and stood near our table, looking at the bill of fare, and then sat down on the opposite side of the room with another gentleman, and ate his dinner. The story of his marriage does him much credit; and indeed I am inclined to like Disraeli, as a man who has made his own place good among a hostile aristocracy, and leads instead of following them.

From the House of Commons we went to Albert Smith's exhibition, or lecture, of the ascent of Mont Blanc, to which Bennoch had orders. It was very amusing, and in some degree instructive. We remained in the saloon at the conclusion of the lecture; and when the audience had dispersed, Mr. Albert Smith made his appearance. . . .

Nothing of moment happened the next day, at least, not till two o'clock, when I went with Mr. Bowman to Birch's eating-house (it is not Birch's now, but this was the name of the original founder, who became an alderman, and has long been dead) for a basin of turtle-soup. It was very rich, very good, better than we had at the Lord Mayor's, and the best I ever ate.

In the evening, Mr. J. B. Davis, formerly our Secretary of Legation, called to take us to dine at Mr. ———'s in Camden Town. Mr. ——— calls his residence Vermont House; but it hardly has a claim to any separate title, being one of the centre houses of a block. I forget whether I mentioned his calling on me. He is a Vermonter, a graduate of Yale College, who has been here several years, and has established a sort of book brokerage, buying libraries for those who want them, and rare works and editions for American collectors. His business naturally brings him into relations with literary people; and he is himself a kindly and pleasant man. On our arrival we found Mr. D——— and one of his sisters already there; and soon came a Mr. Peabody, who, if I mistake not, is one of the Salem Peabodys, and has some connection with the present eminent London Mr. Peabody. At any rate, he is a very sensible, well-instructed, and widely and long travelled man. Mr. Tom Taylor was also expected; but, owing to some accident or mistake, he did not come for above an hour, all which time our host waited. . . . But Mr. Tom Taylor, a wit, a satirist, and a famous diner out, is too formidable and too valuable a personage to be treated cavalierly.

In the interim Mr. ——— showed us some rare old books, which he has in his private collection, a black-letter edition of Chaucer, and other specimens of the early English printers; and I was impressed, as I have often been, with the idea that we have made few, if any, improvements in the art of printing, though we have greatly facilitated the modes of it. He showed us Dryden's translation of Virgil, with Dr. Johnson's autograph in it and a large collection of Bibles, of all dates,—church Bibles, family Bibles of the common translation, and older ones. He says he has written or is writing a history of the Bible (as a printed work, I presume). Many of these Bibles had, no doubt, been in actual and daily use from generation to generation; but they were now all splendidly bound, and were likewise very clean and smooth,—in fact, every leaf had been cleansed by a delicate process, a part of which consisted in soaking the whole book in a tub of water, during several days. Mr. ——— is likewise rich in manuscripts, having a Spanish document with the signature of the son of Columbus; a whole little volume in Franklin's handwriting, being the first specimen of it; and the original manuscripts of many of the songs of Burns. Among these I saw "Auld Lang Syne," and "Bruce's Address to his Army." We amused ourselves with these matters as long as we could; but at last, as there was to be a party in the evening, dinner could no longer be put off; so we took our seats at table, and immediately afterwards Mr. Taylor made his appearance with his wife and another lady.

Mr. Taylor is reckoned a brilliant conversationist; but I suppose he requires somebody to draw him out and assist him; for I could hear nothing that I thought very remarkable on this occasion. He is not a kind of man whom I can talk with, or greatly help to talk; so, though I sat next to him, nothing came of it. He told me some stories of his life in the Temple,—little funny incidents, that he afterwards wrought into his dramas; in short, a sensible, active-minded, clearly perceptive man, with a humorous way of showing up men and matters. . . . I wish I could know exactly what the English style good conversation. Probably it is something like plum-pudding,—as heavy, but seldom so rich.

After dinner Mr. Tom Taylor and Mr. D———, with their respective ladies, took their leave; but when we returned to the drawing-room, we found it thronged with a good many people. Mr. S. C. Hall was there with his wife, whom I was glad to see again, for this was the third time of meeting her, and, in this whirl of new acquaintances, I felt quite as if she were an old friend. Mr. William Howitt was also there, and introduced me to his wife,—a very natural, kind, and pleasant lady; and she presented me to one or two daughters. Mr. Marston, the dramatist, was also introduced to me; and Mr. Helps, a thin, scholarly, cold sort of a man. Dr. Mackay and his wife were there, too; and a certain Mr. Jones, a sculptor,—a jolly, large, elderly person, with a twinkle in his eye. Also a Mr. Godwin, who impressed me as quite a superior person, gentlemanly, cultivated, a man of sensibility; but it is quite impossible to take a clear imprint from any one character, where so many are stamped upon one's notice at once. This Mr. Godwin, as we were discussing Thackeray, said that he is most beautifully tender and devoted to his wife, whenever she can be sensible of his attentions. He says that Thackeray, in his real self, is a sweet, sad man. I grew weary of so many people, especially of the ladies, who were rather superfluous in their oblations, quite stifling me, indeed, with the incense that they burnt under my nose. So far as I could judge, they had all been invited there to see me. It is ungracious, even hoggish, not to be gratified with the interest they expressed in me; but then it is really a bore, and one does not know what to do or say. I felt like the hippopotamus, or— to use a more modest illustration—like some strange insect imprisoned under a tumbler, with a dozen eyes watching whatever I did. By and by, Mr. Jones, the sculptor, relieved me by standing up against the mantel-piece, and telling an Irish story, not to two or three auditors, but to the whole drawing-room, all attentive as to a set exhibition. It was very funny.

The next day after this I went with Mr. Bowman to call on our minister, and found that he, and four of the ladies of his family, with his son, had gone to the Queen's Drawing-room. We lunched at the Wellington; and spent an hour or more in looking out of the window of that establishment at the carriages, with their pompous coachmen and footmen, driving to and from the Palace of St. James, and at the Horse Guards, with their bright cuirasses, stationed along the street. . . . Then I took the rail for Liverpool. . . . While I was still at breakfast at the Waterloo, J——- came in, ruddy-cheeked, smiling, very glad to see me, and looking, I thought, a good deal taller than when I left him. And so ended my London excursion, which has certainly been rich in incident and character, though my account of it be but meagre.

SCOTLAND.—GLASGOW.

May 10th.—Last Friday, May 2d, I took the rail, with Mr. Bowman, from the Lime Street station, for Glasgow. There was nothing of much interest along the road, except that, when we got beyond Penrith, we saw snow on the tops of some of the hills. Twilight came on as we were entering Scotland; and I have only a recollection of bleak and bare hills and villages dimly seen, until, nearing Glasgow, we saw the red blaze of furnace-lights at frequent iron-founderies. We put up at the Queen's Hotel, where we arrived about ten o'clock; a better hotel than I have anywhere found in England,—new, well arranged, and with brisk attendance.

In the morning I rambled largely about Glasgow, and found it to be chiefly a modern-built city, with streets mostly wide and regular, and handsome houses and public edifices of a dark gray stone. In front of our hotel, in an enclosed green space, stands a tall column surmounted by a statue of Sir Walter Scott,—a good statue, I should think, as conveying the air and personal aspect of the man. There is a bronze equestrian statue of the Queen in one of the streets, and one or two more equestrian or other statues of eminent persons. I passed through the Trongate and the Gallow-Gate, and visited the Salt-Market, and saw the steeple of the Tolbooth, all of which Scott has made interesting; and I went through the gate of the University, and penetrated into its enclosed courts, round which the College edifices are built. They are not Gothic, but of the age, I suppose, of James I.,—with odd-looking, conical-roofed towers, and here and there the bust of a benefactor in niches round the courts, and heavy stone staircases ascending from the pavement, outside the buildings, all of dark gray granite, cold, hard, and venerable. The University stands in High Street, in a dense part of the town, and a very old and shabby part, too. I think the poorer classes of Glasgow excel even those in Liverpool in the bad eminence of filth, uncombed and unwashed children, drunkenness, disorderly deportment, evil smell, and all that makes city poverty disgusting. In my opinion, however, they are a better-looking people than the English (and this is true of all classes), more intelligent of aspect, with more regular features. I looked for the high cheek-bones, which have been attributed, as a characteristic feature, to the Scotch, but could not find them. What most distinguishes them front the English is the regularity of the nose, which is straight, or sometimes a little curved inward; whereas the English nose has no law whatever, but disports itself in all manner of irregularity. I very soon learned to recognize the Scotch face, and when not too Scotch, it is a handsome one.

In another part of the High Street, up a pretty steep slope, and on one side of a public green, near an edifice which I think is a medical college, stands St. Mungo's Cathedral. It is hardly of cathedral dimensions, though a large and fine old church. The price of a ticket of admittance is twopence; so small that it might be as well to make the entrance free. The interior is in excellent repair, with the nave and side aisles, and clustered pillars, and intersecting arches, that belong to all these old churches; and a few monuments along the walls. I was going away without seeing any more than this; but the verger, a friendly old gentleman, with a hearty Scotch way of speaking, told me that the crypts were what chiefly interested strangers; and so he guided me down into the foundation-story of the church, where there is an intricacy and entanglement of immensely massive and heavy arches, supporting the structure above. The view through these arches, among the great shafts of the columns, was very striking. In the central part is a monument; a recumbent figure, if I remember rightly, but it is not known whom it commemorates. There is also a monument to a Scotch prelate, which seems to have been purposely defaced, probably in Covenant times. These intricate arches were the locality of one of the scenes in "Rob Roy," when Rob gives Frank Osbaldistone some message or warning, and then escapes from him into the obscurity behind. In one corner is St. Mungo's well, secured with a wooden cover; but I should not care to drink water that comes from among so many old graves.

After viewing the cathedral, I got back to the hotel just in time to go from thence to the steamer wharf, and take passage up the Clyde. There was nothing very interesting in this little voyage. We passed many small iron steamers, and some large ones; and green fields along the river-shores, villas, villages, and all such suburban objects; neither am I quite sure of the name of the place we landed at, though I think it was Bowling. Here we took the railway for Balloch; and the only place or thing I remember during this transit was a huge bluff or crag, rising abruptly from a river-side, and looking, in connection with its vicinity to the Highlands, just such a site as would be taken for the foundation of a castle. On inquiry it turned out that this abrupt and double-headed hill (for it has two summits, with a cleft between) is the site of Dumbarton Castle, for ages one of the strongest fortresses in Scotland, and still kept up as a garrisoned place. At the distance and point of view at which we passed it, the castle made no show.

Arriving at Balloch, we found it a small village, with no marked features, and a hotel, where we got some lunch, and then we took a stroll over the bridge across the Levers, while waiting for the steamer to take us up Loch Lomond. It was a beautiful afternoon, warm and sunny; and after walking about a mile, we had a fine view of Loch Lomond, and of the mountains around and beyond it,—Ben Lomond among the rest. It is vain, at a week's distance, to try to remember the shapes of mountains; so I shall attempt no description of them, and content myself with saying that they did not quite come up to my anticipations. In due time we returned to our hotel, and found in the coffee-room a tall, white-haired, venerable gentleman, and a pleasant-looking young lady, his daughter. They had been eating lunch, and the young lady helped her father on with his outside garment, and his comforter, and gave him his stick, just as any other daughter might do,—all of which I mention because he was a nobleman; and, moreover, had engaged all the post-horses at the inn, so that we could not continue our travels by land, along the side of Loch Lomond, as we had first intended. At four o'clock the railway train arrived again, with a very moderate number of passengers, who (and we among them) immediately embarked on board a neat little steamer which was waiting for us.

The day was bright and cloudless; but there was a strong, cold breeze blowing down the lake, so that it was impossible, without vast discomfort, to stand in the bow of the steamer and look at the scenery. I looked at it, indeed, along the sides, as we passed, and on our track behind; and no doubt it was very fine; but from all the experience I have had, I do not think scenery can be well seen from the water. At any rate, the shores of Loch Lomond have faded completely out of my memory; nor can I conceive that they really were very striking. At a year's interval, I can recollect the cluster of hills around the head of Lake Windermere; at twenty years' interval, I remember the shores of Lake Champlain; but of the shores of this Scottish lake I remember nothing except some oddly shaped rocks, called "The Cobbler and his Daughter," on a mountain-top, just before we landed. But, indeed, we had very imperfect glimpses of the hills along the latter part of the course, because the wind had grown so very cold that we took shelter below, and merely peeped at Loch Lomond's sublimities from the cabin-windows.

The whole voyage up Loch Lomond is, I think, about thirty-two miles; but we landed at a place called Tarbet, much short of the ultimate point. There is here a large hotel; but we passed it, and walked onward a mile or two to Arroquhar, a secluded glen among the hills, where is a new hotel, built in the old manor-house style, and occupying the site of what was once a castle of the chief of the MacFarlanes. Over the portal is a stone taken from the former house, bearing the date 1697. There is a little lake near the house, and the hills shut in the whole visible scene so closely that there appears no outlet nor communication with the external world; but in reality this little lake is connected with Loch Long, and Loch Long is an arm of the sea; so that there is water communication between Arroquhar and Glasgow. We found this a very beautiful place; and being quite sheltered from all winds that blew, we strolled about late into the prolonged twilight, and admired the outlines of the surrounding hills, and fancied resemblances to various objects in the shapes of the crags against the evening sky. The sun had not set till nearly, if not quite, eight o'clock; and before the daylight had quite gone, the northern lights streamed out, and I do not think that there was much darkness over the glen of Arroquhar that night. At all events, before the darkness came, we withdrew into the coffee-room.

We had excellent beds and sleeping-rooms in this new hotel, and I remember nothing more till morning, when we were astir betimes, and had some chops for breakfast. Then our host, Mr. Macregor, who is also the host of our hotel at Glasgow, and has many of the characteristics of an American landlord, claiming to be a gentleman and the equal of his guests, took us in a drosky, and drove us to the shore of Loch Lomond, at a point about four miles from Arroquhar. The lake is here a mile and a half wide, and it was our object to cross to Inversnaid, on the opposite shore; so first we waved a handkerchief, and then kindled some straw on the beach, in order to attract the notice of the ferryman at Inversnaid. It was half an hour before our signals and shoutings resulted in the putting off of a boat, with two oarsmen, who made the transit pretty speedily; and thus we got across Loch Lomond. At Inversnaid there is a small hotel, and over the rock on which it stands a little waterfall tumbles into the lake,—a very little one, though I believe it is reckoned among the other picturesque features of the scene.

We were now in Rob Roy's country, and at the distance of a mile or so, along the shore of the lake, is Rob Roy's cave, where he and his followers are supposed to have made their abode in troublous times. While lunch was getting ready, we again took the boat, and went thither. Landing beneath a precipitous, though not very lofty crag, we clambered up a rude pathway, and came to the mouth of the cave, which is nothing but a fissure or fissures among some great rocks that have tumbled confusedly together. There is hardly anywhere space enough for half a dozen persons to crowd themselves together, nor room to stand upright. On the whole, it is no cave at all, but only a crevice; and, in the deepest and darkest part, you can look up and see the sky. It may have sheltered Rob Roy for a night, and might partially shelter any Christian during a shower.

Returning to the hotel, we started in a drosky (I do not know whether this is the right name of the vehicle, or whether it has a right name, but it is a carriage in which four persons sit back to back, two before and two behind) for Aberfoyle. The mountain-side ascends very steeply from the inn door, and, not to damp the horse's courage in the outset, we went up on foot. The guide-book says that the prospect from the summit of the ascent is very fine; but I really believe we forgot to turn round and look at it. All through our drive, however, we had mountain views in plenty, especially of great Ben Lomond, with his snow-covered head, round which, since our entrance into the Highlands, we had been making a circuit. Nothing can possibly be drearier than the mountains at this season; bare, barren, and bleak, with black patches of withered heath variegating the dead brown of the herbage on their sides; and as regards trees the hills are perfectly naked. There were no frightful precipices, no boldly picturesque features, along our road; but high, weary slopes, showing miles and miles of heavy solitude, with here and there a highland hut, built of stone and thatched; and, in one place, an old gray, ruinous fortress, a station of the English troops after the rebellion of 1715; and once or twice a village of hills, the inhabitants of which, old and young, ran to their doors to stare at us. For several miles after we left Inversnaid, the mountain-stream which makes the waterfall brawled along the roadside. All the hills are sheep-pastures, and I never saw such wild, rough, ragged-looking creatures as the sheep, with their black faces and tattered wool. The little lambs were very numerous, poor things, coming so early in the season into this inclement region; and it was laughable to see how invariably, when startled by our approach, they scampered to their mothers, and immediately began to suck. It would seem as if they sought a draught from the maternal udder, wherewith to fortify and encourage their poor little hearts; but I suppose their instinct merely drove them close to their dams, and, being there, they took advantage of their opportunity. These sheep must lead a hard life during the winter; for they are never fed nor sheltered.

The day was sunless, and very uncomfortably cold; and we were not sorry to walk whenever the steepness of the road gave us cause. I do not remember what o'clock it was, but not far into the afternoon, when we reached the Baillie Nicol-Jarvie Inn at Aberfoyle; a scene which is much more interesting in the pages of Rob Roy than we found it in reality. Here we got into a sort of cart, and set out, over another hill-path, as dreary as or drearier than the last, for the Trosachs. On our way, we saw Ben Venue, and a good many other famous Bens, and two or three lochs; and when we reached the Trosachs, we should probably have been very much enraptured if our eyes had not already been weary with other mountain shapes. But, in truth, I doubt if anybody ever does really see a mountain, who goes for the set and sole purpose of seeing it. Nature will not let herself be seen in such cases. You must patiently bide her time; and by and by, at some unforeseen moment, she will quietly and suddenly unveil herself, and for a brief space allow you to look right into the heart of her mystery. But if you call out to her peremptorily, "Nature! unveil yourself this very moment!" she only draws her veil the closer; and you may look with all your eyes, and imagine that you see all that she can show, and yet see nothing. Thus, I saw a wild and confused assemblage of heights, crags, precipices, which they call the Trosachs, but I saw them calmly and coldly, and was glad when the drosky was ready to take us on to Callender. The hotel at the Trosachs, by the by, is a very splendid one, in the form of an old feudal castle, with towers and turrets. All among these wild hills there is set preparation for enraptured visitants; and it seems strange that the savage features do not subside of their own accord, and that there should still be cold winds and snow on the top of Ben Lomond, and rocks and heather, and ragged sheep, now that there are so many avenues by which the commonplace world is sluiced in among the Highlands. I think that this fashion of the picturesque will pass away.

We drove along the shore of Lake Vennachar, and onward to Callender, which I believe is either the first point in the Lowlands or the last in the Highlands. It is a large village on the river Teith. We stopped here to dine, and were some time in getting any warmth into our benumbed bodies; for, as I said before, it was a very cold day. Looking from the window of the hotel, I saw a young man in Highland dress, with bare thighs, marching through the village street towards the Lowlands, with a martial and elastic step, as if he were going forth to conquer and occupy the world. I suppose he was a soldier who had been absent on leave, returning to the garrison at Stirling. I pitied his poor thighs, though he certainly did not look uncomfortable.

After dinner, as dusk was coming on and we had still a long drive before us (eighteen miles, I believe), we took a close carriage and two horses, and set off for Stirling. The twilight was too obscure to show many things along the road, and by the time we drove into Stirling we could but dimly see the houses in the long street in which stood our hotel. There was a good fire in the coffee-room, which looked like a drawing-room in a large old-fashioned mansion, and was hung round with engravings of the portraits of the county members, and a master of fox-hounds, and other pictures. We made ourselves comfortable with some tea, and retired early.

In the morning we were stirring betimes, and found Stirling to be a pretty large town, of rather ancient aspect, with many gray stone houses, the gables of which are notched on either side, like a flight of stairs. The town stands on the slope of a hill, at the summit of which, crowning a long ascent, up which the paved street reaches all the way to its gate, is Stirling Castle. Of course we went thither, and found free entrance, although the castle is garrisoned by five or six hundred men, among whom are barelegged Highlanders (I must say that this costume is very fine and becoming, though their thighs did look blue and frost-bitten) and also some soldiers of other Scotch regiments, with tartan trousers. Almost immediately on passing the gate, we found an old artillery-man, who undertook to show us round the castle. Only a small portion of it seems to be of great antiquity. The principal edifice within the castle wall is a palace, that was either built or renewed by James VI.; and it is ornamented with strange old statues, one of which is his own. The old Scottish Parliament House is also here. The most ancient part of the castle is the tower, where one of the Earls of Douglas was stabbed by a king, and afterwards thrown out of the window. In reading this story, one imagines a lofty turret, and the dead man tumbling headlong from a great height; but, in reality, the window is not more than fifteen or twenty feet from the garden into which he fell. This part of the castle was burned last autumn; but is now under repair, and the wall of the tower is still stanch and strong. We went up into the chamber where the murder took place, and looked through the historic window.

Then we mounted the castle wall, where it broods over a precipice of many hundred feet perpendicular, looking down upon a level plain below, and forth upon a landscape, every foot of which is richly studded with historic events. There is a small peep-hole in the wall, which Queen Mary is said to have been in the habit of looking through. It is a most splendid view; in the distance, the blue Highlands, with a variety of mountain outlines that I could have studied unweariably; and in another direction, beginning almost at the foot of the Castle Hill, were the Links of Forth, where, over a plain of miles in extent the river meandered, and circled about, and returned upon itself again and again and again, as if knotted into a silver chain, which it was difficult to imagine to be all one stream. The history of Scotland might be read from this castle wall, as on a book of mighty page; for here, within the compass of a few miles, we see the field where Wallace won the battle of Stirling, and likewise the battle-field of Bannockburn, and that of Falkirk, and Sheriffmuir, and I know not how many besides.

Around the Castle Hill there is a walk, with seats for old and infirm persons, at points sheltered from the wind. We followed it downward, and I think we passed over the site where the games used to be held, and where, this morning, some of the soldiers of the garrison were going through their exercises. I ought to have mentioned, that, passing through the inner gateway of the castle, we saw the round tower, and glanced into the dungeon, where the Roderic Dhu of Scott's poem was left to die. It is one of the two round towers, between which the portcullis rose and fell.

EDINBURGH.—THE PALACE OF HOLYROOD.

At eleven o'clock we took the rail for Edinburgh, and I remember nothing more, except that the cultivation and verdure of the country were very agreeable, after our experience of Highland barrenness and desolation, until we found the train passing close at the base of the rugged crag of Edinburgh Castle. We established ourselves at Queen's Hotel, in Prince's Street, and then went out to view the city. The monument to Sir Walter Scott—a rather fantastic and not very impressive affair, I thought— stands almost directly in front of a hotel. We went along Prince's Street, and thence, by what turns I know not, to the Palace of Holyrood, which stands on a low and sheltered site, and is a venerable edifice. Arthur's Seat rises behind it,—a high hill, with a plain between. As we drew near the Palace, Mr. Bowman, who has been here before, pointed out the windows of Queen Mary's apartments, in a circular tower on the left of the gateway. On entering the enclosed quadrangle, we bought tickets for sixpence each, admitting us to all parts of the Palace that are shown to visitors; and first we went into a noble hall or gallery, a long and stately room, hung with pictures of ancient Scottish kings; and though the pictures were none of them authentic, they, at least, answer an excellent purpose in the way of upholstery. It was here that the young Pretender gave the ball which makes one of the scenes in Waverley.

Thence we passed into the old historic rooms of the Palace,—Darnley's and Queen Mary's apartments, which everybody has seen and described. They are very dreary and shabby-looking rooms, with bare floors, and here and there a piece of tapestry, faded into a neutral tint; and carved and ornamented ceilings, looking shabbier than plain whitewash. We saw Queen Mary's old bedstead, low, with four tall posts,—and her looking-glass, which she brought with her from France, and which has often reflected the beauty that set everybody mad,—and some needlework and other womanly matters of hers; and we went into the little closet where she was having such a cosey supper-party with two or three friends, when the conspirators broke in, and stabbed Rizzio before her face. We saw, too, the blood-stain at the threshold of the door in the next room, opening upon the stairs. The body of Rizzio was flung down here, and the attendant told us that it lay in that spot all night. The blood-stain covers a large space,—much larger than I supposed,—and it gives the impression that there must have been a great pool and sop of blood on all the spot covered by Rizzio's body, staining the floor deeply enough never to be washed out. It is now of a dark brown hue; and I do not see why it may not be the genuine, veritable stain. The floor, thereabouts, appears not to have been scrubbed much; for I touched it with my finger, and found it slightly rough; but it is strange that the many footsteps should not have smoothed it, in three hundred years.

One of the articles shown us in Queen Mary's apartments was the breastplate supposed to have been worn by Lord Ruthven at the murder, a heavy plate of iron, and doubtless a very uncomfortable waistcoat.

HOLYROOD ABBEY.

From the Palace, we passed into the contiguous ruin of Holyrood Abbey; which is roofless, although the front, and some broken columns along the nave, and fragments of architecture here and there, afford hints of a magnificent Gothic church in bygone times. It deserved to be magnificent; for here have been stately ceremonials, marriages of kings, coronations, investitures, before the high altar, which has now been overthrown or crumbled away; and the floor—so far as there is any floor —consists of tombstones of the old Scottish nobility. There are likewise monuments, bearing the names of illustrious Scotch families; and inscriptions, in the Scotch dialect, on the walls.

In one of the front towers,—the only remaining one, indeed,—we saw the marble tomb of a nobleman, Lord Belhaven, who is represented reclining on the top,—with a bruised nose, of course. Except in Westminster Abbey, I do not remember ever to have seen an old monumental statue with the nose entire. In all political or religious outbreaks, the mob's first impulse is to hit the illustrious dead on their noses.

At the other end of the Abbey, near the high altar, is the vault where the old Scottish kings used to be buried; but, looking in through the window, I saw only a vacant space,—no skull, nor bone, nor the least fragment of a coffin. In fact, I believe the royal dead were turned out of their last home, on occasion of the Revolutionary movements, at the accession of William III.

HIGH STREET AND THE GRASS-MARKET.

Quitting the Abbey and the Palace, we turned into the Canongate, and passed thence into High Street, which, I think, is a continuation of the Canongate; and being now in the old town of Edinburgh, we saw those immensely tall houses, seven stories high, where the people live in tiers, all the way from earth to middle air. They were not so quaint and strange looking as I expected; but there were some houses of very antique individuality, and among them that of John Knox, which looks still in good repair. One thing did not in the least fall short of my expectations,—the evil odor, for which Edinburgh has an immemorial renown,—nor the dirt of the inhabitants, old and young. The town, to say the truth, when you are in the midst of it, has a very sordid, grimy, shabby, upswept, unwashen aspect, grievously at variance with all poetic and romantic associations.

From the High Street we turned aside into the Grass-Market, the scene of the Porteous Mob; and we found in the pavement a cross on the site where the execution of Porteous is supposed to have taken place.

THE CASTLE.

Returning thence to the High Street, we followed it up to the Castle, which is nearer the town, and of more easy access from it, than I had supposed. There is a large court or parade before the castle gate, with a parapet on the abrupt side of the hill, looking towards Arthur's Seat and Salisbury Crags, mud overhanging a portion of the old town. As we leaned over this parapet, my nose was conscious of the bad odor of Edinburgh, although the streets, whence it must have come, were hundreds of feet below. I have had some experience of this ugly smell in the poor streets of Liverpool; but I think I never perceived it before crossing the Atlantic. It is the odor of an old system of life; the scent of the pine forests is still too recent with us for it to be known in America.

The Castle of Edinburgh is free (as appears to be the case with all garrisoned places in Great Britain) to the entrance of any peaceable person. So we went in, and found a large space enclosed within the walls, and dwellings for officers, and accommodation for soldiers, who were being drilled, or loitering about; and as the hill still ascends within the external wall of the castle, we climbed to the summit, and there found an old soldier whom we engaged to be our guide. He showed us Mons Meg, a great old cannon, broken at the breech, but still aimed threateningly from the highest ramparts; and then he admitted us into an old chapel, said to have been built by a Queen of Scotland, the sister of Harold, King of England, and occupying the very highest part of the hill. It is the smallest place of worship I ever saw, but of venerable architecture, and of very solid construction. The old soldier had not much more to show us; but he pointed out the window whence one of the kings of Scotland is said, when a baby, to have been lowered down, the whole height of the castle, to the bottom of the precipice on which it stands,—a distance of seven hundred feet.

After the soldier had shown us to the extent of his jurisdiction, we went into a suite of rooms, in one of which I saw a portrait of Queen Mary, which gave me, for the first time, an idea that she was really a very beautiful woman. In this picture she is wonderfully so,—a tender womanly grace, which was none the less tender and graceful for being equally imbued with queenly dignity and spirit. It was too lovely a head to be cut off. I should be glad to know the authenticity of this picture.

I do not know that we did anything else worthy of note, before leaving Edinburgh. There is matter enough, in and about the town, to interest the visitor for a very long time; but when the visit is calculated on such brevity as ours was, we get weary of the place, before even these few hours come to an end. Thus, for my part, I was not sorry when, in the course of the afternoon, we took the rail for Melrose, where we duly arrived, and put up at the George Inn.

MELROSE.

Melrose is a village of rather antique aspect, situated on the slope and at the bottom of the Eildon Hills, which, from this point of view, appear like one hill, with a double summit. The village, as I said, has an old look, though many of the houses have at least been refronted at some recent date; but others are as ancient, I suppose, as the days when the Abbey was in its splendor,—a rustic and peasant-like antiquity, however, low-roofed, and straw-thatched. There is an aged cross of stone in the centre of the town.

Our first object, of course, was to see the Abbey, which stands just on the outskirts of the village, and is attainable only by applying at a neighboring house, the inhabitant of which probably supports himself, and most comfortably, too, as a showman of the ruin. He unlocked the wooden gate, and admitted us into what is left of the Abbey, comprising only the ruins of the church, although the refectory, the dormitories, and the other parts of the establishment, formerly covered the space now occupied by a dozen village houses. Melrose Abbey is a very satisfactory ruin, all carpeted along its nave and transepts with green grass; and there are some well-grown trees within the walls. We saw the window, now empty, through which the tints of the painted glass fell on the tombstone of Michael Scott, and the tombstone itself, broken in three pieces, but with a cross engraven along its whole length. It must have been the monument of an old monk or abbot, rather than a wizard. There, too, is still the "marble stone" on which the monk and warrior sat them down, and which is supposed to mark the resting-place of Alexander of Scotland. There are remains, both without and within the Abbey, of most curious and wonderfully minute old sculpture,—foliage, in places where it is almost impossible to see them, and where the sculptor could not have supposed that they would be seen, but which yet are finished faithfully, to the very veins of each leaf, in stone; and there is a continual variety of this accurate toil. On the exterior of the edifice there is equal minuteness of finish, and a great many niches for statues; all of which, I believe, are now gone, although there are carved faces at some points and angles. The graveyard around the Abbey is still the only one which the village has, and is crowded with gravestones, among which I read the inscription of one erected by Sir Walter Scott to the memory of Thomas Pardy, one of his servants. Some sable birds—either rooks or jackdaws— were flitting about the ruins, inside and out.

Mr. Bowman and I talked about revisiting Melrose by moonlight; but, luckily, there was to be no moon that evening. I do not myself think that daylight and sunshine make a ruin less effective than twilight or moonshine. In reference to Scott's description, I think he deplorably diminishes the impressiveness of the scene by saying that the alternate buttresses, seen by moonlight, look as if made of ebon and ivory. It suggests a small and very pretty piece of cabinet-work; not these gray, rough walls, which Time has gnawed upon for a thousand years, without eating them away.

Leaving the Abbey, we took a path or a road which led us to the river Tweed, perhaps a quarter of a mile off; and we crossed it by a foot-bridge,—a pretty wide stream, a dimpling breadth of transparent water flowing between low banks, with a margin of pebbles. We then returned to our inn, and had tea, and passed a quiet evening by the fireside. This is a good, unpretentious inn; and its visitors' book indicates that it affords general satisfaction to those who come here.

In the morning we breakfasted on broiled salmon, taken, no doubt, in the neighboring Tweed. There was a very coarse-looking man at table with us, who informed us that he owned the best horse anywhere round the Eildon Hills, and could make the best cast for a salmon, and catch a bigger fish than anybody,—with other self-laudation of the same kind. The waiter afterwards told us that he was the son of an Admiral in the neighborhood; and soon, his horse being brought to the door, we saw him mount and ride away. He sat on horseback with ease and grace, though I rather suspect, early as it was, that he was already in his cups. The Scotch seem to me to get drunk at very unseasonable hours. I have seen more drunken people here than during all my residence in England, and, generally, early in the day. Their liquor, so far as I have observed, makes them good-natured and sociable, imparting a perhaps needed geniality to their cold natures.

After breakfast we took a drosky, or whatever these fore-and-aft-seated vehicles are called, and set out for three miles distant. It was a cold though rather bright morning, with a most shrewd and bitter wind, which blew directly in my face as I sat beside the driver. An English wind is bad enough, but methinks a Scotch one, is rather worse; at any rate, I was half frozen, and wished Dryburgh Abbey in Tophet, where it would have been warmer work to go and see it. Some of the border hills were striking, especially the Cowden Knowe, which ascends into a prominent and lofty peak. Such villages as we passed did not greatly differ from English villages. By and by we came to the banks of the Tweed, at a point where there is a ferry. A carriage was on the river-bank, the driver waiting beside it; for the people who came in it had already been ferried across to see the Abbey.

The ferryman here is a young girl; and, stepping into the boat, she shoved off, and so skilfully took advantage of the eddies of the stream, which is here deep and rapid, that we were soon on the other side. She was by no means an uncomely maiden, with pleasant Scotch features, and a quiet intelligence of aspect, gleaming into a smile when spoken to; much tanned with all kinds of weather, and, though slender, yet so agile and muscular that it was no shame for a man to let himself be rowed by her.

From the ferry we had a walk of half a mile, more or less, to a cottage, where we found another young girl, whose business it is to show the Abbey. She was of another mould than the ferry-maiden,—a queer, shy, plaintive sort of a body,—and answered all our questions in a low, wailing tone. Passing through an apple-orchard, we were not long in reaching the Abbey, the ruins of which are much more extensive and more picturesque than those of Melrose, being overrun with bushes and shrubbery, and twined about with ivy, and all such vegetation as belongs, naturally, to old walls. There are the remains of the refectory, and other domestic parts of the Abbey, as well as the church, and all in delightful state of decay,—not so far gone but that we had bits of its former grandeur in the columns and broken arches, and in some portions of the edifice that still retain a roof.

In the chapter-house we saw a marble statue of Newton, wofully maltreated by damps and weather; and though it had no sort of business there, it fitted into the ruins picturesquely enough. There is another statue, equally unauthorized; both having been placed here by a former Earl of Buchan, who seems to have been a little astray in his wits.

On one side of the church, within an arched recess, are the monuments of Sir Walter Scott and his family,—three ponderous tombstones of Aberdeen granite, polished, but already dimmed and dulled by the weather. The whole floor of the recess is covered by these monuments, that of Sir Walter being the middle one, with Lady (or, as the inscription calls her, Dame) Scott beyond him, next to the church wall, and some one of his sons or daughters on the hither side. The effect of his being buried here is to make the whole of Dryburgh Abbey his monument. There is another arched recess, twin to the Scott burial-place, and contiguous to it, in which are buried a Pringle family; it being their ancient place of sepulture. The spectator almost inevitably feels as if they were intruders, although their rights here are of far older date than those of Scott.

Dryburgh Abbey must be a most beautiful spot of a summer afternoon; and it was beautiful even on this not very genial morning, especially when the sun blinked out upon the ivy, and upon the shrubberied paths that wound about the ruins. I think I recollect the birds chirruping in this neighborhood of it. After viewing it sufficiently,—sufficiently for this one time,—we went back to the ferry, and, being set across by the same Undine, we drove back to Melrose. No longer riding against the wind, I found it not nearly so cold as before. I now noticed that the Eildon Hills, seen from this direction, rise from one base into three distinct summits, ranged in a line. According to "The Lay of the Last Minstrel," they were cleft into this shape by the magic of Michael Scott. Reaching Melrose . . . . without alighting, we set off for three miles off. The neighborhood of Melrose, leading to Abbotsford, has many handsome residences of modern build and very recent date,—suburban villas, each with its little lawn and garden ground, such as we see in the vicinity of Liverpool. I noticed, too, one castellated house, of no great size, but old, and looking as if its tower were built, not for show, but for actual defence in the old border warfare.

We were not long in reaching Abbotsford. The house, which is more compact, and of considerably less extent than I anticipated, stands in full view from the road, and at only a short distance from it, lower down towards the river. Its aspect disappointed me; but so does everything. It is but a villa, after all; no castle, nor even a large manor-house, and very unsatisfactory when you consider it in that light. Indeed, it impressed me, not as a real house, intended for the home of human beings,—a house to die in or to be born in,—but as a plaything,— something in the same category as Horace Walpole's Strawberry Hill. The present owner seems to have found it insufficient for the actual purposes of life; for he is adding a wing, which promises to be as extensive as the original structure.

We rang at the front door (the family being now absent), and were speedily admitted by a middle-aged or somewhat elderly man,—the butler, I suppose, or some upper servant,—who at once acceded to our request to be permitted to see the house. We stepped from the porch immediately into the entrance-hall; and having the great Hall of Battle Abbey in my memory, and the ideal of a baronial hall in my mind, I was quite taken aback at the smallness and narrowness and lowness of this; which, however, is a very fine one, on its own little scale. In truth, it is not much more than a vestibule. The ceiling is carved; and every inch of the walls is covered with claymores, targets, and other weapons and armor, or old-time curiosities, tastefully arranged, many of which, no doubt, have a history attached to them,—or had, in Sir Walter's own mind. Our attendant was a very intelligent person, and pointed out much that was interesting; but in such a multitudinous variety it was almost impossible to fix the eye upon any one thing. Probably the apartment looked smaller than it really was, on account of being so wainscoted and festooned with curiosities. I remember nothing particularly, unless it be the coal-grate in the fireplace, which was one formerly used by Archbishop Sharpe, the prelate whom Balfour of Burley murdered. Either in this room or the next one, there was a glass case containing the suit of clothes last worn by Scott,—a short green coat, somewhat worn, with silvered buttons, a pair of gray tartan trousers, and a white hat. It was in the hall that we saw these things; for there too, I recollect, were a good many walking-sticks that had been used by Scott, and the hatchet with which he was in the habit of lopping branches from his trees, as he walked among them.

From the hall we passed into the study;—a small room, lined with the books which Sir Walter, no doubt, was most frequently accustomed to refer to; and our guide pointed out some volumes of the Moniteur, which he used while writing the history of Napoleon. Probably these were the driest and dullest volumes in his whole library. About mid-height of the walls of the study there is a gallery, with a short flight of steps for the convenience of getting at the upper books. A study-table occupied the centre of the room, and at one end of the table stands an easy-chair, covered with morocco, and with ample space to fling one's self back. The servant told me that I might sit down in this chair, for that Sir Walter sat there while writing his romances, "and perhaps," quoth the man, smiling, "you may catch some inspiration." What a bitter word this would have been if he had known me to be a romance-writer! "No, I never shall be inspired to write romances!" I answered, as if such an idea had never occurred to me. I sat down, however. This study quite satisfied me, being planned on principles of common-sense, and made to work in, and without any fantastic adaptation of old forms to modern uses.

Next to the study is the library, an apartment of respectable size, and containing as many books as it can hold, all protected by wire-work. I did not observe what or whose works were here; but the attendant showed us one whole compartment full of volumes having reference to ghosts, witchcraft, and the supernatural generally. It is remarkable that Scott should have felt interested in such subjects, being such a worldly and earthly man as he was; but then, indeed, almost all forms of popular superstition do clothe the ethereal with earthly attributes, and so make it grossly perceptible.

The library, like the study, suited me well,—merely the fashion of the apartment, I mean,—and I doubt not it contains as many curious volumes as are anywhere to be met with within a similar space. The drawing-room adjoins it; and here we saw a beautiful ebony cabinet, which was presented to Sir Walter by George IV.; and some pictures of much interest,—one of Scott himself at thirty-five, rather portly, with a heavy face, but shrewd eyes, which seem to observe you closely. There is a full-length of his eldest son, an officer of dragoons, leaning on his charger; and a portrait of Lady Scott,—a brunette, with black hair and eyes, very pretty, warm, vivacious, and un-English in her aspect. I am not quite sure whether I saw all these pictures in the drawing-room, or some of them in the dining-room; but the one that struck me most—and very much indeed—was the head of Mary, Queen of Scots, literally the head cut off and lying on a dish. It is said to have been painted by an Italian or French artist, two days after her death. The hair curls or flows all about it; the face is of a death-like hue, but has an expression of quiet, after much pain and trouble,—very beautiful, very sweet and sad; and it affected me strongly with the horror and strangeness of such a head being severed from its body. Methinks I should not like to have it always in the room with me. I thought of the lovely picture of Mary that I had seen at Edinburgh Castle, and reflected what a symbol it would be,—how expressive of a human being having her destiny in her own hands,—if that beautiful young Queen were painted as carrying this dish, containing her own woful head, and perhaps casting a curious and pitiful glance down upon it, as if it were not her own.

Also, in the drawing-room, there was a plaster cast of Sir Walter's face, taken after death; the only one in existence, as our guide assured us. It is not often that one sees a homelier set of features than this; no elevation, no dignity, whether bestowed by nature or thrown over them by age or death; sunken cheeks, the bridge of the nose depressed, and the end turned up; the mouth puckered, and no chin whatever, or hardly any. The expression was not calm and happy; but rather as if he were in a perturbed slumber, perhaps nothing short of nightmare. I wonder that the family allow this cast to be shown,—the last record that there is of Scott's personal reality, and conveying such a wretched and unworthy idea of it.

Adjoining the drawing-room is the dining-room, in one corner of which, between two windows, Scott died. It was now a quarter of a century since his death; but it seemed to me that we spoke with a sort of hush in our voices, as if he were still dying here, or had but just departed. I remember nothing else in this room. The next one is the armory, which is the smallest of all that we had passed through; but its walls gleam with the steel blades of swords, and the barrels of pistols, matchlocks, firelocks, and all manner of deadly weapons, whether European or Oriental; for there are many trophies here of East Indian warfare. I saw Rob Roy's gun, rifled and of very large bore; and a beautiful pistol, formerly Claverhouse's; and the sword of Montrose, given him by King Charles, the silver hilt of which I grasped. There was also a superb claymore, in an elaborately wrought silver sheath, made for Sir Walter Scott, and presented to him by the Highland Society, for his services in marshalling the clans when George IV. came to Scotland. There were a thousand other things, which I knew must be most curious, yet did not ask nor care about them, because so many curiosities drive one crazy, and fret one's heart to death. On the whole, there is no simple and great impression left by Abbotsford; and I felt angry and dissatisfied with myself for not feeling something which I did not and could not feel. But it is just like going to a museum, if you look into particulars; and one learns from it, too, that Scott could not have been really a wise man, nor an earnest one, nor one that grasped the truth of life; he did but play, and the play grew very sad toward its close. In a certain way, however, I understand his romances the better for having seen his house; and his house the better for having read his romances. They throw light on one another.

We had now gone through all the show-rooms; and the next door admitted us again into the entrance-hall, where we recorded our names in the visitors' book. It contains more names of Americans, I should judge, from casting my eyes back over last year's record, than of all other people in the world, including Great Britain.

Bidding farewell to Abbotsford, I cannot but confess a sentiment of remorse for having visited the dwelling-place—as just before I visited the grave of the mighty minstrel and romancer with so cold a heart and in so critical a mood,—his dwelling-place and his grave whom I had so admired and loved, and who had done so much for my happiness when I was young. But I, and the world generally, now look at him from a different point of view; and, besides, these visits to the actual haunts of famous people, though long dead, have the effect of making us sensible, in some degree, of their human imperfections, as if we actually saw them alive. I felt this effect, to a certain extent, even with respect to Shakespeare, when I visited Stratford-on-Avon. As for Scott, I still cherish him in a warm place, and I do not know that I have any pleasanter anticipation, as regards books, than that of reading all his novels over again after we get back to the Wayside.

[This Mr. Hawthorne did, aloud to his family, the year following his return to America.—ED.]

It was now one or two o'clock, and time for us to take the rail across the borders. Many a mile behind us, as we rushed onward, we could see the threefold Eildon Hill, and probably every pant of the engine carried us over some spot of ground which Scott has made fertile with poetry. For Scotland—cold, cloudy, barren little bit of earth that it is—owes all the interest that the world feels in it to him. Few men have done so much for their country as he. However, having no guide-book, we were none the wiser for what we saw out of the window of the rail-carriage; but, now and then, a castle appeared, on a commanding height, visible for miles round, and seemingly in good repair,—now, in some low and sheltered spot, the gray walls of an abbey; now, on a little eminence, the ruin of a border fortress, and near it the modern residence of the laird, with its trim lawn and shrubbery. We were not long in coming to

BERWICK,

a town which seems to belong both to England and Scotland, or perhaps is a kingdom by itself, for it stands on both sides of the boundary river, the Tweed, where it empties into the German Ocean. From the railway bridge we had a good view over the town, which looks ancient, with red roofs on all the gabled houses; and it being a sunny afternoon, though bleak and chill, the sea-view was very fine. The Tweed is here broad, and looks deep, flowing far beneath the bridge, between high banks. This is all that I can say of Berwick (pronounced Berrick), for though we spent above an hour at the station waiting for the train, we were so long in getting our dinner, that we had not time for anything else. I remember, however, some gray walls, that looked like the last remains of an old castle, near the railway station. We next took the train for

NEWCASTLE,

the way to which, for a considerable distance, lies within sight of the sea; and in close vicinity to the shore we saw Holy Isle, on which are the ruins of an abbey. Norham Castle must be somewhere in this neighborhood, on the English shore of the Tweed. It was pretty late in the afternoon—almost nightfall—when we reached Newcastle, over the roofs of which, as over those of Berwick, we had a view from the railway, and like Berwick, it was a congregation of mostly red roofs; but, unlike Berwick (the atmosphere over which was clear and transparent), there came a gush of smoke from every chimney, which made it the dimmest and smokiest place I ever saw. This is partly owing to the iron founderies and furnaces; but each domestic chimney, too, was smoking on its own account,—coal being so plentiful there, no doubt, that the fire is always kept freshly heaped with it, reason or none. Out of this smoke-cloud rose tall steeples; and it was discernible that the town stretched widely over an uneven surface, on the banks of the Tyne, which is navigable up hither ten miles from the sea for pretty large vessels.

We established ourselves at the Station Hotel, and then walked out to see something of the town; but I remember only a few streets of duskiness and dinginess, with a glimpse of the turrets of a castle to which we could not find our way. So, as it was getting twilightish and very cold, we went back to the hotel, which is a very good one, better than any one I have seen in the South of England, and almost or quite as good as those of Scotland. The coffee-room is a spacious and handsome apartment, adorned with a full-length portrait of Wellington, and other pictures, and in the whole establishment there was a well-ordered alacrity and liberal provision for the comfort of guests that one seldom sees in English inns. There are a good many American guests in Newcastle, and through all the North.

An old Newcastle gentleman and his friend came into the smoking-room, and drank three glasses of hot whiskey-toddy apiece, and were still going on to drink more when we left them. These respectable persons probably went away drunk that night, yet thought none the worse of themselves or of one another for it. It is like returning to times twenty years gone by for a New-Englander to witness such simplicity of manners.

The next morning, May 8th, I rose and breakfasted early, and took the rail soon after eight o'clock, leaving Mr. Bowman behind; for he had business in Newcastle, and would not follow till some hours afterwards. There is no use in trying to make a narrative of anything that one sees along an English railway. All I remember of this tract of country is that one of the stations at which we stopped for an instant is called "Washington," and this is, no doubt, the old family place, where the De Wessyngtons, afterwards the Washingtons, were first settled in England. Before reaching York, first one old lady and then another (Quaker) lady got into the carriage along with me; and they seemed to be going to York, on occasion of some fair or celebration. This was all the company I had, and their advent the only incident. It was about eleven o'clock when I beheld York Cathedral rising huge above the old city, which stands on the river Ouse, separated by it from the railway station, but communicating by a ferry (or two) and a bridge. I wandered forth, and found my way over the latter into the ancient and irregular streets of crooked, narrow, or of unequal width, puzzling, and many of them bearing the name of the particular gate in the old walls of the city to which they lead. There were no such fine, ancient, stately houses as some of those in Shrewsbury were, nor such an aspect of antiquity as in Chester; but still York is a quaint old place, and what looks most modern is probably only something old, hiding itself behind a new front, as elsewhere in England.

I found my way by a sort of instinct, as directly as possible, to

YORK MINSTER.

It stands in the midst of a small open space,—or a space that looks small in comparison with the vast bulk of the cathedral. I was not so much impressed by its exterior as I have usually been by Gothic buildings; because it is rectangular in its general outline and in its towers, and seems to lack the complexity and mysterious plan which perplexes and wonder-strikes me in most cathedrals. Doubtless, however, if I had known better how to admire it, I should have found it wholly admirable. At all events, it has a satisfactory hugeness. Seeking my way in, I at first intruded upon the Registry of Deeds, which occupies a building patched up against the mighty side of the cathedral, and hardly discernible, so small the one and so large the other. I finally hit upon the right door, and I felt no disappointment in my first glance around at the immensity of enclosed space;—I see now in my mind's eye a dim length of nave, a breadth in the transepts like a great plain, and such an airy height beneath the central tower that a worshipper could certainly get a good way towards heaven without rising above it. I only wish that the screen, or whatever they call it, between the choir and nave, could be thrown down, so as to give us leave to take in the whole vastitude at once. I never could understand why, after building a great church, they choose to sunder it in halves by this mid-partition. But let me be thankful for what I got, and especially for the height and massiveness of the clustered pillars that support the arches on which rests the central tower. I remember at Furness Abbey I saw two tall pillars supporting a broken arch, and thought it, the most majestic fragment of architecture that could possibly be. But these pillars have a nobler height, and these arches a greater sweep. What nonsense to try to write about a cathedral!

There is a great, cold bareness and bleakness about the interior; for there are very few monuments, and those seem chiefly to be of ecclesiastical people. I saw no armed knights, asleep on the tops of their tombs; but there was a curious representation of a skeleton, at full length, under the table-slab of one of the monuments. The walls are of a grayish hue, not so agreeable as the rich dark tint of the inside of Westminster Abbey; but a great many of the windows are still filled with ancient painted glass, the very small squares and pieces of which are composed into splendid designs of saints and angels, and scenes from Scripture.

There were a few watery blinks of sunshine out of doors, and whenever these came through the old painted windows, some of the more vivid colors were faintly thrown upon the pavement of the cathedral,—very faintly, it is true; for, in the first place, the sunshine was not brilliant; and painted glass, too, fades in the course of the ages, perhaps, like all man's other works. There were two or three windows of modern manufacture, and far more magnificent, as to brightness of color and material beauty, than the ancient ones; but yet they looked vulgar, glaring, and impertinent in comparison, because such revivals or imitations of a long-disused art cannot have the good faith and earnestness of the originals. Indeed, in the very coloring, I felt the same difference as between heart's blood and a scarlet dye. It is a pity, however, that the old windows cannot be washed, both inside and out, for now they have the dust of centuries upon them.

The screen or curtain between the nave and choir has eleven carved figures, at full length, which appeared to represent kings, some of them wearing crowns, and bearing sceptres or swords. They were in wood, and wrought by some Gothic hand. These carvings, and the painted windows, and the few monuments, are all the details that the mind can catch hold of in the immensity of this cathedral; and I must say that it was a dreary place on that cold, cloudy day. I doubt whether a cathedral is a sort of edifice suited to the English climate. The first buildings of the kind were probably erected by people who had bright and constant sunshine, and who desired a shadowy awfulness—like that of a forest, with its arched wood-paths—into which to retire in their religious moments.

In America, on a hot summer's day, how delightful its cool and solemn depths would be! The painted windows, too, were evidently contrived, in the first instance, by persons who saw how effective they would prove when a vivid sun shone through them. But in England, the interior of a cathedral, nine days out of ten, is a vast sullenness, and as chill as death and the tomb.

At any rate, it was so to-day, and so thought one of the old vergers, who kept walking as briskly as he could along the width of the transepts. There were several of these old men when I first came in, but they went off, all but this one, before I departed. None of them said a word to me, nor I to them; and admission to the Minster seems to be entirely free.

After emerging from this great gloom, I wandered to and fro about York, and contrived to go astray within no very wide space. If its history be authentic, it is an exceedingly old city, having been founded about a thousand years before the Christian era. There used to be a palace of the Roman emperors here, and the Emperor Severus died here, as did some of his successors; and Constantine the Great was born here. I know not what, if any, relics of those earlier times there may be; but York is still partly surrounded with a wall, and has several gates, which the city authorities take pains to keep in repair. I grow weary in my endeavor to find my way back to the railway, and inquired it of one of the good people of York,—a respectable, courteous, gentlemanly person,— and he told me to walk along the walls. Then he went on a considerable distance; but seemed to repent of not doing more for me; so he waited till I came up, and, walking along by my side, pointed out the castle, now the jail, and the place of execution, and directed me to the principal gateway of the city, and instructed me how to reach the ferry. The path along the wall leads, in one place, through a room over the arch of a gateway,—a low, thick-walled, stone apartment, where doubtless the gatekeeper used to lodge, and to parley with those who desired entrance.

I found my way to the ferry over the Ouse, according to this kind Yorkist's instructions. The ferryman told me that the fee for crossing was a halfpenny, which seemed so ridiculously small that I offered him more; but this unparalleled Englishman declined taking anything beyond his rightful halfpenny. This seems so wonderful to me that I can hardly trust my own memory.

Reaching the station, I got some dinner, and at four o'clock, just as I was starting, came Mr. Bowman, my very agreeable and sensible travelling companion. Our journeying together was ended here; for he was to keep on to London, and I to return to Liverpool. So we parted, and I took the rail westward across England, through a very beautiful, and in some degree picturesque, tract of country, diversified with hills, through the valleys and vistas of which goes the railroad, with dells diverging from it on either hand, and streams and arched bridges, and old villages, and a hundred pleasant English sights. After passing Rochdale, however, the dreary monotony of Lancashire succeeded this variety. Between nine and ten o'clock I reached the Tithebarn station in Liverpool. Ever since until now, May 17th, I have employed my leisure moments in scribbling off the journal of my tour; but it has greatly lost by not having been written daily, as the scenes and occurrences were fresh. The most picturesque points can be seized in no other way, and the hues of the affair fade as quickly as those of a dying dolphin; or as, according to Audubon, the plumage of a dead bird.

One thing that struck me as much as anything else in the Highlands I had forgotten to put down. In our walk at Balloch, along the road within view of Loch Lomond and the neighboring hills, it was a brilliant sunshiny afternoon, and I never saw any atmosphere so beautiful as that among the mountains. It was a clear, transparent, ethereal blue, as distinct as a vapor, and yet by no means vaporous, but a pure, crystalline medium. I have witnessed nothing like this among the Berkshire hills nor elsewhere.

York is full of old churches, some of them very antique in appearance, the stones weather-worn, their edges rounded by time, blackened, and with all the tokens of sturdy and age-long decay; and in some of them I noticed windows quite full of old painted glass, a dreary kind of minute patchwork, all of one dark and dusty hue, when seen from the outside. Yet had I seen them from the interior of the church, there doubtless would have been rich and varied apparitions of saints, with their glories round their heads, and bright-winged angels, and perhaps even the Almighty Father himself, so far as conceivable and representable by human powers. It requires light from heaven to make them visible. If the church were merely illuminated from the inside,—that is, by what light a man can get from his own understanding,—the pictures would be invisible, or wear at best but a miserable aspect.

LIVERPOOL.

May 24th.—Day before yesterday I had a call at the Consulate from one of the Potentates of the Earth,—a woolly-haired negro, rather thin and spare, between forty and fifty years of age, plainly dressed; at the first glimpse of whom, I could readily have mistaken him for some ship's steward, seeking to enter a complaint of his captain. However, this was President Roberts, of Liberia, introduced by a note from Mrs. O'Sullivan, whom he has recently met in Madeira. I was rather favorably impressed with him; for his deportment was very simple, and without any of the flourish and embroidery which a negro might be likely to assume on finding himself elevated from slavery to power. He is rather shy, reserved, at least, and undemonstrative, yet not harshly so,—in fine, with manners that offer no prominent points for notice or criticism; although I felt, or thought I felt, that his color was continually before his mind, and that he walks cautiously among men, as conscious that every new introduction is a new experiment. He is not in the slightest degree an interesting man (so far as I discovered in a very brief interview), apart from his position and history; his face is not striking, nor so agreeable as if it were jet black; but there may be miles and miles of depth in him which I know nothing of. Our conversation was of the most unimportant character; for he had called merely to deliver the note, and sat only a few minutes, during which he merely responded to my observations, and originated no remarks. Intelligence, discretion, tact—these are probably his traits; not force of character and independence.

The same day I took the rail from the Little Street station for

MANCHESTER,

to meet Bennoch, who had asked me thither to dine with him. I had never visited Manchester before, though now so long resident within twenty miles of it; neither is it particularly worth visiting, unless for the sake of its factories, which I did not go to see. It is a dingy and heavy town, with very much the aspect of Liverpool, being, like the latter, built almost entirely within the present century. I stopped at the Albion Hotel, and, as Bennoch was out, I walked forth to view the city, and made only such observations as are recorded above. Opposite the hotel stands the Infirmary,—a very large edifice, which, when erected, was on the outskirts, or perhaps in the rural suburbs, of the town, but it is now almost in its centre. In the enclosed space before it stands the statue of Peel, and sits a statue of Dr. Dalton, the celebrated chemist, who was a native of Manchester.

Returning to the hotel, I sat down in the room where we were to dine, and in due time Bennoch made his appearance, with the same glow and friendly warmth in his face that I had left burning there when we parted in London. If this man has not a heart, then no man ever had. I like him inexpressibly for his heart and for his intellect, and for his flesh and blood; and if he has faults, I do not know them, nor care to know them, nor value him the less if I did know them. He went to his room to dress; and in the mean time a middle-aged, dark man, of pleasant aspect, with black hair, black eyebrows, and bright, dark eyes came in, limping a little, but not much. He seemed not quite a man of the world, a little shy in manner, yet he addressed me kindly and sociably. I guessed him to be Mr. Charles Swain, the poet, whom Mr. Bennoch had invited to dinner. Soon came another guest whom Mr. Swain introduced to me as Mr. ———, editor of the Manchester Examiner. Then came Bennoch, who made us all regularly acquainted, or took for granted that we were so; and lastly appeared a Mr. W———, a merchant in Manchester, and a very intelligent man; and the party was then complete. Mr. Swain, the poet, is not a man of fluent conversation; he said, indeed, very little, but gave me the impression of amiability and simplicity of character, with much feeling.

Mr. W——— is a very sensible man. He has spent two or three years in America, and seems to have formed juster conclusions about us than most of his countrymen do. He is the only Englishman, I think, whom I have met, who fairly acknowledges that the English do cherish doubt, jealousy, suspicion, in short, an unfriendly feeling, towards the Americans. It is wonderful how every American, whatever class of the English he mingles with, is conscious of this feeling, and how no Englishman, except this sole Mr. W———, will confess it. He expressed some very good ideas, too, about the English and American press, and the reasons why the Times may fairly be taken as the exponent of British feeling towards us, while the New York Herald, immense as its circulation is, can be considered, in no similar degree or kind, the American exponent.

We sat late at table, and after the other guests had retired, Bennoch and I had some very friendly talk, and he proposed that on my wife's return we should take up our residence in his house at Blackheath, while Mrs. Bennoch and himself were absent for two months on a trip to Germany. If his wife and mine ratify the idea, we will do so.

The next morning we went out to see the Exchange, and whatever was noticeable about the town. Time being brief, I did not visit the cathedral, which, I believe, is a thousand years old. There are many handsome shops in Manchester; and we went into one establishment, devoted to pictures, engravings, and decorative art generally, which is most perfect and extensive. The firm, if I remember, is that of the Messrs. Agnew, and, though originating here, they have now a house in London. Here I saw some interesting objects, purchased by them at the recent sale of the Rogers collection; among other things, a slight pencil and water-color sketch by Raphael. An unfinished affair, done in a moment, as this must have been, seems to bring us closer to the hand that did it than the most elaborately painted picture can. Were I to see the Transfiguration, Raphael would still be at the distance of centuries. Seeing this little sketch, I had him very near me. I know not why,— perhaps it might be fancied that he had only laid down the pencil for an instant, and would take it up again in a moment more. I likewise saw a copy of a handsome, illustrated edition of Childe Harold, presented by old John Murray to Mr.

Rogers, with an inscription on the fly-leaf, purporting that it was a token of gratitude from the publisher, because, when everybody else thought him imprudent in giving four hundred guineas for the poem, Mr. Rogers told him it would turn out the best bargain he ever made.

There was a new picture by Millais, the distinguished Pre-Raphaelite artist, representing a melancholy parting between two lovers. The lady's face had a great deal of sad and ominous expression; but an old brick wall, overrun with foliage, was so exquisitely and elaborately wrought that it was hardly possible to look at the personages of the picture. Every separate leaf of the climbing and clustering shrubbery was painfully made out; and the wall was reality itself, with the weather-stains, and the moss, and the crumbling lime between the bricks. It is not well to be so perfect in the inanimate, unless the artist can likewise make man and woman as lifelike, and to as great a depth, too, as the Creator does.

Bennoch left town for some place in Yorkshire, and I for Liverpool. I asked him to come and dine with me at the Adelphi, meaning to ask two or three people to meet him; but he had other engagements, and could not spare a day at present, though he promises to come before long.

Dining at Mr. Rathbone's one evening last week (May 21st), it was mentioned that

BORROW,

author of the Bible in Spain, is supposed to be of gypsy descent by the mother's side. Hereupon Mr. Martineau mentioned that he had been a schoolfellow of Borrow, and though he had never heard of his gypsy blood, he thought it probable, from Borrow's traits of character. He said that, Borrow had once run away from school, and carried with him a party of other boys, meaning to lead a wandering life.

If an Englishman were individually acquainted with all our twenty-five millions of Americans, and liked every one of them, and believed that each man of those millions was a Christian, honest, upright, and kind, he would doubt, despise, and hate them in the aggregate, however he might love and honor the individuals.

Captain ——— and his wife Oakum; they spent all evening at Mrs. B———'s. The Captain is a Marblehead man by birth, not far from sixty years old; very talkative and anecdotic in regard to his adventures; funny, good-humored, and full of various nautical experience. Oakum (it is a nickname which he gives his wife) is an inconceivably tall woman,— taller than he,— six feet, at least, and with a well-proportioned largeness in all respects, but looks kind and good, gentle, smiling,—and almost any other woman might sit like a baby on her lap. She does not look at all awful and belligerent, like the massive English women one often sees. You at once feel her to be a benevolent giantess, and apprehend no harm from her. She is a lady, and perfectly well mannered, but with a sort of naturalness and simplicity that becomes her; for any the slightest affectation would be so magnified in her vast personality that it would be absolutely the height of the ridiculous. This wedded pair have no children, and Oakum has so long accompanied her husband on his voyages that I suppose by this time she could command a ship as well as he. They sat till pretty late, diffusing cheerfulness all about them, and then, "Come, Oakum," cried the Captain, "we must hoist sail!" and up rose Oakum to the ceiling, and moved tower-like to the door, looking down with a benignant smile on the poor little pygmy women about her. "Six feet," did I say? Why, she must be seven, eight, nine; and, whatever be her size, she is as good as she is big.

June 11th.—Monday night (9th), just as I was retiring, I received a telegraphic message announcing my wife's arrival at

SOUTHAMPTON.

So, the next day, I arranged the consular business for an absence of ten days, and set forth with J——-, and reached Birmingham, between eight and nine, evening. We put up at the Queen's Hotel, a very large establishment, contiguous to the railway. Next morning we left Birmingham, and made our first stage to Leamington, where we had to wait nearly an hour, which we spent in wandering through some of the streets that had been familiar to us last year. Leamington is certainly a beautiful town, new, bright, clean, and as unlike as possible to the business towns of England. However, the sun was burning hot, and I could almost have fancied myself in America. From Leamington we took tickets for Oxford, where we were obliged to make another stop of two hours; and these we employed to what advantage we could, driving up into town, and straying hither and thither, till J——-'s weariness weighed upon me, and I adjourned with him to a hotel. Oxford is an ugly old town, of crooked and irregular streets, gabled houses, mostly plastered of a buff or yellow hue; some new fronts; and as for the buildings of the University, they seem to be scattered at random, without any reference to one another. I passed through an old gateway of Christ Church, and looked at its enclosed square, and that is, in truth, pretty much all I then saw of the University of Oxford. From Christ Church we rambled along a street that led us to a bridge across the Isis; and we saw many row-boats lying in the river,—the lightest craft imaginable, unless it were an Indian canoe. The Isis is but a narrow stream, and with a sluggish current. I believe the students of Oxford are famous for their skill in rowing.

To me as well as to J——- the hot streets were terribly oppressive; so we went into the Roebuck Hotel, where we found a cool and pleasant coffee-room. The entrance to this hotel is through an arch, opening from High Street, and giving admission into a paved court, the buildings all around being part of the establishment,—old edifices with pointed gables and old-fashioned projecting windows, but all in fine repair, and wearing a most quiet, retired, and comfortable aspect. The court was set all round with flowers, growing in pots or large pedestalled vases; on one side was the coffee-room, and all the other public apartments, and the other side seemed to be taken up by the sleeping-chambers and parlors of the guests. This arrangement of an inn, I presume, is very ancient, and it resembles what I have seen in the hospitals, free schools, and other charitable establishments in the old English towns; and, indeed, all large houses were arranged on somewhat the same principle.

By and by two or three young men came in, in wide-awake hats, and loose, blouse-like, summerish garments; and from their talk I found them to be students of the University, although their topics of conversation were almost entirely horses and boats. One of them sat down to cold beef and a tankard of ale; the other two drank a tankard of ale together, and went away without paying for it,—rather to the waiter's discontent. Students are very much alike, all the world over, and, I suppose, in all time; but I doubt whether many of my fellows at college would have gone off without paying for their beer.

We reached Southampton between seven and eight o'clock. I cannot write to-day.

June 15th.—The first day after we reached Southampton was sunny and pleasant; but we made little use of the fine weather, except that S——- and I walked once along the High Street, and J——- and I took a little ramble about town in the afternoon. The next day there was a high and disagreeable wind, and I did not once stir out of the house. The third day, too, I kept entirely within doors, it being a storm of wind and rain. The Castle Hotel stands within fifty yards of the water-side; so that this gusty day showed itself to the utmost advantage,—the vessels pitching and tossing at their moorings, the waves breaking white out of a tumultuous gray surface, the opposite shore glooming mistily at the distance of a mile or two; and on the hither side boatmen and seafaring people scudding about the pier in waterproof clothes; and in the street, before the hotel door, a cabman or two, standing drearily beside his horse. But we were sunny within doors.

Yesterday it was breezy, sunny, shadowy, showery; and we ordered a cab to take us to Clifton Villa, to call on Mrs. ———, a friend of B———'s, who called on us the day after our arrival. Just, as we were ready to start, Mrs. ——— again called, and accompanied us back to her house. It is in Shirley, about two miles from Southampton pier, and is a pleasant suburban villa, with a pretty ornamented lawn and shrubbery about it. Mrs. ——— is an instructress of young ladies; and at B———'s suggestion, she is willing to receive us for two or three weeks, during the vacation, until we are ready to go to London. She seems to be a pleasant and sensible woman, and to-morrow we shall decide whether to go there. There was nothing very remarkable in this drive; and, indeed, my stay hereabouts thus far has been very barren of sights and incidents externally interesting, though the inner life has been rich.

Southampton is a very pretty town, and has not the dinginess to which I have been accustomed in many English towns. The High Street reminds me very much of American streets in its general effect; the houses being mostly stuccoed white or light, and cheerful in aspect, though doubtless they are centuries old at heart. The old gateway, which I presume I have mentioned in describing my former visit to Southampton, stands across High Street, about in the centre of the town, and is almost the only token of antiquity that presents itself to the eye.

June 17th.—Yesterday morning, June 16th, S——, Mrs. ———, and I took the rail for Salisbury, where we duly arrived without any accident or anything noticeable, except the usual verdure and richness of an English summer landscape. From the railway station we walked up into Salisbury, with the tall spire (four hundred feet high) of the cathedral before our eyes. Salisbury is an antique city, but with streets more regular than I have seen in most old towns, and the houses have a more picturesque aspect than those of Oxford, for instance, where almost all are mean-looking alike,—though I could hardly judge of Oxford on that hot, weary day. Through one or more of the streets there runs a swift, clear little stream, which, being close to the pavement, and bordered with stone, may be called, I suppose, a kennel, though possessing the transparent purity of a rustic rivulet. It is a brook in city garb. We passed under the pointed arch of a gateway, which stands in one of the principal streets, and soon came in front of

THE CATHEDRAL.

I do not remember any cathedral with so fine a site as this, rising up out of the centre of a beautiful green, extensive enough to show its full proportions, relieved and insulated from all other patchwork and impertinence of rusty edifices. It is of gray stone, and looks as perfect as when just finished, and with the perfection, too, that could not have come in less than six centuries of venerableness, with a view to which these edifices seem to have been built. A new cathedral would lack the last touch to its beauty and grandeur. It needs to be mellowed and ripened, like some pictures; although I suppose this awfulness of antiquity was supplied, in the minds of the generation that built cathedrals, by the sanctity which they attributed to them. Salisbury Cathedral is far more beautiful than that of York, the exterior of which was really disagreeable to my eye; but this mighty spire and these multitudinous gray pinnacles and towers ascend towards heaven with a kind of natural beauty, not as if man had contrived them. They might be fancied to have grown up, just as the spires of a tuft of grass do, at the same time that they have a law of propriety and regularity among themselves. The tall spire is of such admirable proportion that it does not seem gigantic; and indeed the effect of the whole edifice is of beauty rather than weight and massiveness. Perhaps the bright, balmy sunshine in which we saw it contributed to give it a tender glory, and to soften a little its majesty.

When we went in, we heard the organ, the forenoon service being near conclusion. If I had never seen the interior of York Cathedral, I should have been quite satisfied, no doubt, with the spaciousness of this nave and these side aisles, and the height of their arches, and the girth of these pillars; but with that recollection in my mind they fell a little short of grandeur. The interior is seen to disadvantage, and in a way the builder never meant it to be seen; because there is little or no painted glass, nor any such mystery as it makes, but only a colorless, common daylight, revealing everything without remorse. There is a general light hue, moreover, like that of whitewash, over the whole of the roof and walls of the interior, pillars, monuments, and all;

whereas, originally, every pillar was polished, and the ceiling was ornamented in brilliant colors, and the light came, many-hued, through the windows, on all this elaborate beauty, in lieu of which there is nothing now but space.

Between the pillars that separate the nave from the side aisles, there are ancient tombs, most of which have recumbent statues on them. One of these is Longsword, Earl of Salisbury, son of Fair Rosamond, in chain mail; and there are many other warriors and bishops, and one cross-legged Crusader, and on one tombstone a recumbent skeleton, which I have likewise seen in two or three other cathedrals. The pavement of the aisles and nave is laid in great part with flat tombstones, the inscriptions on which are half obliterated, and on the walls, especially in the transepts, there are tablets, among which I saw one to the poet Bowles, who was a canon of this cathedral. The ecclesiastical dignitaries bury themselves and monument themselves to the exclusion of almost everybody else, in these latter times; though still, as of old, the warrior has his place. A young officer, slain in the Indian wars, was memorialized by a tablet, and may be remembered by it, six hundred years hence, as we now remember the old Knights and Crusaders. It deserves to be mentioned that I saw one or two noses still unbroken among these recumbent figures. Most of the antique statues, on close examination, proved to be almost, entirely covered with names and initials, scratched over the once polished surface. The cathedral and its relics must have been far less carefully watched, at some former period, than now.

Between the nave and the choir, as usual, there is a screen that half destroys the majesty of the building, by abridging the spectator of the long vista which he might otherwise have of the whole interior at a glance. We peeped through the barrier, and saw some elaborate monuments in the chancel beyond; but the doors of the screen are kept locked, so that the vergers may raise a revenue by showing strangers through the richest part of the cathedral. By and by one of these vergers came through the screen, with a gentleman and lady whom he was taking round, and we joined ourselves to the party. He showed us into the cloisters, which had long been neglected and ruinous, until the time of Bishop Dennison, the last prelate, who has been but a few years dead. This Bishop has repaired and restored the cloisters in faithful adherence to the original plan; and they now form a most delightful walk about a pleasant and verdant enclosure, in the centre of which sleeps good Bishop Dennison, with a wife on either side of him, all three beneath broad flat stones. Most cloisters are darksome and grim; but these have a broad paved walk beneath the vista of arches, and are light, airy, and cheerful; and from one corner you can get the best possible view of the whole height and beautiful proportion of the cathedral spire. One side of this cloistered walk seems to be the length of the nave of the cathedral. There is a square of four such sides; and of places for meditation, grave, yet not too sombre, it seemed to me one of the best. While we stayed there, a jackdaw was walking to and fro across the grassy enclosure, and haunting around the good Bishop's grave. He was clad in black, and looked like a feathered ecclesiastic; but I know not whether it were Bishop Dennison's ghost, or that of some old monk.

On one side of the cloisters, and contiguous to the main body of the cathedral, stands the chapter-house. Bishop Dennison had it much at heart to repair this part of the holy edifice; and, if I mistake not, did begin the work; for it had been long ruinous, and in Cromwell's time his dragoons stationed their horses there. Little progress, however, had been made in the repairs when the Bishop died; and it was decided to restore the building in his honor, and by way of monument to him. The repairs are now nearly completed; and the interior of this chapter-house gave me the first idea, anywise adequate, of the splendor of these Gothic church edifices. The roof is sustained by one great central pillar of polished marble,—small pillars clustered about a great central column, which rises to the ceiling, and there gushes out with various beauty, that overflows all the walls; as if the fluid idea had sprung out of that fountain, and grown solid in what we see. The pavement is elaborately ornamented; the ceiling is to be brilliantly gilded and painted, as it was of yore, and the tracery and sculptures around the walls are to be faithfully renewed from what remains of the original patterns.

After viewing the chapter-house, the verger—an elderly man of grave, benign manner, clad in black and talking of the cathedral and the monuments as if he loved them—led us again into the nave of the cathedral, and thence within the screen of the choir. The screen is as poor as possible,—mere barren wood-work, without the least attempt at beauty. In the chancel there are some meagre patches of old glass, and some of modern date, not very well worth looking at. We saw several interesting monuments in this part of the cathedral,—one belonging to the ducal family of Somerset, and erected in the reign of James I.; it is of marble, and extremely splendid and elaborate, with kneeling figures and all manner of magnificence,—more than I have seen in any monument except that of Mary of Scotland in Westminster Abbey. The more ancient tombs are also very numerous, and among them that of the Bishop who founded the cathedral. Within the screen, against the wall, is erected a monument, by Chantrey, to the Earl of Malmesbury; a full-length statue of the Earl in a half-recumbent position, holding an open volume and looking upward,—a noble work,—a calm, wise, thoughtful, firm, and not unbenignant face. Beholding its expression, it really was impossible not to have faith in the high character of the individual thus represented; and I have seldom felt this effect from any monumental bust or statue, though I presume it is always aimed at.

I am weary of trying to describe cathedrals. It is utterly useless; there is no possibility of giving the general effect, or any shadow of it, and it is miserable to put down a few items of tombstones, and a bit of glass from a painted window, as if the gloom and glory of the edifice were thus to be reproduced. Cathedrals are almost the only things (if even those) that have quite filled out my ideal here in this old world; and cathedrals often make me miserable from my inadequacy to take them wholly in; and, above all, I despise myself when I sit down to describe them.

We now walked around the Close, which is surrounded by some of the quaintest and comfortablest ecclesiastical residences that can be imagined. These are the dwelling-houses of the Dean and the canons, and whatever other high officers compose the Bishop's staff; and there was one large brick mansion, old, but not so ancient as the rest, which we took to be the Bishop's palace. I never beheld anything—I must say again so cosey, so indicative of domestic comfort for whole centuries together,—houses so fit to live in or to die in, and where it would be so pleasant to lead a young wife beneath the antique portal, and dwell with her till husband and wife were patriarchal,—

as these delectable old houses. They belong naturally to the cathedral, and have a necessary relation to it, and its sanctity is somehow thrown over them all, so that they do not quite belong to this world, though they look full to overflowing of whatever earthly things are good for man. These are places, however, in which mankind makes no progress; the rushing tumult of human life here subsides into a deep, quiet pool, with perhaps a gentle circular eddy, but no onward movement. The same identical thought, I suppose, goes round in a slow whirl from one generation to another, as I have seen a withered leaf do in the vortex of a brook. In the front of the cathedral there is a most stately and beautiful tree, which flings its verdure upward to a very lofty height; but far above it rises the tall spire, dwarfing the great tree by comparison.

When the cathedral had sufficiently oppressed us with its beauty, we returned to sublunary matters, and went wandering about Salisbury in search of a luncheon, which we finally took in a confectioner's shop. Then we inquired hither and thither, at various livery-stables, for a conveyance to Stonehenge, and at last took a fly from the Lamb Hotel. The drive was over a turnpike for the first seven miles, over a bare, ridgy country, showing little to interest us. We passed a party of seven or eight men, in a coarse uniform dress, resembling that worn by convicts and apparently under the guardianship of a stout, authoritative, yet rather kindly-looking man with a cane. Our driver said that they were lunatics from a neighboring asylum, out for a walk.

Seven miles from Salisbury, we turned aside from the turnpike, and drove two miles across Salisbury Plain, which is an apparently boundless extent of unenclosed land, treeless and houseless. It is not exactly a plain, but a green sea of long and gentle swells and subsidences, affording views of miles upon miles to a very far horizon. We passed large flocks of sheep, with the shepherds watching them; but the dogs seemed to take most of the care of the flocks upon their own shoulders, and would scamper to turn the sheep when they inclined to stray whither they should not; and then arose a thousand-fold bleating, not unpleasant to the ear; for it did not apparently indicate any fear or discomfort on the part of the flock. The sheep and lambs are all black-faced, and have a very funny expression. As we drove over the plain (my seat was beside the driver), I saw at a distance a cluster of large gray stones, mostly standing upright, and some of them slightly inclined towards each other, —very irregular, and so far off forming no very picturesque or noteworthy spectacle. Of course I knew at once that this was and also knew that the reality was going to dwindle wofully within my ideal, as almost everything else does. When we reached the spot, we found a picnic-party just finishing their dinner, on one of the overthrown stones of the druidical temple; and within the sacred circle an artist was painting a wretched daub of the scene, and an old shepherd —the very Shepherd of Salisbury Plain sat erect in the centre of the ruin.

There never was a ruder thing than Stonehenge made by mortal hands. It is so very rude that it seems as if Nature and man had worked upon it with one consent, and so it is all the stranger and more impressive from its rudeness. The spectator wonders to see art and contrivance, and a regular and even somewhat intricate plan, beneath all the uncouth simplicity of this arrangement of rough stones; and certainly, whatever was the intellectual and scientific advancement of the people who built Stonehenge, no succeeding architects will ever have a right to triumph over them; for nobody's work in after times is likely to endure till it becomes a mystery as to who built it, and how, and for what purpose. Apart from the moral considerations suggested by it, Stonehenge is not very well worth seeing. Materially, it is one of the poorest of spectacles, and when complete, it must have been even less picturesque than now,—a few huge, rough stones, very imperfectly squared, standing on end, and each group of two supporting a third large stone on their tops; other stones of the same pattern overthrown and tumbled one upon another; and the whole comprised within a circuit of about a hundred feet diameter; the short, sheep-cropped grass of Salisbury Plain growing among all these uncouth bowlders. I am not sure that a misty, lowering day would not have better suited Stonehenge, as the dreary midpoint of the great, desolate, trackless plain; not literally trackless, however, for the London and Exeter Road passes within fifty yards of the ruins, and another road intersects it.

After we had been there about an hour, there came a horseman within the Druid's circle,—evidently a clerical personage by his white neckcloth, though his loose gray riding pantaloons were not quite in keeping. He looked at us rather earnestly, and at last addressed Mrs. ———, and announced himself as Mr. Hinchman,—a clergyman whom she had been trying to find in Salisbury, in order to avail herself of him as a cicerone; and he had now ridden hither to meet us. He told us that the artist whom we found here could give us more information than anybody about Stonehenge; for it seems he has spent a great many years here, painting and selling his poor sketches to visitors, and also selling a book which his father wrote about the remains. This man showed, indeed, a pretty accurate, acquaintance with these old stones, and pointed out, what is thought to be the altar-stone, and told us of some relation between this stone and two other stones, and the rising of the sun at midsummer, which might indicate that Stonehenge was a temple of solar worship. He pointed out, too, to how little depth the stones were planted in the earth, insomuch that I have no doubt the American frosts would overthrow Stonehenge in a single winter; and it is wonderful that it should have stood so long, even in England. I have forgotten what else he said; but I bought one of his books, and find it a very unsatisfactory performance, being chiefly taken up with an attempt to prove these remains to be an antediluvian work, constructed, I think the author says, under the superintendence of Father Adam himself! Before our departure we were requested to write our names in the album which the artist keeps for the purpose; and he pointed out Ex-President Fillmore's autograph, and those of one or two other Americans who have been here within a short time. It is a very curious life that this artist leads, in this great solitude, and haunting Stonehenge like the ghost of a Druid; but he is a brisk little man, and very communicative on his one subject.

Mr. Hinchman rode with us over the plain, and pointed out Salisbury spire, visible close to Stonehenge. Under his guidance we returned by a different road from that which brought us thither,—and a much more delightful one. I think I never saw such continued sylvan beauty as this road showed us, passing through a good deal of woodland scenery,—fine old trees, standing each within its own space, and thus having full liberty to outspread itself, and wax strong and broad for ages, instead of being crowded, and thus stifled and emaciated, as human beings are here, and forest-trees are in America. Hedges, too, and the rich, rich verdure of England; and villages full of picturesque old houses, thatched, and ivied, or perhaps overrun with roses,—and a stately mansion in the Elizabethan style; and a quiet stream, gliding onward without a ripple from its own motion, but rippled by a large fish darting across it; and over all this scene a gentle, friendly sunshine, not ardent enough to crisp a single leaf or blade of grass. Nor must the village church be forgotten, with its square, battlemented tower, dating back to the epoch of the Normans. We called at a house where one of Mrs. ———'s pupils was residing with her aunt,—a thatched house of two stories high, built in what was originally a sand-pit, but which, in the course of a good many years, has been transformed into the most delightful and homelike little nook almost that can be found in England. A thatched cottage suggests a very rude dwelling indeed; but this had a pleasant parlor and drawing-room, and chambers with lattice-windows, opening close beneath the thatched roof; and the thatch itself gives an air to the place as if it were a bird's nest, or some such simple and natural habitation. The occupants are an elderly clergyman, retired from professional duty, and his sister; and having nothing else to do, and sufficient means, they employ themselves in beautifying this sweet little retreat—planting new shrubbery, laying out new walks around it, and helping Nature to add continually another charm; and Nature is certainly a more genial playfellow in England than in my own country. She is always ready to lend her aid to any beautifying purpose.

Leaving these good people, who were very hospitable, giving tea and offering wine, we reached Salisbury in time to take the train for Southampton.

June 18th.—Yesterday we left the Castle Hotel, after paying a bill of twenty pounds for a little more than a week's board. In America we could not very well have lived so simply, but we might have lived luxuriously for half the money. This Castle Hotel was once an old Roman castle, the landlord says, and the circular sweep of the tower is still seen towards the street, although, being painted white, and built up with modern additions, it would not be taken for an ancient structure. There is a dungeon beneath it, in which the landlord keeps his wine.

J——- and I, quitting the hotel, walked towards Shinley along the water-side, leaving the rest of the family to follow in a fly. There are many traces, along the shore, of the fortifications by which Southampton was formerly defended towards the water, and very probably their foundations may be as ancient as Roman times. Our hotel was no doubt connected with this chain of defences, which seems to have consisted of a succession of round towers, with a wall extending from one to another. We saw two or three of these towers still standing, and likely to stand, though ivy-grown and ruinous at the summit, and intermixed and even amalgamated with pot-houses and mean dwellings; and often, through an antique arch, there was a narrow doorway, giving access to the house of some sailor or laborer or artisan, and his wife gossiping at it with her neighbor, or his children playing about it.

After getting beyond the precincts of Southampton our walk was not very interesting, except to J——-, who kept running down to the verge of the water, looking for shells and sea-insects.

June 29th.—Yesterday, 28th, I left Liverpool from the Lime Street station; an exceedingly hot day for England, insomuch that the rail carriages were really uncomfortable. I have now passed over the London and Northwestern Railway so often that the northern part of it is very wearisome, especially as it has few features of interest even to a new observer. At Stafford—no, at Wolverhampton—we diverged to a track which I have passed over only once before. We stopped an hour and a quarter at Wolverhampton, and I walked up into the town, which is large and old,—old, at least, in its plan, or lack of plan,—the streets being irregular, and straggling over an uneven surface. Like many of the English towns, it reminds me of Boston, though dingier. The sun was so hot that I actually sought the shady sides of the streets; and this, of itself, is one long step towards establishing a resemblance between an English town and an American one.

English railway carriages seem to me more tiresome than any other; and I suppose it is owing to the greater motion, arising from their more elastic springs. A slow train, too, like that which I was now in, is more tiresome than a quick one, at least to the spirits, whatever it may be to the body. We loitered along through afternoon and evening, stopping at every little station, and nowhere getting to the top of our speed, till at last, in the late dusk, we reached

GLOUCESTER,

and I put up at the Wellington Hotel, which is but a little way from the station. I took tea and a slice or two of ham in the coffee-room, and had a little talk with two people there; one of whom, on learning that I was an American, said, "But I suppose you have now been in England some time?" He meant, finding me not absolutely a savage, that I must have been caught a good while ago. . . .

The next morning I went into the city, the hotel being on its outskirts, and rambled along in search of the cathedral. Some church-bells were chiming and clashing for a wedding or other festal occasion, and I followed the sound, supposing that it might proceed from the cathedral, but this was not the case. It was not till I had got to a bridge over the Severn, quite out of the town, that I saw again its tower, and knew how to shape my course towards it.

I did not see much that was strange or interesting in Gloucester. It is old, with a good many of those antique Elizabethan houses with two or three peaked gables on a line together; several old churches, which always cluster about a cathedral, like chickens round a hen; a hospital for decayed tradesmen; another for bluecoat boys; a great many butcher's shops, scattered in all parts of the town, open in front, with a counter or dresser on which to display the meat, just in the old fashion of Shakespeare's house. It is a large town, and has a good deal of liveliness and bustle, in a provincial way. In short, judging by the sheep, cattle, and horses, and the people of agricultural aspect that I saw about the streets, I should think it must have been market-day. I looked here and there for the old Bell Inn, because, unless I misremember, Fielding brings Tom Jones to this inn, while he and Partridge were travelling together. It is still extant; for, on my arrival the night before, a runner from it had asked me to go thither; but I forgot its celebrity at the moment. I saw nothing of it in my rambles about Gloucester, but at last I found

THE CATHEDRAL,

though I found no point from which a good view of the exterior can be seen.

It has a very beautiful and rich outside, however, and a lofty tower, very large and ponderous, but so finished off, and adorned with pinnacles, and all manner of architectural devices,—wherewith these old builders knew how to alleviate their massive structures,—that it seems to sit lightly in the air. The porch was open, and some workmen were trundling barrows into the nave; so I followed, and found two young women sitting just within the porch, one of whom offered to show me round the cathedral. There was a great dust in the nave, arising from the operations of the workmen. They had been laying a new pavement, and scraping away the plaster, which had heretofore been laid over the pillars and walls. The pillars come out from the process as good as new,—great, round, massive columns, not clustered like those of most cathedrals; they are twenty-one feet in circumference, and support semicircular arches. I think there are seven of these columns, on each side of the nave, which did not impress me as very spacious; and the dust and racket of the work-people quite destroyed the effect which should have been produced by the aisles and arches; so that I hardly stopped to glance at this part, though I saw some mural monuments and recumbent statues along the walls.

The choir is separated from the nave by the usual screen, and now by a sail-cloth or something of that kind, drawn across, in order to keep out the dust, while the repairs are going on. When the young woman conducted me hither, I was at once struck by the magnificent eastern window, the largest in England, which fills, or looks vast enough to fill, all that end of the cathedral,—a most splendid window, full of old painted glass, which looked as bright as sunshine, though the sun was not really shining through it. The roof of the choir is of oak and very fine, and as much as ninety feet high. There are chapels opening from the choir, and within them the monuments of the eminent people who built them, and of benefactors or prelates, or of those otherwise illustrious in their day. My recollection of what I saw here is very dim and confused; more so than I anticipated. I remember somewhere within the choir the tomb of Edward II. with his effigy upon the top of it, in a long robe, with a crown on his head, and a ball and sceptre in his hand; likewise, a statue of Robert, son of the Conqueror, carved in Irish oak and painted. He lolls in an easy posture on his tomb, with one leg crossed lightly over the other, to denote that he was a Crusader. There are several monuments of mitred abbots who formerly presided over the cathedral. A Cavalier and his wife, with the dress of the period elaborately represented, lie side by side in excellent preservation; and it is remarkable that though their noses are very prominent, they have come down from the past without any wear and tear. The date of the Cavalier's death is 1637, and I think his statue could not have been sculptured until after the Restoration, else he and his dame would hardly have come through Cromwell's time unscathed. Here, as in all the other churches in England, Cromwell is said to have stabled his horses, and broken the windows, and belabored the old monuments.

There is one large and beautiful chapel, styled the Lady's Chapel, which is, indeed, a church by itself, being ninety feet long, and comprising everything that appertains to a place of worship. Here, too, there are monuments, and on the floor are many old bricks and tiles, with inscriptions on them, or Gothic devices, and flat tombstones, with coats of arms sculptured on them; as, indeed, there are everywhere else, except in the nave, where the new pavement has obliterated them. After viewing the choir and the chapels, the young woman led me down into the crypts below, where the dead persons who are commemorated in the upper regions were buried. The low ponderous pillars and arches of these crypts are supposed to be older than the upper portions of the building. They are about as perfect, I suppose, as when new, but very damp, dreary, and darksome; and the arches intersect one another so intricately, that, if the girl had deserted me, I might easily have got lost there. These are chapels where masses used to be said for the souls of the deceased; and my guide said that a great many skulls and bones had been dug up here. No doubt a vast population has been deposited in the course of a thousand years. I saw two white skulls, in a niche, grinning as skulls always do, though it is impossible to see the joke. These crypts, or crypts like these, are doubtless what Congreve calls the "aisles and monumental caves of Death," in that passage which Dr. Johnson admired so much. They are very singular,—something like a dark shadow or dismal repetition of the upper church below ground.

Ascending from the crypts, we went next to the cloisters, which are in a very perfect state, and form an unbroken square about the green grass-plot, enclosed within. Here also it is said Cromwell stabled his horses; but if so, they were remarkably quiet beasts, for tombstones, which form the pavement, are not broken, nor cracked, nor bear any hoof-marks. All around the cloisters, too, the stone tracery that shuts them in like a closed curtain, carefully drawn, remains as it was in the days of the monks, insomuch that it is not easy to get a glimpse of the green enclosure. Probably there used to be painted glass in the larger apertures of this stone-work; otherwise it is perfect. These cloisters are very different from the free, open, and airy ones of Salisbury; but they are more in accordance with our notions of monkish habits; and even at this day, if I were a canon of Gloucester, I would put that dim ambulatory to a good use. The library is adjacent to the cloisters, and I saw some rows of folios and quartos. I have nothing else to record about the cathedral, though if I were to stay there a month, I suppose it might then begin to be understood. It is wicked to look at these solemn old churches in a hurry. By the by, it was not built in a hurry; but in full three hundred years, having been begun in 1188 and only finished in 1498, not a great many years before Papistry began to go out of vogue in England.

From Gloucester I took the rail for Basingstoke before noon. The first part of the journey was through an uncommonly beautiful tract of country, hilly, but not wild; a tender and graceful picturesqueness,—fine, single trees and clumps of trees, and sometimes wide woods, scattered over the landscape, and filling the nooks of the hills with luxuriant foliage. Old villages scattered frequently along our track, looking very peaceful, with the peace of past ages lingering about them; and a rich, rural verdure of antique cultivation everywhere. Old country-seats—specimens of the old English hall or manor-house—appeared on the hillsides, with park-scenery surrounding the mansions; and the gray churches rose in the midst of all the little towns.

The beauty of English scenery makes me desperate, it is so impossible to describe it, or in any way to record its impression, and such a pity to leave it undescribed; and, moreover, I always feel that I do not get from it a hundredth or a millionth part of the enjoyment that there really is in it, hurrying past it thus. I was really glad when we rumbled into a tunnel, piercing for a long distance through a hill; and, emerging on the other side, we found ourselves in a comparatively level and uninteresting tract of country, which lasted till we reached Southampton. English scenery, to be appreciated and to be reproduced with pen and pencil, requires to be dwelt upon long, and to be wrought out with the nicest touches. A coarse and hasty brush is not the instrument for such work.

July 6th.—Monday, June 30th, was a warm and beautiful day, and my wife and I took a cab from Southampton and drove to about three or four miles. The remains of the Abbey stand in a sheltered place, but within view of Southampton Water; and it is a most picturesque and perfect ruin, all ivy-grown, of course, and with great trees where the pillars of the nave used to stand, and also in the refectory and the cloister court; and so much soil on the summit of the broken walls, that weeds flourish abundantly there, and grass too; and there was a wild rosebush, in full bloom, as much as thirty or forty feet from the ground. S——- and I ascended a winding stair, leading up within a round tower, the steps much foot-worn; and, reaching the top, we came forth at the height where a gallery had formerly run round the church, in the thickness of the wall. The upper portions of the edifice were now chiefly thrown down; but I followed a foot-path, on the top of the remaining wall, quite to the western entrance of the church. Since the time when the Abbey was taken from the monks, it has been private property; and the possessor, in Henry VIII.'s days, or subsequently, built a residence for himself within its precincts out of the old materials. This has now entirely disappeared, all but some unsightly old masonry, patched into the original walls. Large portions of the ruin have been removed, likewise, to be used as building-materials elsewhere; and this is the Abbey mentioned, I think, by Dr. Watts, concerning which a Mr. William Taylor had a dream while he was contemplating pulling it down. He dreamed that a part of it fell upon his head; and, sure enough, a piece of the wall did come down and crush him. In the nave I saw a large mass of conglomerated stone that had fallen from the wall between the nave and cloisters, and thought that perhaps this was the very mass that killed poor Mr. Taylor.

The ruins are extensive and very interesting; but I have put off describing them too long, and cannot make a distinct picture of them now. Moreover, except to a spectator skilled in architecture, all ruined abbeys are pretty much alike. As we came away, we noticed some women making baskets at the entrance, and one of them urged us to buy some of her handiwork; for that she was the gypsy of Netley Abbey, and had lived among the ruins these thirty years. So I bought one for a shilling. She was a woman with a prominent nose, and weather-tanned, but not very picturesque or striking.

TO BLACKHEATH.

On the 6th July, we left the Villa, with our enormous luggage, and took our departure from Southampton by the noon train. The main street of Southampton, though it looks pretty fresh and bright, must be really antique, there being a great many projecting windows, in the old-time style, and these make the vista of the street very picturesque. I have no doubt that I missed seeing many things more interesting than the few that I saw. Our journey to London was without any remarkable incident, and at the Waterloo station we found one of Mr. Bennoch's clerks, under whose guidance we took two cabs for the East Kent station at London Bridge, and there railed to Blackheath, where we arrived in the afternoon.

On Thursday I went into London by one of the morning trains, and wandered about all day,—visiting the Exhibition of the Royal Academy, and Westminster Abbey and St. Paul's, the two latter of which I have already written about in former journals. On Friday, S——, J——, and I walked over the heath, and through the Park to Greenwich, and spent some hours in the Hospital. The painted hall struck me much more than at my first view of it; it is very beautiful indeed, and the effect of its frescoed ceiling most rich and magnificent, the assemblage of glowing hues producing a general result of splendor. . . .

In the evening I went with Mr. and Mrs. ——— to a conversazione at Mrs. Newton Crosland's, who lives on Blackheath. . . . I met with one person who interested me,—Mr. Bailey, the author of Festus; and I was surprised to find myself already acquainted with him. It is the same Mr. Bailey whom I met a few months ago, when I first dined at Mr. ——'s,—a dark, handsome, rather picturesque-looking man, with a gray beard, and dark hair, a little dimmed with gray. He is of quiet and very agreeable deportment, and I liked him and believed in him. . . . There is sadness glooming out of him, but no unkindness nor asperity. Mrs. Crosland's conversazione was enriched with a supper, and terminated with a dance, in which Mr. ——— joined with heart and soul, but Mrs. ——— went to sleep in her chair, and I would gladly have followed her example if I could have found a chair to sit upon. In the course of the evening I had some talk with a pale, nervous young lady, who has been a noted spiritual medium.

Yesterday I went into town by the steamboat from Greenwich to London Bridge, with a nephew of Mr. ———'s, and, calling at his place of business, he procured us an order from his wine-merchants, by means of which we were admitted into

THE WINE-VAULTS OF THE LONDON DOCKS.

We there found parties, with an acquaintance, who was going, with two French gentlemen, into the vaults. It is a good deal like going down into a mine, each visitor being provided with a lamp at the end of a stick; and following the guide along dismal passages, running beneath the streets, and extending away interminably,—roughly arched overhead with stone, from which depend festoons of a sort of black fungus, caused by the exhalations of the wine. Nothing was ever uglier than this fungus. It is strange that the most ethereal effervescence of rich wine can produce nothing better.

The first series of vaults which we entered were filled with port-wine, and occupied a space variously estimated at from eleven to sixteen acres,—which I suppose would hold more port-wine than ever was made. At any rate, the pipes and butts were so thickly piled that in some places we could hardly squeeze past them. We drank from two or three vintages; but I was not impressed with any especial excellence in the wine. We were not the only visitors, for, far in the depths of the vault, we passed a gentleman and two young ladies, wandering about like the ghosts of defunct wine-bibhers, in a Tophet specially prepared for then. People employed here sometimes go astray, and, their lamps being extinguished, they remain long in this everlasting gloom. We went likewise to the vaults of sherry-wine, which have the same characteristics as those just described, but are less extensive.

It is no guaranty for the excellence or even for the purity of the wine, that it is kept in these cellars, under the lock and key of the government; for the merchants are allowed to mix different vintages, according to their own pleasure, and to adulterate it as they like. Very little of the wine probably comes out as it goes in, or is exactly what it pretends to be. I went back to Mr. ———'s office, and we drove together to make some calls jointly and separately. I went alone to Mrs. Heywood's; afterwards with Mr. ——— to the American minister's, whom we found at home; and I requested of him, on the part of the Americans at Liverpool, to tell me the facts about the

American gentleman being refused admittance to the Levee. The ambassador did not seem to me to make his point good for having withdrawn with the rejected guest.

July 9th. (Our wedding-day.)—We were invited yesterday evening to Mrs. S. C. Hall's, where Jenny Lind was to sing; so we left Blackheath at about eight o'clock in a brougham, and reached Ashley Place, as the dusk was gathering, after nine. The Halls reside in a handsome suite of apartments, arranged on the new system of flats, each story constituting a separate tenement, and the various families having an entrance-hall in common. The plan is borrowed from the Continent, and seems rather alien to the traditionary habits of the English; though, no doubt, a good degree of seclusion is compatible with it. Mr. Hall received us with the greatest cordiality before we entered the drawing-room. Mrs. Hall, too, greeted us with most kindly warmth. Jenny Lind had not yet arrived; but I found Dr. Mackay there, and I was introduced to Miss Catherine Sinclair, who is a literary lady, though none of her works happen to be known to me. Soon the servant announced Madam Goldschmidt, and this famous lady made her appearance, looking quite different from what I expected. Mrs. Hall established her in the inner drawing-room, where was a piano and a harp; and shortly after, our hostess came to me, and said that Madam Goldschmidt wished to be introduced to me. There was a gentle peremptoriness in the summons, that made it something like being commanded into the presence of a princess; a great favor, no doubt, but yet a little humbling to the recipient. However, I acquiesced with due gratitude, and was presented accordingly. She made room for me on the sofa, and I sat down, and began to talk.

Jenny Lind is rather tall,—quite tall, for a woman,—certainly no beauty, but with sense and self-reliance in her aspect and manners. She was suffering under a severe cold, and seemed worn down besides, so probably I saw her under disadvantages. Her conversation is quite simple, and I should have great faith in her sincerity; and there is about her the manner of a person who knows the world, and has conquered it. She said something or other about The Scarlet Letter; and, on my part, I paid her such compliments as a man could pay who had never heard her sing. . . . Her conversational voice is an agreeable one, rather deep, and not particularly smooth. She talked about America, and of our unwholesome modes of life, as to eating and exercise, and of the ill-health especially of our women; but I opposed this view as far as I could with any truth, insinuating my opinion that we are about as healthy as other people, and affirming for a certainty that we live longer. In good faith, so far as I have any knowledge of the matter, the women of England are as generally out of health as those of America; always something has gone wrong with them; and as for Jenny Lind, she looks wan and worn enough to be an American herself. This charge of ill-health is almost universally brought forward against us nowadays,—and, taking the whole country together, I do not believe the statistics will bear it out.

The rooms, which were respectably filled when we arrived, were now getting quite full. I saw Mr. Stevens, the American man of libraries, and had some talk with him; and Durham, the sculptor; and Mr. and Mrs. Hall introduced me to various people, some of whom were of note,—for instance, Sir Emerson Tennent, a man of the world, of some parliamentary distinction, wearing a star; Mr. Samuel Lover, a most good-natured, pleasant Irishman, with a shining and twinkling visage; Miss Jewsbury, whom I found very conversable. She is known in literature, but not to me. We talked about Emerson, whom she seems to have been well acquainted with while he was in England; and she mentioned that Miss Martineau had given him a lock of hair; it was not her own hair, but a mummy's.

After our return, Mrs. ——— told us that Miss Jewsbury had written, among other things, three histories, and as she asked me to introduce her to S———, and means to cultivate our acquaintance, it would be well to know something of them. We were told that she is now employed in some literary undertaking of Lady Morgan's, who, at the age of ninety, is still circulating in society, and is as brisk in faculties as ever. I should like to see her ladyship, that is, I should not be sorry to see her; for distinguished people are so much on a par with others, socially, that it would be foolish to be overjoyed at seeing anybody whomsoever.

Leaving out the illustrious Jenny Lind, I suspect that I was myself the greatest lion of the evening; for a good many persons sought the felicity of knowing me, and had little or nothing to say when that honor and happiness was conferred on them. It is surely very wrong and ill-mannered in people to ask for an introduction unless they are prepared to make talk; it throws too great an expense and trouble on the wretched lion, who is compelled, on the spur of the moment, to convert a conversable substance out of thin air, perhaps for the twentieth time that evening. I am sure I did not say—and I think I did not hear said— one rememberable word in the course of this visit; though, nevertheless, it was a rather agreeable one. In due season ices and jellies were handed about; and some ladies and gentlemen—professional, perhaps—were kind enough to sing songs, and play on the piano and harp, while persons in remote corners went on with whatever conversation they had in hand. Then came supper; but there were so many people to go into the supper-room that we could not all crowd thither together, and, coming late, I got nothing but some sponge-cake and a glass of champagne, neither of which I care for. After supper, Mr. Lover sang some Irish songs, his own in music and words, with rich, humorous effect, to which the comicality of his face contributed almost as much as his voice and words. The Lord Mayor looked in for a little while, and though a hard-featured Jew enough, was the most picturesque person there.

July 10th.—Mrs. Heywood had invited me to dinner last evening. . . . Her house is very finely situated, overlooking Hyde Park, and not a great way from where Tyburn tree used to stand. When I arrived, there were no guests but Mr. and Mrs. D———; but by and by came Mr. Monckton Milnes and lady, the Bishop of Lichfield, Mr. Tom Taylor, Mr. Ewart, M. P., Sir Somebody Somerville, Mr. and Mrs. Musgrave, and others. Mr. Milnes, whom I had not seen for more than a year, greeted me very cordially, and so did Mr. Taylor. I took Mrs. Musgrave in to dinner. She is an Irish lady, and Mrs. Heywood had recommended her to me as being very conversable; but I had a good deal more talk with Mrs. M———, with whom I was already acquainted, than with her. Mrs. M——— is of noble blood, and therefore not snobbish,—quite unaffected, gentle, sweet, and easy to get on with, reminding me of the best-mannered American women. But how can anything characteristic be said or done among a dozen people sitting at table in full dress? Speaking of full dress, the Bishop wore small-clothes and silk stockings, and entered the drawing-room with a three-cornered hat, which he kept flattened out under his arm. He asked the briefest blessing possible, and, sitting at the ultra end of the table, I heard nothing further from him till he officiated as briefly before the cloth was withdrawn. Mrs. M——— talked about Tennyson, with whom her husband was at the University, and whom he continues to know intimately. She says that he considers Maud his best poem. He now lives in the Isle of Wight, spending all the year round there, and has recently bought the place on which he resides. She was of opinion that he would have been gratified by my calling on him, which I had wished to do, while we were at Southampton; but this is a liberty which I should hardly venture upon with a shy man like Tennyson,—more especially as he might perhaps suspect me of doing it on the score of my own literary character.

But I should like much to see him Mr. Tom Taylor, during dinner, made some fun for the benefit of the ladies on either side of him. I liked him very well this evening.

When the ladies had not long withdrawn, and after the wine had once gone round, I asked Mr. Heywood to make my apologies to Mrs. Heywood, and took leave; all London lying betwixt me and the London Bridge station, where I was to take the rail homeward. At the station I found Mr. Bennoch, who had been dining with the Lord Mayor to meet Sir William Williams, and we railed to Greenwich, and reached home by midnight. Mr. and Mrs. Bennoch have set out on their Continental journey to-day,—leaving us, for a little space, in possession of what will be more like a home than anything that we shall hereafter find in England.

This afternoon I had taken up the fourth volume of Jerdan's Autobiography,—wretched twaddle, though it records such constant and apparently intimate intercourse with distinguished people,—and was reading it, between asleep and awake, on the sofa, when Mr. Jerdan himself was announced. I saw him, in company with Mr. Bennoch, nearly three years ago, at Rock Park, and wondered then what there was in so uncouth an individual to get him so freely into polished society. He now looks rougher than ever,—time-worn, but not reverend; a thatch of gray hair on his head; an imperfect set of false teeth; a careless apparel, checked trousers, and a stick, for he had walked a mile or two from his own dwelling.

I suspect—and long practice at the Consulate has made me keen-sighted— that Mr. Jerdan contemplated some benefit from my purse; and, to the extent of a sovereign or so, I would not mind contributing to his comfort. He spoke of a secret purpose of Mr. ——— and himself to obtain me a degree or diploma in some Literary Institution,—what one I know not, and did not ask; but the honor cannot be a high one, if this poor old fellow can do aught towards it. I am afraid he is a very disreputable senior, but certainly not the less to be pitied on that account; and there was something very touching in his stiff and infirm movement, as he resumed his stick and took leave, waving me a courteous farewell, and turning upon me a smile, grim with age, as he went down the steps. In that gesture and smile I fancied some trace of the polished man of society, such as he may have once been; though time and hard weather have roughened him, as they have the once polished marble pillars which I saw so rude in aspect at Netley Abbey.

Speaking of Dickens last evening, Mr. ——— mentioned his domestic tastes,—how he preferred home enjoyments to all others, and did not willingly go much into society. Mrs. ———, too, the other day told us of his taking on himself all possible trouble as regards his domestic affairs. . . . There is a great variety of testimony, various and varied, as to the character of Dickens. I must see him before I finally leave England.

July 13th.—On Friday morning (11th), at nine o'clock, I took the rail into town to breakfast with Mr. Milnes. As he had named a little after ten as the hour, I could not immediately proceed to his house, and so walked moderately over London Bridge and into the city, meaning to take a cab from Charing Cross, or thereabouts. Passing through some street or other, contiguous to Cheapside, I saw in a court-yard the entrance to the Guildhall, and stepped in to look at it. It is a spacious hall, about one hundred and fifty feet long, and perhaps half as broad, paved with flagstones which look worn and some of them cracked across; the roof is very lofty and was once vaulted, but has been shaped anew in modern times. There is a vast window partly filled with painted glass, extending quite along each end of the hall, and a row of arched windows on either side, throwing their light from far above downward upon the pavement. This fashion of high windows, not reaching within twenty or thirty feet of the floor, serves to give great effect to the large enclosed space of an antique hall. Against the walls are several marble monuments; one to the Earl of Chatham, a statue of white marble, with various allegorical contrivances, fronting an obelisk or pyramid of dark marble; and another to his son, William Pitt, of somewhat similar design and of equal size; each of them occupying the whole space, I believe, between pavement and ceiling. There is likewise a statue of Beckford, a famous Lord Mayor,—the most famous except Whittington, and that one who killed Wat Tyler; and like those two, his fame is perhaps somewhat mythological, though he lived and bustled within less than a century. He is said to have made a bold speech to the King; but this I will not believe of any Englishman—at least, of any plebeian Englishman—until I hear it. But there stands his statue in the Guildhall in the act of making his speech, as if the monstrous attempt had petrified him.

Lord Nelson, too, has a monument, and so, I think, has some other modern worthy. At one end of the hall, under one of the great painted windows, stand three or four old statues of mediaeval kings, whose identities I forget; and in the two corners of the opposite end are two gigantic absurdities of painted wood, with grotesque visages, whom I quickly recognized as Gog and Magog. They stand each on a pillar, and seem to be about fifteen feet high, and look like enormous playthings for the children of giants; and it is strange to see them in this solemn old hall, among the memorials of dead heroes and statesmen. There is an annual banquet in the Guildhall, given by the Lord Mayor and sheriffs, and I believe it is the very acme of civic feasting.

After viewing the hall, as it still lacked something of ten, I continued my walk through that entanglement of city streets, and quickly found myself getting beyond my reckoning. I cannot tell whither I went, but I passed through a very dirty region, and I remember a long, narrow, evil-odored street, cluttered up with stalls, in which were vegetables and little bits of meat for sale; and there was a frowzy multitude of buyers and sellers. Still I blundered on, and was getting out of the density of the city into broader streets, but still shabby ones, when, looking at my watch, I found it to be past ten, and no cab-stand within sight. It was a quarter past when I finally got into one;

and the driver told me that it would take half an hour to go from thence to Upper Brook Street; so that I was likely to exceed the license implied in Mr. Milnes's invitation. Whether I was quite beyond rule I cannot say; but it did not lack more than ten minutes of eleven when I was ushered up stairs, and I found all the company assembled. However, it is of little consequence, except that if I had come early, I should have been introduced to many of the guests, whom now I could only know across the table. Mrs. Milnes greeted me very kindly, and Mr. Milnes came towards me with an elderly gentleman in a blue coat and gray pantaloons,—with a long, rather thin, homely visage, exceedingly shaggy eyebrows, though no great weight of brow, and thin gray hair, and introduced me to the Marquis of Lansdowne. The Marquis had his right hand wrapped up in a black-silk handkerchief; so he gave me his left, and, from some awkwardness in meeting it, when I expected the right, I gave him only three of my fingers,—a thing I never did before to any person, and it is droll that I should have done it to a Marquis. He addressed me with great simplicity and natural kindness, complimenting me on my works, and speaking about the society of Liverpool in former days. Lord Lansdowne was the friend of Moore, and has about him the aroma communicated by the memories of many illustrious people with whom he has associated.

Mr. Ticknor, the Historian of Spanish Literature, now greeted me. Mr. Milnes introduced me to Mrs. Browning, and assigned her to me to conduct into the breakfast-room. She is a small, delicate woman, with ringlets of dark hair, a pleasant, intelligent, and sensitive face, and a low, agreeable voice. She looks youthful and comely, and is very gentle and lady-like. And so we proceeded to the breakfast-room, which is hung round with pictures; and in the middle of it stood a large round table, worthy to have been King Arthur's, and here we seated ourselves without any question of precedence or ceremony. On one side of me was an elderly lady, with a very fine countenance, and in the course of breakfast I discovered her to be the mother of Florence Nightingale. One of her daughters (not Florence) was likewise present. Mrs. Milnes, Mrs. Browning, Mrs. Nightingale, and her daughter were the only ladies at table; and I think there were as many as eight or ten gentlemen, whose names—as I came so late—I was left to find out for myself, or to leave unknown.

It was a pleasant and sociable meal, and, thanks to my cold beef and coffee at home, I had no occasion to trouble myself much about the fare; so I just ate some delicate chicken, and a very small cutlet, and a slice of dry toast, and thereupon surceased from my labors. Mrs. Browning and I talked a good deal during breakfast, for she is of that quickly appreciative and responsive order of women with whom I can talk more freely than with any man; and she has, besides, her own originality, wherewith to help on conversation, though, I should say, not of a loquacious tendency. She introduced the subject of spiritualism, which, she says, interests her very much; indeed, she seems to be a believer. Mr. Browning, she told me, utterly rejects the subject, and will not believe even in the outward manifestations, of which there is such overwhelming evidence. We also talked of Miss Bacon; and I developed something of that lady's theory respecting Shakespeare, greatly to the horror of Mrs. Browning, and that of her next neighbor,—a nobleman, whose name I did not hear. On the whole, I like her the better for loving the man Shakespeare with a personal love. We talked, too, of Margaret Fuller, who spent her last night in Italy with the Brownings; and of William Story, with whom they have been intimate, and who, Mrs. Browning says, is much stirred about spiritualism. Really, I cannot help wondering that so fine a spirit as hers should not reject the matter, till, at least, it is forced upon her. I like her very much.

Mrs. Nightingale had been talking at first with Lord Lansdowne, who sat next her, but by and by she turned to nee, and began to speak of London smoke Then, there being a discussion about Lord Byron on the other side of the table, she spoke to me about Lady Byron, whom she knows intimately, characterizing her as a most excellent and exemplary person, high-principled, unselfish, and now devoting herself to the care of her two grandchildren,—their mother, Byron's daughter, being dead. Lady Byron, she says, writes beautiful verses. Somehow or other, all this praise, and more of the same kind, gave me an idea of an intolerably irreproachable person; and I asked Mrs. Nightingale if Lady Byron were warm-hearted. With some hesitation, or mental reservation,—at all events, not quite outspokenly,—she answered that she was.

I was too much engaged with these personal talks to attend much to what was going on elsewhere; but all through breakfast I had been more and more impressed by the aspect of one of the guests, sitting next to Milnes. He was a man of large presence,—a portly personage, gray-haired, but scarcely as yet aged; and his face had a remarkable intelligence, not vivid nor sparkling, but conjoined with great quietude,—and if it gleamed or brightened at one time more than another, it was like the sheen over a broad surface of sea. There was a somewhat careless self-possession, large and broad enough to be called dignity; and the more I looked at him, the more I knew that he was a distinguished person, and wondered who. He might have been a minister of state; only there is not one of them who has any right to such a face and presence. At last,—I do not know how the conviction came,—but I became aware that it was Macaulay, and began to see some slight resemblance to his portraits. But I have never seen any that is not wretchedly unworthy of the original. As soon as I knew him, I began to listen to his conversation, but he did not talk a great deal, contrary to his usual custom; for I am told he is apt to engross all the talk to himself. Probably he may have been restrained by the presence of Ticknor, and Mr. Palfrey, who were among his auditors and interlocutors; and as the conversation seemed to turn much on American subjects, he could not well have assumed to talk them down. I am glad to have seen him,—a face fit for a scholar, a man of the world, a cultivated intelligence.

After we left the table, and went into the library, Mr. Browning introduced himself to me,—a younger man than I expected to see, handsome, with brown hair. He is very simple and agreeable in manner, gently impulsive, talking as if his heart were uppermost. He spoke of his pleasure in meeting me, and his appreciation of my books; and—which has not often happened to me—mentioned that The Blithedale Romance was the one he admired most. I wonder why. I hope I showed as much pleasure at his praise as he did at mine; for I was glad to see how pleasantly it moved him. After this, I talked with Ticknor and Miles, and with Mr. Palfrey, to whom I had been introduced very long ago by George Hillard, and had never seen him since. We looked at some autographs, of which Mr. Milnes has two or three large volumes. I recollect a leaf from Swift's Journal to Stella; a letter from Addison; one from

Chatterton, in a most neat and legible hand; and a characteristic sentence or two and signature of Oliver Cromwell, written in a religious book. There were many curious volumes in the library, but I had not time to look at them.

I liked greatly the manners of almost all,—yes, as far as I observed,—all the people at this breakfast, and it was doubtless owing to their being all people either of high rank or remarkable intellect, or both. An Englishman can hardly be a gentleman, unless he enjoy one or other of these advantages; and perhaps the surest way to give him good manners is to make a lord of him, or rather of his grandfather or great-grandfather. In the third generation, scarcely sooner, he will be polished into simplicity and elegance, and his deportment will be all the better for the homely material out of which it is wrought and refined. The Marquis of Lansdowne, for instance, would have been a very commonplace man in the common ranks of life; but it has done him good to be a nobleman. Not that his tact is quite perfect. In going up to breakfast, he made me precede him; in returning to the library, he did the same, although I drew back, till he impelled me up the first stair, with gentle persistence. By insisting upon it, he showed his sense of condescension much more than if, when he saw me unwilling to take precedence, he had passed forward, as if the point were not worth either asserting or yielding. Heaven knows, it was in no humility that I would have trodden behind him. But he is a kind old man; and I am willing to believe of the English aristocracy generally that they are kind, and of beautiful deportment; for certainly there never can have been mortals in a position more advantageous for becoming so. I hope there will come a time when we shall be so; and I already know a few Americans, whose noble and delicate manners may compare well with any I have seen.

I left the house with Mr. Palfrey. He has cone to England to make some researches in the State Paper Office, for the purposes of a work which he has in hand. He mentioned to me a letter which he had seen, written from New England in the time of Charles II. and referring to the order sent by the minister of that day for the appearance of Governor Bellingham and my ancestor on this side of the water. The signature of this letter is an anagram of my ancestor's name. The letter itself is a very bold and able one, controverting the propriety of the measure above indicated; and Mr. Palfrey feels certain that it was written by my aforesaid ancestor. I mentioned my wish to ascertain the place in England whence the family emigrated; and Mr. Palfrey took me to the Record Office, and introduced me to Mr. Joseph Hunter,—a venerable and courteous gentleman, of antiquarian pursuits. The office was odorous of musty parchments, hundreds of years old. Mr. Hunter received me with great kindness, and gave me various old records and rolls of parchment, in which to seek for my family name; but I was perplexed with the crabbed characters, and soon grew weary and gave up the quest. He says that it is very seldom that an American family, springing from the early settlers, can be satisfactorily traced back to their English ancestry.

July 16th.—Monday morning I took the rail from Blackheath to London. It is a very pleasant place, Blackheath, and far more rural than one would expect, within five or six miles of London,—a great many trees, making quite a mass of foliage in the distance; green enclosures; pretty villas, with their nicely kept lawns, and gardens, with grass-plots and flower borders; and village streets, set along the sidewalks with ornamental trees; and the houses standing a little back, and separated one from another,—all this within what is called the Park, which has its gateways, and the sort of semi-privacy with which I first became acquainted at Rock Park.

From the London Bridge station I took a cab for Paddington, and then had to wait above two hours before a train started for Birkenhead. Meanwhile I walked a little about the neighborhood, which is very dull and uninteresting; made up of crescents and terraces, and rows of houses that have no individuality, and second-rate shops,—in short, the outskirts of the vast city, when it begins to have a kind of village character but no rurality or sylvan aspect, as at Blackheath. My journey, when at last we started, was quite unmarked by incident, and extremely tedious; it being a slow train, which plods on without haste and without rest. At about ten o'clock we reached Birkenhead, and there crossed the familiar and detestable Mersey, which, as usual, had a cloudy sky brooding over it. Mrs. Blodgett received me most hospitably, but was impelled, by an overflow of guests, to put me into a little back room, looking into the court, and formerly occupied by my predecessor, General Armstrong. . . . She expressed a hope that I might not see his ghost,—nor have I, as yet.

Speaking of ghosts, Mr. H. A. B——— told me a singular story to-day of an apparition that haunts the Times Office, in Printing-House Square. A Mr. W——— is the engineer of the establishment, and has his residence in the edifice, which is built, I believe, on the site of Merchant Taylor's school,—an old house that was no longer occupied for its original purpose, and, being supposed haunted, was left untenanted. The father-in-law of Mr. W———, an old sea-captain, came on a visit to him and his wife, and was put into their guest-chamber, where he passed the night. The next morning, assigning no very satisfactory reason, he cut his visit short and went away. Shortly afterwards, a young lady came to visit the W———'s; but she too went away the next morning,—going first to make a call, as she said, to a friend, and sending thence for her trunks. Mrs. W——— wrote to this young lady, asking an explanation. The young lady replied, and gave a singular account of an apparition,— how she was awakened in the night by a bright light shining through the window, which was parallel to the bed; then, if I remember rightly, her curtains were withdrawn, and a shape looked in upon her,—a woman's shape, she called it; but it was a skeleton, with lambent flames playing about its bones, and in and out among the ribs. Other persons have since slept in this chamber, and some have seen the shape, others not. Mr. W——— has slept there himself without seeing anything. He has had investigations by scientific people, apparently under the idea that the phenomenon might have been caused by some of the Times's work-people, playing tricks on the magic-lantern principle; but nothing satisfactory has thus far been elucidated. Mr. B——— had this story from Mrs. Gaskell. . . . Supposing it a ghost, nothing else is so remarkable as its choosing to haunt the precincts of the Times newspaper.

July 29th.—On Saturday, 26th, I took the rail from the Lime Street station for London, via the Trent Valley, and reached Blackheath in the evening. . . .

Sunday morning my wife and I, with J——, railed into London, and drove to the Essex Street Chapel, where Mr. Channing was to preach. The

Chapel is the same where Priestley and Belsham used to preach,—one of the plainest houses of worship I was ever in, as simple and undecorated as the faith there inculcated. They retain, however, all the form and ceremonial of the English Established Church, though so modified as to meet the doctrinal views of the Unitarians. There may be good sense in this, inasmuch as it greatly lessens the ministerial labor to have a stated form of prayer, instead of a necessity for extempore outpourings; but it must be, I should think, excessively tedious to the congregation, especially as, having made alterations in these prayers, they cannot attach much idea of sanctity to them.

[Here follows a long record of Mr. Hawthorne's visit to Miss Bacon,—condensed in Our Old Hone, in the paper called "Recollections of a Gifted Woman."]

August 2d.—On Wednesday (30th July) we went to Marlborough House to see the Vernon gallery of pictures. They are the works, almost entirely of English artists of the last and present century, and comprise many famous paintings; and I must acknowledge that I had more enjoyment of them than of those portions of the National Gallery which I had before seen,— including specimens of the grand old masters. My comprehension has not reached their height. I think nothing pleased me more than a picture by Sir David Wilkie,—The Parish Beadle, with a vagrant boy and a monkey in custody; it is exceedingly good and true throughout, and especially the monkey's face is a wonderful production of genius, condensing within itself the whole moral and pathos of the picture.

Marlborough House was the residence of the Great Duke, and is to be that of the Prince of Wales, when another place is found for the pictures. It adjoins St. James's Palace. In its present state it is not a very splendid mansion, the rooms being small, though handsomely shaped, with vaulted ceilings, and carved white-marble fireplaces. I left S——- here after an hour or two, and walked forth into the hot and busy city with J——-. . . . I called at Routledge's bookshop, in hopes to make an arrangement with him about Miss Bacon's business. But Routledge himself is making a journey in the north, and neither of the partners was there, so that I shall have to go thither some other day. Then we stepped into St. Paul's Cathedral to cool ourselves, and it was delightful so to escape from the sunny, sultry turmoil of Fleet Street and Ludgate, and find ourselves at once in this remote, solemn, shadowy seclusion, marble-cool. O that we had cathedrals in America, were it only for the sensuous luxury! We strolled round the cathedral, and I delighted J——- much by pointing out the monuments of three British generals, who were slain in America in the last war,—the naughty and bloodthirsty little man! We then went to Guildhall, where I thought J——- would like to see Gog and Magog; but he had never heard of those illustrious personages, and took no interest in them. . . . But truly I am grateful to the piety of former times for raising this vast, cool canopy of marble [St. Paul's] in the midst of the feverish city. I wandered quite round it, and saw, in a remote corner, a monument to the officers of the Coldstream Guards, slain in the Crimea. It was a mural tablet, with the names of the officers on an escutcheon; and two privates of the Guards, in marble bas-relief, were mourning over them. Over the tablet hung two silken banners, new and glossy, with the battles in which the regiment has been engaged inscribed on them,—not merely Crimean but Peninsular battles. These banners will bang there till they drop away in tatters.

After thus refreshing myself in the cathedral, I went again to Routledge's in Farrington Street, and saw one of the firm. He expressed great pleasure at seeing me, as indeed he might, having published and sold, without any profit on my part, uncounted thousands of my books. I introduced the subject of Miss Bacon's work; and he expressed the utmost willingness to do everything in his power towards bringing it before the world, but thought that his firm—it being their business to publish for the largest circle of readers—was not the most eligible for the publication of such a book. Very likely this may be so. At all events, however, I am to send him the manuscript, and he will at least give me his advice and assistance in finding a publisher. He was good enough to express great regret that I had no work of my own to give him for publication; and, truly, I regret it too, since, being a resident in England, I could now have all the publishing privileges of a native author. He presented me with a copy of an illustrated edition of Longfellow's Poems, and I took my leave.

Thence I went to the Picture Gallery at the British Institution, where there are three rooms full of paintings by the first masters, the property of private persons. Every one of them, no doubt, was worth studying for a long, long time; and I suppose I may have given, on an average, a minute to each. What an absurdity it would seem, to pretend to read two or three hundred poems, of all degrees between an epic and a ballad, in an hour or two! And a picture is a poem, only requiring the greater study to be felt and comprehended; because the spectator must necessarily do much for himself towards that end. I saw many beautiful things,—among them some landscapes by Claude, which to the eye were like the flavor of a rich, ripe melon to the palate.

August 7th.—Yesterday we took the rail for London, it being a fine, sunny day, though not so very warm as many of the preceding days have been. . . . We went along Piccadilly as far as the Egyptian Hall. It is quite remarkable how comparatively quiet the town has become, now that the season is over. One can see the difference in all the region west of Temple Bar; and, indeed, either the hot weather or some other cause seems to have operated in assuaging the turmoil in the city itself. I never saw London Bridge so little thronged as yesterday. At the Egyptian Hall, or in the same edifice, there is a gallery of pictures, the property of Lord Ward, who allows the public to see them, five days of the week, without any trouble or restriction,—a great kindness on his Lordship's part, it must be owned. It is a very valuable collection, I presume, containing specimens of many famous old masters; some of the early and hard pictures by Raphael and his master and fellow-pupils,—very curious, and nowise beautiful; a perfect, sunny glimpse of Venice, by Canaletto; and saints, and Scriptural, allegorical, and mythological people, by Titian, Guido, Correggio, and many more names than I can remember. There is likewise a dead Magdalen by Canova, and a Venus by the same, very pretty, and with a vivid light of joyous expression in her face; . . . . also Powers's Greek Slave, in which I see little beauty or merit; and two or three other statues.

We then drove to Ashley Place, to call on Mrs. S. C. Hall, whom we found at home. In fact, Wednesday is her reception-day; although, as now everybody is out of town, we were the only callers. She is an agreeable and kindly woman. She told us that her husband and herself propose going to America next year, and I heartily wish they may meet with a warm and friendly reception. I have been seldom more assured of the existence of a heart than in her; also a good deal of sentiment. She had been visiting Bessie, the widow of Moore, at Sloperton, and gave S—— a rose from his cottage. Such things are very true and unaffected in her. The only wonder is that she has not lost such girlish freshness of feeling as prompts them. We did not see Mr. Hall, he having gone to the Crystal Palace.

Taking our leave, we returned along Victoria Street—a new street, penetrating through what was recently one of the worst parts of the town, and now bordered with large blocks of buildings, in a dreary, half-finished state, and left so for want of funds—till we came to Westminster Abbey. We went in and spent an hour there, wandering all round the nave and aisles, admiring the grand old edifice itself, but finding more to smile at than to admire in the monuments. . . . The interior view of the Abbey is better than can be described; the heart aches, as one gazes at it, for lack of power and breadth enough to take its beauty and grandeur in. The effect was heightened by the sun shining through the painted window in the western end, and by the bright sunshine that came through the open portal, and lay on the pavement,—that space so bright, the rest of the vast floor so solemn and sombre. At the western end, in a corner from which spectators are barred out, there is a statue of Wordsworth, which I do not recollect seeing at any former visit. Its only companion in the same nook is Pope's friend, Secretary Craggs.

Downing Street, that famous official precinct, took its name from Sir George Downing, who was proprietor or lessee of property there. He was a native of my own old native town, and his descendants still reside there,—collateral descendants, I suppose,—and follow the drygoods business (drapers).

August 10th.—I journeyed to Liverpool via Chester. . . . One sees a variety of climate, temperature, and season in a ride of two hundred miles, north and south, through England. Near London, for instance, the grain was reaped, and stood in sheaves in the stubble-fields, over which girls and children might be seen gleaning; farther north, the golden, or greenish-golden, crops were waving in the wind. In one part of our way the atmosphere was hot and dry; at another point it had been cooled and refreshed by a heavy thunder-shower, the pools of which still lay along our track. It seems to me that local varieties of weather are more common in this island, and within narrower precincts, than in America. . . . I never saw England of such a dusky and dusty green before,—almost sunbrowned, indeed. Sometimes the green hedges formed a marked framework to a broad sheet of golden grain-field. As we drew near Oxford, just before reaching the station I had a good view of its domes, towers, and spires,—better, I think, than when J——- and I rambled through the town a month or two ago.

Mr. Frank Scott Haydon, of the Record Office, London, writes me that he has found a "Henry Atte Hawthorne" on a roll which he is transcribing, of the first Edward III. He belonged to the Parish of Aldremeston, in the hundred of Blakenhurste, Worcester County.

August 21st.—Yesterday, at twelve o'clock, I took the steamer for Runcorn, from the pier-head. In the streets, I had noticed that it was a breezy day; but on the river there was a very stiff breeze from the northeast, right ahead, blowing directly in our face the whole way; and truly this river Mersey is never without a breeze, and generally in the direction of its course,—an evil-tempered, unkindly, blustering wind, that you cannot meet without being exasperated by it. As it came straight against us, it was impossible to find a shelter anywhere on deck, except it were behind the stove-pipe; and, besides, the day was overcast and threatening rain.

I have undergone very miserable hours on the Mersey, where, in the space of two years, I voyaged thousands of miles,—and this trip to Runcorn reminded me of them, though it was less disagreeable after more than a twelvemonth's respite. We had a good many passengers on board, most of whom were of the second class, and congregated on the forward deck; more women than men, I think, and some of them with their husbands and children. Several produced lunch and bottles, and refreshed themselves very soon after we started. By and by the wind became so disagreeable that I went below, and sat in the cabin, only occasionally looking out, to get a peep at the shores of the river, which I had never before seen above Eastham. However, they are not worth looking at; level and monotonous, without trees or beauty of any kind,—here and there a village, and a modern church, on the low ridge behind; perhaps, a windmill, which the gusty day had set busily to work. The river continues very wide—no river indeed, but an estuary—during almost the whole distance to Runcorn; and nearly at the end of our voyage we approached some abrupt and prominent hills, which, many a time, I have seen on my passages to Rock Ferry, looking blue and dim, and serving for prophets of the weather; for when they can be distinctly seen adown the river, it is a token of coming rain. We met many vessels, and passed many which were beating up against the wind, and which keeled over, so that their decks must have dipped,—schooners and vessels that come from the Bridgewater Canal. We shipped a sea ourselves, which gave the fore-deck passengers a wetting.

Before reaching Runcorn, we stopped to land some passengers at another little port, where there was a pier and a lighthouse, and a church within a few yards of the river-side,—a good many of the river-craft, too, in dock, forming quite a crowd of masts. About ten minutes' further steaming brought us to Runcorn, where were two or three tall manufacturing chimneys, with a pennant of black smoke from each; two vessels of considerable size on the stocks; a church or two; and a meagre, uninteresting, shabby, brick-built town, rising from the edge of the river, with irregular streets,—not village-like, but paved, and looking like a dwarfed, stunted city. I wandered through it till I came to a tall, high-pedestalled windmill on the outer verge, the vans of which were going briskly round. Thence retracing my steps, I stopped at a poor hotel, and took lunch, and, finding that I was in time to take the steamer back, I hurried on board, and we set sail (or steam) before three. I have heard of an old castle at Runcorn, but could discover nothing of it. It was well that I returned so promptly, for we had hardly left the pier before it began to rain, and there was a heavy downfall throughout the voyage homeward. Runcorn is fourteen miles from Liverpool, and is the farthest point to which a steamer runs. I had intended to come home by rail,—a circuitous route,—but the advice of the landlady of the hotel, and the aspect of the weather, and a feeling of general discouragement prevented me.

An incident in S. C. Hall's Ireland, of a stone cross, buried in Cromwell's time, to prevent its destruction by his soldiers. It was forgotten, and became a mere doubtful tradition, but one old man had been told by his father, and he by his father, etc., that it was buried near a certain spot; and at last, two hundred years after the cross was buried, the vicar of the parish dug in that spot and found it. In my (English) romance, an American might bring the tradition from over the sea, and so discover the cross, which had been altogether forgotten.

August 24th.—Day before yesterday I took the rail for Southport,—a cool, generally overcast day, with glimmers of faint sunshine. The ride is through a most uninteresting tract of country, at first, glimpses of the river, with the thousands of masts in the docks; the dismal outskirts of a great town, still spreading onward, with beginnings of streets, and insulated brick buildings and blocks; farther on, a wide monotony of level plain, and here and there a village and a church; almost always a windmill in sight, there being plenty of breeze to turn its vans on this windy coast. The railway skirts along the sea the whole distance, but is shut out from the sight of it by the low sand-hills, which seem to have been heaped up by the waves. There are one or two lighthouses on the shore. I have not seen a drearier landscape, even in Lancashire.

Reaching Southport at three, I rambled about, with a view to discover whether it be a suitable residence for my family during September. It is a large village, or rather more than a village, which seems to be almost entirely made up of lodging-houses, and, at any rate, has been built up by the influx of summer visitors,—a sandy soil, level, and laid out with well-paved streets, the principal of which are enlivened with bazaars, markets, shops, hotels of various degrees, and a showy vivacity of aspect. There are a great many donkey-carriages,—large vehicles, drawn by a pair of donkeys; bath-chairs, with invalid ladies; refreshment-rooms in great numbers,—a place where everybody seems to be a transitory guest, nobody at home. The main street leads directly down to the sea-shore, along which there is an elevated embankment, with a promenade on the top, and seats, and the toll of a penny. The shore itself, the tide being then low, stretched out interminably seaward, a wide waste of glistering sands; and on the dry border, people were riding on donkeys, with the drivers whipping behind; and children were digging with their little wooden spades; and there were donkey-carriages far out on the sands,—a pleasant and breezy drive. A whole city of bathing-machines was stationed near the shore, and I saw others in the seaward distance. The sea-air was refreshing and exhilarating, and if S—— needs a seaside residence, I should think this might do as well as any other.

I saw a large brick edifice, enclosed within a wall, and with somewhat the look of an almshouse or hospital; and it proved to be an Infirmary, charitably established for the reception of poor invalids, who need sea-air and cannot afford to pay for it. Two or three of such persons were sitting under its windows. I do not think that the visitors of Southport are generally of a very opulent class, but of the middle rank, from Manchester and other parts of this northern region. The lodging-houses, however, are of sufficiently handsome style and arrangement.

OXFORD.

[Mr. Hawthorne extracted from his recorded Oxford experiences his excursion to Blenheim, but left his observations of the town itself untouched,—and these I now transcribe.—ED.]

August 31st.—. . . . Yesterday we took the rail for London, and drove across the city to the Paddington station, where we met Bennoch, and set out with him for Oxford. I do not quite understand the matter, but it appears that we were expected guests of Mr. Spiers, a very hospitable gentleman, and Ex-Mayor of Oxford, and a friend of Bennoch and of the Halls. Mr. S. C. Hall met us at the Oxford station, and under his guidance we drove to a quiet, comfortable house in St. Giles Street, where rooms had been taken for us. Durham, the sculptor, is likewise of the party.

After establishing ourselves at these lodgings, we walked forth to take a preliminary glimpse of the city, and Mr. Hall, being familiar with the localities, served admirably as a guide. If I remember aright, I spoke very slightingly of the exterior aspect of Oxford, as I saw it with J—— during an hour or two's stay here, on my way to Southampton (to meet S—— on her return from Lisbon). I am bound to say that my impressions are now very different; and that I find Oxford exceedingly picturesque and rich in beauty and grandeur and in antique stateliness. I do not remember very particularly what we saw,—time-worn fronts of famous colleges and halls of learning everywhere about the streets, and arched entrances; passing through which, we saw bits of sculpture from monkish hands,—the most grotesque and ludicrous faces, as if the slightest whim of these old carvers took shape in stone, the material being so soft and manageable by them; an ancient stone pulpit in the quadrangle of Maudlin College (Magdalen), one of only three now extant in England; a splendid—no, not splendid, but dimly magnificent—chapel, belonging to the same College, with painted windows of rare beauty, not brilliant with diversified hues, but of a sombre tint. In this chapel there is an alabaster monument,—a recumbent figure of the founder's father, as large as life,—which, though several centuries old, is as well preserved as if fresh from the chisel.

In the High Street, which, I suppose, is the noblest old street in England, Mr. Hall pointed out, the Crown Inn, where Shakespeare used to spend the night, and was most hospitably welcomed by the pretty hostess (the mother of Sir William Davenant) on his passage between Stratford and London. It is a three-story house, with other houses contiguous,—an old timber mansion, though now plastered and painted of a yellowish line. The ground-floor is occupied as a shoe-shop; but the rest of the house is still kept as a tavern. . . .

It is not now term time, and Oxford loses one of its most characteristic features by the absence of the gownsmen; but still there is a good deal of liveliness in the streets. We walked as far as a bridge beyond Maudlin College, and then drove homeward.

At six we went to dine with the hospitable Ex-Mayor, across the wide, tree-bordered street; for his house is nearly opposite our lodgings. He is an intelligent and gentlemanly person, and was Mayor two years ago, and has done a great deal to make peace between the University and the town, heretofore bitterly inimical. His house is adorned with pictures and drawings, and he has an especial taste for art. . . . The dinner-table was decorated with pieces of plate, vases, and other things, which were presented to him as tokens of public or friendly regard and approbation of his action in the Mayoralty. After dinner, too, he produced a large silver snuff-box, which had been given him on the same account; in fact, the inscription affirmed that it was one of five pieces of plate so presented. The vases are really splendid,—one of them two feet high, and richly ornamented. It will hold five or six bottles of wine, and he said that it had been filled, and, I believe, sent round as a loving-cup at some of his entertainments. He cordially enjoys these things, and his genuine benevolence produces all this excellent hospitality. . . . But Bennoch proposed a walk, and we set forth. We rambled pretty extensively about the streets, sometimes seeing the shapes of old edifices dimly and doubtfully, it being an overcast night; or catching a partial view of a gray wall, or a pillar, or a Gothic archway, by lamplight. . . . The clock had some time ago struck eleven, when we were passing under a long extent of antique wall and towers, which were those of Baliol College. Mr. D——— led us into the middle of the street, and showed us a cross, which was paved into it, on a level with the rest of the road. This was the spot where Latimer and Ridley and another Bishop were martyred in Bloody Mary's time. There is a memorial to them in another street; but this, where I set my foot at nearly midnight, was the very spot where their flesh burned to ashes, and their bones whitened. It has been a most beautiful morning, and I have seen few pleasanter scenes than this street in which we lodge, with its spacious breadth, its two rows of fine old trees, with sidewalks as wide as the whole width of some streets; and, on the opposite side, the row of houses, some of them ancient with picturesque gables, partially disclosed through the intervening foliage. . . . From our window we have a slantwise glimpse, to the right, of the walls of St. John's College, and the general aspect of St. Giles. It is of an antiquity not to shame those mediaeval halls. Our own lodgings are in a house that seems to be very old, with panelled walls, and beams across the ceilings, lattice-windows in the chambers, and a musty odor such as old houses inevitably have. Nevertheless, everything is extremely neat, clean, and comfortable; and in term time our apartments are occupied by a Mr. Stebbing, whose father is known in literature by some critical writings, and who is a graduate and an admirable scholar. There is a bookcase of five shelves, containing his books, mostly standard works, and indicating a safe and solid taste.

After lunch to-day we (that is, Mrs. Hall, her adopted daughter, S———, and I, with the Ex-Mayor) set forth, in an open barouche, to see the remarkables of Oxford, while the rest of the guests went on foot. We first drew up at New College (a strange name for such an old place, but it was new some time since the Conquest), and went through its quiet and sunny quadrangles, and into its sunny and shadowy gardens. I am in despair about the architecture and old edifices of these Oxford colleges, it is so impossible to express them in words. They are themselves—as the architect left them, and as Time has modified and improved them—the expression of an idea which does not admit of being otherwise expressed, or translated into anything else. Those old battlemented walls around the quadrangles; many gables; the windows with stone pavilions, so very antique, yet some of them adorned with fresh flowers in pots,—a very sweet contrast; the ivy mantling the gray stone; and the infinite repose, both in sunshine and shadow,—it is as if half a dozen bygone centuries had set up their rest here, and as if nothing of the present time ever passed through the deeply recessed archway that shuts in the College from the street. Not but what people have very free admittance; and many parties of young men and girls and children came into the gardens while we were there.

These gardens of New College are indescribably beautiful,—not gardens in an American sense, but lawns of the richest green and softest velvet grass, shadowed over by ancient trees, that have lived a quiet life here for centuries, and have been nursed and tended with such care, and so sheltered from rude winds, that certainly they must have been the happiest of all trees. Such a sweet, quiet, sacred, stately seclusion— so age-long as this has been, and, I hope, will continue to be—cannot exist anywhere else. One side of the garden wall is formed by the ancient wall of the city, which Cromwell's artillery battered, and which still retains its pristine height and strength. At intervals, there are round towers that formed the bastions; that is to say, on the exterior they are round towers, but within, in the garden of the College, they are semicircular recesses, with iron garden-seats arranged round them. The loop-holes through which the archers and musketeers used to shoot still pierce through deep recesses in the wall, which is here about six feet thick. I wish I could put into one sentence the whole impression of this garden, but it could not be done in many pages.

We looked also at the outside of the wall, and Mr. Parker, deeply skilled in the antiquities of the spot, showed us a weed growing,—here in little sprigs, there in large and heavy festoons,—hanging plentifully downward from a shallow root. It is called the Oxford plant, being found only here, and not easily, if at all, introduced anywhere else. It bears a small and pretty blue flower, not altogether unlike the forget-me-not, and we took some of it away with us for a memorial. We went into the chapel of New College, which is in such fresh condition that I think it must be modern; and yet this cannot be, since there are old brasses inlaid into tombstones in the pavement, representing mediaeval ecclesiastics and college dignitaries; and busts against the walls, in antique garb; and old painted windows, unmistakable in their antiquity. But there is likewise a window, lamentable to look at, which was painted by Sir Joshua Reynolds, and exhibits strikingly the difference between the work of a man who performed it merely as a matter of taste and business, and what was done religiously and with the whole heart; at least, it shows that the artists and public of the last age had no sympathy with Gothic art. In the chancel of this church there are more painted windows, which I take to be modern, too, though they are in much better taste, and have an infinitely better effect, than Sir Joshua's. At any rate, with the sunshine through them, they looked very beautiful, and tinted the high altar and the pavement with brilliant lines.

The sacristan opened a tall and narrow little recess in the wall of the chancel, and showed it entirely filled with the crosier of William of Wickham. It appears to be made of silver gilt, and is a most rich and elaborate relic, at least six feet high. Modern art cannot, or does not, equal the chasing and carving of this splendid crosier, which is enriched with figures of saints and, apostles, and various Gothic devices,—very minute, but all executed as faithfully as if the artist's salvation had depended upon every notch he made in the silver. . . .

Leaving New College, Bennoch and I, under Mr. Parker's guidance, walked round Christ Church meadows, part of our way lying along the banks of the Cherwell, which unites with the Isis to form the Thames, I believe. The Cherwell is a narrow and remarkably sluggish stream; but is deep in spots, and capriciously so,—so that a person may easily step from knee-deep to fifteen feet in depth. A gentleman present used a queer expression in reference to the drowning of two college men; he said "it was an awkward affair." I think this is equal to Longfellow's story of the Frenchman who avowed himself very much "displeased" at the news of his father's death. At the confluence of the Cherwell and Isis we saw a good many boats, belonging to the students of the various colleges; some of them being very large and handsome barges, capable of accommodating a numerous party, with room on board for dancing and merry-making. Some of them are calculated to be drawn by horses, in the manner of canal-boats; others are propellable by oars. It is practicable to perform the voyage between Oxford and London—a distance of about one hundred and thirty miles—in three days. The students of Oxford are famous boatmen; there is a constant rivalship, on this score, among the different colleges; and annually, I believe, there is a match between Oxford and Cambridge. The Cambridge men beat the Oxonians in this year's trial.

On our return into the city, we passed through Christ Church, which, as regards the number of students, is the most considerable college of the University. It has a stately dome; but my memory is confused with battlements, towers, and gables, and Gothic staircases and cloisters. If there had been nothing else in Oxford but this one establishment, my anticipations would not have been disappointed. The bell was tolling for worship in the chapel; and Mr. Parker told us that Dr. Pusey is a canon, or in some sort of dignity, in Christ Church, and would soon probably make his appearance in the quadrangle, on his way to chapel; so we walked to and fro, waiting an opportunity to see him. A gouty old dignitary, in a white surplice, came hobbling along from one extremity of the court; and by and by, from the opposite corner, appeared Dr. Pusey, also in a white surplice, and with a lady by his side. We met him, and I stared pretty fixedly at him, as I well might; for he looked on the ground, as if conscious that he would be stared at. He is a man past middle life, of sufficient breadth and massiveness, with a pale, intellectual, manly face. He was talking with the lady, and smiled, but not jollily. Mr. Parker, who knows him, says that he is a man of kind and gentle affections. The lady was his niece.

Thence we went through High Street and Broad Street, and passing by Baliol College,—a most satisfactory pile and range of old towered and gabled edifices,—we came to the cross on the pavement, which is supposed to mark the spot where the bishops were martyred. But Mr. Parker told us the mortifying fact, that he had ascertained that this could not possibly have been the genuine spot of martyrdom, which must have taken place at a point within view, but considerably too far off to be moistened by any tears that may be shed here. It is too bad. We concluded the rambles of the day by visiting the gardens of St. John's College; and I desire, if possible, to say even more in admiration of them than of those of New College,—such beautiful lawns, with tall, ancient trees, and heavy clouds of foliage, and sunny glimpses through archways of leafy branches, where, to-day, we could see parties of girls, making cheerful contrast with the sombre walls and solemn shade. The world, surely, has not another place like Oxford; it is a despair to see such a place and ever to leave it, for it would take a lifetime and more than one, to comprehend and enjoy it satisfactorily.

At dinner, to-day, the golden vases were all ranged on the table, the largest and central one containing a most magnificent bouquet of dahlias and other bright-hued flowers.

On Tuesday, our first visit was to Christ Church, where we saw the large and stately hall, above a hundred feet long by forty wide, and fifty to the top of its carved oaken roof, which is ornamented with festoons, as it were, and pendants of solid timber. The walls are panelled with oak, perhaps half-way upward, and above are the rows of arched windows on each side; but, near the upper end, two great windows come nearly to the floor. There is a dais, where the great men of the College and the distinguished guests sit at table, and the tables of the students are arranged along the length of the hall. All around, looking down upon those who sit at meat, are the portraits of a multitude of illustrious personages who were members of the learned fraternity in times past; not a portrait being admitted there (unless it he a king, and I remember only Henry VIII.) save those who were actually students on the foundation, receiving the eleemosynary aid of the College. Most of them were divines; but there are likewise many statesmen, eminent during the last three hundred years, and, among many earlier ones, the Marquis of Wellesley and Canning. It is an excellent idea, for their own glory, and as examples to the rising generations, to have this multitude of men, who have done good and great things, before the eyes of those who ought to do as well as they, in their own time. Archbishops, Prime Ministers, poets, deep scholars,—but, doubtless, an outward success has generally been their claim to this position, and Christ Church may have forgotten a better man than the best of them. It is not, I think, the tendency of English life, nor of the education of their colleges, to lead young men to high moral excellence, but to aim at illustrating themselves in the sight of mankind.

Thence we went into the kitchen, which is arranged very much as it was three centuries ago, with two immense fireplaces. There was likewise a gridiron, which, without any exaggeration, was large enough to have served for the martyrdom of St. Lawrence. The college dinners are good, but plain, and cost the students one shilling and eleven pence each, being rather cheaper than a similar one could be had at an inn. There is no provision for breakfast or supper in commons; but they can have these meals sent to their rooms from the buttery, at a charge proportioned to the dishes they order. There seems to be no necessity for a great expenditure on the part of Oxford students.

From the kitchen we went to the chapel, which is the cathedral of Oxford, and well worth seeing, if there had not been so many other things to see. It is now under repair, and there was a great heap of old wood-work and panelling lying in one of the aisles, which had been stripped away from some of the ancient pillars, leaving them as good as new. There is a shrine of a saint, with a wooden canopy over it; and some painted glass, old and new; and a statue of Cyril Jackson, with a face of shrewdness and insight; and busts, as mural monuments.

Our next visit was to

MERTON COLLEGE,

which, though not one of the great colleges, is as old as any of them, and looks exceedingly venerable. We were here received by a friend of Mr. Spiers, in his academic cap, but without his gown, which is not worn, except in term time. He is a very civil gentleman, and showed us some antique points of architecture,—such as a Norman archway, with a passage over it, through which the Queen of Charles I. used to go to chapel; and an edifice of the thirteenth century, with a stone roof, which is considered to be very curious.

How ancient is the aspect of these college quadrangles! so gnawed by time as they are, so crumbly, so blackened, and so gray where they are not black,—so quaintly shaped, too, with here a line of battlement and there a row of gables; and here a turret, with probably a winding stair inside; and lattice-windows, with stone mullions, and little panes of glass set in lead; and the cloisters, with a long arcade, looking upon the green or pebbled enclosure. The quality of the stone has a great deal to do with the apparent antiquity. It is a stone found in the neighborhood of Oxford, and very soon begins to crumble and decay superficially, when exposed to the weather; so that twenty years do the work of a hundred, so far as appearances go. If you strike one of the old walls with a stick, a portion of it comes powdering down. The effect of this decay is very picturesque, and is especially striking, I think, on edifices of classic architecture, such as some of the Oxford colleges are, greatly enriching the Grecian columns, which look so cold when the outlines are hard and distinct. The Oxford people, however, are tired of this crumbly stone, and when repairs are necessary, they use a more durable material, which does not well assort with the antiquity into which it is intruded.

Mr. E——— showed us the library of Merton College. It occupies two sides of an old building, and has a very delightful fragrance of ancient books. The halls containing it are vaulted, and roofed with oak, not carved and ornamented, but laid flat, so that they look very like a grand and spacious old garret. All along, there is a row of alcoves on each side, with rude benches and reading-desks, in the simplest style, and nobody knows how old. The books look as old as the building. The more valuable were formerly chained to the bookcases; and a few of them have not yet broken their chains. It was a good emblem of the dark and monkish ages, when learning was imprisoned in their cloisters, and chained in their libraries, in the days when the schoolmaster had not yet gone abroad. Mr. E——— showed us a very old copy of the Bible; and a vellum manuscript, most beautifully written in black-letter and illuminated, of the works of Duns Scotus, who was a scholar of Merton College.

He then showed us the chapel, a large part of which has been renewed and ornamented with pictured windows and other ecclesiastical splendor, and paved with encaustic tiles, according to the Puseyite taste of the day; for Merton has adopted the Puseyite doctrines, and is one of their chief strongholds in Oxford. If they do no other good, they at least do much for the preservation and characteristic restoration of the old English churches; but perhaps, even here, there is as much antiquity spoiled as retained. In the portion of the chapel not yet restored, we saw the rude old pavement, inlaid with gravestones, in some of which were brasses, with the figures of the college dignitaries, whose dust slumbered beneath; and I think it was here that I saw the tombstone of Anthony-a-Wood, the gossiping biographer of the learned men of Oxford.

From the chapel we went into the college gardens, which are very pleasant, and possess the advantage of looking out on the broad verdure of Christ Church meadows and the river beyond. We loitered here awhile, and then went to Mr. ———'s rooms, to which the entrance is by a fine old staircase. They had a very comfortable, aspect,—a wainscoted parlor and bedroom, as nice and cosey as a bachelor could desire, with a good collection of theological books; and on a peg hung his gown, with a red border about it, denoting him to be a proproctor. He was kind enough to order a lunch, consisting of bread and cheese, college ale, and a certain liquor called "Archdeacon." . . . . We ate and drank, ... and, bidding farewell to good Mr. E———, we pursued our way to the

RATCLIFFE LIBRARY.

This is a very handsome edifice, of a circular shape; the lower story consisting altogether of arches, open on all sides, as if to admit anybody to the learning here stored up. I always see great beauty and lightsomeness in these classic and Grecian edifices, though they seem cold and intellectual, and not to have had their mortar moistened with human life-blood, nor to have the mystery of human life in them, as Gothic structures do. The library is in a large and beautiful room, in the story above the basement, and, as far as I saw, consisted chiefly or altogether of scientific works. I saw Silliman's Journal on one of the desks, being the only trace of American science, or American learning or ability in any department, which I discovered in the University of Oxford. After seeing the library, we went to the top of the building, where we had an excellent view of Oxford and the surrounding country. Then we went to the Convocation Hall, and afterwards to the theatre, where S——- sat down in the Chancellor's chair, which is very broad, and ponderously wrought of oak. I remember little here, except the amphitheatre of benches, and the roof, which seems to be supported by golden ropes, and on the wall, opposite the door, some full-length portraits, among which one of that ridiculous coxcomb, George IV., was the most prominent. These kings thrust themselves impertinently forward by bust, statue, and picture, on all occasions, and it is not wise in them to show their shallow foreheads among men of mind.

THE BODLEIAN LIBRARY.

Mr. Spiers tried to get us admittance to the Bodleian Library; but this is just the moment when it is closed for the purpose of being cleaned; so we missed seeing the principal halls of this library, and were only admitted into what was called the Picture Gallery. This, however, satisfied all my desires, so far as the backs of books are concerned, for they extend through a gallery, running round three sides of a quadrangle, making an aggregate length of more than four hundred feet,—a solid array of bookcases, full of books, within a protection of open iron-work. Up and down the gallery there are models of classic temples; and about midway in its extent stands a brass statue of Earl Pembroke, who was Chancellor of the University in James I's time; not in scholarly garb, however, but in plate and mail, looking indeed like a thunderbolt of war. I rapped him with my knuckles, and he seemed to be solid metal, though, I should imagine, hollow at heart. A thing which interested me very much was the lantern of Guy Fawkes. It was once tinned, no doubt, but is now nothing but rusty iron, partly broken. As this is called the Picture Gallery, I must not forget the pictures, which are ranged in long succession over the bookcases, and include almost all Englishmen whom the world has ever heard of, whether in statesmanship or literature, I saw a canvas on which had once been a lovely and unique portrait of Mary of Scotland; but it was consigned to a picture-cleaner to be cleansed, and, discovering that it was painted over another picture, he had the curiosity to clean poor Mary quite away, thus revealing a wishy-washy woman's face, which now hangs in the gallery. I am so tired of seeing notable things that I almost wish that whatever else is remarkable in Oxford could be obliterated in some similar manner.

From the Bodleian we went to

THE TAYLOR INSTITUTE,

which was likewise closed; but the woman who had it in charge had formerly been a servant of Mr. Spiers, and he so overpersuaded her that she finally smiled and admitted us. It would truly have been a pity to miss it; for here, on the basement floor, are the original models of Chantrey's busts and statues, great and small; and in the rooms above are a far richer treasure,—a large collection of original drawings by Raphael and Michael Angelo. These are far better for my purpose than their finished pictures,—that is to say, they bring me much closer to the hands that drew them and the minds that imagined them. It is like looking into their brains, and seeing the first conception before it took shape outwardly (I have somewhere else said about the same thing of such sketches). I noticed one of Raphael's drawings, representing the effect of eloquence; it was a man speaking in the centre of a group, between whose ears and the orator's mouth connecting lines were drawn. Raphael's idea must have been to compose his picture in such a way that their auricular organs should not fail to be in a proper relation with the eloquent voice; and though this relation would not have been individually traceable in the finished picture, yet the general effect—that of deep and entranced attention—would have been produced.

In another room there are some copies of Raphael's cartoons, and some queer mediaeval pictures, as stiff and ugly as can well be conceived, yet successful in telling their own story. We looked a little while at these, and then, thank Heaven! went home and dressed for dinner. I can write no more to-day. Indeed, what a mockery it is to write at all!

[Here follows the drive to Cumnor Place, Stanton Harcourt, Nuneham Courtney, Godstowe, etc.,—already published in Our Old Home.—ED.]

September 9th.—The morning after our excursion on the Thames was as bright and beautiful as many preceding ones had been. After breakfast S—— and I walked a little about the town, and bought Thomas a Kempis, in both French and English, for U——. . . . Mr. De la Motte, the photographer, had breakfasted with us, and Mr. Spiers wished him to take a photograph of our whole party. So, in the first place, before the rest were assembled, he made an experimental group of such as were there; and I did not like my own aspect very much. Afterwards, when we were all come, he arranged us under a tree in the garden,—Mr. and Mrs. Spiers, with their eldest son, Mr. and Mrs. Hall and Fanny, Mr. Addison, my wife and me,—and stained the glass with our figures and faces in the twinkling of an eye; not S——-'s face, however, for she turned it away, and left only a portion of her bonnet and dress,—and Mrs. Hall, too, refused to countenance the proceeding. But all the rest of us were caught to the life, and I was really a little startled at recognizing myself so apart from myself, and done so quickly too.

This was the last important incident of our visit to Oxford, except that Mr. Spiers was again most hospitable at lunch. Never did anybody attend more faithfully to the comfort of his friends than does this good gentleman. But he has shown himself most kind in every possible way, and I shall always feel truly grateful. No better way of showing our sense of his hospitality, and all the trouble he has taken for us (and our memory of him), has occurred to us, than to present him with a set of my Tales and Romances; so, by the next steamer, I shall write to Ticknor and Fields to send them, elegantly bound, and S——- will emblazon his coat of arms in each volume. He accompanied us and Mr. and Mrs. Hall to the railway station, and we left Oxford at two o'clock.

It had been a very pleasant visit, and all the persons whom we met were kind and agreeable, and disposed to look at one another in a sunny aspect. I saw a good deal of Mr. Hall. He is a thoroughly genuine man, of kind heart and true affections, a gentleman of taste and refinement, and full of humor.

On the Saturday after our return to Blackheath, we went to

HAMPTON COURT,

about which, as I have already recorded a visit to it, I need say little here. But I was again impressed with the stately grandeur of Wolsey's great Hall, with its great window at each end, and one side window, descending almost to the floor, and a row of windows on each side, high towards the roof, and throwing down their many-colored light on the stone pavement, and on the Gobelin tapestry, which must have been gorgeously rich when the walls were first clothed with it. I fancied, then, that no modern architect could produce so fine a room; but oddly enough, in the great entrance-hall of the Euston station, yesterday, I could not see how this last fell very much short of Wolsey's Hall in grandeur. We were quite wearied in passing through the endless suites of rooms in Hampton Court, and gazing at the thousands of pictures; it is too much for one day,—almost enough for one life, in such measure as life can be bestowed on pictures. It would have refreshed us had we spent half the time in wandering about the grounds, which, as we glimpsed at them from the windows of the Palace, seemed very beautiful, though laid out with an antique formality of straight lines and broad gravelled paths. Before the central window there is a beautiful sheet of water, and a fountain upshooting itself and plashing into it, with a continuous and pleasant sound. How beautifully the royal robe of a monarchy is embroidered! Palaces, pictures, parks! They do enrich life; and kings and aristocracies cannot keep these things to themselves, they merely take care of them for others. Even a king, with all the glory that can be shed around him, is but the liveried and bedizened footman of his people, and the toy of their delight. I am very glad that I came to this country while the English are still playing with such a toy.

Yesterday J——- and I left Blackheath, and reached Liverpool last night. The rest of my family will follow in a few days; and so finishes our residence in Bennoch's house, where I, for my part, have spent some of the happiest hours that I have known since we left our American home. It is a strange, vagabond, gypsy sort of life,—this that we are leading; and I know not whether we shall finally be spoiled for any other, or shall enjoy our quiet Wayside, as we never did before, when once we reach it again.

The evening set in misty and obscure; and it was dark almost when J——- and I arrived at the landing stage on our return. I was struck with the picturesque effect of the high tower and tall spire of St. Nicholas, rising upward, with dim outline, into the duskiness; while midway of its height the dial-plates of an illuminated clock blazed out, like two great eyes of a giant.

September 13th.—On Saturday my wife, with all her train, arrived at Mrs. B———'s; and on Tuesday—vagabonds as we are—we again struck our tent, and set out for

SOUTHPORT.

I do not know what sort of character it will form in the children,—this unsettled, shifting, vagrant life, with no central home to turn to, except what we carry in ourselves. It was a windy day, and, judging by the look of the trees, on the way to Southport, it must be almost always windy, and with the blast in one prevailing direction; for invariably their branches, and the whole contour and attitude of the tree, turn from seaward, with a strangely forlorn aspect. Reaching Southport, we took an omnibus, and under the driver's guidance came to our tall stone house, fronting on the sands, and styled "Brunswick Terrace." . . . .

The English system of lodging-houses has its good points; but it is, nevertheless, a contrivance for bearing the domestic cares of home about with you whithersoever you go; and immediately you have to set about producing your own bread and cheese. However, Fanny took most of this trouble off our hands, though there was inevitably the stiffness and discomfort of a new housekeeping on the first day of our arrival; besides that, it was cool, and the wind whistled and grumbled and eddied into the chinks of the house.

Meanwhile, in all my experience of Southport, I have never yet seen the sea, but only an interminable breadth of sands, looking pooly or plashy in some places, and barred across with drier reaches of sand, but no expanse of water. It must be miles and miles, at low water, to the veritable sea-shore. We are about twenty miles north of Liverpool, on the border of the Irish Sea; and Ireland and, I suppose, the Isle of Man intervene betwixt us and the ocean, not much to our benefit; for the air of the English coast, under ocean influences, is said to be milder than when it comes across the land,—milder, therefore, above or below Ireland, because then the Gulf Stream ameliorates it.

Betimes, the forenoon after our arrival, I had to take the rail to Liverpool, but returned, a little after five, in the midst of a rain,— still low water and interminable sands; still a dreary, howling blast. We had a cheerful fireside, however, and should have had a pleasant evening, only that the wind on the sea made us excessively drowsy. This morning we awoke to hear the wind still blustering, and blowing up clouds, with fitful little showers, and soon blowing them away again, and letting the brightest of sunshine fall over the plashy waste of sand. We have already walked forth on the shore with J——- and R——-, who pick up shells, and dig wells in the sand with their little wooden spades; but soon we saw a rainbow on the western sky, and then a shower came spattering down upon us in good earnest. We first took refuge under the bridge that stretches between the two portions of the promenade; but as there was a chill draught there, we made the best of our way home. The sun has now again come out brightly, though the wind is still tumbling a great many clouds about the sky.

Evening.—Later, I walked out with U——, and, looking seaward, we saw the foam and spray of the advancing tide, tossed about on the verge of the horizon,—a long line, like the crests and gleaming helmets of an army. In about half an hour we found almost the whole waste of sand covered with water, and white waves breaking out all over it; but, the bottom being so nearly level, and the water so shallow, there was little of the spirit and exultation of the sea in a strong breeze. Of the long line of bathing-machines, one after another was hitched to a horse, and trundled forth into the water, where, at a long distance from shore, the bathers found themselves hardly middle deep.

September 19th.—The wind grumbled and made itself miserable all last night, and this morning it is still howling as ill-naturedly as ever, and roaring and rumbling in the chimneys. The tide is far out, but, from an upper window, I fancied, at intervals, that I could see the plash of the surf-wave on the distant limit of the sand; perhaps, however, it was only a gleam on the sky. Constantly there have been sharp spatters of rain, hissing and rattling against the windows, while a little before or after, or perhaps simultaneously, a rainbow, somewhat watery of texture, paints itself on the western clouds. Gray, sullen clouds hang about the sky, or sometimes cover it with a uniform dulness; at other times, the portions towards the sun gleam almost lightsomely; now, there may be an airy glimpse of clear blue sky in a fissure of the clouds;

now, the very brightest of sunshine comes out all of a sudden, and gladdens everything. The breadth of sands has a various aspect, according as there are pools, or moisture enough to glisten, or a drier tract; and where the light gleams along a yellow ridge or bar, it is like sunshine itself. Certainly the temper of the day shifts; but the smiles come far the seldomest, and its frowns and angry tears are most reliable. By seven o'clock pedestrians began to walk along the promenade, close buttoned against the blast; later, a single bathing-machine got under way, by means of a horse, and travelled forth seaward; but within what distance it finds the invisible margin I cannot say,—at all events, it looks like a dreary journey. Just now I saw a sea-gull, wheeling on the blast, close in towards the promenade.

September 21st.—Yesterday morning was bright, sunny and windy, and cool and exhilarating. I went to Liverpool at eleven, and, returning at five, found the weather still bright and cool. The temperature, methinks, must soon diminish the population of Southport, which, judging from appearances, must be mainly made up of temporary visitors. There is a newspaper, The Southport Visitor, published weekly, and containing a register of all the visitants in the various hotels and lodging-houses. It covers more than two sides of the paper, to the amount of some hundreds. The guests come chiefly from Liverpool, Manchester, and the neighboring country-towns, and belong to the middle classes. It is not a fashionable watering-place. Only one nobleman's name, and those of two or three baronets, now adorn the list. The people whom we see loitering along the beach and the promenade have, at best, a well-to-do, tradesmanlike air. I do not find that there are any public amusements; nothing but strolling on the sands, donkey-riding, or drives in donkey-carts; and solitary visitors must find it a dreary place. Yet one or two of the streets are brisk and lively, and, being well thronged, have a holiday aspect. There are no carriages in town save donkey-carts; some of which are drawn by three donkeys abreast, and are large enough to hold a whole family. These conveyances will take you far out on the sands through wet and dry. The beach is haunted by The Flying Dutchman, —a sort of boat on wheels, schooner-rigged with sails, and which sometimes makes pretty good speed, with a fair wind.

This morning we have been walking with J—— and R—— out over the "ribbed sea sands," a good distance from shore. Throughout the week, the tides will be so low as not to cover the shallow basin of this bay, if a bay it be. The weather was sullen, with now and then a faint gleam of sunshine, lazily tracing our shadows on the sand; the wind rather quieter than on preceding days. . . . In the sunshine the sands seem to be frequented by great numbers of gulls, who begin to find the northern climate too wintry. You see their white wings in the sunlight, but they become almost or quite invisible in the shade. We shall soon have an opportunity of seeing how a watering-place looks when the season is quite over; for we have concluded to remain here till December, and everybody else will take flight in a week or two.

A short time ago, in the evening, in a street of Liverpool, I saw a decent man, of the lower orders, taken much aback by being roughly brushed against by a rowdy fellow. He looked after him, and exclaimed indignantly, "Is that a Yankee?" It shows the kind of character we have here.

October 7th.—On Saturday evening, I gave a dinner to Bennoch, at the Adelphi Hotel. The chief point or characteristic of English customs was, that Mr. Radley, our landlord, himself attended at table, and officiated as chief waiter. He has a fortune of 100,000 pounds,—half a million of dollars,—and is an elderly man of good address and appearance. In America, such a man would very probably be in Congress; at any rate, he would never conceive the possibility of changing plates, or passing round the table with hock and champagne. Some of his hock was a most rich and imperial wine, such as can hardly be had on the Rhine itself. There were eight gentlemen besides Bennoch.

A donkey, the other day, stubbornly refusing to come out of a boat which had brought him across the Mersey; at last, after many kicks had been applied, and other persecutions of that kind, a man stepped forward, addressing him affectionately, "Come along, brother,"—and the donkey obeyed at once.

October 26th.—On Thursday, instead of taking the rail for Liverpool, I set out, about eleven, for a long walk. It was an overcast morning, such as in New England would have boded rain; but English clouds are not nearly so portentous as American in that respect. Accordingly, the sun soon began to peep through crevices, and I had not gone more than a mile or two when it shone a little too warmly for comfort, yet not more than I liked. It was very much like our pleasant October days at home; indeed, the climates of the two countries more nearly coincide during the present month than at any other season of the year. The air was almost perfectly still; but once in a while it stirred, and breathed coolly in my face; it is very delightful, this latent freshness, in a warm atmosphere.

The country about Southport has as few charms as it is possible for any region to have. In the close neighborhood of the shore, it is nothing but sand-hillocks, covered with coarse grass; and this is the original nature of the whole site on which the town stands, although it is now paved, and has been covered with soil enough to make gardens, and to nourish here and there a few trees. A little farther inland the surface seems to have been marshy, but has been drained by ditches across the fields and along the roadside; and the fields are embanked on all sides with parapets of earth which appear as if intended to keep out inundations. In fact, Holland itself cannot be more completely on a level with the sea. The only dwellings are the old, whitewashed stone cottages, with thatched roofs, on the brown straw of which grow various weeds and mosses, brightening it with green patches, and sprouting along the ridgepole,—the homeliest hovels that ever mortals lived in, and which they share with pigs and cows at one end. Hens, too, run in and out of the door. One or two of these hovels bore signs, "Licensed to sell beer, ale, and tobacco," and generally there were an old woman and some children visible. In all cases there was a ditch, full of water, close at hand, stagnant, and often quite covered with a growth of water-weeds,—very unwholesome, one would think, in the neighborhood of a dwelling; and, in truth, the children and grown people did look pale.

In the fields, along the roadside, men and women were harvesting their carrots and other root-crops, especially digging potatoes,—the pleasantest of all farm labor, in my opinion, there being such a continual interest in opening the treasures of each hill. As I went on, the country began to get almost imperceptibly less flat, and there was some little appearance of trees.

I had determined to go to Ormskirk, but soon got out of the way, and came to a little hamlet that looked antique and picturesque, with its small houses of stone and brick, built, with the one material and repaired with the other perhaps ages afterward. Here I inquired my way of a woman, who told me, in broad Lancashire dialect, "that I main go back, and turn to my left, till I came to a finger-post"; and so I did, and found another little hamlet, the principal object in which was a public-house, with a large sign, representing a dance round a Maypole. It was now about one o'clock; so I entered, and, being ushered into what, I suppose, they called the coffee-room, I asked for some cold neat and ale. There was a jolly, round, rather comely woman for a hostess, with a free, hospitable, yet rather careless manner.

The coffee-room smelt rather disagreeably of bad tobacco-smoke, and was shabbily furnished with an old sofa and flag-bottomed chairs, and adorned with a print of "Old Billy," a horse famous for a longevity of about sixty years; and also with colored engravings of old-fashioned hunting-scenes, conspicuous with scarlet coats. There was a very small bust of Milton on the mantel-piece. By and by the remains of an immense round of beef, three quarters cut away, were put on the table; then some smoking-hot potatoes; and finally the hostess told me that their own dinner was just ready, and so she had brought me in some hot chops, thinking I might prefer them to the cold meat. I did prefer them; and they were stewed or fried chops, instead of broiled, and were very savory. There was household bread too, and rich cheese, and a pint of ale, home brewed, not very mighty, but good to quench thirst, and, by way of condiment, some pickled cabbage; so, instead of a lunch, I made quite a comfortable dinner. Moreover, there was a cold pudding on the table, and I called for a clean plate, and helped myself to some of it. It was of rice, and was strewn over, rather than intermixed, with some kinds of berries, the nature of which I could not exactly make out.

I then set forth again. It was still sunny and warm, and I walked more slowly than before dinner; in fact, I did little more than lounge along, sitting down, at last, on the stone parapet of a bridge.

The country grew more pleasant, more sylvan, and, though still of a level character, not so drearily flat. Soon appeared the first symptom that

I had seen of a gentleman's residence,—a lodge at a park gate, then a long stretch of wall, with a green lawn, and afterwards an extent of wooded land; then another gateway, with a neat lodge on each side of it, and, lastly, another extent of wood. The Hall or Mansion-house, however, was nowhere apparent, being, doubtless, secluded deep and far within its grounds. I inquired of a boy who was the owner of the estate, and he answered, "Mr. Scarisbrick"; and no doubt it is a family of local eminence.

Along the road,—an old inn; some aged stone houses, built for merely respectable occupants; a canal, with two canal-boats, heaped up with a cargo of potatoes; two little girls, who were watching lest some cows should go astray, and had their two little chairs by the roadside, and their dolls and other playthings, and so followed the footsteps of the cows all day long. I met two boys, coming from Ormskirk, mounted on donkeys, with empty panniers, on which they had carried vegetables to market. Finally, between two and three o'clock, I saw the great tower of Ormskirk Church, with its spire, not rising out of the tower, but sprouting up close beside it; and, entering the town, I directed my steps first to this old church.

ORMSKIRK CHURCH.

It stands on a gentle eminence, sufficient to give it a good site, and has a pavement of flat gravestones in front. It is doubtless, as regards its foundation, a very ancient church, but has not exactly a venerable aspect, being in too good repair, and much restored in various parts; not ivy-grown, either, though green with moss here and there. The tower is square and immensely massive, and might have supported a very lofty spire; so that it is the more strange that what spire it has should be so oddly stuck beside it, springing out of the church wall. I should have liked well enough to enter the church, as it is the burial-place of the Earls of Derby, and perhaps may contain some interesting monuments; but as it was all shut up, and even the iron gates of the churchyard closed and locked, I merely looked at the outside.

From the church, a street leads to the market-place, in which I found a throng of men and women, it being market-day; wares of various kinds, tin, earthen, and cloth, set out on the pavements; droves of pigs; ducks and fowls; baskets of eggs; and a man selling quack medicines, recommending his nostrums as well as he could. The aspect of the crowd was very English,—portly and ruddy women; yeomen with small-clothes and broad-brimmed hats, all very quiet and heavy and good-humored. Their dialect was so provincial that I could not readily understand more than here and there a word.

But, after all, there were few traits that could be made a note of. I soon grew weary of the scene, and so I went to the railway station, and waited there nearly an hour for the train to take me to Southport. Ormskirk is famous for its gingerbread, which women sell to the railway passengers at a sixpence for a rouleau of a dozen little cakes.

November 30th.—A week ago last Monday, Herman Melville came to see me at the Consulate, looking much as he used to do, and with his characteristic gravity and reserve of manner. . . . We soon found ourselves on pretty much our former terms of sociability and confidence. . . . He is thus far on his way to Constantinople. I do not wonder that he found it necessary to take an airing through the world, after so many years of toilsome pen-labor, following upon so wild and adventurous a youth as his was. I invited him to come and stay with us at Southport, as long as he might remain in this vicinity, and accordingly he did come the next day. . . . . On Wednesday we took a pretty long walk together, and sat down in a hollow among the sand-hills, sheltering ourselves from the high cool wind. Melville, as he always does, began to reason of Providence and futurity, and of everything else that lies beyond human ken. . . . He has a very high and noble nature, and is better worth immortality than the most of us. . . . On Saturday we went to Chester together. I love to take every opportunity of going to Chester; it being the one only place, within easy reach of Liverpool, which possesses any old English interest.

We went to

THE CATHEDRAL.

Its gray nave impressed me more than at any former visit. Passing into the cloisters, an attendant took possession of us, and showed us about.

Within the choir there is a profusion of very rich oaken carving, both on the screen that separates it from the nave, and on the seats and walls; very curious and most elaborate, and lavished (one would say) most wastefully, where nobody would think of looking for it,—where, indeed, amid the dimness of the cathedral, the exquisite detail of the elaboration could not possibly be seen. Our guide lighted some of the gas-burners, of which there are many hundreds, to help us see them; but it required close scrutiny, even then. It must have been out of the question, when the whole means of illumination were only a few smoky torches or candles. There was a row of niches, where the monks used to stand, for four hours together, in the performance of some of their services; and to relieve them a little, they were allowed partially to sit on a projection of the seats, which were turned up in the niche for that purpose; but if they grew drowsy, so as to fail to balance themselves, the seat was so contrived as to slip down, thus bringing the monk to the floor. These projections on the seats are each and all of them carved with curious devices, no two alike. The guide showed us one, representing, apparently, the first quarrel of a new-married couple, wrought with wonderful expression. Indeed, the artist never failed to bring out his idea in the most striking manner,—as, for instance, Satan, under the guise of a lion, devouring a sinner bodily; and again in the figure of a dragon, with a man halfway down his gullet, the legs hanging out. The carver may not have seen anything grotesque in this, nor intended it at all by way of joke; but certainly there would appear to be a grim mirthfulness in some of the designs. One does not see why such fantasies should be strewn about the holy interior of a cathedral, unless it were intended to contain everything that belongs to the heart of man, both upward and downward.

In a side aisle of the choir, we saw a tomb, said to be that of the Emperor Henry IV. of Germany, though on very indistinct authority. This is an oblong tomb, carved, and, on one side, painted with bright colors and gilded. During a very long period it was built and plastered into the wall, and the exterior side was whitewashed; but, on being removed, the inner side was found to have been ornamented with gold and color, in the manner in which we now see it. If this were customary with tombs, it must have added vastly to the gorgeous magnificence, to which the painted windows and polished pillars and ornamented ceilings contributed so much. In fact, a cathedral in its fresh estate seems to have been like a pavilion of the sunset, all purple and gold; whereas now it more resembles deepest and grayest twilight.

Afterwards, we were shown into the ancient refectory, now used as the city grammar-school, and furnished with the usual desks and seats for the boys. In one corner of this large room was the sort of pulpit or elevated seat, with a broken staircase of stone ascending to it, where one of the monks used to read to his brethren, while sitting at their meals. The desks were cut and carved with the scholars' knives, just as they used to be in the school-rooms where I was a scholar. Thence we passed into the chapter-house, but, before that, we went through a small room, in which Melville opened a cupboard, and discovered a dozen or two of wine-bottles; but our guide told us that they were now empty, and never were meant for jollity, having held only sacramental wine. In the chapter-house, we saw the library, some of the volumes of which were antique folios. There were two dusty and tattered banners hanging on the wall, and the attendant promised to make us laugh by something that he would tell us about them. The joke was that these two banners had been in the battle of Bunker Hill; and our countrymen, he said, always smiled on hearing this. He had discovered us to be Americans by the notice we took of a mural tablet in the choir, to the memory of a Lieutenant-Governor Clarke, of New York, who died in Chester before the Revolution. From the chapter-house he ushered us back into the nave, ever and anon pointing out some portion of the edifice more ancient than the rest, and when I asked him how he knew this, he said that he had learnt it from the archaeologists, who could read off such things like a book. This guide was a lively, quick-witted man, who did his business less by rote, and more with a vivacious interest, than any guide I ever met.

After leaving the cathedral we sought out the Yacht Inn, near the water-gate. This was, for a long period of time, the principal inn of Chester, and was the house at which Swift once put up, on his way to Holyhead, and where he invited the clergy to come and sup with him. We sat down in a small snuggery, conversing with the landlord. The Chester people, according to my experience, are very affable, and fond of talking with strangers about the antiquities and picturesque characteristics of their town. It partly lives, the landlord told us, by its visitors, and many people spend the summer here on account of the antiquities and the good air. He showed us a broad, balustraded staircase, leading into a large, comfortable, old-fashioned parlor, with windows looking on the street and on the Custom House that stood opposite. This was the room where Swift expected to receive the clergy of Chester; and on one of the window-panes were two acrid lines, written with the diamond of his ring, satirizing those venerable gentlemen, in revenge for their refusing his invitation. The first line begins rather indistinctly; but the writing grows fully legible, as it proceeds.

The Yacht Tavern is a very old house, in the gabled style. The timbers and framework are still perfectly sound. In the same street is the Bishop's house (so called as having been the residence of a prelate long ago), which is covered with curious sculpture, representing Scriptural scenes. And in the same neighborhood is the county court, accessible by an archway, through which we penetrated, and found ourselves in a passage, very ancient and dusky, overlooked from the upper story by a gallery, to which an antique staircase ascended, with balustrades and square landing-places. A printer saw us here, and asked us into his printing-office, and talked very affably; indeed, he could have hardly been more civil, if he had known that both Melville and I have given a good deal of employment to the brethren of his craft.

December 15th.—An old gentleman has recently paid me a good many visits,—a Kentucky man, who has been a good deal in England and Europe generally without losing the freshness and unconventionality of his earlier life. He was a boatman, and afterwards captain of a steamer on the Ohio and Mississippi; but has gained property, and is now the owner of mines of coal and iron, which he is endeavoring to dispose of here in England. A plain, respectable, well-to-do-looking personage, of more than seventy years; very free of conversation, and beginning to talk with everybody as a matter of course; tall, stalwart, a dark face, with white curly hair and keen eyes; and an expression shrewd, yet kindly and benign. He fought through the whole War of 1812, beginning with General Harrison at the battle of Tippecanoe, which he described to me. He says that at the beginning of the battle, and for a considerable time, he heard Tecumseh's voice, loudly giving orders. There was a man named Wheatley in the American camp, a strange, incommunicative person,—a volunteer, making war entirely on his own book, and seeking revenge for some relatives of his, who had been killed by the Indians. In the midst of the battle this Wheatley ran at a slow trot past R——— (my informant), trailing his rifle, and making towards the point where Tecumseh's voice was heard. The fight drifted around, and R——— along with it; and by and by he reached a spot where Wheatley lay dead, with his head on Tecumseh's breast. Tecumseh had been shot with a rifle, but, before expiring, appeared to have shot Wheatley with a pistol, which he still held in his hand. R——— affirms that Tecumseh was flayed by the Kentucky men on the spot, and his skin converted into razor-straps. I have left out the most striking point of the narrative, after all, as R——— told it, viz. that soon after Wheatley passed him, he suddenly ceased to hear Tecumseh's voice ringing through the forest, as he gave his orders. He was at the battle of New Orleans, and gave me the story of it from beginning to end; but I remember only a few particulars in which he was personally concerned. He confesses that his hair bristled upright—every hair in his head—when he heard the shouts of the British soldiers before advancing to the attack. His uncomfortable sensations lasted till he began to fire, after which he felt no more of them. It was in the dusk of the morning, or a little before sunrise, when the assault was made; and the fight lasted about two hours and a half, during which R——— fired twenty-four times; and said he, "I saw my object distinctly each time, and I was a good rifle-shot." He was raising his rifle to fire the twenty-fifth time, when an American officer, General Carroll, pressed it down, and bade him fire no more. "Enough is enough," quoth the General. For there needed no more slaughter, the British being in utter rout and confusion. In this retreat many of the enemy would drop down among the dead, then rise, run a considerable distance, and drop again, thus confusing the riflemen's aim. One fellow had thus got about four hundred and fifty yards from the American line, and, thinking himself secure, he made a derisive gesture. "I'll have a shot at him anyhow," cried a rifleman; so he fired, and the poor devil dropped.

R——— himself, with one of his twenty-four shots, hit a British officer, who fell forward on his face, about thirty paces from our line, and as the enemy were then retreating (they advanced and were repelled two or three times) he ran out, and turned him over on his back. The officer was a man about thirty-eight, tall and fine-looking; his eyes were wide open, clear and bright, and were fixed full on R——— with a somewhat stern glance, but there was the sweetest and happiest smile over his face that could be conceived. He seemed to be dead;—at least, R——— thinks that he did not really see him, fixedly as he appeared to gaze. The officer held his sword in his hand, and R——— tried in vain to wrest it from him, until suddenly the clutch relaxed. R——— still keeps the sword hung up over his mantel-piece. I asked him how the dead man's aspect affected him. He replied that he felt nothing at the time; but that ever since, in all trouble, in uneasy sleep, and whenever he is out of tune, or waking early, or lying awake at night, he sees this officer's face, with the clear bright eyes and the pleasant smile, just as distinctly as if he were bending over him. His wound was in the breast, exactly on the spot that R——— had aimed at, and bled profusely. The enemy advanced in such masses, he says, that it was impossible not to hit them unless by purposely firing over their heads.

After the battle, R——— leaped over the rampart, and took a prisoner who was standing unarmed in the midst of the slain, having probably dropped down during the heat of the action, to avoid the hail-storm of rifle-shots. As he led him in, the prisoner paused, and pointed to an officer who was lying dead beside his dead horse, with his foot still in the stirrup. "There lies our General," said he. The horse had been killed by a grape-shot, and Pakenham himself, apparently, by a six-pounder ball, which had first struck the earth, covering him from head to foot with mud and clay, and had then entered his side, and gone upward through his breast. His face was all besmirched with the moist earth. R——— took the slain General's foot out of the stirrup, and then went to report his death.

Much more he told me, being an exceedingly talkative old man, and seldom, I suppose, finding so good a listener as myself. I like the man,—a good-tempered, upright, bold and free old fellow; of a rough breeding, but sufficiently smoothed by society to be of pleasant intercourse. He is as dogmatic as possible, having formed his own opinions, often on very disputable grounds, and hardened in them; taking queer views of matters and things, and giving shrewd and not ridiculous reasons for them; but with a keen, strong sense at the bottom of his character.

A little while ago I met an Englishman in a railway carriage, who suggests himself as a kind of contrast to this warlike and vicissitudinous backwoodsman. He was about the same age as R———, but had spent, apparently, his whole life in Liverpool, and has long occupied the post of Inspector of Nuisances,—a rather puffy and consequential man; gracious, however, and affable, even to casual strangers like myself. The great contrast betwixt him and the American lies in the narrower circuit of his ideas; the latter talking about matters of history of his own country and the world,—glancing over the whole field of politics, propounding opinions and theories of his own, and showing evidence that his mind had operated for better or worse on almost all conceivable matters; while the Englishman was odorous of his office, strongly flavored with that, and otherwise most insipid. He began his talk by telling me of a dead body which he had lately discovered in a house in Liverpool, where it had been kept about a fortnight by the relatives, partly from want of funds for the burial, and partly in expectation of the arrival of some friends from Glasgow. There was a plate of glass in the coffin-lid, through which the Inspector of Nuisances, as he told me, had looked and seen the dead man's face in an ugly state of decay, which he minutely described. However, his conversation was not altogether of this quality; for he spoke about larks, and how abundant they are just now, and what a good pie they make, only they must be skinned, else they will have a bitter taste. We have since had a lark-pie ourselves, and I believe it was very good in itself; only the recollection of the Nuisance-man's talk was not a very agreeable flavor. A very racy and peculiarly English character might be made out of a man like this, having his life-concern wholly with the disagreeables of a great city. He seemed to be a good and kindly person, too, but earthy,—even as if his frame had been moulded of clay impregnated with the draining of slaughter-houses.

December 21st.—On Thursday evening I dined for the first time with the new Mayor at the Town Hall. I wish to preserve all the characteristic traits of such banquets, because, being peculiar to England, these municipal feasts may do well to picture in a novel. There was a big old silver tobacco-box, nearly or quite as large round as an ordinary plate, out of which the dignitaries of Liverpool used to fill their pipes, while sitting in council or after their dinners. The date "1690" was on the lid. It is now used as a snuff-box, and wends its way, from guest to guest, round the table. We had turtle, and, among other good things, American canvasback ducks. . . . These dinners are certainly a good institution, and likely to be promotive of good feeling; the Mayor giving them often, and inviting, in their turn, all the respectable and eminent citizens of whatever political bias. About fifty gentlemen were present that evening. I had the post of honor at the Mayor's right hand; and France, Turkey, and Austria were toasted before the Republic, for, as the Mayor whispered me, he must first get his allies out of the way. The Turkish Consul and the Austrian both made better English speeches than any Englishman, during the evening; for it is inconceivable what shapeless and ragged utterances Englishmen are content to put forth, without attempting anything like a wholeness; but inserting a patch here and a patch there, and finally getting out what they wish to say, indeed, but in most disorganized guise. . . . I can conceive of very high enjoyment in making a speech; one is in such a curious sympathy with his audience, feeling instantly how every sentence affects them, and wonderfully excited and encouraged by the sense that it has gone to the right spot. Then, too, the imminent emergency, when a man is overboard, and must sink or swim, sharpens, concentrates, and invigorates the mind, and causes matters of thought and sentiment to assume shape and expression, though, perhaps, it seemed hopeless to express them, just before you rose to speak. Yet I question much whether public speaking tends to elevate the orator, intellectually or morally; the effort, of course, being to say what is immediately received by the audience, and to produce an effect on the instant. I don't quite see how an honest man can be a good and successful orator; but I shall hardly undertake to decide the question on my merely post-prandial experience.

The Mayor toasted his guests by their professions,—the merchants, for instance, the bankers, the solicitors,—and while one of the number responded, his brethren also stood up, each in his place, thus giving their assent to what he said. I think the very worst orator was a major of Artillery, who spoke in a meek, little, nervous voice, and seemed a good deal more discomposed than probably he would have been in the face of the enemy. The first toast was "The Ladies," to which an old bachelor responded.

December 31st.—Thus far we have come through the winter, on this bleak and blasty shore of the Irish Sea, where, perhaps, the drowned body of Milton's friend Lycidas might have been washed ashore more than two centuries ago. This would not be very likely, however, so wide a tract of sands, never deeply covered by the tide, intervening betwixt us and the sea. But it is an excessively windy place, especially here on the Promenade; always a whistle and a howl,—always an eddying gust through the corridors and chambers,—often a patter of hail or rain or snow against the windows; and in the long evenings the sounds outside are very much as if we were on shipboard in mid-ocean, with the waves dashing against the vessel's sides. I go to town almost daily, starting at about eleven, and reaching Southport again at a little past live; by which time it is quite dark, and continues so till nearly eight in the morning.

Christmas time has been marked by few characteristics. For a week or two previous to Christmas day, the newspapers contained rich details respecting market-stalls and butchers' shops,—what magnificent carcasses of prize oxen and sheep they displayed. . . .

The Christmas Waits came to us on Christmas eve, and on the day itself, in the shape of little parties of boys or girls, singing wretched doggerel rhymes, and going away well pleased with the guerdon of a penny or two. Last evening came two or three older choristers at pretty near bedtime, and sang some carols at our door. They were psalm tunes, however. Everybody with whom we have had to do, in any manner of service, expects a Christmas-box; but, in most cases, a shilling is quite a satisfactory amount. We have had holly and mistletoe stuck up on the gas-fixtures and elsewhere about the house.

On the mantel-piece in the coroner's court the other day, I saw corked and labelled phials, which it may be presumed contained samples of poisons that have brought some poor wretches to their deaths, either by murder or suicide. This court might be wrought into a very good and pregnant description, with its grimy gloom illuminated by a conical skylight, constructed to throw daylight down on corpses; its greasy Testament covered over with millions of perjured kisses; the coroner himself, whose life is fed on all kinds of unnatural death; its subordinate officials, who go about scenting murder, and might be supposed to have caught the scent in their own garments; its stupid, brutish juries, settling round corpses like flies; its criminals, whose guilt is brought face to face with them here, in closer contact than at the subsequent trial.

O—— P———, the famous Mormonite, called on me a little while ago,—a short, black-haired, dark-complexioned man; a shrewd, intelligent, but unrefined countenance, excessively unprepossessing; an uncouth gait and deportment; the aspect of a person in comfortable circumstances, and decently behaved, but of a vulgar nature and destitute of early culture. I think I should have taken him for a shoemaker, accustomed to reflect in a rude, strong, evil-disposed way on matters of this world and the next, as he sat on his bench. He said he had been residing in Liverpool about six months; and his business with me was to ask for a letter of introduction that should gain him admittance to the British Museum, he intending a visit to London. He offered to refer me to respectable people for his character; but I advised him to apply to Mr. Dallas, as the proper person for his purpose.

March 1st, 1857.—On the night of last Wednesday week, our house was broken into by robbers. They entered by the back window of the breakfast-room, which is the children's school-room, breaking or cutting a pane of glass, so as to undo the fastening. I have a dim idea of having heard a noise through my sleep; but if so, it did not more than slightly disturb me. U—— heard it, she being at watch with R——; and J——, having a cold, was also wakeful, and thought the noise was of servants moving about below. Neither did the idea of robbers occur to U——. J——, however, hearing U—— at her mother's door, asking for medicine for R——, called out for medicine for his cold, and the thieves probably thought we were bestirring ourselves, and so took flight. In the morning the servants found the hall door and the breakfast-room window open; some silver cups and some other trifles of plate were gone from the sideboard, and there were tokens that the whole lower part of the house had been ransacked; but the thieves had evidently gone off in a hurry, leaving some articles which they would have taken, had they been more at leisure.

We gave information to the police, and an inspector and constable soon came to make investigations, taking a list of the missing articles, and informing themselves as to all particulars that could be known. I did not much expect ever to hear any more of the stolen property; but on Sunday a constable came to request my presence at the police-office to identify the lost things. The thieves had been caught in Liverpool, and some of the property found upon them, and some of it at a pawnbroker's where they had pledged it. The police-office is a small dark room, in the basement story of the Town Hall of Southport; and over the mantel-piece, hanging one upon another, there are innumerable advertisements of robberies in houses, and on the highway,—murders, too, and garrotings; and offences of all sorts, not only in this district, but wide away, and forwarded from other police-stations. Bring thus aggregated together, one realizes that there are a great many more offences than the public generally takes note of. Most of these advertisements were in pen and ink, with minute lists of the articles stolen; but the more important were in print; and there, too, I saw the printed advertisement of our own robbery, not for public circulation, but to be handed about privately, among police-officers and pawnbrokers. A rogue has a very poor chance in England, the police being so numerous, and their system so well organized.

In a corner of the police-office stood a contrivance for precisely measuring the heights of prisoners; and I took occasion to measure J———, and found him four feet seven inches and a half high. A set of rules for the self-government of police-officers was nailed on the door, between twenty and thirty in number, and composing a system of constabulary ethics. The rules would be good for men in almost any walk of life; and I rather think the police-officers conform to them with tolerable strictness. They appear to be subordinated to one another on the military plan. The ordinary constable does not sit down in the presence of his inspector, and this latter seems to be half a gentleman; at least, such is the bearing of our Southport inspector, who wears a handsome uniform of green and silver, and salutes the principal inhabitants, when meeting them in the street, with an air of something like equality. Then again there is a superintendent, who certainly claims the rank of a gentleman, and has perhaps been an officer in the army. The superintendent of this district was present on this occasion.

The thieves were brought down from Liverpool on Tuesday, and examined in the Town Hall. I had been notified to be present, but, as a matter of courtesy, the police-officers refrained from calling me as a witness, the evidence of the servants being sufficient to identify the property. The thieves were two young men, not much over twenty,—James and John Macdonald, terribly shabby, dirty, jail-bird like, yet intelligent of aspect, and one of them handsome. The police knew them already, and they seemed not much abashed by their position. There were half a dozen magistrates on the bench,—idle old gentlemen of Southport and the vicinity, who lounged into the court, more as a matter of amusement than anything else, and lounged out again at their own pleasure; for these magisterial duties are a part of the pastime of the country gentlemen of England. They wore their hats on the bench. There were one or two of them more active than their fellows; but the real duty was done by the Clerk of the Court. The seats within the bar were occupied by the witnesses, and around the great table sat some of the more respectable people of Southport; and without the bar were the commonalty in great numbers; for this is said to be the first burglary that has occurred here within the memory of man, and so it has caused a great stir.

There seems to be a strong case against the prisoners. A boy attached to the railway testified to having seen them at Birchdale on Wednesday afternoon, and directed them on their way to Southport; Peter Pickup recognized them as having applied to him for lodgings in the course of that evening; a pawnbroker swore to one of them as having offered my top-coat for sale or pledge in Liverpool; and my boots were found on the feet of one of them,—all this in addition to other circumstances of pregnant suspicion. So they were committed for trial at the Liverpool assizes, to be holden some time in the present month. I rather wished them to escape.

February 27th.—Coming along the promenade, a little before sunset, I saw the mountains of the Welsh coast shadowed very distinctly against the horizon. Mr. Channing told me that he had seen these mountains once or twice during his stay at Southport; but, though constantly looking for them, they have never before greeted my eyes in all the months that we have spent here. It is said that the Isle of Man is likewise discernible occasionally; but as the distance must be between sixty and seventy miles, I should doubt it. How misty is England! I have spent four years in a gray gloom. And yet it suits me pretty well.

TO YORK.

April 10th.—At Skipton. My wife, J——, and I left Southport to-day for a short tour to York and its neighborhood. The weather has been exceedingly disagreeable for weeks past, but yesterday and to-day have been pleasant, and we take advantage of the first glimpses of spring-like weather. We came by Preston, along a road that grew rather more interesting as we proceeded to this place, which is about sixty miles from Southport, and where we arrived between five and six o'clock. First of all, we got some tea; and then, as it was a pleasant sunset, we set forth from our old-fashioned inn to take a walk.

Skipton is an ancient town, and has an ancient though well-repaired aspect, the houses being built of gray stone, but in no picturesque shapes; the streets well paved; the site irregular and rising gradually towards Skipton Castle, which overlooks the town, as an old lordly castle ought to overlook the feudal village which it protects. The castle was built shortly after the Conquest by Robert de Romeli, and was afterwards the property and residence of the famous Cliffords. We met an honest man, as we approached the gateway, who kindly encouraged us to apply for admittance, notwithstanding it was Good Friday; telling us how to find the housekeeper, who would probably show us over the castle. So we passed through the gate, between two embattled towers; and in the castle court we met a flock of young damsels, who had been rambling about the precincts. They likewise directed us in our search for the housekeeper, and S——, being bolder than I in such assaults on feudal castles, led the way down a dark archway, and up an exterior stairway, and, knocking at a door, immediately brought the housekeeper to a parley.

She proved to be a nowise awful personage, but a homely, neat, kindly, intelligent, and middle-aged body. She seemed to be all alone in this great old castle, and at once consented to show us about,—being, no doubt, glad to see any Christian visitors. The castle is now the property of Sir R. Tufton; but the present family do not make it their permanent residence, and have only occasionally visited it. Indeed, it could not well be made an eligible or comfortable residence, according to modern ideas; the rooms occupying the several stories of large round towers, and looking gloomy and sombre, if not dreary,—not the less so for what has been done to modernize them; for instance, modern paper-hangings, and, in some of the rooms, marble fireplaces. They need a great deal more light and higher ceilings; and I rather imagine that the warm, rich effect of glowing tapestry is essential to keep one's spirit cheerful in these ancient rooms. Modern paper-hangings are too superficial and wishy-washy for the purpose. Tapestry, it is true, there is now, completely covering the walls of several of the rooms, but all faded into ghastliness; nor could some of it have been otherwise than ghastly, even in its newness, for it represented persons suffering various kinds of torture, with crowds of monks and nuns looking on. In another room there was the story of Solomon and the Queen of Sheba, and other subjects not to be readily distinguished in the twilight that was gathering in these antique chambers. We saw, too, some very old portraits of the Cliffords and the Thanets, in black frames, and the pictures themselves sadly faded and neglected. The famous Countess Anne of Pembroke, Dorset, and Montgomery was represented on one of the leaves of a pair of folding doors, and one of her husbands, I believe, on the other leaf. There was the picture of a little idiot lordling, who had choked himself to death; and a portrait of Oliver Cromwell, who battered this old castle, together with almost every other English or Welsh castle that I ever saw or heard of. The housekeeper pointed out the grove of trees where his cannon were planted during the siege. There was but little furniture in the rooms; amongst other articles, an antique chair, in which Mary, Queen of Scots, is said to have rested.

The housekeeper next took us into the part of the castle which has never been modernized since it was repaired, after the siege of Cromwell. This is a dismal series of cellars above ground, with immensely thick walls, letting in but scanty light, and dim staircases of stone; and a large hall, with a vast fireplace, where every particle of heat must needs have gone up chimney,—a chill and heart-breaking place enough. Quite in the midst of this part of the castle is the court-yard,—a space of some thirty or forty feet in length and breadth, open to the sky, but shut completely in on every side by the buildings of the castle, and paved over with flat stones. Out of this pavement, however, grows a yew-tree, ascending to the tops of the towers, and completely filling, with its branches and foliage, the whole open space between them. Some small birds—quite a flock of them—were twittering and fluttering among the upper branches. We went upward, through two or three stories of dismal rooms,—among others, through the ancient guard-room,—till we came out on the roof of one of the towers, and had a very fine view of an amphitheatre of ridgy hills which shut in and seclude the castle and the town. The upper foliage was within our reach, close to the parapet of the tower; so we gathered a few twigs as memorials. The housekeeper told us that the yew-tree is supposed to be eight hundred years old, and, comparing it with other yews that I have seen, I should judge that it must measure its antiquity by centuries, at all events. It still seems to be in its prime.

Along the base of the castle, on the opposite side to the entrance, flows a stream, sending up a pleasant murmur from among the trees. The housekeeper said it was not a stream, but only a "wash," whatever that may be; and I conjecture that it creates the motive-power of some factory-looking edifices, which we saw on our first arrival at Skipton.

We now took our leave of the housekeeper, and came homeward to our inn, where I have written the foregoing pages by a bright fire; but I think I write better descriptions after letting the subject lie in my mind a day or two. It is too new to be properly dealt with immediately after coming from the scene.

The castle is not at all crumbly, but in excellent repair, though so venerable. There are rooks cawing about the shapeless patches of their nests, in the tops of the trees. In the castle wall, as well as in the round towers of the gateway, there seem to be little tenements, perhaps inhabited by the servants and dependants of the family. They looked in very good order, with tokens of present domesticity about them. The whole of this old castle, indeed, was as neat as a new, small dwelling, in spite of an inevitable musty odor of antiquity.

April 11th.—This morning we took a carriage and two horses, and set out for a distance of about six miles. The morning was cool, with breezy clouds, intermingled with sunshine, and, on the whole, as good as are nine tenths of English mornings. J——- sat beside the driver, and S——- and I in the carriage, all closed but one window. As we drove through Skipton, the little town had a livelier aspect than yesterday when it wore its Good Friday's solemnity; but now its market-place was thronged, principally with butchers, displaying their meat under little movable pent-houses, and their customers. The English people really like to think and talk of butcher's meat, and gaze at it with delight; and they crowd through the avenues of the market-houses and stand enraptured round a dead ox.

We passed along by the castle wall, and noticed the escutcheon of the Cliffords or the Thanets carved in stone over the portal, with the motto Desormais, the application of which I do not well see; these ancestral devices usually referring more to the past, than to the future. There is a large old church, just at the extremity of the village, and just below the castle, on the slope of the hill. The gray wall of the castle extends along the road a considerable distance, in good repair, with here and there a buttress, and the semicircular bulge of a tower.

The scenery along the road was not particularly striking,—long slopes, descending from ridges; a generally hard outline of country, with not many trees, and those, as yet, destitute of foliage. It needs to be softened with a good deal of wood. There were stone farm-houses, looking ancient, and able to last till twice as old. Instead of the hedges, so universal in other parts of England, there were stone fences of good height and painful construction, made of small stones, which I suppose have been picked up out of the fields through hundreds of years. They reminded me of old Massachusetts, though very unlike our rude stone walls, which, nevertheless, last longer than anything else we build. Another New England feature was the little brooks, which here and there flowed across our road, rippling over the pebbles, clear and bright. I fancied, too, an intelligence and keenness in some of the Yorkshire physiognomies, akin to those characteristics in my countrymen's faces.

We passed an ancient, many-gabled inn, large, low, and comfortable, bearing the name of the Devonshire House, as does our own hotel, for the Duke of Devonshire is a great proprietor in these parts. A mile or so beyond, we came to a gateway, broken through what, I believe, was an old wall of the Priory grounds; and here we alighted, leaving our driver to take the carriage to the inn. Passing through this hole in the wall, we saw the ruins of the Priory at the bottom of the beautiful valley about a quarter of a mile off; and, well as the monks knew how to choose the sites of their establishments, I think they never chose a better site than this,—in the green lap of protecting hills, beside a stream, and with peace and fertility looking down upon it on every side. The view down the valley is very fine, and, for my part, I am glad that some peaceable and comfort-loving people possessed these precincts for many hundred years, when nobody else knew how to appreciate peace and comfort.

The old gateway tower, beneath which was formerly the arched entrance into the domain of the Priory, is now the central part of a hunting-seat of the Duke of Devonshire, and the edifice is completed by a wing of recent date on each side. A few hundred yards from this hunting-box are the remains of the Priory, consisting of the nave of the old church, which is still in good repair, and used as the worshipping-place of the neighborhood (being a perpetual curacy of the parish of Skipton), and the old ruined choir, roofless, with broken arches, ivy-grown, but not so rich and rare a ruin as either Melrose, Netley, or Furness. Its situation makes its charm. It stands near the river Wharfe,—a broad and rapid stream, which hurries along between high banks, with a sound which the monks must have found congenial to their slumberous moods. It is a good river for trout, too; and I saw two or three anglers, with their rods and baskets, passing through the ruins towards its shore. It was in this river Wharfe that the boy of Egremont was drowned, at the Strid, a mile or two higher up the stream.

In the first place, we rambled round the exterior of the ruins; but, as I have said, they are rather bare and meagre in comparison with other abbeys, and I am not sure that the especial care and neatness with which they are preserved does not lessen their effect on the beholder. Neglect, wildness, crumbling walls, the climbing and conquering ivy; masses of stone lying where they fell; trees of old date, growing where the pillars of the aisles used to stand,—these are the best points of ruined abbeys. But, everything here is kept with such trimness that it gives you the idea of a petrifaction. Decay is no longer triumphant; the Duke of Devonshire has got the better of it. The grounds around the church and the ruins are still used for burial, and there are several flat tombstones and altar tombs, with crosiers engraved or carved upon them, which at first I took to be the memorials of bishops or abbots, and wondered that the sculpture should still be so distinct. On one, however, I read the date 1850 and the name of a layman; for the tombstones were all modern, the humid English atmosphere giving them their mossy look of antiquity, and the crosier had been assumed only as a pretty device.

Close beside the ruins there is a large, old stone farm-house, which must have been built on the site of a part of the Priory,—the cells, dormitories, refectory, and other portions pertaining to the monks' daily life, I suppose, and built, no doubt, with the sacred stones. I should imagine it would be a haunted house, swarming with cowled spectres. We wished to see the interior of the church, and procured a guide from this farm-house,—the sexton, probably,—a gray-haired, ruddy, cheery, and intelligent man, of familiar though respectful address. The entrance of the church was undergoing improvement, under the last of the abbots, when the Reformation occurred; and it has ever remained in an unfinished state, till now it is mossy with age, and has a beautiful tuft of wall-flowers growing on a ledge over the Gothic arch of the doorway. The body of the church is of much anterior date, though the oaken roof is supposed to have been renewed in Henry VIII's time. This, as I said before, was the nave of the old Abbey church, and has a one-sided and unbalanced aspect, there being only a single aisle, with its row of sturdy pillars. The pavement is covered with pews of old oak, very homely and unornamental; on the side opposite the aisle there are two or three windows of modern stained glass, somewhat gaudy and impertinent; there are likewise some hatchments and escutcheons over the altar and elsewhere. On the whole, it is not an impressive interior; but, at any rate, it had the true musty odor which I never conceived of till I came to England,—the odor of dead men's decay, garnered up and shut in, and kept from generation to generation; not disgusting nor sickening, because it is so old, and of the past.

On one side of the altar there was a small square chapel,—or what had once been a chapel, separated from the chancel by a partition about a man's height, if I remember aright. Our guide led us into it, and observed that some years ago the pavement had been taken up in this spot, for burial purposes; but it was found that it had already been used in that way, and that the corpses had been buried upright. Inquiring further, I found that it was the Clapham family, and another that was called Morley, that were so buried; and then it occurred to me that this was the vault Wordsworth refers to in one of his poems,—the burial-place of the Claphams and Mauleverers, whose skeletons, for aught I know, were even then standing upright under our feet. It is but a narrow place, perhaps a square of ten feet. We saw little or nothing else that was memorable, unless it were the signature of Queen Adelaide in a visitors' book.

On our way back to Skipton it rained and hailed, but the sun again shone out before we arrived. We took the train for Leeds at half past ten, and arrived there in the afternoon, passing the ruined Abbey of Kirkstall on our way. The ruins looked more interesting than those of Bolton, though not so delightfully situated, and now in the close vicinity of manufactories, and only two or three miles from Leeds. We took a dish of soup, and spent a miserable hour in and about the railway station of Leeds; whence we departed at four, and reached in an hour or two. We put up at the Black Swan, and before tea went out, on the cool bright edge of evening, to get a glimpse of the cathedral, which impressed me more grandly than when I first saw it, nearly a year ago. Indeed, almost any object gains upon me at the second sight. I have spent the evening in writing up my journal,—an act of real virtue.

After walking round the cathedral, we went up a narrow and crooked street, very old and shabby, but with an antique house projecting as much as a yard over the pavement on one side,—a timber house it seemed to be, plastered over and stained yellow or buff. There was no external door, affording entrance into this edifice; but about midway of its front we came to a low, Gothic, stone archway, passing right through the house; and as it looked much time-worn, and was sculptured with untraceable devices, we went through. There was an exceedingly antique, battered, and shattered pair of oaken leaves, which used doubtless to shut up the passage in former times, and keep it secure; but for the last centuries, probably, there has been free ingress and egress. Indeed, the portal arch may never have been closed since the Reformation. Within, we found a quadrangle, of which the house upon the street formed one side, the others being composed of ancient houses, with gables in a row, all looking upon the paved quadrangle, through quaint windows of various fashion. An elderly, neat, pleasant-looking woman now came in beneath the arch, and as she had a look of being acquainted here, we asked her what the place was; and she told us, that in the old Popish times the prebends of the cathedral used to live here, to keep them from doing mischief in the town. The establishment, she said, was now called "The College," and was let in rooms and small tenements to poor people. On consulting the York Guide, I find that her account was pretty correct; the house having been founded in Henry VI.'s time, and called St. William's College, the statue of the patron saint being sculptured over the arch. It was intended for the residence of the parsons and priests of the cathedral, who had formerly caused troubles and scandals by living in the town.

We returned to the front of the cathedral on our way homeward, and an old man stopped us, to inquire if we had ever seen the Fiddler of York. We answered in the negative, and said that we had not time to see him now; but the old gentleman pointed up to the highest pinnacle of the southern front, where stood the Fiddler of York, one of those Gothic quaintnesses which blotch the grandeur and solemnity of this and other cathedrals.

April 12th.—This morning was bleak and most ungenial; a chilly sunshine, a piercing wind, a prevalence of watery cloud,—April weather, without the tenderness that ought to be half revealed in it. This is

EASTER SUNDAY,

and service at the cathedral commenced at half past ten; so we set out betimes and found admittance into the vast nave, and thence into the choir. An attendant ushered S—— and J—— to a seat at a distance from me, and then gave me a place in one of the stalls where the monks used to sit or kneel while chanting the services. I think these stalls are now appropriated to the prebends. They are of carved oaken wood, much less elaborate and wonderfully wrought than those of Chester Cathedral, where all was done with head and heart, each a separate device, instead of cut, by machinery like this. The whole effect of this carved work, however, lining the choir with its light tracery and pinnacles, is very fine. The whole choir, from the roof downward, except the old stones of the outer walls, is of modern renovation, it being but a few years since this part of the cathedral was destroyed by fire. The arches and pillars and lofty roof, however, have been well restored; and there was a vast east window, full of painted glass, which, if it be modern, is wonderfully chaste and Gothic-like. All the other windows have painted glass, which does not flare and glare as if newly painted. But the light, whitewashed aspect of the general interior of the choir has a cold and dreary effect. There is an enormous organ, all clad in rich oaken carving, of similar pattern to that of the stalls. It was communion day, and near the high altar, within a screen, I saw the glistening of the gold vessels wherewith the services were to be performed.

The choir was respectably filled with a pretty numerous congregation, among whom I saw some officers in full dress, with their swords by their sides, and one, old white-bearded warrior, who sat near me, seemed very devout at his religious exercises. In front of me and on the corresponding benches, on the other side of the choir, sat two rows of white-robed choristers, twenty in all, and these, with some women; performed the vocal part of the music. It is not good to see musicians, for they are sometimes coarse and vulgar people, and so the auditor loses faith in any fine and spiritual tones that they may breathe forth.

The services of Easter Sunday comprehend more than the ordinary quantity of singing and chanting; at all events, nearly an hour and a half were thus employed, with some intermixture of prayers and reading of Scriptures; and, being almost congealed with cold, I thought it would never come to an end. The spirit of my Puritan ancestors was mighty within me, and I did not wonder at their being out of patience with all this mummery, which seemed to me worse than papistry because it was a corruption of it. At last a canon gave out the text, and preached a sermon about twenty minutes long,—the coldest, driest, most superficial rubbish; for this gorgeous setting of the magnificent cathedral, the elaborate music, and the rich ceremonies seem inevitably to take the life out of the sermon, which, to be anything, must be all. The Puritans showed their strength of mind and heart by preferring a sermon an hour and a half long, into which the preacher put his whole soul, and lopping away all these externals, into which religious life had first leafed and flowered, and then petrified.

After the service, while waiting for my wife in the nave, I was accosted by a young gentleman who seemed to be an American, and whom I have certainly seen before, but whose name I could not recollect. This, he said, was his first visit to York, and he was evidently inclined to join me in viewing the curiosities of the place, but, not knowing his name, I could not introduce him to my wife, and so made a parting salute.

After dinner, we set forth and took a promenade along the wall, and a ramble through some of the crooked streets, noting the old, jutting-storied houses, story above story, and the old churches, gnawed like a bone by the tooth of Time, till we came suddenly to the Black Swan before we expected it. . . . I rather fancy that I must have observed most of the external peculiarities at my former visit, and therefore need not make another record of them in this journal.

In the course of our walk we saw a procession of about fifty charity-school boys, in flat caps, each with bands under his chin, and a green collar to his coat; all looking unjoyous, and as if they had no home nor parents' love. They turned into a gateway, which closed behind them; and as the adjoining edifice seemed to be a public institution,—at least, not private,—we asked what it was, and found it to be a hospital or residence for Old Maiden ladies, founded by a gentlewoman of York; I know not whether she herself is of the sisterhood. It must be a very singular institution, and worthy of intimate study, if it were possible to make one's way within the portal.

After writing the above, J——- and I went out for another ramble before tea; and, taking a new course, we came to a grated iron fence and gateway, through which we could see the ruins of St. Mary's Abbey. They are very extensive, and situated quite in the midst of the city, and the wall and then a tower of the Abbey seem to border more than one of the streets. Our walk was interesting, as it brought us unexpectedly upon several relics of antiquity,—a loop-holed and battlemented gateway; and at various points fragments of the old Gothic stone-work, built in among more recent edifices, which themselves were old; grimness intermixed with quaintness and grotesqueness; old fragments of religious or warlike architecture mingled with queer domestic structures,—the general effect sombre, sordid, and grimy; but yet with a fascination that makes us fain to linger about such scenes, and come to them again.

We passed round the cathedral, and saw jackdaws fluttering round the pinnacles, while the bells chimed the quarters, and little children played on the steps under the grand arch of the entrance. It is very stately, very beautiful, this minster; and doubtless would be very satisfactory, could I only know it long and well enough,—so rich as its front is, even with almost all the niches empty of their statues; not stern in its effect, which I suppose must be owing to the elaborate detail with which its great surface is wrought all over, like the chasing of a lady's jewel-box, and yet so grand! There is a dwelling-house on one side, gray with antiquity, which has apparently grown out of it like an excrescence; and though a good-sized edifice, yet the cathedral is so large that its vastness is not in the least deformed by it. If it be a dwelling-house, I suppose it is inhabited by the person who takes care of the cathedral. This morning, while listening to the tedious chanting and lukewarm sermon, I depreciated the whole affair, cathedral and all; but now I do more justice, at least to the latter, and am only sorry that its noble echoes must follow at every syllable, and re-reverberate at the commas and semicolons, such poor discourses as the canon's. But, after all, it was the Puritans who made the sermon of such importance in religious worship as we New-Englanders now consider it; and we are absurd in considering this magnificent church and all those embroidered ceremonies only in reference to it.

Before going back to the hotel, I went again up the narrow and twisted passage of College Street, to take another glance at St. William's College. I underestimated the projection of the front over the street; it is considerably more than three feet, and is about eight or nine feet above the pavement. The little statue of St. William is an alto-relievo over the arched entrance, and has an escutcheon of arms on each side, all much defaced. In the interior of the quadrangle, the houses have not gables nor peaked fronts, but have peaked windows on the red-tiled roofs. The doorway, opposite the entrance-arch, is rather stately; and on one side is a large, projecting window, which is said to belong to the room where the printing-press of Charles I. was established in the days of the Parliament.

THE MINSTER.

Monday, April 13th.—This morning was chill, and, worse, it was showery, so that our purposes to see York were much thwarted. At about ten o'clock, however, we took a cab, and drove to the cathedral, where we arrived while service was going on in the choir, and ropes were put up as barriers between us and the nave; so that we were limited to the south transept, and a part of one of the aisles of the choir. It was dismally cold. We crept cheerlessly about within our narrow precincts (narrow, that is to say, in proportion to the vast length and breadth of the cathedral), gazing up into the hollow height of the central tower, and looking at a monumental brass, fastened against one of the pillars, representing a beruffed lady of the Tudor times, and at the canopied tomb of Archbishop de Grey, who ruled over the diocese in the thirteenth century. Then we went into the side aisle of the choir, where there were one or two modern monuments; and I was appalled to find that a sermon was being preached by the ecclesiastic of the day, nor were there any signs of an imminent termination. I am not aware that there was much pith in the discourse, but there was certainly a good deal of labor and earnestness in the preacher's mode of delivery; although, when he came to a close, it appeared that the audience was not more than half a dozen people.

The barriers being now withdrawn, we walked adown the length of the nave, which did not seem to me so dim and vast as the recollection which I have had of it since my visit of a year ago. But my pre-imaginations and my memories are both apt to play me false with all admirable things, and so create disappointments for me, while perhaps the thing itself is really far better than I imagine or remember it. We engaged an old man, one of the attendants pertaining to the cathedral, to be our guide, and he showed us first the stone screen in front of the choir, with its sculptured kings of England; and then the tombs in the north transept,— one of a modern archbishop, and one of an ancient one, behind which the insane person who set fire to the church a few years ago hid himself at nightfall. Then our guide unlocked a side door, and led us into the chapter-house,—an octagonal hall, with a vaulted roof, a tessellated floor, and seven arched windows of old painted glass, the richest that I ever saw or imagined, each looking like an inestimable treasury of precious stories, with a gleam and glow even in the sullen light of this gray morning. What would they be with the sun shining through them! With all their brilliancy, moreover, they were as soft as rose-leaves. I never saw any piece of human architecture so beautiful as this chapter-house; at least, I thought so while I was looking at it, and think so still; and it owed its beauty in very great measure to the painted windows: I remember looking at these windows from the outside yesterday, and seeing nothing but an opaque old crust of conglomerated panes of glass; but now that gloomy mystery was radiantly solved.

Returning into the body of the cathedral, we next entered the choir, where, instead of the crimson cushions and draperies which we had seen yesterday, we found everything folded in black. It was a token of mourning for one of the canons, who died on Saturday night. The great east window, seventy-five feet high, and full of old painted glass in many exquisitely wrought and imagined Scriptural designs, is considered the most splendid object in the Minster. It is a pity that it is partially hidden from view, even in the choir, by a screen before the high altar; but indeed, the Gothic architects seem first to imagine beautiful and noble things, and then to consider how they may best be partially screened from sight. A certain secrecy and twilight effect belong to their plan.

We next went round the side aisles of the choir, which contain many interesting monuments of prelates, and a specimen of the very common Elizabethan design of an old gentleman in a double ruff and trunk breeches, with one of his two wives on either side of him, all kneeling in prayer; and their conjoint children, in two rows, kneeling in the lower compartments of the tomb. We saw, too, a rich marble monument of one of the Strafford family, and the tombstone of the famous Earl himself,—a flat tombstone in the pavement of the aisle, covering the vault where he was buried, and with four iron rings fastened into the four corners of the stone whereby to lift it.

And now the guide led us into the vestry, where there was a good fire burning in the grate, and it really thawed my heart, which was congealed with the dismal chill of the cathedral. Here we saw a good many curious things,—for instance, two wooden figures in knightly armor, which had stood sentinels beside the ancient clock before it was replaced by a modern one; and, opening a closet, the guide produced an old iron helmet, which had been found in a tomb where a knight had been buried in his armor; and three gold rings and one brass one, taken out of the graves, and off the finger-bones of mediaeval archbishops,—one of them with a ruby set in it; and two silver-gilt chalices, also treasures of the tombs; and a wooden head, carved in human likeness, and painted to the life, likewise taken from a grave where an archbishop was supposed to have been buried. They found no veritable skull nor bones, but only this block-head, as if Death had betrayed the secret of what the poor prelate really was. We saw, too, a canopy of cloth, wrought with gold threads, which had been borne over the head of King James I., when he came to York, on his way to receive the English Crown. There were also some old brass dishes, In which pence used to be collected in monkish times. Over the door of this vestry were hung two banners of a Yorkshire regiment, tattered in the Peninsular wars, and inscribed with the names of the battles through which they had been borne triumphantly; and Waterloo was among them. The vestry, I think, occupies that excrescential edifice which I noticed yesterday as having grown out of the cathedral.

After looking at these things, we went down into the crypts, under the choir. These were very interesting, as far as we could see them; being more antique than anything above ground, but as dark as any cellar. There is here, in the midst of these sepulchral crypts, a spring of water, said to be very pure and delicious, owing to the limestone through which the rain that feeds its source is filtered. Near it is a stone trough, in which the monks used to wash their hands.

I do not remember anything more that we saw at the cathedral, and at noon we returned to the Black Swan. The rain still continued, so that S——— could not share in any more of my rambles, but J——— and I went out again, and discovered the Guildhall. It is a very ancient edifice of Richard II.'s time, and has a statue over the entrance which looks time-gnawed enough to be of coeval antiquity, although in reality it is only a representation of George II. in his royal robes. We went in, and found ourselves in a large and lofty hall, with an oaken roof and a stone pavement, and the farther end was partitioned off as a court of justice. In that portion of the hall the Judge was on the bench, and a trial was going forward; but in the hither portion a mob of people, with their hats on, were lounging and talking, and enjoying the warmth of the stoves. The window over the judgment-seat had painted glass in it, and so, I think, had some of the hall windows. At the end of the hall hung a great picture of Paul defending himself before Agrippa, where the Apostle looked like an athlete, and had a remarkably bushy black beard. Between two of the windows hung an Indian bell from Burmah, ponderously thick and massive. Both the picture and the bell had been presented to the city as tokens of affectionate remembrance by its children; and it is pleasant to think that such failings exist in these old stable communities, and that there are permanent localities where such gifts can be kept from generation to generation.

At four o'clock we left the city of York, still in a pouring rain. The Black Swan, where we had been staying, is a good specimen of the old English inn, sombre, quiet, with dark staircases, dingy rooms, curtained beds,—all the possibilities of a comfortable life and good English fare, in a fashion which cannot have been much altered for half a century. It is very homelike when one has one's family about him, but must be prodigiously stupid for a solitary man.

We took the train for Manchester, over pretty much the same route that I travelled last year. Many of the higher hills in Yorkshire were white with snow, which, in our lower region, softened into rain; but as we approached Manchester, the western sky reddened, and gave promise of better weather. We arrived at nearly eight o'clock, and put up at the Palatine Hotel. In the evening I scrawled away at my journal till past ten o'clock; for I have really made it a matter of conscience to keep a tolerably full record of my travels, though conscious that everything good escapes in the process. In the morning we went out and visited the

MANCHESTER CATHEDRAL,

a particularly black and grimy edifice, containing some genuine old wood carvings within the choir. We stayed a good while, in order to see some people married. One couple, with their groomsman and bride's-maid, were sitting within the choir; but when the clergyman was robed and ready, there entered five other couples, each attended by groomsman and bride's-maid. They all were of the lower orders; one or two respectably dressed, but most of them poverty-stricken,—the men in their ordinary loafer's or laborer's attire, the women with their poor, shabby shawls drawn closely about them; faded untimely, wrinkled with penury and care; nothing fresh, virgin-like, or hopeful about them; joining themselves to their mates with the idea of making their own misery less intolerable by adding another's to it. All the six couple stood up in a row before the altar, with the groomsmen and bride's-maids in a row behind them; and the clergyman proceeded to marry them in such a way that it almost seemed to make every man and woman the husband and wife of every other. However, there were some small portions of the service directed towards each separate couple; and they appeared to assort themselves in their own fashion afterwards, each one saluting his bride with a kiss. The clergyman, the sexton, and the clerk all seemed to find something funny in this affair; and the woman who admitted us into the church smiled too, when she told us that a wedding-party was waiting to be married. But I think it was the saddest thing we have seen since leaving home; though funny enough if one likes to look at it from a ludicrous point of view. This mob of poor marriages was caused by the fact that no marriage fee is paid during Easter.

This ended the memorable things of our tour; for my wife and J——— left Manchester for Southport, and I for Liverpool, before noon.

April 19th.—On the 15th, having been invited to attend at the laying of the corner-stone of

MR. BROWNE'S FREE LIBRARY.

I went to the Town Hall, according to the programme, at eleven o'clock. There was already a large number of people (invited guests, members of the Historical Society, and other local associations) assembled in the great hall-room, and one of these was delivering an address to Mr. Browne as I entered. Approaching the outer edge of the circle, I was met and cordially greeted by Monckton Milnes, whom I like, and who always reminds me of Longfellow, though his physical man is more massive. While we were talking together, a young man approached him with a pretty little expression of surprise and pleasure at seeing him there. He had a slightly affected or made-up manner, and was rather a comely person. Mr. Milnes introduced him to me as Lord ———. Hereupon, of course, I observed him more closely; and I must say that I was not long in discovering a gentle dignity and half-imperceptible reserve in his manner; but still my first impression was quite as real as my second one. He occupies, I suppose, the foremost position among the young men of England, and has the fairest prospects of a high course before him; nevertheless, he did not impress me as possessing the native qualities that could entitle him to a high public career. He has adopted public life as his hereditary profession, and makes the very utmost of all his abilities, cultivating himself to a determined end, knowing that he shall have every advantage towards attaining his object. His natural disadvantages must have been, in some respects, unusually great; his voice, for instance, is not strong, and appeared to me to have a more positive defect than mere weakness. Doubtless he has struggled manfully against this defect; and it made me feel a certain sympathy, and, indeed, a friendliness, for which he would not at all have thanked me, had he known it. I felt, in his person, what a burden it is upon human shoulders, the necessity of keeping up the fame and historical importance of an illustrious house; at least, when the heir to its honors has sufficient intellect and sensibility to feel the claim that his country and his ancestors and his posterity all have upon him. Lord ——— is fully capable of feeling these claims; but I would not care, methinks, to take his position, unless I could have considerably more than his strength.

In a little while we formed ourselves into a procession, four in a row, and set forth from the Town Hall, through James Street, Lord Street, Lime Street, all the way through a line of policemen and a throng of people; and all the windows were alive with heads, and I never before was so conscious of a great mass of humanity, though perhaps I may often have seen as great a crowd. But a procession is the best point of view from which to see the crowd that collects together. The day, too, was very fine, even sunshiny, and the streets dry,—a blessing which cannot be overestimated; for we should have been in a strange trim for the banquet, had we been compelled to wade through the ordinary mud of Liverpool. The procession itself could not have been a very striking object. In America, it would have had a hundred picturesque and perhaps ludicrous features,—the symbols of the different trades, banners with strange devices, flower-shows, children, volunteer soldiers, cavalcades, and every suitable and unsuitable contrivance; but we were merely a trail of ordinary-looking individuals, in great-coats, and with precautionary umbrellas. The only characteristic or professional costume, as far as I noticed, was that of the Bishop of Chester, in his flat cap and black-silk gown; and that of Sir Henry Smith, the General of the District, in full uniform, with a star and half a dozen medals on his breast. Mr. Browne himself, the hero of the day, was the plainest and simplest man of all,—an exceedingly unpretending gentleman in black; small, white-haired, pale, quiet, and respectable. I rather wondered why he chose to be the centre of all this ceremony; for he did not seem either particularly to enjoy it, or to be at all incommoded by it, as a more nervous and susceptible man might have been.

The site of the projected edifice is on one of the streets bordering on St. George's Hall; and when we came within the enclosure, the corner-stone, a large square of red freestone, was already suspended over its destined place. It has a brass plate let into it, with an inscription, which will perhaps not be seen again till the present English type has grown as antique as black-letter is now. Two or three photographs were now taken of the site, the corner-stone, Mr. Browne, the distinguished guests, and the crowd at large; then ensued a prayer from the Bishop of Chester, and speeches from Mr. Holme, Mr. Browne, Lord ———, Sir John Pakington, Sir Henry Smith, and as many others as there was time for. Lord ——— acquitted himself very creditably, though brought out unexpectedly, and with evident reluctance. I am convinced that men, liable to be called on to address the public, keep a constant supply of commonplaces in their minds, which, with little variation, can be adapted to one subject about as well as to another; and thus they are always ready to do well enough, though seldom to do particularly well.

From the scene of the corner-stone, we went to St. George's Hall, where a drawing-room and dressing-room had been prepared for the principal guests. Before the banquet, I had some conversation with Sir James Kay Shuttleworth, who had known Miss Bronte very intimately, and bore testimony to the wonderful fidelity of Mrs. Gaskell's life of her. He seemed to have had an affectionate regard for her, and said that her marriage promised to have been productive of great happiness; her husband being not a remarkable man, but with the merit of an exceeding love for her.

Mr. Browne now took me up into the gallery, which by this time was full of ladies; and thence we had a fine view of the noble hall, with the tables laid, in readiness for the banquet. I cannot conceive of anything finer than this hall: it needs nothing but painted windows to make it perfect, and those I hope it may have one day or another.

At two o'clock we sat down to the banquet, which hardly justified that name, being only a cold collation, though sufficiently splendid in its way. In truth, it would have been impossible to provide a hot dinner for nine hundred people in a place remote from kitchens. The principal table extended lengthwise of the hall, and was a little elevated above the other tables, which stretched across, about twenty in all. Before each guest, besides the bill of fare, was laid a programme of the expected toasts, among which appeared my own name, to be proposed by Mr. Monckton Milnes. These things do not trouble me quite as much as they used, though still it sufficed to prevent much of the enjoyment which I might have had if I could have felt myself merely a spectator. My left-hand neighbor was Colonel Campbell of the Artillery; my right-hand one was Mr. Picton, of the Library Committee; and I found them both companionable men, especially the Colonel, who had served in China and in the Crimea, and owned that he hated the French. We did not make a very long business of the eatables, and then came the usual toasts of ceremony, and afterwards those more peculiar to the occasion, one of the first of which was "The House of Stanley," to which Lord ——— responded. It was a noble subject, giving scope for as much eloquence as any man could have brought to bear upon it, and capable of being so wrought out as to develop and illustrate any sort of conservative or liberal tendencies which the speaker might entertain. There could not be a richer opportunity for reconciling and making friends betwixt the old system of society and the new; but Lord ——— did not seem to make anything of it. I remember nothing that he said excepting his statement that the family had been five hundred years connected with the town of Liverpool. I wish I could have responded to "The House of Stanley," and his Lordship could have spoken in my behalf. None of the speeches were remarkably good; the Bishop of Chester's perhaps the best, though he is but a little man in aspect, not at all filling up one's idea of a bishop, and the rest were on an indistinguishable level, though, being all practised speakers, they were less hum-y and ha-y than English orators ordinarily are.

I was really tired to death before my own turn came, sitting all that time, as it were, on the scaffold, with the rope round my neck. At last Monckton Milnes was called up and made a speech, of which, to my dismay, I could hardly hear a single word, owing to his being at a considerable distance, on the other side of the chairman, and flinging his voice, which is a bass one, across the hall, instead of adown it, in my direction. I could not distinguish one word of any allusions to my works, nor even when he came to the toast, did I hear the terms in which he put it, nor whether I was toasted on my own basis, or as representing American literature, or as Consul of the United States. At all events, there was a vast deal of clamor; and uprose peers and bishop, general, mayor, knights and gentlemen, everybody in the hall greeting me with all the honors. I had uprisen, too, to commence my speech; but had to sit down again till matters grew more quiet, and then I got up, and proceeded to deliver myself with as much composure as I ever felt at my own fireside. It is very strange, this self-possession and clear-sightedness which I have experienced when standing before an audience, showing me my way through all the difficulties resulting from my not having heard Monckton Milnes's speech; and on since reading the latter, I do not see how I could have answered it better. My speech certainly was better cheered than any other; especially one passage, where I made a colossus of Mr. Browne, at which the audience grew so tumultuous in their applause that they drowned my figure of speech before it was half out of my mouth.

After rising from table, Lord ——— and I talked about our respective oratorical performances; and he appeared to have a perception that he is not naturally gifted in this respect. I like Lord ———, and wish that it were possible that we might know one another better. If a nobleman has any true friend out of his own class, it ought to be a republican. Nothing further of interest happened at the banquet, and the next morning came out the newspapers with the reports of my speech, attributing to me a variety of forms of ragged nonsense, which, poor speaker as I am, I was quite incapable of uttering.

May 10th.—The winter is over, but as yet we scarcely have what ought to be called spring; nothing but cold east-winds, accompanied with sunshine, however, as east-winds generally are in this country. All milder winds seem to bring rain. The grass has been green for a month,—indeed, it has never been entirely brown,—and now the trees and hedges are beginning to be in foliage. Weeks ago the daisies bloomed, even in the sandy grass-plot bordering on the promenade beneath our front windows; and in the progress of the daisy, and towards its consummation, I saw the propriety of Burns's epithet, "wee, modest, crimson-nipped flower,"—its little white petals in the bud being fringed all round with crimson, which fades into pure white when the flower blooms. At the beginning of this month I saw fruit-trees in blossom, stretched out flat against stone walls, reminding me of a dead bird nailed against the side of a barn. But it has been a backward and dreary spring; and I think Southport, in the course of it, has lost its advantage over the rest of the Liverpool neighborhood in point of milder atmosphere. The east-wind feels even rawer here than in the city.

Nevertheless, the columns, of the Southport Visitor begin to be well replenished with the names of guests, and the town is assuming its aspect of summer life. To say the truth, except where cultivation has done its utmost, there is very little difference between winter and summer in the mere material aspect of Southport; there being nothing but a waste of sand intermixed with plashy pools to seaward, and a desert of sand-hillocks on the land side. But now the brown, weather-hardened donkey-women haunt people that stray along the reaches, and delicate persons face the cold, rasping, ill-tempered blast on the promenade, and children dig in the sands; and, for want of something better, it seems to be determined that this shall be considered spring.

Southport is as stupid a place as I ever lived in; and I cannot but bewail our ill fortune to have been compelled to spend so many months on these barren sands, when almost every other square yard of England contains something that would have been historically or poetically interesting. Our life here has been a blank. There was, indeed, a shipwreck, a month or two ago, when a large ship came ashore within a mile from our windows; the larger portion of the crew landing safely on the hither sands, while six or seven betook themselves to the boat, and were lost in attempting to gain the shore, on the other side of the Ribble. After a lapse of several weeks, two or three of their drowned bodies were found floating in this vicinity, and brought to Southport for burial; so that it really is not at all improbable that Milton's Lycidas floated hereabouts, in the rise and lapse of the tides, and that his bones may still be whitening among the sands.

In the same gale that wrecked the above-mentioned vessel, a portion of a ship's mast was driven ashore, after evidently having been a very long time in and under water; for it was covered with great barnacles, and torn sea-weed, insomuch that there was scarcely a bare place along its whole length; clusters of sea-anemones were sticking to it, and I know not what strange marine productions besides. J—— at once recognized the sea-anemones, knowing them by his much reading of Gosse's Aquarium; and though they must now have been two or three days high and dry out of water, he made an extempore aquarium out of a bowl, and put in above a dozen of these strange creatures. In a little while they bloomed out wonderfully, and even seemed to produce young anemones; but, from some fault in his management, they afterwards grew sickly and died. S—— thinks that the old storm-shattered mast, so studded with the growth of the ocean depths, is a relic of the Spanish Armada which strewed its wrecks along all the shores of England; but I hardly think it would have taken three hundred years to produce this crop of barnacles and sea-anemones. A single summer might probably have done it.

Yesterday we all of us except R—— went to Liverpool to see the performances of an American circus company. I had previously been, a day or two before, with J——, and had been happy to perceive that the fact of its being an American establishment really induced some slight swelling of the heart within me. It is ridiculous enough, to be sure, but I like to find myself not wholly destitute of this noble weakness, patriotism. As for the circus, I never was fond of that species of entertainment, nor do I find in this one the flash and glitter and whirl which I remember in other American exhibitions.

[Here follow the visits to Lincoln and Boston, printed in Our Old Home. —ED.]

May 27th.—We left Boston by railway at noon, and arrived in PETERBOROUGH in about an hour and a quarter, and have put up at the Railway Hotel. After dinner we walked into the town to see

THE CATHEDRAL,

of the towers and arches of which we had already had a glimpse from our parlor window.

Our journey from Boston hitherward was through a perfectly level country,—the fens of Lincolnshire,—green, green, and nothing else, with old villages and farm-houses and old church-towers; very pleasant and rather wearisomely monotonous. To return to Peterborough. It is a town of ancient aspect; and we passed, on our way towards the market-place, a very ancient-looking church, with a very far projecting porch, opening in front and on each side through arches of broad sweep. The street by which we approached from our hotel led us into the market-place, which had what looked like an old Guildhall on one side. On the opposite side, above the houses, appeared the towers of the cathedral, and a street leads from the market-place to its front, through an arched gateway, which used to be the external entrance to the abbey, I suppose, of which the cathedral was formerly the church. The front of the cathedral is very striking, and unlike any other that I have seen; being formed by three lofty and majestic arches in a row, with three gable peaks above them, forming a sort of colonnade, within which is the western entrance of the nave. The towers are massive, but low in proportion to their bulk. There are no spires, but pinnacles and statues, and all the rich detail of Gothic architecture, the whole of a venerable gray line. It is in perfect repair, and has not suffered externally, except by the loss of multitudes of statues, gargoyles, and miscellaneous eccentricities of sculpture, which used to smile, frown, laugh, and weep over the faces of these old fabrics.

We entered through a side portal, and sat down on a bench in the nave, and kept ourselves quiet; for the organ was sounding, and the choristers were chanting in the choir. The nave and transepts are very noble, with clustered pillars and Norman arches, and a great height under the central tower; the whole, however, being covered with plaster and whitewash, except the roof, which is of painted oak. This latter adornment has the merit, I believe, of being veritably ancient; but certainly I should prefer the oak of its native hue, for the effect of the paint is to make it appear as if the ceiling were covered with imitation mosaic-work or an oil-cloth carpet.

After sitting awhile, we were invited by a verger, who came from within the screen, to enter the choir and hear the rest of the service. We found the choristers there in their white garments, and an audience of half a dozen people, and had time to look at the interior of the choir. All the carved wood-work of the tabernacle, the Bishop's throne, the prebends' stalls, and whatever else, is modern; for this cathedral seems to have suffered wofully from Cromwell's soldiers, who hacked at the old oak, and hammered and pounded upon the marble tombs, till nothing of the first and very few of the latter remain. It is wonderful how suddenly the English people lost their sense of the sanctity of all manner of externals in religion, without losing their religion too. The French, in their Revolution, underwent as sudden a change; but they became pagans and atheists, and threw away the substance with the shadow.

I suspect that the interior arrangement of the choir and the chancel has been greatly modernized; for it is quite unlike anything that I have seen elsewhere. Instead of one vast eastern window, there are rows of windows lighting the Lady Chapel, and seen through rows of arches in the screen of the chancel; the effect being, whoever is to have the credit of it, very rich and beautiful. There is, I think, no stained glass in the windows of the nave, though in the windows of the chancel there is some of recent date, and from fragments of veritable antique. The effect of the whole interior is grand, expansive, and both ponderous and airy; not dim, mysterious, and involved, as Gothic interiors often are, the roundness and openness of the arches being opposed to this latter effect.

When the chanting came to a close, one verger took his stand at the entrance of the choir, and another stood farther up the aisle, and then the door of a stall opened, and forth came a clerical dignity of much breadth and substance, aged and infirm, and was ushered out of the choir with a great deal of ceremony. We took him for the bishop, but he proved to be only a cano
We now engaged an attendant to show us through the Lady Chapel ar

other penetralia, which it did not take him long to accomplish. One of the first things he showed us was the tombstone, in the pavement of the southern aisle, beneath which Mary, Queen of Scots, had been originally buried, and where she lay for a quarter of a century, till borne to her present resting-place in Westminster Abbey. It is a plain marble slab, with no inscription. Near this, there was a Saxon monument of the date 870, with sculpture in relief upon it,—the memorial of an Abbot Hedda, who was killed by the Danes when they destroyed the monastery that preceded the abbey and church. I remember, likewise, the recumbent figure of the prelate, whose face has been quite obliterated by Puritanic violence; and I think that there is not a single tomb older than the parliamentary wars, which has not been in like manner battered and shattered, except the Saxon abbot's just mentioned. The most pretentious monument remaining is that of a Mr. Deacon, a gentleman of George I.'s time, in wig and breeches, leaning on his elbow, and resting one hand upon a skull. In the north aisle, precisely opposite to that of Queen Mary, the attendant pointed out to us the slab beneath which lie the ashes of Catharine of Aragon, the divorced queen of Henry VIII.

In the nave there was an ancient font, a venerable and beautiful relic, which has been repaired not long ago, but in such a way as not to lessen its individuality. This sacred vessel suffered especial indignity from Cromwell's soldiers; insomuch that if anything could possibly destroy its sanctity, they would have effected that bad end. On the eastern wall of the nave, and near the entrance, hangs the picture of old Scarlet, the sexton who buried both Mary of Scotland and Catharine of Aragon, and not only these two queens, but everybody else in Peterborough, twice over. I think one feels a sort of enmity and spite against these grave-diggers, who live so long, and seem to contract a kindred and partnership with Death, being boon companions with him, and taking his part against mankind.

In a chapel or some side apartment, there were two pieces of tapestry wretchedly faded, the handiwork of two nuns, and copied from two of Raphael's cartoons.

We now emerged from the cathedral, and walked round its exterior, admiring it to our utmost capacity, and all the more because we had not heard of it beforehand, and expected to see nothing so huge, majestic, grand, and gray. And of all the lovely closes that I ever beheld, that of Peterborough Cathedral is to me the most delightful; so quiet it is, so solemnly and nobly cheerful, so verdant, so sweetly shadowed, and so presided over by the stately minster, and surrounded by ancient and comely habitations of Christian men. The most enchanting place, the most enviable as a residence in all this world, seemed to me that of the Bishop's secretary, standing in the rear of the cathedral, and bordering on the churchyard; so that you pass through hallowed precincts in order to come at it, and find it a Paradise, the holier and sweeter for the dead men who sleep so near. We looked through the gateway into the lawn, which really seemed hardly to belong to this world, so bright and soft the sunshine was, so fresh the grass, so lovely the trees, so trained and refined and mellowed down was the whole nature of the spot, and so shut in and guarded from all intrusion. It is in vain to write about it; nowhere but in England can there be such a spot, nor anywhere but in the close of Peterborough Cathedral.

May 28th.—I walked up into the town this morning, and again visited the cathedral. On the way, I observed the Falcon Inn, a very old-fashioned hostelry, with a thatched roof, and what looked like the barn door or stable door in a side front. Very likely it may have been an inn ever since Queen Elizabeth's time. The Guildhall, as I supposed it to be, in the market-place, has a basement story entirely open on all sides, but from its upper story it communicates with a large old house in the rear. I have not seen an older-looking town than Peterborough; but there is little that is picturesque about it, except within the domain of the cathedral. It was very fortunate for the beauty and antiquity of these precincts, that Henry VIII. did not suffer the monkish edifices of the abbey to be overthrown and utterly destroyed, as was the case with so many abbeys, at the Reformation; but, converting the abbey church into a cathedral, he preserved much of the other arrangement of the buildings connected with it. And so it happens that to this day we have the massive and stately gateway, with its great pointed arch, still keeping out the world from those who have inherited the habitations of the old monks; for though the gate is never closed, one feels himself in a sacred seclusion the instant he passes under the archway. And everywhere there are old houses that appear to have been adapted from the monkish residences, or from their spacious offices, and made into convenient dwellings for ecclesiastics, or vergers, or great or small people connected with the cathedral; and with all modern comfort they still retain much of the quaintness of the olden time,—arches, even rows of arcades, pillars, walls, beautified with patches of Gothic sculpture, not wilfully put on by modern taste, but lingering from a long past; deep niches, let into the fronts of houses, and occupied by images of saints; a growth of ivy, overspreading walls, and just allowing the windows to peep through,—so that no novelty, nor anything of our hard, ugly, and actual life comes into these limits, through the defences of the gateway, without being mollified and modified. Except in some of the old colleges of Oxford, I have not seen any other place that impressed me in this way; and the grounds of Peterborough Cathedral have the advantage over even the Oxford colleges, insomuch that the life is here domestic,—that of the family, that of the affections,—a natural life, which one deludes himself with imagining may be made into something sweeter and purer in this beautiful spot than anywhere else. Doubtless the inhabitants find it a stupid and tiresome place enough, and get morbid and sulky, and heavy and obtuse of head and heart, with the monotony of their life. But still I must needs believe that a man with a full mind, and objects to employ his affection, ought to be very happy here. And perhaps the forms and appliances of human life are never fit to make people happy until they cease to be used for the purposes for which they were directly intended, and are taken, as it were, in a sidelong application. I mean that the monks, probably, never enjoyed their own edifices while they were a part of the actual life of the day, so much as these present inhabitants now enjoy them when a new use has grown up apart from the original one.

Towards noon we all walked into the town again, and on our way went into the old church with the projecting portal, which I mentioned yesterday. A woman came hastening with the keys when she saw us looking up at the door. The interior had an exceeding musty odor, and was very ancient, with side aisles opening by a row of pointed arches into the nave, and a gallery of wood on each side, and built across the two rows of arches. It was paved with tombstones, and I suppose the dead people contributed to the musty odor. Very naked and unadorned it was, except with a few mural monuments of no great interest. We stayed but a little while, and amply rewarded the poor woman with a sixpence. Thence we proceeded to the cathedral, pausing by the way to look at the old Guildhall, which is no longer a Guildhall, but a butter-market; and then we bought some prints of exterior and interior views of the Minster, of which there are a great variety on note-paper, letter-sheets, large engravings, and lithographs. It is very beautiful; there seems to be nothing better than to say this over again. We found the doors most hospitably open, and every part entirely free to us,—a kindness and liberality which we have nowhere else experienced in England, whether as regards cathedrals or any other public buildings. My wife sat down to draw the font, and I walked through the Lady Chapel meanwhile, pausing over the empty bed of Queen Mary, and the grave of Queen Catharine, and looking at the rich and sumptuous roof, where a fountain, as it were, of groins of arches spouts from numberless pilasters, intersecting one another in glorious intricacy. Under the central tower, opening to either transept, to the nave, and to the choir, are four majestic arches, which I think must equal in height those of which I saw the ruins, and one, all but perfect, at Furness Abbey. They are about eighty feet high.

I may as well give up Peterborough here, though I hate to leave it undescribed even to the tufts of yellow flowers, which grow on the projections high out of reach, where the winds have sown their seeds in soil made by the aged decay of the edifice. I could write a page, too, about the rooks or jackdaws that flit and clamor about the pinnacles, and dart in and out of the eyelet-holes, the piercings,—whatever they are called,—in the turrets and buttresses. On our way back to the hotel, J——- saw an advertisement of some knights in armor that were to tilt to-day; so he and I waited, and by and by a procession appeared, passing through the antique market-place, and in front of the abbey gateway, which might have befitted the same spot three hundred years ago. They were about twenty men-at-arms on horseback, with lances and banners. We were a little too near for the full enjoyment of the spectacle; for, though some of the armor was real, I could not help observing that other suits were made of silver paper or gold tinsel. A policeman (a queer anomaly in reference to such a mediaeval spectacle) told us that they were going to joust and run at the ring, in a field a little beyond the bridge.

TO NOTTINGHAM.

May 28th.—We left Peterborough this afternoon, and, however reluctant to leave the cathedral, we were glad to get away from the hotel; for, though outwardly pretentious, it is a wretched and uncomfortable place, with scanty table, poor attendance, and enormous charges. The first stage of our journey to-day was to Grantham, through a country the greater part of which was as level as the Lincolnshire landscapes have been, throughout our experience of them. We saw several old villages, gathered round their several churches; and one of these little communities, "Little Byforth," had a very primitive appearance,—a group of twenty or thirty dwellings of stone and thatch, without a house among them that could be so modern as a hundred years. It is a little wearisome to think of people living from century to century in the same spot, going in and out of the same doors, cultivating the same fields, meeting the same faces, and marrying one another over and over again; and going to the same church, and lying down in the same churchyard,—to appear again, and go through the same monotonous round in the next generation.

At Grantham, our route branches off from the main line; and there was a delay of about an hour, during which we walked up into the town, to take a nearer view of a tall gray steeple which we saw from the railway station. The streets that led from the station were poor and commonplace; and, indeed, a railway seems to have the effect of making its own vicinity mean. We noticed nothing remarkable until we got to the marketplace, in the centre of which there is a cross, doubtless of great antiquity, though it is in too good condition not to have been recently repaired. It consists of an upright pillar, with a pedestal of half a dozen stone steps, which are worn hollow by the many feet that have scraped their hobnailed shoes upon them. Among these feet, it is highly probable, may have been those of Sir Isaac Newton, who was a scholar of the free school of this town; and when J—— scampered up the steps, we told him so. Visible from the market-place also stands the Angel Inn, which seems to be a wonderfully old inn, being adorned with gargoyles and other antique sculpture, with projecting windows, and an arched entrance, and presenting altogether a frontispiece of so much venerable state that I feel curious to know its history. Had I been aware that the chief hotel of Grantham were such a time-honored establishment, I should have arranged to pass the night there, especially as there were interesting objects enough in the town to occupy us pleasantly. The church—the steeple of which is seen over the market-place, but is removed from it by a street or two—is very fine; the tower and spire being adorned with arches, canopies, and niches,—twelve of the latter for the twelve Apostles, all of whom have now vanished,—and with fragments of other Gothic ornaments. The jackdaws have taken up their abodes in the crevices and crannies of the upper half of the steeple.

We left Grantham at nearly seven, and reached

just before eight. The castle, situated on a high and precipitous rock, directly over the edge of which look the walls, was visible, as we drove from the station to our hotel. We followed the advice of a railway attendant in going first to the May Pole, which proved to be a commercial inn, with the air of a drinking-shop, in a by-alley; and, furthermore, they could not take us in. So we drove to the George the Fourth, which seems to be an excellent house; and here I have remained quiet, the size of the town discouraging me from going out in the twilight which was fast coming on after tea. These are glorious long days for travel; daylight fairly between four in the morning and nine at night, and a margin of twilight on either side.

May 29th.—After breakfast, this morning, I wandered out and lost myself; but at last found the post-office, and a letter from Mr. Wilding, with some perplexing intelligence. Nottingham is an unlovely and uninteresting town. The castle I did not see; but, I happened upon a large and stately old church, almost cathedralic in its dimensions. On returning to the hotel, we deliberated on the mode of getting to Newstead Abbey, and we finally decided upon taking a fly, in which conveyance, accordingly, we set out before twelve. It was a slightly overcast day, about half intermixed of shade and sunshine, and rather cool, but not so cool that we could exactly wish it warmer. Our drive to Newstead lay through what was once a portion of Sherwood Forest, though all of it, I believe, has now become private property, and is converted into fertile fields, except where the owners of estates have set out plantations. We have now passed out of the fen-country, and the land rises and falls in gentle swells, presenting a pleasant, but not striking, character of scenery. I remember no remarkable object on the road,—here and there an old inn, a gentleman's seat of moderate pretension, a great deal of tall and continued hedge, a quiet English greenness and rurality, till, drawing near

NEWSTEAD ABBEY.

we began to see copious plantations, principally of firs, larches, and trees of that order, looking very sombre, though with some intermingling of lighter foliage. It was after one when we reached "The Hut,"—a small, modern wayside inn, almost directly across the road from the entrance-gate of Newstead. The post-boy calls the distance ten miles from Nottingham. He also averred that it was forbidden to drive visitors within the gates; so we left the fly at the inn, and set out to walk from the entrance to the house. There is no porter's lodge; and the grounds, in this outlying region, had not the appearance of being very primly kept, but were well wooded with evergreens, and much overgrown with ferns, serving for cover for hares, which scampered in and out of their hiding-places. The road went winding gently along, and, at the distance of nearly a mile, brought us to a second gate, through which we likewise passed, and walked onward a good way farther, seeing much wood, but as yet nothing of the Abbey. At last, through the trees, we caught a glimpse of its battlements, and saw, too, the gleam of water, and then appeared the Abbey's venerable front. It comprises the western wall of the church, which is all that remains of that fabric,—a great, central window, entirely empty, without tracery or mullions; the ivy clambering up on the inside of the wall, and hanging over in front. The front of the inhabited part of the house extends along on a line with this church wall, rather low, with battlements along its top, and all in good keeping with the ruinous remnant. We met a servant, who replied civilly to our inquiries about the mode of gaining admittance, and bade us ring a bell at the corner of the principal porch. We rang accordingly, and were forthwith admitted into a low, vaulted basement, ponderously wrought with intersecting arches, dark and rather chilly, just like what I remember to have seen at Battle Abbey; and, after waiting here a little while, a respectable elderly gentlewoman appeared, of whom we requested to be shown round the Abbey. She courteously acceded, first presenting us to a book in which to inscribe our names.

I suppose ten thousand people, three fourths of them Americans, have written descriptions of Newstead Abbey; and none of them, so far as I have read, give any true idea of the place; neither will my description, if I write one. In fact, I forget very much that I saw, and especially in what order the objects came. In the basement was Byron's bath,—a dark and cold and cellarlike hole, which it must have required good courage to plunge into; in this region, too, or near it, was the chapel, which Colonel Wildman has decorously fitted up, and where service is now regularly performed, but which was used as a dog's kennel in Byron's time.

After seeing this, we were led to Byron's own bedchamber, which remains just as when he slept in it,—the furniture and all the other arrangements being religiously preserved. It was in the plainest possible style, homely, indeed, and almost mean,—an ordinary paper-hanging, and everything so commonplace that it was only the deep embrasure of the window that made it look unlike a bedchamber in a middling-class lodging-house. It would have seemed difficult, beforehand, to fit up a room in that picturesque old edifice so that it should be utterly void of picturesqueness; but it was effected in this apartment, and I suppose it is a specimen of the way in which old mansions used to be robbed of their antique character, and adapted to modern tastes, before mediaeval antiquities came into fashion. Some prints of the Cambridge colleges, and other pictures indicating Byron's predilections at the time, and which he himself had hung there, were on the walls. This, the housekeeper told us, had been the Abbot's chamber, in the monastic time. Adjoining it is the haunted room, where the ghostly monk, whom Byron introduces into Don Juan, is said to have his lurking-place. It is fitted up in the same style as Byron's, and used to be occupied by his valet or page. No doubt in his Lordship's day, these were the only comfortable bedrooms in the Abbey; and by the housekeeper's account of what Colonel Wildman has done, it is to be inferred that the place must have been in a most wild, shaggy, tumble-down condition, inside and out, when he bought it.

It is very different now. After showing us these two apartments of Byron and his servant, the housekeeper led us from one to another and another magnificent chamber fitted up in antique style, with oak panelling, and heavily carved bedsteads, of Queen Elizabeth's time, or of the Stuarts, hung with rich tapestry curtains of similar date, and with beautiful old cabinets of carved wood, sculptured in relief, or tortoise-shell and ivory. The very pictures and realities, these rooms were, of stately comfort; and they were called by the name of kings,—King Edward's, King Charles II's, King Henry VII's chamber; and they were hung with beautiful pictures, many of them portraits of these kings. The chimney-pieces were carved and emblazoned; and all, so far as I could judge, was in perfect keeping, so that if a prince or noble of three centuries ago were to come to lodge at Newstead Abbey, he would hardly know that he had strayed out of his own century. And yet he might have known by some token, for there are volumes of poetry and light literature on the tables in these royal bedchambers, and in that of Henry VII. I saw The House of the Seven Gables and The Scarlet Letter in Routledge's edition.

Certainly the house is admirably fitted up; and there must have been something very excellent and comprehensive in the domestic arrangements of the monks, since they adapt themselves so well to a state of society entirely different from that in which they originated. The library is a very comfortable room, and provocative of studious ideas, though lounging and luxurious. It is long, and rather low, furnished with soft couches, and, on the whole, though a man might dream of study, I think he would be most likely to read nothing but novels there. I know not what the room was in monkish times, but it was waste and ruinous in Lord Byron's. Here, I think, the housekeeper unlocked a beautiful cabinet, and took out the famous skull which Lord Byron transformed into a drinking-goblet. It has a silver rim and stand, but still the ugly skull is bare and evident, and the naked inner bone receives the wine. I should think it would hold at least a quart,—enough to overpower any living head into which this death's-head should transfer its contents; and a man must be either very drunk or very thirsty, before he would taste wine out of such a goblet. I think Byron's freak was outdone by that of a cousin of my own, who once solemnly assured me that he had a spittoon made out of the skull of his enemy. The ancient coffin in which the goblet-skull was found was shown us in the basement of the Abbey.

There was much more to see in the house than I had any previous notion of; but except the two chambers already noticed, nothing remained the least as Byron left it. Yes, another place there was,—his own small dining-room, with a table of moderate size, where, no doubt, the skull-goblet has often gone its rounds. Colonel Wildman's dining-room was once Byron's shooting-gallery, and the original refectory of the monks. It is now magnificently arranged, with a vaulted roof, a music-gallery at one end, suits of armor and weapons on the walls, and mailed arms extended, holding candelabras. There are one or two painted windows, commemorative of the Peninsular war, and the battles in which the Colonel and his two brothers fought,—for these Wildmen seem to have been mighty troopers, and Colonel Wildman is represented as a fierce-looking mustachioed hussar at two different ages. The housekeeper spoke of him affectionately, but says that he is now getting into years, and that they fancy him failing. He has no children. He appears to have been on good terms with Byron, and had the latter ever returned to England, he was under promise to make his first visit to his old home, and it was in such an expectation that Colonel Wildman had kept Byron's private apartments in the same condition in which he found them. Byron was informed of all the Colonel's fittings up and restorations, and when he introduces the Abbey in Don Juan, the poet describes it, not as he himself left it, but as Colonel Wildman has restored it. There is a beautiful drawing-room, and all these apartments are adorned with pictures, the collection being especially rich in portraits by Sir Peter Lely,—that of Nell Gwynn being one, who is one of the few beautiful women whom I have seen on canvas.

We parted with the housekeeper, and I with a good many shillings, at the door by which we entered; and our next business was to see the private grounds and gardens. A little boy attended us through the first part of our progress, but soon appeared the veritable gardener,—a shrewd and sensible old man, who has been very many years on the place. There was nothing of special interest as concerning Byron until we entered the original old monkish garden, which is still laid out in the same fashion as the monks left it, with a large, oblong piece of water in the centre, and terraced banks rising at two or three different stages with perfect regularity around it; so that the sheet of water looks like the plate of an immense looking-glass, of which the terraces form the frame. It seems as if, were there any giant large enough, he might raise up this mirror and set it on end. In the monks' garden, there is a marble statue of Pan, which, the gardener told us, was brought by the "Wicked Lord" (great-uncle of Byron) from Italy, and was supposed by the country people to represent the Devil, and to be the object of his worship,—a natural idea enough, in view of his horns and cloven feet and tail, though this indicates, at all events, a very jolly devil. There is also a female statue, beautiful from the waist upward, but shaggy and cloven-footed below, and holding a little cloven-footed child by the hand. This, the old gardener assured us, was Pandora, wife of the above-mentioned Pan, with her son. Not far from this spot, we came to the tree on which Byron carved his own name and that of his sister Augusta. It is a tree of twin stems,—a birch-tree, I think,—growing up side by side. One of the stems still lives and flourishes, but that on which he carved the two names is quite dead, as if there had been something fatal in the inscription that has made it forever famous. The names are still very legible, although the letters had been closed up by the growth of the bark before the tree died. They must have been deeply cut at first.

There are old yew-trees of unknown antiquity in this garden, and many other interesting things; and among them may be reckoned a fountain of very pure water, called the "Holy Well," of which we drank. There are several fountains, besides the large mirror in the centre of the garden; and these are mostly inhabited by carp, the genuine descendants of those which peopled the fish-ponds in the days of the monks. Coming in front of the Abbey, the gardener showed us the oak that Byron planted, now a vigorous young tree; and the monument which he erected to his Newfoundland dog, and which is larger than most Christians get, being composed of a marble, altar-shaped tomb, surrounded by a circular area of steps, as much as twenty feet in diameter. The gardener said, however, that Byron intended this, not merely as the burial-place of his dog, but for himself too, and his sister. I know not how this may have been, but this inconvenience would have attended his being buried there, that, on transfer of the estate, his mortal remains would have become the property of some other man.

We had now come to the empty space,—a smooth green lawn, where had once been the Abbey church. The length had been sixty-four yards, the gardener said, and within his remembrance there had been many remains of it, but now they are quite removed, with the exception of the one ivy-grown western wall, which, as I mentioned, forms a picturesque part of the present front of the Abbey. Through a door in this wall the gardener now let us out. . . .

In the evening our landlady, who seems to be a very intelligent woman, of a superior class to most landladies, came into our parlor, while I was out, and talked about the present race of Byrons and Lovelaces, who have often been at this house. There seems to be a taint in the Byron blood which makes those who inherit it wicked, mad, and miserable. Even Colonel Wildman comes in for a share of this ill luck, for he has almost ruined himself by his expenditure on the estate, and by his lavish hospitality, especially to the Duke of Sussex, who liked the Colonel, and used often to visit him during his lifetime, and his Royal Highness's gentlemen ate and drank Colonel Wildman almost up. So says our good landlady. At any rate, looking at this miserable race of Byrons, who held the estate so long, and at Colonel Wildman, whom it has ruined in forty years, we might see grounds for believing in the evil fate which is supposed to attend confiscated church property. Nevertheless, I would accept the estate, were it offered me.

. . . . Glancing back, I see that I have omitted some items that were curious in describing the house; for instance, one of the cabinets had been the personal property of Queen Elizabeth. It seems to me that the fashion of modern furniture has nothing to equal these old cabinets for beauty and convenience. In the state apartments, the floors were so highly waxed and polished that we slid on them as if on ice, and could only make sure of our footing by treading on strips of carpeting that were laid down.

June 7th.—We left Nottingham a week ago, and made our first stage to Derby, where we had to wait an hour or two at a great, bustling, pell-mell, crowded railway station. It was much thronged with second and third class passengers, coming and departing in continual trains; for these were the Whitsuntide holidays, which set all the lower orders of English people astir.

This time of festival was evidently the origin of the old "Election" holidays in Massachusetts; the latter occurring at the same period of the year, and being celebrated (so long as they could be so) in very much the same way, with games, idleness, merriment of set purpose, and drunkenness. After a weary while we took the train for

MATLOCK,

via Ambergate, and arrived of the former place late in the afternoon. The village of Matlock is situated on the banks of the Derwent, in a delightful little nook among the hills, which rise above it in steeps, and in precipitous crags, and shut out the world so effectually that I wonder how the railway ever found it out. Indeed, it does make its approach to this region through a long tunnel. It was a beautiful, sunny afternoon when we arrived, and my present impressions are, that I have never seen anywhere else such exquisite scenery as that which surrounds the village. The street itself, to be sure, is commonplace enough, and hot, dusty, and disagreeable; but if you look above it, or on either side, there are green hills descending abruptly down, and softened with woods, amid which are seen villas, cottages, castles; and beyond the river is a line of crags, perhaps three hundred feet high, clothed with shrubbery in some parts from top to bottom, but in other places presenting a sheer precipice of rock, over which tumbles, as it were, a cascade of ivy and creeping plants. It is very beautiful, and, I might almost say, very wild; but it has those characteristics of finish, and of being redeemed from nature, and converted into a portion of the adornment of a great garden, which I find in all English scenery. Not that I complain of this; on the contrary, there is nothing that delights an American more, in contrast with the roughness and ruggedness of his native scenes,—to which, also, he might be glad to return after a while.

We put up at the old Bath Hotel,—an immense house, with passages of such extent that at first it seemed almost a day's journey from parlor to bedroom. The house stands on a declivity, and after ascending one pair of stairs, we came, in travelling along the passageway, to a door that opened upon a beautifully arranged garden, with arbors and grottos, and the hillside rising steep above. During all the time of our stay at Matlock there was brilliant sunshine, and, the grass and foliage being in their freshest and most luxuriant phase, the place has left as bright a picture as I have anywhere in my memory.

The morning after our arrival we took a walk, and, following the sound of a church-bell, entered what appeared to be a park, and, passing along a road at the base of a line of crags, soon came in sight of a beautiful church. I rather imagine it to be the place of worship of the Arkwright family, whose seat is in this vicinity,—the descendants of the famous Arkwright who contributed so much towards turning England into a cotton manufactory. We did not enter the church, but passed beyond it, and over a bridge, and along a road that ascended among the hills and finally brought us out by a circuit to the other end of Matlock village, after a walk of three or four miles. In the afternoon we took a boat across the Derwent,—a passage which half a dozen strokes of the oars accomplished, —and reached a very pleasant seclusion called "The Lovers' Walk." A ferriage of twopence pays for the transit across the river, and gives the freedom of these grounds, which are threaded with paths that meander and zigzag to the top of the precipitous ridge, amid trees and shrubbery, and the occasional ease of rustic seats. It is a sweet walk for lovers, and was so for us; although J———, with his scramblings and disappearances, and shouts from above, and headlong scamperings down the precipitous paths, occasionally frightened his mother. After gaining the heights, the path skirts along the precipice, allowing us to see down into the village street, and, nearer, the Derwent winding through the valley so close beneath us that we might have flung a stone into it. These crags would be very rude and harsh if left to themselves, but they are quite softened and made sweet and tender by the great deal of foliage that clothes their sides, and creeps and clambers over them, only letting a stern face of rock be seen here and there, and with a smile rather than a frown.

The next day, Monday, we went to see the grand cavern. The entrance is high up on the hillside, whither we were led by a guide, of whom there are many, and they all pay tribute to the proprietor of the cavern. There is a small shed by the side of the cavern mouth, where the guide provided himself and us with tallow candles, and then led us into the darksome and ugly pit, the entrance of which is not very imposing, for it has a door of rough pine boards, and is kept under lock and key. This is the disagreeable phase-one of the disagreeable phases—of man's conquest over nature in England,—cavern mouths shut up with cellar doors, cataracts under lock and key, precipitous crags compelled to figure in ornamented gardens,—and all accessible at a fixed amount of shillings or pence. It is not possible to draw a full free breath under such circumstances. When you think of it, it makes the wildest scenery look like the artificial rock-work which Englishmen are so fond of displaying in the little bit of grass-plot under their suburban parlor windows. However, the cavern was dreary enough and wild enough, though in a mean sort of way; for it is but a long series of passages and crevices, generally so narrow that you scrape your elbows, and so low that you hit your head. It has nowhere a lofty height, though sometimes it broadens out into ample space, but not into grandeur, the roof being always within reach, and in most places smoky with the tallow candles that have been held up to it. A very dirty, sordid, disagreeable burrow, more like a cellar gone mad than anything else; but it served to show us how the crust of the earth is moulded. This cavern was known to the Romans, and used to be worked by them as a lead-mine. Derbyshire spar is now taken from it; and in some of its crevices the gleam of the tallow candles is faintly reflected from the crystallizations; but, on the whole, I felt like a mole, as I went creeping along, and was glad when we came into the sunshine again. I rather think my idea of a cavern is taken from the one in the Forty Thieves, or in Gil Blas,—a vast, hollow womb, roofed and curtained with obscurity. This reality is very mean.

Leaving the cavern, we went to the guide's cottage, situated high above the village, where he showed us specimens of ornaments and toys manufactured by himself from Derbyshire spar and other materials. There was very pretty mosaic work, flowers of spar, and leaves of malachite, and miniature copies of Cleopatra's Needle, and other Egyptian monuments, and vases of graceful pattern, brooches, too, and many other things. The most valuable spar is called Blue John, and is only to be found in one spot, where, also, the supply is said to be growing scant. We bought a number of articles, and then came homeward, still with our guide, who showed us, on the way, the Romantic Rocks. These are some crags which have been rent away and stand insulated from the hillside, affording a pathway between it and then; while the places can yet be seen where the sundered rocks would fit into the craggy hill if there were but a Titan strong enough to adjust them again. It is a very picturesque spot, and the price for seeing it is twopence; though in our case it was included in the four shillings which we had paid for seeing the cavern. The representative men of England are the showmen and the policemen; both very good people in their way.

Returning to the hotel, J—— and his mother went through the village to the river, near the railway, where J—— set himself to fishing, and caught three minnows. I followed, after a while, to fetch them back, and we called into one or two of the many shops in the village, which have articles manufactured of the spar for sale. Some of these are nothing short of magnificent. There was an inlaid table, valued at sixty guineas, and a splendid ornament for any drawing-room; another, inlaid with the squares of a chess-board. We heard of a table in the possession of the Marquis of Westminster, the value of which is three hundred guineas. It would be easy and pleasant to spend a great deal of money in such things as we saw there; but all our purchases in Matlock did not amount to more than twenty shillings, invested in brooches, shawl-pins, little vases and toys, which will be valuable to us as memorials on the other side of the water. After this, we visited a petrifying cave, of which there are several hereabouts. The process of petrifaction requires some months, or perhaps a year or two, varying with the size of the article to be operated upon. The articles are placed in the cave, under the drippings from the roof, and a hard deposit is formed upon them, and sometimes, as in the case of a bird's-nest, causes a curious result,— every straw and hair being immortalized and stiffened into stone. A horse's head was in process of petrifaction; and J—— bought a broken eggshell for a penny, though larger articles are expensive. The process would appear to be entirely superficial,—a mere crust on the outside of things,—but we saw some specimens of petrified oak, where the stony substance seemed to be intimately incorporated with the wood, and to have really changed it into stone. These specimens were immensely ponderous, and capable of a high polish, which brought out beautiful streaks and shades.

One might spend a very pleasant summer in Matlock, and I think there can be no more beautiful place in the world; but we left it that afternoon, and railed to Manchester, where we arrived between ten and eleven at night. The next day I left S—— to go to the Art Exhibition, and took J—— with me to Liverpool, where I had an engagement that admitted of no delay. Thus ended our tour, in which we had seen but a little bit of England, yet rich with variety and interest. What a wonderful land! It is our forefathers' land; our land, for I will not give up such a precious inheritance. We are now back again in flat and sandy Southport, which, during the past week, has been thronged with Whitsuntide people, who crowd the streets, and pass to and fro along the promenade, with a universal and monotonous air of nothing to do, and very little enjoyment. It is a pity that poor folks cannot employ their little hour of leisure to better advantage, in a country where the soil is so veined with gold.

These are delightfully long days. Last night, at half past nine, I could read with perfect ease in parts of the room remote from the window; and at nearly half past eleven there was a broad sheet of daylight in the west, gleaming brightly over the plashy sands. I question whether there be any total night at this season.

June 21st.—Southport, I presume, is now in its most vivid aspect; there being a multitude of visitors here, principally of the middling classes, and a frequent crowd, whom I take to be working-people from Manchester and other factory towns. It is the strangest place to come to for the pleasures of the sea, of which we scarcely have a glimpse from month's end to mouth's end, nor any fresh, exhilarating breath from it, but a lazy, languid atmosphere, brooding over the waste of sands; or even if there be a sulky and bitter wind blowing along the promenade, it still brings no salt elixir. I never was more weary of a place in all my life, and never felt such a disinterested pity as for the people who come here for pleasure. Nevertheless, the town has its amusements; in the first place, the daylong and perennial one of donkey-riding along the sands, large parties of men and girls pottering along together; the Flying Dutchman trundles hither and thither when there is breeze enough; an arch cry-man sets up his targets on the beach; the bathing-houses stand by scores and fifties along the shore, and likewise on the banks of the Ribble, a mile seaward; the hotels have their billiard-rooms; there is a theatre every evening; from morning till night comes a succession of organ-grinders, playing interminably under your window; and a man with a bassoon and a monkey, who takes your pennies and pulls off his cap in acknowledgment;

and wandering minstrels, with guitar and voice; and a Highland bagpipe, squealing out a tangled skein of discord, together with a Highland maid, who dances a hornpipe; and Punch and Judy,—in a word, we have specimens of all manner of vagrancy that infests England. In these long days, and long and pleasant ones, the promenade is at its liveliest about nine o'clock, which is but just after sundown; and our little R——- finds it difficult to go to sleep amid so much music as comes to her ears from bassoon, bagpipe, organ, guitar, and now and then a military band. One feature of the place is the sick and infirm people, whom we see dragged along in bath-chairs, or dragging their own limbs languidly; or sitting on benches; or meeting in the streets, and making acquaintance on the strength of mutual maladies,—pale men leaning on their ruddy wives; cripples, three or four together in a ring, and planting their crutches in the centre. I don't remember whether I have ever mentioned among the notabilities of Southport the Town Crier,—a meek-looking old man, who sings out his messages in a most doleful tone, as if he took his title in a literal sense, and were really going to cry, or crying in the world's behalf; one other stroller, a foreigner with a dog, shaggy round the head and shoulders, and closely shaven behind. The poor little beast jumped through hoops, ran about on two legs of one side, danced on its hind legs, or on its fore paws, with its hind ones straight up in the air,—all the time keeping a watch on his master's eye, and evidently mindful of many a beating.

June 25th.—The war-steamer Niagara came up the Mersey a few days since, and day before yesterday Captain Hudson called at my office,—a somewhat meagre, elderly gentleman, of simple and hearty manners and address, having his purser, Mr. Eldredge, with him, who, I think, rather prides himself upon having a Napoleonic profile. The captain is an old acquaintance of Mrs. Blodgett, and has cone ashore principally with a view to calling on her; so, after we had left our cards for the Mayor, I showed these naval gentlemen the way to her house. Mrs. Blodgett and Miss W——— were prodigiously glad to see him and they all three began to talk of old times and old acquaintances; for when Mrs. Blodgett was a rich lady at Gibraltar, she used to have the whole navy-list at her table,—young midshipmen and lieutenants then perhaps, but old, gouty, paralytic commodores now, if still even partly alive. It was arranged that Mrs. Blodgett, with as many of the ladies of her family as she chose to bring, should accompany me on my official visit to the ship the next day; and yesterday we went accordingly, Mrs. Blodgett, Miss W———, and six or seven American captains' wives, their husbands following in another boat. I know too little of ships to describe one, or even to feel any great interest in the details of this or of any other ship; but the nautical people seemed to see much to admire. She lay in the Sloyne, in the midst of a broad basin of the Mersey, with a pleasant landscape of green England, now warm with summer sunshine, on either side, with churches and villa residences, and suburban and rural beauty. The officers of the ship are gentlemanly men, externally very well mannered, although not polished and refined to any considerable extent. At least, I have not found naval men so, in general; but still it is pleasant to see Americans who are not stirred by such motives as usually interest our countrymen,—no hope nor desire of growing rich, but planting their claims to respectability on other grounds, and therefore acquiring a certain nobleness, whether it be inherent in their nature or no. It always seems to me they look down upon civilians with quiet and not ill-natured scorn, which one has the choice of smiling or being provoked at. It is not a true life which they lead, but shallow and aimless; and unsatisfactory it must be to the better minds among them; nor do they appear to profit by what would seem the advantages presented to them in their world-wide, though not world-deep experience. They get to be very clannish too.

After seeing the ship, we landed, all of us, ladies and captain, and went to the gardens of the Rock Ferry Hotel, where J——- and I stayed behind the rest.

TO SCOTLAND.

June 28th.—On the 26th my wife, J——-, and I left Southport, taking the train for Preston, and as we had to stop an hour or two before starting for Carlisle, I walked up into the town. The street through which most of my walk lay was brick-built, lively, bustling, and not particularly noteworthy; but, turning a little way down another street, the town had a more ancient aspect. The day was intensely hot, the sun lying bright and broad as ever I remember it in an American city; so that I was glad to get back again to the shade and shelter of the station. The heat and dust, moreover, made our journey to Carlisle very uncomfortable. It was through very pretty, and sometimes picturesque scenery, being on the confines of the hill-country, which we could see on our left, dim and blue; and likewise we had a refreshing breath from the sea in passing along the verge of Morecambe Bay. We reached Carlisle at about five o'clock, and, after taking tea at the Bush Hotel, set forth to look at the town.

The notable objects were a castle and a cathedral; and we first found our way to the castle, which stands on elevated ground, on the side of the city towards Scotland. A broad, well-constructed path winds round the castle at the base of the wall, on the verge of a steep descent to the plain beneath, through which winds the river Eden. Along this path we walked quite round the castle, a circuit of perhaps half a mile,— pleasant, being shaded by the castle's height and by the foliage of trees. The walls have been so much rebuilt and restored that it is only here and there that we see an old buttress, or a few time-worn stones intermixed with the new facing with which the aged substance is overlaid. The material is red freestone, which seems to be very abundant in this part of the country. We found no entrance to the castle till the path had led us from the free and airy country into a very mean part of the town, where the wretched old houses thrust themselves between us and the castle wall, and then, passing through a narrow street, we walked up what appeared like a by-lane, and the portal of the castle was before us. There was a sentry-box just within the gate, and a sentinel was on guard, for

Carlisle Castle is a national fortress, and has usually been a depot for arms and ammunition. The sergeant, or corporal of the guard, sat reading within the gateway, and, on my request for admittance, he civilly appointed one of the soldiers to conduct us to the castle. As I recollect, the chief gateway of the castle, with the guard-room in the thickness of the wall, is situated some twenty yards behind the first entrance where we met the sentinel.

It was an intelligent young soldier who showed as round the castle, and very civil, as I always find soldiers to be. He had not anything particularly interesting to show, nor very much to say about it; and what he did say, so far as it referred to the history of the castle, was probably apocryphal.

The castle has an inner and outer ward on the descent of the hill; and included within the circuit of the exterior wall. Having been always occupied by soldiers, it has not been permitted to assume the picturesque aspect of a ruin, but the buildings of the interior have either been constantly repaired, as they required it, or have been taken down when past repair. We saw a small part of the tower where Mary, Queen of Scots, was confined on her first coming to England; these remains consist only of a portion of a winding stone staircase, at which we glanced through a window. The keep is very large and massive, and, no doubt, old in its inner substance. We ascended to the castle walls, and looked out over the river towards the Scottish hills, which are visible in the distance,—the Scottish border being not more than eight or nine miles off. Carlisle Castle has stood many sieges, and witnessed many battles under its walls. There are now, on its ramparts, only some half a dozen old-fashioned guns, which our soldier told us had gone quite out of use in these days. They were long iron twelve-pounders, with one or two carronades. The soldier was of an artillery regiment, and wore the Crimean medal. He said the garrison now here consists only of about twenty men, all of whom had served in the Crimea, like himself. They seem to lead a very dull and monotonous life, as indeed it must be, without object or much hope, or any great employment of the present, like prisoners, as indeed they are. Our guide showed us on the rampart a place where the soldiers had been accustomed to drop themselves down at night, hanging by their hands from the top of the wall, and alighting on their feet close beside the path on the outside. The height seemed at least that of an ordinary house, but the soldier said that nine times out of ten the fall might be ventured without harm; and he spoke from experience, having himself got out of the castle in this manner. The place is now boarded up, so as to make egress difficult or impossible.

The castle, after all, was not particularly worth seeing. The soldier's most romantic story was of a daughter of Lord Scroope, a former governor of the castle, when Mary of Scotland was confined here. She attempted to assist the Queen in escaping, but was shot dead in the gateway by the warder; and the soldier pointed out the very spot where the poor young lady fell and died;—all which would be very interesting were there a word of truth in the story. But we liked our guide for his intelligence, simplicity, and for the pleasure which he seemed to take, as an episode of his dull daily life, in talking to strangers. He observed that the castle walls were solid, and, indeed, there was breadth enough to drive a coach and four along the top; but the artillery of the Crimea would have shelled them into ruins in a very few hours. When we got back to the guard-house, he took us inside, and showed the dismal and comfortless rooms where soldiers are confined for drunkenness, and other offences against military laws, telling us that he himself had been confined there, and almost perished with cold. I should not much wonder if he were to get into durance again, through misuse of the fee which I put into his hand at parting.

The cathedral is at no great distance from the castle; and though the streets are mean and sordid in the vicinity, the close has the antique repose and shadowy peace, at once domestic and religious, which seem peculiar and universal in cathedral closes. The foundation of this cathedral church is very ancient, it having been the church portion of an old abbey, the refectory and other remains of which are still seen around the close. But the whole exterior of the building, except here and there a buttress, and one old patch of gray stones, seems to have been renewed within a very few years with red freestone; and, really, I think it is all the more beautiful for being new,—the ornamental parts being so sharply cut, and the stone, moreover, showing various shadings, which will disappear when it gets weatherworn. There is a very large and fine east window, of recent construction, wrought with delicate stone tracery. The door of the south transept stood open, though barred by an iron grate. We looked in, and saw a few monuments on the wall, but found nobody to give us admittance. The portal of this entrance is very lovely with wreaths of stone foliage and flowers round the arch, recently carved; yet not so recently but that the swallows have given their sanction to it, as if it were a thousand years old, and have built their nests in the deeply carved recesses. While we were looking, a little bird flew into the small opening between two of these petrified flowers, behind which was his nest, quite out of sight. After some attempts to find the verger, we went back to the hotel. . . .

In the morning my wife and J—— went back to see the interior of the cathedral, while I strayed at large about the town, again passing round the castle site, and thence round the city, where I found some inconsiderable portions of the wall which once girt it about. It was market-day in Carlisle, and the principal streets were much thronged with human life and business on that account; and in as busy a street as any stands a marble statue, in robes of antique state, fitter for a niche in Westminster Abbey than for the thronged street of a town. It is a statue of the Earl of Lonsdale, Lord Lieutenant of Cumberland, who died about twenty years ago.

[Here follows the record of the visits to the "Haunts of Burns," already published in Our Old Home.—ED.]

GLASGOW.

July 1st.—Immediately after our arrival yesterday, we went out and inquired our way to the cathedral, which we reached through a good deal of Scotch dirt, and a rabble of Scotch people of all sexes and ages. The women of Scotland have a faculty of looking exceedingly ugly as they grow old. The cathedral I have already noticed in the record of my former visit to Scotland. I did it no justice then, nor shall do it any better justice now; but it is a fine old church, although it makes a colder and severer impression than most of the Gothic architecture which I have elsewhere seen. I do not know why this should be so; for portions of it are wonderfully rich, and everywhere there are arches opening beyond arches, and clustered pillars and groined roofs, and vistas, lengthening along the aisles. The person who shows it is an elderly man of jolly aspect and demeanor; he is enthusiastic about the edifice, and makes it the thought and object of his life; and being such a merry sort of man, always saying something mirthfully, and yet, in all his thoughts, words, and actions, having reference to this solemn cathedral, he has the effect of one of the corbels or gargoyles,—those ludicrous, strange sculptures which the Gothic architects appended to their arches.

The upper portion of the minster, though very stately and beautiful, is not nearly so extraordinary as the crypts. Here the intricacy of the arches, and the profound system on which they are arranged, is inconceivable, even when you see them,—a whole company of arches uniting in one keystone; arches uniting to form a glorious canopy over the shrine or tomb of a prelate; arches opening through and beyond one another, whichever way you look,— all amidst a shadowy gloom, yet not one detail wrought out the less beautifully and delicately because it could scarcely be seen. The wreaths of flowers that festoon one of the arches are cut in such relief that they do but just adhere to the stone on which they grow. The pillars are massive, and the arches very low, the effect being a twilight, which at first leads the spectator to imagine himself underground; but by and by I saw that the sunshine came in through the narrow windows, though it scarcely looked like sunshine then. For many years these crypts were used as burial-ground, and earth was brought in, for the purpose of making graves; so that the noble columns were half buried, and the beauty of the architecture quite lost and forgotten. Now the dead men's bones and the earth that covered them have all been removed, leaving the original pavement of the crypt, or a new one in its stead, with only the old relics of saints, martyrs, and heroes underneath, where they have lain so long that they have become a part of the spot. . . . I was quite chilled through, and the old verger regretted that we had not come during the late hot weather, when the everlasting damp and chill of the spot would have made us entirely comfortable. These crypts originated in the necessity of keeping the floor of the upper cathedral on one level, the edifice being built on a declivity, and the height of the crypt being measured by the descent of the site.

After writing the above, we walked out and saw something of the newer portion of Glasgow; and, really, I am inclined to think it the stateliest of cities. The Exchange and other public buildings, and the shops in Buchanan Street, are very magnificent; the latter, especially, excelling those of London. There is, however, a pervading sternness and grimness resulting from the dark gray granite, which is the universal building-material both of the old and new edifices. Later in the forenoon we again walked out, and went along Argyle Street, and through the Trongate and the Salt-Market. The two latter were formerly the principal business streets, and together with High Street, the abode of the rich merchants and other great people of the town. High Street, and, still more, the Salt-Market, now swarm with the lower orders to a degree which I never witnessed elsewhere; so that it is difficult to make one's way among the sullen and unclean crowd, and not at all pleasant to breathe in the noisomeness of the atmosphere. The children seem to have been unwashed from birth. Some of the gray houses appear to have once been stately and handsome, and have their high gable ends notched at the edges, like a flight of stairs. We saw the Tron steeple, and the statue of King William III., and searched for the Old Tolbooth. . . . Wandering up the High Street, we turned once more into the quadrangle of the University, and mounted a broad stone staircase which ascends square, and with right-angular turns on one corner, on the outside of the edifices. It is very striking in appearance, being ornamented with a balustrade, on which are large globes of stone, and a great lion and unicorn curiously sculptured on the opposite side. While we waited here, staring about us, a man approached, and offered to show us the interior. He seemed to be in charge of the College buildings. We accepted his offer, and were led first up this stone staircase, and into a large and stately hall, panelled high towards the ceiling with dark oak, and adorned with elaborately carved cornices, and other wood-work. There was a long reading-table towards one end of the hall, on which were laid pamphlets and periodicals; and a venerable old gentleman, with white head and bowed shoulders, sat there reading a newspaper. This was the Principal of the University, and as he looked towards us graciously, yet as if expecting some explanation of our entrance, I approached and apologized for intruding on the plea of our being strangers and anxious to see the College. He made a courteous response, though in exceedingly decayed and broken accents, being now eighty-six years old, and gave us free leave to inspect everything that was to be seen. This hall was erected two years after the Restoration of Charles II., and has been the scene, doubtless, of many ceremonials and high banquetings since that period; and, among other illustrious personages, Queen Victoria has honored it with her presence. Thence we went into several recitation or lecture rooms in various parts of the buildings; but they were all of an extreme plainness, very unlike the rich old Gothic libraries and chapels and halls which we saw in Oxford. Indeed, the contrast between this Scotch severity and that noble luxuriance, and antique majesty, and rich and sweet repose of Oxford, is very remarkable, both within the edifices and without. But we saw one or two curious things,—for instance, a chair of mahogany, elaborately carved with the arms of Scotland and other devices, and having a piece of the kingly stone of Scone inlaid in its seat. This chair is used by the Principal on certain high occasions, and we ourselves, of course, sat down in it. Our guide assigned to it a date preposterously earlier than could have been the true one, judging either by the character of the carving or by the fact that mahogany has not been known or used much more than a century and a half.

Afterwards he led us into the Divinity Hall, where, he said, there were some old portraits of historic people, and among them an original picture of Mary, Queen of Scots. There was, indeed, a row of old portraits at each end of the apartment,—for instance, Zachariah Boyd, who wrote the rhyming version of the Bible, which is still kept, safe from any critical eye, in the library of the University to which he presented this, besides other more valuable benefactions,—for which they have placed his bust in a niche in the principal quadrangle; also, John Knox makes one of the row of portraits; and a dozen or two more of Scotch worthies, all very dark and dingy. As to the picture of Mary of Scotland, it proved to be not hers at all, but a picture of Queen Mary, the consort of William III., whose portrait, together with that of her sister, Queen Anne, hangs in the same row. We told our guide this, but he seemed unwilling to accept it as a fact. There is a museum belonging to the University; but this, for some reason or other, could not be shown to us just at this time, and there was little else to show. We just looked at the gardens, but, though of large extent, they are so meagre and bare—so unlike that lovely shade of the Oxford gardens—that we did not care to make further acquaintance with them.

Then we went back to our hotel, and if there were not already more than enough of description, both past and to come, I should describe George's Square, on one side of which the hotel is situated. A tall column rises in the grassy centre of it, lifting far into the upper air a fine statue of Sir Walter Scott, which we saw to great advantage last night, relieved against the sunset sky; and there are statues of Sir John Moore, a native of Glasgow, and of James Watt, at corners of the square. Glasgow is certainly a noble city.

After lunch we embarked on board the steamer, and came up the Clyde. Ben Lomond, and other Highland hills, soon appeared on the horizon; we passed Douglas Castle on a point of land projecting into the river; and, passing under the precipitous height of Dumbarton Castle, which we had long before seen, came to our voyage's end at this village, where we have put up at the Elephant Hotel.

July 2d.—After tea, not far from seven o'clock, it being a beautiful decline of day, we set out to walk to

DUMBARTON CASTLE,

which stands apart from the town, and is said to have been once surrounded by the waters of the Clyde. The rocky height on which the castle stands is a very striking object, bulging up out of the Clyde, with abrupt decision, to the elevation of five hundred feet. The summit is cloven in twain, the cleft reaching nearly to the bottom on the side towards the river, but not coming down so deeply on the landward side. It is precipitous all around; and wherever the steepness admits, or does not make assault impossible, there are gray ramparts round the hill, with cannon threatening the lower world. Our path led its beneath one of these precipices several hundred feet sheer down, and with an ivied fragment of ruined wall at the top. A soldier who sat by the wayside told us that this was called the "Lover's Leap," because a young girl, in some love-exigency, had once jumped down from it, and came safely to the bottom. We reached the castle gate, which is near the shore of the Clyde, and there found another artillery soldier, who guided us through the fortress. He said that there were now but about a dozen soldiers stationed in the castle, and no officer.

The lowest battery looks towards the river, and consists of a few twelve-pound cannon; but probably the chief danger of attack was from the land, and the chief pains have been taken to render the castle defensible in that quarter. There are flights of stone stairs ascending up through the natural avenue, in the cleft of the double-summited rock; and about midway there is an arched doorway, beneath which there used to be a portcullis,—so that if an enemy had won the lower part of the fortress, the upper portion was still inaccessible. Where the cleft of the rock widens into a gorge, there are several buildings, old, but not appertaining to the ancient castle, which has almost entirely disappeared. We ascended both summits, and, reaching the loftiest point on the right, stood upon the foundation of a tower that dates back to the fifth century, whence we had a glorious prospect of Highlands and Lowlands; the chief object being Ben Lomond, with its great dome, among a hundred other blue and misty hills, with the sun going down over them; and, in another direction, the Clyde, winding far downward through the plain, with the headland of Dumbeck close at hand, and Douglas Castle at no great distance. On the ramparts beneath us the soldier pointed out the spot where Wallace scaled the wall, climbing an apparently inaccessible precipice, and taking the castle. The principal parts of the ancient castle appear to have been on the other and lower summit of the hill, and thither we now went, and traced the outline of its wall, although none of it is now remaining. Here is the magazine, still containing some powder, and here is a battery of eighteen-pound guns, with pyramids of balls, all in readiness against an assault; which, however, hardly any turn of human affairs can hereafter bring about. The appearance of a fortress is kept up merely for ceremony's sake; and these cannon have grown antiquated. Moreover, as the soldier told us, they are seldom or never fired, even for purposes of rejoicing or salute, because their thunder produces the singular effect of depriving the garrison of water. There is a large tank, and the concussion causes the rifts of the stone to open, and thus lets the water out. Above this battery, and elsewhere about the fortress, there are warders' turrets of stone, resembling great pepper-boxes. When Dr. Johnson visited the castle, he introduced his bulky person into one of these narrow receptacles, and found it difficult to get out again. A gentleman who accompanied him was just stepping forward to offer his assistance, but Boswell whispered him to take no notice, lest Johnson should be offended; so they left him to get out as he could. He did finally extricate himself, else we might have seen his skeleton in the turret. Boswell does not tell this story, which seems to have been handed down by local tradition.

The less abrupt declivities of the rock are covered with grass, and afford food for a few sheep, who scamper about the heights, and seem to have attained the dexterity of goats in clambering. I never knew a purer air than this seems to be, nor a lovelier golden sunset.

Descending into the gorge again, we went into the armory, which is in one of the buildings occupying the space between the two hill-tops. It formerly contained a large collection of arms; but these have been removed to the Tower of London, and there are now only some tattered banners, of which I do not know the history, and some festoons of pistols, and grenades, shells, and grape and canister shot, kept merely as curiosities; and, far more interesting than the above, a few battle-axes, daggers, and spear-heads from the field of Bannockburn; and, more interesting still, the sword of William Wallace. It is a formidable-looking weapon, made for being swayed with both hands, and, with its hilt on the floor, reached about to my chin; but the young girl who showed us the armory said that about nine inches had been broken off the point. The blade was not massive, but somewhat thin, compared with its great length; and I found that I could blandish it, using both hands, with perfect ease. It is two-edged, without any gaps, and is quite brown and lustreless with old rust, from point to hilt.

These were all the memorables of our visit to Dumbarton Castle, which is a most interesting spot, and connected with a long series of historical events. It was first besieged by the Danes, and had a prominent share in all the warfare of Scotland, so long as the old warlike times and manners lasted. Our soldier was very intelligent and courteous, but, as usual with these guides, was somewhat apocryphal in his narrative; telling us that Mary, Queen of Scots, was confined here before being taken to England, and that the cells in which she then lived are still extant, under one of the ramparts. The fact is, she was brought here when a child of six years old, before going to France, and doubtless scrambled up and down these heights as freely and merrily as the sheep we saw.

We now returned to our hotel, a very nice one, and found the street of Dumbarton all alive in the summer evening with the sports of children and the gossip of grown people. There was almost no night, for at twelve o'clock there was still a golden daylight, and Yesterday, before it died, must have met the Morrow.

In the lower part of the fortress there is a large sun-dial of stone, which was made by a French officer imprisoned here during the Peninsular war. It still numbers faithfully the hours that are sunny, and it is a lasting memorial of him, in the stronghold of his enemies.

INVERANNAN.

Evening.—After breakfast at Dumbarton, I went out to look at the town, which is of considerable size, and possesses both commerce and manufactures. There was a screw-steamship at the pier, and many sailor-looking people were seen about the streets. There are very few old houses, though still the town retains an air of antiquity which one does not well see how to account for, when everywhere there is a modern front, and all the characteristics of a street built to-day. Turning from the main thoroughfare I crossed a bridge over the Clyde, and gained from it the best view of the cloven crag of Dumbarton Castle that I had yet found. The two summits are wider apart, more fully relieved from each other, than when seen from other points; and the highest ascends into a perfect pyramid, the lower one being obtusely rounded. There seem to be iron-works, or some kind of manufactory, on the farther side of the bridge; and I noticed a quaint, chateau-like mansion, with hanging turrets standing apart from the street, probably built by some person enriched by business.

We left Dumbarton at noon, taking the rail to Balloch, and the steamer to the head of Loch Lomond.

Wild mountain scenery is not very good to describe, nor do I think any distinct impressions are ever conveyed by such attempts; so I mean to be brief in what I saw about this part of our tour, especially as I suspect that I have said whatever I knew how to say in the record of my former visit to the Highlands. As for Loch Lomond, it lies amidst very striking scenery, being poured in among the gorges of steep and lofty mountains, which nowhere stand aside to give it room, but, on the contrary, do their best to shut it in. It is everywhere narrow, compared with its length of thirty miles; but it is the beauty of a lake to be of no greater width than to allow of the scenery of one of its shores being perfectly enjoyed from the other. The scenery of the Highlands, so far as I have seen it, cannot properly be called rich, but stern and impressive, with very hard outlines, which are unsoftened, mostly, by any foliage, though at this season they are green to their summits. They have hardly flesh enough to cover their bones,—hardly earth enough to lie over their rocky substance,—as may be seen by the minute variety,—the notched and jagged appearance of the profile of their sides and tops; this being caused by the scarcely covered rocks wherewith these great hills are heaped together.

Our little steamer stopped at half a dozen places on its voyage up the lake, most of them being stations where hotels have been established. Morally, the Highlands must have been more completely sophisticated by the invention of railways and steamboats than almost any other part of the world; but physically it can have wrought no great change. These mountains, in their general aspect, must be very much the same as they were thousands of years ago; for their sides never were capable of cultivation, nor even with such a soil and so bleak an atmosphere could they have been much more richly wooded than we see them now. They seem to me to be among the unchangeable things of nature, like the sea and sky; but there is no saying what use human ingenuity may hereafter put them to. At all events, I have no doubt in the world that they will go out of fashion in due time; for the taste for mountains and wild scenery is, with most people, an acquired taste, and it was easy to see to-day that nine people in ten care nothing about them. One group of gentlemen and ladies—at least, men and women—spent the whole time in listening to a trial for murder, which was read aloud by one of their number from a newspaper. I rather imagine that a taste for trim gardens is the most natural and universal taste as regards landscape. But perhaps it is necessary for the health of the human mind and heart that there should be a possibility of taking refuge in what is wild and uncontaminated by any meddling of man's hand, and so it has been ordained that science shall never alter the aspect of the sky, whether stern, angry, or beneficent,— nor of the awful sea, either in calm or tempest,—nor of these rude Highlands. But they will go out of general fashion, as I have said, and perhaps the next fashionable taste will be for cloud land,—that is, looking skyward, and observing the wonderful variety of scenery, that now constantly passes unnoticed, among the clouds.

At the head of the lake, we found that there was only a horse-cart to convey our luggage to the hotel at Inverannan, and that we ourselves must walk, the distance being two miles. It had sprinkled occasionally during our voyage, but was now sunshiny, and not excessively warm; so we set forth contentedly enough, and had an agreeable walk along an almost perfectly level road; for it is one of the beauties of these hills, that they descend abruptly down, instead of undulating away forever. There were lofty heights on each side of us, but not so lofty as to have won a distinctive name; and adown their sides we could see the rocky pathways of cascades, which, at this season, are either quite dry, or mere trickles of a rill. The hills and valleys abound in streams, sparkling through pebbly beds, and forming here and there a dark pool; and they would be populous with trout if all England, with one fell purpose, did not come hither to fish them. A fisherman must find it difficult to gratify his propensities in these days; for even the lakes and streams in Norway are now preserved. J——, by the way, threatens ominously to be a fisherman. He rode the latter portion of the way to the hotel on the luggage-cart; and when we arrived, we found that he had already gone off to catch fish, or to attempt it (for there is as much chance of his catching a whale as a trout), in a mountain stream near the house. I went in search of him, but without success, and was somewhat startled at the depth and blackness of some of the pools into which the stream settled itself and slept. Finally, he came in while we were at dinner. We afterwards walked out with him, to let him play at fishing again, and discovered on the bank of the stream a wonderful oak, with as many as a dozen holes springing either from close to the ground or within a foot or two of it, and looking like twelve separate trees, at least, instead of one.

INVERSNAID.

July 3d.—Last night seemed to close in clear, and even at midnight it was still light enough to read; but this morning rose on us misty and chill, with spattering showers of rain. Clouds momentarily settled and shifted on the hill-tops, shutting us in even more completely than these steep and rugged green walls would be sure to do, even in the clearest weather. Often these clouds came down and enveloped us in a drizzle, or rather a shower, of such minute drops that they had not weight enough to fall. This, I suppose, was a genuine Scotch mist; and as such it is well enough to have experienced it, though I would willingly never see it again. Such being the state of the weather, my wife did not go out at all, but I strolled about the premises, in the intervals of rain-drops, gazing up at the hillsides, and recognizing that there is a vast variety of shape, of light and shadow, and incidental circumstance, even in what looks so monotonous at first as the green slope of a hill. The little rills that come down from the summits were rather more distinguishable than yesterday, having been refreshed by the night's rain; but still they were very much out of proportion with the wide pathways of bare rock adown which they ran. These little rivulets, no doubt, often lead through the wildest scenery that is to be found in the Highlands, or anywhere else, and to the formation and wildness of which they have greatly contributed by sawing away for countless ages, and thus deepening the ravines.

I suspect the American clouds are more picturesque than those of Great Britain, whatever our mountains may be; at least, I remember the Berkshire hills looking grander, under the influence of mist and cloud, than the Highlands did to-day. Our clouds seem to be denser and heavier, and more decided, and form greater contrasts of light and shade. I have remarked in England that the cloudy firmament, even on a day of settled rain, always appears thinner than those I had been accustomed to at home, so as to deceive me with constant expectations of better weather. It has been the same to-day.

Whenever I looked upward, I thought it might be going to clear up; but, instead of that, it began to rain more in earnest after midday, and at half past two we left Inverannan in a smart shower. At the head of the lake, we took the steamer, with the rain pouring more heavily than ever, and landed at Inversnaid under the same dismal auspices. We left a very good hotel behind us, and have come to another that seems also good. We are more picturesquely situated at this spot than at Inverannan, our hotel being within a short distance of the lake shore, with a glen just across the water, which will doubtless be worth looking at when the mist permits us to see it. A good many tourists were standing about the door when we arrived, and looked at us with the curiosity of idle and weather-bound people. The lake is here narrow, but a hundred fathoms deep; so that a great part of the height of the mountains which beset it round is hidden beneath its surface.

July 4th.—This morning opened still misty, but with a more hopeful promise than yesterday, and when I went out, after breakfast, there were gleams of sunshine here and there on the hillsides, falling, one did not exactly see how, through the volumes of cloud. Close beside the hotel of Inversnaid is the waterfall; all night, my room being on that side of the house, I had heard its voice, and now I ascended beside it to a point where it is crossed by a wooden bridge. There is thence a view, upward and downward, of the most striking descents of the river, as I believe they call it, though it is but a mountain-stream, which tumbles down an irregular and broken staircase in its headlong haste to reach the lake. It is very picturesque, however, with its ribbons of white foam over the precipitous steps, and its deep black pools, overhung by black rocks, which reverberate the rumble of the falling water. J—— and I ascended a little distance along the cascade, and then turned aside; he going up the hill, and I taking a path along its side which gave me a view across the lake. I rather think this particular stretch of Loch Lomond, in front of Inversnaid, is the most beautiful lake and mountain view that I have ever seen. It is so shut in that you can see nothing beyond, nor would suspect anything more to exist than this watery vale among the hills; except that, directly opposite, there is the beautiful glen of Inverngl ass, which winds away among the feet of Ben Crook, Ben Ein, Ben Vain, and Ben Voirlich, standing mist-inwreathed together. The mists, this morning, had a very soft and beautiful effect, and made the mountains tenderer than I have hitherto felt them to be; and they lingered about their heads like morning-dreams, flitting and retiring, and letting the sunshine in, and snatching it away again. My wife came up, and we enjoyed it together, till the steamer came smoking its pipe along the loch, stopped to land some passengers, and steamed away again. While we stood there, a Highlander passed by us, with a very dark tartan, and bare shanks, most enormously calved. I presume he wears the dress for the sole purpose of displaying those stalwart legs; for he proves to be no genuine Gael, but a manufacturer, who has a shooting-box, or a share in one, on the hill above the hotel.

We now engaged a boat, and were rowed to Rob Roy's cave, which is perhaps half a mile distant up the lake. The shores look much more striking from a rowboat, creeping along near the margin, than from a steamer in the middle of the loch; and the ridge, beneath which Rob's cave lies, is precipitous with gray rocks, and clothed, too, with thick foliage. Over the cave itself there is a huge ledge of rock, from which immense fragments have tumbled down, ages and ages ago, and fallen together in such a way as to leave a large irregular crevice in Rob Roy's cave. We scrambled up to its mouth by some natural stairs, and scrambled down into its depths by the aid of a ladder. I suppose I have already described this hole in the record of my former visit. Certainly, Rob Roy, and Robert Bruce, who is said to have inhabited it before him, were not to be envied their accommodations; yet these were not so very intolerable when compared with a Highland cabin, or with cottages such as Burns lived in.

J—— had chosen to remain to fish. On our return from the cave, we found that he had caught nothing; but just as we stepped into the boat, a fish drew his float far under water, and J—— tugging at one end of the line, and the fish at the other, the latter escaped, with the hook in his month. J—— avers that he saw the fish, and gives its measurement as about eighteen inches; but the fishes that escape us are always of tremendous size. The boatman thought, however, that it might have been a pike.

THE TROSACHS' HOTEL.—ARDCHEANOCHROCHAN.

July 5th.—Not being able to get a post-chaise, we took places in the omnibus for the bead of Loch Katrine. Going up to pay a parting visit to the waterfall before starting, I met with Miss C———, as she lately was, who is now on her wedding tour as Mrs. B———. She was painting the falls in oil, with good prospect of a successful picture. She came down to the hotel to see my wife, and soon afterwards J——— and I set out to ascend the steep hill that comes down upon the lake of Inversnaid, leaving the omnibus to follow at leisure. The Highlander who took us to Rob Roy's cave had foreboded rain, from the way in which the white clouds hung about the mountain-tops; nor was his augury at fault, for just at three o'clock, the time he foretold, there were a few rain-drops, and a more defined shower during the afternoon, while we were on Loch Katrine. The few drops, however, did not disturb us; and, reaching the top of the hill, J——— and I turned aside to examine the old stone fortress which was erected in this mountain pass to bridle the Highlanders after the rebellion of 1745. It stands in a very desolate and dismal situation, at the foot of long bare slopes, on mossy ground, in the midst of a disheartening loneliness, only picturesque because it is so exceedingly ungenial and unlovely. The chief interest of this spot in the fact that Wolfe, in his earlier military career, was stationed here. The fortress was a very plain structure, built of rough stones, in the form of a parallelogram, one side of which I paced, and found it between thirty and forty of my paces long. The two ends have fallen down; the two sides that remain are about twenty feet high, and have little port-holes for defence, but no openings of the size of windows. The roof is gone, and the interior space overgrown with grass. Two little girls were at play in one corner, and, going round to the rear of the ruin, I saw that a small Highland cabin had been built against the wall. A dog sat in the doorway, and gave notice of my approach, and some hens kept up their peculiarly domestic converse about the door.

We kept on our way, often looking back towards Loch Lomond, and wondering at the grandeur which Ben Vain and Ben Voirlich, and the rest of the Ben fraternity, had suddenly put on. The mists which had hung about them all day had now descended lower, and lay among the depths and gorges of the hills, where also the sun shone softly down among them, and filled those deep mountain laps, as it were, with a dimmer sunshine. Ben Vain, too, and his brethren, had a veil of mist all about them, which seemed to render them really transparent; and they had unaccountably grown higher, vastly higher, than when we viewed them from the shore of the lake. It was as if we were looking at them through the medium of a poet's imagination. All along the road, since we left Inversnaid, there had been the stream, which there formed the waterfall, and which here was brawling down little declivities, and sleeping in black pools, which we disturbed by flinging stones into them from the roadside. We passed a drunken old gentleman, who civilly bade me "good day"; and a man and woman at work in a field, the former of whom shouted to inquire the hour; and we had come in sight of little Loch Arklet before the omnibus came up with us. It was about five o'clock when we reached the head of and went on board the steamer Rob Roy; and, setting forth on our voyage, a Highland piper made music for us the better part of the way.

We did not see Loch Katrine, perhaps, under its best presentment; for the surface was roughened with a little wind, and darkened even to inky blackness by the clouds that overhung it. The hill-tops, too, wore a very dark frown. A lake of this size cannot be terrific, and is therefore seen to best advantage when it is beautiful. The scenery of its shores is not altogether so rich and lovely as I had preimagined; not equal, indeed, to the best parts of Loch Lomond,—the hills being lower and of a more ridgy shape, and exceedingly bare, at least towards the lower end. But they turn the lake aside with headland after headland, and shut it in closely, and open one vista after another, so that the eye is never weary, and, least of all, as we approach the end. The length of the loch is ten miles, and at its termination it meets the pass of the Trosachs, between Ben An and Ben Venue, which are the rudest and shaggiest of hills. The steamer passes Ellen's Isle, but to the right, which is the side opposite to that on which Fitz-James must be supposed to have approached it. It is a very small island, situated where the loch narrows, and is perhaps less than a quarter of a mile distant from either shore. It looks like a lump of rock, with just soil enough to support a crowd of dwarf oaks, birches, and firs, which do not grow so high as to be shadowy trees. Our voyage being over, we landed, and found two omnibuses, one of which took us through the famous pass of the Trosachs, a distance of a mile and a quarter, to a hotel, erected in castellated guise by Lord Willoughby d'Eresby. We were put into a parlor within one of the round towers, panelled all round, and with four narrow windows, opening through deep embrasures. No play-castle was ever more like the reality, and it is a very good hotel, like all that we have had experience of in the Highlands. After tea we walked out, and visited a little kirk that stands near the shore of Loch Achray, at a good point of view for seeing the hills round about.

This morning opened cloudily; but after breakfast I set out alone, and walked through the pass of the Trosachs, and thence by a path along the right shore of the lake. It is a very picturesque and beautiful path, following the windings of the lake,—now along the beach, now over an impending bank, until it comes opposite to Ellen's Isle, which on this side looks more worthy to be the island of the poem than as we first saw it. Its shore is craggy and precipitous, but there was a point where it seemed possible to land, nor was it too much to fancy that there might be a rustic habitation among the shrubbery of this rugged spot. It is foolish to look into these matters too strictly. Scott evidently used as much freedom with his natural scenery as he did with his historic incidents; and he could have made nothing of either one or the other if he had been more scrupulous in his arrangement and adornment of them. In his description of the Trosachs, he has produced something very beautiful, and as true as possible, though certainly its beauty has a little of the scene-painter's gloss on it. Nature is better, no doubt, but Nature cannot be exactly reproduced on canvas or in print; and the artist's only resource is to substitute something that may stand instead of and suggest the truth.

The path still kept onward, after passing Ellen's Isle, and I followed it, finding it wilder, more shadowy with overhanging foliage of trees, old and young,—more like a mountain-path in Berkshire or New Hampshire, yet still with an Old World restraint and cultivation about it,—the farther I went. At last I came upon some bars, and though the track was still seen beyond, I took this as a hint to stop, especially as I was now two or three miles from the hotel, and it just then began to rain. My umbrella was a poor one at best, and had been tattered and turned inside out, a day or two ago, by a gust on Loch Lomond; but I spread it to the shower, and, furthermore, took shelter under the thickest umbrage I could find. The rain came straight down, and bubbled in the loch; the little rills gathered force, and plashed merrily over the stones; the leaves of the trees condensed the shower into large drops, and shed them down upon me where I stood. Still I was comfortable enough in a thick Skye Tweed, and waited patiently till the rain abated; then took my way homeward, and admired the pass of the Trosachs more than when I first traversed it. If it has a fault, it is one that few scenes in Great Britain share with it,—that is, the trees and shrubbery, with which the precipices are shagged, conceal them a little too much. A crag, streaked with black and white, here and there shows its head aloft, or its whole height from base to summit, and suggests that more of such sublimity is bidden than revealed. I think, however, that it is this unusual shagginess which made the scene a favorite with Scott, and with the people on this side of the ocean generally. There are many scenes as good in America, needing only the poet.

July 6th.—We dined yesterday at the table d'hote, at the suggestion of the butler, in order to give less trouble to the servants of the hotel, and afford them an opportunity to go to kirk. The dining-room is in accordance with the rest of the architecture and fittings up of the house, and is a very good reproduction of an old baronial hall, with high panellings and a roof of dark, polished wood. There were about twenty guests at table; and if they and the waiters had been dressed in mediaeval costume, we might have imagined ourselves banqueting in the Middle Ages.

After dinner we all took a walk through the Trosachs' pass again, and by the right-hand path along the lake as far as Ellen's Isle. It was very pleasant, there being gleams of calm evening sunshine gilding the mountain-sides, and putting a golden crown occasionally on the Tread of Ben Venue. It is wonderful how many aspects a mountain has,—how many mountains there are in every single mountain!—how they vary too, in apparent attitude and bulk. When we reached the lake its surface was almost unruffled, except by now and then the narrow pathway of a breeze, as if the wing of an unseen spirit had just grazed it in flitting across. The scene was very beautiful, and, on the whole, I do not know that Walter Scott has overcharged his description, although he has symbolized the reality by types and images which it might not precisely suggest to other minds. We were reluctant to quit the spot, and cherish still a hope of seeing it again, though the hope does not seem very likely to be gratified.

This was a lowering and sullen morning, but soon after breakfast I took a walk in the opposite direction to Loch Katrine, and reached the Brig of Turk, a little beyond which is the new Trosachs' Hotel, and the little rude village of Duncraggan, consisting of a few hovels of stone, at the foot of a bleak and dreary hill. To the left, stretching up between this and other hills, is the valley of Glenfinlas,—a very awful region in Scott's poetry and in Highland tradition, as the haunt of spirits and enchantments. It presented a very desolate prospect. The walk back to the Trosachs showed me Ben Venue and Ben An under new aspects,—the bare summit of the latter rising in a perfect pyramid, whereas from other points of view it looks like quite a different mountain. Sometimes a gleam of sunshine came out upon the rugged side of Ben Venue, but his prevailing mood, like that of the rest of the landscape, was stern and gloomy. I wish I could give an idea of the variety of surface upon one of these hillsides,—so bulging out and hollowed in, so bare where the rock breaks through, so shaggy in other places with heath, and then, perhaps, a thick umbrage of birch, oak, and ash ascending from the base high upward. When I think I have described them, I remember quite a different aspect, and find it equally true, and yet lacking something to make it the whole or an adequate truth.

J—— had gone with me part of the way, but stopped to fish with a pin-hook in Loch Achray, which bordered along our path. When I returned, I found him much elated at having caught a fish, which, however, had got away, carrying his pin-hook along with it. Then he had amused himself with taking some lizards by the tail, and had collected several in a small hollow of the rocks. We now walked home together, and at half past three we took our seats in a genuine old-fashioned stage-coach, of which there are few specimens now to be met with. The coachman was smartly dressed in the Queen's scarlet, and was a very pleasant and affable personage, conducting himself towards the passengers with courteous authority. Inside we were four, including J——, but on the top there were at least a dozen, and I would willingly have been there too, but had taken an inside seat, under apprehension of rain, and was not allowed to change it. Our drive was not marked by much describable incident. On changing horses at Callender, we alighted, and saw Ben Ledi behind us, making a picturesque background to the little town, which seems to be the meeting-point of the Highlands and Lowlands. We again changed horses at Doune, an old town, which would doubtless have been well worth seeing, had time permitted. Thence we kept on till the coach drew up at a spacious hotel, where we alighted, fancying that we had reached Stirling, which was to have been our journey's end; but, after fairly establishing ourselves, we found that it was the

BRIG OF ALLAN.

The place is three miles short of Stirling. Nevertheless, we did not much regret the mistake, finding that the Brig of Allan is the principal Spa of Scotland, and a very pleasant spot, to all outward appearance. After tea we walked out, both up and down the village street, and across the bridge, and up a gentle eminence beyond it, whence we had a fine view of a glorious plain, out of which rose several insulated headlands. One of these was the height on which stands Stirling Castle, and which reclines on the plain like a hound or a lion or a sphinx, holding the castle on the highest part, where its head should be. A mile or two distant from this picturesque hill rises another, still more striking, called the Abbey Craig, on which is a ruin, and where is to be built the monument to William Wallace. I cannot conceive a nobler or more fitting pedestal. The sullenness of the day had vanished, the air was cool but invigorating, and the cloud scenery was as fine as that below it. . . . Though it was nearly ten o'clock, the boys of the village were in full shout and play, for these long and late summer evenings keep the children out of bed interminably.

STIRLING.

July 7th.—We bestirred ourselves early this morning, ... and took the rail for Stirling before eight. It is but a few minutes' ride, so that doubtless we were earlier on the field than if we had slept at Stirling. After our arrival our first call was at the post-office, where I found a large package containing letters from America, but none from U——. We then went to a bookseller's shop, and bought some views of Stirling and the neighborhood; and it is surprising what a quantity and variety of engravings there are of every noted place that we have visited. You seldom find two sets alike. It is rather nauseating to find that what you came to see has already been looked at in all its lights, over and over again, with thousand-fold repetition; and, beyond question, its depictment in words has been attempted still oftener than with the pencil. It will be worth while to go back to America, were it only for the chance of finding a still virgin scene.

We climbed the steep slope of the Castle Hill, sometimes passing an antique-looking house, with a high, notched gable, perhaps with an ornamented front, until we came to the sculptures and battlemented wall, with an archway, that stands just below the castle. . . . A shabby-looking man now accosted us, and could hardly be shaken off. I have met with several such boors in my experience of sight-seeing. He kept along with us, in spite of all hints to the contrary, and insisted on pointing out objects of interest. He showed us a house in Broad Street, below the castle and cathedral, which he said had once been inhabited by Henry Darnley, Queen Mary's husband. There was little or nothing peculiar in its appearance; a large, gray, gabled house standing lengthwise to the street, with three windows in the roof, and connected with other houses on each side. Almost directly across the street, he pointed to an archway, through the side of a house, and, peeping through it, we found a soldier on guard in a court-yard, the sides of which were occupied by an old mansion of the Argyle family, having towers at the corners, with conical tops, like those reproduced in the hotel at the Trosachs. It is now occupied as a military hospital. Shaking off our self-inflicted guide, we now made our way to the castle parade, and to the gateway, where a soldier with a tremendously red nose and two medals at once took charge of us.

Beyond all doubt, I have written quite as good a description of the castle and Carse of Stirling in a former portion of my journal as I can now write. We passed through the outer rampart of Queen Anne; through the old round gate-tower of an earlier day, and beneath the vacant arch where the portcullis used to fall, thus reaching the inner region, where stands the old palace on one side, and the old Parliament House on the other. The former looks aged, ragged, and rusty, but makes a good appearance enough pictorially, being adorned all round about with statues, which may have been white marble once, but are as gray as weather-beaten granite now, and look down from between the windows above the basement story. A photograph would give the idea of very rich antiquity, but as it really stands, looking on a gravelled court-yard, and with "CANTEEN" painted on one of its doors, the spectator does not find it very impressive. The great hall of this palace is now partitioned off into two or three rooms, and the whole edifice is arranged to serve as barracks. Of course, no trace of ancient magnificence, if anywise destructible, can be left in the interior. We were not shown into this palace, nor into the Parliament House, nor into the tower, where King James stabbed the Earl of Douglas. When I was here a year ago, I went up the old staircase and into the room where the murder was committed, although it had recently been the scene of a fire, which consumed as much of it as was inflammable. The window whence the Earl's body was thrown then remained; but now the whole tower seems to have been renewed, leaving only the mullions of the historic window.

We merely looked up at the new, light-colored freestone of the restored tower in passing, and ascended to the ramparts, where we found one of the most splendid views, morally and materially, that this world can show. Indeed, I think there cannot be such a landscape as the Carse of Stirling, set in such a frame as it is,—the Highlands, comprehending our friends, Ben Lomond, Ben Venue, Ben An, and the whole Ben brotherhood, with the Grampians surrounding it to the westward and northward, and in other directions some range of prominent objects to shut it in; and the plain itself, so worthy of the richest setting, so fertile, so beautiful, so written over and over again with histories. The silver Links of Forth are as sweet and gently picturesque an object as a man sees in a lifetime. I do not wonder that Providence caused great things to happen on this plain; it was like choosing a good piece of canvas to paint a great picture upon. The battle of Bannockburn (which we saw beneath us, with the Gillie's Hill on the right) could not have been fought upon a meaner plain, nor Wallace's victory gained; and if any other great historic act still remains to be done in this country, I should imagine the Carse of Stirling to be the future scene of it. Scott seems to me hardly to have done justice—to this landscape, or to have bestowed pains enough to put it in strong relief before the world; although it is from the light shed on it, and so much other Scottish scenery, by his mind, that we chiefly see it, and take an interest in it. . . .

I do not remember seeing the hill of execution before,—a mound on the same level as the castle's base, looking towards the Highlands. A solitary cow was now feeding upon it. I should imagine that no person could ever have been unjustly executed there; the spot is too much in the sight of heaven and earth to countenance injustice.

Descending from the ramparts, we went into the Armory, which I did not see on my former visit. The superintendent of this department is an old soldier of very great intelligence and vast communicativeness, and quite absorbed in thinking of and handling weapons; for he is a practical armorer. He had few things to show us that were very interesting,—a helmet or two, a bomb and grenade from the Crimea; also some muskets from the same quarter, one of which, with a sword at the end, he spoke of admiringly, as the best weapon in the collection, its only fault being its extreme weight. He showed us, too, some Minie rifles, and whole ranges of the old-fashioned Brown Bess, which had helped to win Wellington's victories; also the halberts of sergeants now laid aside, and some swords that had been used at the battle of Sheriffmuir. These latter were very short, not reaching to the floor, when I held one of them, point downward, in my hand. The shortness of the blade and consequent closeness of the encounter must have given the weapon a most dagger-like murderousness. Ranging in the hall of arms, there were two tattered banners that had gone through the Peninsular battles, one of them belonging to the gallant 42d Regiment. The armorer gave my wife a rag from each of these banners, consecrated by so much battle-smoke; also a piece of old oak, half burned to charcoal, which had been rescued from the panelling of the Douglas Tower. We saw better things, moreover, than all these rusty weapons and ragged flags; namely, the pulpit and communion-table of John Knox. The frame of the former, if I remember aright, is complete; but one or two of the panels are knocked out and lost, and, on the whole, it looks as if it had been shaken to pieces by the thunder of his holdings forth,—much worm-eaten, too, is the old oak wood, as well it may be, for the letters MD (1500) are carved on its front. The communion-table is polished, and in much better preservation.

Then the armorer showed us a Damascus blade, of the kind that will cut a delicate silk handkerchief while floating in the air; and some inlaid matchlock guns. A child's little toy-gun was lying on a workbench among all this array of weapons; and when I took it up and smiled, he said that it was his son's. So he called in a little fellow four years old, who was playing in the castle yard, and made him go through the musket exercise, which he did with great good-will. This small Son of a Gun, the father assured us, cares for nothing but arms, and has attained all his skill with the musket merely by looking at the soldiers on parade. . . .

Our soldier, who had resigned the care of us to the armorer, met us again at the door, and led us round the remainder of the ramparts, dismissing us finally at the gate by which we entered. All the time we were in the castle there had been a great discordance of drums and fifes, caused by the musicians who were practising just under the walls; likewise the sergeants were drilling their squads of men, and putting them through strange gymnastic motions. Most, if not all, of the garrison belongs to a Highland regiment, and those whom we saw on duty, in full costume, looked very martial and gallant. Emerging from the castle, we took the broad and pleasant footpath, which circles it about midway on the grassy steep which descends from the rocky precipice on which the walls are built. This is a very beautiful walk, and affords a most striking view of the castle, right above our heads, the height of its wall forming one line with the precipice. The grassy hillside is almost as precipitous as the dark gray rock that rises out of it, to form the foundations of the castle; but wild rose-bushes, both of a white and red variety, are abundant here, and all in bloom; nor are these the only flowers. There is also shrubbery in some spots, tossing up green waves against the precipice; and broad sheets of ivy here and there mantle the headlong rock, which also has a growth of weeds in its crevices. The castle walls above, however, are quite bare of any such growth. Thus, looking up at the old storied fortress, and looking down over the wide, historic plain, we wandered half-way round the castle, and then, retracing our steps, entered the town close by an old hospital.

A hospital it was, or had been intended for; but the authorities of the town had made some convenient arrangement with those entitled to its charity, and had appropriated the ancient edifice to themselves. So said a boy who showed us into the Guildhall,—an apartment with a vaulted oaken roof, and otherwise of antique aspect and furniture; all of which, however, were modern restorations. We then went into an old church or cathedral, which was divided into two parts; one of them, in which I saw the royal arms, being probably for the Church-of-England service, and the other for the Kirk of Scotland. I remember little or nothing of this edifice, except that the Covenanters had uplifted it with pews and a gallery, and whitewash; though I doubt not it was a stately Gothic church, with innumerable enrichments and incrustations of beauty, when it passed from popish hands into theirs. Thence we wandered downward, through a back street, amid very shabby houses, some of which bore tokens of having once been the abodes of courtly and noble personages. We paused before one that displayed, I think, the sign of a spirit-retailer, and looked as disreputable as a house could, yet was built of stalwart stone, and had two circular towers in front, once, doubtless, crowned with conical tops. We asked an elderly man whether he knew anything of the history of this house; and he said that he had been acquainted with it for almost fifty years, but never knew anything noteworthy about it. Reaching the foot of the hill, along whose back the streets of Stirling run, and which blooms out into the Castle Craig, we returned to the railway, and at noon took leave of Stirling.

I forgot to tell of the things that awakened rather more sympathy in us than any other objects in the castle armory. These were some rude weapons— pikes, very roughly made; and old rusty muskets, broken and otherwise out of order; and swords, by no means with Damascus blades— that had been taken from some poor weavers and other handicraft men who rose against the government in 1820. I pitied the poor fellows much, seeing how wretched were their means of standing up against the cannon, bayonets, swords, shot, shell, and all manner of murderous facilities possessed by their oppressors. Afterwards, our guide showed, in a gloomy quadrangle of the castle, the low windows of the dungeons where two of the leaders of the insurrectionists had been confined before their execution. I have not the least shadow of doubt that these men had a good cause to fight for; but what availed it with such weapons! and so few even of those!

. . . . I believe I cannot go on to recount any further this evening the experiences of to-day. It has been a very rich day; only that I have seen more than my sluggish powers of reception can well take in at once. After quitting Stirling, we came in somewhat less than an hour to and, alighting, took up our quarters at the Star and Garter Hotel, which, like almost all the Scottish caravan-saries of which we have had experience, turns out a comfortable one. . . . We stayed within doors for an hour or two, and I busied myself with writing up my journal. At about three, however, the sky brightened a little, and we set forth through the ancient, rusty, and queer-looking town of Linlithgow, towards the palace and the ancient church, which latter was one of St. David's edifices, and both of which stand close together, a little removed from the long street of the village. But I can never describe them worthily, and shall make nothing of the description if I attempt it now.

July 8th.—At about three o'clock yesterday, as I said, we walked forth through the ancient street of Linlithgow, and, coming to the market-place, stopped to look at an elaborate and heavy stone fountain, which we found by an inscription to be the fac-simile of an old one that used to stand on the same site. Turning to the right, the outer entrance to the palace fronts on this market-place, if such it be; and close to it, a little on one side, is the church. A young woman, with a key in her hand, offered to admit us into the latter; so we went in, and found it divided by a wall across the middle into two parts. The hither portion, being the nave, was whitewashed, and looked as bare and uninteresting as an old Gothic church of St. David's epoch possibly could do. The interior portion, being the former choir, is covered with pews over the whole floor, and further defaced by galleries, that unmercifully cut midway across the stately and beautiful arches. It is likewise whitewashed. There were, I believe, some mural monuments of Bailies and other such people stuck up about the walls, but nothing that much interested me, except an ancient oaken chair, which the girl said was the chair of St. Crispin, and it was fastened to the wall, in the holiest part of the church. I know not why it was there; but as it had been the chair of so distinguished a personage, we all sat down in it. It was in this church that the apparition of St. James appeared to King James IV., to warn him against engaging in that war which resulted in the battle of Flodden, where he and the flower of his nobility were slain. The young woman showed us the spot where the apparition spake to him,—a side chapel, with a groined roof, at the end of the choir next the nave. The Covenanters seem to have shown some respect to this one chapel, by refraining from drawing the gallery across its height; so that, except for the whitewash, and the loss of the painted glass in the window, and probably of a good deal of rich architectural detail, it looks as it did when the ghostly saint entered beneath its arch, while the king was kneeling there.

We stayed but a little while in the church, and then proceeded to the palace, which, as I said, is close at hand. On entering the outer enclosure through an ancient gateway, we were surprised to find how entire the walls seemed to be; but the reason is, I suppose, that the ruins have not been used as a stone-quarry, as has almost always been the case with old abbeys and castles. The palace took fire and was consumed, so far as consumable, in 1745, while occupied by the soldiers of General Hawley; but even yet the walls appear so stalwart that I should imagine it quite possible to rebuild and restore the stately rooms on their original plan. It was a noble palace, one hundred and seventy-five feet in length by one hundred and sixty-five in breadth, and though destitute of much architectural beauty externally, yet its aspect from the quadrangle which the four sides enclose is venerable and sadly beautiful. At each of the interior angles there is a circular tower, up the whole height of the edifice and overtopping it, and another in the centre of one of the sides, all containing winding staircases. The walls facing upon the enclosed quadrangle are pierced with many windows, and have been ornamented with sculpture, rich traces of which still remain over the arched entrance-ways; and in the grassy centre of the court there is the ruin and broken fragments of a fountain, which once used to play for the delight of the king and queen, and lords and ladies, who looked down upon it from hall and chamber. Many old carvings that belonged to it are heaped together there; but the water has disappeared, though, had it been a natural spring, it would have outlasted all the heavy stone-work.

As far as we were able, and could find our way, we went through every room of the palace, all round the four sides. From the first floor upwards it is entirely roofless. In some of the chambers there is an accumulation of soil, and a goodly crop of grass; in others there is still a flooring of flags or brick tiles, though damp and moss-grown, and with weeds sprouting between the crevices. Grass and weeds, indeed, have found soil enough to flourish in, even on the highest ranges of the walls, though at a dizzy height above the ground; and it was like an old and trite touch of romance, to see how the weeds sprouted on the many hearth-stones and aspired under the chimney-flues, as if in emulation of the long-extinguished flame. It was very mournful, very beautiful, very delightful, too, to see how Nature takes back the palace, now that kings have done with it, and adopts it as a part of her great garden.

On one side of the quadrangle we found the roofless chamber where Mary, Queen of Scots, was born, and in the same range the bedchamber that was occupied by several of the Scottish Jameses; and in one corner of the latter apartment there is a narrow, winding staircase, down which I groped, expecting to find a door, either into the enclosed quadrangle or to the outside of the palace. But it ends in nothing, unless it be a dungeon; and one does not well see why the bedchamber of the king should be so convenient to a dungeon. It is said that King James III. once escaped down this secret stair, and lay concealed from some conspirators who had entered his chamber to murder him. This range of apartments is terminated, like the other sides of the palace, by a circular tower enclosing a staircase, up which we mounted, winding round and round, and emerging at various heights, until at last we found ourselves at the very topmost point of the edifice; and here there is a small pepper-box of a turret, almost as entire as when the stones were first laid. It is called Queen Margaret's bower, and looks forth on a lovely prospect of mountain and plain, and on the old red roofs of Linlithgow town, and on the little loch that lies within the palace grounds. The cold north-wind blew chill upon us through the empty window-frames, which very likely were never glazed; but it must be a delightful nook in a calmer and warmer summer evening.

Descending from this high perch, we walked along ledges and through arched corridors, and stood, contemplative, in the dampness of the banqueting-hall, and sat down on the seats that still occupy the embrasures of the deep windows. In one of the rooms, the sculpture of a huge fireplace has recently been imitated and restored, so as to give an idea of what the richness of the adornments must have been when the building was perfect. We burrowed down, too, a little way, in the direction of the cells, where prisoners used to be confined; but these were too ugly and too impenetrably dark to tempt us far. One vault, exactly beneath a queen's very bedchamber, was designated as a prison. I should think bad dreams would have winged up, and made her pillow an uncomfortable one.

There seems to be no certain record as respects the date of this palace, except that the most recent part was built by James I., of England, and bears the figures 1620 on its central tower. In this part were the kitchens and other domestic offices. In Robert Bruce's time there was a castle here, instead of a palace, and an ancestor of our friend Bennoch was the means of taking it from the English by a stratagem in which valor went halves. Four centuries afterwards, it was a royal residence, and might still have been nominally so, had not Hawley's dragoons lighted their fires on the floors of the magnificent rooms; but, on the whole, I think it more valuable as a ruin than if it were still perfect. Scotland, and the world, needs only one Holyrood; and Linlithgow, were it still a perfect palace, must have been second in interest to that, from its lack of association with historic events so grand and striking.

After tea we took another walk, and this time went along the High Street, in quest of the house whence Bothwellhaugh fired the shot that killed the Regent Murray. It has been taken down, however; or, if any part of it remain, it has been built into and incorporated with a small house of dark stone, which forms one range with two others that stand a few feet back from the general line of the street. It is as mean-looking and commonplace an edifice as is anywhere to be seen, and is now occupied by one Steele, a tailor. We went under a square arch (if an arch can be square), that goes quite through the house, and found ourselves in a little court; but it was not easy to identify anything as connected with the historic event, so we did but glance about us, and returned into the street. It is here narrow, and as Bothwellhaugh stood in a projecting gallery, the Regent must have been within a few yards of the muzzle of his carbine. The street looks as old as any that I have seen, except, perhaps, a vista here and there in Chester,—the houses all of stone, many of them tall, with notched gables, and with stone staircases going up outside, the steps much worn by feet now dust; a pervading ugliness, which yet does not fail to be picturesque; a general filth and evil odor of gutters and people, suggesting sorrowful ideas of what the inner houses must be, when the outside looks and smells so badly; and, finally, a great rabble of the inhabitants, talking, idling, sporting, staring about their own thresholds and those of dram-shops, the town being most alive in the long twilight of the summer evening. There was nothing uncivil in the deportment of these dirty people, old or young; but they did stare at us most unmercifully.

We walked very late, entering, after all that we had seen, into the palace grounds, and skirting along Linlithgow Loch, which would be very beautiful if its banks were made shadowy with trees, instead of being almost bare. We viewed the palace on the outside, too, and saw what had once been the principal entrance, but now looked like an arched window, pretty high in the wall; for it had not been accessible except by a drawbridge. I might write pages in telling how venerable the ruin, looked, as the twilight fell deeper and deeper around it; but we have had enough of Linlithgow, especially as there have been so many old palaces and old towns to write about, and there will still be more. We left Linlithgow early this morning, and reached Edinburgh in half an hour. To-morrow I suppose I shall try to set down what I see; at least, some points of it.

July 9th.—Arriving at

EDINBURGH,

and acting under advice of the cabman, we drove to Addison's Alma Hotel, which we find to be in Prince's Street, having Scott's monument a few hundred yards below, and the Castle Hill about as much above.

The Edinburgh people seem to be accustomed to climb mountains within their own houses; so we had to mount several staircases before we reached our parlor, which is a very good one, and commands a beautiful view of Prince's Street, and of the picturesque old town, and the valley between, and of the castle on its hill.

Our first visit was to the castle, which we reached by going across the causeway that bridges the valley, and has some edifices of Grecian architecture on it, contrasting strangely with the nondescript ugliness of the old town, into which we immediately pass. As this is my second visit to Edinburgh, I surely need not dwell upon describing it at such length as if I had never been here before. After climbing up through various wards of the castle to the topmost battery, where Mons Meg holds her station, looking like an uncouth dragon,—with a pile of huge stone balls beside her for eggs,—we found that we could not be admitted to Queen Mary's apartments, nor to the crown-room, till twelve o'clock; moreover, that there was no admittance to the crown-room without tickets from the crown-office, in Parliament Square. There being no help for it, I left my wife and J——— to wander through the fortress, and came down through High Street in quest of Parliament Square, which I found after many inquiries of policemen, and after first going to the Justiciary Court, where there was a great throng endeavoring to get in; for the trial of Miss Smith for the murder of her lover is causing great excitement just now. There was no difficulty made about the tickets, and, returning, found S——— and J———; but J——— grew tired of waiting, and set out to return to our hotel, through the great strange city, all by himself. Through means of an attendant, we were admitted into Queen Margaret's little chapel, on the top of the rock; and then we sat down, in such shelter as there was, to avoid the keen wind, blowing through the embrasures of the ramparts, and waited as patiently as we could.

Twelve o'clock came, and we went into the crown-room, with a throng of other visitors,—so many that they could only be admitted in separate groups. The Regalia of Scotland lie on a circular table within an iron railing, round and round which the visitors pass, gazing with all their eyes. The room was dark, however, except for the dim twinkle of a candle or gaslight; and the regalia did not show to any advantage, though there are some rich jewels, set in their ancient gold. The articles consist of a two-handed sword, with a hilt and scabbard of gold, ornamented with gems, and a mace, with a silver handle, all very beautifully made; besides the golden collar and jewelled badge of the Garter, and something else which I forget. Why they keep this room so dark I cannot tell; but it is a poor show, and gives the spectator an idea of the poverty of Scotland, and the minuteness of her sovereignty, which I had not gathered from her royal palaces.

Thence we went into Queen Mary's room, and saw that beautiful portrait— that very queen and very woman—with which I was so much impressed at my last visit. It is wonderful that this picture does not drive all the other portraits of Mary out of the field, whatever may be the comparative proofs of their authenticity. I do not know the history of this one, except that it is a copy by Sir William Gordon of a picture by an Italian, preserved at Dunrobin Castle.

After seeing what the castle had to show, which is but little except itself, its rocks, and its old dwellings of princes and prisoners, we came down through the High Street, inquiring for John Knox's house. It is a strange-looking edifice, with gables on high, projecting far, and some sculpture, and inscriptions referring to Knox. There is a tobacconist's shop in the basement story, where I learned that the house used to be shown to visitors till within three months, but it is now closed, for some reason or other. Thence we crossed a bridge into the new town, and came back through Prince's Street to the hotel, and had a good dinner, as preparatory to fresh wearinesses; for there is no other weariness at all to be compared to that of sight-seeing.

In mid afternoon we took a cab and drove to Holyrood Palace, which I have already described, as well as the chapel, and do not mean to meddle with either of them again. We looked at our faces in the old mirrors that Queen Mary brought from France with her, and which had often reflected her own lovely face and figure; and I went up the winding stair through which the conspirators ascended. This, I think, was not accessible at my former visit. Before leaving the palace, one of the attendants advised us to see some pictures in the apartments occupied by the Marquis of Breadalbane during the queen's residence here. We found some fine old portraits and other paintings by Vandyke, Sir Peter Lely, Sir Godfrey Kneller, and a strange head by Rubens, amid all which I walked wearily, wishing that there were nothing worth looking at in the whole world. My wife differs altogether from me in this matter; . . . . but we agreed, on this occasion, in being tired to death. Just as we got through with the pictures, I became convinced of what I had been dimly suspecting all the while, namely, that at my last visit to the palace I had seen these selfsame pictures, and listened to the selfsame woman's civil answers, in just the selfsame miserable weariness of mood.

We left the palace, and toiled up through the dirty Canongate, looking vainly for a fly, and employing our time, as well as we could, in looking at the squalid mob of Edinburgh, and peeping down the horrible vistas of the closes, which were swarming with dirty life, as some mouldy and half-decayed substance might swarm with insects,—vistas down alleys where sin, sorrow, poverty, drunkenness, all manner of sombre and sordid earthly circumstances, had imbued the stone, brick, and wood of the habitations for hundreds of years. And such a multitude of children too; that was a most striking feature.

After tea I went down into the valley between the old town and the new, which is now laid out as an ornamental garden, with grass, shrubbery, flowers, gravelled walks, and frequent seats. Here the sun was setting, and gilded the old town with its parting rays, making it absolutely the most picturesque scene possible to be seen. The mass of tall, ancient houses, heaped densely together, looked like a Gothic dream; for there seemed to be towers and all sorts of stately architecture, and spires ascended out of the mass; and above the whole was the castle, with a diadem of gold on its topmost turret. It wanted less than a quarter of nine when the last gleam faded from the windows of the old town, and left the crowd of buildings dim and indistinguishable, to reappear on the morrow in squalor, lifting their meanness skyward, the home of layer upon layer of unfortunate humanity. The change symbolized the difference between a poet's imagination of life in the past—or in a state which he looks at through a colored and illuminated medium—and the sad reality.

This morning we took a cab, and set forth between ten and eleven to see Edinburgh and its environs; driving past the University, and other noticeable objects in the old town, and thence out to Arthur's Seat. Salisbury Crags are a very singular feature of the outskirts. From the heights, beneath Arthur's Seat, we had a fine prospect of the sea, with Leith and Portobello in the distance, and of a fertile plain at the foot of the hill. In the course of our drive our cabman pointed out Dumbiedikes' house; also the cottage of Jeanie Deans,—at least, the spot where it formerly stood; and Muschat's Cairn, of which a small heap of stones is yet remaining. Near this latter object are the ruins of St. Anthony's Chapel, a roofless gable, and other remains, standing on the abrupt hillside. We drove homeward past a parade-ground on which a body of cavalry was exercising, and we met a company of infantry on their route thither. Then we drove near Calton Hill, which seems to be not a burial-ground, although the site of stately monuments. In fine, we passed through the Grass-Market, where we saw the cross in the pavement in the street, marking the spot, as I recorded before, where Porteous was executed. Thence we passed through the Cowgate, all the latter part of our drive being amongst the tall, quaint edifices of the old town, alike venerable and squalid. From the Grass-Market the rock of the castle looks more precipitous than as we had hitherto seen it, and its prisons, palaces, and barracks approach close to its headlong verge, and form one steep line with its descent. We drove quite round the Castle Hill, and returned down Prince's Street to our hotel. There can be no other city in the world that affords more splendid scenery, both natural and architectural, than Edinburgh.

Then we went to St. Giles's Cathedral, which I shall not describe, it having been kirkified into three interior divisions by the Covenanters; and I left my wife to take drawings, while J—— and I went to Short's Observatory, near the entrance of the castle. Here we saw a camera-obscura, which brought before us, without our stirring a step, almost all the striking objects which we had been wandering to and fro to see. We also saw the mites in cheese, gigantically magnified by a solar microscope; likewise some dioramic views, with all which I was mightily pleased, and for myself, being tired to death of sights, I would as lief see them as anything else. We found, on calling for mamma at St. Giles's, that she had gone away; but she rejoined us between four and five o'clock at our hotel, where the next thing we did was to dine. Again after dinner we walked out, looking at the shop-windows of jewellers, where ornaments made of cairngorm pebbles are the most peculiar attraction. As it was our wedding-day, ... I gave S—— a golden and amethyst-bodied cairngorm beetle with a ruby head; and after sitting awhile in Prince's Street Gardens, we came home.

July 10th.—Last evening I walked round the castle rock, and through the Grass-Market, where I stood on the inlaid cross in the pavement, thence down the High Street beyond John Knox's house. The throng in that part of the town was very great. There is a strange fascination in these old streets, and in the peeps down the closes; but it doubtless would be a great blessing were a fire to sweep through the whole of ancient Edinburgh. This system of living on flats, up to I know not what story, must be most unfavorable to cleanliness, since they have to fetch their water all that distance towards heaven, and how they get rid of their rubbish is best known to themselves.

My wife has gone to Roslin this morning, and since her departure it has been drizzly, so that J—— and I, after a walk through the new part of the town, are imprisoned in our parlor with little resource except to look across the valley to the castle, where Mons Meg is plainly visible on the upper platform, and the lower ramparts, zigzagging about the edge of the precipice, which nearly in front of us is concealed or softened by a great deal of shrubbery, but farther off descends steeply down to the grass below. Somewhere on this side of the rock was the point where Claverhouse, on quitting Edinburgh before the battle of Killiecrankie, clambered up to hold an interview with the Duke of Gordon. What an excellent thing it is to have such striking and indestructible landmarks and time-marks that they serve to affix historical incidents to, and thus, as it were, nail down the Past for the benefit of all future ages!

The old town of Edinburgh appears to be situated, in its densest part, on the broad back of a ridge, which rises gradually to its termination in the precipitous rock, on which stands the castle. Between the old town and the new is the valley, which runs along at the base of this ridge, and which, in its natural state, was probably rough and broken, like any mountain gorge. The lower part of the valley, adjacent to the Canongate, is now a broad hollow space, fitted up with dwellings, shops, or manufactories; the next portion, between two bridges, is converted into an ornamental garden free to the public, and contains Scott's beautiful monument,—a canopy of Gothic arches and a fantastic spire, beneath which he sits, thoughtful and observant of what passes in the contiguous street; the third portion of the valley, above the last bridge, is another ornamental garden, open only to those who have pass-keys. It is an admirable garden, with a great variety of surface, and extends far round the castle rock, with paths that lead up to its very base, among leafy depths of shrubbery, and winds beneath the sheer, black precipice. J—— and I walked there this forenoon, and took refuge from a shower beneath an overhanging jut of the rock, where a bench had been placed, and where a curtain of hanging ivy helped to shelter us. On our return to the hotel, we found mamma just alighting from a cab. She had had very bad fortune in her excursion to Roslin, having had to walk a long distance to the chapel, and being caught in the rain; and, after all, she could only spend seven minutes in viewing the beautiful Roslin architecture.

MELROSE.

July 11th.—We left Edinburgh, where we had found at Addison's, 87 Prince's Street, the most comfortable hotel in Great Britain, and went to Melrose, where we put up at the George. This is all travelled ground with me, so that I need not much perplex myself with further description, especially as it is impossible, by any repetition of attempts, to describe Melrose Abbey. We went thither immediately after tea, and were shown over the ruins by a very delectable old Scotchman, incomparably the best guide I ever met with. I think he must take pains to speak the Scotch dialect, he does it with such pungent felicity and effect, and it gives a flavor to everything he says, like the mustard and vinegar in a salad. This is not the man I saw when here before. The Scotch dialect is still, in a greater or less degree, universally prevalent in Scotland, insomuch that we generally find it difficult to comprehend the answers to our questions, though more, I think, from the unusual intonation than either from strange words or pronunciation. But this old man, though he spoke the most unmitigated Scotch, was perfectly intelligible,—perhaps because his speech so well accorded with the classic standard of the Waverley Novels. Moreover, he is thoroughly acquainted with the Abbey, stone by stone; and it was curious to see him, as we walked among its aisles, and over the grass beneath its roofless portions, pick up the withered leaves that had fallen there, and do other such little things, as a good housewife might do to a parlor. I have met with two or three instances where the guardian of an old edifice seemed really to love it, and this was one, although the old man evidently had a Scotch Covenanter's contempt and dislike of the faith that founded the Abbey. He repeated King David's dictum that King David the First was "a sair saint for the crown," as bestowing so much wealth on religious edifices; but really, unless it be Walter Scott, I know not any Scotchman who has done so much for his country as this same St. David. As the founder of Melrose and many other beautiful churches and abbeys, he left magnificent specimens of the only kind of poetry which the age knew how to produce; and the world is the better for him to this day,—which is more, I believe, than can be said of any hero or statesman in Scottish annals.

We went all over the ruins, of course, and saw the marble stone of King Alexander, and the spot where Bruce's heart is said to be buried, and the slab of Michael Scott, with the cross engraved upon it; also the exquisitely sculptured kail-leaves, and other foliage and flowers, with which the Gothic artists inwreathed this edifice, bestowing more minute and faithful labor than an artist of these days would do on the most delicate piece of cabinet-work. We came away sooner than we wished, but we hoped to return thither this morning; and, for my part, I cherish a presentiment that this will not be our last visit to Scotland and Melrose. . . . J——- and I then walked to the Tweed, where we saw two or three people angling, with naked legs, or trousers turned up, and wading among the rude stones that make something like a dam over the wide and brawling stream. I did not observe that they caught any fish, but J——- was so fascinated with the spectacle that he pulled out his poor little fishing-line, and wished to try his chance forthwith. I never saw the angler's instinct stronger in anybody. We walked across the foot-bridge that here spans the Tweed; and J—— observed that he did not see how William of Deloraine could have found so much difficulty in swimming his horse across so shallow a river. Neither do I. It now began to sprinkle, and we hastened back to the hotel.

It was not a pleasant morning; but we started immediately after breakfast for

ABBOTSFORD,

which is but about three miles distant. The country between Melrose and that place is not in the least beautiful, nor very noteworthy,—one or two old irregular villages; one tower that looks principally domestic, yet partly warlike, and seems to be of some antiquity; and an undulation, or rounded hilly surface of the landscape, sometimes affording wide vistas between the slopes. These hills, which, I suppose, are some of them on the Abbotsford estate, are partly covered with woods, but of Scotch fir, or some tree of that species, which creates no softened undulation, but overspreads the hill like a tightly fitting wig. It is a cold, dreary, disheartening neighborhood, that of Abbotsford; at least, it has appeared so to me at both of my visits,—one of which was on a bleak and windy May morning, and this one on a chill, showery morning of midsummer.

The entrance-way to the house is somewhat altered since my last visit; and we now, following the direction of a painted finger on the wall, went round to a side door in the basement story, where we found an elderly man waiting as if in expectation of visitors. He asked us to write our names in a book, and told us that the desk on the leaf of which it lay was the one in which Sir Walter found the forgotten manuscript of Waverley, while looking for some fishing-tackle. There was another desk in the room, which had belonged to the Colonel Gardiner who appears in Waverley. The first apartment into which our guide showed us was Sir Walter's study, where I again saw his clothes, and remarked how the sleeve of his old green coat was worn at the cuff,—a minute circumstance that seemed to bring Sir Walter very near me. Thence into the library; thence into the drawing-room, whence, methinks, we should have entered the dining-room, the most interesting of all, as being the room where he died. But this room seems not to be shown now. We saw the armory, with the gun of Rob Roy, into the muzzle of which I put my finger, and found the bore very large; the beautifully wrought pistol of Claverhouse, and a pair of pistols that belonged to Napoleon; the sword of Montrose, which I grasped, and drew half out of the scabbard; and Queen

Mary's iron jewel-box, six or eight inches long, and two or three high, with a lid rounded like that of a trunk, and much corroded with rust. There is no use in making a catalogue of these curiosities. The feeling in visiting Abbotsford is not that of awe; it is little more than going to a museum. I do abhor this mode of making pilgrimages to the shrines of departed great men. There is certainly something wrong in it, for it seldom or never produces (in me, at least) the right feeling. It is an odd truth, too, that a house is forever after spoiled and ruined as a home, by having been the abode of a great man. His spirit haunts it, as it were, with a malevolent effect, and takes hearth and hall away from the nominal possessors, giving all the world the right to enter there because he had such intimate relations with all the world.

We had intended to go to Dryburgh Abbey; but as the weather more than threatened rain, ... we gave up the idea, and so took the rail for Berwick, after one o'clock. On our road we passed several ruins in Scotland, and some in England,—one old castle in particular, beautifully situated beside a deep-banked stream. The road lies for many miles along the coast, affording a fine view of the German Ocean, which was now blue, sunny, and breezy, the day having risen out of its morning sulks. We waited an hour or more at Berwick, and J—— and I took a hasty walk into the town. It is a rough and rude assemblage of rather mean houses, some of which are thatched. There seems to have been a wall about the town at a former period, and we passed through one of the gates. The view of the river Tweed here is very fine, both above and below the railway bridge, and especially where it flows, a broad tide, and between high banks, into the sea. Thence we went onward along the coast, as I have said, pausing a few moments in smoky Newcastle, and reaching Durham about eight o'clock.

DURHAM.

I wandered out in the dusk of the evening,—for the dusk comes on comparatively early as we draw southward,—and found a beautiful and shadowy path along the river-side, skirting its high banks, up and adown which grow noble elms. I could not well see, in that obscurity of twilight boughs, whither I was going, or what was around me; but I judged that the castle or cathedral, or both, crowned the highest line of the shore, and that I was walking at the base of their walls. There was a pair of lovers in front of me, and I passed two or three other tender couples. The walk appeared to go on interminably by the river-side, through the same sweet shadow; but I turned and found my way into the cathedral close, beneath an ancient archway, whence, issuing again, I inquired my way to the Waterloo Hotel, where we had put up.

ITEMS.—We saw the Norham Castle of Marmion, at a short distance from the station of the same name. Viewed from the railway, it has not a very picturesque appearance,—a high, square ruin of what I suppose was the keep.—At Abbotsford, treasured up in a glass case in the drawing-room, were memorials of Sir Walter Scott's servants and humble friends,—for instance, a brass snuff-box of Tom Purdie,—there, too, among precious relics of illustrious persons.—In the armory, I grasped with some interest the sword of Sir Adam Ferguson, which he had worn in the Peninsular war. Our guide said, of his own knowledge, that "he was a very funny old gentleman." He died only a year or two since.

July 11th.—The morning after our arrival in Durham being Sunday, we attended service in the cathedral. . . . We found a tolerable audience, seated on benches, within and in front of the choir; and people continually strayed in and out of the sunny churchyard and sat down, or walked softly and quietly up and down the side aisle. Sometimes, too, one of the vergers would come in with a handful of little boys, whom he had caught playing among the tombstones.

DURHAM CATHEDRAL

has one advantage over the others which I have seen, there being no organ-screen, nor any sort of partition between the choir and nave; so that we saw its entire length, nearly five hundred feet, in one vista. The pillars of the nave are immensely thick, but hardly of proportionate height, and they support the round Norman arch; nor is there, as far as I remember, a single pointed arch in the cathedral. The effect is to give the edifice an air of heavy grandeur. It seems to have been built before the best style of church architecture had established itself; so that it weighs upon the soul, instead of helping it to aspire. First, there are these round arches, supported by gigantic columns; then, immediately above, another row of round arches, behind which is the usual gallery that runs, as it were, in the thickness of the wall, around the nave of the cathedral; then, above all, another row of round arches, enclosing the windows of the clere-story. The great pillars are ornamented in various ways,—some with a great spiral groove running from bottom to top; others with two spirals, ascending in different directions, so as to cross over one another; some are fluted or channelled straight up and down; some are wrought with chevrons, like those on the sleeve of a police-inspector. There are zigzag cuttings and carvings, which I do not know how to name scientifically, round the arches of the doors and windows; but nothing that seems to have flowered out spontaneously, as natural incidents of a grand and beautiful design. In the nave, between the columns of the side aisles, I saw one or two monuments. . . .

The cathedral service is very long; and though the choral part of it is pleasant enough, I thought it not best to wait for the sermon, especially as it would have been quite unintelligible, so remotely as I sat in the great space. So I left my seat, and after strolling up and down the aisle a few times, sallied forth into the churchyard. On the cathedral door there is a curious old knocker, in the form of a monstrous face, which was placed there, centuries ago, for the benefit of fugitives from justice, who used to be entitled to sanctuary here. The exterior of the cathedral, being huge, is therefore grand;

it has a great central tower, and two at the western end; and reposes in vast and heavy length, without the multitude of niches, and crumbling statues, and richness of detail, that make the towers and fronts of some cathedrals so endlessly interesting. One piece of sculpture I remember,—a carving of a cow, a milk-maid, and a monk, in reference to the legend that the site of the cathedral was, in some way, determined by a woman bidding her cow go home to Dunholme. Cadmus was guided to the site of his destined city in some such way as this.

It was a very beautiful day, and though the shadow of the cathedral fell on this side, yet, it being about noontide, it did not cover the churchyard entirely, but left many of the graves in sunshine. There were not a great many monuments, and these were chiefly horizontal slabs, some of which looked aged, but on closer inspection proved to be mostly of the present century. I observed an old stone figure, however, half worn away, which seemed to have something like a bishop's mitre on its head, and may perhaps have lain in the proudest chapel of the cathedral before occupying its present bed among the grass. About fifteen paces from the central tower, and within its shadow, I found a weather-worn slab of marble, seven or eight feet long, the inscription on which interested me somewhat. It was to the memory of Robert Dodsley, the bookseller, Johnson's acquaintance, who, as his tombstone rather superciliously avers, had made a much better figure as an author than "could have been expected in his rank of life." But, after all, it is inevitable that a man's tombstone should look down on him, or, at all events, comport itself towards him "de haut en bas." I love to find the graves of men connected with literature. They interest me more, even though of no great eminence, than those of persons far more illustrious in other walks of life. I know not whether this is because I happen to be one of the literary kindred, or because all men feel themselves akin, and on terms of intimacy, with those whom they know, or might have known, in books. I rather believe that the latter is the case.

My wife had stayed in the cathedral, but she came out at the end of the sermon, and told me of two little birds, who had got into the vast interior, and were in great trouble at not being able to find their way out again. Thus, two winged souls may often have been imprisoned within a faith of heavy ceremonials.

We went round the edifice, and, passing into the close, penetrated through an arched passage into the crypt, which, methought, was in a better style of architecture than the nave and choir. At one end stood a crowd of venerable figures leaning against the wall, being stone images of bearded saints, apostles, patriarchs, kings,—personages of great dignity, at all events, who had doubtless occupied conspicuous niches in and about the cathedral till finally imprisoned in this cellar. I looked at every one, and found not an entire nose among them, nor quite so many heads as they once had.

Thence we went into the cloisters, which are entire, but not particularly interesting. Indeed, this cathedral has not taken hold of my affections, except in one aspect, when it was exceedingly grand and beautiful.

After looking at the crypt and the cloisters, we returned through the close and the churchyard, and went back to the hotel through a path by the river-side. This is the same dim and dusky path through which I wandered the night before, and in the sunshine it looked quite as beautiful as I knew it must,— a shadow of elm-trees clothing the high bank, and overarching the paths above and below; some of the elms growing close to the water-side, and flinging up their topmost boughs not nearly so high as where we stood, and others climbing upward and upward, till our way wound among their roots; while through the foliage the quiet river loitered along, with this lovely shade on both its banks, to pass through the centre of the town. The stately cathedral rose high above us, and farther onward, in a line with it, the battlemented walls of the old Norman castle, gray and warlike, though now it has become a University. This delightful walk terminates at an old bridge in the heart of the town; and the castle hangs immediately over its busiest street. On this bridge, last night, in the embrasure, or just over the pier, where there is a stone seat, I saw some old men seated, smoking their pipes and chatting. In my judgment, a river flowing through the centre of a town, and not too broad to make itself familiar, nor too swift, but idling along, as if it loved better to stay there than to go, is the pleasantest imaginable piece of scenery; so transient as it is, and yet enduring,—just the same from life's end to life's end; and this river Wear, with its sylvan wildness, and yet so sweet and placable, is the best of all little rivers,—not that it is so very small, but with a bosom broad enough to be crossed by a three-arched bridge. Just above the cathedral there is a mill upon its shore, as ancient as the times of the Abbey.

We went homeward through the market-place and one or two narrow streets; for the town has the irregularity of all ancient settlements, and, moreover, undulates upward and downward, and is also made more unintelligible to a stranger, in its points and bearings, by the tortuous course of the river.

After dinner J—— and I walked along the bank opposite to that on which the cathedral stands, and found the paths there equally delightful with those which I have attempted to describe. We went onward while the river gleamed through the foliage beneath us, and passed so far beyond the cathedral that we began to think we were getting into the country, and that it was time to return; when all at once we saw a bridge before us, and beyond that, on the opposite bank of the Wear, the cathedral itself! The stream had made a circuit without our knowing it. We paused upon the bridge, and admired and wondered at the beauty and glory of the scene, with those vast, ancient towers rising out of the green shade, and looking as if they were based upon it. The situation of Durham Cathedral is certainly a noble one, finer even than that of Lincoln, though the latter stands even at a more lordly height above the town. But as I saw it then, it was grand, venerable, and sweet, all at once; and I never saw so lovely and magnificent a scene, nor, being content with this, do I care to see a better. The castle beyond came also into the view, and the whole picture was mirrored in the tranquil stream below. And so, crossing the bridge, the path led us back through many a bower of hollow shade; and we then quitted the hotel, and took the rail for

YORK,

where we arrived at about half past nine. We put up at the Black Swan, with which we had already made acquaintance at our previous visit to York. It is a very ancient hotel; for in the coffee-room I saw on the wall an old printed advertisement, announcing that a stage-coach would leave the Black Swan in London, and arrive at the Black Swan in York, with God's permission, in four days. The date was 1706; and still, after a hundred and fifty years, the Black Swan receives travellers in Coney Street. It is a very good hotel, and was much thronged with guests when we arrived, as the Sessions come on this week. We found a very smart waiter, whose English faculties have been brightened by a residence of several years in America.

In the morning, before breakfast, I strolled out, and walked round the cathedral, passing on my way the sheriff's javelin-men, in long gowns of faded purple embroidered with gold, carrying halberds in their hands; also a gentleman in a cocked hat, gold-lace, and breeches, who, no doubt, had something to do with the ceremonial of the Sessions. I saw, too, a procession of a good many old cabs and other carriages, filled with people, and a banner flaunting above each vehicle. These were the piano-forte makers of York, who were going out of town to have a jollification together.

After breakfast we all went to the cathedral, and no sooner were we within it than we found how much our eyes had recently been educated, by our greater power of appreciating this magnificent interior; for it impressed us both with a joy that we never felt before. J—— felt it too, and insisted that the cathedral must have been altered and improved since we were last here. But it is only that we have seen much splendid architecture since then, and so have grown in some degree fitted to enjoy it. York Cathedral (I say it now, for it is my present feeling) is the most wonderful work that ever came from the hands of man. Indeed, it seems like "a house not made with hands," but rather to have come down from above, bringing an awful majesty and sweetness with it and it is so light and aspiring, with all its vast columns and pointed arches, that one would hardly wonder if it should ascend back to heaven again by its mere spirituality. Positively the pillars and arches of the choir are so very beautiful that they give the impression of being exquisitely polished, though such is not the fact; but their beauty throws a gleam around them. I thank God that I saw this cathedral again, and I thank him that he inspired the builder to make it, and that mankind has so long enjoyed it, and will continue to enjoy it.

July 14th.—We left York at twelve o'clock, and were delayed an hour or two at Leeds, waiting for a train. I strolled up into the town, and saw a fair, with puppet-shows, booths of penny actors, merry-go-rounds, clowns, boxers, and other such things as I saw, above a year ago, at Greenwich fair, and likewise at Tranmere, during the Whitsuntide holidays.

We resumed our journey, and reached Southport in pretty good trim at about nine o'clock. It has been a very interesting tour. We find Southport just as we left it, with its regular streets of little and big lodging-houses, where the visitors perambulate to and fro without any imaginable object. The tide, too, seems not to have been up over the waste of sands since we went away; and far seaward stands the same row of bathing-machines, and just on the verge of the horizon a gleam of water, —even this being not the sea, but the mouth of the river Ribble, seeking the sea amid the sandy desert. But we shall soon say good-by to Southport.

OLD TRAFFORD, MANCHESTER.

July 22d.—We left Southport for good on the 20th, and have established ourselves in this place, in lodgings that had been provided for us by Mr. Swain; our principal object being to spend a few weeks in the proximity of the Arts' Exhibition. We are here, about three miles from the Victoria Railway station in Manchester on one side, and nearly a mile from the Exhibition on the other. This is a suburb of Manchester, and consists of a long street, called the Stratford Road, bordered with brick houses two stories high, such as are usually the dwellings of tradesmen or respectable mechanics, but which are now in demand for lodgings, at high prices, on account of the Exhibition. It seems to be rather a new precinct of the city, and the houses, though ranged along a continuous street, are but a brick border of the green fields in the rear. Occasionally you get a glimpse of this country aspect between two houses; but the street itself, even with its little grass-plots and bits of shrubbery under the front windows, is as ugly as it can be made. Some of the houses are better than I have described; but the brick used here in building is very unsightly in hue and surface.

Betimes in the morning the Exhibition omnibuses begin to trundle along, and pass at intervals of two and a half minutes through the day,—immense vehicles constructed to carry thirty-nine passengers, and generally with a good part of that number inside and out. The omnibuses are painted scarlet, bordered with white, have three horses abreast, and a conductor in a red coat. They perform the journey from this point into town in about half an hour; and yesterday morning, being in a hurry to get to the railway station, I found that I could outwalk them, taking into account their frequent stoppages.

We have taken the whole house (except some inscrutable holes, into which the family creeps), of respectable people, who never took lodgers until this juncture. Their furniture, however, is of the true lodging-house pattern, sofas and chairs which have no possibility of repose in them; rickety tables;

an old piano and old music, with "Lady Helen Elizabeth" somebody's name written on it. It is very strange how nothing but a genuine home can ever look homelike. They appear to be good people; a little girl of twelve, a daughter, waits on table; and there is an elder daughter, who yesterday answered the door-bell, looking very like a young lady, besides five or six smaller children, who make less uproar of grief or merriment than could possibly be expected. The husband is not apparent, though I see his hat in the hall. The house is new, and has a trim, light-colored interior of half-gentility. I suppose the rent, in ordinary times, might be 25 pounds per annum; but we pay at the rate of 335 pounds for the part which we occupy. This, like all the other houses in the neighborhood, was evidently built to be sold or let; the builder never thought of living in it himself, and so that subtile element, which would have enabled him to create a home, was entirely left out.

This morning, J—— and I set forth on a walk, first towards the palace of the Arts' Exhibition, which looked small compared with my idea of it, and seems to be of the Crystal Palace order of architecture, only with more iron to its glass. Its front is composed of three round arches in a row. We did not go in. . . . Turning to the right, we walked onward two or three miles, passing the Botanic Garden, and thence along by suburban villas, Belgrave terraces, and other such prettinesses in the modern Gothic or Elizabethan style, with fancifully ornamented flower-plats before them; thence by hedgerows and fields, and through two or three villages, with here and there an old plaster and timber-built thatched house, among a street full of modern brick-fronts,—the alehouse, or rural inn, being generally the most ancient house in the village. It was a sultry, heavy day, and I walked without much enjoyment of the air and exercise. We crossed a narrow and swift river, flowing between deep banks. It must have been either the Mersey, still an infant stream, and little dreaming of the thousand mighty ships that float on its farther tide, or else the Irwell, which empties into the Mersey. We passed through the village beyond this stream, and went to the railway station, and then were brought back to Old Trafford, and deposited close by the Exhibition.

It has showered this afternoon; and I beguiled my time for half an hour by setting down the vehicles that went past; not that they were particularly numerous, but for the sake of knowing the character of the travel along the road.

July 26th.—Day before yesterday we went to the Arts' Exhibition, of which I do not think that I have a great deal to say. The edifice, being built more for convenience than show, appears better in the interior than from without,—long vaulted vistas, lighted from above, extending far away, all hung with pictures; and, on the floor below, statues, knights in armor, cabinets, vases, and all manner of curious and beautiful things, in a regular arrangement. Scatter five thousand people through the scene, and I do not know how to make a better outline sketch. I was unquiet, from a hopelessness of being able to enjoy it fully. Nothing is more depressing to me than the sight of a great many pictures together; it is like having innumerable books open before you at once, and being able to read only a sentence or two in each. They bedazzle one another with cross lights. There never should be more than one picture in a room, nor more than one picture to be studied in one day. Galleries of pictures are surely the greatest absurdities that ever were contrived, there being no excuse for them, except that it is the only way in which pictures can be made generally available and accessible.

We went first into the Gallery of British Painters, where there were hundreds of pictures, every one of which would have interested me by itself; but I could not fix nay mind on one more than another, so I wandered about, to get a general idea of the Exhibition. Truly it is very fine; truly, also, every great show is a kind of humbug. I doubt whether there were half a dozen people there who got the kind of enjoyment that it was intended to create,—very respectable people they seemed to be, and very well behaved, but all skimming the surface, as I did, and none of them so feeding on what was beautiful as to digest it, and make it a part of themselves. Such a quantity of objects must be utterly rejected before you can get any real profit from one! It seemed like throwing away time to look twice even at whatever was most precious; and it was dreary to think of not fully enjoying this collection, the very flower of Time, which never bloomed before, and never, by any possibility, can bloom again. Viewed hastily, moreover, it is somewhat sad to think that mankind, after centuries of cultivation of the beautiful arts, can produce no more splendid spectacle than this. It is not so very grand, although, poor as it is, I lack capacity to take in even the whole of it.

What gave me most pleasure (because it required no trouble nor study to come at the heart of it) were the individual relics of antiquity, of which there are some very curious ones in the cases ranged along the principal saloon or nave of the building. For example, the dagger with which Felton killed the Duke of Buckingham,—a knife with a bone handle and a curved blade, not more than three inches long; sharp-pointed, murderous-looking, but of very coarse manufacture. Also, the Duke of Alva's leading staff of iron; and the target of the Emperor Charles V., which seemed to be made of hardened leather, with designs artistically engraved upon it, and gilt. I saw Wolsey's portrait, and, in close proximity to it, his veritable cardinal's hat in a richly ornamented glass case, on which was an inscription to the effect that it had been bought by Charles Kean at the sale of Horace Walpole's collection. It is a felt hat with a brim about six inches wide all round, and a rather high crown; the color was, doubtless, a bright red originally, but now it is mottled with a grayish hue, and there are cracks in the brim, as if the hat had seen a good deal of wear. I suppose a far greater curiosity than this is the signet-ring of one of the Pharaohs, who reigned over Egypt during Joseph's prime ministry,—a large ring to be worn on the thumb, if at all,—of massive gold, seal part and all, and inscribed with some characters that looked like Hebrew. I had seen this before in Mr. Mayer's collection in Liverpool. The mediaeval and English relics, however, interested me more,—such as the golden and enamelled George worn by Sir Thomas More; or the embroidered shirt of Charles I.,—the very one, I presume, which he wore at his execution. There are no blood-marks on it, it being very nicely washed and folded. The texture of the linen cloth—if linen it be—is coarser than any peasant would wear at this day, but the needle-work is exceedingly fine and elaborate. Another relic of the same period,—the Cavalier General Sir Jacob Astley's buff-coat, with his belt and sword; the leather of the buff-coat, for I took it between my fingers, is about a quarter of an inch thick, of the same material as a wash-leather glove, and by no means smoothly dressed, though the sleeves are covered with silver-lace. Of old armor, there are admirable specimens; and it makes one's head ache to look at the iron pots which men used to thrust their heads into. Indeed, at one period they seem to have worn an inner iron cap underneath the helmet. I doubt whether there ever was any age of chivalry. . . . It certainly was no chivalric sentiment that made men case themselves in impenetrable iron, and ride about in iron prisons, fearfully peeping at their enemies through little slits and gimlet-holes. The unprotected breast of a private soldier must have shamed his leaders in those days. The point of honor is very different now.

I mean to go again and again, many times more, and will take each day some one department, and so endeavor to get some real use and improvement out of what I see. Much that is most valuable must be immitigably rejected; but something, according to the measure of my poor capacity, will really be taken into my mind. After all, it was an agreeable day, and I think the next one will be more so.

July 28th.—Day before yesterday I paid a second visit to the Exhibition, and devoted the day mainly to seeing the works of British painters, which fill a very large space,—two or three great saloons at the right side of the nave. Among the earliest are Hogarth's pictures, including the Sigismunda, which I remember to have seen before, with her lover's heart in her hand, looking like a monstrous strawberry; and the March to Finchley, than which nothing truer to English life and character was ever painted, nor ever can be; and a large stately portrait of Captain Coram, and others, all excellent in proportion as they come near to ordinary life, and are wrought out through its forms. All English painters resemble Hogarth in this respect. They cannot paint anything high, heroic, and ideal, and their attempts in that direction are wearisome to look at; but they sometimes produce good effects by means of awkward figures in ill-made coats and small-clothes, and hard, coarse-complexioned faces, such as they might see anywhere in the street. They are strong in homeliness and ugliness, weak in their efforts at the beautiful. Sir Thomas Lawrence attains a sort of grace, which you feel to be a trick, and therefore get disgusted with it. Reynolds is not quite genuine, though certainly he has produced some noble and beautiful heads. But Hogarth is the only English painter, except in the landscape department; there are no others who interpret life to me at all, unless it be some of the modern Pre-Raphaelites. Pretty village scenes of common life,—pleasant domestic passages, with a touch of easy humor in them,—little pathoses and fancynesses, are abundant enough; and Wilkie, to be sure, has done more than this, though not a great deal more. His merit lies, not in a high aim, but in accomplishing his aim so perfectly. It is unaccountable that the English painters' achievements should be so much inferior to those of the English poets, who have really elevated the human mind; but, to be sure, painting has only become an English art subsequently to the epochs of the greatest poets, and since the beginning of the last century, during which England had no poets. I respect Haydon more than I once did, not for his pictures, they being detestable to see, but for his heroic rejection of whatever his countrymen and he himself could really do, and his bitter resolve to achieve something higher,— failing in which, he died.

No doubt I am doing vast injustice to a great many gifted men in what I have here written,—as, for instance, Copley, who certainly has painted a slain man to the life; and to a crowd of landscape-painters, who have made wonderful reproductions of little English streams and shrubbery, and cottage doors and country lanes. And there is a picture called "The Evening Gun" by Danby,—a ship of war on a calm, glassy tide, at sunset, with the cannon-smoke puffing from her porthole; it is very beautiful, and so effective that you can even hear the report breaking upon the stillness, with so grand a roar that it is almost like stillness too. As for Turner, I care no more for his light-colored pictures than for so much lacquered ware or painted gingerbread. Doubtless this is my fault, my own deficiency; but I cannot help it,—not, at least, without sophisticating myself by the effort. The only modern pictures that accomplish a higher end than that of pleasing the eye—the only ones that really take hold of my mind, and with a kind of acerbity, like unripe fruit—are the works of Hunt, and one or two other painters of the Pre-Raphaelite school. They seem wilfully to abjure all beauty, and to make their pictures disagreeable out of mere malice; but at any rate, for the thought and feeling which are ground up with the paint, they will bear looking at, and disclose a deeper value the longer you look. Never was anything so stiff and unnatural as they appear; although every single thing represented seems to be taken directly out of life and reality, and, as it were, pasted down upon the canvas. They almost paint even separate hairs. Accomplishing so much, and so perfectly, it seems unaccountable that the picture does not live; but Nature has an art beyond these painters, and they leave out some medium,—some enchantment that should intervene, and keep the object from pressing so baldly and harshly upon the spectator's eyeballs. With the most lifelike reproduction, there is no illusion. I think if a semi-obscurity were thrown over the picture after finishing it to this nicety, it might bring it nearer to nature. I remember a heap of autumn leaves, every one of which seems to have been stiffened with gum and varnish, and then put carefully down into the stiffly disordered heap. Perhaps these artists may hereafter succeed in combining the truth of detail with a broader and higher truth. Coming from such a depth as their pictures do, and having really an idea as the seed of them, it is strange that they should look like the most made-up things imaginable. One picture by Hunt that greatly interested me was of some sheep that had gone astray among heights and precipices, and I could have looked all day at these poor, lost creatures,—so true was their meek alarm and hopeless bewilderment, their huddling together, without the slightest confidence of mutual help; all that the courage and wisdom of the bravest and wisest of them could do being to bleat, and only a few having spirits enough even for this.

After going through these modern masters, among whom were some French painters who do not interest me at all, I did a miscellaneous business, chiefly among the water-colors and photographs, and afterwards among the antiquities and works of ornamental art. I have forgotten what I saw, except the breastplate and helmet of Henry of Navarre, of steel, engraved with designs that have been half obliterated by scrubbing. I remember, too, a breastplate of an Elector of Saxony, with a bullet-hole through it. He received his mortal wound through that hole, and died of it two days afterwards, three hundred years ago.

There was a crowd of visitors, insomuch that, it was difficult to get a satisfactory view of the most interesting objects. They were nearly all middling-class people; the Exhibition, I think, does not reach the lower classed at all; in fact, it could not reach them, nor their betters either, without a good deal of study to help it out. I shall go to-day, and do my best to get profit out of it.

July 30th.—We all, with R—— and Fanny, went to the Exhibition yesterday, and spent the day there; not J——, however, for he went to the Botanical Gardens. After some little skirmishing with other things, I devoted myself to the historical portraits, which hang on both sides of the great nave, and went through them pretty faithfully. The oldest are pictures of Richard II. and Henry IV. and Edward IV. and Jane Shore, and seem to have little or no merit as works of art, being cold and stiff, the life having, perhaps, faded out of them; but these older painters were trustworthy, inasmuch as they had no idea of making a picture, but only of getting the face before them on canvas as accurately as they could. All English history scarcely supplies half a dozen portraits before the time of Henry VIII.; after that period, and through the reigns of Elizabeth and James, there are many ugly pictures by Dutchmen and Italians; and the collection is wonderfully rich in portraits of the time of Charles I. and the Commonwealth. Vandyke seems to have brought portrait-painting into fashion; and very likely the king's love of art diffused a taste for it throughout the nation, and remotely suggested, even to his enemies, to get their pictures painted. Elizabeth has perpetuated her cold, thin visage on many canvases, and generally with some fantasy of costume that makes her ridiculous to all time. There are several of Mary of Scotland, none of which have a gleam of beauty; but the stiff old brushes of these painters could not catch the beautiful. Of all the older pictures, the only one that I took pleasure in looking at was a portrait of Lord Deputy Falkland, by Vansomer, in James I.'s time,—a very stately, full-length figure in white, looking out of the picture as if he saw you. The catalogue says that this portrait suggested an incident in Horace Walpole's Castle of Otranto; but I do not remember it.

I have a haunting doubt of the value of portrait-painting; that is to say, whether it gives you a genuine idea of the person purporting to be represented. I do not remember ever to have recognized a man by having previously seen his portrait. Vandyke's pictures are full of grace and nobleness, but they do not look like Englishmen,—the burly, rough, wine-flushed and weather-reddened faces, and sturdy flesh and blood, which we see even at the present day, when they must naturally have become a good deal refined from either the country gentleman or the courtier of the Stuarts' age. There is an old, fat portrait of Gervoyse Holles, in a buff-coat,—a coarse, hoggish, yet manly man. The painter is unknown; but I honor him, and Gervoyse Holles too,—for one was willing to be truly rendered, and the other dared to do it. It seems to be the aim of portrait-painters generally, especially of those who have been most famous, to make their pictures as beautiful and noble as can anywise consist with retaining the very slightest resemblance to the person sitting to them. They seldom attain even the grace and beauty which they aim at, but only hit some temporary or individual taste. Vandyke, however, achieved graces that rise above time and fashion, and so did Sir Peter Lely, in his female portraits; but the doubt is, whether the works of either are genuine history. Not more so, I suspect, than the narrative of a historian who should seek to make poetry out of the events which he relates, rejecting those which could not possibly be thus idealized.

I observe, furthermore, that a full-length portrait has seldom face enough; not that it lacks its fair proportion by measurement, but the artist does not often find it possible to make the face so intellectually prominent as to subordinate the figure and drapery. Vandyke does this, however. In his pictures of Charles I., for instance, it is the melancholy grace of the visage that attracts the eye, and it passes to the rest of the composition only by an effort. Earlier and later pictures are but a few inches of face to several feet of figure and costume, and more insignificant than the latter because seldom so well done; and I suspect the same would generally be the case now, only that the present simplicity of costume gives the face a chance to be seen.

I was interrupted here, and cannot resume the thread; but considering how much of his own conceit the artist puts into a portrait, how much affectation the sitter puts on, and then again that no face is the same to any two spectators; also, that these portraits are darkened and faded with age, and can seldom be more than half seen, being hung too high, or somehow or other inconvenient, on the whole, I question whether there is much use in looking at them. The truest test would be, for a man well read in English history and biography, and himself an observer of insight, to go through the series without knowing what personages they represented, and write beneath each the name which the portrait vindicated for itself.

After getting through the portrait-gallery, I went among the engravings and photographs, and then glanced along the old masters, but without seriously looking at anything. While I was among the Dutch painters, a gentleman accosted me. It was Mr. J———, whom I once met at dinner with Bennoch. He told me that "the Poet Laureate" (as he called him) was in the Exhibition rooms; and as I expressed great interest, Mr. J——— was kind enough to go in quest of him. Not for the purpose of introduction, however, for he was not acquainted with Tennyson. Soon Mr. J——— returned, and said that he had found the Poet Laureate,—and, going into the saloon of the old masters, we saw him there, in company with Mr. Woolner, whose bust of him is now in the Exhibition.

Gazing at him with all my eyes, I liked him well, and rejoiced more in him than in all the other wonders of the Exhibition.

How strange that in these two or three pages I cannot get one single touch that may call him up hereafter!

I would most gladly have seen more of this one poet of our day, but forbore to follow him; for I must own that it seemed mean to be dogging him through the saloons, or even to look at him, since it was to be done stealthily, if at all.

He is as un-English as possible; indeed an Englishman of genius usually lacks the national characteristics, and is great abnormally. Even the great sailor, Nelson, was unlike his countrymen in the qualities that constituted him a hero; he was not the perfection of an Englishman, but a creature of another kind,—sensitive, nervous, excitable, and really more like a Frenchman.

Un-English as he was, Tennyson had not, however, an American look. I cannot well describe the difference; but there was something more mellow in him,—softer, sweeter, broader, more simple than we are apt to be. Living apart from men as he does would hurt any one of us more than it does him. I may as well leave him here, for I cannot touch the central point.

August 2d.—Day before yesterday I went again to the Exhibition, and began the day with looking at the old masters. Positively, I do begin to receive some pleasure from looking at pictures; but as yet it has nothing to do with any technical merit, nor do I think I shall ever get so far as that. Some landscapes by Ruysdael, and some portraits by Murillo, Velasquez, and Titian, were those which I was most able to appreciate; and I see reason for allowing, contrary to my opinion, as expressed a few pages back, that a portrait may preserve some valuable characteristics of the person represented. The pictures in the English portrait-gallery are mostly very bad, and that may be the reason why I saw so little in them. I saw too, at this last visit, a Virgin and Child, which appeared to me to have an expression more adequate to the subject than most of the innumerable virgins and children, in which we see only repetitions of simple maternity; indeed, any mother, with her first child, would serve an artist for one of them. But, in this picture the Virgin had a look as if she were loving the infant as her own child, and at the same time rendering him an awful worship, as to her Creator.

While I was sitting in the central saloon, listening to the music, a young man accosted me, presuming that I was so-and-so, the American author. He himself was a traveller for a publishing firm; and he introduced conversation by talking of Uttoxeter, and my description of it in an annual. He said that the account had caused a good deal of pique among the good people of Uttoxeter, because of the ignorance which I attribute to them as to the circumstance which connects Johnson with their town. The spot where Johnson stood can, it appears, still be pointed out. It is on one side of the market-place, and not in the neighborhood of the church. I forget whether I recorded, at the time, that an Uttoxeter newspaper was sent me, containing a proposal that a statue or memorial should be erected on the spot. It would gratify me exceedingly if such a result should come from my pious pilgrimage thither.

My new acquaintance, who was cockneyish, but very intelligent and agreeable, went on to talk about many literary matters and characters; among others, about Miss Bronte, whom he had seen at the Chapter Coffee-House, when she and her sister Anne first went to London. He was at that time connected with the house of ——— and ———, and he described the surprise and incredulity of Mr.———, when this little, commonplace-looking woman presented herself as the author of Jane Eyre. His story brought out the insignificance of Charlotte Bronte's aspect, and the bluff rejection of her by Mr. ———, much more strongly than Mrs. Gaskell's narrative.

Chorlton Road, August 9th.—We have changed our lodgings since my last date, those at Old Trafford being inconvenient, and the landlady a sharp, peremptory housewife, better fitted to deal with her own family than to be complaisant to guests. We are now a little farther from the Exhibition, and not much better off as regards accommodation, but the housekeeper is a pleasant, civil sort of a woman, auspiciously named Mrs. Honey. The house is a specimen of the poorer middle-class dwellings as built nowadays,—narrow staircase, thin walls, and, being constructed for sale, very ill put together indeed,—the floors with wide cracks between the boards, and wide crevices admitting both air and light over the doors, so that the house is full of draughts. The outer walls, it seems to me, are but of one brick in thickness, and the partition walls certainly no thicker; and the movements, and sometimes the voices, of people in the contiguous house are audible to us. The Exhibition has temporarily so raised the value of lodgings here that we have to pay a high price for even such a house as this.

Mr. Wilding having gone on a tour to Scotland, I had to be at the Consulate every day last week till yesterday; when I absented myself from duty, and went to the Exhibition. U—— and I spent an hour together, looking principally at the old Dutch masters, who seem to me the most wonderful set of men that ever handled a brush. Such lifelike representations of cabbages, onions, brass kettles, and kitchen crockery; such blankets, with the woollen fuzz upon them; such everything I never thought that the skill of man could produce! Even the photograph cannot equal their miracles. The closer you look, the more minutely true the picture is found to be, and I doubt if even the microscope could see beyond the painter's touch. Gerard Dow seems to be the master among these queer magicians. A straw mat, in one of his pictures, is the most miraculous thing that human art has yet accomplished; and there is a metal vase, with a dent in it, that is absolutely more real than reality. These painters accomplish all they aim at,—a praise, methinks, which can be given to no other men since the world began. They must have laid down their brushes with perfect satisfaction, knowing that each one of their million touches had been necessary to the effect, and that there was not one too few nor too many. And it is strange how spiritual and suggestive the commonest household article—an earthen pitcher, for example— becomes, when represented with entire accuracy. These Dutchmen got at the soul of common things, and so made them types and interpreters of the spiritual world.

Afterwards I looked at many of the pictures of the old masters, and found myself gradually getting a taste for them; at least, they give me more and more pleasure the oftener I come to see them. Doubtless, I shall be able to pass for a man of taste by the time I return to America. It is an acquired taste, like that for wines; and I question whether a man is really any truer, wiser, or better for possessing it. From the old masters, I went among the English painters, and found myself more favorably inclined towards some of them than at my previous visits; seeing something wonderful even in Turner's lights and mists and yeasty waves, although I should like him still better if his pictures looked in the least like what they typify. The most disagreeable of English painters is Etty, who had a diseased appetite for woman's flesh, and spent his whole life, apparently, in painting them with enormously developed busts. I do not mind nudity in a modest and natural way; but Etty's women really thrust their nudity upon you with malice aforethought, ... and the worst of it is they are not beautiful.

Among the last pictures that I looked at was Hogarth's March to Finchley; and surely nothing can be covered more thick and deep with English nature than that piece of canvas. The face of the tall grenadier in the centre, between two women, both of whom have claims on him, wonderfully expresses trouble and perplexity; and every touch in the picture meant something and expresses what it meant.

The price of admission, after two o'clock, being sixpence, the Exhibition was thronged with a class of people who do not usually come in such large numbers. It was both pleasant and touching to see how earnestly some of them sought to get instruction from what they beheld. The English are a good and simple people, and take life in earnest.

August 14th.—Passing by the gateway of the Manchester Cathedral the other morning, on my way to the station, I found a crowd collected, and, high overhead, the bells were chiming for a wedding. These chimes of bells are exceedingly impressive, so broadly gladsome as they are, filling the whole air, and every nook of one's heart with sympathy. They are good for a people to rejoice with, and good also for a marriage, because through all their joy there is something solemn,—a tone of that voice which we have heard so often at funerals. It is good to see how everybody, up to this old age of the world, takes an interest in weddings, and seems to have a faith that now, at last, a couple have come together to make each other happy. The high, black, rough old cathedral tower sent out its chime of bells as earnestly as for any bridegroom and bride that came to be married five hundred years ago. I went into the churchyard, but there was such a throng of people on its pavement of flat tombstones, and especially such a cluster along the pathway by which the bride was to depart, that I could only see a white dress waving along, and really do not know whether she was a beauty or a fright. The happy pair got into a post-chaise that was waiting at the gate, and immediately drew some crimson curtains, and so vanished into their Paradise. There were two other post-chaises and pairs, and all three had postilions in scarlet. This is the same cathedral where, last May, I saw a dozen couples married in the lump.

In a railway carriage, two or three days ago, an old merchant made rather a good point of one of the uncomfortable results of the electric telegraph. He said that formerly a man was safe from bad news, such as intelligence of failure of debtors, except at the hour of opening his letters in the morning; and then he was in some degree prepared for it, since, among (say) fifteen letters, he would be pretty certain to find some "queer" one. But since the telegraph has come into play, he is never safe, and may be hit with news of failure, shipwreck, fall of stocks, or whatever disaster, at all hours of the day.

I went to the Exhibition on Wednesday with U——, and looked at the pencil sketches of the old masters; also at the pictures generally, old and new. I particularly remember a spring landscape, by John Linnell the younger. It is wonderfully good; so tender and fresh that the artist seems really to have caught the evanescent April and made her permanent. Here, at least, is eternal spring.

I saw a little man, behind an immense beard, whom I take to be the Duke of Newcastle; at least, there was a photograph of him in the gallery, with just such a beard. He was at the Palace on that day.

August 16th.—I went again to the Exhibition day before yesterday, and looked much at both the modern and ancient pictures, as also at the water-colors. I am making some progress as a connoisseur, and have got so far as to be able to distinguish the broader differences of style,— as, for example, between Rubens and Rembrandt. I should hesitate to claim any more for myself thus far. In fact, however, I do begin to have a liking for good things, and to be sure that they are good. Murillo seems to me about the noblest and purest painter that ever lived, and his "Good Shepherd" the loveliest picture I have seen. It is a hopeful symptom, moreover, of improving taste, that I see more merit in the crowd of painters than I was at first competent to acknowledge. I could see some of their defects from the very first; but that is the earliest stage of connoisseurship, after a formal and ignorant admiration. Mounting a few steps higher, one sees beauties. But how much study, how many opportunities, are requisite to form and cultivate a taste! The Exhibition must be quite thrown away on the mass of spectators.

Both they and I are better able to appreciate the specimens of ornamental art contained in the Oriental Room, and in the numerous cases that are ranged up and down the nave. The gewgaws of all Time are here, in precious metals, glass, china, ivory, and every other material that could be wrought into curious and beautiful shapes; great basins and dishes of embossed gold from the Queen's sideboard, or from the beaufets of noblemen; vessels set with precious stones; the pastoral staffs of prelates, some of them made of silver or gold, and enriched with gems, and what have been found in the tombs of the bishops; state swords, and silver maces; the rich plate of colleges, elaborately wrought,—great cups, salvers, tureens, that have been presented by loving sons to their Alma Mater; the heirlooms of old families, treasured from generation to generation, and hitherto only to be seen by favored friends; famous historical jewels, some of which are painted in the portraits of the historical men and women that hang on the walls; numerous specimens of the beautiful old Venetian glass, some of which looks so fragile that it is a wonder how it could bear even the weight of the wine, that used to be poured into it, without breaking. These are the glasses that tested poison, by being shattered into fragments at its touch. The strangest and ugliest old crockery, pictured over with monstrosities,—the Palissy ware, embossed with vegetables, fishes, lobsters, that look absolutely real; the delicate Sevres china, each piece made inestimable by pictures from a master's hand;—in short, it is a despair and misery to see so much that is curious and beautiful, and to feel that far the greater portion of it will slip out of the memory, and be as if we had never seen it. But I mean to look again and again at these things. We soon perceive that the present day does not engross all the taste and ingenuity that has ever existed in the mind of man; that, in fact, we are a barren age in that respect.

August 20th.—I went to the Exhibition on Monday, and again yesterday, and measurably enjoyed both visits. I continue to think, however, that a picture cannot be fully enjoyed except by long and intimate acquaintance with it, nor can I quite understand what the enjoyment of a connoisseur is. He is not usually, I think, a man of deep, poetic feeling, and does not deal with the picture through his heart, nor set it in a poem, nor comprehend it morally. If it be a landscape, he is not entitled to judge of it by his intimacy with nature; if a picture of human action, he has no experience nor sympathy of life's deeper passages. However, as my acquaintance with pictures increases, I find myself recognizing more and more the merit of the acknowledged masters of the art; but, possibly, it is only because I adopt the wrong principles which may have been laid down by the connoisseurs. But there can be no mistake about Murillo,— not that I am worthy to admire him yet, however.

Seeing the many pictures of Holy Families, and the Virgin and Child, which have been painted for churches and convents, the idea occurs, that it was in this way that the poor monks and nuns gratified, as far as they could, their natural longing for earthly happiness. It was not Mary and her heavenly Child that they really beheld, or wished for; but an earthly mother rejoicing over her baby, and displaying it probably to the world as an object worthy to be admired by kings,—as Mary does, in the Adoration of the Magi. Every mother, I suppose, feels as if her first child deserved everybody's worship.

I left the Exhibition at three o'clock, and went to Manchester, where I sought out Mr. C S——— in his little office. He greeted me warmly, and at five we took the omnibus for his house, about four miles from town. He seems to be on pleasant terms with his neighbors, for almost everybody that got into the omnibus exchanged kindly greetings with him, and indeed his kindly, simple, genial nature comes out so evidently that it would be difficult not to like him. His house stands, with others, in a green park,—a small, pretty, semi-detached suburban residence of brick, with a lawn and garden round it. In close vicinity, there is a deep clough or dell, as shaggy and wild as a poet could wish, and with a little stream running through it, as much as five miles long.

The interior of the house is very pretty, and nicely, even handsomely and almost sumptuously, furnished; and I was very glad to find him so comfortable. His recognition as a poet has been hearty enough to give him a feeling of success, for he showed me various tokens of the estimation in which he is held,—for instance, a presentation copy of Southey's works, in which the latter had written "Amicus amico,—poeta poetae." He said that Southey had always been most kind to him. . . . There were various other testimonials from people of note, American as well as English. In his parlor there is a good oil-painting of himself, and in the drawing-room a very fine crayon sketch, wherein his face, handsome and agreeable, is lighted up with all a poet's ecstasy; likewise a large and fine engraving from the picture. The government has recognized his poetic merit by a pension of fifty pounds,—a small sung, it is true, but enough to mark him out as one who has deserved well of his country. . . . The man himself is very good and lovable. . . . I was able to gratify him by saying that I had recently seen many favorable notices of his poems in the American newspapers; an edition having been published a few months since on our side of the ocean. He was much pleased at this, and asked me to send him the notices. . . .

August 30th.—I have been two or three times to the Exhibition since my last date, and enjoy it more as I become familiar with it. There is supposed to be about a third of the good pictures here which England contains; and it is said that the Tory nobility and gentry have contributed to it much more freely and largely than the Whigs. The Duke of Devonshire, for instance, seems to have sent nothing. Mr. Ticknor, the Spanish historian, whom I met yesterday, observed that we should not think quite so much of this Exhibition as the English do after we have been to Italy, although it is a good school in which to gain a preparatory knowledge of the different styles of art. I am glad to hear that there are better things still to be seen. Nevertheless, I should suppose that certain painters are better represented here than they ever have been or will be elsewhere. Vandyke, certainly, can be seen nowhere else so well; Rembrandt and Rubens have satisfactory specimens; and the whole series of English pictorial achievement is shown more perfectly than within any other walls. Perhaps it would be wise to devote myself to the study of this latter, and leave the foreigners to be studied on their own soil. Murillo can hardly have done better than in the pictures by him which we see here. There is nothing of Raphael's here that is impressive. Titian has some noble portraits, but little else that I care to see. In all these old masters, Murillo only excepted, it is very rare, I must say, to find any trace of natural feeling and passion; and I am weary of naked goddesses, who never had any real life and warmth in the painter's imagination,—or, if so, it was the impure warmth of an unchaste woman, who sat for him.

Last week I dined at Mr. F. Heywood's to meet Mr. Adolphus, the author of a critical work on the Waverley Novels, published long ago, and intended to prove, from internal evidence, that they were written by Sir Walter Scott. . . . His wife was likewise of the party, ... and also a young Spanish lady, their niece, and daughter of a Spaniard of literary note. She herself has literary tastes and ability, and is well known to Prescott, whom, I believe, she has assisted in his historical researches, and also to Professor Ticknor; and furthermore she is very handsome and unlike an English damsel, very youthful and maiden-like; and her manners have all ardor and enthusiasm that were pleasant to see, especially as she spoke warmly of my writings; and yet I should wrong her if I left the impression of her being forthputting and obtrusive, for it was not the fact in the least. She speaks English like a native, insomuch that I should never have suspected her to be anything else.

My nerves recently have not been in an exactly quiet and normal state. I begin to weary of England and need another clime.

September 6th.—I think I paid my last visit to the Exhibition, and feel as if I had had enough of it, although I have got but a small part of the profit it might have afforded me. But pictures are certainly quite other things to me now from what they were at my first visit; it seems even as if there were a sort of illumination within them, that makes me see them more distinctly. Speaking of pictures, the miniature of Anne of Cleves is here, on the faith of which Henry VIII. married her; also, the picture of the Infanta of Spain, which Buckingham brought over to Charles I. while Prince of Wales. This has a delicate, rosy prettiness.

One rather interesting portion of the Exhibition is the Refreshment-room, or rather rooms; for very much space is allowed both to the first and second classes. I have looked most at the latter, because there John Ball and his wife may be seen in full gulp aid guzzle, swallowing vast quantities of cold boiled beef, thoroughly moistened with porter or bitter ale; and very good meat and drink it is.

At my last visit, on Friday, I met Judge Pollock of Liverpool, who introduced me to a gentleman in a gray slouched hat as Mr. Du Val, an artist, resident in Manchester; and Mr. Du Val invited me to dine with him at six o'clock. So I went to Carlton Grove, his residence, and found it a very pretty house, with its own lawn and shrubbery about it. . . . There was a mellow fire in the grate, which made the drawing-room very cosey and pleasant, as the dusk came on before dinner. Mr. Du Val looked like an artist, and like a remarkable man. . . . We had very good talk, chiefly about the Exhibition, and Du Val spoke generously and intelligently of his brother-artists. He says that England might furnish five exhibitions, each one as rich as the present. I find that the most famous picture here is one that I have hardly looked at, "The Three Marys," by Annibal Caracci. In the drawing-room there were several pictures and sketches by Du Val, one of which I especially liked,—a misty, moonlight picture of the Mersey, near Seacombe. I never saw painted such genuine moonlight. . . .

I took my leave at half past ten, and found my cab at the door, and my cabman snugly asleep inside of it; and when Mr. Du Val awoke him, he proved to be quite drunk, insomuch that I hesitated whether to let him clamber upon the box, or to take post myself, and drive the cabman home. However, I propounded two questions to him: first, whether his horse would go of his own accord; and, secondly, whether he himself was invariably drunk at that time of night, because, if it were his normal state, I should be safer with him drunk than sober. Being satisfied on these points, I got in, and was driven home without accident or adventure; except, indeed, that the cabman drew up and opened the door for me to alight at a vacant lot on Stratford Road, just as if there had been a house and home and cheerful lighted windows in that vacancy. On my remonstrance he resumed the whip and reins, and reached Boston Terrace at last; and, thanking me for an extra sixpence as well as he could speak, he begged me to inquire for "Little John" whenever I next wanted a cab. Cabmen are, as a body, the most ill-natured and ungenial men in the world; but this poor little man was excellently good-humored.

Speaking of the former rudeness of manners, now gradually refining away, of the Manchester people, Judge ——— said that, when he first knew Manchester, women, meeting his wife in the street, would take hold of her dress and say, "Ah, three and sixpence a yard!" The men were very rough, after the old Lancashire fashion. They have always, however, been a musical people, and this may have been a germ of refinement in them. They are still much more simple and natural than the Liverpool people, who love the aristocracy, and whom they heartily despise. It is singular that the great Art-Exhibition should have come to pass in the rudest great town in England.

LEAMINGTON.

Lansdowne Cirrus, September 10th.—We have become quite weary of our small, mean, uncomfortable, and unbeautiful lodgings at Chorlton Road, with poor and scanty furniture within doors, and no better prospect from the parlor windows than a mud-puddle, larger than most English lakes, on a vacant building-lot opposite our house. The Exhibition, too, was fast becoming a bore; for you must really love a picture, in order to tolerate the sight of it many times. Moreover, the smoky and sooty air of that abominable Manchester affected my wife's throat disadvantageously; so, on a Tuesday morning, we struck our tent and set forth again, regretting to leave nothing except the kind disposition of Mrs. Honey, our housekeeper. I do not remember meeting with any other lodging-house keeper who did not grow hateful and fearful on short acquaintance; but I attribute this, not so much to the people themselves, as, primarily, to the unfair and ungenerous conduct of some of their English guests, who feel so sure of being cheated that they always behave as if in an enemy's country, and therefore they find it one.

The rain poured down upon us as we drove away in two cabs, laden with mountainous luggage to the London Road station; and the whole day was grim with cloud and moist with showers. We went by way of Birmingham, and stayed three hours at the great dreary station there, waiting for the train to Leamington, whither Fanny had gone forward the day before to secure lodgings for us (as she is English, and understands the matter) We all were tired and dull by the time we reached the Leamington station, where a note from Fanny gave us the address of our lodgings. Lansdowne Circus is really delightful after that ugly and grimy suburb of Manchester. Indeed, there could not possibly be a greater contrast than between Leamington and Manchester,—the latter built only for dirty uses, and scarcely intended as a habitation for man; the former so cleanly, so set out with shade trees, so regular in its streets, so neatly paved, its houses so prettily contrived and nicely stuccoed, that it does not look like a portion of the work-a-day world.

KENILWORTH.

September 13th.—The weather was very uncertain through the last week, and yesterday morning, too, was misty and sunless; notwithstanding which we took the rail for Kenilworth before eleven. The distance from Leamington is less than five miles, and at the Kenilworth station we found a little bit of an omnibus, into which we packed ourselves, together with two ladies, one of whom, at least, was an American. I begin to agree partly with the English, that we are not a people of elegant manners. At all events there is sometimes a bare, hard, meagre sort of deportment, especially in our women, that has not its parallel elsewhere. But perhaps what sets off this kind of behavior, and brings it into alto relievo, is the fact of such uncultivated persons travelling abroad, and going to see sights that would not be interesting except to people of some education and refinement.

We saw but little of the village of Kenilworth, passing through it sidelong fashion, in the omnibus; but I learn that it has between three and four thousand inhabitants, and is of immemorial antiquity. We saw a few old, gabled, and timber-framed houses; but generally the town was of modern aspect, although less so in the immediate vicinity of the castle gate, across the road from which there was an inn, with bowling-greens, and a little bunch of houses and shops. Apart from the high road there is a gate-house, ancient, but in excellent repair, towered, turreted, and battlemented, and looking like a castle in itself. Until Cromwell's time, the entrance to the castle used to be beneath an arch that passed through this structure; but the gate-house being granted to one of the Parliament officers, he converted it into a residence, and apparently added on a couple of gables, which now look quite as venerable as the rest of the edifice. Admission within the outer grounds of the castle is now obtained through a little wicket close beside the gate-house, at which sat one or two old men, who touched their hats to us in humble willingness to accept a fee. One of them had guide-books for sale; and, finding that we were not to be bothered by a cicerone, we bought one of his books.

The ruins are perhaps two hundred yards from the gate-house and the road, and the space between is a pasture for sheep, which also browse in the inner court, and shelter themselves in the dungeons and state apartments of the castle. Goats would be fitter occupants, because they would climb to the tops of the crumbling towers, and nibble the weeds and shrubbery that grow there. The first part of the castle which we reach is called Caesar's Tower, being the oldest portion of the ruins, and still very stalwart and massive, and built of red freestone, like all the rest. Caesar's Tower being on the right, Leicester's Buildings, erected by the Earl of Leicester, Queen Elizabeth's favorite, are on the left; and between these two formerly stood other structures which have now as entirely disappeared as if they had never existed; and through the wide gap, thus opened, appears the grassy inner court, surrounded on three sides by half-fallen towers and shattered walls. Some of these were erected by John of Gaunt; and among these ruins is the Banqueting-Hall,— or rather was,— for it has now neither floor nor roof, but only the broken stone-work of some tall, arched windows, and the beautiful, old ivied arch of the entrance-way, now inaccessible from the ground. The ivy is very abundant about the ruins, and hangs its green curtains quite from top to bottom of some of the windows. There are likewise very large and aged trees within the castle, there being no roof nor pavement anywhere, except in some dungeon-like nooks; so that the trees having soil and air enough, and being sheltered from unfriendly blasts, can grow as if in a nursery. Hawthorn, however, next to ivy, is the great ornament and comforter of these desolate ruins. I have not seen so much nor such thriving hawthorn anywhere else,—in the court, high up on crumbly heights, on the sod that carpets roofless rooms,—everywhere, indeed, and now rejoicing in plentiful crops of red berries. The ivy is even more wonderfully luxuriant; its trunks being, in some places, two or three feet in diameter, and forming real buttresses against the walls, which are actually supported and vastly strengthened by this parasite, that clung to them at first only for its own convenience, and now holds them up, lest it should be ruined by their fall. Thus an abuse has strangely grown into a use, and I think we may sometimes see the same fact, morally, in English matters. There is something very curious in the close, firm grip which the ivy fixes upon the wall, closer and closer for centuries. Neither is it at all nice as to what it clutches, in its necessity for support. I saw in the outer court an old hawthorn-tree, to which a plant of ivy had married itself, and the ivy trunk and the hawthorn trunk were now absolutely incorporated, and in their close embrace you could not tell which was which.

At one end of the Banqueting-Hall, there are two large bay-windows, one of which looks into the inner court, and the other affords a view of the surrounding country. The former is called Queen Elizabeth's Dressing-room. Beyond the Banqueting-Hall is what is called the Strong Tower, up to the top of which we climbed principally by the aid of the stones that have tumbled down from it. A lady sat half-way down the crumbly descent, within the castle, on a camp-stool, and before an easel, sketching this tower, on the summit of which we sat. She said it was Amy Robsart's Tower; and within it, open to the day, and quite accessible, we saw a room that we were free to imagine had been occupied by her. I do not find that these associations of real scenes with fictitious events greatly heighten the charm of them.

By this time the sun had come out brightly, and with such warmth that we were glad to sit down in the shadow. Several sight-seers were now rambling about, and among them some school-boys, who kept scrambling up to points whither no other animal, except a goat, would have ventured. Their shouts and the sunshine made the old castle cheerful; and what with the ivy and the hawthorn, and the other old trees, it was very beautiful and picturesque. But a castle does not make nearly so interesting and impressive a ruin as an abbey, because the latter was built for beauty, and on a plan in which deep thought and feeling were involved; and having once been a grand and beautiful work, it continues grand and beautiful through all the successive stages of its decay. But a castle is rudely piled together for strength and other material conveniences; and, having served these ends, it has nothing left to fall back upon, but crumbles into shapeless masses, which are often as little picturesque as a pile of bricks. Without the ivy and the shrubbery, this huge Kenilworth would not be a pleasant object, except for one or two window-frames, with broken tracery, in the Banqueting-Hall. . . .

We stayed from eleven till two, and identified the various parts of the castle as well as we could by the guide-book. The ruins are very extensive, though less so than I should have imagined, considering that seven acres were included within the castle wall. But a large part of the structures have been taken away to build houses in Kenilworth village and elsewhere, and much, too, to make roads with, and a good deal lies under the green turf in the court-yards, inner and outer. As we returned to the gate, my wife and U—— went into the gate-house to see an old chimney-piece, and other antiquities, and J—— and I proceeded a little way round the outer wall, and saw the remains of the moat, and Lin's Tower,—a real and shattered fabric of John of Gaunt.

The omnibus now drove up, and one of the old men at the gate came hobbling up to open the door, and was rewarded with a sixpence, and we drove down to the King's Head. . . . We then walked out and bought prints of the castle, and inquired our way to the church and to the ruins of the Priory. The latter, so far as we could discover them, are very few and uninteresting; and the church, though it has a venerable exterior, and an aged spire, has been so modernized within, and in so plain a fashion, as to have lost what beauty it may once have had. There were a few brasses and mural monuments, one of which was a marble group of a dying woman and her family by Westmacott. The sexton was a cheerful little man, but knew very little about his church, and nothing of the remains of the Priory. The day was spent very pleasantly amid this beautiful green English scenery, these fine old Warwickshire trees, and broad, gently swelling fields.

LIVERPOOL.

September 17th.—I took the train for Rugby, and thence to Liverpool. The most noticeable character at Mrs. Blodgett's now is Mr. T———, a Yankee, who has seen the world, and gathered much information and experience already, though still a young man,—a handsome man, with black curly hair, a dark, intelligent, bright face, and rather cold blue eyes, but a very pleasant air and address. His observing faculties are very strongly developed in his forehead, and his reflective ones seem to be adequate to making some, if not the deepest, use of what he sees. He has voyaged and travelled almost all over the world, and has recently published a book of his peregrinations, which has been well received. He is of exceeding fluent talk, though rather too much inclined to unfold the secret springs of action in Louis Napoleon, and other potentates, and to tell of revolutions that are coming at some unlooked-for moment, but soon. Still I believe in his wisdom and foresight about as much as in any other man's. There are no such things. He is a merchant, and meditates settling in London, and making a colossal fortune there during the next ten or twenty years; that being the period during which London is to hold the exchanges of the world, and to continue its metropolis. After that, New York is to be the world's queen city.

There is likewise here a young American, named A———, who has been at a German University, and favors us with descriptions of his student life there, which seems chiefly to have consisted in drinking beer and fighting duels. He shows a cut on his nose as a trophy of these combats. He has with him a dog of St. Bernard, who is a much more remarkable character than himself,—an immense dog, a noble and gentle creature; and really it touches my heart that his master is going to take him from his native snow-mountain to a Southern plantation to die. Mr. A——— says that there are now but five of these dogs extant at the convent; there having, within two or three years, been a disease among them, with which this dog also has suffered. His master has a certificate of his genuineness, and of himself being the rightful purchaser; and he says that as he descended the mountain, every peasant along the road stopped him, and would have compelled him to give up the dog had he not produced this proof of property. The neighboring mountaineers are very jealous of the breed being taken away, considering them of such importance to their own safety. This huge animal, the very biggest dog I ever saw, though only eleven months old, and not so high by two or three inches as he will be, allows Mr. ——— to play with him, and take him on his shoulders (he weighs, at least, a hundred pounds), like any lapdog.

LEAMINGTON.

Lansdowne Circus, October 10th.—I returned hither from Liverpool last week, and have spent the time idly since then, reposing myself after the four years of unnatural restraint in the Consulate. Being already pretty well acquainted with the neighborhood of Leamington, I have little or nothing to record about the prettiest, cheerfullest, cleanest of English towns.

On Saturday we took the rail for Coventry, about a half-hour's travel distant. I had been there before, more than two years ago. . . . No doubt I described it on my first visit; and it is not remarkable enough to be worth two descriptions,—a large town of crooked and irregular streets and lanes, not looking nearly so ancient as it is, because of new brick and stuccoed fronts which have been plastered over its antiquity; although still there are interspersed the peaked gables of old-fashioned, timber-built houses; or an archway of worn stone, which, if you pass through it, shows like an avenue from the present to the past; for just in the rear of the new-fangled aspect lurks the old arrangement of court-yards, and rustiness, and grimness, that would not be suspected from the exterior.

Right across the narrow street stands St. Michael's Church with its tall, tall tower and spire. The body of the church has been almost entirely recased with stone since I was here before; but the tower still retains its antiquity, and is decorated with statues that look down from their lofty niches seemingly in good preservation. The tower and spire are most stately and beautiful, the whole church very noble. We went in, and found that the vulgar plaster of Cromwell's time has been scraped from the pillars and arches, leaving them all as fresh and splendid as if just made.

We looked also into Trinity Church, which stands close by St. Michael's, separated only, I think, by the churchyard. We also visited St. John's Church, which is very venerable as regards its exterior, the stone being worn and smoothed—if not roughened, rather—by centuries of storm and fitful weather. This wear and tear, however, has almost ceased to be a charm to my mind, comparatively to what it was when I first began to see old buildings. Within, the church is spoiled by wooden galleries, built across the beautiful pointed arches.

We saw nothing else particularly worthy of remark except Ford's Hospital, in Grey Friars' Street. It has an Elizabethan front of timber and plaster, facing on the street, with two or three peaked gables in a row, beneath which is a low, arched entrance, giving admission into a small paved quadrangle, open to the sky above, but surrounded by the walls, lozenge-paned windows, and gables of the Hospital. The quadrangle is but a few paces in width, and perhaps twenty in length; and, through a half-closed doorway, at the farther end, there was a glimpse into a garden. Just within the entrance, through an open door, we saw the neat and comfortable apartment of the Matron of the Hospital; and, along the quadrangle, on each side, there were three or four doors, through which we glanced into little rooms, each containing a fireplace, a bed, a chair or two,—a little, homely, domestic scene, with one old woman in the midst of it; one old woman in each room. They are destitute widows, who have their lodging and home here,—a small room for each one to sleep, cook, and be at home in,—and three and sixpence a week to feed and clothe themselves with,—a cloak being the only garment bestowed on them. When one of the sisterhood dies each old woman has to pay twopence towards the funeral; and so they slowly starve and wither out of life, and claim each their twopence contribution in turn. I am afraid they have a very dismal time.

There is an old man's hospital in another part of the town, on a similar plan. A collection of sombre and lifelike tales might be written on the idea of giving the experiences of these Hospitallers, male and female; and they might be supposed to be written by the Matron of one, who had acquired literary taste and practice as a governess,—and by the Master of the other, a retired school-usher.

It was market-day in Coventry, and far adown the street leading from it there were booths and stalls, and apples, pears, toys, books, among which I saw my Twice-Told Tales, with an awful portrait of myself as frontispiece,—and various country produce, offered for sale by men, women, and girls. The scene looked lively, but had not much vivacity in it.

October 27th.—The autumn has advanced progressively, and is now fairly established, though still there is much green foliage, in spite of many brown trees, and an enormous quantity of withered leaves, too damp to rustle, strewing the paths,—whence, however, they are continually swept up and carried off in wheelbarrows, either for neatness or for the agricultural worth, as manure, of even a withered leaf. The pastures look just as green as ever,—a deep, bright verdure, that seems almost sunshine in itself, however sombre the sky may be. The little plats of grass and flowers, in front of our circle of houses, might still do credit to an American midsummer; for I have seen beautiful roses here within a day or two; and dahlias, asters, and such autumnal flowers, are plentiful; and I have no doubt that the old year's flowers will bloom till those of the new year appear. Really, the English winter is not so terrible as ours.

October 30th.—Wednesday was one of the most beautiful of all days, and gilded almost throughout with the precious English sunshine,—the most delightful sunshine ever made, both for its positive fine qualities and because we seldom get it without too great an admixture of water. We made no use of this lovely day, except to walk to an Arboretum and Pinetum on the outskirts of the town. U—— and Mrs. Shepard made an excursion to Guy's Cliff.

[Here comes in the visit to Leicester's Hospital and Redfern's Shop, and St. Mary's Church, printed in Our Old Home.—ED.]

From Redfern's we went back to the market-place, expecting to find J—— at the Museum, but the keeper said he had gone away. We went into this museum, which contains the collections in Natural History, etc., of a county society. It is very well arranged, and is rich in specimens of ornithology, among which was an albatross, huge beyond imagination. I do not think that Coleridge could have known the size of the fowl when he caused it to be hung round the neck of his Ancient Mariner. There were a great many humming-birds from various parts of the world, and some of their breasts actually gleamed and shone as with the brightest lustre of sunset. Also, many strange fishes, and a huge pike taken from the river Avon, and so long that I wonder how he could turn himself about in such a little river as the Avon is near Warwick. A great curiosity was a bunch of skeleton leaves and flowers, prepared by a young lady, and preserving all the most delicate fibres of the plant, looking like inconceivably fine lace-work, white as snow, while the substance was quite taken away. In another room there were minerals, shells, and a splendid collection of fossils, among which were remains of antediluvian creatures, several feet long. In still another room, we saw some historical curiosities,—the most interesting of which were two locks of reddish-brown hair, one from the head and one from the beard of Edward IV. They were fastened to a manuscript letter which authenticates the hair as having been taken from King Edward's tomb in 1739. Near these relics was a seal of the great Earl of Warwick, the mighty kingmaker; also a sword from Bosworth Field, smaller and shorter than those now in use; for, indeed, swords seem to have increased in length, weight, and formidable aspect, now that the weapon has almost ceased to be used in actual warfare. The short Roman sword was probably more murderous than any weapon of the same species, except the bowie-knife. Here, too, were Parliamentary cannon-balls, etc. . . .

[The visit to Whitnash intervenes here.—ED.]

LONDON.

24 Great Russell Street, November 10th.—We have been thinking and negotiating about taking lodgings in London lately, and this morning we left Leamington and reached London with no other misadventure than that of leaving the great bulk of our luggage behind us,—the van which we hired to take it to the railway station having broken down under its prodigious weight, in the middle of the street. On our journey we saw nothing particularly worthy of note,—but everywhere the immortal verdure of England, scarcely less perfect than in June, so far as the fields are concerned, though the foliage of the trees presents pretty much the same hues as those of our own forests, after the gayety and gorgeousness have departed from them.

Our lodgings are in close vicinity to the British Museum, which is the great advantage we took them for.

I felt restless and uncomfortable, and soon strolled forth, without any definite object, and walked as far as Charing Cross. Very dull and dreary the city looked, and not in the least lively, even where the throng was thickest and most brisk. As I trudged along, my reflection was, that never was there a dingier, uglier, less picturesque city than London; and that it is really wonderful that so much brick and stone, for centuries together, should have been built up with so poor a result. Yet these old names of the city—Fleet Street, Ludgate Hill, the Strand-used to throw a glory over these homely precincts when I first saw them, and still do so in a less degree. Where Farrington Street opens upon Fleet Street, moreover, I had a glimpse of St. Paul's, along Ludgate Street, in the gathering dimness, and felt as if I saw an old friend. In that neighborhood—speaking of old friends—I met Mr. Parker of Boston, who told me sad news of a friend whom I love as much as if I had known him for a lifetime, though he is, indeed, but of two or three years' standing. He said that my friend's bankruptcy is in to-day's Gazette. Of all men on earth, I had rather this misfortune should have happened to any other; but I hope and think he has sturdiness and buoyancy enough to rise up beneath it. I cannot conceive of his face otherwise than with a glow on it, like that of the sun at noonday.

Before I reached our lodgings, the dusk settled into the streets, and a mist bedewed and bedamped me, and I went astray, as is usual with me, and had to inquire my way; indeed, except in the principal thoroughfares, London is so miserably lighted that it is impossible to recognize one's whereabouts. On my arrival I found our parlor looking cheerful with a brisk fire; . . . . but the first day or two in new lodgings is at best an uncomfortable time. Fanny has just come in with more unhappy news about ———. Pray Heaven it may not be true! . . . . Troubles are a sociable brotherhood; they love to come hand in hand, or sometimes, even, to come side by side, with long looked-for and hoped-for good fortune. . . .

November 11th.—This morning we all went to the British Museum, always a most wearisome and depressing task to me. I strolled through the lower rooms with a good degree of interest, looking at the antique sculptures, some of which were doubtless grand and beautiful in their day. . . . The Egyptian remains are, on the whole, the more satisfactory; for, though inconceivably ugly, they are at least miracles of size and ponderosity,—for example, a hand and arm of polished granite, as much as ten feet in length. The upper rooms, containing millions of specimens of Natural History, in all departments, really made my heart ache with a pain and woe that I have never felt anywhere but in the British Museum, and I hurried through them as rapidly as I could persuade J—— to follow me. We had left the rest of the party still intent on the Grecian sculptures; and though J—— was much interested in the vast collection of shells, he chose to quit the Museum with me in the prospect of a stroll about London. He seems to have my own passion for thronged streets, and the utmost bustle of human life.

We went first to the railway station, in quest of our luggage, which we found. Then we made a pretty straight course down to Holborn, and through Newgate Street, stopping a few moments to look through the iron fence at the Christ's Hospital boys, in their long blue coats and yellow petticoats and stockings. It was between twelve and one o'clock; and I suppose this was their hour of play, for they were running about the enclosed space, chasing and overthrowing one another, without their caps, with their yellow petticoats tucked up, and all in immense activity and enjoyment. They were eminently a healthy and handsome set of boys.

Then we went into Cheapside, where I called at Mr. Bennett's shop, to inquire what are the facts about ———. When I mentioned his name, Mr. Bennett shook his head and expressed great sorrow; but, on further talk, I found that he referred only to the failure, and had heard nothing about the other rumor. It cannot, therefore, be true; for Bennett lives in his neighborhood, and could not have remained ignorant of such a calamity. There must be some mistake; none, however, in regard to the failure, it having been announced in the Times.

From Bennett's shop—which is so near the steeple of Bow Church that it would tumble upon it if it fell over—we strolled still eastward, aiming at London Bridge; but missed it, and bewildered ourselves among many dingy and frowzy streets and lanes. I bore towards the right, however, knowing that that course must ultimately bring me to the Thames; and at last I saw before me ramparts, towers, circular and square, with battlemented summits, large sweeps and curves of fortification, as well as straight and massive walls and chimneys behind them (all a great confusion—to my eye), of ancient and more modern structure, and four loftier turrets rising in the midst; the whole great space surrounded by a broad, dry moat, which now seemed to be used as an ornamental walk, bordered partly with trees. This was the Tower; but seen from a different and more picturesque point of view than I have heretofore gained of it. Being so convenient for a visit, I determined to go in. At the outer gate, which is not a part of the fortification, a sentinel walks to and fro, besides whom there was a warder, in the rich old costume of Henry VIII's time, looking very gorgeous indeed,—as much so as scarlet and gold can make him.

As J—— and I were not going to look at the Jewel-room, we loitered about in the open space, before the White Tower, while the tall, slender, white-haired, gentlemanly warder led the rest of the party into that apartment. We found what one might take for a square in a town, with gabled houses lifting their peaks on one side, and various edifices enclosing the other sides, and the great White Tower,—now more black than white,—rising venerable, and rather picturesque than otherwise, the most prominent object in the scene. I have no plan nor available idea of it whatever in my mind, but it seems really to be a town within itself, with streets, avenues, and all that pertains to human life. There were soldiers going through their exercise in the open space, and along at the base of the White Tower lay a great many cannon and mortars, some of which were of Turkish manufacture, and immensely long and ponderous. Others, likewise of mighty size, had once belonged to the famous ship Great Harry, and had lain for ages under the sea. Others were East-Indian. Several were beautiful specimens of workmanship. The mortars—some so large that a fair-sized man might easily be rammed into them—held their great mouths slanting upward to the sky, and mostly contained a quantity of rain-water. While we were looking at these warlike toys,—for I suppose not one of them will ever thunder in earnest again,—the warder reappeared with his ladies, and, leading us all to a certain part of the open space, he struck his foot on the small stones with which it is paved, and told us that we were standing on the spot where Anne Boleyn and Catharine Parr were beheaded. It is not exactly in the centre of the square, but on a line with one of the angles of the White Tower. I forgot to mention that the middle of the open space is occupied by a marble statue of Wellington, which appeared to me very poor and laboriously spirited.

Lastly, the warder led us under the Bloody Tower, and by the side of the Wakefield Tower, and showed us the Traitor's Gate, which is now closed up, so as to afford no access to the Thames. No; we first visited the Beauchamp Tower, famous as the prison of many historical personages. Some of its former occupants have left their initials or names, and inscriptions of piety and patience, cut deep into the freestone of the walls, together with devices—as a crucifix, for instance—neatly and skilfully done. This room has a long, deep fireplace; it is chiefly lighted by a large window, which I fancy must have been made in modern times; but there are four narrow apertures, throwing in a little light through deep alcoves in the thickness of the octagon wall. One would expect such a room to be picturesque; but it is really not of striking aspect, being low, with a plastered ceiling,—the beams just showing through the plaster,—a boarded floor, and the walls being washed over with a buff color. A warder sat within a railing, by the great window, with sixpenny books to sell, containing transcripts of the inscriptions on the walls.

We now left the Tower, and made our way deviously westward, passing St. Paul's, which looked magnificently and beautifully, so huge and dusky as it was, with here and there a space on its vast form where the original whiteness of the marble came out like a streak of moonshine amid the blackness with which time has made it grander than it was in its newness. It is a most noble edifice; and I delight, too, in the statues that crown some of its heights, and in the wreaths of sculpture which are hung around it.

November 12th.—This morning began with such fog, that at the window of my chamber, lighted only from a small court-yard, enclosed by high, dingy walls, I could hardly see to dress. It kept alternately darkening, and then brightening a little, and darkening again, so much that we could but just discern the opposite houses; but at eleven or thereabouts it grew so much clearer that we resolved to venture out. Our plan for the day was to go in the first place to Westminster Abbey; and to the National Gallery, if we should find time. . . . The fog darkened again as we went down Regent Street, and the Duke of York's Column was but barely visible, looming vaguely before us; nor, from Pall Mall, was Nelson's Pillar much more distinct, though methought his statue stood aloft in a somewhat clearer atmosphere than ours. Passing Whitehall, however, we could scarcely see Inigo Jones's Banqueting-House, on the other side of the street; and the towers and turrets of the new Houses of Parliament were all but invisible, as was the Abbey itself; so that we really were in some doubt whither we were going. We found our way to Poets' Corner, however, and entered those holy precincts, which looked very dusky and grim in the smoky light. . . . I was strongly impressed with the perception that very commonplace people compose the great bulk of society in the home of the illustrious dead. It is wonderful how few names there are that one cares anything about a hundred years after their departure; but perhaps each generation acts in good faith in canonizing its own men. . . . But the fame of the buried person does not make the marble live,—the marble keeps merely a cold and sad memory of a man who would else be forgotten. No man who needs a monument ever ought to have one.

The painted windows of the Abbey, though mostly modern, are exceedingly rich and beautiful; and I do think that human art has invented no other such magnificent method of adornment as this.

Our final visit to-day was to the National Gallery, where I came to the conclusion that Murillo's St. John was the most lovely picture I have ever seen, and that there never was a painter who has really made the world richer, except Murillo.

November 12th.—This morning we issued forth, and found the atmosphere chill and almost frosty, tingling upon our cheeks. . . . The gateway of Somerset House attracted us, and we walked round its spacious quadrangle, encountering many government clerks hurrying to their various offices. At least, I presumed them to be so. This is certainly a handsome square of buildings, with its Grecian facades and pillars, and its sculptured bas-reliefs, and the group of statuary in the midst of the court. Besides the part of the edifice that rises above ground, there appear to be two subterranean stories below the surface. From Somerset House we pursued our way through Temple Bar, but missed it, and therefore entered by the passage from what was formerly Alsatia, but which now seems to be a very respectable and humdrum part of London. We came immediately to the Temple Gardens, which we walked quite round. The grass is still green, but the trees are leafless, and had an aspect of not being very robust, even at more genial seasons of the year. There were, however, large quantities of brilliant chrysanthemums, golden, and of all hues, blooming gorgeously all about the borders; and several gardeners were at work, tending these flowers, and sheltering them from the weather. I noticed no roses, nor even rose-bushes, in the spot where the factions of York and Lancaster plucked their two hostile flowers.

Leaving these grounds, we went to the Hall of the Middle Temple, where we knocked at the portal, and, finding it not fastened, thrust it open. A boy appeared within, and the porter or keeper, at a distance, along the inner passage, called to us to enter; and, opening the door of the great hall, left us to view it till he should be at leisure to attend to us. Truly it is a most magnificent apartment; very lofty,—so lofty, indeed, that the antique oak roof was quite hidden, as regarded all its details, in the sombre gloom that brooded under its rafters. The hall was lighted by four great windows, I think, on each of the two sides, descending half-way from the ceiling to the floor, leaving all beneath enclosed by oaken panelling, which, on three sides, was carved with escutcheons of such members of the society as have held the office of reader. There is likewise, in a large recess or transept, a great window, occupying the full height of the hall, and splendidly emblazoned with the arms of the Templars who have attained to the dignity of Chief Justices. The other windows are pictured, in like manner, with coats of arms of local dignitaries connected with the Temple; and besides all these there are arched lights, high towards the roof, at either end full of richly and chastely colored glass, and all the illumination that the great hall had come through these glorious panes, and they seemed the richer for the sombreness in which we stood. I cannot describe, or even intimate, the effect of this transparent glory, glowing down upon us in that gloomy depth of the hall. The screen at the lower end was of carved oak, very dark and highly polished, and as old as Queen Elizabeth's time. The keeper told us that the story of the Armada was said to be represented in these carvings, but in the imperfect light we could trace nothing of it out. Along the length of the apartment were set two oaken tables for the students of law to dine upon; and on the dais, at the upper end, there was a cross-table for the big-wigs of the society; the latter being provided with comfortable chairs, and the former with oaken benches. From a notification, posted near the door, I gathered that the cost of dinners is two shillings to each gentleman, including, as the attendant told me, ale and wine. I am reluctant to leave this hall without expressing how grave, how grand, how sombre, and how magnificent I feel it to be. As regards historical association, it was a favorite dancing-hall of Queen Elizabeth, and Sir Christopher Hatton danced himself into her good graces here.

We next went to the Temple Church, and, finding the door ajar, made free to enter beneath its Norman arches, which admitted us into a circular vestibule, very ancient and beautiful. In the body of the church beyond we saw a boy sitting, but nobody either forbade or invited our entrance. On the floor of the vestibule lay about half a score of Templars,—the representatives of the warlike priests who built this church and formerly held these precincts,—all in chain armor, grasping their swords, and with their shields beside them.

Except two or three, they lay cross-legged, in token that they had really fought for the Holy Sepulchre. I think I have seen nowhere else such well-preserved monumental knights as these. We proceeded into the interior of the church, and were greatly impressed with its wonderful beauty,—the roof springing, as it were, in a harmonious and accordant fountain, out of the clustered pillars that support its groined arches; and these pillars, immense as they are, are polished like so many gems. They are of Purbeck marble, and, if I mistake not, had been covered with plaster for ages until latterly redeemed and beautified anew. But the glory of the church is its old painted windows; and, positively, those great spaces over the chancel appeared to be set with all manner of precious stones,—or it was as if the many-colored radiance of heaven were breaking upon us,—or as if we saw the wings of angels, storied over with richly tinted pictures of holy things. But it is idle to talk of this marvellous adornment; it is to be seen and wondered at, not written about. Before we left the church, the porter made his appearance, in time to receive his fee,— which somebody, indeed, is always ready to stretch out his hand for. And so ended our visit to the Temple, which, by the by, though close to the midmost bustle of London, is as quiet as if it were always Sunday there.

We now went to St. Paul's. U—— and Miss Shepard ascended to the Whispering Gallery, and we, sitting under the dome, at the base of one of the pillars, saw them far above us, looking very indistinct, for those misty upper-depths seemed almost to be hung with clouds. This cathedral, I think, does not profit by gloom, but requires cheerful sunshine to show it to the best advantage. The statues and sculptures in St. Paul's are mostly covered with years of dust, and look thereby very grim and ugly; but there are few memories there from which I should care to brush away the dust, they being, in nine cases out of ten, naval and military heroes of second or third class merit. I really remember no literary celebrity admitted solely on that account, except Dr. Johnson. The Crimean war has supplied two or three monuments, chiefly mural tablets; and doubtless more of the same excrescences will yet come out upon the walls. One thing that I newly noticed was the beautiful shape of the great, covered marble vase that serves for a font.

From St. Paul's we went down Cheapside, and, turning into King Street, visited Guildhall, which we found in process of decoration for a public ball, to take place next week. It looked rather gewgawish thus gorgeous, being hung with flags of all nations, and adorned with military trophies; and the scene was repeated by a range of looking-glasses at one end of the room. The execrably painted windows really shocked us by their vulgar glare, after those of the Temple Hall and Church; yet, a few years ago, I might very likely have thought them beautiful. Our own national banner, I must remember to say, was hanging in Guildhall, but with only ten stars, and an insufficient number of stripes.

November 15th.—Yesterday morning we went to London Bridge and along Lower Thames Street, and quickly found ourselves in Billingsgate Market, —a dirty, evil-smelling, crowded precinct, thronged with people carrying fish on their heads, and lined with fish-shops and fish-stalls, and pervaded with a fishy odor. The footwalk was narrow,—as indeed was the whole street,—and filthy to travel upon; and we had to elbow our way among rough men and slatternly women, and to guard our heads from the contact of fish-trays; very ugly, grimy, and misty, moreover, is Billingsgate Market, and though we heard none of the foul language of which it is supposed to be the fountain-head, yet it has its own peculiarities of behavior. For instance, U—— tells me that one man, staring at her and her governess as they passed, cried out, "What beauties!"—another, looking under her veil, greeted her with, "Good morning, my love!" We were in advance, and heard nothing of these civilities. Struggling through this fishy purgatory, we caught sight of the Tower, as we drew near the end of the street; and I put all my party under charge of one of the Trump Cards, not being myself inclined to make the rounds of the small part of the fortress that is shown, so soon after my late visit.

When they departed with the warder, I set out by myself to wander about the exterior of the Tower, looking with interest at what I suppose to be Tower Hill,—a slight elevation of the large open space into which Great Tower Street opens; though, perhaps, what is now called Trinity Square may have been a part of Tower Hill, and possibly the precise spot where the executions took place. Keeping to the right, round the Tower, I found the moat quite surrounded by a fence of iron rails, excluding me from a pleasant gravel-path, among flowers and shrubbery, on the inside, where I could see nursery-maids giving children their airings. Possibly these may have been the privileged inhabitants of the Tower, which certainly might contain the population of a large village. The aspect of the fortress has so much that is new and modern about it that it can hardly be called picturesque, and yet it seems unfair to withhold that epithet from such a collection of gray ramparts. I followed the iron fence quite round the outer grounds, till it approached the Thames, and in this direction the moat and the pleasure-ground terminate in a narrow graveyard, which extends beneath the walls, and looks neglected and shaggy with long grass. It appeared to contain graves enough, but only a few tombstones, of which I could read the inscription of but one; it commemorated a Mr. George Gibson, a person of no note, nor apparently connected with the place. St. Katharine's Dock lies along the Thames, in this vicinity; and while on one side of me were the Tower, the quiet gravel-path, and the shaggy graveyard, on the other were draymen and their horses, dock-laborers, sailors, empty puncheons, and a miscellaneous spectacle of life,—including organ-grinders, men roasting chestnuts over small ovens on the sidewalk, boys and women with boards or wheelbarrows of apples, oyster-stands, besides pedlers of small wares, dirty children at play, and other figures and things that a Dutch painter would seize upon.

I went a little way into St. Katharine's Dock, and found it crowded with great ships; then, returning, I strolled along the range of shops that front towards this side of the Tower. They have all something to do with ships, sailors, and commerce; being for the sale of ships' stores, nautical instruments, arms, clothing, together with a tavern and grog-shop at every other door; bookstalls, too, covered with cheap novels and song-books; cigar-shops in great numbers; and everywhere were sailors, and here and there a soldier, and children at the doorsteps, and women showing themselves at the doors or windows of their domiciles. These latter figures, however, pertain rather to the street up which I walked, penetrating into the interior of this region, which, I think, is Blackwall—no, I forget what its name is. At all events, it has an ancient and most grimy and rough look, with its old gabled houses, each of them the seat of some petty trade and business in its basement story. Among these I saw one house with three or four peaks along its front,—a second story projecting over the basement, and the whole clapboarded over. . . . There was a butcher's stall in the lower story, with a front open to the street, in the ancient fashion, which seems to be retained only by butchers' shops. This part of London having escaped the Great Fire, I suppose there may be many relics of architectural antiquity hereabouts.

At the end of an hour I went back to the Refreshment-room, within the outer gate of the Tower, where the rest of us shortly appeared. We now returned westward by way of Great Tower Street, Eastcheap, and Cannon Street, and, entering St. Paul's, sat down beneath the misty dome to rest ourselves. The muffled roar of the city, as we heard it there, is very soothing, and keeps one listening to it, somewhat as the flow of a river keeps us looking at it. It is a grand and quiet sound; and, ever and anon, a distant door slammed somewhere in the cathedral, and reverberated long and heavily, like the roll of thunder or the boom of cannon. Every noise that is loud enough to be heard in so vast an edifice melts into the great quietude. The interior looked very sombre, and the dome hung over us like a cloudy sky. I wish it were possible to pass directly from St. Paul's into York Minster, or from the latter into the former; that is, if one's mind could manage to stagger under both in the same day. There is no other way of judging of their comparative effect.

Under the influence of that grand lullaby,—the roar of the city,—we sat for some time after we were sufficiently rested; but at last plunged forth again, and went up Newgate Street, pausing to look through the iron railings of Christ's Hospital. The boys, however, were not at play; so we went onward, in quest of Smithfield, and on our way had a greeting from Mr. Silsbee, a gentleman of our own native town. Parting with him, we found Smithfield, which is still occupied with pens for cattle, though I believe it has ceased to be a cattle-market. Except it be St. Bartholomew's hospital on one side, there is nothing interesting in this ugly square; though, no doubt, a few feet under the pavement there are bones and ashes as precious as anything of the kind on earth. I wonder when men will begin to erect monuments to human error; hitherto their pillars and statues have only been for the sake of glorification. But, after all, the present fashion may be the better and wholesomer. . . .

November 16th.—Mr. Silsbee called yesterday, and talked about matters of art, in which he is deeply interested, and which he has had good opportunities of becoming acquainted with, during three years' travel on the Continent. He is a man of great intelligence and true feeling, and absolutely brims over with ideas,—his conversation flowing in a constant stream, which it appears to be no trouble whatever to him to keep up. . . . He took his leave after a long call, and left with us a manuscript, describing a visit to Berlin, which I read to my wife in the evening. It was well worth reading. He made an engagement to go with us to the Crystal Palace, and came rather for that purpose this morning.

We drove to the London Bridge station, where we bought return tickets that entitled us to admission to the Palace, as well as conveyance thither, for half a crown apiece. On our arrival we entered by the garden front, thus gaining a fine view of the ornamental grounds, with their fountains and stately pathways, bordered with statues; and of the edifice itself, so vast and fairy-like, looking as if it were a bubble, and might vanish at a touch. There is as little beauty in the architecture of the Crystal Palace, however, as was possible to be with such gigantic use of such a material. No doubt, an architectural order of which we have as yet little or no idea is to be developed from the use of glass as a building-material, instead of brick and stone. It will have its own rules and its own results; but, meanwhile, even the present Palace is positively a very beautiful object. On entering we found the atmosphere chill and comfortless,—more so, it seemed to me, than the open air itself. It was not a genial day; though now and then the sun gleamed out, and once caused fine effects in the glasswork of a crystal fountain in one of the courts.

We were under Mr. Silshee's guidance for the day, ... and first we looked at the sculpture, which is composed chiefly of casts or copies of the most famous statues of all ages, and likewise of those crumbs and little fragments which have fallen from Time's jaw,—and half-picked bones, as it were, that have been gathered up from spots where he has feasted full,—torsos, heads and broken limbs, some of them half worn away, as if they had been rolled over and over in the sea. I saw nothing in the sculptural way, either modern or antique, that impressed me so much as a statue of a nude mother by a French artist. In a sitting posture, with one knee over the other, she was clasping her highest knee with both hands; and in the hollow cradle thus formed by her arms lay two sweet little babies, as snug and close to her heart as if they had not yet been born,—two little love-blossoms,—and the mother encircling them and pervading them with love. But an infinite pathos and strange terror are given to this beautiful group by some faint bas-reliefs on the pedestal, indicating that the happy mother is Eve, and Cain and Abel the two innocent babes.

Then we went to the Alhambra, which looks like an enchanted palace. If it had been a sunny day, I should have enjoyed it more; but it was miserable to shiver and shake in the Court of the Lions, and in those chambers which were contrived as places of refuge from a fervid temperature. Furthermore, it is not quite agreeable to see such clever specimens of stage decoration; they are so very good that it gets to be past a joke, without becoming actual earnest. I had not a similar feeling in respect to the reproduction of mediaeval statues, arches, doorways, all brilliantly colored as in the days of their first glory; yet I do not know but that the first is as little objectionable as the last. Certainly, in both cases, scenes and objects of a past age are here more vividly presented to the dullest mind than without such material facilities they could possibly be brought before the most powerful imagination. Truly, the Crystal Palace, in all its departments, offers wonderful means of education. I marvel what will come of it. Among the things that I admired most was Benvenuto Cellini's statue of Perseus holding the head of Medusa, and standing over her headless and still writhing body, out of which, at the severed neck, gushed a vast exuberance of snakes. Likewise, a sitting statue, by Michel Angelo, of one of the Medici, full of dignity and grace and reposeful might. Also the bronze gate of a baptistery in Florence, carved all over with relieves of Scripture subjects, executed in the most lifelike and expressive manner. The cast itself was a miracle of art. I should have taken it for the genuine original bronze.

We then wandered into the House of Diomed, which seemed to me a dismal abode, affording no possibility of comfort. We sat down in one of the rooms, on an iron bench, very cold.

It being by this time two o'clock, we went to the Refreshment-room and lunched; and before we had finished our repast, my wife discovered that she had lost her sable tippet, which she had been carrying on her arm. Mr. Silsbee most kindly and obligingly immediately went in quest of it, ... but to no purpose. . . .

Upon entering the Tropical Saloon, we found a most welcome and delightful change of temperature among those gigantic leaves of banyan-trees, and the broad expanse of water-plants, floating on lakes, and spacious aviaries, where birds of brilliant plumage sported and sang amid such foliage as they knew at home. Howbeit, the atmosphere was a little faint and sickish, perhaps owing to the odor of the half-tepid water. The most remarkable object here was the trunk of a tree, huge beyond imagination, —a pine-tree from California. It was only the stripped-off bark, however, which had been conveyed hither in segments, and put together again beyond the height of the palace roof; and the hollow interior circle of the tree was large enough to contain fifty people, I should think. We entered and sat down in all the remoteness from one another that is attainable in a good-sized drawing-room. We then ascended the gallery to get a view of this vast tree from a more elevated position, and found it looked even bigger from above. Then we loitered slowly along the gallery as far as it extended, and afterwards descended into the nave; for it was getting dusk, and a horn had sounded, and a bell rung a warning to such as delayed in the remote regions of the building. Mr. Silsbee again most kindly went in quest of the sables, but still without success. . . . I have not much enjoyed the Crystal Palace, but think it a great and admirable achievement.

November 19th.—On Tuesday evening Mr. Silsbee came to read some letters which he has written to his friends, chiefly giving his observations on Art, together with descriptions of Venice and other cities on the Continent. They were very good, and indicate much sensibility and talent. After the reading we had a little oyster-supper and wine.

I had written a note to ———, and received an answer, indicating that he was much weighed down by his financial misfortune. . . . However, he desired me to come and see him; so yesterday morning I wended my way down into the city, and after various reluctant circumlocutions arrived at his house. The interior looked confused and dismal.

It seems to me nobody else runs such risks as a man of business, because he risks everything. Every other man, into whatever depth of poverty he may sink, has still something left, be he author, scholar, handicraftman, or what not; the merchant has nothing.

We parted with a long and strong grasp of the hand, and ——— promised to come and see us soon. . . .

On my way home I called at Truebner's in Pater Noster Row. . . . I waited a few minutes, he being busy with a tall, muscular, English-built man, who, after he had taken leave, Truebner told me was Charles Reade. I once met him at an evening party, but should have been glad to meet him again, now that I appreciate him so much better after reading Never too Late to Mend.

December 6th.—All these days, since my last date, have been marked by nothing very well worthy of detail and description. I have walked the streets a great deal in the dull November days, and always take a certain pleasure in being in the midst of human life,—as closely encompassed by it as it is possible to be anywhere in this world; and in that way of viewing it there is a dull and sombre enjoyment always to be had in Holborn, Fleet Street, Cheapside, and the other busiest parts of London. It is human life; it is this material world; it is a grim and heavy reality. I have never had the same sense of being surrounded by materialisms and hemmed in with the grossness of this earthly existence anywhere else; these broad, crowded streets are so evidently the veins and arteries of an enormous city. London is evidenced in every one of them, just as a megatherium is in each of its separate bones, even if they be small ones. Thus I never fail of a sort of self-congratulation in finding myself, for instance, passing along Ludgate Hill; but, in spite of this, it is really an ungladdened life to wander through these huge, thronged ways, over a pavement foul with mud, ground into it by a million of footsteps; jostling against people who do not seem to be individuals, but all one mass, so homogeneous is the street-walking aspect of them; the roar of vehicles pervading me,—wearisome cabs and omnibuses; everywhere the dingy brick edifices heaving themselves up, and shutting out all but a strip of sullen cloud, that serves London for a sky,—in short, a general impression of grime and sordidness; and at this season always a fog scattered along the vista of streets, sometimes so densely as almost to spiritualize the materialism and make the scene resemble the other world of worldly people, gross even in ghostliness. It is strange how little splendor and brilliancy one sees in London,—in the city almost none, though some in the shops of Regent Street. My wife has had a season of indisposition within the last few weeks, so that my rambles have generally been solitary, or with J——- only for a companion. I think my only excursion with my wife was a week ago, when we went to Lincoln's Inn Fields, which truly are almost fields right in the heart of London, and as retired and secluded as if the surrounding city were a forest, and its heavy roar were the wind among the branches. We gained admission into the noble Hall, which is modern, but built in antique style, and stately and beautiful exceedingly. I have forgotten all but the general effect, with its lofty oaken roof, its panelled walls, with the windows high above, and the great arched window at one end full of painted coats of arms, which the light glorifies in passing through them, as if each were the escutcheon of some illustrious personage. Thence we went to the chapel of Lincoln's Inn, where, on entering, we found a class of young choristers receiving instruction from their music-master, while the organ accompanied their strains. These young, clear, fresh, elastic voices are wonderfully beautiful; they are like those of women, yet have something more birdlike and aspiring, more like what one conceives of the singing of angels. As for the singing of saints and blessed spirits that have once been human, it never can resemble that of these young voices; for no duration of heavenly enjoyments will ever quite take the mortal sadness out of it.

In this chapel we saw some painted windows of the time of James I., a period much subsequent, to the age when painted glass was in its glory; but the pictures of Scriptural people in these windows were certainly very fine,—the figures being as large as life, and the faces having much expression. The sunshine came in through some of them, and produced a beautiful effect, almost as if the painted forms were the glorified spirits of those holy personages.

After leaving Lincoln's Inn, we looked at Gray's Inn, which is a great, quiet domain, quadrangle beyond quadrangle, close beside Holborn, and a large space of greensward enclosed within it. It is very strange to find so much of ancient quietude right in the monster city's very jaws, which yet the monster shall not eat up,—right in its very belly, indeed, which yet, in all these ages, it shall not digest and convert into the same substance as the rest of its bustling streets. Nothing else in London is so like the effect of a spell, as to pass under one of these archways, and find yourself transported from the jumble, mob, tumult, uproar, as of an age of week-days condensed into the present hour, into what seems an eternal sabbath. Thence we went into Staple Inn, I think it was,—which has a front upon Holborn of four or five ancient gables in a row, and a low arch under the impending story, admitting you into a paved quadrangle, beyond which you have the vista of another. I do not understand that the residences and chambers in these Inns of Court are now exclusively let to lawyers; though such inhabitants certainly seem to preponderate there.

Since then J——— and I walked down into the Strand, and found ourselves unexpectedly mixed up with a crowd that grew denser as we approached Charing Cross, and became absolutely impermeable when we attempted to make our way to Whitehall. The wicket in the gate of Northumberland House, by the by, was open, and gave me a glimpse of the front of the edifice within,—a very partial glimpse, however, and that obstructed by the solid person of a footman, who, with some women, were passing out from within. The crowd was a real English crowd, perfectly undemonstrative, and entirely decorous, being composed mostly of well-dressed people, and largely of women. The cause of the assemblage was the opening of Parliament by the Queen, but we were too late for any chance of seeing her Majesty. However, we extricated ourselves from the multitude, and, going along Pall Mall, got into the Park by the steps at the foot of the Duke of York's Column, and thence went to the Whitehall Gateway, outside of which we found the Horse Guards drawn up,—a regiment of black horses and burnished cuirasses. On our way thither an open carriage came through the gateway into the Park, conveying two ladies in court dresses; and another splendid chariot pressed out through the gateway,—the coachman in a cocked hat and scarlet and gold embroidery, and two other scarlet and gold figures hanging behind. It was one of the Queen's carriages, but seemed to have nobody in it. I have forgotten to mention what, I think, produced more effect on me than anything else, namely, the clash of the bells from the steeple of St. Martin's Church and those of St. Margaret. Really, London seemed to cry out through them, and bid welcome to the Queen.

December 7th.—This being a muddy and dismal day, I went only to the

BRITISH MUSEUM,

which is but a short walk down the street (Great Russell Street). I have now visited it often enough to be on more familiar terms with it than at first, and therefore do not feel myself so weighed down by the many things to be seen. I have ceased to expect or hope or wish to devour and digest the whole enormous collection; so I content myself with individual things, and succeed in getting now and then a little honey from them. Unless I were studying some particular branch of history or science or art, this is the best that can be done with the British Museum.

I went first to-day into the Townley Gallery, and so along through all the ancient sculpture, and was glad to find myself able to sympathize more than heretofore with the forms of grace and beauty which are preserved there,—poor, maimed immortalities as they are,—headless and legless trunks, godlike cripples, faces beautiful and broken-nosed,— heroic shapes which have stood so long, or lain prostrate so long, in the open air, that even the atmosphere of Greece has almost dissolved the external layer of the marble; and yet, however much they may be worn away, or battered and shattered, the grace and nobility seem as deep in them as the very heart of the stone. It cannot be destroyed, except by grinding them to powder. In short, I do really believe that there was an excellence in ancient sculpture, which has yet a potency to educate and refine the minds of those who look at it even so carelessly and casually as I do. As regards the frieze of the Parthenon, I must remark that the horses represented on it, though they show great spirit and lifelikeness, are rather of the pony species than what would be considered fine horses now. Doubtless, modern breeding has wrought a difference in the animal. Flaxman, in his outlines, seems to have imitated these classic steeds of the Parthenon, and thus has produced horses that always appeared to me affected and diminutively monstrous.

From the classic sculpture, I passed through an Assyrian room, where the walls are lined with great slabs of marble sculptured in bas-relief with scenes in the life of Senmacherib, I believe; very ugly, to be sure, yet artistically done in their own style, and in wonderfully good preservation. Indeed, if the chisel had cut its last stroke in them yesterday, the work could not be more sharp and distinct. In glass cases, in this room, are little relics and scraps of utensils, and a great deal of fragmentary rubbish, dug up by Layard in his researches,—things that it is hard to call anything but trash, but which yet may be of great significance as indicating the modes of life of a long-past race. I remember nothing particularly just now, except some pieces of broken glass, iridescent with certainly the most beautiful hues in the world,—indescribably beautiful, and unimaginably, unless one can conceive of the colors of the rainbow, and a thousand glorious sunsets, and the autumnal forest-leaves of America, all condensed upon a little fragment of a glass cup,—and that, too, without becoming in the least glaring or flagrant, but mildly glorious, as we may fancy the shifting lines of an angel's wing may be. I think this chaste splendor will glow in my memory for years to come. It is the effect of time, and cannot be imitated by any known process of art. I have seen it in specimens of old Roman glass, which has been famous here in England; but never in anything is there the brilliancy of these Oriental fragments. How strange that decay, in dark places, and underground, and where there are a billion chances to one that nobody will ever see its handiwork, should produce these beautiful effects! The glass seems to become perfectly brittle, so that it would vanish, like a soap-bubble, if touched.

Ascending the stairs, I went through the halls of fossil remains,—which I care little for, though one of them is a human skeleton in limestone,— and through several rooms of mineralogical specimens, including all the gems in the world, among which is seen, not the Koh-i-noor itself, but a fac-simile of it in crystal. I think the aerolites are as interesting as anything in this department, and one piece of pure iron, laid against the wall of the room, weighs about fourteen hundred pounds. Whence could it have come? If these aerolites are bits of other planets, how happen they to be always iron? But I know no more of this than if I were a philosopher.

Then I went through rooms of shells and fishes and reptiles and tortoises, crocodiles and alligators and insects, including all manner of butterflies, some of which had wings precisely like leaves, a little withered and faded, even the skeleton and fibres of the leaves represented; and immense hairy spiders, covering, with the whole circumference of their legs, a space as big as a saucer; and centipedes little less than a foot long; and winged insects that look like jointed twigs of a tree. In America, I remember, when I lived in Lenox, I found an insect of this species, and at first really mistook it for a twig. It was smaller than these specimens in the Museum. I suppose every creature, almost, that runs or creeps or swims or flies, is represented in this collection of Natural History; and it puzzles me to think what they were all made for, though it is quite as mysterious why man himself was made.

By and by I entered the room of Egyptian mummies, of which there are a good many, one of which, the body of a priestess, is unrolled, except the innermost layer of linen. The outline of her face is perfectly visible. Mummies of cats, dogs, snakes, and children are in the wall-cases, together with a vast many articles of Egyptian manufacture and use,—even children's toys; bread, too, in flat cakes; grapes, that have turned to raisins in the grave; queerest of all, methinks, a curly wig, that is supposed to have belonged to a woman,—together with the wooden box that held it. The hair is brown, and the wig is as perfect as if it had been made for some now living dowager.

From Egypt we pass into rooms containing vases and other articles of Grecian and Roman workmanship, and funeral urns, and beads, and rings, none of them very beautiful. I saw some splendid specimens, however, at a former visit, when I obtained admission to a room not indiscriminately shown to visitors. What chiefly interested me in that room was a cast taken from the face of Cromwell after death; representing a wide-mouthed, long-chinned, uncomely visage, with a triangular English nose in the very centre. There were various other curiosities, which I fancied were safe in my memory, but they do not now come uppermost.

To return to my to-day's progress through the Museum;—next to the classic rooms are the collections of Saxon and British and early English antiquities, the earlier portions of which are not very interesting to me, possessing little or no beauty in themselves, and indicating a kind of life too remote from our own to be readily sympathized with. Who cares for glass beads and copper brooches, and knives, spear-heads, and swords, all so rusty that they look as much like pieces of old iron hoop as anything else? The bed of the Thames has been a rich treasury of antiquities, from the time of the Roman Conquest downwards; it seems to preserve bronze in considerable perfection, but not iron.

Among the mediaeval relics, the carvings in ivory are often very exquisite and elaborate. There are likewise caskets and coffers, and a thousand other Old World ornamental works; but I saw so many and such superior specimens of them at the Manchester Exhibition, that I shall say nothing of them here. The seal-ring of Mary, Queen of Scots, is in one of the cases; it must have been a thumb-ring, judging from its size, and it has a dark stone, engraved with armorial bearings. In another case is the magic glass formerly used by Dr. Doe, and in which, if I rightly remember, used to be seen prophetic visions or figures of persons and scenes at a distance. It is a round ball of glass or crystal, slightly tinged with a pinkish hue, and about as big as a small apple, or a little bigger than an egg would be if perfectly round. This ancient humbug kept me looking at it perhaps ten minutes; and I saw my own face dimly in it, but no other vision. Lastly, I passed through the Ethnographical Rooms; but I care little for the varieties of the human race,—all that is really important and interesting being found in our own variety. Perhaps equally in any other. This brought me to the head of one of the staircases, descending which I entered the library.

Here—not to speak of the noble rooms and halls—there are numberless treasures beyond all price; too valuable in their way for me to select any one as more curious and valuable than many others. Letters of statesmen and warriors of all nations, and several centuries back,—among which, long as it has taken Europe to produce them, I saw none so illustrious as those of Washington, nor more so than Franklin's, whom America gave to the world in her nonage; and epistles of poets and artists, and of kings, too, whose chirography appears to have been much better than I should have expected from fingers so often cramped in iron gauntlets. In another case there were the original autograph copies of several famous works,—for example, that of Pope's Homer, written on the backs of letters, the direction and seals of which appear in the midst of "the Tale of Troy divine," which also is much scratched and interlined with Pope's corrections; a manuscript of one of Ben Jonson's masques; of the Sentimental Journey, written in much more careful and formal style than might be expected, the book pretending to be a harum-scarum; of Walter Scott's Kenilworth, bearing such an aspect of straightforward diligence that I shall hardly think of it again as a romance;—in short, I may as well drop the whole matter here.

All through the long vista of the king's library, we come to cases in which—with their pages open beneath the glass—we see books worth their weight in gold, either for their uniqueness or their beauty, or because they have belonged to illustrious men, and have their autographs in them. The copy of the English translation of Montaigne, containing the strange scrawl of Shakespeare's autograph, is here. Bacon's name is in another book; Queen Elizabeth's in another; and there is a little devotional volume, with Lady Jane Grey's writing in it. She is supposed to have taken it to the scaffold with her. Here, too, I saw a copy, which was printed at a Venetian press at the time, of the challenge which the Admirable Crichton caused to be posted on the church doors of Venice, defying all the scholars of Italy to encounter him. But if I mention one thing, I find fault with myself for not putting down fifty others just as interesting,—and, after all, there is an official catalogue, no doubt, of the whole.

As I do not mean to fill any more pages with the British Museum, I will just mention the hall of Egyptian antiquities on the ground-floor of the edifice, though I did not pass through it to-day. They consist of things that would be very ugly and contemptible if they were not so immensely magnified; but it is impossible not to acknowledge a certain grandeur, resulting from the scale on which those strange old sculptors wrought. For instance, there is a granite fist of prodigious size, at least a yard across, and looking as if it were doubled in the face of Time, defying him to destroy it. All the rest of the statue to which it belonged seems to have vanished; but this fist will certainly outlast the Museum, and whatever else it contains, unless it be some similar Egyptian ponderosity. There is a beetle, wrought out of immensely hard black stone, as big as a hogshead. It is satisfactory to see a thing so big and heavy.

Then there are huge stone sarcophagi, engraved with hieroglyphics within and without, all as good as new, though their age is reckoned by thousands of years. These great coffins are of vast weight and mass, insomuch that when once the accurately fitting lids were shut down, there might have seemed little chance of their being lifted again till the Resurrection. I positively like these coffins, they are so faithfully made, and so black and stern,—and polished to such a nicety, only to be buried forever; for the workmen, and the kings who were laid to sleep within, could never have dreamed of the British Museum.

There is a deity named Pasht, who sits in the hall, very big, very grave, carved of black stone, and very ludicrous, wearing a dog's head. I will just mention the Rosetta Stone, with a Greek inscription, and another in Egyptian characters which gave the clew to a whole field of history; and shall pretermit all further handling of this unwieldy subject.

In all the rooms I saw people of the poorer classes, some of whom seemed to view the objects intelligently, and to take a genuine interest in them. A poor man in London has great opportunities of cultivating himself if he will only make the best of them; and such an institution as the British Museum can hardly fail to attract, as the magnet does steel, the minds that are likeliest to be benefited by it in its various departments. I saw many children there, and some ragged boys.

It deserves to be noticed that some small figures of Indian Thugs, represented as engaged in their profession and handiwork of cajoling and strangling travellers, have been removed from the place which they formerly occupied in the part of the Museum shown to the general public. They are now in the more private room, and the reason of their withdrawal is, that, according to the Chaplain of Newgate, the practice of garroting was suggested to the English thieves by this representation of Indian Thugs. It is edifying, after what I have written in the preceding paragraph, to find that the only lesson known to have been inculcated here is that of a new mode of outrage.

December 8th.—This morning, when it was time to rise, there was but a glimmering of daylight, and we had candles on the breakfast-table at nearly ten o'clock. All abroad there was a dense dim fog brooding through the atmosphere, insomuch that we could hardly see across the street. At eleven o'clock I went out into the midst of the fog-bank, which for the moment seemed a little more interfused with daylight; for there seem to be continual changes in the density of this dim medium, which varies so much that now you can but just see your hand before you, and a moment afterwards you can see the cabs dashing out of the duskiness a score of yards off. It is seldom or never, moreover, an unmitigated gloom, but appears to be mixed up with sunshine in different proportions; sometimes only one part sun to a thousand of smoke and fog, and sometimes sunshine enough to give the whole mass a coppery line. This would have been a bright sunny day but for the interference of the fog; and before I had been out long, I actually saw the sun looking red and rayless, much like the millionth magnification of a new halfpenny.

I was bound towards Bennoch's; for he had written a note to apologize for not visiting us, and I had promised to call and see him to-day.

I went to Marlborough House to look at the English pictures, which I care more about seeing, here in England, than those of foreign artists, because the latter will be found more numerously and better on the Continent. I saw many pictures that pleased me; nothing that impressed me very strongly. Pictorial talent seems to be abundant enough, up to a certain point; pictorial genius, I should judge, is among the rarest of gifts. To be sure, I very likely might not recognize it where it existed; and yet it ought to have the power of making itself known even to the uninstructed mind, as literary genius does. If it exist only for connoisseurs, it is a very suspicious matter. I looked at all Turner's pictures, and at many of his drawings; and must again confess myself wholly unable to understand more than a very few of them. Even those few are tantalizing. At a certain distance you discern what appears to be a grand and beautiful picture, which you shall admire and enjoy infinitely if you can get within the range of distinct vision. You come nearer, and find only blotches of color and dabs of the brush, meaning nothing when you look closely, and meaning a mystery at the point where the painter intended to station you. Some landscapes there were, indeed, full of imaginative beauty, and of the better truth etherealized out of the prosaic truth of Nature; only it was still impossible actually to see it. There was a mist over it; or it was like a tract of beautiful dreamland, seen dimly through sleep, and glimmering out of sight, if looked upon with wide-open eyes. These were the more satisfactory specimens. There were many others which I could not comprehend in the remotest degree; not even so far as to conjecture whether they purported to represent earth, sea, or sky. In fact, I should not have known them to be pictures at all, but might have supposed that the artist had been trying his brush on the canvas, mixing up all sorts of hues, but principally white paint, and now and then producing an agreeable harmony of color without particularly intending it. Now that I have done my best to understand them without an interpreter, I mean to buy Ruskin's pamphlet at my next visit, and look at them through his eyes. But I do not think that I can be driven out of the idea that a picture ought to have something in common with what the spectator sees in nature.

Marlborough House may be converted, I think, into a very handsome residence for the young Prince of Wales. The entrance from the court-yard is into a large, square central hall, the painted ceiling of which is at the whole height of the edifice, and has a gallery on one side, whence it would be pleasant to look down on a festal scene below. The rooms are of fine proportions, with vaulted ceilings, and with fireplaces and mantel-pieces of great beauty, adorned with pillars and terminal figures of white and of variegated marble; and in the centre of each mantel-piece there is a marble tablet, exquisitely sculptured with classical designs, done in such high relief that the figures are sometimes almost disengaged from the background. One of the subjects was Androcles, or whatever was his name, taking the thorn out of the lion's foot. I suppose these works are of the era of the first old Duke and Duchess. After all, however, for some reason or other, the house does not at first strike you as a noble and princely one, and you have to convince yourself of it by examining it more in detail.

On leaving Marlborough House, I stepped for a few moments into the National Gallery, and looked, among other things, at the Turners and Claudes that hung there side by side. These pictures, I think, are quite the most comprehensible of Turner's productions; but I must say I prefer the Claudes. The latter catches "the light that never was on sea or land" without taking you quite away from nature for it. Nevertheless, I will not be quite certain that I care for any painter except Murillo, whose St. John I should like to own. As far as my own pleasure is concerned, I could not say as much for any other picture; for I have always found an infinite weariness and disgust resulting from a picture being too frequently before my eyes. I had rather see a basilisk, for instance, than the very best of those old, familiar pictures in the Boston Athenaeum; and most of those in the National Gallery might soon affect me in the same way.

From the Gallery I almost groped my way towards the city, for the fog seemed to grow denser and denser as I advanced; and when I reached St. Paul's, the sunny intermixture above spoken of was at its minimum, so that, the smoke-cloud grew really black about the dome and pinnacles, and the statues of saints looked down dimly from their standpoints on high. It was very grand, however, to see the pillars and porticos, and the huge bulk of the edifice, heaving up its dome from an obscure foundation into yet more shadowy obscurity; and by the time I reached the corner of the churchyard nearest Cheapside, the whole vast cathedral had utterly vanished, leaving "not a wrack behind," unless those thick, dark vapors were the elements of which it had been composed, and into which it had again dissolved. It is good to think, nevertheless,—and I gladly accept the analogy and the moral,—that the cathedral was really there, and as substantial as ever, though those earthly mists had hidden it from mortal eyes.

I found ——— in better spirits than when I saw him last, but his misfortune has been too real not to affect him long and deeply. He was cheerful, however, and his face shone with almost its old lustre. It has still the cheeriest glow that I ever saw in any human countenance.

I went home by way of Holborn, and the fog was denser than ever,—very black, indeed more like a distillation of mud than anything else; the ghost of mud,—the spiritualized medium of departed mud, through which the dead citizens of London probably tread in the Hades whither they are translated. So heavy was the gloom, that gas was lighted in all the shop-windows; and the little charcoal-furnaces of the women and boys, roasting chestnuts, threw a ruddy, misty glow around them. And yet I liked it. This fog seems an atmosphere proper to huge, grimy London; as proper to London as that light neither of the sun nor moon is to the New Jerusalem.

On reaching home, I found the same fog diffused through the drawing-room, though how it could have got in is a mystery. Since nightfall, however, the atmosphere is clear again.

December 20th.—Here we are still in London, at least a month longer than we expected, and at the very dreariest and dullest season of the year. Had I thought of it sooner, I might have found interesting people enough to know, even when all London is said to be out of town; but meditating a stay only of a week or two (on our way to Rome), it did not seem worth while to seek acquaintances.

I have been out only for one evening; and that was at Dr. ———'s, who had been attending all the children in the measles. (Their illness was what detained us.) He is a homoeopathist, and is known in scientific or general literature; at all events, a sensible and enlightened man, with an un-English freedom of mind on some points. For example, he is a Swedenborgian, and a believer in modern spiritualism. He showed me some drawings that had been made under the spiritual influence by a miniature-painter who possesses no imaginative power of his own, and is merely a good mechanical and literal copyist; but these drawings, representing angels and allegorical people, were done by an influence which directed the artist's hand, he not knowing what his next touch would be, nor what the final result. The sketches certainly did show a high and fine expressiveness, if examined in a trustful mood. Dr. ——— also spoke of Mr. Harris, the American poet of spiritualism, as being the best poet of the day; and he produced his works in several volumes, and showed me songs, and paragraphs of longer poems, in support of his opinion. They seemed to me to have a certain light and splendor, but not to possess much power, either passionate or intellectual. Mr. Harris is the medium of deceased poets, Milton and Lord Byron among the rest; and Dr. ——— said that Lady Byron—who is a devoted admirer of her husband, in spite of their conjugal troubles—pronounced some of these posthumous strains to be worthy of his living genius. Then the Doctor spoke of various strange experiences which he himself has had in these spiritual matters;

for he has witnessed the miraculous performances of Home, the American medium, and he has seen with his own eyes, and felt with his own touch, those ghostly hands and arms the reality of which has been certified to me by other beholders. Dr. ——— tells me that they are cold, and that it is a somewhat awful matter to see and feel them. I should think so, indeed. Do I believe in these wonders? Of course; for how is it possible to doubt either the solemn word or the sober observation of a learned and sensible man like Dr. ———? But again, do I really believe it? Of course not; for I cannot consent to have heaven and earth, this world and the next, beaten up together like the white and yolk of an egg, merely out of respect to Dr. ———'s sanity and integrity. I would not believe my own sight, nor touch of the spiritual hands; and it would take deeper and higher strains than those of Mr. Harris to convince me. I think I might yield to higher poetry or heavenlier wisdom than mortals in the flesh have ever sung or uttered.

Meanwhile, this matter of spiritualism is surely the strangest that ever was heard of; and yet I feel unaccountably little interest in it,—a sluggish disgust, and repugnance to meddle with it,—insomuch that I hardly feel as if it were worth this page or two in my not very eventful journal. One or two of the ladies present at Dr. ———'s little party seemed to be mediums.

I have made several visits to the picture-galleries since my last date; and I think it fair towards my own powers of appreciation to record that I begin to appreciate Turner's pictures rather better than at first. Not that I have anything to recant as respects those strange, white-grounded performances in the chambers at the Marlborough House; but some of his happier productions (a large landscape illustrative of Childe Harold, for instance) seem to me to have more magic in them than any other pictures. I admire, too, that misty, morning landscape in the National Gallery; and, no doubt, his very monstrosities are such as only he could have painted, and may have an infinite value for those who can appreciate the genius in them.

The shops in London begin to show some tokens of approaching Christmas; especially the toy-shops, and the confectioners',—the latter ornamenting their windows with a profusion of bonbons and all manner of pygmy figures in sugar; the former exhibiting Christmas-trees, hung with rich and gaudy fruit. At the butchers' shops, there is a great display of fat carcasses, and an abundance of game at the poulterers'. We think of going to the Crystal Palace to spend the festival day, and eat our Christmas dinner; but, do what we may, we shall have no home feeling or fireside enjoyment. I am weary, weary of London and of England, and can judge now how the old Loyalists must have felt, condemned to pine out their lives here, when the Revolution had robbed them of their native country. And yet there is still a pleasure in being in this dingy, smoky, midmost haunt of men; and I trudge through Fleet Street and Ludgate Street and along Cheapside with an enjoyment as great as I ever felt in a wood-path at home; and I have come to know these streets as well, I believe, as I ever knew Washington Street in Boston, or even Essex Street in my stupid old native town. For Piccadilly or for Regent Street, though more brilliant promenades, I do not care nearly so much.

December 27th.—Still leading an idle life, which, however, may not be quite thrown away, as I see some things, and think many thoughts.

The other day we went to Westminster Abbey, and through the chapels; and it being as sunny a day as could well be in London, and in December, we could judge, in some small degree, what must have been the splendor of those tombs and monuments when first erected there.

I presume I was sufficiently minute in describing my first visit to the chapels, so I shall only mention the stiff figure of a lady of Queen Elizabeth's court, reclining on the point of her elbow under a mural arch through all these dusty years; . . . . and the old coronation-chair, with the stone of Scone beneath the seat, and the wood-work cut and scratched all over with names and initials. . . .

I continue to go to the picture-galleries. I have an idea that the face of Murillo's St. John has a certain mischievous intelligence in it. This has impressed me almost from the first. It is a boy's face, very beautiful and very pleasant too, but with an expression that one might fairly suspect to be roguish if seen in the face of a living boy.

About equestrian statues, as those of various kings at Charing Cross, and otherwhere about London, and of the Duke of Wellington opposite

Apsley House, and in front of the Exchange, it strikes me as absurd, the idea of putting a man on horseback on a place where one movement of the steed forward or backward or sideways would infallibly break his own and his rider's neck. The English sculptors generally seem to have been aware of this absurdity, and have endeavored to lessen it by making the horse as quiet as a cab-horse on the stand, instead of rearing rampant, like the bronze group of Jackson at Washington. The statue of Wellington, at the Piccadilly corner of the Park, has a stately and imposing effect, seen from far distances, in approaching either through the Green Park, or from the Oxford Street corner of Hyde Park.

January 3d, 1858.—On Thursday we had the pleasure of a call from Mr. Coventry Patmore, to whom Dr. Wilkinson gave me a letter of introduction, and on whom I had called twice at the British Museum without finding him. We had read his Betrothal and Angel in the House with unusual pleasure and sympathy, and therefore were very glad to make his personal acquaintance. He is a man of much more youthful aspect than I had expected, ... a slender person to be an Englishman, though not remarkably so had he been an American; with an intelligent, pleasant, and sensitive face,—a man very evidently of refined feelings and cultivated mind. . . . He is very simple and agreeable in his manners; a little shy, yet perfectly frank, and easy to meet on real grounds. . . . He said that his wife had proposed to come with him, and had, indeed, accompanied him to town, but was kept away. . . . We were very sorry for this, because Mr. Patmore seems to acknowledge her as the real "Angel in the House," although he says she herself ignores all connection with the poem. It is well for her to do so, and for her husband to feel that the character is her real portrait; and both, I suppose, are right. It is a most beautiful and original poem,—a poem for happy married people to read together, and to understand by the light of their own past and present life; but I doubt whether the generality of English people are capable of appreciating it. I told Mr. Patmore that I thought his popularity in America would be greater than at home, and he said that it was already so; and he appeared to estimate highly his American fame, and also our general gift of quicker and more subtle recognition of genius than the English public. . . . We mutually gratified each other by expressing high admiration of one another's works, and Mr. Patmore regretted that in the few days of our further stay here we should not have time to visit him at his home. It would really give me pleasure to do so. . . . I expressed a hope of seeing him in Italy during our residence there, and he seemed to think it possible, as his friend, and our countryman, Thomas Buchanan Read, had asked him to come thither and be his guest. He took his leave, shaking hands with all of us because he saw that we were of his own people, recognizing him as a true poet. He has since given me the new edition of his poems, with a kind rote.

We are now making preparations for our departure, which we expect will take place on Tuesday; and yesterday I went to our Minister's to arrange about the passport. The very moment I rang at his door, it swung open, and the porter ushered me with great courtesy into the anteroom; not that he knew me, or anything about me, except that I was an American citizen. This is the deference which an American servant of the public finds it expedient to show to his sovereigns. Thank Heaven, I am a sovereign again, and no longer a servant; and really it is very singular how I look down upon our ambassadors and dignitaries of all sorts, not excepting the President himself. I doubt whether this is altogether a good influence of our mode of government.

I did not see, and, in fact, declined seeing, the Minister himself, but only his son, the Secretary of Legation, and a Dr. P———, an American traveller just from the Continent. He gave a fearful account of the difficulties that beset a person landing with much luggage in Italy, and especially at Civita Vecchia, the very port at which we intended to debark. I have been so long in England that it seems a cold and shivery thing to go anywhere else.

Bennoch came to take tea with us on the 5th, it being his first visit since we came to London, and likewise his farewell visit on our leaving for the Continent.

On his departure, J——- and I walked a good way down Oxford Street and Holborn with him, and I took leave of him with the kindest wishes for his welfare.

END OF VOL. II.

About Author

Nathaniel Hawthorne (Hathorne; July 4, 1804 – May 19, 1864) was an American novelist, dark romantic, and short story writer. His works often focus on history, morality, and religion.

He was born in 1804 in Salem, Massachusetts, to Nathaniel Hathorne and the former Elizabeth Clarke Manning. His ancestors include John Hathorne, the only judge involved in the Salem witch trials who never repented of his actions. He entered Bowdoin College in 1821, was elected to Phi Beta Kappa in 1824, and graduated in 1825. He published his first work in 1828, the novel Fanshawe; he later tried to suppress it, feeling that it was not equal to the standard of his later work. He published several short stories in periodicals, which he collected in 1837 as Twice-Told Tales. The next year, he became engaged to Sophia Peabody. He worked at the Boston Custom House and joined Brook Farm, a transcendentalist community, before marrying Peabody in 1842. The couple moved to The Old Manse in Concord, Massachusetts, later moving to Salem, the Berkshires, then to The Wayside in Concord. The Scarlet Letter was published in 1850, followed by a succession of other novels. A political appointment as consul took Hawthorne and family to Europe before their return to Concord in 1860. Hawthorne died on May 19, 1864, and was survived by his wife and their three children.

Much of Hawthorne's writing centers on New England, many works featuring moral metaphors with an anti-Puritan inspiration. His fiction works are considered part of the Romantic movement and, more specifically, dark romanticism. His themes often center on the inherent evil and sin of humanity, and his works often have moral messages and deep psychological complexity. His published works include novels, short stories, and a biography of his college friend Franklin Pierce, the 14th President of the United States.

Biography

Early life

Nathaniel Hawthorne was born on July 4, 1804, in Salem, Massachusetts;

his birthplace is preserved and open to the public. William Hathorne was the author's great-great-great-grandfather. He was a Puritan and was the first of the family to emigrate from England, settling in Dorchester, Massachusetts, before moving to Salem. There he became an important member of the Massachusetts Bay Colony and held many political positions, including magistrate and judge, becoming infamous for his harsh sentencing. William's son and the author's great-great-grandfather John Hathorne was one of the judges who oversaw the Salem witch trials. Hawthorne probably added the "w" to his surname in his early twenties, shortly after graduating from college, in an effort to dissociate himself from his notorious forebears. Hawthorne's father Nathaniel Hathorne Sr. was a sea captain who died in 1808 of yellow fever in Suriname; he had been a member of the East India Marine Society. After his death, his widow moved with young Nathaniel and two daughters to live with relatives named the Mannings in Salem, where they lived for 10 years. Young Hawthorne was hit on the leg while playing "bat and ball" on November 10, 1813, and he became lame and bedridden for a year, though several physicians could find nothing wrong with him.

In the summer of 1816, the family lived as boarders with farmers before moving to a home recently built specifically for them by Hawthorne's uncles Richard and Robert Manning in Raymond, Maine, near Sebago Lake. Years later, Hawthorne looked back at his time in Maine fondly: "Those were delightful days, for that part of the country was wild then, with only scattered clearings, and nine tenths of it primeval woods." In 1819, he was sent back to Salem for school and soon complained of homesickness and being too far from his mother and sisters. He distributed seven issues of The Spectator to his family in August and September 1820 for the sake of having fun. The homemade newspaper was written by hand and included essays, poems, and news featuring the young author's adolescent humor.

Hawthorne's uncle Robert Manning insisted that the boy attend college, despite Hawthorne's protests. With the financial support of his uncle, Hawthorne was sent to Bowdoin College in 1821, partly because of family connections in the area, and also because of its relatively inexpensive tuition rate. Hawthorne met future president Franklin Pierce on the way to

Bowdoin, at the stage stop in Portland, and the two became fast friends. Once at the school, he also met future poet Henry Wadsworth Longfellow, future congressman Jonathan Cilley, and future naval reformer Horatio Bridge. He graduated with the class of 1825, and later described his college experience to Richard Henry Stoddard:

> I was educated (as the phrase is) at Bowdoin College. I was an idle student, negligent of college rules and the Procrustean details of academic life, rather choosing to nurse my own fancies than to dig into Greek roots and be numbered among the learned Thebans.

Early career

In 1836, Hawthorne served as the editor of the American Magazine of Useful and Entertaining Knowledge. At the time, he boarded with poet Thomas Green Fessenden on Hancock Street in Beacon Hill in Boston. He was offered an appointment as weigher and gauger at the Boston Custom House at a salary of $1,500 a year, which he accepted on January 17, 1839. During his time there, he rented a room from George Stillman Hillard, business partner of Charles Sumner. Hawthorne wrote in the comparative obscurity of what he called his "owl's nest" in the family home. As he looked back on this period of his life, he wrote: "I have not lived, but only dreamed about living." He contributed short stories to various magazines and annuals, including "Young Goodman Brown" and "The Minister's Black Veil", though none drew major attention to him. Horatio Bridge offered to cover the risk of collecting these stories in the spring of 1837 into the volume Twice-Told Tales, which made Hawthorne known locally.

Marriage and family

While at Bowdoin, Hawthorne wagered a bottle of Madeira wine with his friend Jonathan Cilley that Cilley would get married before Hawthorne did. By 1836, he had won the bet, but he did not remain a bachelor for life. He had public flirtations with Mary Silsbee and Elizabeth Peabody, then he began pursuing Peabody's sister, illustrator and transcendentalist Sophia Peabody. He joined the transcendentalist Utopian community at Brook Farm in 1841, not because he agreed with the experiment but because it helped him save money to marry Sophia. He paid a $1,000 deposit and was put in charge of shoveling the hill of manure referred to as "the Gold Mine". He left later that year, though his Brook Farm adventure became an inspiration for his novel The Blithedale Romance. Hawthorne married Sophia Peabody on July 9, 1842, at a ceremony in the Peabody parlor on West Street in Boston. The couple moved to The Old Manse in Concord, Massachusetts, where they lived for three years. His neighbor Ralph Waldo Emerson invited him into his social circle, but Hawthorne was almost pathologically shy and stayed silent at gatherings. At the Old Manse, Hawthorne wrote most of the tales collected in Mosses from an Old Manse.

Like Hawthorne, Sophia was a reclusive person. Throughout her early life, she had frequent migraines and underwent several experimental medical treatments. She was mostly bedridden until her sister introduced her to Hawthorne, after which her headaches seem to have abated. The Hawthornes enjoyed a long and happy marriage. He referred to her as his "Dove" and wrote that she "is, in the strictest sense, my sole companion; and I need no other—there is no vacancy in my mind, any more than in my heart ... Thank God that I suffice for her boundless heart!" Sophia greatly admired her husband's work. She wrote in one of her journals:

> I am always so dazzled and bewildered with the richness, the depth, the ... jewels of beauty in his productions that I am always looking forward to a second reading where I can ponder and muse and fully take in the miraculous wealth of thoughts.

Poet Ellery Channing came to the Old Manse for help on the first anniversary of the Hawthornes' marriage. A local teenager named Martha Hunt had drowned herself in the river and Hawthorne's boat Pond Lily was needed to find her body. Hawthorne helped recover the corpse, which he described as "a spectacle of such perfect horror ... She was the very image of death-agony". The incident later inspired a scene in his novel The Blithedale Romance.

The Hawthornes had three children. Their first was daughter Una, born March 3, 1844; her name was a reference to The Faerie Queene, to the displeasure of family members. Hawthorne wrote to a friend, "I find it a very sober and serious kind of happiness that springs from the birth of a child ... There is no escaping it any longer. I have business on earth now, and must look about me for the means of doing it." In October 1845, the Hawthornes moved to Salem. In 1846, their son Julian was born. Hawthorne wrote to his sister Louisa on June 22, 1846: "A small troglodyte made his appearance here at ten minutes to six o'clock this morning, who claimed to be your nephew." Daughter Rose was born in May 1851, and Hawthorne called her his "autumnal flower".

Middle years

In April 1846, Hawthorne was officially appointed the Surveyor for the District of Salem and Beverly and Inspector of the Revenue for the Port of Salem at an annual salary of $1,200. He had difficulty writing during this period, as he admitted to Longfellow:

> I am trying to resume my pen ... Whenever I sit alone, or walk alone, I find myself dreaming about stories, as of old; but these forenoons in the Custom House undo all that the afternoons and evenings have done. I should be happier if I could write.

This employment, like his earlier appointment to the custom house in Boston, was vulnerable to the politics of the spoils system. Hawthorne was a Democrat and lost this job due to the change of administration in Washington after the presidential election of 1848. He wrote a letter of protest to the Boston Daily Advertiser which was attacked by the Whigs and supported by the Democrats, making Hawthorne's dismissal a much-talked about event in New England. He was deeply affected by the death of his mother in late July, calling it "the darkest hour I ever lived". He was appointed the corresponding secretary of the Salem Lyceum in 1848. Guests who came to speak that season included Emerson, Thoreau, Louis Agassiz, and Theodore Parker.

Hawthorne returned to writing and published The Scarlet Letter in mid-March 1850, including a preface that refers to his three-year tenure in the Custom House and makes several allusions to local politicians—who did not appreciate their treatment. It was one of the first mass-produced books in America, selling 2,500 volumes within ten days and earning Hawthorne $1,500 over 14 years. The book was pirated by booksellers in London and became a best-seller in the United States; it initiated his most lucrative period as a writer. Hawthorne's friend Edwin Percy Whipple objected to the novel's "morbid intensity" and its dense psychological details, writing that the book "is therefore apt to become, like Hawthorne, too painfully anatomical in his exhibition of them", though 20th-century writer D. H. Lawrence said that there could be no more perfect work of the American imagination than The Scarlet Letter.

Hawthorne and his family moved to a small red farmhouse near Lenox, Massachusetts, at the end of March 1850. He became friends with Herman Melville beginning on August 5, 1850, when the authors met at a picnic hosted by a mutual friend. Melville had just read Hawthorne's short story collection Mosses from an Old Manse, and his unsigned review of the collection was printed in The Literary World on August 17 and August 24 titled "Hawthorne and His Mosses". Melville wrote that these stories revealed a dark side to Hawthorne, "shrouded in blackness, ten times black". He was composing his novel Moby-Dick at the time, and dedicated the work in 1851 to Hawthorne: "In token of my admiration for his genius, this book is inscribed to Nathaniel Hawthorne."

Hawthorne's time in the Berkshires was very productive. While there, he wrote The House of the Seven Gables (1851), which poet and critic James Russell Lowell said was better than The Scarlet Letter and called "the most valuable contribution to New England history that has been made." He also wrote The Blithedale Romance (1852), his only work written in the first person. He also published A Wonder-Book for Girls and Boys in 1851, a collection of short stories retelling myths which he had been thinking about writing since 1846. Nevertheless, poet Ellery Channing reported that Hawthorne "has suffered much living in this place". The family enjoyed the scenery of the Berkshires, although Hawthorne did not enjoy the winters in their small house. They left on November 21, 1851. Hawthorne noted, "I am sick to death of Berkshire ... I have felt languid and dispirited, during almost my whole residence."

The Wayside and Europe

In May 1852, the Hawthornes returned to Concord where they lived until July 1853. In February, they bought The Hillside, a home previously inhabited by Amos Bronson Alcott and his family, and renamed it The Wayside. Their neighbors in Concord included Emerson and Henry David Thoreau.That year, Hawthorne wrote The Life of Franklin Pierce, the campaign biography of his friend which depicted him as "a man of peaceful pursuits". Horace Mann said, "If he makes out Pierce to be a great man or a brave man, it will be the greatest work of fiction he ever wrote." In the biography, Hawthorne depicts Pierce as a statesman and soldier who had accomplished no great feats because of his need to make "little noise" and so "withdrew into the background". He also left out Pierce's drinking habits, despite rumors of his alcoholism, and emphasized Pierce's belief that slavery could not "be remedied by human contrivances" but would, over time, "vanish like a dream".

With Pierce's election as President, Hawthorne was rewarded in 1853 with the position of United States consul in Liverpool shortly after the publication of Tanglewood Tales.The role was considered the most lucrative foreign service position at the time, described by Hawthorne's wife as "second in dignity to the Embassy in London". His appointment ended in 1857 at the close of the Pierce administration, and the Hawthorne family toured France and Italy. During his time in Italy, the previously clean-shaven Hawthorne grew a bushy mustache.

The family returned to The Wayside in 1860, and that year saw the publication of The Marble Faun, his first new book in seven years. Hawthorne admitted that he had aged considerably, referring to himself as "wrinkled with time and trouble".

Later years and death

At the outset of the American Civil War, Hawthorne traveled with William D. Ticknor to Washington, D.C., where he met Abraham Lincoln and other notable figures. He wrote about his experiences in the essay "Chiefly About War Matters" in 1862.

Failing health prevented him from completing several more romance novels. Hawthorne was suffering from pain in his stomach and insisted on a recuperative trip with his friend Franklin Pierce, though his neighbor Bronson Alcott was concerned that Hawthorne was too ill. While on a tour of the White Mountains, he died in his sleep on May 19, 1864, in Plymouth, New Hampshire. Pierce sent a telegram to Elizabeth Peabody asking her to inform Mrs. Hawthorne in person. Mrs. Hawthorne was too saddened by the news to handle the funeral arrangements herself. Hawthorne's son Julian was a freshman at Harvard College, and he learned of his father's death the next day; coincidentally, he was initiated into the Delta Kappa Epsilon fraternity on the same day by being blindfolded and placed in a coffin.Longfellow wrote a tribute poem to Hawthorne published in 1866 called "The Bells of Lynn". Hawthorne was buried on what is now known as "Authors' Ridge" in Sleepy Hollow Cemetery, Concord, Massachusetts. Pallbearers included Longfellow, Emerson, Alcott, Oliver Wendell Holmes Sr., James Thomas Fields, and Edwin Percy Whipple. Emerson wrote of the funeral: "I thought there was a tragic element in the event, that might be more fully rendered—in the painful solitude of the man, which, I suppose, could no longer be endured, & he died of it."

His wife Sophia and daughter Una were originally buried in England. However, in June 2006, they were reinterred in plots adjacent to Hawthorne.

Writings

Hawthorne had a particularly close relationship with his publishers William Ticknor and James Thomas Fields. Hawthorne once told Fields, "I care more for your good opinion than for that of a host of critics." In fact, it was Fields who convinced Hawthorne to turn The Scarlet Letter into a novel rather than a short story. Ticknor handled many of Hawthorne's personal matters, including the purchase of cigars, overseeing financial accounts, and even purchasing clothes. Ticknor died with Hawthorne at his side in Philadelphia in 1864; according to a friend, Hawthorne was left "apparently dazed".

Literary style and themes

Hawthorne's works belong to romanticism or, more specifically, dark romanticism, cautionary tales that suggest that guilt, sin, and evil are the most inherent natural qualities of humanity. Many of his works are inspired by Puritan New England, combining historical romance loaded with symbolism and deep psychological themes, bordering on surrealism. His depictions of the past are a version of historical fiction used only as a vehicle to express common themes of ancestral sin, guilt and retribution. His later writings also reflect his negative view of the Transcendentalism movement.

Hawthorne was predominantly a short story writer in his early career. Upon publishing Twice-Told Tales, however, he noted, "I do not think much of them," and he expected little response from the public. His four major romances were written between 1850 and 1860: The Scarlet Letter (1850), The House of the Seven Gables (1851), The Blithedale Romance (1852) and The Marble Faun (1860). Another novel-length romance, Fanshawe, was published anonymously in 1828. Hawthorne defined a romance as being radically different from a novel by not being concerned with the possible or probable course of ordinary experience. In the preface to The House of the Seven Gables, Hawthorne describes his romance-writing as using "atmospherical medium as to bring out or mellow the lights and deepen and enrich the shadows of the picture". The picture, Daniel Hoffman found, was one of "the primitive energies of fecundity and creation."

Critics have applied feminist perspectives and historicist approaches to Hawthorne's depictions of women. Feminist scholars are interested particularly in Hester Prynne: they recognize that while she herself could not be the "destined prophetess" of the future, the "angel and apostle of the coming revelation" must nevertheless "be a woman." Camille Paglia saw Hester as mystical, "a wandering goddess still bearing the mark of her Asiatic origins ... moving serenely in the magic circle of her sexual nature". Lauren Berlant termed Hester "the citizen as woman [personifying] love as a quality of the body that contains the purest light of nature," her resulting "traitorous political theory" a "Female Symbolic" literalization of futile Puritan metaphors. Historicists view Hester as a protofeminist and avatar of the self-reliance and responsibility that led to women's suffrage and reproductive emancipation. Anthony Splendora found her literary genealogy among other archetypally fallen but redeemed women, both historic and mythic. As examples, he offers Psyche of ancient legend; Heloise of twelfth-century France's tragedy involving world-renowned philosopher Peter Abelard; Anne Hutchinson (America's first heretic, circa 1636), and Hawthorne family friend Margaret Fuller. In Hester's first appearance, Hawthorne likens her, "infant at her bosom", to Mary, Mother of Jesus, "the image of Divine Maternity". In her study of Victorian literature, in which such "galvanic outcasts" as Hester feature prominently, Nina Auerbach went so far as to name Hester's fall and subsequent redemption, "the novel's one unequivocally religious activity". Regarding Hester as a deity figure, Meredith A. Powers found in Hester's characterization "the earliest in American fiction that the archetypal Goddess appears quite graphically," like a Goddess "not the wife of traditional marriage, permanently subject to a male overlord"; Powers noted "her syncretism, her flexibility, her inherent ability to alter and so avoid the defeat of secondary status in a goal-oriented civilization".

Aside from Hester Prynne, the model women of Hawthorne's other novels—from Ellen Langton of Fanshawe to Zenobia and Priscilla of The Blithedale Romance, Hilda and Miriam of The Marble Faun and Phoebe and Hepzibah of The House of the Seven Gables—are more fully realized than his male characters, who merely orbit them. This observation is equally true of his short-stories, in which central females serve as allegorical figures: Rappaccini's beautiful but life-altering, garden-bound, daughter; almost-perfect Georgiana of "The Birthmark"; the sinned-against (abandoned) Ester of "Ethan Brand"; and goodwife Faith Brown, linchpin of Young Goodman Brown's very belief in God. "My Faith is gone!" Brown exclaims in despair upon seeing his wife at the Witches' Sabbath. Perhaps the most sweeping statement of Hawthorne's impetus comes from Mark Van Doren: "Somewhere, if not in the New England of his time, Hawthorne unearthed the image of a goddess supreme in beauty and power."

Hawthorne also wrote nonfiction. In 2008, the Library of America selected Hawthorne's "A show of wax-figures" for inclusion in its two-century retrospective of American True Crime.

Criticism

In "Hawthorne and His Mosses", Herman Melville wrote a passionate argument for Hawthorne to be among the burgeoning American literary canon, "He is one of the new, and far better generation of your writers." In this review of Mosses from an Old Manse, Melville describes an affinity for Hawthorne that would only increase: "I feel that this Hawthorne has dropped germinous seeds into my soul. He expands and deepens down, the more I contemplate him; and further, and further, shoots his strong New-England roots into the hot soil of my Southern soul." Edgar Allan Poe wrote important reviews of both Twice-Told Tales and Mosses from an Old Manse. Poe's assessment was partly informed by his contempt of allegory and moral tales, and his chronic accusations of plagiarism, though he admitted,

> The style of Mr. Hawthorne is purity itself. His tone is singularly effective—wild, plaintive, thoughtful, and in full accordance with his themes ... We look upon him as one of the few men of indisputable genius to whom our country has as yet given birth.

Ralph Waldo Emerson wrote, "Nathaniel Hawthorne's reputation as a writer is a very pleasing fact, because his writing is not good for anything, and this is a tribute to the man." Henry James praised Hawthorne, saying, "The fine thing in Hawthorne is that he cared for the deeper psychology, and that, in his way, he tried to become familiar with it." Poet John Greenleaf Whittier wrote that he admired the "weird and subtle beauty" in Hawthorne's tales. Evert Augustus Duyckinck said of Hawthorne, "Of the American writers destined to live, he is the most original, the one least indebted to foreign models or literary precedents of any kind."

Contemporary response to Hawthorne's work praised his sentimentality and moral purity while more modern evaluations focus on the dark psychological complexity. Beginning in the 1950s, critics have focused on symbolism and didacticism.

The critic Harold Bloom opined that only Henry James and William Faulkner challenge Hawthorne's position as the greatest American novelist, although he admitted that he favored James as the greatest American novelist.

Bloom saw Hawthorne's greatest works to be principally The Scarlet Letter, followed by The Marble Faun and certain short stories, including "My Kinsman, Major Molineux", "Young Goodman Brown", "Wakefield", and "Feathertop". (Source: Wikipedia)

NOTABLE WORKS

NOVELS

Fanshawe (published anonymously, 1828)

The Scarlet Letter (1850)

The House of the Seven Gables (1851)

The Blithedale Romance (1852)

The Marble Faun: Or, The Romance of Monte Beni (1860) (as Transformation: Or, The Romance of Monte Beni, UK publication, same year)

The Dolliver Romance (1863) (unfinished)

Septimius Felton; or, the Elixir of Life (unfinished, published in the Atlantic Monthly, 1872)

Doctor Grimshawe's Secret: A Romance (unfinished, with preface and notes by Julian Hawthorne, 1882)

SHORT STORY COLLECTIONS

Twice-Told Tales (1837)

Grandfather's Chair (1840)

Mosses from an Old Manse (1846)

A Wonder-Book for Girls and Boys (1851)

The Snow-Image, and Other Twice-Told Tales (1852)

Tanglewood Tales (1853)

The Dolliver Romance and Other Pieces (1876)

The Great Stone Face and Other Tales of the White Mountains (1889)

SELECTED SHORT STORIES

"The Hollow of the Three Hills" (1830)

"Roger Malvin's Burial" (1832)

"My Kinsman, Major Molineux" (1832)

"The Minister's Black Veil" (1832)

"Young Goodman Brown" (1835)

"The Gray Champion" (1835)

"The White Old Maid" (1835)

"Wakefield" (1835)

"The Ambitious Guest" (1835)

"The Man of Adamant" (1837)

"The May-Pole of Merry Mount" (1837)

"The Great Carbuncle" (1837)

"Dr. Heidegger's Experiment" (1837)

"A Virtuoso's Collection" (May 1842)

"The Birth-Mark" (March 1843)

"The Celestial Railroad" (1843)

"Egotism; or, The Bosom-Serpent" (1843)

"Earth's Holocaust" (1844)

"Rappaccini's Daughter" (1844)

"P.'s Correspondence" (1845)

"The Artist of the Beautiful" (1846)

"Fire Worship" (1846)

"Ethan Brand" (1850)

"The Great Stone Face" (1850)

"Feathertop" (1852)

NONFICTION

Twenty Days with Julian & Little Bunny (written 1851, published 1904)

Our Old Home (1863)

Passages from the French and Italian Notebooks (1871)

CPSIA information can be obtained
at www.ICGtesting.com
Printed in the USA
LVHW030500140720
660560LV00012B/568

9 789390 170531